SAVING PARADISE

SAVING
PARADISE

How Christianity Traded
Love of This World for
Crucifixion and Empire

RITA NAKASHIMA BROCK
REBECCA ANN PARKER

Beacon Press

BOSTON

BEACON PRESS
25 Beacon Street
Boston, Massachusetts 02108-2892
www.beacon.org

Beacon Press books
are published under the auspices of
the Unitarian Universalist Association of Congregations.

11 10 09 08   8 7 6 5 4 3 2 1

Composition by Wilsted & Taylor Publishing Services
All photographs by the authors

This book is printed on acid-free paper that meets
the uncoated paper ANSI/NISO specifications
for permanence as revised in 1992.

Library of Congress Cataloging-in-Publication Data
Brock, Rita Nakashima.
Saving paradise : how Christianity traded love of this world for crucifixion and empire /
Rita Nakashima Brock, Rebecca Ann Parker.
p. cm.
Includes bibliographical references and index.
ISBN 978-0-8070-6750-5 (alk. paper)
1. Theology—History—Early church, ca. 30–600. 2. Theology—History—Middle Ages,
600–1500. 3. Paradise—Christianity—History of doctrines. 4. Nature—Religious aspects—
Christianity. 5. Creation. I. Parker, Rebecca Ann. II. Title.
BT23.B76 2008
230.09—dc22
2007038363

Grateful acknowledgment is made to translators and publishers for kind permission to reproduce
material in this book. Samuel Kramer, *Sumerian Mythology: A Study of Spiritual and Literary
Achievement*, 1972, reprinted by permission of the University of Pennsylvania Press, Philadelphia;
Sebastian Brock, translator and editor, *Saint Ephrem: Hymns on Paradise*, 1990, reprinted by permission of St Vladimir's Seminary Press, Crestwood, NY 10707, www.svspress.com; Sebastian
Brock, *The Luminous Eye: The Spiritual World Vision of Saint Ephrem*, 1992, reprinted by permission of Cistercian Publications, Kalamazoo, MI; Kathleen E. McVey, *Ephrem the Syrian: Hymns*,
1989, reprinted by permission of Paulist Press, New York; Stephen Cox, *The New Testament and
Literature: A Guide to Literary Patterns*, 2006, reprinted by permission of Carus Publishing Company, Chicago; Ronald Murphy, *The Heliand: The Saxon Gospel*, 1992, reprinted by permission of
Oxford University Press, New York; Peter Dronke, *Women Writers of the Middle Ages: A Critical Study
of Texts from Perpetua (d. 203) to Marguerite Porete (d. 1310)*, 1984, reprinted by permission of Cambridge University Press, New York; and Dhuoda, *Liber Manualis: Handbook for her Warrior Son*,
Cambridge Medieval Classics 8, ed. and trans. Marcelle Thiébaux, 1998, reprinted by permission
of Cambridge University Press, New York.

In Memoriam

Dorothy Eleanore Cooper Hartshorne

1904–1995

CONTENTS

Prologue

It took Jesus a thousand years to die. Images of his corpse did not appear in churches until the tenth century. Why not? This question set us off on a five-year pilgrimage that led to this book.

Initially, we didn't believe it could be true. Surely the art historians were wrong. The crucified Christ was too important to Western Christianity. How could it be that images of Jesus's suffering and death were absent from early churches? We had to see for ourselves and consider what this might mean.

In July 2002, we traveled to the Mediterranean in search of the dead body of Jesus. We began in Rome, descending from the blaze of the summer sun into the catacombs where underground tunnels and tombs are carved into soft tufa rock. The earliest surviving Christian art is painted onto the plaster-lined walls of tombs or carved onto marble sarcophagi as memorials to the interred.

In the cool, dimly lit caverns, we saw a variety of biblical images. Many of them suggested rescue from danger. For example, Abraham and Isaac stood side by side in prayer with a ram bound next to them. Jonah, the recalcitrant prophet who was swallowed and coughed up by a sea monster, reclined peacefully beneath the shade of a vine. Daniel stood alive and well between two pacified lions. Other images suggested baptism and healing, such as the Samaritan woman drawing water from a well, John the Baptist dousing Jesus, depicted as a child, and

Jesus raising Lazarus from the dead. Jesus also appeared as a shepherd carrying a lamb on his shoulders like Orpheus.

We could not find a dead Jesus, not even one. It was just as the angel had said to the women looking for Jesus at his tomb, "Why do you look for the living among the dead?" (Luke 24:5). "He is not here" (Mark 16:6). He most certainly was not.

Emerging from the underworld, we traipsed the dusty streets of the city to continue our investigation of the mystery of the missing corpse. Some art historians said there was a Crucifixion carved on the doors of St. Sabina Church, so we trudged up the hill from the Tiber to see it late one sweltering afternoon. Under the church's covered entrance were two huge, fifteen-hundred-year-old cypress doors with thirty-two scenes from the Bible. Each carved relief panel was about eighteen by twelve inches. Among them, we were told, would be one of the oldest known representations of the Crucifixion, created around 425.

We spotted it in the far upper left corner. Three robust, bearded men faced forward: a large central figure flanked by two smaller ones. They wore loincloths and stood firmly, unwounded and unbowed. They raised their stout, strong arms to the side, elbows slightly bent, hands shoulder high. We'd seen this familiar stance in the catacombs. Art historians call it the *orant,* the ancient position for prayer, a posture of both strength and openness, as if the arms were ready to embrace the viewer. Abraham, Isaac, and Daniel had stood in such a position in the catacombs. In this image on the door, the open palms of Christ and the two thieves were nailed to small blocks of wood behind their hands. The blocks were the only trace of crosses. They stood before what appeared to be a brick wall with an open window on the upper left side. Their wide-open eyes gazed at the viewer. This image, we realized, depicted victory over death. Jesus was definitely not dead.

From Rome we went to Istanbul and then to a remote part of northeastern Turkey where the crumbling remains of ninth- to eleventh-century monastery churches could be found upon high mountains. We failed to find even one dead Jesus. Returning to Italy, we lingered for several days in Ravenna to examine its beautifully restored fifth- and sixth-century mosaics.

In the sixth-century St. Apollinare Nuovo Church, at the edge of the old city, we found the earliest surviving life story of Jesus depicted in images. Near the ceiling on both sides of the basilica nave, thirteen rectangular mosaics marched from the chancel toward the main door. We examined each of the twenty-six panels closely. On the right wall near the chancel, an image of the Last Supper began the thirteen scenes of his Passion. At panel ten we encountered Simon of Cyrene carrying the cross for Jesus to Golgotha. We expected to see the Crucifixion on panel eleven. Instead, we were confronted by an angel who sat before a tomb. The apparition spoke to two women swaying forward like Gospel choir singers. We too leaned forward in astonishment and remembered what the angel had said: "I know that you are looking for Jesus who was crucified. He is not here" (Matt. 28:5–6). The remaining panels showed the risen Christ visiting his followers in the stories of doubting Thomas (John 20:19–29) and the road to Emmaus (Luke 24:13–43).

We found no Crucifixions in any of Ravenna's early churches. The death of Jesus, it seemed, was not a key to meaning, not an image of devotion, not a ritual symbol of faith for the Christians who worshipped among the churches' glittering mosaics. The Christ they saw was the incarnate, risen Christ, the child of baptism, the healer of the sick, the teacher of his friends, and the one who defeated death and transfigured the world with the Spirit of life.

Why were we looking for the living among the dead? Like most Western Christians, we were accustomed to images of a Christ who died in agony. We had learned in church and in graduate school that Christians believed the crucifixion of Jesus Christ saved the world and that this idea was the core of Christian faith. In our book *Proverbs of Ashes,* we challenged this idea because we saw that it contributed to sanctioning intimate violence and war. It uses Jesus's death as the supreme model of self-sacrificing love and encourages those who want to follow him to love in the same way. It places victims of violence in harm's way and absolves perpetrators of their responsibility for unethical behavior. The idea deeply troubled us, but we never questioned its centrality to Christianity.

After our book was published, we discovered that the idea troubled many Christians. We were invited to discuss our book on Christian radio stations and had lively, engaged conversations with many listeners who were also concerned that this idea might encourage domestic violence and the sexual abuse of children. Rita's sister-in-law, the daughter of Christian missionaries, wrote us a long letter of gratitude because the book made her think more deeply about her faith. We were gratified that so many were willing to listen to what we had to say and to think about what they believed about the Crucifixion. Even so, we were unprepared for the possibility that Christians did not focus on the death of Jesus for a thousand years.

After we investigated early Christian art, we stepped back, astonished at the weight of the reality: Jesus's dead body was just not there. We could not find it in the catacombs or Rome's early churches, in Istanbul's great sixth-century cathedral Hagia Sophia, in the monastery churches in northeastern Turkey, or in Ravenna's mosaics. The mystery of its absence deepened. We searched as many sources of early Christian art as we could find; we studied with an expert on first-millennium art at the University of California in Berkeley, and we consulted several times with a distinguished scholar of Christian art.[1]

After we realized that the Crucifixion was absent, we began to pay attention to what *was* present in early Christian art. We found one arresting image in an unlikely place, the most important church in Western Christendom and still the *cathedra* (seat) of the bishop of Rome, St. Giovanni in Laterano. The basilica was donated to the church by Constantine (274–337). Though the pope now resides at the Vatican, this church is still his official seat. What we saw in the apse of this basilica astonished us. Though the apse mosaic image has changed and been restored over the centuries, parts of it likely date to the fourth to sixth centuries.[2]

We arrived at St. Giovanni during Mass. It was conducted from a high baroque altar—residue, to modern eyes, of one of the more incongruent restorations of the seventeenth century—placed where the nave and transept intersect. The altar displayed a triptych painting with the

Crucifixion in the center. It completely hid the apse. We walked quietly down the right aisle, tiptoed up the transept stairs, ignored the velvet rope blocking further progress, and sneaked behind the altar. When we spotted the apse, we gasped in wonder. At the top of its curve, a bust of Jesus gazed down, serious and dignified. His golden nimbus outlined his countenance against a dark blue background strewn with white, red, and blue clouds. Winged seraphim hovered at the upper edges of the image, four on a side. A single seraphim hovered directly above him upside down, wings spread out.

Below this upper blue crescent of sky, the apse sparkled in gold, like the light in a dawn sky. Immediately below Jesus's bust, a dove emerged head down in the golden sky, like the seraphim above his head, with wings similarly spread. From its beak, a pale stream of water poured downward. Below the dove was a gold, segmented cross, with a large jewel in the center of each segment. The stream of water fell behind the cross, slowly widening until it formed a translucent pool around its base. In the center of the cross was an oval medallion. It showed Jesus standing in water, his head slightly bowed while John the Baptist on the shore poured water over his head.

At the base of the golden cross, next to the pool, two delicate six-pointed deer, one on either side, stood atop a hill of grass and flowers. They turned toward the cross, heads lowered, and gazed at the viewer. "As a deer longs for flowing streams, so my soul longs for you, O God" (Ps. 42:1). Below the pool, four rivers flowed out below the tree like roots, two curving left and two curving right, so that the rivers seemed to lift the cross out of the meadow below. They were carefully labeled Pishon, Gihon, Tigris, and Euphrates, the rivers of paradise in Genesis 2:11–14. Three snow-white sheep on either side, slightly smaller than the deer and directly beneath them, drank from the streams. "The Lord is my shepherd, I shall not want" (Ps. 23:1).

Where the rivers split left and right, they made a triangle in the meadow. Inside the triangle, directly below the cross, a small golden city nestled as if protected by the rivers. A saint stood before the city. Behind his head, above the city, waved a palm tree in whose fronds a peacock perched, both images of immortality. Busts of Peter and Paul peered above the city towers. At the base of the entire apse, the rivers merged with the Jordan. The great river flowed laterally across the bottom of the apse, with a lush meadow, dotted with birds and flowers, as its bank. In the river itself, swans paddled serenely in pairs, a couple of cherubs fished from a boat, one cherub rode a swan, another swam in the waves, and a fifth wind-surfed across them.

This image penetrated our consciousness until, at last, we understood: we stood in paradise. The image depicted a vision found in a popular third-century Christian text called the *Apocalypse of Paul*:

I entered Paradise and saw the beginning of waters, and the angel beckoned me. . . . And when I had gone inside I saw a tree planted from whose roots water flowed out, and from this was the beginning of the four rivers. And the Spirit of God rested on that tree, and when the Spirit blew, the waters flowed forth, and I said, "My Lord, is it this tree itself which makes the waters flow?" And he said to me, "From the beginning, before the heavens and earth appeared, the Spirit has been resting upon this tree; wherefore, whenever the Spirit blows, the waters flow forth from the tree."[3]

As we looked at other early church interiors, we saw more clearly how each captured dimensions of paradise. The spaces placed Christians in a lush visual environment: a cosmos of stars in midnight skies, golden sunlight, sparkling waters teeming with fish, exuberant fauna, and verdant meadows filled with flowers and fruit trees. Punctuating such scenes were images of the great cloud of witnesses, many dressed in purple robes of nobility. Others wore white robes of baptism as brides of Christ. They wore or carried wreaths of victory. Many apse images included exactly four rivers flowing from a lamb, globe, or golden cross.

Paradise, we realized, was the dominant image of early Christian sanctuaries. This both disconcerted and intrigued us. On the one hand, we were dismayed to think that early Christians appeared to be obsessed with the afterlife. On the other hand, we wondered why they covered every inch of church walls with such beautiful sights. We contemplated what it felt like to worship in such spaces. We studied ancient liturgies, ritual practices, prayers, and hymns that may have been used in these churches. We tried, in other words, to feel and sense our way into their visual and liturgical worlds. We also explored early commentaries on Genesis. Reading early church texts on paradise, we sought to understand the ideas worshippers held as they daily prayed, processed, stood, sang, and partook of the Eucharist in such spaces.

To our surprise and delight, we discovered that early Christian paradise was something other than "heaven" or the afterlife. Our modern views of heaven and paradise think of them as a world after death. However, in the early church, paradise—first and foremost—was this world, permeated and blessed by the Spirit of God. It was on the earth. Images of it in Rome and Ravenna captured the craggy, scruffy pastoral landscape, the orchards, the clear night skies, and teeming waters of the Mediterranean world, as if they were lit by a power from within. Sparkling mosaics in vivid colors captured the world's luminosity. The images filled the walls of spaces in which liturgies fostered aesthetic, emotional, spiritual, and intellectual experiences of life in the present, in a world created as good and delightful.

Like the breathing of a human body, the images said that God blessed the earth with the breath of Spirit. It permeated the entire cosmos and made paradise the salvation that baptism in the Spirit offered. As the most blessed place imaginable, paradise was also where the departed saints rested from their earthly labors and returned to visit those who loved them. In early Christian understandings, even heaven was a dimension of this life; it was the mysterious abode of God from which blessings flowed upon the earth. Nearby to heaven, the dead rested in their own neighborhood of paradise.

After thirty years of working in religion and theology, we had stumbled inadvertently into paradise. Like most scholars of Christian history and theology, we had studied the texts of creeds and councils, chronicling the many struggles over doctrine. We were taught to regard Chris-

tian theology as the gradual unfolding of the truth of orthodox Christianity. Some misguided and infamous heretics contested this truth, but
the church "fathers" had vigorously defended it and triumphed. We
have been skeptical of such a limited and apologist version of the faith,
but we have had to find our own resources for alternative understandings to derail this juggernaut.[4]

Nearly everything we had previously understood about Christian
history, theology, and ritual began to shift as we delved deeper into the
meaning of paradise. We felt as if we had been climbing a long, steep
mountain trail. We could see behind us the terrain we had trudged
through—an arid Golgotha landscape of sharp, barren rocks that had
left us thirsty, sore, and spent. At a sudden turn, the switchbacks
opened onto a new vista. Opening before us were vast meadows, lush
and green. When we began to look at early Christianity through the lens
of its visual and ritual worlds, we found that much of what we'd been
taught had to be reexamined—beginning with our modern assumptions that doctrinal texts provided a primary orientation to early Christian faith. We worked to understand the world of early Christianity not
as the literate few knew it but as the visually literate many knew it when
they worshipped in churches and recited memorized scriptures and
creeds. For them, visual art and poetic and narrative literature, found
in prayers, stories, psalms, and hymns, shaped Christian life and sustained it.

Beauty and art—in all its forms—engage the more holistic, emotional, and sensory-laden dimensions of experience and memory. They
capture multilayered experiences of imagination, feeling, perceiving,
and thinking. Through art, the aesthetic, emotional, sensory, and intellectual dimensions of life can come together and be mixed in fresh
ways. Throughout this book, and especially in Part I, we have tried to
capture the experience of the liturgical spaces of the early Christian
world. We include descriptions of some of the images, selections from
liturgical poetry and stories, and concrete details of rituals. Though we
recognize that these are inadequate to convey the sensory spaces and
experiences of a distant time, we have sought to communicate something of the aesthetic experience of paradise.

In addition to these forms of beauty and liturgy, we have drawn on a variety of early thinkers in creating a picture of the early church and its understandings of paradise. We have reached across a wide terrain of resources for understanding early Christianity, including thinkers in Asia, Europe, and Africa who used Latin, Greek, or Syriac as their main language. Although contemporary Christians separate the heretics from the orthodox leaders, at the time these disputes arose such clean divides were not always so obvious. Some heretics, such as Origen of Alexandria (c. 185–c. 254), had great influence on orthodox thinkers. On occasion, we have lifted up voices or texts we believe merit greater attention—some of which may surprise the reader. Finally, in some cases, with well-known thinkers such as Augustine of Hippo and texts such as the Gospel of John and the Martyrdom of Perpetua, we offer alternative ways of reading them in terms of paradise. We reach across such a vast spectrum of thinkers and traditions for two reasons. First, the spectrum allows us to demonstrate how pervasive an idea paradise was in early Christianity, and, second, it reveals how thinkers adapted their views of paradise in relation to the specificities of their own cultures and geographies.

Part I of this book is a genealogy of paradise, showing how it was understood to be in this world and on the earth. We examine the earliest roots of paradise in chapter 1, reaching back nearly four thousand years to explore how the ancient people of West Asia imagined paradise as the best that life could be, long before it was written about in Genesis 1–2. We show how the Bible's Hebrew prophets invoked the Garden of Eden to raise ethical questions about the exploitation and carnage of empires—even to challenge the kings of Israel. We note how biblical authors periodically rewrite the stories of Creation and paradise in new ways to highlight the importance of their times and places to the fate of God's world. In chapter 2, we examine how stories of Jesus in the Gospels develop this prophetic tradition during times of Roman oppression, using the idea of the kingdom, or reign, of God. We show how they reinterpret Genesis 1–2 in the first century. In addition, we discuss the meaning of the Passion stories and the Crucifixion in relation to the church's claim that this world is paradise. We unlock a form of Christianity that affirmed life in this world as the place of salvation. Within their church communities, Christians sought to help life flourish in the face of imperial power, violence, and death. Though persecuted, they refused to surrender their identity as members of the church, and the empire executed them for it. In chapter 3, we explore the meaning of martyrdom in relation to paradise, as well as the emergence of apocalyptic ideas as resistance to Rome.

The church's fortunes changed significantly starting in the early fourth century under the Emperor Constantine. In chapter 4, we discuss the church's power struggle with Rome, as emperors attempted, with little success, to inflict uniformity of belief upon the culturally diverse and disputatious world of early churches. We find that struggle especially evident in the flourishing of ideas of the church as paradise in this world. In claiming the space of paradise, Christians staked out ground separate from the rule of Christian emperors and made their spaces superior to any place that marked imperial power. We also examine how, in this pivotal century, church teachers shifted gender ideas to favor more masculine models, established uniformity of belief as the basis of church, and created a deeply fractured relationship to Judaism. Christians understood that they failed often to live as they should. Their failures, however, were not a sign to them of paradise lost, but a sign of their failure to live ethically in it.

The subject of chapter 5 is the intense training that Christians received to prepare them to be initiated into paradise in this life. Through baptism, Christians learned to resist the forces of sin and evil and become wise about how good and evil work in the world, especially the oppressive powers of empires. In becoming ever wiser, Christians were expected to take responsibility for the power they received through the church, a power we call "ethical grace." Christians undertook spiritual disciplines together and looked to Jesus as the model of their own divinity and of their own agency in life. As savior, Jesus enabled their adoption into God's family of divinity. He embodied Spirit in human flesh, he transfigured the world, and he reopened the paradise garden on this earth, created by God as the home of humanity. In this examination of spiritual practices, we focus on the Jerusalem church in the second half of the fourth century as an example of what initiates to Christian baptism undertook in learning lifelong disciplines.

Spiritual disciplines were essential to being at home in the world as paradise. To experience the Spirit of God in all things and the beauties of this world, early Christians cultivated acute attunement to the life around them. We conclude Part I with a twofold discussion of the new humanity the church envisioned and the power of beauty as humanity's ethical basis. We examine how Christians struggled to stay grounded in love, in justice, in nonviolence, in wisdom, and in freedom, to live together as humanity in the garden of God. Church communities helped everyone to share resources, to cultivate wisdom and honesty, to understand ideas and doctrines, and to care for each other in sickness and need. They created systems of restitution, rehabilitation, and restoration that acknowledged human failure and expected all to take responsibility for their uses of power. These practices did not lead early Christians to idealize themselves or this world. They saw life as an arena of struggle to gain wisdom and to live ethically and responsibly toward others, so that love might flourish in their communities and so that they might live now in paradise together.

As the paradise of early Christianity entered our vision and seeped into our consciousness, crucifixion-centered Christianity seemed increasingly strange to us. We wondered what had happened to the understanding of this world as paradise. When and why did Christianity shift to an obsession with atoning death and redemption through violence? What led Western Christianity to replace resurrection and life with a crucifixion-centered salvation and to relegate paradise to a distant afterlife?

In Part II, we unravel the mystery of paradise expelled from this world in the Christian West, especially in the ninth to thirteenth centuries. Like detectives in search of a murder victim, we followed a trail of clues that led us, finally, to a body. We found the corpse of Jesus for the first time at a considerable distance from the Mediterranean world, in the forests of the far north of Europe, where the Rhine wends its way

from the Alps to the North Sea. Saxon artists carved the first Crucifixions—life-size three-dimensional wooden figures—in the tenth century. Their ninth-century ancestors were forced by Charlemagne's
soldiers to be baptized at the point of a sword, so that Latin Christianity came to them accompanied by death. The oldest crucifix to survive,
the Gero Cross, was created around 965 and is found in the Cathedral of St. Peter and Maria in Cologne, Germany. Chapter 9 tells this
tragic tale.

Chapter 10 describes the decisive turning point toward violence,
which arrived in 1095, when Pope Urban the II launched the First Crusade in an attempt to quell the feudal violence plaguing Europe. Urban
declared that war was not only just, it was holy—it was a pilgrimage that
served God and that enacted love for one's kin. Crusaders who killed
Jews and Muslims earned forgiveness for all their sins and were assured
of a place in paradise *after* death, not after baptism. This moral confu-
sion about violence postponed paradise and made it a reward for killing. Holy war became the route to paradise. In chapter 11, we examine
the theological innovations that supported the Crusades, especially
an explicit theology of atonement, which proposed that God became
human in Jesus in order to die on the cross and pay the penalty for
humanity's sins, a death pleasing to God. We show how the erotic joy
of paradise was transformed into a union of eros and torture, worship
of violence and victims, and self-inflicted harm.

In chapter 12, we expose the impoverishment of spiritual resources
and the tragedy of the Christian turn to a piety of Crucifixion during
the disasters that afflicted western Europe in the fourteenth century. As
a response to the reclosing of paradise and a piety of suffering, western
Europe devised various escape routes from this world. We describe a
number that emerged in the fifteenth and sixteenth centuries and led to
the transatlantic slave trade, the Protestant Reformation, and the conquest and colonization of North America.

Chapter 13 tells the story of the early history of New England first
from the perspective of the natives who lived there, then from the perspective of the Calvinist Europeans seeking to build paradise free of the
corrupting influences of Europe. Calvinist approaches to paradise re-

main important in both conservative and liberal expression of white American Christianity. In the wake of the worst war in the history of the last five hundred years in North America, King Philip's War of 1675–76, we describe the emergence of an "American" identity, developed through the Great Awakening and the myth of the extinct American Indian.

Finally, in chapter 14, we discuss the nineteenth- and twentieth-century reforming impulses of American Christianity that sought to reclaim the value of life in this world and salvation *on earth,* as it is in heaven. Some nineteenth-century thinkers returned humanity to an appreciation for nature and individual spiritual development. Among their acts of reclaiming the goodness of this world, Christians challenged the medieval atonement theology holding that Jesus's death saved the world. They also exposed the narrow, self-centered piety of personal sin and salvation and involved themselves in the struggle for the abolition of slavery and the fight for women's suffrage. They argued that socially organized sin was a far greater evil than personal sins; then they set to work to create justice for the poor, imprisoned, and oppressed. We examine the strengths and the limitations of these reform movements as partial ways to recover the sensibility that paradise is in this life and in this world.

This book is a work of love for this life, in all its tragedies and stunning beauty. As we pieced together the forgotten history of paradise, we discovered how life-affirming forms of Christianity succumbed to the focus on redemptive violence that marks the second millennium of the Christian West. Without such understanding, the Christian West will carry forward fatal errors as though they were damaged genetic codes: invisible, silent killers. We conclude with a meditation on what life in the twenty-first century will require of Christians. In reflecting on the meaning of paradise for our world now, we offer no final solution to the dilemmas of our times. Instead we suggest fresh ways of understanding our dilemmas so that new spiritual guideposts become clearer as we struggle for social change for the common good.

Christians have always sought to see their faith, history, future, and relationship to the world and to other faiths in ways relevant to their concrete historical lives. We recover here a life-giving, life-affirming Christianity, rooted in an ancient Mesopotamian past, that has survived despite many attempts to repress or destroy it and despite theological shifts that have betrayed it. We offer our study of this world as paradise as a way to retrieve a faith that affirms the many ways that people love one another, themselves, and the earth. Such faith remains deeply skeptical of the human will to power and the need to think of the saved as innocent and good. As inheritors of Western Christianity and citizens of a New World stolen from those who still live upon this land, we believe we must stand again at the open doors of paradise and bless this world as sacred soil, as holy ground, and as a home which all must learn to inhabit together.

We seek to rekindle Christian traditions that hold fast to love and thereby teach Christian people how, in the midst of horror and tragedy and loss, to resist violence, to honor the earth, and to humanize life. We offer an understanding of freedom and human agency that calls for responsible uses of power to create just relationships—the cultivation of ethical grace through a love of beauty. This activity of love, embodied in heart, soul, mind, and bodily strength, lies at the core of our work for justice, freedom, human rights, sustainable life, and peace. We invite you now to return home to paradise with us so that, together, we can save it.

PART ONE

FIGURE 1. *Cathedral of St. Giovanni in Laterano, Rome, Italy. Apse, mosaic. Fourth to thirteenth centuries. Baptism cross.*

CHAPTER ONE

In the Beginning...
Paradise on the Earth

In the day that the Lord God made the earth and the heavens, when no plant of the field was yet in the earth and no herb of the field had yet sprung up—for the Lord God had not caused it to rain upon the earth, and there was no one to till the ground; but a stream would rise from the earth, and water the whole face of the ground—then the Lord God formed an earth-creature [*adam*] from the dust of the ground [*adamah*], and breathed into his nostrils the breath of life and the earth-creature became a living being. And the Lord God planted a garden of delight [*gan-eden*], in the east, and there he put the earth-creature he had formed. Out of the ground the Lord God made every tree that is pleasant to the sight and good for food, the tree of life also in the midst of the garden of delight, and the tree of the knowledge of good and evil.

A river flows out of the place of delight [*eden*] to water the garden and from there it divides and becomes four branches. The name of the first is Pishon; it is the one that flows around the whole land of Havilah, where there is gold; and the gold of that land is good; bdellium and onyx stone are there. The name of the second river is Gihon; it is one that flows around the whole land of Cush. The name of the third river is Tigris, which flows east of Assyria. And the fourth river is the Euphrates.

The Lord God took the earth-creature and put him in the

garden of delight to till it and keep it. And the Lord God commanded the earth-creature. "You may freely eat of every tree of
the garden; but of the tree of the knowledge of good and evil
you shall not eat, for in the day that you eat of it you shall die."

GENESIS 2:4–17

The four rivers were the visual clue that told us we were in paradise.
In the apse mosaic of St. Giovanni in Rome, water poured from the
dove, flowed down behind the cross, and became the four streams that
fed the meadows of paradise. Seeing images such as this sent us to the
library to discover what early Christian sources said about paradise. We
knew that this image in St. Giovanni drew on the ancient Genesis text
to picture the world blessed by the Spirit, and we discovered that the
Genesis story drew on even older sources. Those ancient sources went
all the way back to one of the first written languages in West Asia,
Sumerian. Sumerian stories of paradise placed it on the earth and described how life was at its most fertile, just, enjoyable, and beautiful. In
this chapter, we explore the ancient wellsprings of the Bible's stories and
images of the garden of delight as they emerge in Genesis and elsewhere
in the Hebrew Bible.[1]

Just as in Genesis, however, Sumerian stories of paradise are accompanied by stories of what can go wrong: violence, competition,
greed, and environmental catastrophes. The Sumerian paradise, called
Dilmun, existed to the east somewhere nearby, as did Eden in Genesis.
Because it could not be clearly located, it could not be conquered or destroyed. Instead, it was always there so that humanity would remember
the ethical requirements of living in paradise and so that those requirements would hold accountable those who threatened it. Hence paradise
functioned not only to describe life on earth, but also to provide the ethical measure of life. In this long multicultural genealogy of paradise, we
trace various streams of its meanings. Most important, we show how stories of paradise place it on the earth and how they raise ethical implications about how humanity should live.

BETWEEN THE RIVERS

The genealogy of paradise begins in Mesopotamia (literally, "between the rivers"). The Tigris and the Euphrates originate within fifty miles of each other from the far western edge of the Himalayas in eastern Turkey. The two rivers diverge and wander a thousand miles southeast until they meet again in the Persian Gulf. This landscape generated a literature of paradise associated with mountains, rivers, and gardens, beginning with that of the Sumerians.

The Sumerians, a people of mysterious origins, migrated south from the mountains in Turkey in prehistoric times and settled in the hot, flat, fertile delta between the rivers. Around the fifth millennium BCE they began to master flood control and irrigation and built walled settlements. Their stories, first passed on in oral traditions, come to us as texts pressed on clay tablets that date to around 2100 BCE, near the end of their history. They recorded their myths in a phonetic script they invented, called *cuneiform* ("wedge-shaped"). One of the oldest written languages on earth, Sumerian became the scientific, sacred, ceremonial, and literary language for the Assyrians, Babylonians, Persians, and many other surrounding cultures for centuries, despite the fact that it was related to no other language in the region and that, to become fluent, one had to master its separate dialects for men and women.[2]

For subsequent cultures, Sumerian, the language and the culture, was the equivalent of Greek in Roman society or Latin in medieval Europe: the much admired classical language and culture of antiquity. Sumerians encouraged this view with stories of the glories of their rulers and gods. Their conquerors borrowed Sumer's stories in creating their own myths and used its script to write their very different languages just as, today, English is written with Latin script.[3] The Bible itself indicates the importance of Sumer; Abram and Sarai (renamed Abraham and Sarah) trace their lineage back to Ur, the last capital of Sumer, from which they migrated westward to Canaan (Gen. 11:26–13:12).[4]

It is easy to see the traces of Sumerian stories in Genesis. Long before Genesis 1:2 came to speak of God's Spirit hovering over the deep waters, the Sumerians began their stories of creation with Nammu, the goddess of the watery abyss or primordial sea and mother of all the gods. Out of her depths, she created the god An, heavens, and the goddess Ki, earth. *An-ki* meant universe or cosmos. A great cosmic mountain united An and Ki in one solid block. The base of the mountain Anki was in the bottom of the earth with the underworld of the dead and its top was in the heavens with the gods. This cosmic mountain held a three-tiered universe: the heavens of the gods, the earth of all living things, and the underworld of the dead. An and Ki had a son, Enlil, god of air, who separated the lapis lazuli dome of the heavens from the flat disk of the earth and created the world in the space between them. As we find later in Genesis, life on earth in Sumerian myths began with breath, wind, spirit—all translations of the Hebrew *ruah,* "a *wind* from God swept over the face of the waters" (Gen. 1:2). Enlil mated with his wife, Ninlil, goddess of air, to give birth to the celestial gods such as the moon and sun.[5]

Dilmun, the Sumerians' paradise, was without conflict, blessed with abundant fresh water, thick forests, and gardens. There Nammu's son Enki, god of sweet water, mated with her daughter Ninhursag, another name for Ki (earth), goddess of the sacred mountain, to create the deities of earth and healing.[6]

> *The land Dilmun is a pure place,*
> *The place, after Enki had laid himself by his wife.*
> *That place is clean, that place is bright.*
> *In Dilmun the raven uttered no cries,*
> *The lion killed not,*
> *The wolf snatched not the lamb,*
> *Unknown was the kid-killing dog,*
> *Unknown was the grain-devouring boar.*
> *The singer utters no wail,*
> *By the side of the city he utters no lament.*[7]

Also unknown were disease, hunger, war, death, and sorrow. The exact location of Dilmun was a bit mysterious. It was not Sumer itself, but was located just east of it on a sacred mountain. This combination of specificity of description and vagueness of location gave it both a sense of reality and of inaccessibility—a place true and real but belonging to no ruler, city, or civilization. Dilmun continued to be a synonym for paradise long after Sumer ceased to exist.[8]

The Sumerians built ziggurats to replicate their cosmic mountain, complete with paradise: they united An and Ki (heavens and earth) linking the gods, humanity, and paradise. Rising from the river delta, ziggurats were rectangular towers, stepped to look like a mountain, with trees and shrines at every level. At the peak, one or more temples were constructed with a main sanctuary and multiple side rooms with altars for making sacrifices. The temples were lavishly decorated, with vividly colored mosaics and frescoes showing the whole range of life-giving community activities, such as planting, harvesting, herding, and processions to the temples. Beautiful flowers, guardian animals such as leopards and bulls, and mythical beasts such as eagles with lion heads and bulls with human faces adorned porticoes and sanctuaries. These centers of ritual, towering above the deltas, grew to contain housing for the community's priests, artists, engineers, scribes, and other tradespeople.[9]

Sumer's stories and art celebrated the goodness of ordinary life in ways we can still understand, depicted as activities of paradise. Their myths tell of gods enjoying sexual pleasure, making music, dancing, traveling about and having adventures, and encouraging the fertility of the land. They also waged wars in defense of the land against its enemies and mourned the deaths of those they loved. Inanna, a goddess who lost her shepherd husband, Dumuzi, to the underworld, played the greatest role in Sumer's epics of all the gods and behaved like any powerful deity.[10] On many cylinder seals, she and other deities are shown riding in flat reed boats or striding up stepped mountains. All wear wide-brimmed hats with tall conical crowns—even Utu, the sun, wears a hat. Enki—the god who separated the sweet and salty waters—can be identified by the waves of water cascading from his hands or shoulders, which often contain fish.

A creative, resourceful, and practical people who figured out how to flourish on a hot, flat river delta, the Sumerians tell stories of gods who take pride in such inventions as the pickaxes they used to build canals that protected them from spring floods. Remains of their cities show they cultivated carefully planned gardens and created public architecture. Tablets found in temples give evidence that they held the resources essential to survival, what we might call public utilities—water, fields, orchards, flocks, and herds—as a community trust. Through their temple systems, which replicated the great cosmic mountain and its earthly paradise, they managed these resources by keeping written records of things held in trust and tracking how they were distributed.[11]

The Sumerians told their stories of creation and paradise as a preface to their stories of the many gods. The prefaces were a literary formula such as "once upon a time when..." or "in the beginning when God created..." These recitations established the way the world was at its best, as a contrast to the stories they told of disasters, conflicts, violence, and war. The Sumerians loved their rivers, but a rare deluge could deposit as much as fifteen feet of silt in one spring season, so they had a story about a great flood with only one human survivor, Ziusudra, who gained "life like a god...breath eternal." Ziusudra subsequently dwelt on a mountain in the land of Dilmun, the Sumerian paradise, somewhere east of the Tigris.[12] Later biblical traditions pictured Noah landing his ark on Mount Ararat—the highest peak in the mountains at the headwaters of the Tigris and the Euphrates.

The Sumerians pondered the problems that accompanied centralized city-states and the rise of empires. Their stories spoke of inequality in the distribution of resources and the exploitation of forced labor, and they even suggested some of the problems of male dominance over women. Humanity was created, they said, because the gods were tired of all the work involved in farming the fields and digging canals. At a drunken banquet of the gods, Enki and Ninhursag, using clay, created six flawed humans to do the work. Enki created one human so feeble that Ninhursag was the only one capable of feeding it. Ninhursag cursed Enki and indicted him as a remote god who did not understand life on the land. She accused him of abandoning her when her city was attacked, her temple was destroyed, her son the king was taken captive, and she was made a refugee. Instead of helping her, she said, he tried to dominate her. Though the full contents of this curse are not entirely clear, Enki seemed to accept it as his due.[13]

Early in the third millennium BCE, rulers rose up from the most powerful Sumerian city-states, centralized their control, and expanded their territories. Nippur became the center of the Sumerian temple system. Its patron deity, Enlil, the god of air, superceded older city-state deities, such as An, Ki, and Nammu, and his temple in Nippur collected tributes from them. Eventually, a king system existed alongside of or, in some cases, instead of priests to rule the city-states. Cylinder seals began to show kings approaching deities without being accompanied by priests, and the kings began to be seen as divine themselves.[14]

By the time Sumer's myths were recorded, the Sumerians had experienced the rise and fall of several kings, who had consolidated power by unifying some of the city-states into a monarchy and conquered territories as far east as Syria. The last empire fell within a century or two of the time of the recording of the myths. The stories reflect on the costs and dangers of empires and the talents and liabilities of various kings. Arguments among the patron gods symbolize wars among city-states. The Sumerian hymns extolled their ideal king as like the shepherd Dumuzi, consort of Inanna, and they may have been sung by way of contrast with the real thing. The ideal king filled the granaries, protected the city, and was distinguished-looking, intelligent, daring, eloquent, learned, astute, courageous, just, kind, and pious.[15]

In contrast to the centralized power associated with Sumer's actual empires and the glorification of its kings, the stories of Dilmun suggested that the deities of old held council meetings, and women and men held relatively equal power. The powers of the gods were limited to their spheres of influence, and they governed their spheres for the good and security of the whole. Dilmun's peace required the interactive functioning of all the powers, not the independent actions of heroic gods or one god lording it over all the others. The gods were capable of both good and evil, and the council managed the will to power of any one deity with humor, cajoling, negotiation, trickery, seduction, competition, scolding, and distraction. The council, when effective, maintained life at its best, and the stories of the gods of Dilmun contrast with life in the city-states. Dilmun depicts an image of Sumerian life as a confederacy of interdependent city-states or as a distant land no longer so easily accessed, even by the gods.

The Sumerians lived in Mesopotamia for several thousand years before a Semitic tongue began to supplant their language. During their later history, they saw a number of centralized kingdoms come and go, and powerful empires formed at their borders. The Babylonians conquered them for the last time around 2050 BCE, adapted their myths, and re-created their ziggurats. Babylonia transformed Sumer's myths into more aggressive tales of war, conquest, and male dominance. Nammu's creation of the heavens and earth became a deadly contest between the Babylonian dragon Tiamat, the sea, and her son Marduk, the warrior and chief hero of the gods who had been one of the minor sons of Enki in Sumer. Marduk slew Tiamat in fury. From this matricide, he took the two halves of his mother's body to create the heavens and the earth.[16]

Sumer became the lost primordial culture of West Asia. By the time Genesis was written, the Sumerians' myths had been adapted and edited through more than a millennium of history in Canaan, where the legendary immigrants from Sumer, Abram and Sarai, had migrated. The kingdom of Israel emerged in Canaan under Saul (1029–1000 BCE) and David (1000–961 BCE). The Davidic dynasty collapsed with the death of David's son Solomon (961–922 BCE). The one nation Israel, composed of twelve tribes, became two kingdoms in 921. The Assyrians conquered and annexed the northern nation of ten tribes, called Israel, in 722 (2 Kings 17:5–6). The Babylonian king Nebuchadnezzar defeated the southern kingdom of Judah in 586 BCE and kidnapped its leaders, initiating five decades of exile for Judah's people. The term "Jews" was later derived from its name.

The Persians and Jews had a long period of contact beginning with King Cyrus the Great (ca. 576–529 BCE), who conquered Babylonia in 539, ending its domination of Mesopotamia. Persia, today's Iran, was a blend of ancient peoples that Cyrus consolidated into a vast empire with territory from the Aegean and North Africa to India. He created the first empire of many languages and cultures ruled by one administration and one language, Persian, a modern form of which is now called Farsi and which remained a common language of the diverse peoples of India for many centuries. The word "paradise" comes into Persian through Median, *paridaeza*, *pari* (around), and *daeza* (wall), meaning a garden surrounded by a wall. Persian, an Indo-European language like Sanskrit and Greek, uses *paridaida* to refer to vineyards, orchards, forests, tree nurseries, and stables. Greek borrowed it as *paradeisos*, and Latin as *paradisos*. *Paridaeza* also appears as a loan word in the Semitic languages of Babylonian, as *pardēsu*, and Hebrew, as *pardès*.[17]

The Persian kings constructed huge *paridaida*, walled gardens with trees, streams, vegetation, and animals for hunting. One ancient tribute paid to kings by client countries were rare, exotic animals, which Persian kings kept in their paradises as something like private zoos. By hunting in their paradises, they practiced the arts of war.[18] Cyrus the Great was known for his vast *paridaida*. The Persians prized the trees in their *paridaida* and cultivated them carefully. Lysander, a Spartan guest of King Cyrus the Younger, described "the grandeur of the trees, the uniform distances at which they were planted, the straightness of the rows of the trees, the beautiful regularity of all the angles and the number and sweetness of the odours that accompanied them as they walked around." Persian paradises would become a model for grand gardens across their empire.[19]

Cyrus the Great was somewhat unusual for his time. Although he was a great military strategist who amassed a powerful army and waged brutal wars, he preferred to keep the loyalty of subjugated people by offering religious tolerance and rebuilding what his predecessors had destroyed. He freed the Jews from their captivity by the Babylonian Empire and assisted them in the rebuilding of Jerusalem (Ezra 1:2–11, 6:3–5). With such benevolence, he elicited cooperation and support from conquered peoples. The post-exilic prophet, third Isaiah (the book of Isaiah has three separate authors: the pre-exilic first Isaiah, second Isaiah of the exile, and the post-exilic third Isaiah), enthusiastically referred to Cyrus, a gentile, as God's Messiah, an anointed one, translated in Greek as Christ (Isa. 44:28–45:1–8). Sometimes he was more popular with peoples he conquered than their own rulers were.

Cyrus was likely a Zoroastrian, practicing a Persian religion founded by the prophet Zarathustra (Zoroaster in Greek), who lived around the beginning of the first millennium BCE. Scholars of the history of Zoroastrianism link its early roots to Hindu ideas, but it became more monotheistic. Zoroaster preached a form of monotheism with lesser spirits and demons. He also developed a postmortem dimension of paradise tied to a strong dualism of good and evil. Upon death, human beings would be judged for their deeds by Ahura Mazda, Lord Wisdom, and enter a heavenly paradise or fall into hell. The arrival of three saviors and a final battle to annihilate evil would bring the new perfect age and would defeat Angra Mainyu, evil spirit. Humans could save the world by defending Wisdom with reason and insight. The new age, purified by holy fire, would be similar to the one in the distant past that preceded the current age of evil. While Cyrus's religious ideas are harder to determine, his son Darius left inscriptions naming Ahura Mazda as creator of the universe.[20]

Today, it may be tempting to read this apocalyptic vision of paradise as kin to the hope that motivates suicide bombers or that leads Christian Zionists to pray for an intensification of war in Israel to hasten Armageddon. However, Zoroaster lived at a time when empires were relatively new in human history. Their wars of expansion had devastated human societies and the environment, and the idea of capricious gods or the hand of fate encouraged humans to see themselves as pawns of greater powers. They also often saw their kings as divinities. Zoroaster offered a vision of good and evil that affirmed human free will and called for human ethical responsibility. Only those who were ethical be-longed in paradise. The responsibility of humanity was not to serve the exploitive, capricious gods or fate, but to take the side of good and to be ethical. He challenged the ideas that those with extraordinary power had the right to decide right and wrong and that kings were divine. He said, instead, that the carnage and injustices of earthly empires would not go unnoticed or unpunished by a greater power that ruled from heaven. The self-defeating contradiction in this vision was the sugges-tion that a cosmic war would put an end to human wars. Violence can beget fear, stalemate, annihilation, dominance, or more violence, but it cannot beget love, justice, abundant life, community, or peace.

Zoroastrian apocalyptic ideas probably entered Jewish thinking in the post-exilic time of contact with Persia, since they do not appear in Jewish literature until after this time—for example, in the book of Daniel. The Hebrew Bible generally follows Sumerian traditions in imagining life after death as an underworld that is mysterious, cold, and dark. It depicts the cosmos as a three-tiered universe: heavens, earth with paradise, and the underworld, united by the cosmic sacred moun-tain. Zoroastrian apocalypticism assuredly influenced Christianity, which we discuss in chapter 3, but a divide of the afterlife into heaven and hell is absent from Christianity's visual world until the medieval period.

PARADISE IN THE HEBREW BIBLE

Genesis reflects the long history of Israelite and Jewish contact with Sumer and Persia. It pictures paradise with Sumer's geography of the Tigris and Euphrates rivers, and it echoes Sumer's stories. Like them, it tells the story of Creation first, beginning with the chaos of the wa-tery, deep abyss. God, or Elohim—who speaks in the plural—bears some resemblance to Enlil and Ninlil, the god and goddess of air. Like Enlil and Ninlil, God created with wind and made breathing space for earthly life between the heavens and the primordial waters.[21] The or-derly progression moved from cosmic to geologic to vegetative and animal forms and, finally, to humanity, male and female in the image of Elohim, a plural noun. The formulaic endings of divine delight after each day lend themselves to oral recitation. Alternate translations for "it was good" include it was delightful, it was blessed, and it was beautiful—Creation is all these things: joy, blessings, and beauty.

Though biblical scholars have shown how the account of Creation in Genesis 1 is separate from that in chapter 2, most interpretations have read them in relation to each other, just as stories of Dilmun can be read as a second stage of the story of the creation of the cosmic mountain. In Genesis 2, God—called Yahweh—shaped the muddy earth into a human creature. Yahweh breathed air into its nostrils to give it life. This story was often interpreted as an elaboration on Genesis 1:26–30:

> Then God [Elohim] said, "Let us make humankind [*adam*] in our image, according to our likeness; and let them have dominion over the fish of the sea, and over the birds of the air, and over the cattle, and over all the wild animals of the earth, and every creeping thing that creeps upon the earth."
> And God created humankind [*ha-adam*] in-his-image,
> in-the-image-of God created-he him;
> male-and-female [*zakar un ʿqeba*] created-he them.[22]
> God blessed them, and God said to them, "Be fruitful and multiply, and fill the earth and subdue it. . . . See, I have given you every plant yielding seed that is upon the face of all the earth, and every tree with seed in its fruit; you shall have them for food. . . ." God saw everything that he had made, and indeed, it was very good.

In Genesis 1, humanity, male and female, shared in the divine image. They were not the flawed grunt labor for the gods in the Sumerian stories—not slaves, but gods. Instead of being impaired by exploitation, humanity was empowered and given agency to act ethically. Jewish tradition has understood "be fruitful and multiply" as the first commandment given to humanity. As in the Sumerian stories, the productivity of agriculture and animal husbandry were greatly valued in the Genesis account. Modern technologies of mass destruction make the command-

ment to subdue the earth sound sinister, and the command for humanity to assume godlike responsibilities has been taken as license to abuse
the earth for the gratification of human consumption. But four thousand
years or more ago, creating a garden and cities of abundance, safety,
beauty, and peace were monumental achievements. In Genesis, humanity was instructed to be vegetarian, as were the animals, rather than
rapacious or predatory.

> God said, "See I have given you every plant yielding seed that is
> upon the face of all the earth, and every tree with seed in its fruit;
> you shall have them for food. And to every beast of the earth, and
> to every bird of the air, and to everything that creeps on the earth,
> everything that has the breath of life, I have given every green plant
> for food." And it was so. (Gen. 1:29–30)

Humanity, like God, was responsible for making life flourish, so that joy
and beauty might bless the world. Immediately upon finishing the
whole Creation, God rested and hallowed Sabbath rest as holy. As an
image of divine life, this conclusion, on the seventh day, suggests that
taking delight in Creation and stopping work regularly to restore the energies of life are also human values.[23]

In Genesis 2, we arrive in the beautiful garden of delight. Like
Dilmun, this garden is hard to locate, but it is on the earth. It has one
great river, which later tradition identified with the Jordan. Because
great rivers originate in mountains, early biblical commentators often
suggested a mountaintop as the location of the garden—perhaps the
legendary mountain on which Noah docked his ark, the seventeen
thousand-foot-high Mt. Ararat. This one river divides into four: two unknown rivers and two identifiable rivers, the Tigris and Euphrates,
the boundaries of Sumer. The jewels and precious metals found in the
lands of the Gihon and Pishon were just those elements that the river
delta of Sumer lacked but that the culture highly prized.

In Genesis, the tone of God's care for humanity contrasts with the
cavalier attitude of the Sumerian gods, who create indifferently as a
contest of power. Yahweh worried that the earth-creature, unique in the

garden, was lonely. "It is not good that the *adam* should be alone" (Gen. 2:18). God creates the animals to keep it company, but they are not adequate friends. The creature is therefore compelled to sleep and is separated into two parts, male and female, bone of bone, flesh of flesh, partners and friends. In human life in paradise, gender diversity provided the blessing of companionship—it was not a source of strife, and the dreams of sleep accessed divine touch and creativity.

Biblical scholar Phyllis Trible notes that in Genesis 2, God made a creature from clay. The Hebrew word, *adam* (earthling), is not a proper name for a male individual, but a generic noun that designates a being made of *ha-ᵃdama* (earth). As in Genesis 1, *adam* was a generic human being, encompassing male and female. Trible notes that this reading is necessary if the woman is to be held accountable for knowing God's warning to avoid eating of the tree of knowledge. If the earthling contained both male and female, she would have known the commandment. If the earthling was male, then God created the female only after God gave the commandment. Either *adam* meant all humanity, and therefore, the woman was accountable to the command, or *adam* meant male, and the female did not receive the command to avoid the tree of knowledge. The Christian tradition has repeatedly tried to make Eve responsible for humanity's sin while claiming Adam was made first and Eve was made later (a bit like wanting to eat your apple and have it, too).[24] When God explained to the earthling that not all the trees were safe to eat, the story suggested that Creation had boundaries that should not be crossed and that acquiring knowledge carried risks.

Like the Sumerian stories, the book of Genesis set the stage with "at the beginning of Creation," and then told of things going wrong. Humanity failed the requirements of life in paradise. Disasters followed. God exiled the woman and man from the garden. Childbirth became arduous. Men dominated women. Brothers murdered and deceived one another, wrangling over their inheritance and fighting over blessings. Fathers raped their daughters. Tribes invaded and colonized lands, killing or oppressing their inhabitants. Somewhere, paradise remained in the world, haunting every tale of folly, injustice, or greed.

PARADISE RENEWED

The actual Hebrew word *pardès* rarely occurs in the Bible. One place it is used is in the Song of Solomon (also called the Song of Songs), which was compiled from earlier sources, probably in the fourth century BCE. It uses *pardès* to capture the eros of a beautiful garden:

> *A garden locked is my sister, my bride,*
> *   a garden locked, a fountain sealed.*
> *Your channel is an orchard [*pardès*] of pomegranates*
> *   with all choicest fruits,*
> *henna with nard,*
> *   nard and saffron, calamus and cinnamon,*
> *with all trees of frankincense, myrrh and aloes,*
> *   with all chief spices—*
> *a garden fountain, a well of living water,*
> *   and flowing streams from Lebanon. (Song of Sol. 4:12–14)*

Phyllis Trible suggests that these references to a paradise garden harken back to Genesis and recapture the delight in the earth and human life in paradise. This celebration of love and joy provides the antidote to the banishment of Adam and Eve. This return to the garden nullified the curse of male dominance, hard work, and shame about vulnerability and sexuality.[25]

Passages from the Song of Songs commonly appeared in early Christian liturgies. Images of vines, fountains, and abundant fruits and flowers adorned churches. Prayers and songs repeated:

> *The flowers appear on the earth,*
> *   the time of singing has come,*
> *And the voice of the turtledove,*
> *   is heard in our land.*
> *The fig tree puts forth its figs,*
> *   and the vines are in blossom;*
> *they give forth fragrance. (Song of Sol. 2:12–13)*

Though the word *pardès* appears only in the Song of Songs and two other places, the Hebrew Bible refers frequently to pastures, gardens, vineyards, orchards, and holy mountains. These references became synonyms for paradise because of the spread of the Greek language. Alexander the Great conquered Persia in the late fourth century BCE, after which the Hebrew Bible was translated into the Greek, called the Septuagint. Wherever the Hebrew word for garden, *gan* or *gan-Eden,* appeared, the Septuagint substituted *paradeisos,* including in Genesis 2. This importation of the word "paradise" heightened its importance for both Jewish and Christian interpreters, since many used the Septuagint. The intermingling of Persian, North African, and West Asian cultures and ideas with Greek culture and language began in this period of Hellenization. In addition, texts written originally in Greek, found in the apocryphal literature from the third century BCE through the third century CE made much greater use of *paradeisos.* Discussion and speculation about paradise increased, as apocryphal texts such as I Enoch described journeys to paradise and heaven.

PARADISE IN CRISIS

Just as the Sumerians told stories of paradise to remind themselves of life at its best and in contrast to the devastations of empires, the prophets of Israel evoked images of paradise in times of crisis. Amos, the earliest written prophet, warned the northern kingdom of Israel in the middle of the eighth century BCE that its habits of violence and greed were unjust and unsustainable. He called upon the leaders of Israel to change their ways, prefacing his demand with an invocation to the God of Creation, "the one who made the Pleiades and Orion, and turns deep darkness into the morning . . . who calls for the waters of the sea, and pours them out on the surface of the earth" (Amos 5:8). God as Creator and judge against injustice formed the context for Amos's outcry against the exploitation of the poor by the wealthy. Repeatedly, in vivid images of horror, he cited the devastating consequences of injustice that would be visited upon cities, kings, and nature. "You trample on the poor and take from them levies of grain, you have built houses of hewn stone, but you shall not live in them, you have planted pleasant vineyards, but you shall not drink their wine" (Amos 5:11). He promised that the gifts of paradise could be restored to them if they would "establish justice" and "seek good and not evil."

> *Let justice roll down like waters*
> *And righteousness like an everflowing stream. (Amos 5:24)*

The book concludes with Edenic images of an abundant mountain and fruitful gardens, and a final promise: "I shall plant them on their own soil, they shall never again be uprooted from the soil I have given them."[26] The poetry of Amos captures something of the gestalt of paradise in upholding the struggle for justice, mercy, and peace by anchoring them in the life-giving waters of earth. This image of justice as the cascading streams that renew paradise was invoked by Martin Luther King Jr. in his famous speech "I Have a Dream" and memorialized in the Civil Rights Monument in Montgomery, Alabama, designed by Maya Lin. There water flows over a sheet of black granite. On its polished surface are carved the important moments of the Civil Rights Movement and the names of forty people who died in the struggle.[27]

The book of Isaiah contains many references to paradise. First Isaiah was written between 742 and 687 BCE, when the Assyrian Empire threatened Judah. It expressed hope by describing a world where animals lived in harmony, as they did with Adam and Eve in Eden. Echoing descriptions of Dilmun, Isaiah pictured peace: "The wolf shall dwell with the lamb, the leopard shall lie down with the kid. . . . They will not hurt or destroy on all my holy mountain; for earth will be full of the knowledge of the Lord as the waters cover the sea" (Isa. 11:6, 9). During the Exile, after King Nebuchadnezzar took Jerusalem in 586 and deported its leaders to Babylonia, second Isaiah used images of paradise to promise divine deliverance:

> *For the Lord will comfort Zion;*
> *he will comfort all her waste places,*
> *and will make her wilderness like Eden,*
> *her desert like the garden of the Lord. (Isa. 51:3)*

The Exile haunted the prophets. If God was mightier than all kings and foreign gods, were the devastation of the land, the slaughter of the people, and the kidnapping of their leaders recompense for Israel's sin? Did God indiscriminately use an empire more evil than God's own to punish Israel by harming even the poor and innocent? Why keep covenant with such a God as this? Or were other gods more powerful? Different Judean factions had their own answers. Some exiles, sent to Egypt, believed the hard, exclusivist monotheism of King Josiah caused Judah to fall (Jer. 44:15-19). Isaiah, writing on the eve of the Exile's end, said the time of anguish was over. He chose not to lay blame and rejected devastation as divine punishment. He said that the people's suffering far surpassed any sin they might have committed.

> *Have you not known? Have you not heard?*
> *The Lord is the everlasting God,*
> *the Creator of the ends of the earth.*
> *He does not faint or grow weary;*
> *his understanding is unsearchable.*
> *He gives power to the faint,*
> *and strengthens the powerless .*
> *Those who wait for the Lord shall renew their strength,*
> *they shall mount up with wings like eagles,*
> *they shall run and not be weary,*
> *they shall walk and not faint.*
> *Do not fear, for I am with you*
> *I will strengthen you, I will help you*
> *I will uphold you with my victorious right hand.*
> *(Isa. 40:28-41:13, excerpts)*

Though Isaiah asserted a form of monotheism, it was grounded in justice, rather than in favoritism or nationalism. God cared for the suffering and oppressed, and faithful people who were committed to the welfare of all would restore and sustain paradise.

> *Loose the bonds of injustice,*
> *Undo the thongs of the yoke,*

Let the oppressed go free,
bring the homeless poor into your house,
offer your food to the hungry,
and satisfy the needs of the afflicted,
then your light shall rise in the dawn,
you shall be like a watered garden,
like a spring whose waters never fail. (Isa. 58:6—11, excerpts)

Luke 4:18–21 later used Isaiah's vision of paradise to define the mission of Jesus:

The spirit of the Lord God is upon me,
because the Lord has anointed me;
he has sent me to bring good news to the oppressed,
to bind up the brokenhearted,
They will be called oaks of righteousness,
the planting of the Lord, to display his glory.
For as the earth brings forth its shoots,
and as a garden causes what is sown in it to spring up,
so the Lord God will cause righteousness and praise
to spring up before all the nations. (Isa. 61:1, 11)

These prophetic texts are not, however, unambiguous. While they proclaimed peace, they often imagined God as a warrior who would defeat the foes of Israel and slaughter the unrighteous. They sometimes hoped for the restoration of their monarchy, built on justice. Then, all nations would pay tribute to their nation. Such sentiments about restoration lent themselves to a nostalgic view of the conquest and colonization of Canaan and the establishment of Israel. That kingdom had established itself like other empires, was no more virtuous than those empires, and ended in civil war. Nostalgia about the fallen kingdom carried the dangers of an arrogant and naïve sense of national exceptionalism, the idea that one group of people or one nation was special to God. In addition, the prophets depicted religious apostasy as harlotry and adultery, using images of marriage between a dominant male God and a subordinate people. This metaphor of female sexuality inscribed misogyny and gender inequality in holy terms. Biblical scholar Renita Weems reveals how this metaphor of love, sex, and marriage sanctioned domestic violence by depicting God as an angry, abusive husband.[28] In contrast to prophets who often pictured God as a dominant male requiring obedience and using violence to punish, the Genesis paradise story presented these characteristics as a curse that accompanied the loss of paradise. The Song of Songs proclaimed that the end of such dominance brought the return of joy, delights, and unshakeable love as strong as death.

Readers of the Bible must carefully weigh the prophetic texts against each other, not as infallible commands but as a range of human responses to crisis. Listening to the Bible requires testing various texts in light of moral questions that the Bible itself raises about its own traditions. The Bible described no form of governance or divine favor that absolved human beings from responsibility for the right use of power. I Samuel 8 warned against the establishment of a kingdom. Isaiah said all rulers must answer to the ethics of justice—neither kings nor nations possessed divine rights; they were accountable to the standards of righteousness that were the will of God. God did not will disasters, but justice; the horrors visited upon the land and its people were the consequences of injustice and misused power. The gift of freedom required moral responsibility. Only ethical uses of power, not domination, coercion, and war, could sustain and renew paradise.

Ezekiel, the sixth-century BCE prophet, wrote in Babylon during the Exile and reflected on the conflicts among the empires that dominated his time. His highly symbolic book begins with the fall of Jerusalem to the Babylonians in 586 BCE and ends with a plan for the rebuilding of the Jerusalem temple. The first chapter opens with a theophany, an appearance of God. In this theophany, Ezekiel, among his fellow exiles along a river, looks up to see a thunderstorm. Four living creatures emerge from the clouds and lightning, each with human form but four faces: a human, lion, ox, and eagle. Each has four wings, and hooves that shine as though bronzed. Wheels spin beside them in the midst of a rainbow. This vision likely reflected the impressive stone carvings of totem animals that decorated Babylonian palaces.[29] Elements of Ezekiel's theophany—the rainbow, clouds, and four creatures —appear in early Christian art to show the presence of God. The elements often hover in a golden sky, just above the risen Christ and the meadows of paradise to indicate divine blessing on the world. Instead of four faces, the four winged creatures in the art came to have one face each: human, lion, ox, and eagle. These creatures eventually became the symbols of the four Gospel writers, with each holding a book.[30]

In chapter 28, describing the fall of the king of Tyre to Babylon in 606 BCE, Ezekiel alluded to Eden to explain the rise and fall of his kingdom:

You were the signet of perfection, full of wisdom, and perfect in beauty. You were in Eden, the garden of God. . . . You were on the holy mountain of God . . . until iniquity was found in you. . . . You were filled with violence . . . so I cast you as a profane thing from the mountain of God. . . . I turned you to ashes on the earth. (Ezek. 28:12–16)

Similarly, Ezekiel likened the growth of the great empire of Egypt to a flowering tree in Eden that was nourished by abundant water. The tree became too proud and God razed it (Ezek. 31). Ezekiel contrasted the blessed garden of God with the political ambitions, environmental devastations, and carnage of kings, and he promised a renewal of paradise for the nation that repents:

On the day that I cleanse you from all your iniquities, I will cause the towns to be inhabited, and the waste places shall be rebuilt. . . . And they will say, "This land that was desolate has become like the garden of Eden; and the waste and desolate and ruined towns are now inhabited and fortified." (Ezek. 36:33–35)

In his oracles of comfort and hope to the exiles, Ezekiel pictured the restoration of paradise as abundant pasturelands tended by a shepherd.

In chapter 34, he described the traits of a good shepherd that would inform early Christian images of Jesus and, later, models of leadership in the church. Ezekiel said the shepherd sought out missing sheep and rescued them from danger. He fed them on mountains and led them to good water and grazing land. He cared for the sick and injured and gave strength to the weak. Then, the prophet linked the work of the shepherd to God's care for the people. He said the good shepherd fed people with justice, made a covenant of peace, helped them flourish, and protected them. "I will send down the showers in their season; they shall be showers of blessing. The trees of the field shall yield their fruit, and the earth shall yield its increase. They shall be secure on their soil... when I break the bars of their yoke, and save them from the hand of those who enslaved them" (Ezek. 34:25-27).

Near the end of the book, Ezekiel detailed his vision of the rebuilt temple on Mt. Zion (Ezek. 40-47). He described being transported to the eastern gate, the direction of paradise: "The glory of the God of Israel was coming from the east; the sound was like the sound of mighty waters, and the earth shone with his glory" (43:2). A great river welled up from below the threshold of the temple, flowing east and south. "And where the river goes every living creature which swarms will live, and there will be very many fish... everything will live where the river goes. People will stand fishing... on the banks of both sides of the river, there will grow all kinds of trees... their fruit will be for food and their leaves for healing" (Ezek. 47:9-12).[31] Ezekiel said Jerusalem must be called "The Lord is there" (48:35). For Ezekiel, the temple on the mountain renewed paradise. It was an earthly place where God drew near to human beings, and from which waters of life cascaded down to bring life to all the earth. It was not a place created after the apocalyptic destruction of this world, but it could be threatened by war and imperial domination.[32] From his dwelling place in the temple, God announced, "Enough, O princes of Israel. Put away violence and oppression, and do what is just and right" (Ezek. 45:9).

Some exiles, liberated by the Persian king Cyrus the Great, returned to Jerusalem and eventually built the second temple in Jerusalem under his son King Darius. They completed it in 516 BCE. The books of Ezra and Nehemiah describe the controversies with local inhabitants and difficulties that accompanied this time of restoration, as well as the modest proportions of this new temple. Some leaders began to identify the second temple and Mt. Zion as the actual location of paradise.[33] The determination of a precise spot for paradise, however, risked narrowing it to the territory of one kingdom, to the exclusion of all others. This specificity made paradise more vulnerable to cooptation by imperial dynasties and corrupt priests. Other books such as Leviticus, Proverbs, Ecclesiastes, I Enoch, and Jubilees, maintained the mysterious location of paradise, suggesting that it suffused the entire land of Israel or even the whole Creation.[34]

One of the mysteries of Dilmun and Eden was their precise location. Whether in the direction of the rising sun or between four great rivers, paradise confused any attempts to pin it on a map. It eluded the control, captivity, or ownership of any one nation, people, religion, or time. In direct contrast to the wars, economic exploitation, fratricidal divisions, and environmental devastations of empires, it offered experiences and visions of justice, of the goodness of ordinary life, and of a vibrant peace. Paradise was described in terms recognizable as earthly life at its best. In these descriptions, it could be experienced as real—not as a permanent state of being but as aspects of life itself. It flourished where people took responsibility for the well-being of all and respected and protected the great cycles of life that sustain human life.

Many of the Psalms date from the second temple period. They praise God's creativity, justice, and healing, using images of paradise.[35] They begin with a hymn to the virtuous and wise, who are rooted in God "like trees planted by streams of water" (Ps. 1:3). Green pastures and still waters are the abode of those tended by the divine shepherd in Psalm 23, who face their enemies and death with equanimity. Psalm 48:1 says, "[God's] holy mountain, beautiful in elevation, is the joy of all the earth." Psalm 104, a version of the Creation story, sings with joy for God's creative power and greatness, "From your lofty abode you water the mountains; the earth is satisfied with the fruit of your work" (Ps.

104:13). In Psalm 36, the unjust flatter themselves and plot mischief, but those who seek shelter under God's wings of love and righteousness receive blessing:

> *They feast on the abundance of your house,*
> *and you give them drink from the river of your delights.*
> *For with you is the fountain of life;*
> *in your light we see light. (Ps. 36:8–9)*

The Psalms affirm that the gifts of paradise are tangible in this life. "O taste and see that the Lord is good" (Ps. 34:8). They speak of respite from weariness, pleasure in companionship, freedom from oppression, comfort in sorrow, delight in beauty, satisfaction of hunger, and protection from danger. Though these precious aspects of life can be lost or compromised, they are real dimensions of human experience on the earth, not imaginary ideals. This is what it means to say that paradise is in this world: the actual tastes, sights, fragrances, and textures of paradise touch our lives. They call us to resist the principalities and powers that deny the goodness of ordinary life, threaten to destroy it, or seek to secure its blessings for a few at the expense of many.

The descendants of the exiles who rebuilt the temple in Jerusalem did not enjoy a long peace. The Persian Empire gave them breathing space for a time, until the Greeks conquered the region and brought them once again under oppressive imperial domination. Then in c. 63 BCE, the Romans occupied Galilee and Judea. They maintained a line of client Jewish kings who heavily taxed the people for Rome and for their own gain. Herod (c. 74–4 BCE) was notoriously profligate and violent. He massively expanded the Jerusalem temple as a monument to his dynasty and put a Roman eagle over the main entrance. Many Jewish resistance movements protested Herodian and Roman abuses— often with nonviolent acts and sometimes in armed revolt. The Romans suppressed opposition by crucifying dissident leaders and burning towns to the ground. Jewish opposition intensified until the Romans destroyed the second temple in 70 CE. They finally leveled Jerusalem in

139, rebuilt it as a pagan city, and renamed the region Palestine in honor of Israel's enemies, the Philistines. A hundred years later, the Roman governor of Palestine did not even know the name Jerusalem.

In Galilee, the legacy of paradise would feed a movement of resistance, led by a rabbi named Jesus of Nazareth. Like a tree planted by the water, his movement took root, moistened by the waters of paradise and shaded by its trees and vines. In the long genealogy of paradise and its call to humanity to live justly and ethically, Jesus was yet another branch of this great, sheltering tree.

CHAPTER TWO

In the Beginning . . .
God So Generously Loved

Truly I tell you, today,
you will be with me in Paradise.

LUKE 23:43

The Bible opens with Creation and with the Garden of Delight in Genesis 1–2 and closes with the last words of Revelation 22, "Let everyone who is thirsty, come. Let anyone who wishes take the water of life as a gift." In this chapter, we explore how the gospels use paradise themes to depict Jesus, his mission, and his community, and we reveal how paradise grounds the struggle to live wisely and justly in a world of complex and conflicting powers. The paradise themes in the gospels come into focus when we read the miracle stories, the Gospel of John, and the Passion and Resurrection narratives through the lens of Genesis 1–2. Such a reading illuminates deeper meanings of the texts. We show how the stories and teachings of Jesus use paradise to present his work as resistance to and critique of the Roman Empire.[1]

The Gospels echo prophetic uses of paradise and justice. In Luke, for example, Jesus announces his mission in the world by reading a paradise text from the book of Isaiah.

The Spirit of the Lord is upon me,
because he has anointed me to bring good news to the poor.

He has sent me to proclaim release to the captives
and recovery of sight to the blind,
to let the oppressed go free,
to proclaim the year of the Lord's favor.
(Luke 4:18-19 and Isa. 61:1-2)

The Isaiah passage concludes with an image of the earth flourishing as a renewed garden. With the arrival of the year of the Lord's favor—a jubilee year of justice—God will cause "what is sown in [the garden] to spring up ... righteousness and praise to spring up before all the nations" (Isa. 61:11). Isaiah wrote his words to exiles suffering under the Babylonian Empire; in Luke, Jesus reads these words to the poor of Galilee who were struggling with a new empire. "Today," Jesus announces to them, "this scripture has been fulfilled in your hearing" (Luke 4:21). In echoing the vision of Isaiah, Jesus says the Spirit of God in the world assures a flowering of righteousness, a concept we call "ethical grace." By using the terms "ethical" and "grace" together, we want to suggest that the idea of paradise carries both the grace of the core goodness of life on earth, and humanity's responsibility for sustaining it.

Jesus shows ethical grace in action: love and generosity in community, care for all who have need, healing of the sick, appreciation for life, confrontation with powers of injustice and exploitation, and advocacy for freedom of the imprisoned. The New Testament presents him as the model or forerunner of a restored human community that saw its mission as sustaining ethical grace. In John's Gospel he says, "I came that they may have life, and have it abundantly" (10:10), and he speaks frequently of the promise of "eternal life" to his disciples. The Gospel defines three dimensions of this eternal life: knowing God; receiving the one sent by God to proclaim abundant life to all; and loving each other as he had loved them. Eternal life, in all three meanings, relates to how life is lived on earth. The concrete acts of care Jesus has shown his disciples are the key to eternal life. By following his example of love, the disciples enter eternal life now. Eternal life is thus much more than a hope for postmortem life: it is earthly existence grounded in ethical grace.

The most oft-told story in the Christian scriptures is the miracle of loaves and fish, and this ordinary act of feeding the hungry is a consummate example of ethical grace. It appears no fewer than six times in the Gospels.[2] In Mark's first version, Jesus and his disciples sailed to a deserted place, but a crowd followed them on foot from the nearby towns, arriving there first. Setting foot on shore before the vast crowd, Jesus felt compassion for them because "they were like sheep without a shepherd." He taught them until it grew late. His disciples urged him to tell the crowd to disperse and find food. Jesus, however, urged his disciples to feed them. They protested the expense and work involved. He told them to survey the crowd to see what food was available, which came to five loaves of bread and two fish.

> Then he ordered them to get all the people to sit down in groups on the green grass. So they sat down in groups of hundreds and of fifties. Taking the five loaves and the two fish, he looked up to heaven, and blessed and broke the loaves, and gave them to his disciples to set before the people; and he divided the two fish among them all. And all ate and were filled; and they took up twelve baskets full of broken pieces and of the fish. Those who had eaten the loaves numbered five thousand men. (Mark 6:32–44)

When Jesus prayed to heaven to bless the food, he paid tribute to the divine source of the food he offered, and he symbolically stood against the Roman Empire. The Roman emperors maintained their power by distributing bread to the poor. Jesus's feeding of the multitude suggested that he—not Rome—was the true source of life.

In the Christian catacombs in Rome, images of the loaves and fish are frequent motifs. Large baskets of bread and platters of fish are set around a table with seven people enjoying the food. One delightful image in the Priscilla catacombs shows a table of women. In another, an inscription says the women call, "Bring it warm!" The early church framed its most important ritual meal as this act of feeding. They called it the Eucharist, the Great Thanksgiving, the meal that celebrated the bread of earth, blessed by heaven, and shared in community.[3] Biblical scholar John Dominic Crossan notes the significance of this practice: *"It is in food and drink offered equally to everyone that the presence of God and Jesus is found.* But food and drink are the material bases of life, so the Lord's Supper is political criticism and economic challenge as well as sacred rite and liturgical worship."[4]

BREAD OF HEAVEN COME DOWN

In the time of Jesus, the Roman Empire used *oikoumenē,* Greek for "household," as shorthand for its self-aggrandizing claim that it controlled the world, *orbis terrarum* in Latin. Images of Roman officials depicted them holding orbs in their hands or, as in the case of Julius Caesar, treading on a globe. *Oikoumenē* is related to the words "economics," "ecumenical," and *oikos* (people). The usual translation of *oikoumenē* in the gospels is "this world." *Gē* (earth) was different. God created *gē,* but Rome controlled *oikoumenē.*[5]

The Gospels refer to the *basileia* (realm) of God as not of "this world." In saying this, they place Jesus and his movement in direct conflict with Rome's claims of power. When Jesus spoke of heaven, he referred to the world of God, not the world of Rome. The heavens were the dwelling place of God and all the heavenly hosts, such as the council of gods and the angels. Heavenly beings descended to earth to help humanity. The use of the plural, heavens, conveyed the magnitude and inclusiveness of the heavens. The surface of the dome of the heavens was the great vault of sky and clouds, above which the heavenly hosts dwelled, and its vastness encompassed everything on the earth.[6] When Christians developed their iconography of paradise in the fourth to sixth centuries, they pictured the heavens as a night sky filled with stars, or a golden dawn sky with clouds of pink, blue, and white. Sometimes angels appeared, but God was shown, if at all, only as a hand reaching down from the clouds.[7]

The sky is the most mysterious part of the cosmos, and it is the most regular and reliable in its patterns. The sun, moon, and stars make their rhythmic courses, marking the pace of planting and harvesting and generating the flow of time within the space of the great cosmos. The heavens bring sweet water to earth in the rain and fill the mountain storehouses of snow that feed the great rivers. Thus the heavens were, for the ancients, the wellspring of spiritual power. They were not something out of this world, but were the locus of life-giving power within this world, a realm of constancy from which humanity received many blessings. Their spiritual messengers visited those who awaited them in dreams and visions, and their earthly emissaries brought illumination and life.

In Matthew 2, the heavens shine on the earth with special favor in the star of Bethlehem. The magi, from Persia, the direction of paradise, follow the star to find the heavenly visitation revealed beneath its glow. Rome had outlawed the magic and astrology of its nemesis Persia, the unconquerable empire in the east. That the Gospel of Matthew brought these magi to the cradle of Jesus was no accident, for they were the observers of the heavens, and they demonstrated that Rome did not govern heavenly portents. No matter how vast or potent, the empire was impotent wherever the Spirit of God was active in this world.[8]

In the bread of heaven, God blessed ordinary food for ordinary people. The multitudes who came to Jesus from the countryside and towns of the area around the Sea of Galilee would have been peasants. As a number of biblical scholars have noted, peasants were forced to bear the burdens of a tax system that maintained the sumptuous lifestyles of the rulers and their military powers.[9] During the time of Jesus, ordinary people were driven into destitution and homelessness by King Herod's extravagant building projects, including an ambitious rebuilding of the second temple. To stave off riots and resistance, Roman officials distributed wheat imported from Egypt, North Africa, and Asia throughout the empire. Shipments from the fertile Nile delta were so crucial to Rome that protection of them from piracy was a major function of its navy—the Mediterranean was commonly referred to as the "Roman Lake."

In the miracle of the bread and fish, large crowds flock to Jesus, hungry in spirit and body, and they depart filled. His act of feeding offered compassion for the needy, encouraged generosity for the good of all, even among those with little, and affirmed life abundant for everyone, regardless of status or need. This value system undermined the paternalism of Rome, which was built on an elite and powerful few having so much that they might scatter their largess, distributing 20 percent of their grain as a dole to the vast masses. The poor and powerless were expected to be grateful to the empire for acts of charity that maintained its domination.[10] Jesus, on the other hand, belonged to the peasant class and working poor, and his relentless judgments against the rich and powerful revealed how injustice betrayed God's desire for all to have abundant life. He challenged this paternalistic system by offering food blessed by heaven and not by Rome.

> When the people saw the sign he had done, they began to say. "This is indeed the prophet who is to come into the world." Jesus answered them, "Very truly, I tell you, it was not Moses who gave you the bread from heaven, but it is my Father who gives you the true bread from heaven. For the bread of God is that which comes down from heaven and gives life to the world.... I am the bread of life. Whoever comes to me will never be hungry, and whoever believes in me will never be thirsty... for I have come down from heaven, not to do my will, but the will of him who sent me." (John 6:14, 26–38)

The modern world has a tendency to divide the sacred and the secular and to disconnect the spiritual from the physical. This makes it easy to neglect the relationship between material life and spiritual power. We can fall into the habit of thinking that people who must worry about material things are less noble than those who meditate on intangible ideas and inner spiritual truth. The nineteenth-century transcendentalist Ralph Waldo Emerson, for example, extolled the virtues of his own "self-reliance" as an enlightened soul who needed only God, not other people. He forgot to mention that he depended daily upon his wife, his mother, three servants, and a gardener. And our complex modern economies result, often, in a lack of connection with the material sources of life. Many of us have no relationship to the plants we eat, how they were grown and what is sprayed on them, or to the people whose back-breaking, toxic, poorly paid labors allow us to load our groaning tables. Lacking ethical awareness about how even basic acts of sustenance, much less excess consumption, affect others, we continue to live oblivious to how material life must be part of spiritual and ethical awareness. We live in self-deception and perpetuate harm we do not intend. The Bible is often interpreted through such modern separations of the spiritual and material. But as the feeding of the multitude illustrates, the Bible understands heaven as infusing the practical and ordinary rather than being separated from it.

In offering "that which comes down from heaven and gives life to the world," Jesus, like the Hebrew prophets, connected paradise—abundant life—to the practical needs of human beings, who require a sustainable and sustaining life free from economic exploitation and political oppression. The spiritual and material are inseparable, as are grace and ethics. Those who feast on the bread of heaven must pray that "Give us this day our daily bread" is answered for all, and they must work to make such bread real. This is why, at the end of John's Gospel, Jesus addresses Peter, a leader among the disciples, by saying, repeatedly, "If you love me, feed my sheep."

IN THE BEGINNING, WISDOM'S WORD

The Gospel of John introduces a revised version of "in the beginning" that linked Creation and paradise to Jesus Christ and influenced early Christian ideas about him.

> In the beginning was the Word, and the Word was with God, and the Word was God. He was in the beginning with God. All things came into being through him, and without him not one thing came into being. What has come into being in him was life, and the life was the light of all people. (John 1:1–4)

In first-century understandings, the *logos* (Word) was a divine being who coexisted with God and who created all things in the *kosmos* (world). Many branches of the Israelite tree shared the concept of the divine Logos.[11] It emerged from the Hellenization process—the mingling of Greek ideas with Hebrew and Persian cultures in West Asia and North Africa. Philo of Alexandria (20 BCE–50 CE), a Jew who used Platonic philosophy to interpret the books of Moses, associated God's acts of Creation with Logos.[12]

In the Septuagint, the Hebrew feminine noun *Hokmah* (Wisdom) in Proverbs became *Sophia* (Wisdom), which was linked to Word, as the principle of Creation. John retells the Creation story found in Proverbs 8 and fleshes out the connection between Logos and Sophia as synonyms for creativity.[13]

> *Ages ago I [Wisdom] was set up,*
> *at the first, before the beginning of the earth.*
> *When there were no depths I was brought forth,*
> *when there were no springs abounding with water.*
> *Before the mountains had been shaped,*
> *before the hills, I was brought forth—*
> *when he had not yet made earth,*
> *when he marked out the foundations of the earth,*
> *then I was beside him, like a master worker;*
> *and I was daily his delight,*
> *rejoicing before him always,*
> *rejoicing in his inhabited world*
> *and delighting in the human race.*
> *Wisdom has built her house,*
> *she has also set her table.*
> *To those without sense she says,*
> *"Come, eat of my bread*
> *and drink of the wine I have mixed.*
> *Lay aside immaturity, and live,*
> *and walk in the way of insight." (Prov. 8:23–9:6, excerpts)*

The early church shared the Jewish identification of Word with Wisdom and named many churches Hagia Sophia, Holy Wisdom. Christian personifications of Wisdom resembled figures such as Inanna of Sumer, Isis of Egypt, and Ishtar of Canaan.[14] Wisdom wandered the streets offering the joy and delight of the paradise garden, "Her paths are peace. She is a tree of life to those who lay hold of her" (Prov. 3:17–18). The fruits of her labors were bread and wine, both of which required human care and attention to mature. Though available to all, Wisdom could not give power to those too gullible and naïve to receive her. Those who understood Wisdom's power could enlist her help and explain how she works; they knew her name, could claim her attention, and draw others into her world.[15]

Wisdom's fate in the world was not, however, secured. She was often ignored, as was Logos.[16] John explains, "He was in the world, and the world came into being through him; yet the world did not know him. He came to what was his own, and his own people did not accept him." The world could ignore, disregard, or even oppose the life-giving ways of Logos. But John's Creation story asserted the persistence of Logos, despite the world's inhospitality: "The light shines in the darkness, and the darkness has not overcome it." All who received Logos were given power "to become children of God" (John 1:5, 12).

The prologue of John culminates with the creation of a human being who bore the image of God in the flesh:

> And the Word became flesh and lived among us, and we have seen his glory, the glory as of a father's only son, full of grace and truth.... From his fullness we have all received, grace upon grace. The law indeed was given through Moses; grace and truth came through Jesus Christ. No one has ever seen God. It is God the only Son, who is close to the Father's heart, who has made him known.

For John, Jesus marked the descent of Sophia/Logos again into the world. Scholar Daniel Boyarin comments that Wisdom did not abandon earth for the heavens. Instead, God, in an extraordinary act, incarnated Logos in flesh and blood, "coming into the world as an avatar and teacher of the Word." Boyarin notes, "When the incarnate Logos speaks, he speaks Torah."[17]

Throughout, the Gospel of John employs dynamic images of descent and ascent, echoing Moses's ascent and descent of sacred mountains, and Jacob's dream of a ladder of angels descending and ascending from heaven and earth.[18] Jesus calls his first disciples by saying, "You will see heaven opened and the angels of God ascending and descending upon the Son of Man" (John 1:51). As in other sacred mountain stories, the Spirit descends from the heavens to bring blessings, help, and guidance to humanity. Without those who bring the Spirit of God into the world, in the flesh, humanity will be bereft of the power of life, the breath of divine Spirit that makes creation possible. At the Jordan River, Jesus approaches John the Baptist, and John testifies:

> I saw the Spirit descending from heaven like a dove, and it remained on him. I myself did not know him, but the one who sent me to baptize with water said to me, "He on whom you see the Spirit descend and remain is the one who baptizes with the Holy Spirit." And I myself have seen and have testified that this is the Son of God. (John 1:32–34)

Early church teachers, drawing on John, spoke of the incarnation as the re-creation of humanity in the image of God—a renewal of Wisdom's presence in the world and the reopening of paradise. They said Christ, as the glory of the Word made flesh, restored to humanity its original glory in Eden. The Greek word for "glory," *doxa,* connotes luminous beauty, or shining presence, similar to the Hebrew word *shekinah,* the shining face of God. Some interpreters taught that Adam and Eve had originally been cloaked in garments or skins of light that they had lost when they were sent out of the Garden. With the incarnation, Jesus regained the garments of light, becoming a luminous sign of divine presence. He opened the way for the restoration of humanity's divine powers.[19] Baptism "in the name of Jesus" placed humanity in paradise on earth and bestowed on his disciples the power of Logos/Sophia. Paul wrote to the Colossians church, "He is the image of the invisible

God, the firstborn of all creation.... [You] have clothed yourselves with the new self, which is being renewed in knowledge according to the image of its creator" (Col. 1:15; 3:9–10).

John's Gospel, like Genesis 1, suggested that God creates in the company of other powers. In Genesis 1:26, God said, "Let *us* make humanity in *our* image," and a number of biblical books refer to a council of gods. For example, "God stands in the divine council: in the midst of the gods he passes judgment" (Ps. 82:1).[20] Why, we might wonder, did monotheistic religions such as Zoroastrianism, Judaism, or Christianity have so many spirits or divine beings, such as the Logos and Sophia? Although our modern perspective regards monotheism as belief in a single, monopolizing, omnipotent divine being, the fundamental question in the ancient world was not whether one all-powerful God controlled the universe. The question was how to negotiate a world of many powers and access the right ones. The will of God guided the powers and human wills; it did not control them. Paul spoke of this plurality of unseen forces as angels, principalities, and powers (Rom. 8:38). Many powers were at work in life, which was why Jesus taught that it was important to be wise as serpents and gentle as doves instead of being innocent and unwitting. Freedom of choice gave humanity the capacity to gain wisdom and to embody the creative power of God, but people had to learn to discern the spirits, and they had to choose what spirits they would serve.

Spiritual powers came from an invisible source, usually imagined as heaven. They were manifested in earthly, material life. Speaking of divinities or spirits was a way to describe invisible powers, experienced in observable and diverse material forms. As historian Peter Brown notes, even philosophers did not regard the gods as imaginary or "airy abstractions." Philosophers assigned themselves the most superior gods and demoted to lesser status the average gods of average people, who hovered closer to earth or shared the same physical space with human beings. For ordinary people, gods were "vibrant beings" who touched all aspects of the natural world and human society and "were ready to maximize and to maintain, in return for due observance, the good things of life."²¹ People sought to know the spirits that would help them and avoid those that caused harm. The Christian scriptures claimed that the Spirit of God—the creativity, wisdom, and power of life—dwelled in human beings. This Spirit descended and took up residence in the flesh, inhabiting this life in all its diversity, as different in manifestations as we are different from one another. Jesus was the sign of this reality. His very name came to signify the power of life lived in the Spirit. To be baptized in his name was to possess the same power.

THE WEDDING OF SPIRIT AND WATER IN PARADISE

Genesis begins with Creation and moves to the garden of paradise in its second chapter. John's Gospel follows the same pattern. In chapter 2 it introduces a marriage feast. The Song of Songs in the Hebrew Bible, as well as the prophets, makes the link between paradise and the joys of an erotic union. Isaiah 61—the passage quoted by Jesus in Luke as the announcement of his purpose in the world—anticipates the joy of paradise renewed:

> *My whole being shall exult in my God;*
> *for he has clothed me with the garments of salvation . . .*
> *as a bridegroom decks himself with a garland,*
> *and as a bride adorns herself with jewels. (Isa. 61:10)*

John's story of the wedding in Cana and its wine suggests the vineyard of the Song of Songs (John 2:1–11). The drama begins when the wine runs out before the festivities have ended. Prompted to act by his mother and assisted by the household servants, Jesus turns six jars of water into wine. The wedding has already taken place offstage; the story focuses on the guests enjoying the banquet. Until Jesus acts, the existence of paradise—symbolized by wine, the fruit of the garden—is uncertain. The miracle of water into wine "revealed his glory" and demonstrated that, at that moment, the joys of the garden flowed into the world. A chapter later, John the Baptist testifies to this joy by speaking of Jesus as the bridegroom and himself as the best man at the wedding: "The friend of the bridegroom, who stands and hears him, rejoices greatly at the bridegroom's voice. For this reason my joy has been fulfilled" (John 3:29). With Jesus, the wait is over. The wedding has happened. Paradise is here.

Following the miracle of water turned into "spirits," Nicodemus, a Pharisaic leader, approaches Jesus alone at night and in secret (John 3:1–21). He confesses that "we know that you are a teacher who has come from God; for no one can do these signs that you do apart from the presence of God" (John 3:2). Jesus responds that "no one can see the Kingdom of God without being born from above . . . born of water and spirit." Nicodemus asks how such a birth could be possible for one who was already born. Jesus, astonished that Nicodemus was baffled, explains that the one who ascended and descended from heaven offered eternal life. Jesus goes on to say:

> God so generously loved the world [*kosmos*] that he placed [*edo-ken*] his only Son here, so that everyone who has confidence in him may not be lost or be destroyed but may have eternal life. God did not send the Son into the world to put the world on trial, but so the world might be rescued through him. (John 3:16, author paraphrase from the Greek)

Today this passage is invariably interpreted to mean that God placed Jesus in the world to die on the cross,[22] but at no point does this story mention death. It does not use the Greek verb *paradidomai,* the word that John's Gospel specifically uses to describe the action of those who "gave" or "handed over" Jesus to be crucified.[23] John 19:16 makes clear that Pilate, not God, "handed him over to them to be crucified." Jesus's words to Nicodemus are about birth and life, not death and the afterlife. They reiterate the themes of Creation and the power to be born of God that we spoke of in chapter 1. God loves the world, the *kosmos,* and loves the Son, to whom he gives "the Spirit without measure" (John 3:34).

As Jesus elaborates the meaning of God's love for the world, Nicodemus disappears from the story. When Jesus next appears, he is baptizing in the Judean countryside. Nicodemus is nowhere to be found.

The departure of Nicodemus provides some clues about what baptism meant at the time of John and Jesus. Baptism was more than a personal choice about one's beliefs. It was a ritual that incorporated initiates into a community and its sources of power. As such, it was inseparable from social and political issues. John the Baptist and Jesus came from groups that were critical of the ruling aristocracy in Jerusalem. The baptizing sects offered a path by which people separated and purified themselves from the corruptions of the Roman occupation and its client-king. To be baptized was to renounce allegiance to the polluting and false powers of Rome and to join movements that drew on different wellsprings—Wisdom, Word, Torah, and Spirit. As a Pharisee, Nicodemus was a member of a community of scholars who were not at ease with the ruling elite but were implicated in it. By the time of Jesus's ministry, the Pharisees' power and authority in the society had been significantly curtailed, but as teachers of the law they were expected to administer aspects of the government's policies.[24] When human life is embedded in this kind of ambiguity—simultaneously complicit in and troubled by a social system—questions tend to arise in the sleepless hours of midnight. Negotiating such crosscurrents requires wisdom about which powers command loyalty and which require resistance. Nicodemus may have been drawn to Jesus's community, but we are not told if he joined it. At the end of the Gospel, he appears publicly for the first time, to bury Jesus.

Jesus's next encounter ends differently. He left the Judean countryside and traveled through Samaria, the hill country between Jerusalem and Galilee. There he meets a Samaritan woman drawing water at Jacob's well (John 4:1–42). The Samaritans were northern Israelites whose religious practices centered on the five books of Moses. They lived at odds with the Jews who dominated the Jerusalem temple.[25] They had their own sacred mountain and temple at Gerizim, which the

Judean Maccabeans had destroyed after their revolt against Greek rule. The Samaritans did not share the hope of Jews that a Messiah would restore the Davidic kingdom. Instead, they looked for a Messiah who would be the return of Moses as promised in Deuteronomy 18:18. Their Messiah would vindicate the oppressed and inaugurate a season of "refreshment"—a renewal of God's presence and blessing. He would possess the power of the name of God revealed to Moses, which was "the original creative agent, by which the world was created and sustained."[26]

The story of the Samaritan woman occurs just after the failed conversation between Jesus and Nicodemus. Jesus and the woman meet at midday at a community well. The Samaritan woman, unlike Nicodemus, asks astute questions and makes comments that reveal deeper layers of meaning shared between Jews and Samaritans. Her theological disputation with Jesus is the longest in the New Testament. Because of enmity between their peoples, Jews usually avoided traveling through Samaritan territory. Yet Jesus, a Jew and a man, requests a drink of water from this stranger, a Samaritan and a woman. She challenges his unusual request. Her interrogation opens an extended conversation about ordinary water and the living water of eternal life. Using a paradise image of the "well of living water" first mentioned in Song of Songs 4:15, Jesus tells her he has living water to offer:

> Those who drink of the water that I will give them will never be thirsty. The water that I will give will become in them a spring of water gushing up to eternal life. (John 4:13–14)

She says she would be glad to have some of his water, but rejoins that Samaritans have their own sacred mountain, different from Jews who claim all people ought to worship in their temple in Jerusalem. With this brief comment, she alludes to the biblical stories of fratricidal enmity among the twelve tribes of Israel and the civil war that split them north and south. The ten tribes of the northern kingdom of Israel, the "Samaritans," had built their capital of Samaria on Mount Gerizim and the two southern tribes in Judah, the "Jews," had their capital in Jerusalem on Mount Zion. As we noted in chapter 1, the Samaritans had long rejected the Jews and their temple. Her comment about their differences can be seen as a test of Jesus's loyalties to that temple. Jesus rejects it, identifying himself as a friend of the Samaritans. He says that he embraces all who worship God "in spirit and truth." She concedes that her people awaited a Messiah who would "proclaim all things to us."[27] Jesus replies, "I am he, the one who is speaking to you" (John 4:24–26).

In saying "I am," *egō eimi,* Jesus invokes Moses, the Samaritan's most important religious figure. When God called Moses from the burning bush, Moses asked for God's name. "I am who I am," God replied (Exod. 3:14). By echoing these words, Jesus announces to the Samaritan woman that he, like Moses, possesses the power of the Name and embodies God's life-giving presence. He is the fulfillment of her people's hopes. This "I am" statement is the first of many in John's Gospel. He would go on to say,

> *I am the bread.*
> *I am the light.*
> *I am the good shepherd.*
> *I am the resurrection and the life.*
> *I am the way.*
> *I am the vine.*[28]

These "I am" statements about abundant life identify Jesus with the return of Moses and with earthly paradise. Each "I am" statement lifts up Jesus as the one who shows the way to paradise, with its pastoral landscape, rich vegetation, and abundant harvests.

Jesus's "I am" left the Samaritan woman wondering. Their conversation is interrupted by the arrival of his disciples, astonished to see him talking to her. She goes to her community to discuss her experience, "Come and see a man who told me everything I have ever done! He cannot be the Messiah, can he?" (John 4:29). From her report, many believe he is the prophet they expected, but others go to see for themselves.

While the Samaritans are on the way, Jesus has a conversation with the disciples who questioned his speaking to a Samaritan woman. He tells his disciples that they benefit from others who have labored to sow a harvest and that he has come to unite sowers and harvesters, breaking down divisions through an ethic of sharing and generosity. "I sent you to reap that for which you did not labor. Others have labored, and you have entered into their labor" (John 4:38). The Samaritans invite Jesus and his disciples to be their guests. After his visit, the skeptics say to the woman, "It is no longer because of what you said that we believe, for we have heard for ourselves, and we know that this is truly the Savior of the world."

The Samaritan woman would become one of the most popular figures in early Christian art. She appeared in the mid-third-century Dura Europas baptistery, in the Roman catacombs, and in early church mosaics. Usually wearing a striped dress, she stood at the well, bucket in hand, while Jesus sat nearby, speaking to her. Her boldness in disputation suggests that one way paradise flows into the world as living water is through those who raise questions, probe answers, and stay in the conversation.

PARADISE AND POWER

Though his disciples believed in Jesus, John said, "the world did not know him"; even his own people did not accept who he was (John 1:10–11). The Gospel introduced this conflict again in 2:13–22, immediately on the heels of the wedding in Cana. Jesus took on the epicenter of Roman domination in Palestine, the Jerusalem temple. He used a whip of cords to drive the animals and the moneychangers off the temple grounds. He poured out their coins and overturned their tables, shouting, "Stop making my Father's house a marketplace!"

All the Gospels told a version of this demonstration against the temple. More than any other, this offense put his life on a collision course with Rome, for it challenged the economic and political basis of their control of Galilee and Judea. To underscore this tension with the Roman Empire, the Gospels set him at odds with Rome in other ways as well.[29] In Luke 2, the nativity of Jesus occurred during the registration for Roman taxation, a hated system that benefited the rich. In the story of an exorcism, the Gospel of Mark called demons "legion," the name of the largest Roman military unit, and Jesus turned them into pigs (Mark 5:1–14). John, chapter 11, accused Jesus's enemies in Jerusalem of plotting to sacrifice him to Caesar to propitiate imperial wrath.

> "If we let him go on like this, everyone will believe in him, and the Romans will come and destroy both our holy place and our nation." But one of them, Caiaphas, who was high priest that year, said to them, "You know nothing at all! You do not understand that it is better for you to have one man die for the people than to have the whole nation destroyed." (John 11:48–50)

The Gospels challenged systems of domination wherever they manifested themselves, including gender relationships. Genesis 1–2 and the Song of Songs had established the prototype for equal relationships among women and men. Though the stories of women in the Gospels cannot be called feminist, they do present women as ordinary people exercising power and agency beyond the social structures that might have constrained them. They were a sign that Jesus's community did not follow Roman hierarchies of power and exclusion. Jesus had women friends, shared communal meals that transgressed social divisions, and refuted dogmatic applications of sacred scripture.[30] The Gospels report that these practices threatened even the male disciples, who complained that Jesus spoke with women and was too generous to outcasts.

At the time of his impending death, Jesus ate supper with his community and delivered an extended farewell sermon about how they should live together after he leaves them (John 13:12–17:26). "Love one another as I have loved you," he said, and described their community as one of friends who shared in his power and in his joy in life. He explained that he had been a true friend to them and that they were to do likewise for one another. They were to value each other's lives as much as their own. They were to "abide in him" as he did in them, not as servants submissive to a master but as mutual friends whose life-giving relationship was an organic one. "I am the vine, you are the branches." In these passages, John's Gospel reflects knowledge of the Greek literature of true and false friendship, but the Greek ethic regarded friendship as possible only between independent men.[31] Friendship excluded women, slaves, servants—all social inferiors or dependents. Jesus's circle of friends included women, such as Mary and Martha, and a number of scholars have noted the social and political importance of the gender-disrupting idea implied by his model of friendship.[32]

At this farewell gathering, Jesus told his friends that he had given them the wisdom and knowledge he had received from God and would leave an advocate and comforter to be with them forever. He prayed,

> Father, the hour has come; glorify your Son so that the Son may glorify you, since you have given him authority over all people, to give eternal life to all whom you have given him. And this is eternal life, that they may know you, the only true God, and Jesus Christ whom you have sent. I glorified you on earth by finishing the work that you gave me to do. So now, Father, glorify me in your own presence with the glory that I had in your presence before the world existed.
>
> Holy Father, protect them in your name that you have given me, so that they may be one, as we are one. I made your name known to them, and I will make it known, so that the love with which you have loved me may be in them, and I in them. (John 17:1–26, excerpts)

This theme of eternal life—a variation on the concept of paradise—reverberated throughout the Gospel. On this last night of his life, Jesus delivered his most extended explanation of its meaning. Eternal life consisted of knowing God and loving one another—in this life and in God's world. "I am not asking you to take them out of the world," Jesus says (John 17:15). Eternal life was possible here and now because of the presence of divinity in the world, come down from heaven to bless this earthly life. The blessing of Spirit in the world, this power of love in community, this companionship of Wisdom, was the infinite source of life. Jesus, in contrast to "the world" that did not know God, offered "true life." Life "in truth" noticed the shining face of divine presence—glory. This *kosmos*, this world, was the dwelling place of God, whose luminous fire was not extinguished even in the deepest night. Those who loved, who cared generously for human needs and treated others as friends, were born of the Spirit, as he was. They knew and saw God in this life now, as well as in the life to come. They possessed the power to resist unjust powers. They lived deeply rooted in holy ground, in paradise.

Defiant of Rome to the end, Jesus spoke directly to Pontius Pilate of the power he served. Pilate, interrogating Jesus at his trial about his title of king of the Jews, asked, "What have you done?" Jesus replied, "My kingdom is not from this world. If my kingdom were from this world, my followers would be fighting to keep me from being handed over to the Jews. But as it is, my kingdom is not from here" (John 18:35–37). Jesus's use of "this world" distinguished imperial strategies of war, torture, and state terrorism from an ethic of nonviolent resistance to injustice. "This world" was the empire occupying Jerusalem. Jesus's realm had a different source. Metaphors of Creation and paradise evoked it: wind, water, bread, vines, and a good shepherd. Jesus's realm was the world generously loved by God—what the other Gospels distinguished as *gē*, earth, not *oikoumenē*, the household of Rome. The world of Pilate was imperial violence; the world of Jesus was life-giving truth. Jesus's response to Pilate was like someone today saying, "You are from Mars, I am from Venus."

"For this I was born, and for this I came into the world," Jesus told Pilate, "to testify to the truth. Everyone who belongs to the truth listens to my voice" (John 18:37). When Pilate interrogated Jesus a second time, Jesus's response was silence. Jesus refused to answer Pilate's questions, for to admit or deny the charges against him would have been to accept that Pilate's authority was the frame of their discussion. At this resistance to his authority, Pilate threatened that he determined whether Jesus lived or died. Jesus replied, "You would have no power over me unless it had been given you from above; therefore the one who handed me over to you is guilty of a greater sin" (John 19:11). The Greek word translated here as "power" signified authority conferred from a source beyond the individual.[33] Jesus's response denied that Pilate had any authority conferred by God. Pilate's power came from Rome, not God. Rome, contrary to God, operated through violence and extortion. Imperial, totalitarian control lacked the power of truth, love, generosity, or ethical grace. It served an elite few and left many destitute. Those who turned Jesus over to Rome had committed the greater sin because they had professed allegiance to God but had ceded their power to Rome.

In John's Gospel, Jesus's response to religious opposition was different from his response to imperial challenges. In controversies with his religious kin, Jesus employed the sources of religious authority honored by Samaritans and Jews—he did not reject them. He rejected only Rome's authority. When the Samaritan woman interrogated him about their religious differences, he replied by invoking the traditions that Jews and Samaritans shared in Moses. When Jews accused him of blasphemy for claiming to be God's Son, he replied by quoting Psalm 82, using scripture sacred to the Jews to make the case that God has many children—he was not unique (John 10:34–38). The point of such a claim was not self-aggrandizement or idolatry. It was to undermine the power of empire with the work of justice. His arguments with his Jewish opponents, however, had an acute and vitriolic tone unlike the stoic calm exhibited in his defiance of Pilate. His stoicism with Pilate reflected Roman standards of masculinity and made him Pilate's peer. The caustic intensity of his conflicts with the Jews reflected connection and passionate expectation rather than cool distance. The Gospel of John, as many have observed, is simultaneously the most Jewish and the most anti-Jewish of the Gospels. Jesus called Jews children of the devil, murderers, and liars for plotting his execution. He charged that they were not authentic descendants of Abraham. He heatedly condemned

Jews who do not believe in him by saying that they loved darkness and that their deeds were evil (3:19), that they would receive God's wrath instead of eternal life (3:36), that they would die in their sins (8:24), and that they would be pruned away and burned (15:2, 6). The Gospel accused Jews of calling for his crucifixion and portrayed Pilate as a pawn of Jewish power. Though Rome reserved the exclusive right to use capital punishment, the Gospel blamed unbelieving Jews for murdering Jesus. The Gospel inflated Jesus's conflict with his religious kin into cosmic proportions. It arrayed believers and nonbelievers on opposite poles of light and darkness, life and death, survival and destruction.[34]

The scriptures must be read critically and carefully for religious and ethical guidance, using principles that the Bible itself provides. John's Gospel should be weighed against its own report that Jesus, a Jew, said, "I came that they might have life." The Gospel is clear that the will of God is that life should flourish. It also recognizes that God's will is not the only force operating in the world. Humans, created in God's image, also have power and freedom—this is the meaning of Genesis 1–3. The decisive question is whether human beings align themselves with the Spirit of life, the power of God, or use their power to collaborate with destructive principalities and powers. Christians have used John's Gospel to generate and justify violence against Jews. It has also been used to condemn "nonbelieving" Muslims, pagans, humanists, and "heretical" Christians. But the Gospels do not kill people, interpreters do. Interpreters have used the Bible to aid and abet the enemies of life, just as others have used it to advocate justice and peace. Sacred scripture alone cannot protect the world from injustice and war. Those for whom the Bible is sacred text must exercise discernment and wisdom, accepting both power and responsibility. How believers imagine God's power shapes how they conceive of and handle their own. Most early church teachers believed God worked through the Spirit of wisdom, the flow of justice, the strength of truth, acts of love, and the lure of beauty. This ethical grace requires rejecting the enmities that John's Gospel entertains, since the Gospel itself says, "God did not send the Son into the world to condemn the world, but in order that the world might be saved through him" (John 3:17).

THE CRUCIFIXION OF JESUS

Jesus's suffering on the cross and his corpse did not appear in Christian art until the tenth century. We began this book because we were puzzled about this absence. After all, the Gospels commit significant portions to describing the Crucifixion in detail.[35] They tell about Jesus's betrayal, trial, torture, execution, and burial in a cave. They expose how his male disciples abandoned him while women stayed with him to the end. They place words about prayer, thirst, love, forgiveness, paradise, and despair on his dying lips. How should we read this testimony to his torture and his dying exclamations?

Crucifixion was designed to destroy both bodies and identities. It was Rome's most horrifying and humiliating form of capital punishment. The Romans used it to discourage people from joining dissident movements, escaping slavery or military service, or conducting magical arts. In the slave rebellion of Spartacus that was defeated in 71 BCE, six thousand crucified bodies rotted along the Appian Way from Capua to Rome.[36] Roman soldiers erected crosses in public places, often at the site of the crime, to terrorize subject peoples. Victims were usually tortured, and then they died in slow agony, sometimes over days. A quick death was a mercy. Dead bodies were left hanging to rot and be eaten by scavengers; broken or scattered fragments were usually all that remained of a person's identity.[37]

Crucifixion required no trial and was more akin to lynching than formal execution. Seneca was one of the few ancient writers to discuss its uses and methods, and he spared no words in describing its humiliations and horrors. Crucifixion was used against the underclasses and slaves and was regarded as so shameful that even victims' families would not speak of it. It functioned to fragment communities, tearing the fabric of even the strongest bonds of connection and commitment. The one surviving early image of crucifixion, from a third-century military barracks in Rome, was crudely scratched on the wall like graffiti. The image depicted an ass hanging backwards on a cross, and the caption reads, "Alessameno worships his god."[38]

In speaking explicitly about Jesus's crucifixion, the Gospels used words of lament from the Psalms and prophets. In doing so, they tied his death to earlier imperial carnage visited upon his people. In their descriptions of Jesus's corpse, they said he had no broken bones, was removed intact, and was properly buried by members of his community. These details indicate that Rome was impotent to erase Jesus from memory.

The authors of the Passion narratives constructed an innovative strategy to resist public torture and execution. They created a literature of disclosure and wove the killing of Jesus into the fabric of a long history of violence against those who spoke for justice. In placing the opening of Psalm 22 on Jesus's lips, they evoked the bitter lament of grief and struggle that runs through the whole Psalm:

> *My God, my God, why have you forsaken me?*
> *Why are you so far from helping me, from the words of*
>   *my groaning? . . .*
> *I am poured out like water,*
>   *and all my bones are out of joint;*
> *my heart is like wax;*
>   *it is melted within my breast;*
> *my mouth is dried up like a potsherd,*
>   *and my tongue sticks to my jaws . . .*
> *For dogs are all around me;*
>   *a company of evildoers encircles me.*
> *My hands and feet have shriveled;*
> *I can count all my bones.*
> *They stare and gloat over me . . .*
>   *and for my clothing they cast lots. (Ps. 22:1–2, 14–18)*

The Passion narratives broke silence about the shame and fear that crucifixion instilled. To lament was to claim powers that crucifixion was designed to destroy: dignity, courage, love, creativity, and truth-telling. In telling his story, his community remembered his name and claimed the death-defying power of saying his name aloud. In using an-

cient literature to expose what torture did to the soul and to communities, the Passion stories brought testimony before a higher court of appeals than the bogus trial of Jesus they indict.[39] The purpose of such
writing is assuredly not to valorize victims, to praise their suffering as
redemptive, to reveal "true love" as submission and self-sacrifice, or to
say that God requires the passive acceptance of violence. Such interpretations mistakenly answer the abusive use of power with an abnegation of power.[40] The story of Jesus's crucifixion, in marked contrast,
asserted that the answer to abusive power is the courageous and decisive employment of the powers of life—to do deeds in Jesus's name.

The Passion narratives would not exist without the agency of
women. From ancient times, women have tended the bodies of the
dead, and they have carried the public role of grieving. "Call for the
mourning women to come . . . let them raise a dirge over us, so that our
eyes may run down with tears," Jeremiah cried (Jer. 9:17–18). As professional mourners, women also composed the words of lamentation.
The long history of women's lament-poetry expressed sorrow, outrage,
and resistance. In the Bible, lamentation protested God's absence and
reported the effects of violence:

> *Look, and see our disgrace!*
> *Our inheritance has been turned over to strangers,*
> > *our homes to aliens.*
> *We must pay for the water we drink;*
> > *the wood we get must be bought.*
> *With a yoke on our necks we are hard driven;*
> > *we are weary, we are given no rest.*
> *We get our bread at the peril of our lives.*
> *Women are raped in Zion,*
> > *virgins in the towns of Judah.*
> *Princes are hung up by their hands;*
> > *no respect is shown to the elders.*
> *The joy of our hearts has ceased.*
> *Why have you forgotten us completely?*
> > *Why have you forsaken us these many days?*
> *(Lam. 5:2–20, excerpts)*

The women who mourned Jesus preserved the memory of how he died and drew on ancient practices of keening. The Gospels reflect women's roles in public lamentation, in the construction of literatures of lament, in the careful attention to detail, and in the elegiac emotional quality of those who hold to life against all odds and every power arrayed against them. In her study of women's poetry of lamentation, Constantina-Nadia Seremetakis concludes that lament is "a prelude to the staging of women's reentry (as individuals and as a collectivity) into the social order on their own terms."[41] It is, in other words, an assertion of life-giving power in the face of unjust structures that suppress, exclude, violate, and control life.

Telling the truth about Jesus's crucifixion has abiding importance. To break silence whenever violence is used to shame, instill fear, fragment human community, or suppress those who advocate for justice is life-giving. Just as Jesus, in John's Gospel, stood before Pilate and said, "You have no power over me," the Passion narratives defied the power of crucifixion to silence Jesus's movement. In doing so, they placed before his movement the choice to tell the truth and live by ethical grace. They said life is found in surviving the worst a community can imagine, in lamenting the consequences of imperialism, and in holding fast to the core goodness of this world, blessed by divine justice and abundant life. By the fourth century, the church recited the stories of lamentation every year in the week before Easter. Remembering the sorrows that injustice and violence inflicted, the early Christians filled their churches with images of the life that lamentation allowed to break free, the life of ethical grace, the life of paradise on earth.

RESURRECTION

The final disclosure of paradise in John comes with the Resurrection. Golgotha, the place of the Crucifixion, had a garden. There two of Jesus's secret Jewish followers—one of whom was Nicodemus—took his body to a new tomb and buried him according to Jewish custom (John 19:38–42). At dawn on the first day of the week, Mary found two angels in the tomb instead of a body. Jesus appeared to her in the garden at dawn (John 20:1–18) and asked why she was weeping. Seeing him, Mary mistook him for the gardener until he called to her by name. In recognition, she called him "teacher." Another Resurrection appearance described Jesus directing a miraculous catch of fish. He used them for a feast with his disciples; then he interrogated Simon's love for him. He asked Simon to show that love by feeding and tending his lambs and sheep (John 21:1–19).

The Resurrection appearances in all four Gospels have the quality of visions and dreams, the way people are surprised by apparitions of the departed. They often do not immediately recognize what they are seeing. Until Jesus established his familiarity with them, through enacting familiar rituals, saying personal names, or disclosing his identity to them, he remained an unrecognized stranger. In Luke, it was when an unknown visitor broke bread with the disciples that "their eyes were opened and they recognized him." When Thomas heard reports of his appearances, he refused to believe them and accepted them only when he saw for himself that it was really Jesus and not an imposter. His appearances are called "signs" and were received with the feelings of skepticism, astonishment, joy, and gratitude that often accompany visitations of the dead. Such visitations come to those who mourn. The women at the tomb, carrying out their rites of care for the dead, wept at the tomb. "Their eyes were full of tears when the realization hit them that Jesus was not in the grave. Grief may also be a precondition for resurrection, and tears for permitting the eyes to see," observes Marianne Sawicki.[42]

The Resurrection was the gift of persistent love, stronger than death: "life in his name" (John 20:31). It was not, however, a panacea or a final solution to life's struggles and conflicts. It did not quell conflict within the community of Jesus. The Gospel of John concluded with a challenge by Simon Peter to the unnamed disciple, "the one whom Jesus loved" (John 21:20), whose testimony informed the writing of the Gospel. This closing coda reiterates the subtext of dispute and controversy in the communities found throughout the Christian scriptures.

In Luke 23:43, when Jesus said to the thief hanging next to him on the cross, "Today, you will be with me in paradise," Christians believed he meant it. They understood that in extremities of repression and pain, "Many waters cannot quench love, neither can floods drown it . . . for love is strong as death" (Song of Sol. 8:7, 6). Rage, protest, and lamentation carried the energy of this power, as did acts of compassion, generosity, and justice. Those who loved him, comforted by the ancient words of scripture, the choreography of well-known rituals, and the prayers of many, resided with Jesus in paradise, the space of resistance to the death-dealing powers of Rome and its many legions.

In the cross-cultural brew that produced early Christianity, the assurance of paradise was an inebriating grace, a life-giving recipe drawn from many ancient sources. This assurance of salvation fueled Christian resistance to Roman oppression and sustained love for the world, despite its many difficulties. When Christians gathered to share of the bread of heaven, partaking in the Eucharist feast, they entered the most concentrated form of paradise on earth, where living and dead communed with the risen Christ, and the banquet of abundance was spread for all. From feasting in paradise, they took strength to embody ethical grace in the world—the world that God so generously loved.

So Great a Cloud

Therefore, since we are surrounded by so great a cloud of
witnesses, let us also lay aside every weight and the sin that
clings so closely, and let us run with perseverance the race that
is set before us, looking to Jesus the pioneer and perfecter of
our faith, who for the sake of the joy that was set before him
endured the cross, disregarding its shame, and has taken
his seat at the right hand of the throne of God.

Consider him who endured such hostility against himself
from sinners, so that you may not grow weary or lose heart.

HEBREWS 12:1–3

The dead and the living remain connected. Communities tell stories
of the dead not only to remember those who have died, but to hold on
to what love has created and what cannot be destroyed. The beloved
dead return in dreams, visions, memories, and stories told to their descendants. The literature of lamentation that grounded the Gospels
offered a remembrance of Jesus brought to life for his friends. In their
retelling, the stories were shaped and reshaped by those who told them
—and who tell them still.

Where and how the dead live on can be experienced in many ways.
The book of Hebrews pictured the assembly of departed saints as a
"great cloud of witnesses" who surround the living. When Christians
gathered to worship—breaking bread and sharing in the feast of life—

they entered the region of God's holy mountain encompassed by this cloud:

You have come to Mount Zion, and to the city of the living God, the heavenly Jerusalem, and to innumerable angels in festal gathering, and to the assembly of the firstborn who are enrolled in heaven, and to God the judge of all, and to the spirits of the righteous made perfect, and to Jesus. (Heb. 12:22–23)

THE LIFE OF THE DEAD

The idea that the righteous live on after death and inhabit a realm from which they could visit the living is an ancient one. The New Testament says that Jesus's disciples saw him, spoke with him, and shared meals with him, before and after he rose from the dead. In testifying to the presence of the risen Christ, Christians reflected a mix of ideas about the realm of the dead that emerged from the cultures that influenced the Hebrew Bible, as well as from Greek and Roman traditions. Visitations from the dead were a familiar experience, as they continue to be for many today.[1]

For oppressed people, it was especially important to affirm that those killed by repressive regimes were not exiled to a distant, cold realm, isolated from the living. By affirming the resurrection of the dead, as Jewish texts began to do during the war-torn centuries of foreign occupation from 200 BCE to 200 CE, survivors of imperial violence defied the power of their persecutors and solaced their grief. They pictured their righteous dead in a place of consolation and vindication. The book of I Enoch, a Jewish apocryphal text composed during the third to first centuries BCE, described the abode of the righteous as a version of Eden—a garden of delight and abundance located on the earth. There, the first-century Testament of Abraham said, the dead rested "where there is no toil, no sadness, no sighing, but peace and joy and endless life." Fourth Maccabees, from the same era, told the story of heroes who defied tyrants and kept faith with God, even when threatened by death. God took them up into heaven.[2] The story memorialized a mother and her sons killed "because of the violence of the tyrant who wished to destroy the way of life of the Hebrews."

> The moon in heaven, with the stars, does not stand so august as you, who, after lighting the way of your star-like seven sons to piety, stand in honor before God and are firmly set in heaven with them. (4 Macc. 17:5)

Through traditions such as these, Christians drew the idea that God would preserve the faithful beyond the reach of their oppressors and tormentors. The faithful would live on in a place of honor and protection, imagined variously as heaven, as celestial Jerusalem, or as a zone of earthly paradise inhabited by the righteous. From their abodes, they might still touch, bless, and guide the living. Like the visionary, dreamlike visitations of the dead, the realms from which they came could be indefinite and vague or vivid and clear, but the realm of the dead was within this world, as the *Didascalia* explained:

> God Almighty raises us up from the dead.... Indeed, though we be thrown into the depth of the sea, or scattered by the winds like chaff, we are still within the world, and the whole world itself is enclosed beneath the hand of God.[3]

By the third century, the Christian realm of the dead had become a place of beauty and peace. The departed rested close by in a region of earthly paradise, a mysterious dimension of this world with green meadows, streams, and fragrant flowers and fruits. The dead could rest because Satan could not enter, and they no longer had to wrestle with sin, evil, or oppression. They did not, however, rest so far away that they could not visit the living to give advice, comfort, or guidance. In their realm of paradise, resurrected saints were restored to the divine presence and gained spiritual power to assist the living. They were like relatives who had retired from New York to Florida. The living could feast with them in sacred meals and could experience their presence in dreams and visions.

Memorial feasts with the dead were common and popular. The meals were usually held in the evening, often outdoors under covered arbors near the entrance to tombs. Participants spread tables with special foods and wine and invited the dead to join the meal. Catacomb frescoes of funeral banquets have preserved phrases used to greet the dead, "May God refresh you . . . enjoy refreshment with the Holy Spirit." Small stone chairs have survived on which a lighted candle would be placed to signify the presence of the dead. Through such practices, Christians welcomed the departed into life and affirmed that neither suffering nor persecution could sever the bonds of love. The living gained strength for "the race set before them." Following such banquets, it was traditional to distribute food or coins to the poor—extending the grace of the feast to benefit others.[4]

In the fourth century, some Christian bishops began to preach against these banquets—apparently appalled that the living indulged with too much enthusiasm on occasion. Bishop Ambrose of Milan (339–397) instructed Augustine's mother, Monica, to stop attending the feasts, but they continued well into the fifth century. Teachers in the fourth century also disputed where and how the dead visited the living. Augustine argued against the possibility of nocturnal visitations by the dead. His evidence: Monica had never visited his dreams. He found it unimaginable that she no longer wished to see him, which meant such visitations were impossible. His was an unpopular view.[5]

Christians held memorial feasts with the dead in the catacombs outside of Rome. Romans required that Jews and Christians inter their dead outside the walls of the city, where areas of soft underground tufa rock lent itself to the digging of burial caverns. Most pagans cremated their dead, though some also began burying them around the second century. The catacombs were dug along major roads leading to Rome. Sections for the poor were crammed floor to ceiling with body-size cavities, while better-off families had separate chambers dug for them.

Two-thirds of graves were for infants and children. Memorial inscriptions reveal the deep and personal affections parents held for their children and spouses for their partners. Their sense of loss is still palpable.

Early death plagued the Roman world. Life expectancy in the first century CE was twenty-five. Though violence took its toll, natural causes and accidents were the greatest threats to survival. Men lived longer than women, who bore the brunt of high pregnancy rates and poor medical care. Barely a third of children survived. The median marriage age for women was fourteen. Less than 3 percent of men lived beyond the age of fifty. To keep the population from shrinking and undermining the financial base of the empire, every woman needed to have at least five children before she died. Rome penalized citizens who did not marry and bear as many children as possible.[6]

The catacombs were religiously diverse burial sites, reflecting close relationships among Jews, Christians, and pagans. Burial images depict stories from the Hebrew scriptures shared by Christians and Jews and from pagan mythology as well. For example, frescoes of Hercules and Jesus, as well as Moses and Abraham, adorn the walls of the Via Latina Catacomb. These heroes appear on the walls of vaults leading to different chambers of a catacomb that probably belonged to one large wealthy family for several generations.[7] Determining the religious affiliation of the deceased in the catacombs is often difficult. Religiously mixed images indicate, perhaps, that the living wished to visit the spirits of their beloved departed and commune with them all together—even if the dead belonged to different religions. Or, family ritual practices may have encompassed a variety of traditions. Inclusivity and connection, rather than separation, appear to have been the rule. Catacomb art contains no images related to judgment and hell.[8]

In the third century, empirewide persecutions of Christians erupted several times. The first identifiably Christian images appear around the same time in the catacombs. The images highlight the power of God to protect the life of the faithful in times of violent repression. Though the catacombs were not secret gathering places, many catacomb images depict biblical stories about resistance to empires. Shadrach, Meshach, and Abednego are shown standing in a fiery furnace without being burned. These three youths defied imperial coercion successfully because of divine protection (Dan. 3:12–97). Daniel, possessed of the same power, stands confidently between two lions without a scratch (Dan. 6:17–25, 14:31–42). The virtuous Susanna prays gratefully after escaping her tormentors' false charges of adultery and the threat of death (Sus. 1). Scenes from the popular story of Jonah appear frequently in frescoes and relief carvings. Sailors toss him overboard as he flees the call to preach against the Assyrian Empire. A scaly sea monster swallows him and then spits him up on the shore. The end of Jonah's story is idealized in the images. According to the book of Jonah, he eventually preaches the destruction of the empire, just as God commanded him. The Assyrian Empire repents, at which point Jonah becomes furious with God for sparing its destruction. He pouts under the shade of a gourd vine that springs up miraculously and wilts just as quickly. The catacomb images gloss his bad behavior and show him resting languidly in a lush vineyard. His casual recline imitates the iconography of the Roman god Endymion, who slept peacefully in paradise until his monthly mating with the moon goddess, Selena.[9]

Other Roman-influenced scenes depict shepherds; meadows with trees, flowers, birds, and animals; and springs of water.[10] These images had a long history in the funerary art of the Romans, who venerated the dead to keep their ancestors alive. In addition, Rome had an extensive navy and a vast coastline ringing the Mediterranean, so symbols of sailing and the sea are common in the catacombs. Images of dolphins and fish are ubiquitous—for Christians they represented the baptized "born of water and spirit." Dolphins rescued drowning sailors and so also may have signified Christ's saving help.[11]

The catacombs include no images of Jesus's crucifixion, but they show his birth. Among the Nativity stories, the tale of the three magi is the most commonly depicted (Matt. 2:1–12). The Gospel of Matthew said they were from the east, the direction of paradise. They were, by legend, Persian astrologers and magicians. Persia, favorably remem-

FIGURE 2. *British Museum, London, England, Marble sarcophagus. Fifth to sixth centuries. Jonah. At the bottom of the image, the serpent waits to swallow the prophet, then spits him up on land. On the right, he reclines under his vine.*

bered in Isaiah, was Rome's unconquerable, hated nemesis on its eastern frontier. The earliest catacomb images of the magi dress them in Phrygian attire, a style associated with Persia. The magi wear short tunics, pantaloons, capes, and puffy, knobbed hats—a swank signature look that continued for more than a millennium. Roman men wore togas, not pants, or battle armor, not flowing capes. They also cut their hair short, whereas the magi often are shown with tresses peeking from their hats. The three cool youths in the fiery furnace share the magi's fashion taste and suspicion of evil kings (Dan. 3:8–30).

Jesus appears in the catacomb images as a miracle worker and healer. He and Moses are both shown using a magic wand and performing water miracles. Jesus uses his wand to raise Lazarus from his tomb and to heal the paralytic. Though the story of the crossing of the Red Sea in Exodus 14–15 makes no explicit mention of the pharoah drowning, the catacombs show Moses waving his wand to close the sea over his watery grave. Origen of Alexandria (c. 185–c. 254), a Greek theologian born in Egypt, said that the Egyptians maligned Moses as a magician and that the Romans slandered Jesus Christ on similar charges. Origen defended Jesus as a legitimate physician. Jesus is also shown feeding people with fish and bread. Other Gospel figures include the Samaritan woman drawing water from the well and John the Baptist in his cloak of animal skins baptizing Jesus as a small boy.[12]

Most often, Jesus has the look of a shepherd. He occasionally milks a sheep. Sometimes he even wears a puffy hat, like the magi. He is often young and beardless with long hair, quite at odds with the cropped, mature, masculine look of an emperor. One of the most famous shepherd images, now in the Vatican Museum, is a marble statue from around 300. Jesus holds a lamb across his shoulders and turns his head to gaze at its face. Youthful and strong, he wears a short tunic and sandals and is coiffed in loose, curly locks. Art historian Thomas Mathews notes, "One dainty tress reaches almost to the nipple of his naked chest—a style hardly suited to the rugged outdoor life of a shepherd."[13]

The shepherd was a model of Christian leadership drawn especially from the prophet Ezekiel and the Gospel of John. It contrasted sharply with imperial authority, military culture, and pagan sacerdotal power. A Roman emperor was, first and foremost, a warrior who held office by winning wars, and he governed through regional procurators who managed local client kings. The emperor served the personal deities of his household, as well as the gods of war, and his priests performed the prescribed rituals of the imperial household cults and of military victory. The household rites were inaccessible to the masses, who were free to follow their own family cults. Other pagan priests presided over rituals and festivals of their local deities.

The attentive, personal care of a shepherd differed from the remote imperial model of military control and delegated political authority. Church leaders were expected to model themselves on the shepherd— the bishop's staff is a shepherd's crook. They saw to the care of the sick, ministered to those in prison, offered hospitality to strangers, managed commonly held resources and distributed them to the poor and elderly, and settled disputes and conflicts. In addition, they taught the basic ideas of the faith, explained the stories in the scriptures, prophesied, initiated converts, and organized community participation in the rituals. By the third century, these community practices of leadership and care created a Christian social welfare network in cities throughout the empire.[14]

The success of the church's system of networked communities increasingly threatened the empire's bread and circuses, strategies of welfare and violent entertainment designed to pacify the unruly masses. Rome responded to the threats by killing Christian leaders, which led to speculation about who or what survived death in the afterlife. Two North Africans of the early third century, one Latin and one Greek, offered divergent explanations. Tertullian of Carthage (c. 160–225), one of the earliest Latin theologians of the church, highly valued the body and argued that paradise was found in the material life of Creation. Death would bring an even greater union of flesh and spirit, which the cycles of renewal in nature already revealed. To be restored to paradise after death required a resurrection of flesh and spirit, since there could be no residence in paradise without a body.

> The flesh shall rise again, wholly in every man, in its own identity, in its absolute integrity. Wherever it may be, it is in safe keeping in God's presence, through that most faithful "Mediator between God and man, (the man) Jesus Christ," who shall reconcile both God to man, and man to God; the spirit to the flesh, and the flesh to the spirit.[15]

Because he thought paradise continued after death, Tertullian argued that it was better to die than to give in to Rome's persecutions: "Nothing matters to us in this age but to escape from it with all speed."[16] He was, however, rather obsessed with the body and how it was treated in this life; he wrote an entire fashion treatise justifying his decision to change from a Roman toga to Greek philosopher's pallium.[17]

Origen of Alexandria, who was a neo-Platonist, argued that spiritual power lay in the soul's immateriality. As was typical in Roman society, he saw the body as a lesser reality in need of discipline and control by civilization. He understood paradise as a spiritual journey of the soul to God, in which material existence would be left behind.[18] He described martyrdom as liberation from the body, "Bring wild beasts, bring crosses, bring fire, bring tortures. I know that as soon as I die, I come forth from the body, I rest with Christ."[19] Souls possessed an ineffable body of light and could transcend physical torture and death. His own father was martyred in 202; legend said his mother saved Origen's life by hiding his clothes so that he wouldn't go out. Origen's intellectual tradition valued reason, the quelling of unruly passions, and the acquisition of knowledge and wisdom through the search for truth. The realm of the dead, he believed, was a paradise of learning, something like graduating from life into a perpetual college, without the exams and grades. He imagined a place of instruction for what "the divine scripture calls 'paradise.' " He described it as "a lecture room (auditorium) or school for souls, in which they may be taught about all that they had seen on earth."[20]

Though Tertullian and Origen held contrasting views of resurrection, they affirmed that persecution could not sever the connection between the living and the dead. "[The deceased are] as it were present and reclining at the banquet held for them," Tertullian wrote. Origen pictured the dead joining with the living whenever Christians gathered for worship. In fact, the dead would be the first to arrive: "Souls come more rapidly than living persons to the places of worship."[21] The living received the blessing of paradise when the dead visited them.

THE WITNESSES

Martyrs were buried in the catacombs, and members of their community sought to be interred with them. Martyrs' tombs became points of contact with those who had faced the threats of Roman violence at its worst and remained unbowed. Their deaths carried special potency, and their remains held traces of the power that Rome could not overcome or take away.

The word "martyr" literally means witness. Anyone who was willing to risk death and who withstood the trials of persecution could be counted a martyr. Even when a renowned martyr died of old age, her or

his burial site became a major pilgrimage destination. When people today use the word "martyr," they are referring either to someone with
suicidal impulses who wants to suffer and die for the faith or to a victim. These views, however, capture neither the understandings of
power and moral agency that martyrs themselves experienced nor how
deeply a passionate love for this life grounded their commitments.[22]

Early Christians did not regard martyrs as victims, but as people who
manifested the power of God. When faced with Rome's coercive
threats, the martyrs held fast to their freedom and their relationships
within their Christian community. They would not surrender these to
an oppressive power. Rome chose to kill them, but they chose to preserve life in paradise. They had already experienced paradise in their
earthly life, and they knew death would not take that from them. Their
witness encouraged others to trust that violence in the worst forms
imaginable could not separate them from their beloved community or
cut them off from their source of life and power. A martyr's death was a
paradox; in refusing to submit to unjust power, the martyr witnessed to
the true power that generated paradise on earth. The martyr's testimony to the power of God exposed the impotence of Rome. Historian
Peter Brown notes that martyrs turned cities into religiously contested
spaces. Both the empire and the church viewed the contest as a "public clash of gods." Unlike contemporary ideas of martyrs as lone, heroic
individuals, early Christian accounts did not emphasize "their purely
human courage." Instead, their heroic deaths revealed that they had a
"mighty God in them," and demonstrated the impotence of the ancient
gods of the city. Brown asserts, "Those few who died for Christ made
the power of their God seem overwhelmingly present to the many."[23]

Christians who resisted Rome unto death were actually few and far
between. The Romans usually selected leaders as examples to instill fear
in their followers, which heightened the importance of the valorous
few. Persecutions were episodic and mostly limited in scope. They
waxed and waned based on decisions by local governors. Even with
empirewide bans against Christians, the effectiveness of the bans depended on the cooperation of the local rulers. Martyrdom was controversial. Martyrs created problems for church leaders who sought to

avoid antagonizing the empire, and they condemned martyrdom as foolhardy. Some leaders either accommodated imperial demands to surrender texts or, when ordered to prove they had made sacrifices, paid for forged documents. They objected not to Rome per se but to the violent excesses of some of its rulers and cautioned against provoking it.

As a cosmopolitan movement, Christianity benefited from the empire's infrastructures. The Apostle Paul, who traveled the empire's roads and was a citizen, advocated respect for political authority even though he was persecuted. Other Christians thought martyrdom was sometimes necessary, but only under extreme circumstances. The empire provided some social stability in cities and, in towns near frontiers, protection from invasions. Greek presbyter Irenaeus (c. 130–c. 200), who replaced the martyred bishop in Lyon and was probably martyred himself, led a community of Greek-speaking Anatolian merchants and immigrants in Gaul. Though members of his Christian community were forbidden to appear in public places, the merchants in his community relied on the imperial system of roads, and he prayed for Rome to keep the roads safe.

Whether Christians were circumspect or enthusiastic about martyrdom, martyrs came to be important inspirations of faith for many Christians. One of the most vivid accounts of martyrdom is the story of Perpetua. Unlike many stories of martyrs written by their admirers and recorded long after the events occurred, this account contains elements of a journal probably written by Perpetua herself, though the final version of her story was put together by an editor. Perpetua's words illustrate both the support that martyrs received from their communities and the conflicts they faced in choosing to die. She was killed on March 7 in the year 203 in Carthage, Tunisia. The city had been devastated by Rome in the Punic Wars (264–146 BCE), and the empire was widely hated, especially by the non-Latin Berbers. Resistance to Rome had deep roots in North Africa, and Rome responded with severe persecutions against Christians. In addition, only a century before Perpetua's slaying, the city had outlawed the sacrifice of infants and the commission of suicides in the arena. This legacy of ritual public death may have left a social pattern of community bonding through violence.[24]

On that day in March, gladiators killed five Christians in the arena at a festival to honor the birthday of the son of Emperor Septimus Severus. The group consisted of Perpetua, who was around age 20, married, and the mother of an infant son; her pregnant slave, Felicitas; another slave named Revocatus; and two free men, Saturus and Saturninus. Another man, Secundulus, was arrested with them, but he was killed in prison by a guard.[25]

Perpetua's prison account creates a counterpoint to the editor's heroic, valorizing portrait of the martyrs in the arena. She begins her notes with an encounter with her elderly father, who threatened her before leaving in anger at her refusal to deny her Christian identity. This is the first of several confrontations between them. These encounters highlight the power of her decision to maintain her freedom as a Christian woman in the face of the *pater familias,* the quintessential symbol of Rome's domination and authority. At the last meeting with her father, she stood erect while he tore out his beard and lay prostrate before her. She felt pity for him in his unhappy old age but refused to succumb to his "diabolical" manipulations.

The imprisoned Christians, Perpetua noted, were anxious. They loved their families and their Christian community. Perpetua struggled with the wretched state of the hot, crowded, unlit pit used to confine them, and she worried about her son, who was still nursing. Members of the Christian community bribed guards to improve conditions for the imprisoned Christians and took care of them throughout their confinement. Saturus asked Perpetua, a gifted seer, to pray for a vision that might reveal if their trial "is to be suffering unto death or a passing thing." Perpetua dreamed of a dangerous metal ladder with a "serpent of wondrous size" guarding its base and weapons for tearing flesh on its rungs. In her vision, Saturus (who, as a fellow Christian, was her "brother" in Christ) ascended the ladder first and warned her about the bite of the serpent. Confident and calm, she ascended safely:

At the summit I saw an immense garden, in the center of which sat a tall, gray-haired man dressed like a shepherd, milking sheep.

Standing around him were several thousand white-robed people. As he raised his head he noticed me and said, "Welcome, my child." Then he beckoned me to approach and gave me a small morsel of the cheese he was making. I accepted it with cupped hands and ate it. When all those surrounding us said "Amen," I awoke, still tasting the sweet cheese. I immediately told my brother [Saturus] about the vision, and we both realized that we were to experience the sufferings of martyrdom. From then on we gave up having any hope in this world.[26]

Elements of Perpetua's dream echo the Christian ritual of baptism, in which the newly baptized were given white robes and welcomed into earthly paradise in their first Eucharist feast. Her ascent to a garden was probably the most important sign that she and Saturus would soon enter the realm of the departed, where the great shepherd welcomed them. But this paradise was not just a hope or promise; it was a realm she already had tasted and seen in her Christian community's ritual practices. At the Eucharist, they prayed for their beloved dead, welcoming them as the cloud of witnesses who communed with them and the risen Christ at the breaking of the bread. The martyrs celebrated such a meal together the night before they died. The paradise of the dead existed simultaneously with this life, and it could be accessed through rituals and altered states of consciousness. In her dream, Perpetua ascended to an upper region, connected to this life by a ladder of ascent and descent. The shepherd in her dream appeared around the same time in Christian catacomb art. Saturus, too, dreamed of paradise. He saw

a great open space, which looked like a park, with roses as high as trees and all kinds of flowers. The trees were as high as cypresses and their leaves were constantly singing.... Then we came near a place whose walls seemed to be constructed of light. And in front of the gate stood four angels, who dressed those who entered in white garments. We also entered and heard the sound of voices in unison chanting endlessly: 'Holy, holy, holy.'. . . [and] recognized many of our brethren, martyrs among them. All of us were sustained by an indescribable fragrance that satisfied us.[27]

Their visions traversed the permeable boundaries between the paradise of the living and of the departed. The two experienced a world that already existed, where beloved friends awaited their arrival.

Perpetua visited the realms of the dead twice more. She dreamed of her younger brother, who had died at age seven of a disease that left his face disfigured. She saw him sick, hot, dirty, and thirsty in a place she could not go. She worried about him and prayed for him. She subsequently had a vision in which he drank from a golden bowl. He was healed, happy, and playing. She awakened certain that he was relieved of his suffering.

The day before her execution, Perpetua had a vision of her victory. In her dream, Pomponius, a deacon dressed in gleaming white, said, "Don't be afraid; here I am, beside you, sharing your toil." Supported by assistants from her community, she entered a contest against "an Egyptian, foul of aspect." To combat him, she dreamed that she was stripped naked and had become a man. Before they dueled,

> a man of amazing size came out—he towered even over the vault of the amphitheatre. He was wearing the purple, loosely, with two stripes crossing his chest, and patterned sandals made of gold and silver, carrying a baton like a fencing-master and a green bough laden with golden apples. He . . . said: "This Egyptian, if he defeats her, will kill her with his sword; she, if she defeats him, will receive this bough."
>
> And we joined in combat, and fists began to fly. He tried to grab my feet, but I struck him in the face with my heels. . . . He fell on his face, and I trod upon his head. . . . And I went to the fencing-master and received the bough. He kissed me and said: "Daughter, peace be with you!" . . . I knew the victory would be mine.[28]

Christ in noble dress described the stakes: capitulation to the empire's gladiator led to death; the saint's victory was paradise. Here, we see a gender-crossing pattern that was enacted in Christian baptism of the time: during the ritual, all took on a male persona for confronting the devil and a female persona for union with Christ.[29]

The editor picked up the story with the day of their execution and depicted them with the typical heroism of martyrs, returning Perpetua and Felicitas to more conventional and subservient gender roles. When the young women are hauled naked in nets into the arena, the shocked crowd requires them to be covered. The editor described Perpetua as struggling to hold on to proper female decorum by keeping her gown over her thighs as a wild cow mauled her. After the beasts failed to kill the martyrs, gladiators arrived to slit their throats.

> [The martyrs] voluntarily arose and moved where the crowd wanted them. Before doing so they kissed each other so that their martyrdom would be completely perfected by ... the kiss of peace. ... Saturus ... to be Perpetua's encouragement, was the first to die. ... Perpetua, in order to feel some of the pain, groaning as she was struck between the ribs, took the gladiator's trembling hand [and] guided it to her throat.[30]

According to the editor, the gladiator tried to stab Perpetua in the breast, as men were slain. But she guided his hand to her throat, a woman's death.

In the ritual of arena games, criminals were expected to die ignominiously, without "virtue." Perpetua and the other martyrs died, instead, with dignity, defying the empire. Perpetua, the editor said, entered the arena "with shining face and quiet poise, as the beloved of God [*Dei delicata*], as a wife of Christ [*Matrona Christi*], beating back the gaze of the crowd with the power of her eyes."[31] Their power carried the martyrs to the realms of paradise where others who had gone before awaited them.

Perpetua and her community may have belonged to the New

Prophecy movement. Perpetua received cheese from the shepherd in her vision of paradise, and opponents of New Prophecy groups pejoratively called them "bread and cheesers" because they used cheese in their Eucharist.[32] Also called Montanists, they claimed legitimacy through their legacies of martyrs and their apocalyptic visions of a transformed world that would descend from the heavens. The New Prophecy was led by the women Priscilla and Maxmilla, prophets and ecstatic visionaries, and by the man Montanus. The movement stressed ecstatic visions of the Holy Spirit speaking through their prophets and practiced fasting and chastity.

The men in her community recognized Perpetua as a leader. As scholars of religion have noticed, women who are excluded from male-dominated church leadership often gain authority through charismatic power granted by the inspiration of the Holy Spirit, usually via ecstatic visions and dreams. Followers of the New Prophecy believed they lived near the time of fulfillment of the Holy Spirit. The movement's female prophets, bishops, and priests represent a Christian ideal found in Galatians 3:28, which proclaimed that in Christ there is neither slave nor free, male nor female, Jew nor Gentile. A strong this-worldly sensibility governed their apocalyptic imagination. Christ appeared to them in female form, and she prophesied that the New Jerusalem would descend into their village of Pepouza in central Anatolia, today's Turkey. The movement endured until around the fifth century.[33]

Tertullian may have been the editor of the Perpetua story—he was probably in Carthage at the time of the executions. A master polemicist and satirist, Tertullian maintained an uncompromising support of martyrdom and ridiculed Rome for persecuting Christians.

If the Tiber rises so high it floods the walls, or the Nile so low it doesn't flood the fields, if the earth opens, or the heavens don't, if there is famine, if there is plague, instantly the howl goes up, "The Christians to the lion!" What, all of them? to a single lion?[34]

Tertullian, born and raised in Carthage, began his jurist career in Rome as a pagan, where he lived a licentious life, a typical young adulthood for Roman men. Tradition claimed that he converted to Christianity after observing Christian slaves being slain in gladiator games in Rome. He asserted that the church was born from the seeds of its martyrs. His turn to Christianity was accompanied by purist moral sensibilities and his sharp, ironic wit. Sometimes, in his most outrageous writings, one easily imagines him winking at the reader. He is notorious for calling women the "gateway of the devil" and proposing the term "original sin."[35] Tertullian eventually turned his acid polemics and wit against other Christian leaders, who he thought compromised with the empire too much. Tertullian eventually joined the New Prophecy movement, one of the great ironies of his life—women as the gateway to paradise, perhaps.

REVELATION: WHAT IT LEFT BEHIND

Persecuted Christians faced a dramatic choice of life or death: hold fast to the power "not of this world" and dwell in paradise, or deny it and succumb to the unjust and oppressive power of Rome, losing paradise here and paradise beyond the grave. The New Prophecy martyrs had clear apocalyptic expectations about the transformation of the world, but their vision of change differed from early Christianity's most famous version of apocalypticism, the book of Revelation. Revelation envisions the total destruction of the earth, rather than the descent of heavenly power into a beloved place.

"Apocalypse" means unveiling. Revelation unveiled the principalities and powers of *oikoumene*—the household of Rome—and described their destruction. To Rome's tortured, conquered, persecuted, and exploited peoples, it refused to speak of *oikoumene* as anything but hell.[36] The text exposed how empires inflate appearances of power by fomenting fear and terrorizing people into submission. The author's outrage is worthy of Amos. Like the prophets, it too proclaimed that the savage bloodletting, environmental catastrophes, and cataclysmic horrors of empires carried the seeds of their own destruction.

Revelation unveils by veiling. The book disguised the past as the future, making memory—the destruction of Babylonia—into a foretelling, as if to say history was fated to repeat itself. With the passage of centuries, however, Revelation's coded message left open speculation about what would be destroyed. Stillborn predictions have plagued those who read the coded text as a foretelling rather than as a remembrance and warning. Revelation's visions of a final cosmic battle of good against evil and the creation of a new heaven and earth came to dominate later Christian readings of the future. Scripts about the end of the world became a compulsive, self-fulfilling prophecy. They fed what theologian Catherine Keller calls the West's "apocalyptic habit," the predilection to see the impending end of history in one's own time and to act it out. Mesmerized by stark, apocalyptic either/or choices in a complex world, people drive toward solutions that seek salvation through destruction.[37]

Revelation, in its original context, responded to—rather than provoked—devastating violence. During the troubled first century in Galilee and Judea, religious movements fomented many forms of resistance to Rome, which had taken over the territory in 63 BCE. Rome governed with a brutal and exploitive hand, epitomized by Herod the Great. It co-opted the Jerusalem temple system to extract heavy taxes, and it crucified dissidents. Leaders of resistance movements condemned Rome and frequently also denounced Jerusalem and the temple. The words of Jesus, son of Hananiah, a mid-first-century prophet, provide an example:

> *A voice from the east, a voice from the west,*
> *A voice from the four winds.*
> *A voice against Jerusalem and the temple,*
> *A voice against the bridegroom and the brides,*
> *A voice against the whole people.*[38]

After decades of internal turmoil and struggle against Roman oppression, Jews rose up in revolt in 66–70 CE. Rome responded with massive force, sending troops into Jerusalem to raze its temple. Three years later at Masada, a fortress on a mesa along the southwestern shore of the Dead Sea, a thousand Jewish resisters and their families were the last holdouts against the empire. Their situation hopeless, they thought death at their own hands to be preferable to capture. To avoid capture, the men drew lots and a dozen of them killed the entire group and one another until the last man left committed suicide. A woman and her children had hidden during the killings, and they survived to tell the story to the stunned Roman soldiers who were greeted by eerie silence after they breached the walls of the fortress the next morning.

Undeterred, Jews organized a second revolt in 139 CE. This time Rome sent in its Tenth Legion. The legion destroyed villages and Jewish strongholds of resistance throughout the countryside. It felled the forests surrounding Jerusalem, laid siege to the city, overran its walls, killed or enslaved its inhabitants, and burned the city to the ground. Describing the wars that led to the final obliteration of Jerusalem, Cassius Dio's *Roman History* reported the destruction of "50 Jewish fortresses, 985 villages and the death *in battle alone* of 580,000 Jewish men."[39] Over the ruins of Jerusalem, Rome built a pagan city from which it banned all Jews on penalty of death. The book of Revelation was probably written around this time.

In Revelation, Babylonia represents the Roman Empire, just as it does in the catacomb depictions of stories from the book of Daniel. The whore of Babylon, its corrupt capital city, symbolizes not Rome but Jerusalem. Harlotry was used by the Hebrew prophets as a metaphor for apostasy. Pagan Rome was not an apostate city, but Herod's Jerusalem was. The author of Revelation depicted scenes of destruction worthy of what Rome did to Jerusalem when its legion devastated the city in 139 CE: the clash of swords, the rivers of blood, the scorched earth, the piles of rubble, and, finally, the cold ashes drifting across the desolated hills. He told his people to purify themselves and their communities, to trust in God, and to await the arrival of a new heaven and new earth. Jerusalem was to blame for her own destruction. What else was left to hope for but an entirely new beginning?[40]

The author of Revelation drew on Ezekiel's visions in constructing his prophecy. He was steeped in the prophet's images of mythical beasts and cosmic wonders, and he added his own fantastic nightmares, inspired by Zoroastrian images of heaven and, especially, hell. He saw the empire's rapacious, violent legions. He envisioned the cosmetically obsessed, seductive Jerusalem, "the great whore who is seated on many waters, with whom the kings of the earth have committed fornication, and with the wine of whose fornication the inhabitants of the earth have become drunk" (Rev. 17:1–2). He pictured himself writing his vision down and sending it to seven churches that shared "the persecution and the kingdom and the patient endurance" (Rev. 1:9–11). He affirmed the various strengths of the seven churches, warned them of their particular failings, and promised they would receive the blessings of God if they conquered their problems (Rev. 2–3).

Their failings sound almost modern. They were to stop consuming poisonous foods and harming themselves. They were to reject the poverty of riches, the hollowness of soulless consumerism. Instead of gazing inward, they were to wake up and pay attention to what was happening in the world. They should condemn those who betrayed truth. They should expel false prophets. The author told his listeners to hold fast in times of trial, to uphold truth, and to overcome self-satisfied mediocrity and lukewarm equivocating. He told the church at Ephesus, hardworking and patient, that its intolerance of evildoers had stolen its capacity to love. If it repented and found its love, the author promised, "To everyone who conquers I will give permission to eat from the tree of life that is in the paradise of God" (Rev. 2:7).

Many Christians have found Revelation a troubling text. It threatened terrifying punishments for those who picked the wrong side. Why populate heaven with those driven out of their wits by fear of hell? As anthropologist Margaret Mead once noted, when people are motivated by fear of eternal punishment, it might be more accurate to understand such behavior not as ethical but as cowardly. But this is not a cowardly text. It is a fatalistic one. The author enjoined the churches to maintain ethical practices while waiting for God to destroy evil, a holding pattern to guarantee them safe passage and rest until God brought the end and delivered a new beginning. Its images of terrifying doom and its passive fatalism make much better emotional and religious sense as a recitation of traumatic events its recipients already had witnessed than as predictions of future events. Among the most devastating destructive forces in the text, and those that have generated no end of speculation about end times, are the natural disasters evoked by the angels of God. Rome used environmental destruction, such as salting their enemies' fields, as a tactic of warfare and claimed to rule the world, including the natural world. The writer of Revelation begs to differ and presents the natural disasters—earthquakes, plagues, storms, and fires—as commanded by heaven to destroy the violent, rapacious empire and its claims of world domination.

With his images of Jezebel and the whore of Babylon, the writer of Revelation perpetuated the use of female promiscuity as a symbol for religious apostasy, reinforcing the mandate of violence against women and describing it. "She will be burned with fire; for mighty is the Lord God who judges her...and he has avenged on her the blood of his slaves" (Rev. 18:8, 19:2). Revelation's evil women were powerful. Their virtuous corollaries, two "good" women, had to rely on the power of others. One was pregnant and clothed in the sun, moon, and stars; the other was the bride of the Lamb. The former, crying in agony, delivered a son who was destined to rule with a rod of iron. Under divine protection, his mother hid from the forces of evil in the wilderness (Rev. 12). The bride emerged near the end of the book, joined with the victorious lamb. Her main role was to make a fashion statement. "To her it has been granted to be clothed with fine linen, bright and pure—for the fine linen is the righteous deeds of the saints" (Rev. 19:7–8).[41]

Revelation's image of a wrathful, punishing God was a major reason it was frequently left behind when Christians assembled lists of their sacred books. It had difficulty being included in the Christian canon and has remained controversial since. Yet it also criticized its own fantasy of destruction. Sometimes, when it spoke of victory, it advocated a power different from the violence used in "this world," a power that scholar Barbara Rossing describes as "lamb power."[42] This power was what Jesus said was not of "this world," and it was the power of the enthroned lamb in paradise. The book did not counsel the churches to take up arms or wage wars. It advised them to purify their communities, to be faithful unto death, and to wait for God to restore life.

Revelation promised paradise renewed to those who persevered. The author saw, in the annihilation of empire, a new earth and heaven and a new Jerusalem which descended from heaven. A voice said:

> *See, the home of God is among mortals.*
> *He will dwell with them;*
> *they will be his peoples,*
> *and God himself will be with them;*
> *he will wipe every tear from their eyes.*
> *Death will be no more;*
> *mourning and crying and pain will be no more,*
> *for the first things have passed away.*
> *See, I am making all things new. (Rev. 21:3–5, excerpts)*

This new Jerusalem would have no temple, and it would have no celestial lights; it would have, perpetually, the divine radiance and the lamp of the Lamb. This new earthly city would have

> the river of the water of life, bright as crystal, flowing from the throne of God and of the Lamb through the middle of the street of the city. On either side of the river is the tree of life with its twelve kinds of fruit, producing its fruit each month; and the leaves of the tree are for the healings of the nations. Nothing accursed will be found there any more.... And there will be no more night. (Rev. 22:1–3, 5)

What would such a vision of Jerusalem have meant to those who remembered its ashes? Surely, there is some echo of Ezekiel's valley of dry bones brought to life and his vision of Mt. Zion as paradise. And surely, somewhere behind the ecstatic vision of the heavenly city come down to earth, there were years of grief and lamentation. "The roads to Zion mourn, for no one comes to the festivals; all her gates are desolate, her priests groan; her young girls grieve, and her lot is bitter....

Her downfall was appalling, with none to comfort her" (Lam. 1:4, 9). But the text had no time for sorrow, just as it had no imagination for women's power as good. Between the last wisps of sulfur and the new heaven and new earth, there is no hint of mourning for what is left behind: no anguish for the webs of life and relationships forever incinerated, no grief for what might have been loved and lost, no reflection on the cost of the final solution and its cataclysmic war between good and evil.

Revelation asks its readers to believe that the murderous powers of war and catastrophe are instruments of good when wielded by the heavenly opponents of apostasy. Its idol is the sheer power of destruction, which dissolves moral distinctions between good and evil, between the legions of Satan and the forces of God. As philosopher Alfred North Whitehead noted, "The church gave unto God the attributes which belonged exclusively to Caesar."[43] The idea of an omnipotent God who is not accountable to moral questions but defines his own morality is still common in Christian circles today. In the face of the last two centuries of genocide, natural disasters, wars, and accumulations of weapons of mass destruction, an increasing number of religious people of conscience have concluded that an omnipotent God is neither good nor moral. If the power of God is no different from Satan, where is goodness to be found?

Revelation has more words devoted to paradise than does any other text in the scriptures. But Revelation's paradise is too thin and meager to carry the weight of its fury. In being obsessed with the dualism of good and evil and galvanizing its attention on empire, it closes the door, finally, on any possibility of forgiveness, and it envisions a denatured new Jerusalem that is out of this world. It loses its grounding in the world as a gift of God. Once its volcanic heat is blown, it can only offer a crystalline, cold comfort. It promises a glittering antiworld, a place absent meadows, night, dreams, animals, companionship, and pleasure. Its paradise resembles Doris Lessing's description of hell in a locked psychiatric ward—the lights are on all the time, and nowhere can one find tender mercies or the warmth of love.[44]

THE EMPIRE STRIKES BACK

Rome did not dissolve in a vast lake of fire as Revelation imagined it would. Its slow demise came as it rotted from within and was nibbled to death by invasions. The emperor Diocletian took control of the empire in 284, and for nineteen years he worked to save it from a century of runaway inflation and bankruptcy, a military stretched too thin, civil wars, urban riots, plagues, invasions, and the dropout members of the ruling and wealthy classes, who had found the burdens of empire more than they wanted to bear. Diocletian created a bureaucracy with more effective administrative control of the empire. He divided it into quarters and ruled them autocratically from his capital in Nicea, Turkey. Dissident religions gained popularity during the century of crises, so he used his pagan cult to enforce his empirewide administrative system. He called himself Lord and God and required supplicants to lie prostrate before him.[45]

During the third century of disasters and failed emperors, Christian churches formed regional systems with presbyters and deacons, headed by a bishop, with the bishop of the largest city leading the region. By the middle of the third century, Rome had 155 priests, and North Africa had more than ninety bishops. Using this system, churches cooperated in sharing resources and caring for members.[46] Teachers of the early third century, such as Tertullian and Justin Martyr of Rome, commented on how Christians renounced personal wealth and status by donating their holdings to the community and sharing them in common, a practice described in the book of Acts and letters of Paul. By the mid–third century, the church in Rome was reported to be supporting about fifteen hundred widows, orphans, elderly men, shipwrecked sailors, miners, prisoners, and sick people.[47]

In 303, Diocletian turned his attention to Christianity and issued a series of bans against it. He began by confiscating property and destroying churches. Reluctant to fuel resistance by creating more martyrs, he first tortured Christian leaders by blinding them or disabling them in other ways. Some he banished to brutal slave labor in mines, which usually killed them within a year. With each ban that failed to quash the churches, he escalated his crackdown. His ten-year, empirewide persecution was the worst in the church's history and is often called the Great Persecution.[48]

In the small town of Cirta in North Africa, a Roman public slave wrote an account of one incident. On May 19, 303, Felix, the local high priest for Diocletian, took a delegation to the Christian house church and seized its leaders. Felix demanded that they surrender their sacred objects. "Bring forth the scriptures of your law and anything else you have here, as has been ordered by the edict." The Christian bishop Paul, fearing for his life, responded, "The lectors have the scriptures, but we surrender what we have got here." The Romans confiscated two gold chalices, six each silver chalices and dishes, a silver bowl, seven silver lamps, eighteen bronze lamps, four baskets, six casks, one book, eighty-two women's and sixteen men's baptismal tunics, thirty-eight veils, thirteen men's and forty-seven women's pairs of slippers, and eighteen pairs of clogs. Paul sat on his bishop seat in silence, surrounded by the other officers of the church, as they watched the sacred objects carted away. Historian Gregory Dix notes that in a few short minutes, they had committed apostasy, which, for church leaders at the time, could not be forgiven, ever. "And they knew it; Felix knew it; even the grinning public slaves knew it. They had saved their lives—but they had all irremediably forfeited their orders in that quarter of an hour."[49]

When asked for the names of the lectors, already publicly known by the Romans, two sub-deacons refused. "We are not informers. Here we stand. Command us to be executed." They were arrested, tortured, and sent to the mines.

HOLDING TO PARADISE

There are worse things than dying. One is having to live with the knowledge that you, by your own choice, have surrendered to forces you abhor and been complicit in the destruction of what you most love. To submit to Rome's demands was, for many, a different kind of death sentence. Apostate leaders severed their connection to the Spirit, relinquished their freedom and moral agency, and abandoned their community.

Those who held fast during times of trial—even if it meant their deaths—joined hands with those who had gone on before. The cloud of witnesses had surrounded them in life and would carry them across the threshold of death. Martyrs stayed connected against all odds to those who, for love of life, had resisted oppression while they lived, and now they dwelt in paradise. Not isolated heroism, self-denial, or self-sacrifice, martyrdom was an act of participation in the communion of saints.

Christians cherished the remains of martyr's bodies, holding to tatters of cloth and fragments of bone as talismans of life-giving power. "We collect the bones [of the martyrs] as if they were gold and precious stones and see to their burial."[50] They interred them in the catacombs or built small octagonal or round buildings to hold the remains of martyrs near where they died. Eventually, beautiful reliquaries were crafted to hold the saint's relics. Churches were built on or next to the martyria, and the lives of martyrs in paradise were depicted on the walls in vivid mosaics. Such places became major pilgrimage sites, where the faithful could come and experience the power of the Spirit and gain access to energies of resistance, healing, and life. As Peter Brown notes, a relic was an enduring physical remnant of "a fully redeemed person, a saint, who now dwelt in God's Paradise." Such relics brought this paradise to the world of the living, as a world of lush flora and radiant color. "To come to the tomb of a major saint . . . was to breathe in a little of the healing air of Paradise."[51]

Relics and rituals associated with them linked the living to the martyred dead and defied oppressive powers. They created bonds that bridged the chasm of death and harnessed forces of life and love. Such energies are still needed in struggles against violence and injustice, struggles that continue to the present day. Resistance cannot be measured by one life or one lifetime alone. It requires solidarity across the generations. In our time, the righteous dead call us to keep faith with their witness and carry on their legacy of commitment to life. As a contemporary memorial prayer expresses it, "Those who lived before us, who struggled for justice and suffered injustice before us, have not melted into the dust, and have not disappeared. They are with us still."[52] Their devotion to life is a sustaining inheritance. When we choose to hold fast to love as they did, we enter with them into paradise, now.

CHAPTER FOUR

The Church as Paradise
in This World

The Church has been planted
as a *paradisus* in this world.

IRENAEUS, BISHOP OF LYON

(C. 130–C. 200)

Theodore of Euchaita, a Christian, was conscripted into the Roman
army in 306. He refused to worship the emperor and was burned at the
stake for it. "I have been, am, and shall be with my Christ," Theodore
had replied when the Roman governor asked him to choose whether to
"be with us or be with your Christ."[1] According to legend, Theodore's
body was unharmed by the flames. Gregory of Nyssa (c. 330–c. 395) described the martyrium built to commemorate his witness. The shrine
was filled with images: "wood, in the shape of animals, beautiful flowers illustrating nature, the elaborate mosaic floor that is like a prayer in
tiny stones to the martyr, polished stones that are as smooth as silver."
A painting depicted Theodore's contest with the empire; Christ himself presided over the scene. Pilgrims came to the shrine, Gregory said,
"like ants all year long, since it was known especially as a healing shrine
for all sorts of diseases, a storehouse for those in need, an inn for the
weary, and an incessant festival for those celebrating." This shrine
raised the dead. "Those who see the body see it as living and thriving,

and they embrace it [with arms] and with eyes, by mouth [with kisses], with ears, with all the senses they come to it."[2] Shrines to martyrs became prototypes for the expansion of Christian art and architecture that began in the fourth century.

The fourth and fifth centuries of Christianity were among the most transformative in its history. After Diocletian's reign (284–305), the Emperors Constantine (306–337) and Licinius (308–324) issued the Edict of Milan in 313, which decriminalized Christianity and established religious tolerance.[3] Constantine also became a major patron of the church; he followed Diocletian's example and used religious networks to administrate a sprawling empire, substituting Christianity for paganism. After the edict, church leaders responded to Christianity's favored status in several ways. They accommodated imperial demands; they struggled to hold a power base separate from the empire; and they used their newfound clout to fight their Jewish and pagan opponents. Imperial favor lasted barely a half-century. Constantine's nephew Julian, who took power in 361 and was slain in battle in 363, briefly reinstated paganism, patronized Judaism, and persecuted Christians. His was the last attempt to reclaim the old pagan Rome. Christianity eventually emerged from this process as the favored religion under the empire. The Theodosian Codes of 429–438 CE transformed some church canons, passed at councils of bishops, into Roman civil laws.[4]

In the midst of this century of changing fortunes, Christian leaders produced an extensive literature about paradise. They advanced ideas and practices already developed over three previous centuries of resistance to imperialism, and they forged new patterns of dissidence. They also accepted imperial patronage, which expanded their capacities to care for the sick and needy and funded the building of churches filled with lush visual environments of paradise. The church maintained its tensions with empire by insisting that paradise in this world was most concretely realized in the church and that Jesus Christ incarnated God and returned humanity to paradise.

IMAGES OF SALVATION

Artists and architects took the iconography of the martyr's shrines and developed it into large-scale public worship spaces. Most artwork from the fourth century has been lost, but mosaics from the fifth and sixth centuries have survived in Ravenna, Italy, which holds the richest store of church art from early Christianity. In Ravenna's mosaics, we see a continuity of images from the catacombs, as well as the emergence of a full-blown iconography of paradise and Jesus Christ as *Pantokrator* (all-holding), All Sustaining, Just Presence.[5]

As soon as congregants entered ancient churches, they stood in a three-tiered sacred cosmos. A starry night sky or multihued clouds represented the first tier, the heavens; from this mysterious realm, the right hand of God emerged to bless the world, and celestial beings hovered in golden skies. The second tier was an intermediary space over which the living Christ presided. The departed saints stood with him in the meadows of paradise and visited to bless the living. The third tier was the floor of the church where worshippers stood in God's garden on earth.

We saw this sacred cosmos in the mausoleum of Galla Placidia in Ravenna, Italy, a small, cross-shaped building. Built around 430 as a martyrium commemorating St. Lawrence, the interior central dome displays a midnight blue sky that teems with gold stars. A simple Latin cross marks the center apex of the sky, and the winged creatures of Ezekiel's heavenly vision—a lion, ox, eagle, and man—emerge from red and white clouds in the corners of the dome. Below the celestial heavens, arches support the areas of the four arms of the cross and frame half-moon lunettes. The arches and lunettes depict paradise: spiraling grape and acanthus vines grow abundantly, bushes are laden with fruit, deer and doves drink at fountains and pools, and saints stand in green meadows. In one lunette, Lawrence, a deacon executed in Rome in 258, stands in his white robe of glory and gold nimbus. He became the patron saint of librarians because legend says he was burned for defending sacred books. In the image, his cabinet of books stands next to him.[6] In the facing lunette, Christ appears as a good shepherd, the last existing early image of him as a shepherd. He sits on a pile of stones in a shrub-covered, rugged landscape. His beardless, boyish face, framed by wavy shoulder-length hair, turns across his right shoulder toward a sheep who gazes at him, one of six arrayed around him on the rocky out-croppings. With his left hand, he holds a shepherd's staff in the form of a cross-shaped labarum, and his right hand extends to touch the uplifted face of a sheep. Ancient visitors to this shrine would have stood, as we did, one level below on the stone floor looking up at the canopy of the heavens, and around at the paradise that was home to Christ and the departed saints.

In this three-tiered universe, paradise had both a "here" and "not here" quality. Christians taught that paradise had always been here on earth. Sin had once closed its portals, but Jesus Christ had reopened them for the living. While Christians could taste, see, and feel the traces of it in ordinary life, they arrived most fully in paradise in community

FIGURE 3. *Mausoleum of Galla Placidia, Ravenna, Italy. Lunette, mosaic. Fifth century. Jesus as the Good Shepherd.*

worship. With its art and buildings, the church created a space that united the living on earth with the heavenly beings and departed saints, who surrounded and blessed the living. The risen Christ and clouds of witnesses embraced this life and lifted it to touch the heavens at every Eucharist. In that holy ritual, the community stood within the sacred cosmos, blessed by the fruits of the earth and the power of the saints.

Early church sensibilities about salvation were oriented to space—to a world of many dimensions, blessed by the all-permeating Spirit. However, the modern Western religious consciousness imagines salvation almost entirely in temporal terms. Theologians speak of sacred and profane time, of salvation history, and of hope. They interpret the expulsion of Adam and Eve from paradise as the beginning of salvation history: the world runs along a hard arrow of time, beginning with human sin and culminating in a final New Age, kingdom of God, Second Coming, or New Heaven and Earth. Humanity lives "between the times," awaiting a future yet to be consummated. Christ will return to fulfill God's promise of salvation, which the faithful will receive after death, after God destroys this evil world, or after God creates a just world and has beaten all swords into plowshares. While these future-oriented themes are present among early Christian ideas, they did not delay salvation until after death or in an indefinite future time. They pictured salvation as the landscape of paradise, an environment full of life that was entered here and now through the church. Theodore of Euchaita had said, "I have been, am, and shall be with my Christ." His salvation was ever present.

Salvation in paradise was an experience and a place, as well as work yet to be completed. The early church understood that paradise encompassed many dimensions—material and spiritual, awaited and fulfilled. Perception and knowledge connected these dimensions, and Christians gained them through their lifelong training of perception and spiritual practices in worship that developed ethical discernment about good and evil. To know how to distinguish good and evil required acute attunement to the present and reflection about ethical behavior. Through such wisdom, Christians sought to live joyfully and enact justice, nonviolence, and love.

THE GENESIS COMMENTARIES

Long before the full-blown iconography of paradise emerged in churches, Christians wrote profusely and taught extensively about paradise. Paradise was important enough that virtually every early theologian of the church remarked at length on Genesis 1–3. Some even wrote entire commentaries to describe the Creation, paradise, and the relationship of humanity to God. Church teachers asserted that even in a conflict-ridden, difficult world, paradise existed on the earth. They suggested that its most concrete, realized form was lived out in the social practices and spiritual training of the church.

Early on, teachers spoke of the church itself as the renewed paradise of God. Bishop Irenaeus of Lyon exhorted those who might be misled by unsound, heretical ideas to

flee to the Church, and be brought up in her bosom, and be nourished with the Lord's scriptures. For the Church has been planted as a *paradisus* in this world; therefore says the Spirit of God (Genesis 2:16), "Thou mayest freely eat from every tree of the garden," that is, Eat ye from every Scripture of the Lord.[7]

Irenaeus did not blame Adam and Eve for sinning and threatening human destiny. He thought they were like naïve children who made a huge mistake. Because their sin affected human life as a consequence, Irenaeus said death was a necessary mercy to deliver humanity to a realm of paradise where evil could not follow. Irenaeus taught that paradise existed in the next life and also in this life because Christ reversed the Fall and restored Creation. "For God is rich in all things, and all things are his. It is right, therefore, for this created order to be restored to its pristine state."[8] Christians, like Christ, would "receive the Spirit of God." As spiritual fruit "planted in the paradise of God . . . [they would] arrive at the pristine nature of man—that which was created after the image and likeness of God."[9] In other words, Jesus Christ incarnated the Spirit and restored to humanity the divinity that Adam and Eve lost.

Theophilus of Antioch, another theologian of the second century, taught that humanity was not intrinsically good or evil but had the freedom to become divine. To assist humanity with this possibility, God gave Adam and Eve a place to learn:

> God transferred [humanity] out of the earth from which he was made into paradise, giving him an opportunity for progress so that by growing and becoming mature, and furthermore having been declared a god, he might also ascend into heaven . . . possessing immortality.[10]

Origen of Alexandria agreed that the church offered paradise in some form in this life and that Eden existed somewhere as a real place. However, as a neo-Platonist, he disliked literal interpretations of paradise: "What is so silly as to believe that God . . . set in it a visible and palpable 'tree of life,' of such sort that anyone who tasted its fruit with his bodily teeth would gain life?"[11] Interpreting the Genesis story as an allegory for the soul's spiritual ascent to divinity, he taught that the world of ideas was superior to material life and that the soul preexisted the body. Humanity would ultimately join with the world soul, God, from which it had descended into this life. In contrast to Origen, other early Christians emphasized the material dimensions of paradise, as well as its metaphorical or allegorical significance. Origen's contemporary, Cyprian (c. 200–258), a bishop of Carthage martyred in the same persecution that killed Lawrence, taught that the church was the *paradisus cum fructus pomorum* (the garden with abundant fruit) described in the Song of Songs and the place of miraculous waters in the desert recalled in Isaiah 48:21. These metaphors affirmed that the church provided both material and spiritual nourishment.

The Greek Septuagint and Latin Vulgate versions of Genesis supported material understandings of the earth as paradise. These versions translated the Hebrew word *gan-eden* (garden of delight) in generic terms rather than as the proper name Eden with one location. The Septuagint used *paradeisos truphes* (luxurious paradise) for *gan-*

eden; the Vulgate used *paradisum voluptatis* (pleasure paradise). These translations suggested paradise was an earthly garden in a general way. The church's teachers ran with this idea. They scattered paradise throughout the earth and concentrated it, especially, in any church anywhere. In their musings, Christian commentators tended to follow second temple ideas about the river that flowed from Eden, identifying it as the Jordan. From the gates of the garden, it split into the Gihon, Pishon, Tigris, and Euphrates; circulated under and around the world; and returned to the garden. This cyclical flow permeated the earth with the moist, rejuvenating qualities of paradise, since all the waters of the earth shared in this original source and final destination.[12] Hippolytus of Rome (c. 170–c. 236) observed:

> Some persons claim that paradise is in heaven and is not a created thing. But when one sees with one's own eyes the rivers that flow from it and that can still be seen today, one must conclude that paradise is not heavenly but part of creation.[13]

Many theologians speculated about how much paradise infused this life and in what ways it was known. Some placed it on top of a remote mountain in Mesopotamia, since the Tigris and Euphrates flowed from there. Attempts to identify the other two rivers, the Gihon and Pishon, shifted the placement. The Gihon was usually the Nile, but the Pishon could be the Ganges, the Danube, or even the Arabian Sea. Those who preferred the Ganges placed paradise east of India, somewhere off the coast of China. The Danube led to musings that paradise might be near the Arctic. Wherever it was, if it could be located, it would be at the top of a mountain, since most great rivers originate in mountains. Basil the Great (c. 330–379) concluded that remnants of paradise existed on the heights of virtually any mountain.[14]

Early church discussions of paradise tended to be pastoral, poetic, and meandering. The teachers of the church asserted that, wherever paradise was, humanity's first parents had once lived harmoniously in the garden of delight with each other and with the animals and environment. They had direct access to God in the verdant beauties of paradise. Whether or not Adam and Eve had sex in Eden was disputed —most thought not, but Augustine insisted they did, but without lust. He wrote three commentaries on Genesis during the course of his career (which is not to say he got it right).

Early Christian theologians incorporated Greek and Roman ideas into their musings about paradise. Hesiod described a golden age when humanity "lived like gods without sorrow of heart, remote and free from toil and grief." After death, "they dwelt in ease and peace upon their lands, with many good things, rich in flocks and loved by the blessed gods." Homer's *Odyssey* told of a great orchard island with two abundant springs. He also explained that the immortals sent persons to the Elysian plain, a theme reiterated in the *Aeneid,* in which the Elysian Fields were a natural earthly paradise in a lower world. Virgil, Ovid, and Horace were among other writers who described a golden past, Happy Isles, or other places in which, in their native state, human beings "kept faith and did the right."[15]

The cross-cultural, multireligious origins of paradise were enough to make pagans accuse Christians of stealing their ideas. In the face of such criticism, the second-century convert and apologist for Christianity Justin Martyr (c. 100–c. 165) justified these influences by claiming that Homer borrowed his ideas of paradise from Moses, the designated author of Genesis. Philo of Alexandria, a Jewish theologian, had mounted a similar defense in the first century about the relationship of Plato and Moses. Justin Martyr's *Exhortation to the Greeks* argued that Homer found the five books of Moses in Egypt, translated the paradise texts into Greek, and cribbed them for his own use. In Justin's time, borrowing a good idea or using a great writer's words paid tribute not only to the writer but to the education, skill, and astuteness of the borrower. However, primacy went to the one from whom one borrowed. In addition, he lived at a time that prized novelty in military matters but not in religion. Ideas with gravitas that were more likely to earn respect needed the patina of antiquity. Their age proved their veracity through the vicissitudes of time.[16]

In addressing the question of whether paradise was a physical place on earth or the spiritual journey of souls, a number of influential fourth-century theologians—Ephrem, Ambrose, and Augustine, among others —said it was both a real place on earth and an allegory for human spiritual development. This both/and approach allowed them to speak about paradise on the earth in a diffuse way and to locate its most concentrated form in the church. The church as the concentration of paradise united aesthetic appreciation for the material goodness of the world God created with ethical responsiveness to this gift, what we call ethical grace.

Ephrem

Ephrem the Syrian (c. 306–373), a poet, teacher, and lay ascetic from Nisibis, Syria, was the greatest writer of his century on paradise. Nisibis, located in conflicted borderlands between the Roman and Persian empires, was a major crossroads that attracted Asian, African, and European residents, and their cultural influences inform Ephrem's writing.[17] The rabbinic community there offered him instruction in Jewish commentaries and the models and methods of Hebrew poetry. He was rooted in the religious and cultural symbol systems of Mesopotamia and Persia, and he was exposed to Greek science and philosophy. His work reflects a rich cross-cultural education, and gives us a complex picture of fourth-century Christian ideas about paradise, especially how paradise functioned to offer prophetic critiques of empires.

Ephrem's contemporaries regarded him as their foremost writer of poetry. His hymns, written in Syriac—the language used by Christians throughout Asia—were translated into many languages and sung throughout the Christian world from the fourth to sixth centuries.[18] He was acquainted with Basil the Great, whose brother Gregory of Nyssa wrote a biography of Ephrem. Other Greek and Latin Christian theologians commented on Ephrem appreciatively; the Latin Jerome (c. 342–420) valued his eloquence and recognized in him "the acumen of a lofty intellect."[19] The early-fifth-century Greek historian Sozomen praised both the quality and quantity of his literary output:

His style of writing was so filled with splendid oratory and with richness and temperateness of thought that he surpassed the most approved writers of Greece . . . It is said he wrote three hundred thousand verses, and that he had many disciples who were zealously attached to his doctrines.[20]

Through his lyric poetry, Ephrem engaged in theological debate with other religious viewpoints. He wrote poems that argued against the [Manicheans,] who promised release for souls trapped in the earthly "realm of darkness." Their prophet Mani taught that souls could merge after death into the "paradise of light" by practicing a strict asceticism during this life. Though he was a voluntary lay ascetic who had taken a vow of celibacy, Ephrem affirmed the body and sex. He regarded earthly existence as a good realm in which paradise could be found and entered through rituals, spiritual disciplines, and ethical practices. He also opposed the Marcionites, who rejected the Hebrew Bible and its God.[21] Ephrem saw the Hebrew Bible as sacred scripture, and he described his study of it as a transporting pleasure. On reading the opening chapters of Genesis 1–2, he said, the texts filled him with joy:

> *The verses and lines*
> *spread out their arms to welcome me;*
> *the first rushed out and kissed me,*
> *and led me on to its companions.*
> *and when I reached that line*
> *where the story*
> *of Paradise is written, it lifted me up*
> *and transported me*
> *from the bosom of the Book*
> *to the very bosom of Paradise.*[22]

In his commentary on Genesis, Ephrem identified the four rivers of paradise as the Danube, Nile, Tigris, and Euphrates, and he noted, "In between these we live." Ephrem said Eden tamed the waters of chaos and was the site of the holy mountain on which Noah landed his ark.

His placement of Eden at the top of his world's highest peak echoed
Jewish ideas in the second-century BCE *Book of Jubilees*. From this
mountaintop, Ephrem said, the waters of Eden flowed down and divided so that "the blessing of Paradise should be mingled by means of
water as it issues forth to irrigate the world."[23]

Ephrem's most extensive reflections on paradise were recorded in
his *Hymns on Paradise*, a book comprising fifteen long poems. In these
poems, Ephrem spoke of paradise as a landscape that called humanity
to live ethical, just, and joyous lives and to journey toward God. He pictured paradise as a great cosmic mountain that encompassed the earth
and the ocean. "Gloriously entwined is the wreath of Paradise that en-
circles the whole of creation."[24] The baptized entered paradise now and
lived within the embrace of this mountain. Its foothills were the home
of the repentant; its slopes housed the just. Its higher regions, past the
tree of knowledge, were the abode of the glorious, the children of light.
The summit, beyond the tree of life, was the dwelling place of the Shekinah, the shining presence of God. From these heights, "Divinity flew
down to draw humanity up."[25] The descent of Christ and the ascent of
humanity took place on the holy mountain of paradise. This exchange
restored humanity to Eden.

All dimensions of life—heart, mind, soul, and strength—belonged in
paradise. In Ephrem's symbolism, different zones of the mountain also
represented dimensions of human existence. The base was the body;
the rising slopes were the soul, the spirit, and the intellect; and the summit was humanity's divine nature. Ephrem used erotic images from the
Song of Songs to describe these zones. The delights of the garden filled
the lowest regions; the summit was the bridal chamber. In the church,
humanity gained access to all the zones of paradise and its inebriating
pleasures:

> *Paradise surrounds the limbs*
> *with its many delights;*
> *the eyes, with its handiwork*
> *the hearing, with its sounds,*

the mouth and the nostrils,
with its tastes and scents . . .
Paradise raised me up as I perceived it,
it enriched me as I meditated upon it;
I forgot my poor estate,
for it had made me drunk with its fragrance.[26]

Ephrem's joy in paradise stands in contrast to the many difficulties his Christian communities faced under two powerful empires. Born into a Christian family during the Great Persecution, his life was marked by the wars of Rome and Persia. When Constantine conquered the eastern half of the Roman Empire in 324, the Christians in Nisibis, which was located on the easternmost edge of the empire, enjoyed security for a time. However, peace was short-lived. Beginning in 335, King Shapur II of Persia began a long campaign to reconquer Mesopotamia. In the period 337–350, the Persians repeatedly attacked Nisibis. In 350, Shapur besieged the city, using elephants—one of the great weapons of ancient warfare. He diverted the River Mydonius in an effort to flood the city and topple its walls. The inhabitants resisted the attack and rebuilt their city.

In 361, the emperor Julian, Constantine's pagan nephew, seized power and tried once again to suppress Christianity. He confiscated Christian property and destroyed churches, schools, and civic spaces, building pagan temples on their ruins. Employing a double-pronged strategy, he simultaneously mimicked and maligned the work of the Christian community, instructing pagan priests to replace Christian networks of social welfare while accusing Christians of misleading people into baptism by seducing them with bread and false promises of networks of care. Julian also assassinated Christian leaders in his army and wrote vitriolic treatises against the false teachings of the "Galileans," especially the veneration of martyrs and the offensive teaching that Jesus was God.[27] He offered patronage to Jews—a divide-and-conquer strategy that strained relationships among Christians and Jews who were close kin in places like Nisibis.

Julian also waged war against Persia. He was decisively overwhelmed in 363 and slain in battle. Nisibis's Christians fled the city because they feared the Persians, who harshly persecuted Christians within their realm. Ephrem lamented this exile in his *Carmina Nisibena* (Songs on Nisibis).[28]

> *My Lord, my children have fled like chicks*
> *pursued by an eagle. They are hidden in a refuge!*
> *Let your Peace return to them.*
> *I have lifted up my eyes to all the squares; they are deserted.*[29]

Ephrem also wrote four *Hymns against Julian,* in which he blamed Julian for the fall of his beloved city. He described the war between Rome and Persia as a vicious fight between wild animals. Echoing the Hebrew prophets, he denounced Julian as a faithless ruler and warned against the disasters that come when people abandon the way of life taught by the true prophets. He condemned the Jews in Nisibis who had welcomed Julian's imperial favor, and he called on Christians to remain firmly rooted in paradise. Speaking of Julian's death, he rejoiced that "the lance of Justice passed through the belly of him who despised Him Who made the lance of paradise pass away."[30] The lance of paradise was the flaming sword of the cherubim, which kept it closed. Jesus removed the lance. Paradise was a realm of life and safety that could be trusted, even when the clash of empires threatened on all sides. Ephrem consoled his people with an image of Jesus as the True Vine which could not be cut down. Its roots were firmly planted in heaven, and its branches sheltered life on earth. Ephrem reassured his people that God had not deserted them. "He is the power on Whom depend the creation and its inhabitants."[31] After the fall of Nisibis, Ephrem made a new life in exile in Edessa, a city known as the "Athens of the East."[32] There, he taught biblical commentary, founded choirs, and kept writing poetry. When a famine struck Edessa in 372, leaders of the city's church asked Ephrem to lead the effort to alleviate it. His writings and actions during this famine and the epidemics that followed it demonstrate his understanding of what living in paradise required. Ephrem organized food distribution and set up hospitals to care for the sick. He enlisted the cooperation of the healthy to maintain the community and extended the church's care to the entire city. His poetry and hymns on paradise show us that he encouraged those under his care to savor the mystery of the goodness of life until their last breath:

The breath that wafts
  from some blessed corner of Paradise
gives sweetness
  to the bitterness of this region,
it tempers the curse
  on this earth of ours.
That Garden is   n̄ṭ duqlijun
  the life-breath
of this diseased world.[33]

Ephrem's verses also extolled the power of the ordinary: familiar music, lovely fragrances, tasty morsels of food, and beauties for the eyes.[34] His poetic corpus, read in tandem with his life and deeds, reveals a person actively working to ease the injustices, dangers, and hungers of this life through the healing balms of the church. In the face of imperial violence, natural disasters, and disease, the church held the doors of paradise open, offering love against all odds.[35]

The assembly of saints
  bears resemblance to Paradise:
In it each day is plucked
  the fruit of Him who gives life to all;
in it . . . is trodden
  the cluster of grapes, to be the medicine of life.[36]

The term "medicine of life" was a popular Syriac image for Christ as the physician who healed diseases of the body and the soul and who was even the cure for death. He dispensed his medicine through the Eucharist bread and wine and through the anointing of healing oil given at baptism. Such rituals and the mutuality of care within the Christian community were activities within paradise. Christians, Ephrem said, were grafted onto Christ, the tree of life, through their responsiveness to one another's needs. Even Christ had need of human care. With his nativity, "the Provisioner of all entered—and experienced hunger; He who gives drink to all entered—and experienced thirst." Life required reciprocity, the richness of one supplying the wants of another: "The inhabitants of the world fill in the common need from the common excess. We should rejoice in this need on that part of us all. . . . Our need for everything binds us with a love for everything."[37] Sharing vulnerability and using one's power to help others kept the circle of love complete. To ask for help was a sign of the generosity of allowing another to demonstrate love:

> *One person falls sick—and so another can visit and help him;*
> *one person starves—and so another can provide him with*
>   *food and give him life;*
> *one person does something stupid—*
> *but he can be instructed by another and thereby grow.*
> *In this way the world can recover:*
> *tens of thousands of hidden ways are to be found,*
> *ready to assist us.*[38]

For Ephrem, paradise was a reality that infused the church through works of love and rituals of sensual joy. He perceived proofs of paradise in communities that struggled to live with ethical grace: to care for one another, to live nonviolently and wisely, to resist empires when necessary, and to appreciate the beauties and pleasures of ordinary life. Though paradise was only partially realized in the church, it could still be tasted and experienced there. After a year, the famine and epidemics in Edessa ended, and Ephrem settled back into his life as a teacher. He lived another year before he died. For his many theological insights, captured in thousands of poems and hymns, the Eastern church affectionately calls him, still, "the Songbird of Paradise."

Ambrose

Ambrose of Milan (c. 339-397) was born in Gaul, where his father was governor of one of the four vast prefectures of Rome. His Christian mother raised him in Rome upon the death of his father during his adolescence. Ambrose trained in law, became governor of Liguria and

Emilia in 370, and moved to Milan, the capital of the provinces he governed and of the Roman Empire. In 374, controversy erupted about who should replace the recently deceased bishop as competing factions struggled for control of the church. Ambrose was drafted to be the bishop of Milan, which made him the emperor's bishop. Ambrose had to be baptized, ordained, and consecrated in eight days; this was after the community caught him trying to leave town. Ambrose commented that his lack of education in theology required him to teach in the morning what he had learned overnight. Unlike most of the Latin theologians of the church, Ambrose was fluent in Greek, and Philo, Origen, and Basil the Great deeply influenced his teaching and writing. His *Hexameron,* a commentary on the six days of Creation in Genesis 1, evidenced a deep debt to Basil especially.

Ambrose wrote an extensive commentary on Genesis 2-3 that he called *Paradise.* The book begins with great enthusiasm: "In approaching this subject I seem to be possessed by an unusual eagerness in my quest to clarify the facts about Paradise, its place, and its nature to those who are desirous of this knowledge." However, after writing an entire book on the subject, Ambrose still could not pin down where and what paradise was exactly. He explained that even Paul, who was "caught up in paradise," could not remember if he experienced paradise "in or out of the body" (2 Cor. 12:2-4). This left all possibilities open. Ambrose affirmed that paradise had a physical location replete with vigorous trees and delightful waters, but paradise was also the spiritual state of a "fertile soul" who produced "good fruits." He described each of the four rivers of Paradise as flowing through geographical regions of the earth such as India and Ethiopia, but at the same time the Great River, or fount of paradise, was Jesus Christ, or Wisdom. "In your soul there exists a fount" he wrote, from which virtue and gladness flowed, making life abundant and happy.[39]

In his thinking, the four rivers signified virtues, from *virtus* (manliness) which epitomized a Christian model of pious, stoic, and assertive masculinity that emerged in the fourth century, exemplified by Ambrose himself.[40] The Tigris represented fortitude: "Fortitude in its rapid course tosses aside everything standing in its path and like this river is not hindered by any material obstacle." The Euphrates, justice, was the concord and mother of all virtues because it was indivisible; justice was "the nourishment of every soul." The name Euphrates, Ambrose noted, came from "the Greek [for] . . . a 'feeling of gladness,' because the human race rejoices in nothing more than it does in Justice and Equity." The Pishon was prudence, and the Gihon was chastity, which washed away carnal sin.[41]

After Ambrose established a power base of churches in northern Italy, he had the audacity and political acumen in 390 to excommunicate the Roman emperor Theodosius, who had ordered a massacre in Thessalonica after rioters there killed one of his generals. The historian Theodoret (c. 393–466) wrote of the massacre: "Seven thousand perished without any forms of law, and without even having judicial sentence passed upon them; but that, like ears of wheat in the time of harvest, they were alike cut down."[42] Ambrose, in keeping with the church's teaching that shedding human blood was a sin, forbade the emperor from participating in the Eucharist until he had performed sufficient penance. If the emperor insisted on attending the Eucharist, Ambrose would withhold the Eucharist from the entire community. In other words, the entire community would be unable to "feast in paradise" if the emperor did not repent or renounce his baptism and leave the community. Because the sin was public, Ambrose told Theodosius, he had to act publicly:

There was not one who did not lament it, not one who thought lightly of it; your being in fellowship with Ambrose was no excuse for your deed. Blame for what had been done would have been heaped more and more on me, had no one said that your reconciliation to our God was necessary.[43]

Theodosius accepted the discipline of his bishop and his Christian community, and he undertook penance for approximately eight months. He attended worship with other penitents, in plain clothes without any trappings of his office, and he practiced austerities such as fasting and almsgiving. Theodoret also records Theodosius prostrating himself in the church, praying with tears, and tearing his hair as acts of lamentation and repentance.[44] At the time of the emperor's penance, Augustine was in Milan:

> What could be more admirable than his religious humility, when ...being laid hold of by the discipline of the church, [he] did penance in such a way that the sight of his imperial loftiness prostrated made the people who were interceding for him weep.[45]

In compelling the repentance of the emperor for shedding human blood, Ambrose showed the extent to which a bishop of the church had authority over a baptized emperor, and he demonstrated that life in paradise had ethical requirements that could call even an emperor's behavior into question. His stance contrasted with that of other Christian leaders in the fourth century, most notably Eusebius of Caesarea (c. 260–c. 340), who had exulted when the Emperor Constantine converted to Christianity. In writing his *Church History* and his *Life of Constantine,* Eusebius imagined that a Christianized empire would embody paradise on earth, which he equated with the zone of victory in which Christ, via war, crushed his enemies.[46] Ambrose, who was a bishop a half-century later, sanctioned wars in some cases, based on biblical examples of victorious kings who fought with God's assistance, but he maintained tension between the church and the empire. Paradise was a corrective and counterpoint; it was not to be equated with empire.

Augustine

Augustine (354–430), who grew up in Roman North Africa, converted to Christianity largely because of Ambrose, who trained and baptized him. His mentor's sophisticated allegorical interpretations of the Hebrew scriptures especially impressed Augustine. His mother, Monica, had attempted to raise him in the Christian faith, but he found it simple and inadequate. As a young adult, he became a Manichaean dualist and rejected the Jewish scriptures. He trained in rhetoric and lived for fifteen years with a common-law wife, with whom he raised a son. He sought to make his fame and fortune as a teacher in Rome, and at the age of thirty he achieved one of the highest academic positions in the Latin world: teacher to the imperial court in Milan. There he encountered the preaching of Ambrose, whose ability to read silently also impressed him; Augustine had never before observed this skill. Ambrose baptized him in 387. Deeming him ready, Monica betrothed him to a girl from a wealthy family, which required him to send the mother of his son away. Then, rather than marry the wealthy young girl whom Monica selected for him, he chose celibacy and the priesthood. He returned to North Africa after a half-decade in Italy and served as the bishop of Hippo, about sixty miles west of Carthage, from 395 to the end of his long life. In leaving behind a decade as a Manichaean dualist, a pessimistic philosophy based in Persian ideas of good and evil, Augustine rejected the idea that the world was the "displeasing" product of an evil source hostile to God. He found that such dualism could "see not Thy works through Thy Spirit, nor recognize Thee in them."[47]

Augustine turned to Creation and paradise as alternatives; these themes permeate his work. He concluded his *Confessions* with an extended meditation on the seven days of Creation. The Spirit had breathed over the depths of humanity's fallen state and the voice of God had called, "Let there be light." God's Spirit had come to rest in humanity, enabling us "to live more and more by the fountain of life, and in His light to see light, and to be perfected, and enlightened, and made happy." God helped troubled souls. "Displeased with our darkness, we turned unto Thee, and there was light." Augustine associated the light of Creation with deeds of justice and mercy:

> Let us break our bread to the hungry, and let us bring the houseless poor to our house. Let us clothe the naked, and despise not those of our own flesh. . . . Let us appear as lights in the world. . . . Run ye to and fro everywhere, ye holy fires, ye beautiful fires; for ye are the light of the world.[48]

In his third commentary on Genesis, Augustine explained how Genesis 1, the story of the Creation, related to Genesis 2 and paradise. He pointed out that Creation in chapter 1 was the same world from which God created in chapter 2. The trees, having once been planted in paradise, grew out of the same materials as the rest of earth. Not only that, but earth still possessed this power of paradise and "puts forth similar trees to be seen in their own time." In noting the earth's creative powers, Augustine believed that the causal origin of all plants and trees could be traced to the Creation, which was the material basis for paradise. Hence, paradise was hidden within the earth from the beginning of time, and spiritual transformation was buried in Creation itself, like seeds waiting for the light of justice and mercy. The regenerated soul saw the goodness of the created world and praised God for its beauty.[49]

Augustine called the world "a smiling place."[50] He suggested that "paradise" had multiple, interconnected meanings:

The word "paradise" properly means any wooded place, but figuratively it can also be used for any spiritual region, as it were, whatever it is (and it is, indeed, something wonderfully and singularly sublime), is Paradise; and so also certain joy springing from a good conscience within man himself is Paradise. Hence the Church also, in the saints who live temperately and justly and devoutly, is rightly called Paradise, vigorous as it is with an abundance of graces and with pure delights.[51]

The church responded to Creation with praise and joy and sought to yield fruits of love, justice, and compassion.

When the Vandals sacked Rome in 410 and the church's critics accused Christianity of weakening the empire and making it vulnerable, Augustine wrote *The City of God* to distinguish the "city of the world," Rome, from the "city of God," the church.[52] In this book, which many consider his greatest, Augustine again affirmed paradise as a real place on the earth, and also as an allegory for the church's mission in the world:

Paradise is the Church, as it is called in the [Song of Songs]; the four rivers of Paradise are the four gospels; the fruit-trees the saints, and the fruit their work; the tree of life is the holy of holies, Christ; the tree of the knowledge of good and evil, the will's free choice.[53]

The church was an imperfect embodiment of paradise on earth, but its presence was an alternative to the city of Rome. Augustine rejected Eusebius's enthusiastic and confident embrace of the empire.[54] He understood that the church benefited when the empire was at peace and prospered, but the church had its own life and mission in the world. The city of God existed eternally as the critic and judge of transient imperial powers, not as the sanction for them. It served to trouble, not palliate, empires. Self-love and vice ruled Rome, not love of God and virtue. An earthly embodiment of the city of God existed only in the church. Even there, its citizens had to contend with temptation, sin, and imperfection, but in God's paradise, such struggle was for the good of the whole, not an elite few, and for joy, for life, and for beauty.

As part of his critique of the empire, Augustine wrestled with Rome's history of wars. A number of early Christian teachers insisted that Christians should never take up arms—a topic we will discuss more fully in chapter 7. In the *City of God*, Augustine grappled with the question of whether killing in war could ever be justified and laid the groundwork for a shift in Christian ethics that undermined its prohibition on shedding human blood. However, while introducing principles for a theory of just war, Augustine expressed grave reservations about most wars. He was clear that the deeds of the empire, especially its wars, were almost entirely unjust and should not be confused with the church and the will of God. He abhorred civil war, decried the disasters and calamities of the Punic Wars, and denounced the folly of imperial ambition. He condemned the use of the words "glory" or "victory" in the context of war as "disguises of wild delusion." He said, "Look at the naked deeds: weigh them naked, judge them naked." He said that the empire's motivation for waging most wars was "restless ambition" and that its calamitous history of wars and lust for power "disturbs and consumes the human race." He refused to consider emperors and soldiers great men simply because they had the might and skill to conquer others: "I think it were better to take the consequences of any sloth, than to seek the glory won by such arms."[55]

In sum, the early church—before and after Constantine—taught that paradise was a place, a way of life, even an ecosystem. The church as a community that dispensed "the medicine of life" nourished human life in paradise. The church was a concentration of paradise, a place where the strengths, weakness, needs, and contributions of each member could complement the others. Their life in paradise was a shared accomplishment in which the exercise of human powers and the imperatives of human need worked together to save and sustain life for all members together. People could come to see the value of their own lives and learn that their actions mattered to others, to see power in a personal sense of agency. They could learn to negotiate power and its responsible uses for the good of the whole. Talents and gifts could bless many. Heavy burdens and difficulties that might have crushed individuals could instead be borne on the shoulders of many. No form of governance and no society can thrive without this interstitial zone of human contact and interaction, what the ancient church called the body of Christ, the church of the Holy Spirit, the assembly of saints, and paradise on earth.

THE DIVINITY OF JESUS CHRIST AND OF HUMANITY

Christian thinkers formed their ideas about Jesus Christ over three centuries of resistance to Rome and drew their ideas from many sources. The Gospel of John was a major influence on their theologies. It presented Jesus as the incarnation of Wisdom and Word who existed with God at the beginning of Creation. As such, Jesus had power that transcended the power and authority of earthly rulers—most especially Caesar. Christ, sent from heaven and returned there, conferred upon Christian communities the gift of the Holy Spirit, and those baptized in

Jesus's name shared in this power.[56] The apostle Paul spoke of Christ as the second Adam (I Corinthians 15:45–49). The second-century *Testament of Levi* said the Messiah "shall open the gates of paradise... and shall give to the saints to eat from the tree of life and the Spirit of holiness shall be on them."[57] Christ's incarnation, Irenaeus asserted, restored humanity to its original nature in paradise, created in the image of God. The church, for its part, nourished the ethical and spiritual development of humanity so that Christians might use divine power justly and wisely. In the paradise of the church, the early Syriac *Book of the Cave of Treasures* suggested, every baptized Christian became, like Adam, a prophet, priest, and king.[58]

Disputes about the nature of Jesus, which had marked even early Christianity, escalated in the fourth century. The heated conflicts presented problems for Constantine, who sought to use Christianity to help him govern a vast and nearly unmanageable empire. After he deposed his eastern rival Licinius in 324 CE, Constantine called an empirewide council of bishops, often referred to as the first "universal" council of the church. Although he invited fifteen hundred bishops to his summer palace in Nicaea, Anatolia, in 325, all expenses paid, only about three hundred attended. Among these leaders would have been some who bore the scars of torture from the time of the Great Persecution. The bishops may have been grateful for Constantine's beneficence and careful about expressing any criticisms of the empire, but there had been periods of imperial tolerance before, followed by further persecutions. The beneficence of one emperor did not overcome the bishops' suspicion of Roman imperial power. Bishops from major cities were accustomed to dealing with well-educated pagans and the governing classes, and they were often deft at strategic uses of political power; members of the nobility belonged to some of their churches.

Constantine wanted bishops at the Council of Nicaea to settle disputes about the nature of the divinity of Jesus Christ. Controversy was swirling on just *how* Jesus was divine. Was he "subordinate" to God (*homo-i-ousios*) or "of the same substance" as God (*homo-ousios*)? That *i*, the iota, raised important issues not just for Christ's identity and power, but for the identity and power of baptized Christians who became partakers of Christ's divinity. From Constantine's perspective, the divisiveness of multiple opinions was the problem; he wanted a unified church so it could more efficiently serve the empire. From the bishops' perspective, the debated points of doctrine had subtle implications for their power in relationship to the emperor and for just how subservient they were willing to be. Roman imperial practices viewed the emperor as a son of God who was divinized after death (or occasionally during his lifetime). At issue was whether Christ's divinity was like that of the emperor (who was a subordinate son of God) or something more.[59]

After weeks of intense debate, when the vote was taken, the bishops satisfied Constantine's demand for agreement, but they did so in a subversive way. Virtually unanimously, they jettisoned the iota and resolved that Christ was "of the same substance" as God, rather than "subordinate."[60] In affirming that Christ had this highest possible status, they gave themselves and every baptized Christian who shared in Christ's divinity greater spiritual power and authority than the unbaptized emperor Constantine. Keeping the iota would have made Jesus merely equal to the rulers of the very empire that had tried to destroy the church.

It may seem that the church engaged in heated struggles over inconsequential doctrinal minutiae with only one iota of difference. In the ancient world, however, theology was also always politics (and, of course, it still is). The anti-iota stance would later be called orthodox or Nicene Christianity. The bishops refused to cede their faith-based power to a state that wanted to use the church to buttress its alternative and exploitive system of authority. The Council of Nicaea created a power base for the church that declared the divinity of Jesus Christ higher than the status of the emperor, and by implication, protected the church and the salvation it delivered.[61] This strategy of resistance was not without dangers: its hierarchical placement of Christ above the emperor contributed to a greater emphasis on patriarchal hierarchy within the church, to the detriment of women's leadership.[62] Imperial favor also escalated conflicts between Christians and Jews. Church councils passed policies against Jews, which eventually evolved into imperial legislation. Nevertheless, the Nicene Christ held a tension between the church and imperial domination and established a power struggle between them.

Constantine may have sought to create a less conflict-riven church for his empire. Instead, by forcing a vote on a major controversy, he upped the ante on the conflict and raised the stakes of the outcome. The pro-iota position was associated with the Alexandrian presbyter Arius (250–336) and came to be called Arianism after it lost the vote. Arius, who reportedly popularized his ideas by putting them to music, regarded Jesus as divine, but saw him as a "creature" descended from God, not a creator alongside of God. He held to a strong monotheism, and his teachings emphasized that Christ shared humanity's creaturely struggles and difficulties. For the Arians, the equality of Jesus with God would have capitulated to Roman pagan polytheistic values and compromised the one supreme God.[63] Athanasius of Alexandria (296–373) belonged to the orthodox faction at Nicaea, and he became its most militant spokesperson. He was so militant, in fact, that his fellow bishops charged him with murder, though he was never convicted; he left town instead of appearing at a hearing, and he waited out his opponents. His arguments made clear that humanity's deification was at stake.[64]

The conflict was unrelenting. One bishop complained that he could not even get his hair cut without having to listen to people in the barbershop argue about the nature of Jesus's divinity. Cyril of Jerusalem (c. 310–386) mentioned—in something of an understatement—that "there is much controversy, and the strife is various in its forms." The strife included riots in the streets of Alexandria and the lynching of a bishop. Constantine would waffle, and he eventually consented to baptism as an Arian on his deathbed. He set a precedent, both for the timing of baptism to protect the emperor from the authority of his bishop and for the persistence of the pesky iota, especially among the ruling classes. All his sons were Arians, and most emperors following Constantine were Arians, as were the majority of the highest-ranking members of the Roman aristocracy. The controversy over Nicaea would rage for another century, become an instrument for hunting heretics, and the divinity of Jesus is still debated.[65]

THE GOOD SHEPHERD AND CAESAR

The iconography that emerged after Constantine's reign reflected the church's resistance to co-optation by Rome. In the earliest surviving apse image of Christ, Rome's early-fifth-century St. Pudenziana Church, Christ sat on a throne of Jupiter—a sign that he was higher than Caesar. His apostles were dressed in togas and seated like a council of gods at a time when not even senators were allowed to sit in the presence of the emperor. Christ held a book, not a scepter. Above this scene hovers a large, golden, jeweled cross. The bishop's chair would have been positioned directly under the image of Christ to indicate the divinity of the church as Christ's living body. Art historian Thomas Mathews notes that this arrangement would have shown that the bishop derived his authority directly from Christ, not the empire. Mathews also suggests that the struggle at Nicaea was a struggle against the power of the emperor and that "the victory over Arianism was a vindication of the freedom of the Church from imperial control."[66]

Below the image of Christ, the mosaic originally depicted a lamb standing on a small green hill from which the four rivers of paradise emerged. By the fifth and sixth centuries, Christians had formed a full-blown iconography that placed worshipping Christians in the sacred space of paradise, presided over by the living Christ.

We saw this iconography for ourselves when we visited the Church of St. Vitale in Ravenna, consecrated in 547. Its rough brick exterior contrasted with the elegant interior of tessellated marble walls, alabaster floors, and pillars and arches supporting a high central dome. Across the octagonal nave, the tall, deep presbytery glittered in green and gold mosaics, as if lit by a hidden fire. It was capped by a soaring vault of the heavens—a patch of midnight blue with stars at its peak—and enclosed at its far end by a curved, golden apse. Under the center of the vault was the Eucharist table.

The image at the center of the golden apse was especially intriguing. Christ sat on an enormous blue globe. His boyish, friendly face gazed out benignly. He wore a purple robe of nobility and simple sandals. We had seen his youthful countenance just a few minutes before in the Galla Placidia mausoleum, located across the yard and built about a century before St. Vitale. There he had been the good shepherd holding a staff and tending his sheep lovingly in a craggy Mediterranean landscape. Here he had been promoted to preside over all Creation. Sitting on his enormous orb, he held a golden crown studded with emeralds in his right hand and extended it to St. Vitalis, a martyr who stood nearby. In his left hand, Christ held a scroll with seven seals, which rested on his knee. A bishop stood on this side, presenting him with a model of St. Vitale Church.

A meadow on a small green hill cradled the bottom of the blue orb that formed Christ's seat. From the cliffs on the hill, the four rivers of paradise poured down, two on each side. The rivers flowed out right and left into lush meadows, broken by small green bluffs and dotted with white lilies and red carnations. Christ on the globe linked the heavens with the earth, and the meadow of paradise surrounded the living worshippers celebrating the feast. Blue globes, like the one Christ sat on, appeared frequently in Roman imperial art, usually as a small orb held in the hand of an emperor. The globelike orb symbolized Roman control of the known world. Roman imperial art also used rich landscapes of trees, fields, animals, and rivers to symbolize the breadth of Rome's dominance. But in St. Vitale, the earth belonged to a boyish, nonimperial Christ; the empire had been displaced.[67] A level below Christ, on the walls on either side of the apse, full-length, fancy portraits of the Empress Theodora (500–548) and Emperor Justinian (482–565), with ecclesial and court entourages, processed toward Christ. They carried gifts for the Eucharist meal, and their ostentatious jeweled finery contrasted sharply with the Christ's plain garb. It was clear that imperial power, despite its opulence, was subordinate to Christ.[68]

We stood on the marble floor taking in the images of prophets and saints on the walls and vault above us. When we looked around the arch at the entrance to the chancel area, we could see the bust of the Panto-

FIGURE 4. *St. Vitale Church, Ravenna, Italy. Apse, mosaic.*
Early sixth century. Jesus Pantocrator.

crator Christ at its apex, a bearded teacher holding a codex and framed by leaping green dolphins. On either side down the arch surfaces were similarly framed portraits of the twelve apostles, six on a side, we thought, until we counted. There were actually seven, including Protasio and Gervasius, who were local saints. On the upper surfaces of the chancel walls, we saw lush, spiraling vines, flowers, animals, and laden trees as well as angels and a victorious lamb at the very top of the vault.

When we looked up to our right, we were captivated by a small image of Moses. He posed in front of a blue-green outcropping of rocks, his long white tunic vivid against the dark, mountainous background. He lifted his left knee as his upper torso bent over it, and his arms hung down on either side of his knee, untying his sandal. At the toe of Moses's lifted left sandal, a small bush was on fire, but his eye was not on the bush. He turned his haloed head back across his right shoulder and looked upward toward an inky-blue sky with red and white clouds; the hand of divine blessing emerged from a cloud toward him. We knew the biblical story, just as ancient Christians would have. God was speaking to him, "Remove the sandals from your feet, for the place on which you are standing is holy ground" (Exod. 3:5). The account continues:

I have observed the misery of my people who are in Egypt; I have heard their cry on account of their taskmasters. Indeed, I know their sufferings, and I have come down to deliver them . . . and to bring them up out of that land to a good and broad land, a land flowing with milk and honey. . . . I will send you to Pharaoh to bring my people out of Egypt. (Exod. 3:7–10)

All around Moses, on every rocky outcropping from his feet to the sky overhead, little bushes blazed. All earth was holy ground, illumined by the Spirit. Every ritual in the church took place in this cosmos, this image of paradise in this world. Fourth-century rabbis taught that the presence of God, the Shekinah, had departed from the earth when Adam and Eve sinned, rising higher and higher with the tragedies of human failure told in Genesis. They said that through the righteous, be-

FIGURE 5. *St. Vitale Church, Ravenna, Italy. Right chancel wall. Early sixth century. Moses and the burning bush.*

ginning with Abraham and culminating with Moses on Sinai, God's presence had returned to dwell with humanity, and paradise was regained.[69] The walls of St. Vitale showed many of the saints who restored divinity to human life and to earth, with Jesus Christ as the most important member of that company. Everywhere, the images in St. Vitale said, God's presence assured liberation from[unjust empires]and the opening of paradise for those who had been in exile.

CHAPTER FIVE

The Portal to Paradise

In baptism did Adam find
that glory which had been his
among the trees of paradise.

EPHREM OF SYRIA, *EPIPHANY* 12:1

Baptism was the portal to paradise.[1] Through this ritual, Christians gained entrance into the garden of God, which stood beyond the open doors of every church. The church dipped initiates into lakes, immersed them in rivers, or drenched them from urns to wash them in the living waters of the Jordan, the great river of paradise that flowed throughout the earth and blessed all its waters. "Water was the beginning of the world, and the Jordan the beginning of the Gospel tidings," said Bishop Cyril of Jerusalem.[2]

Christians had begun to use baptisteries, instead of natural bodies of water, by the third century. The oldest surviving Christian baptistery dates from around 230 and was uncovered among ruins in Dura-Europas, Syria, a Roman garrison town that fell to Persia in around 250. The shallow square pool was at one end of a room in a private house. The frescoes on the walls around the pool are the earliest surviving Christian images outside the catacombs.[3] They show the paralytic carrying his bed on his back; Peter and Jesus walking on water; Adam and Eve fleeing bent over while behind them a snake wraps around a tree; and a procession of women in white carrying torches to a sepulcher. This iconographic scheme, linking Adam and Eve to Christ's resurrection, reflected the teachings of the Syrian church and early Christianity. As Ephrem would later write, "From the tomb of the Garden did Christ bring Adam in glory into the marriage feast of the Garden of Paradise."[4] Baptism consummated humanity's restoration to paradise, as the *Odes of Solomon,* a mid-second-century Syrian text expressed it:

> *Then he uncovered my inward being towards Him*
> *And filled me with His love. . . .*
> *And speaking waters touched my lips*
> *From the fountain of the Lord generously,*
> *And so I drank and became intoxicated,*
> *From the living water that does not die. . . .*
> *And He took me to His Paradise,*
> *Wherein is the wealth of the Lord's pleasure. . . .*
> *And I said, Blessed, O Lord, are they*
> *Who are planted in Thy land,*
> *And who have a place in Thy Paradise.*[5]

The images tell the story of the ritual's destination: paradise, here and now.[6]

A circular, waist-deep marble pool dominates the center of the small, octagonal, fifth-century Arian Baptistery in Ravenna. It has channels where fresh water once flowed from a nearby stream. Anyone who stood in that pool and looked up into the dome would have seen an image of Jesus being baptized in the Jordan, the harbinger of their own dousing. A wreath of leaves, a victor's laurel, frames the image. Jesus faces forward and stands visibly naked hip-deep in crystalline waters. Beardless, he is pudgy, like a boy, and his thick hair falls in waves tracing his sloping shoulders. Directly above his head, a dove hovers beak down, spraying water over him. On the viewer's left is a white-haired, bearded river god with a muscular naked torso, who sits on a rock and sports red crab-claw horns (gods of natural phenomena were usually personified according to the gender of the Latin noun). The river pours forth from a flask behind the god and swirls under his body to fill up the lower center of the image. A bearded, muscular John the Baptist, twice Jesus's size, stands on the rocky bank opposite the river god. He holds a small shepherd crook across his left shoulder. Barefoot and wearing knee-length animal skins, he leans toward Jesus and places his right hand near the top of Jesus's head. This scene is encircled by the twelve apostles standing in a meadow punctuated by palm trees, symbols of life everlasting. Holding victors' crowns and dressed in white robes, they surround the baptism scene like daisy petals.

APPLYING FOR ADMISSION

In considering an initiation ritual such as baptism, ancient people would not have asked, "Is this brainwashing?" or "What's in this for me?" They would have asked, "Where has this ritual taken people I know, and do I want to join them?" Completing the ritual process required physical and intellectual effort and ethical and spiritual discipline.[7] It was akin to applying for, attending, and graduating from college while also training for an Olympic team sport and undergoing group therapy. Individual conversion, commitment, and work affected

FIGURE 6. *Arian Baptistery, Ravenna, Italy. Ceiling, mosaic.*
Late fifth century. The baptism of Jesus.

the depth of the transformation, but baptism was not just an individual affair. The entire community helped. The culminating immersion had the celebratory quality of a commencement ceremony. Everyone participated in a process that transported people out of their previous world and into the church, the "paradise in this world," as Irenaeus called it.[8]

The baptismal practices we describe below come from Bishop Cyril of Jerusalem, who used them in the second half of the fourth century. An educated, fourth-century Christian lay woman from Spain named Egeria spent a year in Jerusalem and observed the rituals. Her surviving journal accounts are especially valuable because she was a lively, attentive reporter who wrote to a community of women friends. She shared her observations, without the need to persuade, to condemn, or to instruct. She provides us with an independent account of what other sources of the time claim were the primary features of the ritual.[9]

Baptism began with a formal application. Churches required applicants to appear before the bishop with sponsors who would vouch for their good character and serious intentions. If accepted, applicants became *katechoumenoi*, catechumens (ones being taught).[10] Egeria described the querying of the individuals:

The bishop questions individually the neighbors of each who has come up, asking, "Is the person of good life? Respectful to parents? Not a drunkard or liar?" He also asks the more serious vices in a person. If the person is proved without reproach in all these things about which the bishop has questioned the witnesses present, he notes the person's name with his own hand. If however, someone is accused of anything, the bishop immediately orders the person to leave, saying "Change yourself, and if you do reform, come to the baptismal font." He makes such inquiries about both men and women.[11]

Standing before Cyril, the candidates faced a bishop whose own life had been shaped by the traumas of his city's history. When Cyril was born, Jerusalem was a discarded backwater of the Roman Empire. Many pagans would not have recognized its ancient name, Jerusalem, calling it Aelia Capitolina instead, for the city built on the ruins of the Roman conquest of 139 CE.[12] The Council of Nicaea in 325 brought still another reversal of the city's fortunes. Jerusalem's bishop claimed that the holy sites in the city were dilapidated. The sites became the focus of a dramatic rebuilding program initiated by Constantine and his mother, Helena. She visited Jerusalem around 328 and supervised the building of shrines and churches in the region. She may have gone in response to the bishop's report, but more likely she went as a political ploy. Her trip diverted attention from a scandal surrounding Constantine. In the year after Nicaea, he ordered the murders of his second wife, Fausta, and eldest son, who were allegedly plotting against him. Their assassinations prompted his spiritual adviser, the Christian Hosius of Spain, to resign.

When Eusebius of Caesarea wrote his hagiography of Constantine, he used Helena's journey to allege the Christian virtue of Constantine and his family. He described how Helena's excavations unearthed "the sacred and all-holy memorial of the Saviour's resurrection."[13] What this memorial of the Resurrection was, Eusebius did not say, but by the end of the fourth century legends arose that Helena had discovered the "true cross" buried in the neglected city.[14] Constantine came to the city in 335 to dedicate a new basilica erected near the Anastasis shrine that marked Christ's empty tomb. (*Anastasis* is Greek for "resurrection.") Cyril would likely have witnessed the grand imperial dedication of the new church. Egeria, on her pilgrimage, described the splendor of the decorations in the buildings on a festival day:

You see there nothing but gold and gems and silk. . . . How can I describe or estimate the numbers and weight of candelabra, candles and lamps and other furnishing? What can I say about the decorating of the building itself, which Constantine, under his mother's supervision, honored as much as his empire permitted with gold, mosaics and precious marbles.[15]

Cyril became bishop around 350. Among his first official acts was to write an ingratiating letter to Constantine's successor, Constantius II, soliciting continuing imperial largess. He was well aware that imperial patronage had raised the stature of Jerusalem's Christian community and promoted it as a pilgrimage site. He sought to increase Jerusalem's prestige over the city of Caesarea, the more powerful bishopric. At the same time, he was wary of Roman control. Imperial blessing was not without ambiguities for Christians living in Jerusalem and was highly problematic for Jews, whom Constantine once again had banished from the city. In his instructions to the catechumens, Cyril explained that the traditional teaching of Christianity was that Jesus would come again and destroy the Roman Empire. Christians should be on their guard against the deceptions of the Antichrist, who would take on the guise of an emperor who "will put on a show of mildness and of soberness and benevolence" but will "afterwards characterize himself by all kinds of excesses of cruelty and lawlessness . . . a spirit murderous and ruthless, merciless and crafty." He charged those he trained to "remain unsubdued by Antichrist," and to focus their lives on the good deeds of feeding the hungry, giving water to the thirsty, clothing the naked, and visiting the imprisoned.[16]

Rome punished Cyril for just such acts of mercy. To feed the poor during a famine, Cyril sold Constantine's gifts to the Jerusalem basilica. His rival in Caesarea reported this to Constantius II, who deposed and banished Cyril. Julian the Apostate restored him as part of his plan to fracture the church by bringing back exiled leaders.[17] Julian sought to undo Christianity's privileges, reassert Roman paganism, and enlist Jews as his allies. Though Cyril's Catechetical Lectures record lively debates with Jews over the meaning of scriptures, he despised Julian's plans to rebuild their temple in Jerusalem. The respite for Jews was short-lived, however. When Julian died in 363, Christian dominance of Jerusalem was restored.[18]

Cyril instructed catechumens for admission into the church in the midst of such controversies and their legacies. Candidates for baptism appeared before a bishop whose loyalty to his people was stronger than allegiance to any emperor. He personally examined each candidate for baptism. He knew that their levels of commitment varied and that some came for paltry reasons. Whatever the candidates' starting points, Cyril knew that Christian life was not for the faint of heart. He taught the catechumens to struggle with "principalities and powers." He made clear that to become a Christian was to confront Satan, who operated through despotic empires, but his lessons emphasized joy.

To begin, those who applied were expected to have amended their lives—even to have changed their occupations. Until the time of Constantine, some churches denied baptism to Roman government officials or soldiers. Even after the fourth century, most Roman officials remained catechumens until their deathbeds. Other excluded occupations included artists, many of whom made images of gods and emperors, and those who worked in imperial pagan entertainments, such as actors, charioteers, and gladiators. Occupations prohibited mostly on moral grounds included brothel owners, prostitutes, and charlatans. Also on rejected lists were astrologers and pagan priests (this probably means that some applied).

Catechumens lived in liminal space between the old life they relinquished and the new one they slowly came to know. They attended only the first part of the Eucharist. They heard the lessons and sermon and stood in a special place reserved for them—early churches did not have seats. Their separation indicated their status and allowed the whole community to observe, guide, and encourage them. The congregation taught them the chants and choreography of the rituals. The bishop, presbyters, and lay leaders delivered instruction in theology and biblical interpretation. The catechumens memorized the Psalms and stories. They were to fast one day a week, if they could. They were forbidden to participate in the kiss of peace, and they were dismissed before the blessing and the serving of the food. They were expected to visit the sick, be generous in almsgiving, and they could not shed another's blood—not even if they were soldiers under orders. As the *Apostolic Tradition* ascribed to third-century presbyter Hippolytus of Rome explained:

A soldier who is in authority must be told not to execute men. If he should be ordered to do it, he shall not do it. He must be told not to take the military oath.... If a catechumen or a baptized Christian wishes to become a soldier, let him be cast out. For he has despised God.[19]

When catechumens chose to move to the next stage of preparation, they appeared before the bishop a second time, formally asking to be enrolled as one of the *photizomenoi* (ones being enlightened). If accepted, they began an intense eight-week period of daily instruction, austerities, healings, and exorcism. This would prepare them spiritually, intellectually, and physically for their ritual immersion, which would take place during the Easter vigil.[20] This Lenten period was arduous, and Cyril encouraged them.

> *You are on the right path, and the most beautiful one as well.*
> *Now that you have lit the torches of your faith,*
> *Keep them ever lit in your hands,*
> *So that he who once on holy Golgotha*
> *Opened paradise to the thief in answer to his faith,*
> *May let you also sing the marriage song.*[21]

TRAINING THE FLESH

During Lent, candidates for baptism prepared themselves through physical austerities that included fasting, sexual abstinence, and avoidance of all public entertainments. They were also not to bathe because Roman bathing was public and communal. By the fourth century, men and women customarily bathed together, and the use of public baths was controversial even for the baptized, who should avoid "the lasciviousness of the baths," according to Augustine. The prohibition on bathing may also have provided protection from undue influences by demons when a person was naked and vulnerable. The body's intimate connection to the soul in Christian thought required that it be treated with care, not casually. As Tertullian commented, the two are ultimately inseparable:

The flesh is the very condition on which the soul hinges. And since the soul is, in consequence of its salvation, chosen to the service of God, it is the flesh which actually renders it capable of such service. The flesh, indeed, is washed, in order that the soul may be cleansed.[22]

Training for baptism was designed to teach lifelong ethical and spiritual practices. To support the *photizomenoi*, the bishop, presbyters, and members of the church also practiced the Lenten austerities of fasting and abstinence. Egeria notes:

Some, who have eaten something on the Lord's Day [Sunday] after the dismissal, that is, eleven o'clock or noon, do not eat again for the whole week until the Sabbath [Saturday]. . . . Those are the ones who "keep the week." . . . No one demands that anyone do anything, but all do as they can.[23]

Athanasius extolled the power of fasting. He claimed it cured diseases, dried up "bodily humors," exorcized demons, banished impure thoughts, clarified the mind and heart, sanctified the body, and raised humans to the throne of God.[24] Some groups, such as the New Prophecy movement, explicitly used fasting to induce visions, trances, and ecstatic states, through which their female leaders claimed the power of prophecy and gained spiritual authority outside official ecclesiastical hierarchies of men.

Fasting and other austerities can be misunderstood as a negative attitude toward the "sinful" body or as symbolic identification with Christ's suffering. These interpretations are, however, typical only of medieval Christian spirituality. In the fourth century, Cyril opposed those who taught that the material world was evil and that only the spiritual realm was holy. He taught, instead, that fasting was a positive thing: it prepared Christians to feast on God's goodness experienced in earthly life. Christians, "feasting with thanksgiving, turn towards the Maker of the world an affectionate heart."[25] The body, along with the entire material world, was to be treated with reverence and respect.

> Endure not any of those who say that the body belongs not to God. ... But for what have they condemned this wonderful body? In beauty what lack has it? And what is there of its fashioning not wrought with art? Ought they not to have considered how bright the eyes are; and how the ears placed obliquely receive sounds without hindrance; and how the sense of smell is discriminating in scents, and early discerns incense; and how the tongue is the minister of two things, the faculty of tasting, and the power of speech? ... Be tender then of your body, as being the temple of the Holy Spirit. ... Defile not this your fairest robe; but if you have defiled it, cleanse it now through penitence; while the time allows, wash it.[26]

Periods of fasting and abstinence promoted healthy care of the body. Such discipline taught self-control, physical stamina, emotional maturity, and mental focus—virtues needed for life in paradise. Bishops often encouraged catechumens with sports metaphors. "The priest leads you into the spiritual arena as athletes of Christ," wrote Cyril's near contemporary, John Chrysostom of Constantinople, who was especially fond of explaining preparation for baptism as akin to training for an athletic event.[27] The "athletes of Christ" had to train together to achieve victory. Modern athletes train in much the same way. They find the best coaches and follow their advice and instruction. They monitor when and what they eat, endure extraordinary hours of physical exertion to hone their skills and build strength, and train mentally to think toward victory—psyching themselves up. John Chrysostom encouraged catechumens to be aware of how their preparation would affect each other and emphasized the highly public nature of their baptisms:

Young athletes, the stadium is open, there are the spectators on the tiers of the amphitheater, in front of them is the leader of the games. Then, there is no middle ground, either you fall like a coward and leave covered with shame, or you act bravely and win the crown and the prize.[28]

The Christian community supported everyone's endeavor. The disciplines learned for baptism were encouraged as lifelong practices of faith. Study, prayer, fasting, sexual control, voluntary poverty, and non-violence were methods by which the gifts of God to humanity—first given in the Garden of Eden—were restored to human beings and humanity drew close to God. The leaders—presbyters, deacons, and bishops—functioned as counselors, exorcists, healers, liturgists, advocates, nurses, and political and moral advisers for their community. In his book *On Spiritual Perfection,* Clement of Alexandria (c. 150–c. 215) gave comprehensive instruction for how the Christian is to serve God "by cherishing that which is divine in himself."[29] Such service was to take place "continuously all our life through, and in all possible days." It was strenuous and joyful work. Spiritual practices were a means of "teaching us here the nature of the life we shall hereafter live with gods."[30] They were the ways of paradise. Through "prayers and praises and the reading of the Scriptures before dining, and psalms and hymns during dinner and before going to bed, aye and of prayers again during the night," the Christian "unites himself with the heavenly choir."[31] Such daily attunement to divinity on earth, along with the ethical deeds of justice, fortitude, almsgiving, and intellectual development, transplanted Christians into paradise now.

EMPOWERING THE PSYCHE

From their enrollment for baptism until their immersion, catechumens underwent rituals of healing and exorcism. These physical, psychological, spiritual rituals helped candidates stay healthy. "If anyone is conscious of wounds, let him seek healing! If anyone has fallen, let him get up!" Cyril enjoined the candidates.[32] Exorcism freed them from the principalities and powers that denied them control of their own behavior. During Lent, the *photizomenoi* endured an intense ordeal called "scrutiny." The practice began in the second century as an investigation of the lives of the elect and their progress toward baptism. By the late fourth century, it had become a public rite, including physical examination for diseases and curses, the laying on of hands against demons, and a practice called insufflation—hissing to expel bad spirits and blow the breath of the Holy Spirit into people. Such practices conditioned catechumens for the contest with evil forces. Cyril explained the purpose of the exorcism rituals:

> Hasten to receive the exorcisms. The insufflation and the exorcisms over you bring salvation. Think of yourself as gold that is impure and alloyed, a mixture of various things: copper, tin, iron, or lead. What we want is pure gold!
>
> Without fire, gold cannot be purified of alien elements. So too, without exorcisms the soul cannot be purified.... When goldsmiths fan the flame by directing air upon it with a bellows, they melt the gold that is hidden in the crucible, and they obtain what they are seeking. So too, when exorcisms instill fear by the power of God's Breath and make the soul, which is hidden in the body as in a crucible, pass through the fire, the hostile demon flees.[33]

Late antique society understood that spirits inhabited many aspects of life. To be human was to be a social creature under the sway of powerful forces. Demon possession was a standard explanation for compulsions, addictions, nightmares, mental illnesses, antisocial neighbors, houses with sinister humors, and oppressive provincial governors. Exorcism acknowledged that invisible powers permeated human experience in all its dimensions—social, psychological, intellectual, physical, and spiritual. Demons caused people to lose their reason and self-control, bringing great distress and destruction to body, mind, and spirit. Many physical and mental forces oppressed people, who needed release from their burdens. Such burdens might be as vast as imperial domination or as intimate as the seduction of wealth or personal prestige or the dissipation of trivial entertainments, sexual promiscuity, or addictions.[34]

Educated and uneducated alike experienced demons. Spirits were everywhere. The capricious gods, who had to be appeased with offerings, or the deterministic fates ruled most human lives. Few people in late antiquity beyond an elite class of philosophers had confidence in individual reason for managing demons. Whereas philosophers might pursue intellectual mastery over such beings, they tended to regard lesser mortals as inadequate to the task. Philosophers such as Philo and Plutarch sought to describe demons as an inextricable feature of everyday life, creatures in the netherworld between human and divine realms. Even the highest members of the ruling classes were subject to social and religious forces and had to make sacrifices to the deities that ensured the prosperity of the empire—the best gods blessed the best rulers. Some satirists, such as Lucian of Samosata, ridiculed exorcism. He attacked exorcists as sorcerers or magicians, who brought evil magic from places such as Egypt or Persia, or as charlatans with pecuniary motives. But most people understood that powerful gods and their human servants kept such dangerous forces away. Negotiating a world of them took training and skill. Successful exorcists needed to know which demons afflicted a community to conduct a ritual that guaranteed they would not return.

Christians did not move from a secular, unbelieving world into a world of faith; they moved from being subject to the powers of demons to being free of their powers. Jesus Christ demonstrated God's power over the demonic forces that afflicted human life. His disciples carried on these miraculous powers. The bishops continued this legacy when they prepared candidates for baptism. On the night of their baptism, the *photizomenoi* would take an active role in freeing themselves. Cyril instructed them to imagine Satan chasing them right up to the baptismal font. They would turn to face their pursuer and declare: "I renounce you who lurk in ambush, who pretend friendship but have been the cause of every iniquity, who instigated the sin of our first parents! I renounce you, Satan, author and abettor of every evil."[35] Cyril taught them they would be liberated, just as Moses and the Israelites escaped slavery in Egypt. "[Pharaoh] pursued the people of old as far as the sea, as for you, this shameless, impudent demon, the source of all evil, pursues you as far as the fountain of salvation. The tyrant was submerged in the sea; the demon disappears in the waters of salvation."[36]

Today, most people speak of socialization instead of demons, and they seek therapy to improve their lives. They wonder about the limits of conscious choice and individual responsibility. The law allows an insanity plea, and psychologists offer the disease theory of addiction. Therapists struggle to alleviate the compulsions of sexual offenders, the entrenched cycles of domestic violence, and the suffering of posttraumatic stress. Scientists search for genetic causes of such behaviors, and social scientists study the sexism, racism, and homophobia that spread harm through every society. Demons were the symbol of such forces in ancient times. The usual treatment was not punishment, but exorcism: identifying and expelling the demon and providing social support for healing, self-knowledge, and ethical behavior.[37]

Exorcism freed people from the compulsions of harmful behaviors. They could not become wise without intense attunement to the forces in themselves and in their world that stole their self-control. "Know thyself," Cyril exhorted. "Know thou hast a soul possessed of freedom, the fairest work of God, made after the image of Him who formed it . . . a living thing, reasonable . . . having power to do what it willeth."[38] He taught his students that they had gifts, powers, and options. They needed community support and ritual to reclaim their powers, and they needed to learn to use the good things God had given them. Through baptism, Christians re-formed their whole beings in conformity to the Spirit, which gave them the power to love and respect others.

The Christian initiates received their power through relationships of support and care within the church. Christians took responsibility for one another and for safeguarding the well-being of the whole community. Ephrem of Syria spoke of mutual vulnerability as important to the health of a community and essential to love. The church grounded reciprocity and solidarity in a power greater than all other principalities and powers: Jesus Christ, who was proclaimed as healer, exorcist, and savior to the afflicted and who shared his powers with the community through the ritual of baptism.

The church's practices of scrutiny and exorcism may seem intrusive to modern sensibilities. Deeply ingrained attitudes about privacy, personal choice, and individual liberty, especially about autonomy and self-sufficiency, make many averse to intense public attention to their behavior. This individualistic sensibility guides contemporary Western habits of interaction, and it drives atomistic solutions in medicine, law, psychology, economics, and public policy. Few are inclined to think in terms of social networks and ecological systems when assessing human behavior or what enables it to change. As many observers have noted, these reductionistic and isolating—perhaps even alienating—habits of thinking are characteristic of the West. They are inadequate to the complex social realities of human life from birth to death. They also fail to acknowledge the ecological interdependencies of material life on earth. To create more complex social solutions for such problems would require Westerners to adopt a different value system. Instead of placing individual success, ownership, and power at its pinnacle, a society of ethical grace would measure itself by the well-being of its most vulnerable members, by its enhancements of human sociability and love, and by the creation of sustainable and decent life for all.

The ancient idea of exorcism offered a social perspective on sin and evil. It said that social, cultural, and environmental forces inextricably shape human beings. Though people inherit a great deal by genetics, they also inherit social systems that interact with biology. The absence of the stabilizing, socializing forces of community and the reality of too little love and too few limits results in narcissistic, miserable adults who lack healthy boundaries, self-possession, and self-knowledge. They are often harmful both to themselves and to others. Our unavoidable relationships with one another make violence and hatred morally and emotionally devastating. We mistake hate as separation from relationships, when such negative feelings and behaviors are, in fact, intense forms of emotional enmeshment. By identifying harmful behaviors as sin, the church made it possible for people to confront these within themselves rather than to be resigned to such behaviors as fate or as the work of gods beyond their control. The power of God made it possible for human beings to be free of capricious gods and of the fates.

The modern West has its own collective maladies and life-threatening addictions. The compulsions, stresses, and transpersonal forces that threaten people's lives cannot be addressed by individual willpower or personal lifestyle changes. Societies are collectively captive to disorders that endanger human life, the environment, and future generations. Climate change, patterns of overconsumption, and inequalities of wealth and poverty operate at complex social levels that require collective action to rectify. Facing the facts and recognizing what is wrong do not generate change without social movements and support systems. Exorcism was a way to recognize that social change required social rituals to transform communities. Paradise is not a private realm of personal spirituality—only communal practices and shared endeavors in ritually organized communities can open its gates.

TRAINING THE MIND

Cyril said to his catechumens: "For those then who receive this spiritual or saving Seal, is required a disposition of mind kindred to it: for as a writing-reed or a dart has need of one to use it, so does grace require believing minds."[39] By believing minds, he meant critical, thinking minds. The bishop gave daily lectures in scripture and theology to the *photizomenoi*. They gathered every morning for a three-hour session in the Anastasis. Egeria describes them sitting in a circle. The bishop presented understandings of the faith, and candidates questioned, debated, and discussed them. They were expected to hone their skills of critical thinking, to be conversant with challenges to the faith, and to probe the implications of diverse theological viewpoints.

Egeria reports that instruction was done in Greek while presbyters translated into Latin and Syriac; she speaks as if such a polyglot community and leadership were unremarkable.

Cyril explained that the purpose of the teaching was for the candidates to "have their senses now exercised to discern both good and evil." The intellectually passive or blind were ill-equipped to defend against the deceits of the devil or to see the wonders of God's created world. "We have need . . . of seeing eyes: lest eating tares as wheat, we come to harm out of ignorance; lest taking the wolf for a sheep, we are made his prey; lest imagining the Devil, the Destroyer, to be an Angel of mercy, we are devoured."[40] The ones being enlightened were instructed to recognize the marvel and goodness of life. Their awareness was necessary for them to live justly and joyfully.

The bishop and presbyters expected searching inquiry to ground a lifelong faith that fed mind, body, and soul. According to Egeria, instruction involved extensive discussion.

> God knows ladies and sisters, that the faithful who have come in to hear the catechesis which is explained by the bishop raise their voices [in questioning] more than when the bishop sits and preaches [in church] about each of the things being explained.[41]

The hottest debate in Cyril's time was about the divinity of Jesus and what it meant for the identity of baptized Christians.[42] His catechetical lectures reveal that intense controversy continued to surround the creed voted at the Council of Nicaea. He reported that people were asking, "What reason was there so great, that God should descend to humanity? And can the nature of God have converse with humanity at all?" Cyril explained that humanity was originally created in the image of God, but humanity's divinity was wounded by the devil, who had led Adam and Eve astray. Christ took on the flesh of humanity and renewed humanity's likeness to God. "Christ came that He might be baptized, and that He might sanctify Baptism. . . . The Lord took of us a like nature with us, that He might save human nature."[43]

Today, people tend to use the term "human nature" to refer to something unavoidable, essential, and unchanging across time and culture. Cyril used the term to refer to humanity's transformation and restoration in baptism. Through his incarnation, Christ honored the flesh of all bodies and became the new tree of life. Baptism would graft those who are baptized into this tree:

> If because of the tree of food they were thus cast out of paradise, shall not believers now because of the Tree of Jesus, much more easily enter into paradise? . . . Adam by the Tree fell; you by the Tree are brought to Paradise.[44]

Another controversy in Cyril's community was whether the crucifixion of Christ was shameful. Apparently, as late as the fourth century, the way Jesus died discredited Christian claims of Christ's divinity. The church sought to assign his execution a meaningful place in the scheme of salvation. Cyril argued that the Crucifixion was not shameful because the Resurrection had dispelled its ignominy. In keeping with New Testament texts, he said that Christ's death expiated sin and that his blood could protect against death. He likened Christ to the Passover lamb, which guarded against the angel of death and liberated the oppressed from a cruel tyrant. Cyril refuted those who claimed the Crucifixion was an illusion. He insisted that Christ's death revealed that he was human as well as divine. "Take the cross as an indestructible foundation on which to build the rest of the faith. Do not deny the Crucified," he urged.[45]

Though Cyril had a ready theological explanation for the Crucifixion, he consistently emphasized the Resurrection. "Now that the Resurrection has followed the cross, I am not ashamed to declare it."[46] His church read accounts of Christ's resurrection *every* Sunday of the year, and *every evening* it observed the ritual of the *Lucernare*, the lighting of the lamps from the flame that always burned in the Anastasis. The fire symbolized the presence of the risen Christ.[47] By Egeria's report, the remembrance of the Crucifixion was observed one day a year, on the

Friday of Holy Week. The Passion narratives were read on the legendary site of his Crucifixion. Egeria explained that a piece of the "true cross" was displayed on that day and that congregants came to kiss it. She reported profuse weeping as the stories were recited, lamentation of a magnitude and length she had never before witnessed.

Bishops in Cyril's time were engaged in a struggle over whether baptism should primarily be interpreted in relation to Jesus's death and resurrection or to his baptism in the Jordan River.[48] During Christianity's first centuries, most theologians in the east and the west interpreted baptism in terms of *anamnesis,* the reenactment of Jesus's baptism in the Jordan. They focused on birth and rebirth. Many taught that when Jesus was baptized, he left his cloak of glory in the Jordan River. Those baptized in his name were reclothed in garments of light—the very garments Adam and Eve had lost when they were expelled from paradise. Through immersion in the font, humanity was reborn with divine powers first given in Eden. As Gregory of Nyssa explained: "Because our nature is mixed with the divine nature, our nature is made divine. . . . In the baptism of Jesus all of us, putting off our sins like some poor and patched garment, are clothed in the holy and most fair garment of regeneration."[49]

A less common tradition in the first three centuries of Christianity followed Origen, who compared baptism symbolically to the Passion story—the baptized symbolically died and rose with Christ by being immersed into and rising up out of the waters, as Paul expressed in Romans 6:4. Teaching in Jerusalem, where the shrines marking Jesus's crucifixion and resurrection had become pilgrimage sites, Cyril incorporated themes of "dying and rising with Christ" into his baptismal instruction. When he connected baptism to the death and resurrection of Jesus, he used the Exodus story as a paradigm, making it a ritual of liberation from oppression. However, Cyril resisted making Jesus's death and resurrection the primary model for baptism. Most often, Cyril interpreted baptism in images related to the Jordan River, the descent of the Holy Spirit, the Garden of Eden, the Song of Songs, and the marriage feast. He characteristically offered multiple meanings:

> *Great indeed is the baptism you shall receive!*
> *It brings ransom for the captive, forgiveness of sins, death to*
> *sin, new birth for the soul*
> *It is a garment of light, an indelible seal, a chariot bearing*
> *you to heaven.*
> *It is the delights of paradise, the gift of the kingdom, the grace*
> *of adoptive sonship.*[50]

Baptism effected a "renewal of mind," the birth of discerning thinking. During the final week of Lent, the *photizomenoi* learned a common creed by heart. The creed was an epitome of the theological topics they had covered during their course of study, and they had struggled to understand the creed's meaning. Though they memorized the same words, they were already acquainted with many interpretations of each phrase. People needed sharpness of mind, lest they assent uncritically to ideas that sounded good but were faulty and weak. Intellectual alacrity and discernment were necessary to negotiate harmful forces. Solid grounding in scripture, as illumined by the Holy Spirit, was a test of truth. Cyril enjoined the candidates to judge truth on this basis for themselves: "We ought not . . . be drawn aside by mere probabilities and the artifices of argument. Do not then believe me because I tell you these things, unless you receive from the Holy Scriptures the proof of what is set forth."[51]

Augustine understood that teaching catechumens was a difficult art. His instructions to a catechist on how to conduct the initial training for applicants to baptism reveal an astute, self-critical teacher. He was well aware of the pitfalls and joys of teaching theology, for both the catechist and the pupil. He described his own dissatisfaction with his attempts, knowing that words could not fully capture his intuitions and insights, for he was "sorely disappointed that my tongue has not been able to answer the demands of my mind." Augustine also demonstrated experience in a variety of teaching methods adapted to different types of learners. He noted that a good teacher ascertained the intellectual ability of the learners and taught at a level they could understand. He advised the catechist to treat his pupils as sincere seekers, even when he was certain some sought entry to the church for personal gain or out of fear of injury, which Augustine called "feigned faith." He advised the catechist to teach as best he could because he might transform a feigned faith into an unfeigned faith, for "undoubtedly the mercy of God is often present through the ministry of the catechist."[52] Anyone teaching today can recognize the challenges of facing a class of students who range from the animated and curious to those merely hoping to pass a requirement.

Today, we speak of believing or not believing in religious ideas as if *belief* in a predetermined and authoritative set of ideas were the most defining element of religion. For ancient Christians, intellectual understanding was pursued through careful teaching and lively debate, but assent to particular ideas was only one aspect of a more comprehensive transformation. To believe in Christian ideas without committing to a community and living out those beliefs would be like believing regular exercise is the key to good health and determining the very best regimen for optimal well-being but doing nothing physical. A privately and personally held belief that was not lived out in community and society would be equally useless. Conversely, exercising regularly, without necessarily believing in the benefits of exercise, can bestow health. Many who practice yoga or Buddhist meditation learn that ritual practices, performed regularly and correctly, can gradually transform the whole person. Effective practice does not entirely depend upon belief in ideas or in final goals. Transformative rituals, however, require performing them under the guidance of competent teachers. Early church baptism worked in just such ways.

Cyril explained his role as teacher by picturing himself as a doorkeeper at the gates of paradise. He stood there as a porter, ready to carry the bags of his students as they embarked on their journey to its life-giving spaces. His taught them patiently, knowing that some things must first be learned in experience and practice. He did his part, but the students had to do their part as well. They had to prepare themselves and each other to receive the Holy Spirit, which would regenerate them into new life. The immersion ritual would provide the tangible, final experience that made paradise here and now comprehensible.

THE NIGHT OF TRANSFORMATION

The ritual of baptism usually took place on Saturday of Holy Week. In the dead of night, the *photizomenoi*—children, men, and women—climbed the winding streets to the Church of the Holy Sepulcher. The congregation was already assembled outside to keep vigil and sing psalms. As the candidates arrived, church members surrounded and welcomed them, cheering them on. Augustine described one ritual in which a famous philosopher, Marius Victorinus, came forward for baptism. His name passed like a wave through the astonished crowd as they murmured to each other, "Victorinus! Victorinus!"[53] Then the cheering began.

The *photizomenoi* gathered around the baptismal font. In Jerusalem, a spring-fed pool in the courtyard, surrounded by open porticoes, looked out over the city's mountains. Godparents supported the candidates through the ritual. Cyril, dressed in a white linen robe, invited the *photizomenoi* to complete their journey to paradise.

> *May God deign then to show you this night*
> *the darkness that is as bright as day....*
> *For each man and woman among you*
> *may the door of paradise swing wide!*
> *Enjoy then the perfumed waters;*
> *receive the name of Christ*
> *and the power to do deeds that are divine.*[54]

Night deepened. Bonfires took the chill off the cold air as the candidates removed their clothing. Nakedness signified the stripping away of their burdens and sins, and symbolically placed them in Eden. "What a marvelous thing!" Cyril said to them. "You were naked in the sight of all, yet you did not blush. In very truth, you were an image of the first man, Adam, who in the garden was likewise naked and did not blush."[55]

Just outside the edge of light lurked the dangers of night, of nightmares and demons. Cyril told them to face west, and to imagine Satan "as if he were actually present." West, the direction of the sunset and of night, represented the presence of evil. They raised their hands, as they had been instructed, and shouted:

I renounce you Satan, wicked and cruel tyrant. Henceforth I am no longer in your power. For Christ destroyed that power by sharing with me a nature of flesh and blood. He destroyed death by dying; never again shall I be enslaved to you![56]

The bishop assured them that God was moved by their tribulations and offered them freedom. "When you renounce Satan, you break off every agreement you have entered into with him, every covenant you have established with hell. Then there opens to you the paradise which God planted in the East." Next, facing east, they pledged themselves to be joined to Christ.[57]

The immersion followed. Cyril circumambulated the pool with a censor of incense and recited a prayer to sanctify the waters of paradise. The congregation sang, "Set me as a seal upon your heart, as a seal upon your arms, for, soon, we will be brides of Christ." The assistants rubbed the candidates' naked bodies from head to toe with olive oil, which was also used on gladiators. Warmed and massaged, they were prepared as athletes for Christ, ready to engage in a struggle with the forces of evil. In some versions of the ritual, the assistants or bishop placed salt on their tongues to steady them. Salt signified wisdom, perhaps in reference to Jesus calling his followers the "salt of the earth."

Cyril stepped into the water, and a presbyter or deacon led each naked, oiled candidate to the water, first the children, next the men, and finally the women.[58] Supported by godparents, each descended and approached the bishop. He blew in their faces to replace any evil vapors with the breath of the Spirit. He asked them to confess their faith: Do you believe in God the Father; do you believe in Jesus Christ; do you believe in the Holy Spirit? With an affirmative reply to each question, he lowered the candidates into the water, one immersion for each "I believe." In the waters of the font, the Holy Spirit regenerated them.[59]

And why has He called the grace of the Spirit by the name of water? Because by water all things subsist.... For one fountain watered the whole of the Garden, and one and the same rain comes down upon all the world, yet it becomes white in the lily, and red in the rose, and purple in the violets and pansies, and different and varied in each several kind; so it is one in the palm tree, and another in the vine, and all in all things ... adapting itself to the nature of each thing which receives it, it becomes to each what is suitable.[60]

The deacons and godparents helped the neophytes (which literally means "new natures") out of the pool and anointed them with perfumed oil, first their foreheads, then their ears, their nostrils, and finally their breasts. With this anointing, they were to reflect divine glory, understand God's mysteries, breathe the fragrance of Christ, and be strong of heart. The deacons wrapped each neophyte in a white linen robe; the robe of glory that had belonged to Adam and Eve in paradise was now theirs through Christ. Cyril told them, "You have become like the Son of God.... Yes, you have become christs by receiving the mark of the Holy Spirit ... anointed to bring the Good News to the poor."[61] After every candidate had completed the ritual immersion, the bishop announced:

The Church rejoices in the redemption of many.... The Church prepares a banquet and invokes Christ. "Let my beloved come into the garden and eat the fruit of his apple trees." What are these apple trees? You were made dry wood in Adam, but now through the grace of Christ you flower as apple trees.[62]

The neophytes were given a small clay oil lamp to carry in the First Entrance Processional of the Easter Eucharist from the baptismal font to the Anastasis—the site of Christ's resurrection. In the light of their lamps and the first traces of dawn, their white robes glowed. They chanted a psalm:

The Lord feeds me, and I shall want nothing;
He has set me in a place of pasture;
He has brought me upon the water of refreshment;
He has converted my soul.
He has led me on the paths of justice for his own name's sake.
For though I should walk in the midst of the shadow of death,
I will fear no evils,
for you are with me.
Your rod is power, the staff suffering,
The one created, the other redeemed.
You have prepared a table before me, against them that
*   afflict me.*
You have anointed my head with oil.
And my chalice which inebriates, how goodly is it!
And your mercy shall follow me all the days of my life,
That I may dwell in the house of the Lord for the length
*   of my days.*[63]

As the new Christians arrived, the doors of the church were thrown open, and everyone streamed in. The cantor sang, "Taste and see how good the Lord is" (Ps. 34:9). Cyril announced to them, "I waited till this present season ... that I might take and lead you to the brighter and more fragrant meadow of this present paradise."[64] The bishop, assisted by the presbyters, served them their first Communion—a cup of milk sweetened with honey to break their long fast, a tradition taken from the Exodus story to signify the promised land. Then everyone shared the bread and wine of paradise.[65] Cyril explained to the new Christians that they now were admitted into the mysteries of the Eucharist and were part of the tree of life. "Let us therefore bear fruit as we should!"[66] Communion was followed by prayers exhorting all to live as manifestations of the Spirit that now permeated them.

When all this is finished, each person must hasten to do good work, please God, and live a good life. Let him devote himself to the Church, putting into practice what he has been taught and making progress in the service of God.[67]

At the conclusion of the feast, the golden light of dawn awaited the newly baptized. They had reached Easter. As they walked into the light of paradise, they received the benedictory blessing and made their response:

> *Everything belongs to the God of goodness,*
> *Everything belongs to the God of beauty,*
> *Everything belongs to the God of wisdom,*
> *Everything belongs to the God of justice.*
> *To God, glory now and forever!*[68]

CHAPTER SIX

The Beautiful Feast of Life

The beauty of the heavenly bodies is one kind,
And the beauty of the earthly bodies is another.
The sun has one kind of beauty, the moon another
And the stars another; and star differs from star in beauty.
So it will be with the resurrection of the dead.
The body is raised in beauty.

I CORINTHIANS 15:40–43

The Eucharist took place everywhere on Sunday, the day of resurrection, and in large urban churches with many presbyters on staff it happened more often. The liturgy had two stages. In the first, everyone was present: the catechumens, the teachers, the penitents, and the baptized. They sang psalms, heard scriptures read, prayed, and listened to a homily by the bishop. In the second stage, the catechumens and penitents were dismissed, and the bishop, deacons, and presbyters prepared to serve the holy meal.[1]

THE NOURISHMENTS OF BEAUTY

As the leaders prepared, the people greeted one another in peace and reconciliation by clasping hands, embracing, or kissing. Then the great offertory processional began. Members brought gifts to support the church and offered foods for the Eucharist meal. Heaped on tables, the offering represented the community's shared resources, its common wealth in God.

Different churches allowed their own particular foods, though bread was universally served, as were many other products of harvests. Bishop Hippolytus of Rome (170–236) explained, "In offering fruits, roses and lilies, the believer was celebrating the goodness of the God who had given them to him. He read the name of God in the fruits of the earth, and God read the homage of love in the heart of the offerer."[2] His church banned, however, all vegetables from the ritual:

> The following fruits are blessed: grapes, figs, pomegranates, olives, pears, apples, mulberries, peaches, cherries, almonds, plums; not watermelons, melons, cucumber, mushrooms, garlic, or any other vegetable. But sometimes flowers too are offered; thus roses and lilies are offered, but no other flowers.[3]

Other churches included olive oil, olives, fresh milk, cheese curds dressed with honey, grilled fish, salt, water, or wine in addition to bread.

Red meat was universally banned, a restriction that may reflect a Christian desire to avoid associations with Roman animal sacrifice, since pagan sacrificial meat was sold in public markets. Sometimes water or milk replaced wine because it was also used in pagan rituals, especially those honoring Dionysus. When the Eucharist liturgies referred to sacrifice, they called it "bloodless," which meant that prayer was their holy sacrifice. On the avoidance of meat and wine, scholar Andrew McGowan suggests that these bans may also have been "a conscientious objection of sorts" that protected communicants from being part of any ritual that suggested the blood of Christ or that implicated them in "guilt for Christ's death."[4]

After blessing the offerings, the bishop called the people to "lift up their hearts" and recited the Great Prayer of Thanksgiving, the Eucharist (literally, the giving thanks). Retelling Genesis 1–3, the prayer celebrated the divine origin, the goodness, and the beauty of the cosmos, and it told the story of humanity in paradise.

You are the giver of every good thing
You create the visible world and all it contains
You inebriate it with inexhaustible springs
You said, "Let us make man in our own image"
You gave him a soul endowed with reason and judgment
You gave him a body endowed with five senses and
       with movement
You brought him into this paradise of delights
But he scorned your commandment
You rightly thrust him forth from paradise
But you did not wholly reject him in his lost state
You promised to release him from the bonds of death
So that he might live and rise from the dead.[5]

The prayer recited God's many acts of redemption and named many of the prophets and saints. It also named members of the church's own community who had died, lifting the veil between the living and dead. The congregants stood in the midst of "a great a cloud of witnesses" (Heb. 12:1). After the calling together of all the saints, the Great Thanksgiving prayer moved to its climax, and the bishop gave thanks for Christ's incarnation, teachings, and miraculous assistance to those in need.[6]

The third-century anaphora of Addai and Mari said:

You clothed yourself in our humanity
that you might give us life through your divinity.
You brought our mortal nature back to life
You enlightened our minds
You conquered our enemies
through the abundant mercies of your grace.[7]

Following these words of remembrance, the bishop prayed for the descent of the Holy Spirit. This prayer of consecration, the *epiclesis,* called the Spirit down into the food on the table and into the entire community. It asked that the fire of Spirit sanctify everyone and everything with the blessing of the divine presence.

Cyril of Jerusalem taught that the Spirit's descent reopened paradise. To the flaming sword that barred entrance to paradise he contrasted the tongues of flame in Acts 2:1–4 that appeared over the heads of the community at Pentecost as they preached in many languages: "The fiery sword barred of old the gates of Paradise; the fiery tongue which brought salvation restored the gift."[8] Ephrem, too, used this metaphor of fire:

> *The Fire of compassion descended*
> *And took up residence in the Bread.*
> *See, Fire and Spirit are in the womb of her who bore You;*
> *See, Fire and Spirit are in the river in which You were*
> *baptized.*
> *Fire and Spirit are in our baptismal font,*
> *In the Bread and the Cup are Fire and Holy Spirit.*[9]

The communicants received the power of divinity in their own flesh, just as a body received energy from food. Cyril explained that in partaking of the sacrament, "we become Christ-bearers, as his body and blood are spread around our limbs." The communicants were to take care not to drop a crumb because "it is as if it were a part of your own body that is being lost."[10] Augustine, in a sermon explaining the Eucharist to the newly baptized, asked them to contemplate what they saw when they were admitted to the Eucharist feast for the first time. "You are Christ's body and members, it is your own mystery that lies here upon the table of the Lord, and it is your own mystery you receive. . . . It is what you are yourselves."[11] Ephrem exulted:

> *Christ's body has been newly mingled with our bodies,*
> *His Blood too has been poured out into our veins,*
> *His voice is in our ears,*
> *His brightness in our eyes.*
> *In His compassion the whole of Him has been mingled*
> *in with the whole of us.*[12]

In every celebration of the Eucharist, Christians feasted in paradise. They felt its nourishments and its joy.

The Eucharist trained the whole person—body, soul, mind, and strength—to know the world and the Spirit in it. In fourth-century Jerusalem, the Eucharist included the anointing of the eyes, the ears, and the hands to symbolize a transformation of the senses. In sipping the wine, Cyril invited communicants to touch their wet lips with their fingers and moisten their forehead "and other senses."[13] Anointing renewed and reinforced attention to accurate perception. The Eucharist enacted a way of perceiving the whole created world that recognized it as filled with the Spirit of God.

Ancient Christians believed that this world revealed God's creativity, providence, and beauty. The unique particulars of material life possessed an inner "face" or presence that shone from all things, precisely perceived: this sweet bread, that sharp wine, the cold metal rim of the cup, and the heat sliding down the throat. Augustine knew this when he described how the face of God shone through particular things:

> I said to all things that throng the gateways of the senses: "Tell me of my God, since you are not He. Tell me something of Him." And they cried out in a great voice: "He made us." My question was my gazing upon them, and their answer was their beauty.[14]

The beautiful feast of life returned the senses to an open, joyous experience of the world; it was an encounter with divine presence infusing physical life. The Eucharist thus bound humanity to the glory of divine life in "this present paradise," and through its Eucharists, the church cultivated responsiveness to the power of holy presence in the world. Its beauty opened the heart.

Luke's Gospel reports that after his crucifixion and burial, Jesus approached his disciples and walked with them on the road to Emmaus, but they did not recognize him. Though it is easy to assume that such stories refer to a literal understanding of the senses, the kind of perception described in biblical stories was not just about bodily organs and their functioning. In other words, the disciples' physical eyes worked just fine, but they lacked perception. While the ancient world certainly regarded disability as a difficult fate, it was also clear that those with physical disabilities could perceive with great acuity. The body's capacities, whatever they were, could be in perceptive relationship with the world. In Luke's story, the disciples on the road talked with Jesus and discussed the recent events in Jerusalem and the Crucifixion, but they could see only a stranger as they struggled to understand what had happened. They extended hospitality to him, and, at the evening meal, he blessed the bread, broke it, and shared it. Then "their eyes were opened and they recognized him" (Luke 24:31). Only when he enacted the ritual of feeding could they perceive him accurately—the ritual of nourishment awakened their perception. The story of Emmaus described the ritual's power to restore life-giving perception when tragic events made people unable to see.

In the Sermon on the Mount, Jesus taught that no one could help another without first removing the log from her or his own eye (Matt. 7:4). He asked his disciples to perceive carefully the things of the world—to consider the sparrows and the lilies and learn from them. They must open their senses to the world, with the heart's assistance; then, perceiving the world through many sensory ways, each could become a means of knowing God and loving one's neighbor as oneself. Jesus's miracles, while literally described as restoring the senses, are especially about renewed perception. He promised that perceiving could be rekindled spiritually as well as physically. Such rekindling was, for the church, the key purpose of the Eucharist and its beauty.

Some early Christian teachers held the senses suspect but maintained the importance of beauty. They taught that, after the Fall, the human senses lost their ability to receive the divine presence accurately, but the restored "spiritual senses" could reopen the soul to God and beauty. Origen associated the material, fallen senses with Eve and accorded Adam the more spiritual capacities of mind and intellect, such as sight to "contemplate supernatural things such as the Cherubim and Seraphim," hearing to capture voices without physical sound, taste to savor bread descended from heaven, smell to detect the fragrance of Christ, and touch to hold the Word of Life.[15]

Other church fathers shared Origen's distrust of the material senses. Ambrose, for example, asserted that men were reasonable and women were emotional and sensual, and he blamed the weakness of Eve's senses and emotions for the Fall: "Sin was committed by man because of the pleasure of sense."[16] Augustine, like Origen, was deeply influenced by Platonism and struggled with the contrary motions of material sensuality and spiritual sensuality. For him, the lure of divine beauty could turn the senses to their redemptive, spiritual role—but such turning required spiritual training.[17]

This view of spiritual beauty has both appeal and power. The body and senses can be problematic in many ways. Eyewitnesses to events can have conflicting accounts of what they observed. For those of advanced years, the infirmities of aging can take their toll on spirit as well as flesh, as does sickness, which can strike at any age. Augustine noted that, despite his desire to behave morally, his body's "unruly member" seemed to defy his moral control. However, many ancient theologians understood the importance of integrating thinking, feeling, and perception, and they knew the potential dangers and deceptions of arranging them into a hierarchy that gave control and dominance to one capacity over the others. Tertullian, who is infamous for saying women were the gateway of the devil, strongly objected to arguments that the "spiritual" intellect was superior to the "material" senses (thereby, incidentally, undermining one of the arguments for domination of masculine over feminine). He asserted that the senses were essential for learning, intellectual life, and joy, and he ridiculed intellectual elitists who disparaged the senses:

> O Academics! What impudence you are showing! . . . Whence, do you think, come the various arts, the ingenious developments in business, politics, commerce, medicine? Whence the techniques of prudent advice and consolation, the resources that have made progress in all phases of human life and culture? Without his senses, man's life would be deprived of all joy and satisfaction, the only rational being in creation would thus be incapable of intelligence or learning, or even of founding an Academy! . . . Intellect is not superior to sense.[18]

The disparagement of the senses endangers life, but careful training of perception supports life. Healing the sick requires sensory attunement to symptoms and cures. In situations of chaos, disruption, and emergency, the leadership of those who can think clearly and remain attentive to sensory information can mean the difference between life or death. The cultivation of integrated sensing, feeling, and thinking is vital for human survival and thriving; one needs only to think of post-traumatic stress syndrome for an example of the long-term suffering created by dissociation.[19] Complex interactions of perception, reflection, and feeling deeply determine our behavior, even when we think we have made conscious, rational choices. Ancient Christians understood that there is no naïve sense perception, that all sensory experience is the result of a complex interpretative act. They also understood that ethical action depends on finely tuned, accurate perception. The Eucharist taught such perception.

THE POWER OF BEAUTY

The practices of the Eucharist, in their sensory richness and beauty, were designed to open spiritual perceptions of beauty. Only through beauty, Augustine came to believe, could humanity come to love God:

> Late have I loved Thee, O Beauty so ancient and so new; late have I loved Thee! . . . Thou wert with me and I was not with Thee. . . . Thou didst call and cry to me and break open my deafness: and Thou didst send forth Thy beams and shine upon me and chase away my blindness: Thou didst breathe fragrance upon me, and I drew in my breath and so now pant for Thee: I tasted Thee and now hunger and thirst for Thee: Thou didst touch me, and I have burned for Thy peace.[20]

Without beauty, there was no life. In the rhythms of life, Augustine said, beauty made itself known. A divine rhythm beat its graceful, grace-filled cadence even in a sinful, sin-filled soul. Sin was disharmony, dissonance, an irregular movement that led away from God. A fractured rhythm was less and less beautiful, but it always had some beauty. Augustine believed the myriad manifestations of beauty revealed that God had "arranged that even a sinful and sorrowful soul can be moved by rhythm and can rightly perform it, even down to the lowest corruption of the flesh." Like the involuntary, regular thump of a heartbeat or the rising and falling of breath, beauty kept presence with the soul, even if the soul could not embrace it.

Nothing in human life had as much power as beauty to draw humanity to God. Salvation was always present because divine rhythms and the human capacity to respond were never absent. The spiritual power of life was like the soft swishing in the heart, inaudible to those not listening, but still there.

Beauty compelled attention and elicited desire. The ancients called the power of beauty *eros*, or love. Only love could capture the experience of wholeness that was beauty. The soul's response of delight and pleasure at beauty generated the urge toward right relationship with God. Desire for divine beauty enticed the soul toward the strong and powerful rhythms of virtuous states—justice, courage, prudence, and charity.[21] Today, when people hear the word *eros*, they are likely to think of sex or romance. Many trivialize beauty as a vain preoccupation with physical appearance. Standards for physical appearance can enforce norms that pressure people to conform to celebrity ideals—a disheartening and dehumanizing imperative, since the examples depicted in advertising often starve themselves, undergo surgery, or appear in retouched photos. Love of beauty, furthermore, is often equated with materialistic ambitions, the indulgence of the wealthy, who buy luxurious objects for display. Aesthetic "tastes" can define people's economic and social class, reducing the arts to superficial accessories. Despite Western contemporary biases against beauty, many people remain drawn to it as elemental to their sense of wholeness and well-being. They seek to create and experience beauty in their lives, savoring the nourishment it provides for body and soul and the sensitive, focused attunement to the present it evokes. Through many ordinary pleasures, such as gardening, playing music, walking outdoors, or sharing a meal with friends, people renew their appreciation for life and experience the power of beauty.

The Greek *kallos* (beauty) has its root meaning in "whole" and "vigorous." Beauty lured—by its very existence, it elicited grateful and graceful love. The apostle Paul understood it as the power of many, diverse particulars, each with its own *doxa*, or "beauty." *Doxa* also meant "splendor," "glory," or "shining presence." Beauty was thus not simply an object to perceive and behold, but a shining presence of spirit in all things that called for presence in response. Beauty's ethical power was its ability to educe a loving orientation toward the world. It gathered into a life-giving whole all the fragments of life that the powers of "this world" tore asunder.

The *eros* of beauty was the key to Ephrem's hymns and to his understanding of paradise as the integration of material and spiritual contrasts. His poems made earthly existence sacramental. For him, even ordinary bread, the food of the poor, when eaten in the Eucharist, was holy; the gifts of paradise were drawn from the beauties of the created world:

> *Let us see those things that He does for us every day!*
> *How many tastes for the mouth! How many beauties*
> *   for the eye!*
> *How many melodies for the ear! How many scents for*
> *   the nostrils!*
> *Who is sufficient in comparison to the goodness of these*
> *   little things?*[22]

Beauty is relationship through presence—the immediate qualities of things and beings as they are experienced by other beings. It is not just in the eye of the beholder. Beauty is in the relationship of the beholder to the presence that shines from the many myriad and diverse things.[23] Such differences as movement and stillness, light and dark, sound and silence, hunger and fulfillment, sour and sweet, purple and yellow, or rough and smooth share an architectural substructure of being that holds them together—taste, energy, hearing, color, texture, or another property. When placed in relationship, they magnify one another, making each more fully present, more deeply perceived for being together, the way the heat of sun makes the cool of shade more vivid.

The greater the contrasts that are held in relationships, the greater the beauty. The Eucharist itself, as an experience of beauty, is held in contrast to the world outside the liturgy, a world full of heartbreak and goodness. That world is brought to the Eucharist experience by its participants. The Eucharist's power evokes profound love for the world and deeper, life-affirming relationships with it. Without this contrast with the world, the Eucharist becomes simply an escape into something pleasant and irrelevant to the fullness of life.

Macrina (328–380), the sister and teacher of Basil of Caesarea and Gregory of Nyssa, spoke about the dynamic, fluid, and diverse created world. It revealed the character of divine beauty as a world of contrasts. Gregory wrote his sister's biography and reported her saying:

> We see the universal harmony in the wondrous sky and on the wondrous earth; how elements essentially opposed to each other are all woven together in an ineffable union to serve one common end, each contributing its particular force to maintain the whole . . . how those elements which are naturally buoyant move downwards, the heat of the sun, for instance, descending in the rays, while the bodies which possess weight are lifted by becoming rarefied in vapor, so that water contrary to its nature ascends, being conveyed through the air to the upper regions; how too that fire of the firmament so penetrates the earth that even its abysses feel the heat; how the moisture of the rain infused into the soil generates, one though it be by nature, myriads.[24]

Augustine, too, affirmed that no experiences of life were more powerful or life-giving than beauty. It opened the soul and turned perception, thinking, and feeling outward toward the life of the world. Perceiving beauty was an experience of an intuitive whole that was greater than the sum of its parts. In that wholeness, it offered an experience of transcendence. It made the self anew through its vulnerability to presences beyond itself, and the self received them with deep appreciation and joy. Christ, the one in whom all the fullness of God was pleased to dwell, concentrated the beauty of God, sending God's image into the world with focused intensity.

Irenaeus explained that those who saw God manifested in "the resplendent flesh" of Christ were penetrated by divine fire and transformed. Through Christ, the incarnation of the Word, those who "behold the glory" come fully to life. Irenaeus explained this glory in one of his most famous passages:

> For the glory of God is a living human being; and the life of humanity consists in beholding God. For if the manifestation of God which is made by means of the creation affords life to all living on the earth, much more does that revelation of the Father which comes through the Word, give life to those who see God.[25]

As John 1:14 said, "The Word became flesh, he lived among us, and we saw his *doxa* (beauty)."

The apse mosaic in the sixth-century church of St. Apollinare in Classe, the ancient seaport of Ravenna, Italy, places beauty at the heart of the cosmos. At its center, a sapphire globe rests on an emerald meadow that stretches across the width of the apse. White lilies and daisies, red anemones, and mossy green rocks stud the meadow. Pine, cedar, and olive trees rise from it into a golden sky. Scattered among the flowers and trees are doves, partridges, parakeets, and larks. At the bottom center of the meadow, feet firmly planted in the grass, stands a white-robed saint, labeled "Sanctus Apolenaris" to honor the first bishop of Ravenna. Arms raised in the pose of an orant—the gesture of prayer—he welcomes the worshippers into the paradise around and before them. Six sheep flank him on either side, symbols of apostles. Above him to the right and left, three sheep representing Peter, James, and John gaze at the huge globe. Silver and gold stars fill its blue field.

The globe's gold and red frame is encrusted with emeralds, sapphires, and pearls. A large golden cross, decorated with the same jewels, transects its center. From the middle of the cross, encircled by a small medallion of pearls, the tiny, bearded face of Christ peers directly out at the viewer, intense and grave. Just above the cross is written *Ichthus* (fish), the Greek acrostic for Jesus Christ, God's Son, Savior. Under the cross is written in Latin *Salus mundi* (the world's salvation).

The globe rests on the meadow, but it also seems to float into the gleaming sky that spans the upper portion of the apse. The hand of God peeks out of wispy pink and blue clouds at the top of the sky. Immersed waist deep in the heavenly clouds, two figures, clad in flowing white togas, hover on either side of the orb and point toward it. Their names are inscribed next to their faces: Elijah is on the right, and Moses is on the left.

Elijah and Moses cue the viewer that this mosaic depicts the Transfiguration. As told in the Gospels, the Transfiguration occurs when Jesus, Peter, James, and John climb a high mountain, usually identified as Mt. Tabor (Matt. 17:1–7, Mark. 9:2–8, Luke 9:28–36). There, before the eyes of the others, Jesus changes. His "face shone like the sun and his clothes became dazzling white" (Matt. 17.2). His transfiguration unveils the divinity hidden within the flesh of his humanity. The three apostles see Elijah and Moses talking to him. A cloud of luminous mist rises and encompasses them, and "from the cloud a voice said, 'This is my Son, the Beloved . . . listen to him!' When the disciples heard this they fell to the ground and were overcome by fear. But Jesus came and touched them, saying 'Get up and do not be afraid.' And when they looked up, they saw no one except Jesus himself alone" (Matt. 17:5–7).

The mosaic portrays Jesus Christ as the face at the heart of the cosmos—a presence that shines within the night's stars and the day's sunlit meadows. His radiant companions, Moses and Elijah, who had met God face to face on Mt. Sinai, confirm the revelation. Both had taken refuge in the mountains in fear for their lives. Moses's countenance had gleamed with reflected light after seeing God. Elijah had been transformed when God came to him not in the thunder or the earthquake but in the "still small voice." Their encounters with God changed them. For Jesus's disciples, the mountain mist momentarily changes the whole landscape, opening into the realm of paradise where Moses and Elijah dwell. In that moment, they hear God's voice and see Jesus's divine nature shining forth. The worshipper standing before this image also stood in the presence of God shining forth.

Depictions of the Transfiguration filled many early Christian churches; among the most famous is the sixth-century apse mosaic of St. Catherine's Monastery at Mt. Sinai. There, as in St. Apollinare in Classe, a field of sapphire blue indicates Christ's transfigured presence. The significance of this color relates to Moses, Aaron, and the Seventy Elders who climbed Mt. Sinai and "saw the God of Israel. Under his feet there was something like a pavement of sapphire stone, like the very heaven for clearness" (Exod. 24:9–10). A fourth-century monk, Evagrius the Solitary, taught that all Christians were invited to enter this transfigured place and discover their true nature:

FIGURE 7. *St. Apollinare in Classe, Ravenna, Italy. Apse, mosaic. Sixth century. The Transfiguration. With Moses and Elijah in the clouds.*

When the mind has put off the old [person] and clothed itself with grace, then during prayer it will see its own nature like a sapphire or the color of heaven. In Scripture this is called the dwelling place of God that was seen by the elders on Mt. Sinai.[26]

To this day, theologians of the Eastern church speak of "the transfiguration of the world." They define salvation as an awakening to the whole world illumined by the brilliance of divine presence. Sacred art and ritual initiate people into this life-changing knowledge: God has intertwined the spiritual and the material in Christ, restoring divinity to humanity and returning "the world to the beauty in which it was first created."[27]

THE ETHICS OF BEAUTY

In Western thinking, ethics and aesthetics are often divided, and ethical concerns take priority. The ancient understanding of beauty, however, included both. Beauty integrated goodness with glory, ethics with grace, and spirit with flesh; all were essential to a fully realized humanity. Beauty made ethics possible by evoking deep yearnings for justice, healing, and peace. The ethics of beauty were grounded not in a mental list of rules to be obeyed but in a loving orientation toward the world. Beauty called humanity out into life and invited acute observation and attunement to the here and now. Such cultivated attention grounded ethics in responsive relationship to the world.

Transfigured in the Spirit and opened to beauty, the church did the work of Christ in the world. John Chrysostom, when he was a presbyter in the fourth-century church in Antioch, reported that it fed three thousand widows, orphans, disabled, and poor people every day. It also supported an enormous staff of priests who organized this work. Augustine's congregation in Hippo raised money to buy people out of slavery. Ephrem's church in Edessa created hospitals for the entire city during a yearlong famine. These ethical acts of generosity and justice were inseparable from the Eucharist. Christians received the body of

Christ to become the life-giving presence of God in the world and to recognize it in Creation.[28]

Though this emphasis on ritual beauty as the source of ethics may seem archaic, superstitious, or weak, each of us authors has experienced the Eucharist's ethically transforming power. We have seen it empower a shift that moves the ground of ethics from external rules to a sense of love. In the mid-1980s, a minister in a small Seattle church preached a sermon one Sunday morning about how Christians had once believed that the earth was flat, that women should be kept in their place, and that slavery was ordained by God. But they had been open to the leading of the Spirit of God. When that Spirit challenged traditional interpretations of the Bible, the church had been willing to listen to new ideas. Without openness to truth unfolding through the guidance of the Spirit, the church would become a relic and die. The minister said that the next truth facing the church was that homosexuality was not a sin, not wrong, but one of the many ways human beings loved each other. It was a gift, therefore, of God.

The elder assigned to give the first prayer at the Eucharist table that Sunday was a middle-age woman named Violet, who dyed her hair jet black and was very careful and conscientious about preparing for her church duties. She did not like surprises and left nothing to chance. She always wrote out her prayers ahead of time. As the minister preached, Violet's face grew angrier and angrier. After the sermon, the congregation sat in shocked silence. Finally, the organist played the scheduled music, during which the elders came to the table. People stood and weakly warbled a hymn. When Violet rose for the hymn, it was not clear whether she would walk up to the chancel or out the rear door.

On the last verse, Violet strode angrily to the altar, a ball of paper in her right fist. As all sat and bowed their heads, she uncrumpled the paper and sputtered her prayer through clenched teeth, "Our heavenly Father, we come before your table this morning to give thanks for the gift of life you have given to us. In partaking of this bread, we are grateful for all it represents, both earthly and spiritual nourishment given to us. We affirm that no one is stranger or alien to you, that all are welcome.

Just as you welcome everyone to this table, we too must welcome all who come in faith. For this food of life and for your presence with us at this table, we give eternal thanks. Amen." After the elements were served and the elders returned to their seats, Violet did not sit down. She picked up her purse and coat and walked out the door.[29]

Two months later, the church board responded to the controversies by voting to affirm the minister's position. Those who wanted the minister fired left the church, and for the next few months, the church struggled to survive. Not all who remained were comfortable with what the minister had preached, but they chose to stay in their church and grapple with their faith. Slowly, the church grew as gays, lesbians, bisexuals, and parents of gays and lesbians found a welcoming community. The congregation took on the character of a community of people who had stayed at the table with each other, people who were committed to being together in their differences.

A few months after the board vote, Violet returned to the church. When the service was over, she stopped on her way out to tell the minister that she had wrestled for a long time with her faith. She had finally decided that what she had written on that wad of paper and prayed to God over the Communion table was what she really believed. She did not understand homosexuals and was uncomfortable with them, but her faith required her to welcome them. As she settled back into church life, she began to ask for prayers for her alcoholic son, something she had never done before. She found herself supported by her pastor and others in the church. She seemed less tense and more open, as if something deep within her had relaxed a little. Members who had previously not much cared for Violet began to reach out to her and added her son to their prayer lists. Other members began to share their personal struggles with depression, fear, addiction, and failure. The community slowly knitted itself together through bonds of honesty about their lives and their willingness to care about each other as members of one diverse community. They became a welcoming community, gathered around the Eucharist table as members of one another. They embraced, with respect and honesty, the disagreements in their midst and their efforts to understand each other. In their willingness to be together in struggle, they achieved a greater openness to the diversity of the world in its heartbreaks and its goodness.

The ancient Eucharist was designed to capture the wholeness of beauty and to imprint right relationship to the world. Its design elicited greater capacities for truth, beauty, and goodness in the community, and it guided love to find particular expression in diverse relationships. The ritual feast initiated people into *this* world unveiled as paradise— as the Genesis garden in which God was walking in the cool of the day. There, the tree of life yielded fruits that fed the body and the soul, offering knowledge, discernment, and healing. In the Eucharist, the threat of death lost its sting because those who died returned and visited the living. The risen Christ was a sign of the return of life, appearing to the women at the doors of the tomb, to his disciples on the road, and to his friends in a meal of fish cooked on the beach with a charcoal fire.

RESISTING CRUCIFIXION

Beyond the doors of its sanctuaries, the church sent people out into the world as agents of life, as those who resisted the exploitation and violence of the principalities and powers of the world. To teach them such resistance, the church immersed them in a ritual of life in paradise. Because beauty in such rituals had great power, it could also have dangerous consequences. If beauty was used to valorize or sanctify what was harmful to humanity, its power could be destructive. In this spirit, the early church avoided focusing on the Crucifixion, not only in its art, but also in its Eucharist. Some even avoided mentioning it.

The *Didache,* the oldest surviving Christian liturgical handbook, was written in first-century Syria as early as the Gospels and makes no reference to Jesus's crucifixion. Instead, its Eucharist prayer gave thanks to God "for the life and knowledge which you have revealed to us through Jesus your Child." It explained the cup as a symbol for Jesus, "the holy vine of David," and associated the bread with the life of the church. "Just as the bread broken was first scattered on the hills, then was gathered and become one, so let your Church be gathered from the ends of the earth into your kingdom."[30]

A late-first-century Eucharist prayer reported by Clement of Rome, who according to Irenaeus was the third bishop to follow the apostle Peter, said that Jesus Christ, "the high priest of our offerings" had "opened the eyes of our hearts." The prayer pictured Christ resting among the saints, but like the *Didache,* it does not mention the Crucifixion:

> *Through him you have called us*
> *From darkness to light,*
> *From ignorance to full knowledge of your glorious name*
> *And to a hope in your name,*
> *Which is the origin of all creation.*
> *You alone are the Most High in the heavenly heights,*
> *the Holy One who rests among the saints.*
> *You cast down the insolence of the proud,*
> *You frustrate the plans of the nations,*
> *You raise up the humble and abase the proud.*
> *You enrich and you reduce to poverty*
> *Sole benefactor of spirits and God of all flesh*
> *You have taught us,*
> *Sanctified us and glorified us.*[31]

Justin Martyr's mid-second-century description of the Eucharist mentioned the Gospel account of Jesus saying, "Do this in memory of me; this is my body," and "This is my blood," but he did not include the phrase "broken for you" (which is found in only some ancient versions of I Corinthians 11:24 but not in the four Gospels). Justin also omitted Matthew's phrase for the cup, "poured out for the remission of sins." He said that the "food over which the Eucharist has been spoken becomes the flesh and blood of the incarnate Jesus, in order to nourish and transform our flesh and blood." He explained that the liturgy was to take place on the day of the sun, because Sunday was "the day on which God transformed darkness and matter and created the world, and the day on which Jesus Christ our Savior rose from the dead."[32]

The first example of a Eucharist prayer that included words of brokenness in the *anamnesis* (remembrance) was the mid-third-century prayer of Hippolytus of Rome: "Take, eat, this is my body which is broken for you. . . . This is my blood, which is shed for you; when you do this, you make my remembrance."[33] But church teachers made clear that this remembrance referred to the living body and blood, the incarnate Christ who made the request *before he was broken* and who died "to destroy death . . . to pour out his light upon the just, to establish the covenant and manifest his resurrection." The holy foods on the Eucharist table nourished those who received them to be "filled with the Holy Spirit" and "strengthened in faith."[34]

In early Eucharist prayers, when Jesus's crucifixion was mentioned, it was listed among a series of events. It was not the focus of the liturgy and was not the key to its meaning. The entire story communicated the Spirit in life.[35] The Eucharist foods signified Christ's living body, the union of spirit and flesh in his incarnation, and the abiding power of life, manifested in his resurrection. The foods represented his miracles of feeding and healing and his post-resurrection appearances to the disciples, several of which involved meals. During the fourth century, associating the Eucharist with the Last Supper became commonplace, but even then references to the Last Supper were not universal. The liturgy of Addai and Mari, which originated in Edessa in Anatolia in perhaps the third century, is still in use today by Christians in the Assyrian Church of the East, once called Nestorian by their opponents. It has no words of institution and makes no connection to "the night before he died."

Eucharistic prayers went out of their way to make it clear that the Christian observance was not about shedding blood of any sort. Cyril of Jerusalem repeatedly emphasized that the Eucharist was "the spiritual sacrifice, the worship without blood."[36] The prayers underscored that the Eucharist was a "living sacrifice," a "bloodless offering," a "sacrifice of thanks and praise." Cyril represented a long tradition already in place, and like the Gospel of John, Jerusalem's fourth-century Eucharist liturgy appears to have omitted any reference to Jesus's having instituted the Eucharist on the night before he died.[37] Cyril insisted on accepting the reality of the Crucifixion, but it was not the focus of his Eucharist.

The political, social, and theological meanings of Christian Eucharist prayers varied over regions and diverse Christian sects, but early Christian rituals consistently placed the accent on Jesus's incarnation, his teaching and miracles of healing and feeding, his baptism, and his resurrection.[38] The remembrance of the Crucifixion was not central to what the Eucharist memorialized; instead, the Eucharist focused on incarnation and Resurrection. The feast remembered how Jesus overcame death with life, never to die again.

Some church leaders, however, placed greater focus on the Crucifixion, which sometimes had dangerous consequences. Melito of Sardis argued in his mid-second-century homily *On the Pasch* that Easter should commemorate the Crucifixion as well as the Resurrection. Melito interpreted Jesus's suffering and death as prefigured in the death of Abel, the binding of Isaac, the selling of Joseph, and the "lamb that was sacrificed in the land of Egypt and saved Israel by its blood." Christ endured all of these persecutions, which culminated when he was crucified in Jerusalem:

> *He is the silent Lamb,*
> *He is the Lamb slain,*
> *Who was born of Mary, the noble Lamb.*
> *It is he who was taken from the flock*
> *And led to sacrifice.*[39]

In his sermon, Melito harshly assails Jews for killing Christ. "O Israel, why have you committed this unheard-of crime?" He asserted that Christ's execution and resurrection had superceded the old meaning of the Passover lamb but that the Jews "make clever play of the Lord's sacrifice." He said that when "the Gospel was revealed, then the figure was emptied out. . . . For precious of old was the death of the lamb, but now it has lost its value because of the salvation of the Lord." His sermon shows how easily a focus on the death of Jesus spilled over into the vilification of Jews:

> You put to death him who gave you life! Why did you do this, O Israel? ... You are mistaken, Israel. ... You were not moved to reverence for him. ... You scourged his body, you set upon his head a crown of thorns, you bound his kindly hands that had shaped you from the dust. ... You put your Savior to death during the great feast![40]

Perhaps the early Christians who observed the Eucharist with little or no reference to the Crucifixion sought to avoid this kind of anti-Judaism—a potential present in the Gospels and in Paul, and one that Christians would, in the long haul, fail to resist.

When Christian baptism and Eucharist affix blame for killing Christ, then the rituals function to separate the "forgiven" from the "guilty." Christians become, by definition, those who had been absolved, and Jews and pagans become unrepentant killers. Participating in such rituals embeds remission for the sin of killing Christ as an indelible aspect of Christian identity. History shows that ritually enacting this understanding can fuel a deadly dynamic that separates those worthy to live from those who deserve to die.[41] Such rituals shape who is embraced within the saved community and who must be scapegoated or sacrificed to preserve the community's identity. Whether and how Christians can memorialize Jesus's crucifixion without fomenting hostility to those who hold to a different faith remains a moral issue for those who participate in such rituals.

When the Christian Eucharist was not a memorial to the shedding of Christ's blood, the ritual did not focus on absolving people for the crime of killing Jesus. Instead, the ritual restored humanity's divinity in paradise, providing a basis for relationship rather than division among Christians, pagans, and Jews. The potential was there, even when imperfectly realized, for Christians to recognize all of humanity as created in the image of God. Grafted onto the tree of life and feasting at the wedding banquet through the Eucharist, Christians embraced a world of flesh infused with spirit. They received insight and strength to resist unjust principalities and powers, to live in freedom and responsibility, and to hold to nonviolence in the struggle against evil. They partook of the feast with doxology, praise for beauty and thanks for life. They went forth to live in the world as a life-giving presence. In the Western churches, the Eucharist continued to be understood as a feast of the Resurrection until the ninth century. Eastern Orthodox churches continue to regard it so, and in recent years some Western Christians have revived the ancient understanding and enlarged it in creative new directions.[42]

THE MOVEMENTS OF BEAUTY

Pseudo-Dionysius, a late-fifth-century, neo-Platonist Christian (perhaps of Syrian origin), emphasized that beauty was marked by diversity and creative interactions, not by static hierarchy. Those who knew beauty had moved beyond rigid structures of superiority and inferiority, for movement created beauty. Those who loved beauty aligned themselves with the "great creating cause which bestirs the world." He commented:

From [beauty] derives the existence of everything as beings, what they have in common and what differentiates them ... their sharing of opposites, the way in which their ingredients maintain identity, the providence of the higher ranks of beings, the interrelationship of those of the same rank, the return upward by those of lower status.... Hence, the harmony and the love which are formed between them but which do not obliterate identity. Hence, the innate togetherness of everything. Hence, too, the intermingling of everything, the persistence of things, the unceasing emergence of things. Hence, all rest and hence, the stirrings of mind and spirit and body. There is rest for everything and movement for everything ... traveling in an endless circle through the Good, from the Good, in the Good and to the Good.[43]

While partaking of the Eucharist, communicants examined the images in the church. The mosaics, designed to reflect light from the myriad angled surfaces of colored glass, communicated the *doxa*—the shining presence of God's glory embodied in the Creation and in Christ. We contemplated this *doxa* in the mosaics of the early-sixth-century church of St. Apollinare Nuovo in Ravenna, Italy, about two decades older than the church dedicated to St. Apollinarius in nearby Classe. On the morning of our visit, natural light streamed from the windows that lined the long, elegant nave near the ceiling. Along the length of the nave a dozen marble columns, with Corinthian capitals linked by arches, marched down either side. The stately columns separated the warm glow in the central nave from the darker side aisles.

The upper walls above the columns, nearest the ceiling on either side of the nave, were covered with a row of mosaics. Thirteen on one side showed Jesus teaching and performing miracles of healing and feeding. The other wall displayed his betrayal, arrest, trial, and his resurrection appearances. Actually quite large, perhaps five feet across, they appeared small from where we stood on the floor of the basilica. Each scene featured a few figures against a plain background with key props relating to the story depicted.

For the ancient Christians who worshipped in this space, these were more than illustrations of biblical texts. Images had the power to shape the life and identity of those who encountered them. Macrina taught that seeing beauty allowed the soul to mirror divinity and know itself in truth. "The soul . . . should know herself accurately . . . and should behold the Original Beauty reflected in the mirror and in the figure of her own beauty. For truly herein consists the real assimilation to the Divine—making our own life in some degree a copy of the Supreme Being."[44]

Care with images was especially important in a ritual space. In it, souls were being trained to open their senses to recognize divinity within and around them and to open their hearts to each other and the world. Images transmitted the power of that which they portrayed, and so the liturgical shaping of vulnerable souls required beauty, truth, courage, and grace to fill the space, or they might be wrongly formed. Human beings, the church understood, could resist evil only after becoming deeply attuned to divine presence around them and within them.[45]

We believe the absence of images of the Crucifixion can be understood partly in this light. Since images emitted power, a display of the Crucifixion might have allowed the evil that killed Jesus to gain access to the congregation. Rather than opening the senses and the heart, the presence of violence usually hardens, numbs, or hurts people. Conversely, the scenes of Christ teaching and healing, raising the dead, remaining steadfast through betrayal and trial, and appearing resurrected opened a channel for the power of these events to flow onto the congregation. Though this sense of the power of an image may seem today to be supernatural hocus-pocus, it is not so different from how films, photos of loved ones, and art such as the Vietnam Memorial in Washington, D.C., are experienced as possessing the power to move and to inspire.

We looked carefully at the scenes in the church to discern what they meant. In the Last Supper scene, Jesus reclined on one side of a semicircular table with his twelve disciples reclining around it. The table had a plate with two large fish on it, surrounded by a semicircle of seven small loaves, but no chalice or wine. We realized the moment captured in this scene was when Jesus said, "One of you will betray me." The disciples around the table looked at him and each other in dismay and appeared to be asking him, "Is it I?" This moment in the story was the most common depiction of the Last Supper in early Christian art. It reflects the truth about humanity's capacity to betray sacred presence. It also reflects Christ's steadfastness through trial—offering viewers a reminder that they have power to choose between faithfulness and apostasy, between God and Caesar.[46]

We noticed that the bread and fish we saw in the mosaic of the Last Supper were also present directly across the nave in a depiction of the feeding of the multitude—the only miracle to appear in all four Gospels a total of six times. In John 6, Jesus explained that the bread was his incarnate life: "For the bread of God is that which comes down from heaven, and gives life to the world. . . . I am the bread of life; he who comes to me shall not hunger, and he who believes in me shall never thirst." About the meaning of the bread, Bishop Irenaeus of Lyon, wrote:

> For as the bread, which is produced from the earth, when it receives the invocation of God, is no longer common bread, but the Eucharist, consisting of two realities, earthly and heavenly; so also our bodies, when they receive the Eucharist, are no longer corruptible, having the hope of the resurrection to eternity.[47]

The images of bread and fish reflected to communicants that they too were sanctified bodies who offered bread to the world. Rather than memorializing the execution of Christ, the Eucharist—as the images made clear—celebrated the incarnation and the everlasting life manifested in and through Christ. This meaning of the Eucharist reflected the Gospel of John's discussion of Jesus as "the resurrection and the life" who commanded his disciples to "love one another as I have loved you" (John 15:12). The power of divine love was displayed everywhere on the walls of the church in Ravenna. What they saw of Christ with their eyes, they repeated with their lips in the prayers to God:

> *Show yourself to those in need.*
> *Heal the sick.*
> *Fill the hungry,*
> *Give freedom to our prisoners.*
> *Console the fainthearted.*[48]

As the worshippers in St. Apollinare Nuovo gazed around the church during the Eucharist, they saw the story of their lives in paradise on the walls of the nave. It was a story of divinity in this world. On the walls below the narrative sequence, large images of Jesus and his mother sat on thrones in the meadow of paradise, confirming the power of birth and rebirth into life, celebrated in the feast of the Resurrection and made manifest in deeds of justice, mercy, healing, and compassion. What worshippers saw of Christ on the walls of the church was what they, too, were to do and be to manifest their identity as humanity restored to paradise: they were to heal, teach, dispute and discuss, share bread, pray, put down the sword, and remain steadfast in times of trial. For them, too, the promise of life beyond the grave would be fulfilled. They would rise to eternal life in the company of the resurrected saints.[49]

Ancient Christian rituals empowered participants to become creators—to become artists of life by placing them in beauty. The sensual world of their rituals communicated what Clement of Alexandria meant when he exclaimed: "Everything belongs to the God of beauty, everything subsists in the God of Beauty." Beauty instructed humanity to move beyond narrow self-reference or isolated, individual concerns to a vast, value-filled cosmos.

The Native American scholar and activist Vine Deloria spoke for a culture that was practical and pragmatic and that ritualized many ordinary acts that most of us do thoughtlessly and automatically. He made the plea:

> The lands of the planet call to humankind for redemption. But it is a redemption of sanity, not a supernatural reclamation project at the end of history.... The lands wait for those who can discern their rhythms. The peculiar genius of each continent—each river valley, the rugged mountains, the placid lakes—all call for relief from the constant burden of exploitation.... Who will find peace with the lands? The future of humankind lies waiting for those who will come to understand their lives and take up their responsibilities to all living things. Who will listen to the trees, the animals and birds, the voices of the places of the land?[50]

What does it take to see the Spirit in all of life and embrace the intrinsic value of the world? Interpretative frameworks tell people what matters. Ritual can change those frames, can attune people more acutely to the presence of the world, in its beauty and its difficulty, and can return them to their senses. "Beauty can save the world," Dostoevsky's character Myshkin says in *The Idiot,* reflecting the Eastern Orthodox understanding of salvation as the "transfiguration of the world." Peace with the land and with one another requires astute attention to the sacred presence permeating life. Whether we see or don't see the *doxa,* the glory, the beauty, may determine whether we will save or destroy paradise.

CHAPTER SEVEN

Gods Seeing God

The soul should know herself accurately and should behold
the Original Beauty reflected in the mirror and in the figure of
her own beauty. For truly herein consists the real assimilation
to the Divine—making our own life in some degree a copy of
the Supreme Being.

MACRINA (327–379)

Throughout their lives, Christians were instructed to be the earthly
manifestation of God. Like their forerunner and model, Jesus Christ,
they were to become fully human and fully divine. A Jewish peasant car-
penter and teacher from Galilee had revealed God, and he had left the
Holy Spirit of God with his community. This power of God, found in
an ordinary life and given to ordinary people, exposed the limits of all
other principalities and powers, even the authority of Rome. Christians
shared a power that nothing could destroy, a power that affirmed the
freedom and dignity of humanity. Freedom and dignity grounded their
work together for justice; they did not await the arrival of justice. Instead
of seeing the oppressed as weak or powerless—the oppressor's view of
them—the church offered marginalized and privileged people alike the
power of divinity and supported them to live together as gods in paradise here and now.[1]

   Christians located the story of their divinity in Genesis 1–3. The
serpent in Genesis 3:1–6 had told the woman that eating of the tree of
knowledge of good and evil would open her eyes and make her like God.

Desiring such knowledge, she ate and shared the fruit with the man, who also ate. But the young Eve and Adam were not prepared for this knowledge, and the consequence was loss of paradise, distortion of their likeness to God, inequality, and mortality. Jesus Christ reversed these consequences and gave humanity what they desired. He incarnated God in human flesh and infused humanity with divinity. Ephrem of Syria noted,

> *The Most High knew that Adam wanted to become a god,*
> *so He sent His Son who put him on in order to grant him*
>   *his desire. . . . Divinity flew down*
> *to draw up humanity.*
> *For the Son had made beautiful the deformities of the*
>   *servant,*
> *and so he has become a god, just as he desired.*[2]

Doing the work of Christ and sharing his Spirit, Christians manifested divinity. The community's work was to restore human life in paradise by healing the sick, instructing the ignorant, loving its neighbors, liberating the captives, resisting evil, practicing nonviolence, and appreciating the beauties of life. This understanding of salvation permeated many regions and branches of the first millennium of Christianity, as we were to discover in our examination of Christian art.

THE SUN AND THE SON

Early one morning in July 2002, we boarded a bus in Erzurum, Turkey, the ancient city of Theodosiopolis in Anatolia. Our destination was a region in the rugged Kackar Mountains near the Turkish border with Armenia and Georgia; the headwaters of the Tigris and Euphrates flow from the southwestern shoulders of this range. We had read that ruins of ancient Georgian churches could still be found on their peaks, and we hoped that these ninth- to eleventh-century monastery churches contained traces of art largely untouched by later centuries.

Our bus took us across Turkey's vast, mile-high central plateau, through the Çoruh River gorge, and zigzagged up the mountains along-side the tumbling river to Artvin, the provincial capital on the precipitous slope above the river. The next morning, we headed for the village of Işhan. Its tenth-century church was reportedly the best preserved in the area. After we rode about an hour along the main highway, our *taksi* driver Erçun turned into a range of steep, buff-colored peaks. As we traveled through the mountains, we passed villages of people with red hair and blue eyes and villages of people with black hair and brown eyes and skin. Dodging the remains of mudslides, Erçun left the two-lane gravel road and headed up the side of one of the taller peaks. We bumped along a goat trail passing as a road and ascended the steep slope. As the cab curled around the final vertiginous switchback, we were abruptly delivered into a tree-shaded farm village perched in a wide saddle near the summit. Above the rustling treetops, we saw the cone-capped, cylindrical tower of the great church in Işhan. It reached two hundred feet into the sky. The church had been used as a mosque from the time of the fifteenth-century Ottoman Conquest until the early twentieth century. Muslims, who believe destroying a house of God is a sin, often converted churches by whitewashing the images in their interiors. Their centuries of upkeep had retarded the ravages of time, weather, and earthquakes.

Half the sanctuary's limestone walls had collapsed, along with parts of the roof and most of the apse. Inside and out, relief-work decorated the church walls with zodiacs, vines and leaves, Celtic knotted crosses, and a lion pouncing on a snake. On the lower interior sections of the remaining walls, faint frescoed images of Christian saints bled through the perfunctory whitewashing like ancient ghosts. Above the first twenty feet, untouched portraits and busts of now-anonymous women and men greeted us as if they had awaited our arrival. Some faces were dark brown, and rings of black curly hair surrounded them. Others were pale skinned and had lank reddish hair—a diverse range of humanity. We found no images of the Crucifixion anywhere.

In the center of the cross-shaped sanctuary, four tall stone struts curved gracefully upward, supporting the dome. The walls between the struts had mostly broken away, and sunlight poured down, placing the area under the dome in deep shade. We peered with binoculars a long time before the image in the dome was visible. Finally, we saw that it was painted a vivid blue and was strewn with gold stars. In the center of the dome, four angels held a large round white medallion in the night sky, their luminous robes billowing around them. A golden cross intersected the medallion, but its arms widened outward, so that it appeared to be turning into a sun.

On one side of the blue, star-studded sky, just below the angels, a pale full moon glowed. Below it, a beardless man rode a chariot rightward across the sky, pulled through a turbulent ocean of clouds by two winged horses. The dark-skinned figure wore a white robe, and his curly black hair swirled against the gold of his nimbus. His body turned toward the horses with the reins in his right hand. His face was turned to look at us. What was this charioteer doing up there, traversing the

FIGURE 8. *Church in İşhan, Turkey. Dome, fresco. Tenth century. Charioteer. Feet of angels are at the top; full moon below; charioteer with horses at the bottom.*

space between heaven and earth so deftly? And what did the sunburst cross in the medallion above his head mean?

The sun question was easier for us to answer. Early Christians closely connected the sun with the Son. The weekly Lord's Day and Easter are the days of the sun and Resurrection. The Gospel of John and early church sources associated Jesus with light. Clement of Alexandria said, "Hail, oh light for he who rides over all creation is the 'Sun of Righteousness' who has changed sunset into sunrise, and crucified death into life." Christians prayed toward the direction of the sun, the east, which symbolized "the day of birth."[3] Churches were "oriented," that is, they faced east, the direction of paradise, and baptisteries were often designed to have the newly baptized exit toward the east. Basil the Great likened the sun to the Holy Spirit:

> It seems to everyone who enjoys the sun's warmth that he is the only one receiving it, but the sun's radiance lights up the whole earth and sea and dissolves together with the sky. In the same way the Spirit seems unique to everyone in whom He abides, but all of His grace pours down on everyone. Everyone enjoys this grace to the greatest degree he is capable of, and not to the greatest degree which is possible for the Spirit.[4]

At the time of Jesus, Roman emperors were regularly regarded as sons of their god, such as Jupiter, Sol Invictus, or Mars.[5] Sol Invictus, the god of the sun, had been a primary imperial deity from the time of Julius Caesar (100–44 BCE).

The charioteer was a little more puzzling. We speculated that he might have been a depiction of divinity from an ancient Psalm:

> *Bless the Lord, O my soul*
> *O Lord, you are very great!*
> *You are clothed in honor and majesty,*
> *wrapped in light as with a garment.*
> *You make the clouds your chariot,*
> *You ride on the wings of the wind. (Ps. 104:1–4)*

Inspired human beings also rode chariots into the sky. The prophet Elijah ascended to heaven in a whirlwind riding "a chariot of fire and horses of fire" (2 Kings 2:11). In the ruins of the original necropolis beneath the Vatican's St. Peter, a fourth-century mosaic shows Christ borne aloft on a chariot. Light beams radiate from his head like the crown on the Statue of Liberty.

Deceased emperors rode a chariot into the sky for their *apotheosis* (divinization). Roman rulers declared their predecessors gods and paid obeisance to them as part of the cult of the empire. The nimbus around the emperors' heads imitated the aureole of the sun god, and it became the Christian halo. Constantine portrayed himself as Sol Invictus, and after he died, his sons issued a coin of their father's *apotheosis*. On the coin, the divinized Constantine rode a chariot into heaven where a hand reached down to him from a cloud.

The Işhan charioteer suggested these complex associations of ascent to the heavens and divinity as he rode joyfully above the tumbling white clouds. Though there were various possibilities for his identity—the Christ of the sun, lord of Creation, who radiated light on the worshippers at every Eucharist; Elijah; or Jesus—we concluded that the charioteer was most likely a Christian saint who was completing his divinization. A half-millennium before this image was created, Ephrem had written:

> *The saints have ascended to the firmament and opened it,*
> *One of them cleft the air with his chariot;*
> *The Watchers rejoiced as they met him.*[6]

The image captured the idea that humanity had been granted its desire to become gods.

IN THE IMAGE OF GOD

In John's Gospel, Jesus said he was God's Son. When his opponents challenged this claim, he quoted Psalm 82:6.[7]

Is it not written in your law, "I said, you are gods"? If those to whom the word of God came were called "gods"—and the scripture cannot be annulled—can you say that the one whom the Father has sanctified and sent into the world is blaspheming because I said, "I am God's Son"? If I am not doing the works [*erga*] of my Father, then do not believe me. But if I do them, even though you do not believe me, believe the works, so that you may know and understand that the Father is in me and I am in the Father." (John 10:34–38)

In Psalm 82, God appealed to a council of gods, and by citing the text, Jesus tapped the deeper meaning of being gods. *Erga* (works) is related to *energeia* (energy or activity). To be gods and to do the works of God means:

> *Give justice to the weak and the orphan;*
> *Maintain the right of the lowly and the destitute.*
> *Rescue the weak and the needy;*
> *Deliver them from the hand of the wicked. (Ps. 82:3–4)*

Within a generation of Jesus's death, Christian leaders were teaching that Christians gained the same powers of divinity as Jesus Christ through baptism. They believed that humanity had become "partakers in the divine nature" (2 Pet. 1:4).

In modern Western theology, the idea that human beings incarnate divinity has been largely ignored. Some theologians, such as Adolf Harnack, rejected the idea as a pagan corruption of Christianity's message of salvation because, if the incarnation of the Word was saving, Jesus's atoning death was not necessary.[8] Others, such as Karl Barth and Reinhold Niebuhr, said it was too optimistic about human nature; it led Christians to be naïve about how easily they perpetrate great evil. Western Christians are used to seeing human nature as sinful, weak, or flawed and to regard human nature in individual, rather than collective, terms. Many Western Christians see Jesus's suffering on the cross as revealing his humanity and as demonstrating divine solidarity with human nature in its suffering and sorrow. From this perspective, Christ-likeness is found not in gaining power and using it but in abnegating it through surrender, obedience, and humility.

We found the idea of human divinity pervasive in early Christianity. Theologians of the early church were certainly not credulous about human capacities to do evil, but they did not believe great good could be done without great power. We began to wonder why the idea of human divinity emerged in the early church and what the idea might have meant to ordinary people, such as peasants, women, and those who were poor, imprisoned, or enslaved. We discovered that it addressed questions about how human beings should live in paradise together and that it located spiritual power in the creation of just relationships.

The Greek and Syriac theologians, especially, developed the concept. Clement of Alexandria instructed Christians in the practices of prayer, study, and ethical responsibility that would enable them to perfect their humanity and become enthroned gods. He taught that "rank and honors are assigned to those who are perfected. . . . And the name of gods is given to those that shall hereafter be enthroned with the other gods." He rejoiced that in the perfected saints, "the worth of love shines forth in ever-increasing light."[9] Athanasius of Alexandria placed humanity's deification, *theopoesis* ("God doing"), at the center of Christian theology. He spoke of Christ as "the deifying and enlightening power of the Father" and said that "Christ becomes 'incarnate' that we might be 'ingodded.' "[10]

Gregory of Nazianzus (326–389) used the word *theosis* for human divinity. This term described the community's work to reclaim the image of God found in Genesis 1. Gregory explained that through Christ's incarnation,

> human nature is completely joined with the whole Divinity, not the way that a prophet, divinely inspired, is in communion with God Himself, with something divine, but in essence, so that God has humanity in the way that the sun has rays. . . . God has become human and humanity has been deified.[11]

The other famous Gregory of the fourth century, Gregory of Nyssa, made clear that "the image is not in part of our nature, nor is the divine gift in any single person." Since "any particular man is limited," the gift was given to all, equally. It took a whole community to reflect the image of God.[12]

Many early church thinkers wrote on *theosis*, and it remains important in Eastern Orthodox Christianity. It captured how the Spirit empowered humanity to dwell in paradise according to its originally created nature. Cyril of Alexandria (d. 444) said that through Christ "human nature was refashioned . . . to the original image according to which the first human had been made." God's image "has been stamped upon us," engraving us in light "that comes through His own spirit, that they may be called, like Him, gods and sons of God." The Holy Spirit "makes the divine image gleam" and "shine forth clearly" in sanctified human beings whom the Spirit restores to "our nature's original beauty."[13] Ultimately, the whole Creation was to be made new by its union with God. "Deification is the goal of creation, and for its sake everything which came into being was created. And everything will be deified—God will be everything, and in everything."[14]

Symeon the New Theologian (949–1022), an Eastern Christian monk from the era of the Işhan charioteer, captured the meaning of the image and the integrative power of *theosis* in a hymn:

> *God rises in me, within my lowly heart, like the sun,*
> *like the circle of the sun, appearing spherical, luminous,*
> > *as a flame*
> *thou hast risen at once in my darkened heart.*
> *Thou hast descended even into me,*
> *thou the sun before the ages.*
> *Suddenly I behold thee having come to be wholly in me.*
> *I move my hand, and my hand is the whole Christ,*
> *I move my foot and it shines as he.*
> *Do not say that I blaspheme,*
> *Thou takest us up with thee, wholly shining with thy light,*

and makest us, from being mortals, immortal, and remaining
what we are
we become like thee, Gods seeing God.[15]

THEOSIS AND COMMUNITY

The earliest Christian movements attracted slaves, peasants, women, the disaffected, and other ordinary people. They joined communities that enabled them to be "partakers in divinity," which gave them a status greater than that of those who exploited them. The church expected them to share their goods in common so that every member of the community could have a decent life. Early Christian teachers condemned private wealth as a basis of exploitation. They insisted that material blessings were gifts of God and must be shared. Writing around 200 CE, Tertullian of Carthage said Christians created an alternative social order, which he called "the Christian society," that embraced people of every age and status. Contrary to the imperial taxes used for wars, building projects, and luxuries for the already privileged, Christians, he said, contributed

> to support the destitute, and to pay for their burial expenses; to supply the needs of boys and girls lacking money and power, and of old people confined to the home . . . we do not hesitate to share our earthly goods with one another.[16]

Theosis was a collective activity of the whole church community—embodied in love, which is always a social reality and never an individual achievement. Like the interactions of teaching and learning, *theosis* was a group process. Individual commitment and effort were required, but the divinization of humanity was realized in the common good, not in private salvation. Ephrem described this process as the teamwork of climbing a mountain. As he imagined paradise, children of light, who lived near the summit of the cosmic mountain, descended to the lower regions "where they rejoice in the midst of the world." Here they taught disciples how to ascend and to enjoy the upper reaches of the mountain. He pictured these teachers as chariot riders.

> *The clouds, their chariots fly through the air;*
> *each of them has become the leader of those he has taught;*
> *his chariot corresponds to his labors,*
> *his glory corresponds to his followers.*[17]

The Işhan charioteer may have been such a beloved teacher, memorialized as he was remembered descending from the heights to guide climbers to the summit. Even the earth itself, Ephrem said, helped humanity to achieve *theosis.* The paradise mountain bent to help those who set out to climb it. "From inside, Paradise inclines its whole self to all who ascend it; the whole of its interior gazes upon the just with joy."[18]

The symbolism of ascending and descending reflected the geography of mountains, as well as the hierarchical structures of ancient societies.[19] Ethics, knowledge, and responsibility flowed upward. Those at the highest reaches of leadership had the greatest obligation to live out the ideals of the community and to help others achieve them. Until well after the time of Constantine, churches usually elected their own bishops, and they expected them to use their power to build up the entire community. Leaders had to embody divine care for everyone, especially for those most vulnerable. They were to assure that wealth and benefits were distributed to all who had need. They sought to alleviate suffering as much as possible—not to romanticize or sanctify it as validation of a God who suffered with humanity.

Christians were expected to help the light of divinity radiate throughout their community, by loving each other as God had loved them and "doing deeds that were divine." Misfortune, oppression, enslavement, imprisonment, ignorance, and sickness diminished the light of God that shone from each person. Like Christ, they were anointed to preach the good news to the poor, heal the sick, and liberate the oppressed. *Theosis* revealed humanity to be the glory of God, holy fires of divinity, the light of the world. Irenaeus of Lyon said humanity was "the receptacle of all God's wisdom and power."[20]

Church leaders emphasized the joy and glory of *theosis,* just as they emphasized living in paradise as beautiful and good. At the same time, they warned against gullibility. They understood that the serpent was in the garden before Adam and Eve sinned and that their very innocence defeated them. Irenaeus believed they were children who lacked the wisdom to handle knowledge of good and evil, which left them ill-equipped to detect the deceptions of the serpent. Innocence provided no defense against abuses of power or evil. He blamed Satan for leading them astray, though Adam and Eve repented:

> Adam showed his repentance through covering himself with fig-leaves, while there were many other leaves, which would have irritated his body in a less degree. He, however, adopted a dress conformable to his disobedience (since he had lost his natural disposition and child-like mind, and had come to the knowledge of evil things). Inasmuch as, he says, I have by disobedience lost that robe of sanctity which I had from the Spirit, I do now also acknowledge that I am deserving of a covering of this nature, which affords no gratification, but which gnaws and frets the body.[21]

Irenaeus taught that baptism delivered the spiritual power to resist evil and that the church was the paradise in which the faithful were nurtured as they grew wise and matured in faith. Wisdom was the key to *theosis,* and many early churches were dedicated to Wisdom. Growing old was valued for the gains in insight, experience, and wisdom it brought. Since the Gospels do not specify Jesus's age at his execution, Irenaeus insisted that when he died, he was a wise old man of fifty. He believed that Jesus, in being born human and living through every stage of life, sanctified all aspects of human life, even death, and restored humanity's glory. Every stage of human life had its own beauty because, through each one, humanity grew in wisdom and knowledge of God.[22]

Humanity, to reach its full moral and spiritual potential in paradise, had to develop the insight and knowledge necessary to use power ethically. Ambrose of Milan wrote that such knowledge had to start with a recognition of good and evil alike:

> It is fitting that a person who knows what is good know, also, what is evil, in order that he may know the means to avoid it and, by taking the necessary precautions, that he may act with discretion. Again, it is not sufficient to know merely what is evil. Lest, although you know what is evil, you may find yourself deprived of what is good. It is best, therefore, that we know both so that, since we know what is good, we may avoid evil. . . . Moreover, we ought to know both so that our knowledge may be profound and so that we may put in practice what we know, act and acknowledge to be in perfect balance. Besides, Scripture points out that more is expected of him who has general knowledge of both than of him who is ignorant of them.[23]

For ancient Christians, wisdom about good and evil and moral agency maintained humanity's life in paradise. The Holy Spirit freed Christians to use their new power to create justice, to act with love, and to resist evil. Their churches placed them in beautiful, inspiring spaces and led them through ritual processes so that they could learn and practice ethical responsibility. These contexts and practices honed their creativity, courage, and astuteness about their own uses and misuses of power.

MEDICINE FOR SIN

Freedom in Christ had its dangers. Christians knew that *theosis* could not be fully achieved in this life. Though baptism had washed away all sins, power could be misused, and temptation was pervasive. Tertullian, who had lived a typically sexually profligate life as a young pagan man, argued that desire was the source of *vitium originis* (original sin). His suggestion reflects a fundamental dilemma about life in the church.

How was it possible to commune together in paradise, when so much could go wrong? To those considering baptism, Augustine said,

> I do not tell you that you will live here without sin, but they are venial sins which this life is never without. Baptism was instituted for all sins. For light sins, without which we cannot live, prayer was instituted.[24]

For more serious sins, a Christian could make personal restitution to those wronged, pray, and make offerings as adequate recompense for forgiveness.

Christians, even bishops, could also commit virtually unpardonable sins, sins that cut to the core of their souls, injured their spirits, and harmed the entire community. Such extraordinary violations of life in paradise, such as adultery, apostasy, and shedding human blood, required special handling. Apostasy was an acute problem for the church, partly because persecutions deliberately targeted church leaders to demoralize churches. The aftermath of persecution lingered, and churches gradually formalized a process for its apostates. Church leaders who betrayed their communities could not simply pray privately and return. Church communities needed to decide how to relate to those who had abandoned their baptismal vows of allegiance to God. Following the Decian persecutions (249–51), Cyprian's treatise on "the lapsed" declared that "divinity had come to the rescue" and offered a way for the benefits of baptism to be renewed. Through penitential "confession, fasting, tears, suffering and almsgiving," apostates could return to the Christian community.

Penance began with excommunication, denial of the Eucharist feast. Penitents reverted to the status of catechumens and, like them, stood in their own special section in worship to listen to the proclamation of the Word. They prayed prostrate, indicating their humility and repentance with tears, and they performed the physical gestures of anguish. They were dismissed before the Eucharist, which was akin to being quarantined. They undertook austerities such as fasting, sexual abstinence, simple clothing, and isolation, and they focused on works of justice, love, and mercy, including recompense to those they had wronged, if this was possible. Augustine warned,

> Do not commit those sins on account of which you would have to be separated from the body of Christ. Perish the thought! For those whom you see [at the church] doing penance have committed crimes, either adultery or some other enormities. That is why they are doing penance. [25]

Grave sins required penance because, if unaddressed, they poisoned networks of love, truth, compassion, and justice. While the historical sources make little mention of how the church addressed the harm done to victims of grave sins, the ministry of the church and its leaders included healing harm and taking care of all its members. Excommunication protected victims from being in communion with those who had harmed them. Sin broke relationships, and rehabilitation from sin required penitents to take responsibility for their behavior. Responsibility, in turn, involved committing to one's own well-being as well as to that of the community. Penitents had to make willing restitution for the harm they inflicted. Such restitution might mean, in the case of shedding blood, that the murderer had to provide the support for the victim's family in perpetuity. The sixth-century *Irish Penitentials* prescribed that the penitent live with the victim's family and replace the victim for the rest of her or his life.

The system of penance acknowledged that those who sinned grievously carried in their own souls demons of deceit, cowardice, greed, lust, despair, hatred, or fear. These demons betrayed the Spirit that gave Christians the power to do the work of God, and they were banned from the feast of life. Those who sinned could not rejoin the community while unaware of what they carried inside them or remaining unhealed from harm. The rehabilitation of penance relieved people of burdens such as shame, humiliation, and self-deception.

During Christianity's earliest centuries, leaders such as Origen,

Tertullian, and Justin Martyr taught that Christians could not shed human blood for any reason. As Tertullian explained, "The Lord, by taking away Peter's sword, disarmed every soldier thereafter."[26] Athanasius based the Christian's call to avoid violence on the divinity of humanity: "How does it come about that each one of us has turned away from his brother, despising the peace which we had been given? Yet your brother, your neighbor, is not only a man, but is God himself."[27] War was a consequence of the Fall. Those who lived as "citizens of paradise" were to fight against evil with the instruments of peace, compassion, and justice—not the instruments of violence. However, Athanasius was of two minds. Like many thinkers in the post-Constantine church, Athanasius developed qualifications for some use of war.

Ambrose believed killing Jews and barbarians could be just. His student Augustine, who condemned the "deceitful masks" of war, struggled to define the circumstances under which killing in war could ever be justified.[28] By the fifth century, the Theodosian Code required all soldiers to be Christian. But even after Christian principles of "just war" emerged, the church maintained prohibitions against war.[29] The early-fifth-century *Canons of Hippolytus* instructed:

> A Christian should not voluntarily become a soldier unless compelled to by someone in authority. He should have a sword, but he should not be commanded to shed blood. If it is ascertained that he has done so, he should stay away from the mysteries at least until he has been purified through tears and lamentation.[30]

Clergy and lay servants of the church were forbidden from taking up arms or shedding human blood, and Christians who killed for any reason—including as soldiers—were expected to undergo penance before partaking of the Eucharist. The church knew that even those who killed in self-defense or in a just war suffered what we now call "post-traumatic stress" and needed healing from violence. The church's moral stand on shedding human blood, while never adequately lived out, held for a millennium. As late at the Norman invasion of England in 1066, warriors went to monasteries to do penance for killing.

Penance could only be done once in a lifetime. In the earliest traditions, the length of penance, usually seven years, was often long enough to cease near the end of a person's life. The long sentence allowed those struggling to overcome their demons a way to avoid relapsing and further harming others. The process began with public confession. Until the sixth century, public confession was required for killing, adultery, and apostasy. It enabled church members to know those who sought support and had committed themselves to the process of healing as well as to determine whether or not and when penitents could be absolved. Jerome explained:

If the serpent, the devil, bites someone secretly, he infects that person with the venom of sin. And if the one who has been bitten keeps silence and does not do penance, and does not want to confess his wound . . . then his brother and his master, who have the word [of absolution] that will cure him, cannot very well assist him.[31]

Penance was the medicine that would make them well enough to return to the Eucharist. In Ireland, by the late sixth century, priests were regarded as physicians of the soul (called "soul-friends") who dispensed precise remedies to assist sin-sick souls. The sixth-century *Penitential of St. Columbanus* described this healing work:

Doctors of the body compound their medicines in diverse kinds; thus they heal wounds in one manner, sicknesses in another, boils in another, bruises in another. So also should spiritual doctors treat with diverse kinds of cures the wounds of the soul, their sicknesses, pains, ailments, and infirmities.[32]

The community guided and corrected its members through prayer and social pressures, not by force or threat of punishment. Those who sinned had to accept penance willingly if it was to be an effective cure. John Chrysostom noted:

Christians, more than all people, are not allowed to correct by force the faults of those who sin. Secular judges, indeed, when they have captured wrongdoers under the law, demonstrate that their authority is great by preventing them, even against their own will, from following their own desires; but in our case the wrongdoer must be corrected not by force, but by persuasion.[33]

The freedom to exercise power and make choices did not guarantee that every decision would be ideal or without regret; real moral dilemmas never have unambiguous outcomes. Freedom to make moral choices is, however, the only guarantee that there can be restitution and healing from sin or that there are any moral choices and love at all.

In a world in which solidarity with others, shared knowledge, and community life were essential to survival, reliance on the community was the key to personal strength. When Christians asked for help, they provided their spiritual community an opportunity to demonstrate love and goodness and to participate in building up the body of Christ. Vulnerability was a form of emotional strength—it affirmed the communal power of the Spirit as love. Love could not be coerced; it could only be offered and enabled. Penitential processes of accountability, ethical training, and protection from harm made greater love possible. Penitents received support from those with greater wisdom about good and evil than they possessed themselves. In turning to their godly kin for support, prayers, and absolution, penitents relearned moral discernment, self-knowledge, generosity, and humility. Ambrose appealed to such values in his letter of excommunication to the Emperor Theodosius. Augustine, who witnessed Theodosius's penance, described how the community wept for their fallen emperor and prayed for his rehabilitation. The community was expected not to condemn or judge sinners, but to hold them accountable and pray regularly as one would for a brother or sister. Their support for penitents sustained the power of baptism and affirmed that the Spirit was greater than the principalities and powers of the world, that restoration to the Body of Christ and the Eucharist was still possible.

WOMEN AND MEN IN PARADISE

As thinkers such as Irenaeus, Ambrose, and Augustine understood, the power granted through *theosis* was dangerous. It required both personal discipline and community participation and guidance to be used responsibly and ethically. When it came to women, however, many men carried forward the social attitudes of their time, rather than accepting or seeing the full implications of *theosis*. Gender was a major issue for church leaders because Genesis 1–2, the primary scriptural basis for both paradise and *theosis,* specifically stated that both male and female were made in the image of God. Genesis 3 describes women's subordination and humanity's expulsion from paradise as consequences of the fall. If Jesus Christ overcame the fall, why would he also not remedy women's subordination?

Many male leaders attempted to justify male domination as divinely authorized based on labored interpretations of Genesis 1–3. Ambrose, for example, struggled in circular and convoluted fashion to blame Eve for the fall and, thereby, to justify her subordination to her husband. To make the case, he asserted things not found in Genesis 1–3. He even imagined an offstage conversation between Adam and Eve, based on his assumptions of women's intellectual weakness to explain how Eve was to blame for changing the commandment told to Adam. He then insisted her subordination was the natural state of humanity, rather than being the product of the fall. Hence, Ambrose read the curse after the fall, "Your husband shall rule over you," back into Genesis 1–2.[34]

Ambrose reflected gender values of his time, which based hierarchies on relationships within the *pater familias*. Ambrose mixed literal interpretations of Genesis 2–3 with allegorical ones—unacknowledged doublespeak still common in scriptural interpretation. On the one hand, Ambrose argued that male and female shared one divine nature, which Genesis 1:27 literally said. Then, he applied, literally out of order, the story in Genesis 3, where God cursed Eve, to Genesis 2. Thus, he maintained women's perpetual subordination to men by reading Genesis 2-3 in reverse order, making the curse the "natural" order of Creation in paradise. He applied his view of marriage to rationalize other hierarchies as divinely created. This view allowed him to use the example of one man's service to a more powerful man to discuss the importance of subservient helpers. We note that the women of his congregation, who on more than one occasion sought to remove him from office, may not have shared his view.

Roman ideas about sex universalized hierarchical, heterosexual marriage. The most offensive, unnatural, illegal form of sex was between men who were equals, which undermined the control and dominance of a household's ruling father. Sexual relations between men were acceptable, as long as one was subordinated to the other by age, income, status, and/or role—so the subordinated male performed the wife's role. Only such hierarchical sex counted as real sex. This construction of male sexual behavior as dominance and control made it unremarkable for Ambrose to use a relationship between two unequal men as a parallel to a relationship between husband and wife.[35]

Ambrose, himself the son of a high-ranking Roman official, typified the ways church leaders used *theosis* to support privileged men —despite aspects of the life of Christ that appeared "unmanly" and biblical texts that clearly mandated equality as the condition of sanctified humanity. As elite males entered Christian life, they incorporated the classic Roman virtues into *theosis*. These virtues—from the Latin root *vir* (man)—defined manliness through the ideals of courage, control, and dispassion, and they were often mixed with Greek ideas of the power of masculine *nous* (mind) over feminine *aisthesis* (senses). Christian teachers such as Clement of Alexandria taught that these manly virtues—well matched to military and political rule—could become religious disciplines that advanced the divinization of humanity. These traditional masculine virtues required men to reject their passions and vulnerabilities. Following Platonic and Stoic divisions of the soul into the "hard" masculine virtues and the "soft" feminine passions, Clement encouraged triumph over the passions as a mark of masculinity as well as spiritual maturity. Just as men were to dominate women, the virtues were to rule over the passions. Baptism, in this light, cleansed the soul of the polluting passions and opened it to the spirit of discipline and the control of feeling and desire. Jerome pictured the ideal man as one who regulated his body "as a charioteer does his pace." The body was a chariot, and the mind was the charioteer.[36]

Christians who followed the path of "manly virtue" and *apatheia* (lack of feelings), sought to eliminate or control the passions as incompatible with a sanctified life. They found support in Paul's division of feelings between those "of the spirit" and those "of the flesh." Paul wrote that Christ crucified the passions when he died on the cross, and "those who belong to Christ Jesus have crucified the flesh with its passion and desires" (Gal. 5:24). Some Christian leaders intensified the military masculine virtues. They said the ideal Christian fought evil with the courage and fortitude of a symbolic "soldier of Christ," who, instead of shedding blood, slew the passions.

Historian Virginia Burrus discusses how thoroughly Christian theologies of *theosis* were infected with notions of masculinity as mastery of the body and its desires. Submission to God justified men's efforts to define and control women's bodies and souls. Virtuous women were also to control their emotions, desires, and bodies. They were to display the manly virtues of courage, fortitude, temperance, and justice, and eschew the passions. Nonetheless, they were to submit to men.

After Constantine decriminalized Christianity, more and more elite men joined the church. A new set of virtues to guarantee men's submission to church authority began to be added to the manly virtues. Bishops such as Ambrose offered a new masculinity to privileged Roman men. Not only were they to possess manly virtue in terms of traditional masculinity, but they were also to take on the traditional feminine qualities: submission and humility in relation to God. These new virtues for men had previously been the assigned roles of women, of lower-status men, and of slaves. The new virtues defined men's ideal relationship to God as brides, handmaidens, servants, and even slaves. Accepting and performing these feminine virtues of subordination to God granted men power over others in the church because their submission demonstrated that they enacted the will of God. This symbolic use of marriage as husbands dominating wives, a product of the curse and not an image of life in paradise, became the prototype both for the relationship of Jesus Christ and his bride, the church, and for male leaders in relationship to their communities. Some fourth-century male leaders redefined female virginity as subservience instead of power and freedom, while keeping for themselves the older traditional idea of women's virginity as sovereign power for themselves through ideals of monastic asceticism.[37]

Among the "new males" who incorporated previously feminine virtues into their ideas of sanctified humanity was Augustine. His biographer Peter Brown characterizes him as a critic of the Roman ideals of manliness. The ideals of courage, fortitude, temperance, and justice forced men to reject their weaknesses, their emotions and passions, and their need for others. When Augustine grappled with the imperative to dominate and control his desires and to subjugate his feelings, he failed. He took solace in Romans 8, "The good I would do I cannot do." His struggles led him to conclude that force of will or individual effort could not accomplish ethical virtues. They required the grace of the Holy Spirit and the grace of a sanctified and sanctifying community. He formed an understanding of Christian spirituality that embraced the passions. Desire and delight could lead the soul to God. Fear, distress, and anger could illuminate where sinful acts harmed life, where outcry and reform were needed. He affirmed desire:

Do not cease to long. Your ceaseless longing is your ceaseless voice. You will be silent, if you stop loving . . . the chilling of charity is the heart's silence . . . the burning of charity is the heart's clamour.[38]

This affirmation of the passions did not lead Augustine to regard women as the equals of men. Though elite men might embrace "feminine" qualities as their own, they valorized "the feminine" in themselves while protecting male privilege. Like his teacher Ambrose, Augustine retold the story of Creation at the end of the *Confessions* as a way to show that male dominance was divinely ordained. He praised his own Christian mother's submission to his abusive father, celebrating what he said was her response to "women whose faces were disfigured by blows from their husbands. . . . She told them that ever since they had heard the marriage deed read over to them, they ought to have regarded it as a contract which bound them to serve their husbands . . . and not defy their masters."[39]

Contemporary scholarship about early Christian communities has demonstrated that some did promote egalitarian relationships and that many marginalized or oppressed people belonged to churches. Ephrem, who was of a church tradition different from that of Augustine and Ambrose, respected the spiritual power of women and lauded their courage and boldness. And women themselves did not simply accept their subordination.

THEOSIS AND WOMEN

Women used *theosis* to claim spiritual authority. As "partakers in divinity," they regarded themselves as infused with the Spirit's power and restored to their freedom and dignity in paradise. They established and led churches and became leaders in existing churches, where they disrupted traditional structures of male dominance.[40] Many opted out of marriage and lived in Christian communities instead of in their *pater familias*, the fundamental building block of Roman systems of control. Thecla, for instance, was a famous first-century itinerant preacher and evangelist who rejected a husband chosen by her wealthy family. The *Acts of Thecla*, a second-century text, reported that she baptized herself in the face of her family's opposition and Paul's refusal to do so. Though she was frequently imprisoned and endured threats to her life, she traveled on her own or sometimes with a reluctant Paul over the course of her long career, and she was famous throughout Christianity. Churches in Spain, Egypt, and Anatolia named themselves for her.

Many cities, including Rome, claimed to be the site of her death. Her grave in Seleucia, Anatolia, became a major pilgrimage site, where she was venerated as one of the great early martyrs.

Thecla's life inspired devotional movements of women, many of whom used her example to become church leaders or pilgrims themselves. Tertullian, the satirical and conflicted misogynist, complained that some Christians used Thecla to legitimate women's teaching and baptizing activities. Letters written by Athanasius indicate that Thecla inspired a large community of virgins in Alexandria. Egeria, the fourth-century pilgrim to Jerusalem, may have written her diary reports to such a women's community in fourth-century Spain. She visited Thecla's still popular shrine in Seleucia and participated in its devotional practices. She mentioned, with delight, that a selection from the *Acts of Thecla* was the scripture reading for worship. Some churches and leaders identified Thecla and other notable women leaders as part of the apostolic succession of the church. She is still the "patron" saint—perhaps we should say "matron" saint—of Tarragon, Spain.[41]

Women were priests and bishops, holding office and leadership in early church communities, as scholars of the early church increasingly document.[42] Given the importance of Mary of Magdala in the Gospels, some scholars have suggested she should be counted among the inner circle of the apostles. Among the Gnostic Gospels, which were documents of the Coptic Church in Egypt written between the late first and early fourth centuries, several place her above the apostles and in conflict with Peter for leadership of the community. That she was the first witness to the Resurrection was cited as an indication of her closeness to Jesus Christ, closer than all the men.[43]

The Gospel of Mary, a Christian text dating from around 100 CE, describes Mary Magdalene instructing the male disciples. They were distraught over the Crucifixion: "If even he was not spared, how shall we be spared?" She exhorted them to take heart and be courageous, saying, "Do not mourn or grieve or be irresolute, for his grace will be with you all and will defend you." Mary then explained what she had learned from the risen Christ in a vision: the soul must journey through multi-

ple realms to attain rest in "the time (*kronos*) and season (*kairos*) of the
Aeon in silence." On its journey, the soul must make its way past seven
oppressive powers, including domination, deception, ignorance, and
wrath, that threaten to bind it, challenge its identity, and prevent its ascent. These must be negotiated successfully for the soul to proceed. The
disciples doubted Mary's authority to teach them this, but Levi defended her, saying to Peter, "You are always irate. Now I see that you are
contending against the woman like the adversaries. But if the Saviour
made her worthy, who are you to reject her?" The disciples decided to
follow Mary's teaching and resolved to "put on the Perfect Man, to form
us as he commanded."[44]

The Gospel of Mary's testimony to disputation, modeled on stories
of Jesus and his opponents, supports Mary's authority. Through engaged inquiry, the community negotiated the shoals of doubt rather
than simply submit to a system of domination that brooked no opposition. Through questioning and disputation, deeper truths could be discovered. *The Gospel of Mary* explained that the Spirit gave Christians
power to resist oppression in this world and ascend to God. The soul's
true home was "another world," but the "other world" was what this
world should be and what Christian communities enacted through rituals and by doing the work of God in the world. Christian communities had to develop their powers of divinity by resisting domination and
engaging the active search for truth. In this way, they could ascend to
peace.[45]

In resisting domination, many early Christian women rejected the
curse of women's subordination to men, a status based on heterosexual
sex. Engaging in sex with men required women to accept a subjugated
role. Virginity and chastity gave them power. Virgins chose to remain
so by refusing to marry, and married women left their husbands to live
in women's communities. Sex was legally regulated and restricted and
socially fraught by gender and power, as it still is today. However, today
many tend to regard virginity as a sign of conformity to patriarchal double standards and the disempowerment of women. The popular novel
The DaVinci Code, which suggests that Mary Magdalene was Jesus's

wife and carried his bloodlines through her descendants, might appear to elevate Mary's importance to Christianity. However, early Christians would not have regarded making her Mrs. Jesus as an improvement over her role as a preeminent apostle and teacher with her own divinity. The virginity of early Christian women was a radical statement against male dominance and in favor of women's own power. The only legitimate virgin in a *pater familias* was a daughter, who was owned by her father until she could be transferred to a husband, at which point she was no longer a virgin. For daughters to refuse to marry may have aggravated Roman opposition to Christianity. As a spiritual practice, women's abstinence from marriage granted freedom from male sexual domination. Abstinence ended the curse inflicted upon Eve when she was exiled from the Garden, "your desire shall be for your husband and he shall lord it over you" (Gen. 3:16). Therefore, Christian virginity defied the core power system upon which Rome was built, the *pater familias*.[46]

In Roman culture, females had authority over males in two roles: as their mothers or as goddesses. The Gospels of Matthew and Luke claimed that Mary was the mother of Jesus Christ and a virgin. The second-century *Protoevangelium of James* said that Mary's mother, Anna, was also a virgin.[47] That Mary was mother of Jesus Christ and a virgin gave her extraordinary authority and power. The Council of Ephesus in 431 declared Mary to be Theotokos (the Mother of God). In other words, they said she gave birth both to the humanity and divinity of her son. In early church art, she was often enthroned like her son, resembling images of Isis, the queen of heaven, who is sometimes shown nursing her son Hippolytus, as Mary was shown nursing Jesus.

Mary's dignity and power were reflected in depictions of other mothers. In the arch of the apse of St. Maria Maggiorie, the story of Herod's slaughter of the infants in Matthew 2:1–12 focuses on the mothers. A dozen of them, their hair loosened in grief, hold the bodies of their infants and stand erect, heads unbowed, before Herod upon his throne, indicting him for his crimes and demanding justice. The narthex of the thirteenth-century Chora Church in Istanbul, Turkey, has a series of scenes that tell this same story. In the first fresco, mothers fight fiercely with soldiers, grasping with their bare hands at swords and spears. They hold their sons tightly as the soldiers pull them away and impale the small bodies. Then, a group of mothers sit in a circle on the ground; their hair streaming down their shoulders and backs in mourning. They hug the corpses of their children and weep in lamentation. Finally, their hair still loose and holding their infants, they stand before the enthroned Herod, staring at him face to face, shaming him with their eyes.

Men also practiced sexual abstinence. About a decade before the birth of Jesus, Rome passed marriage laws that inflicted severe tax penalties on citizens who refused to marry and to generate offspring. With an infant mortality rate of more than 60 percent and life expectancy at age twenty-five, Rome needed every woman to begin reproducing at the onset of puberty and bear five children to keep the empire's population at a replacement rate. A shrinking population meant a declining tax base and fewer sons to serve in the military and guard the empire's vast frontiers. The standard marriage involved an adult male, who had proven his ability to provide for a family, and an adolescent female a decade or more younger. People joined dissident religious groups to resist conscription and overtaxation, and asceticism and virginity emerged as ways to defy imperial pressures to reproduce and marry. The Apostle Paul, who, unlike Jesus, was a Roman citizen, advocated a life of celibacy and recommended marriage only for those too weak to avoid fornication.[48]

The church in the West did not declare marriage a sacrament until the medieval period. Marriage often occurred when couples lived together and declared themselves married. The ascetic ideals that challenged imperial systems of heterosexual marriage offered people an alternative to the *pater familias,* and, despite the attempts of bishops to construct virginity according to gender subordination, abstinence from marriage was a pathway to *theosis* and offered spiritual power. According to historian Peter Brown, ascetics "ringed a careworn society with the shimmering hope of Paradise regained."[49]

Ephrem was a voluntary lay ascetic. He saw abstinence as a sanctifying spiritual discipline and advocated it for men as well as women. He praised Mary for her virginity. He emphasized that she freely chose this state. However, this did not mean that Ephrem regarded sex as inherently bad or defiling. Of married women he said, "intercourse is not defiled. . . . Nor is marriage accursed."[50] Like every important human activity, it required moral discernment. Human sexual behavior could be predatory, dominating, and humiliating, or joyous, loving, and uplifting. Sexuality and its uses had powerful social consequences, so engaging in ethical sex required the exercise of free will. Ephrem wrote a great many hymns about the dignity, power, and humanity of women who acted with courage. His view of women as models of humanity affirmed a wide range of female roles and activities.

Ephrem noted how women such as Tamar, Rahab, and Ruth, who used sex to gain justice and bear children, were part of a long legacy of women who brought God into the world. His admiration for such marginalized, courageous women included the Samaritan woman at the well in John 4:1–42. Though she had five husbands, lived with a man she had not married, and appeared to have no children, Ephrem insisted there was nothing shameful about her life. He said that she interrogated Jesus boldly and without apology, and he insisted that no one with a shameful life could have been so forthright. She spoke to Jesus Christ, he said, "as a learned one, as a disputant," and "her voice was authoritative." She was a popular figure in early Christian art. Ephrem extolled her wisdom, saying Christ "labored with you and sanctified you in order to be like His glorious Father." He described her as a "type of our humanity that He leads step by step." She embodied the gifts of a searching heart, astute learning, and lively mind that led her to engage important religious questions.[51]

In claiming their freedom, women found *theosis* in whole-bodied, passionate life. For example, second-century stories of Thecla reveal that Christian women affirmed their capacities to know, to create, to reason, to love, and to bear children. They experienced the spiritual power of their desires, pleasures, and pains.[52] The passions guided the soul toward its likeness to God. While the passions, or even the virtues, could be out of balance, such tyranny of the passions or virtues was a consequence of the Fall. In contrast to theologians such as Ambrose, who valorized Mary for giving birth to Jesus without pain or groans (how he knew this is a mystery), a fourth-century Spanish letter to a woman ascetic, Marcella, exhorts her to "imitate the groans of holy Mary who labors, so that just as within the dark matrix of the womb, so within the secret cell of the monastery something will take form in us which will contribute to our salvation."[53] Mary's labor pains were a sign of the sanctification of women's physical experiences and a model for a spiritual life incarnate in bodies and emotions.

The ascetic and theologian Macrina, according to her brother Gregory of Nyssa, commented that desire "arises only when the thing missing is not found." It remembers good things and hopes for them again. When desire is satisfied, the soul finds equanimity and

offers no harbour within itself either for hope or for memory. It holds the object of the one; the other is extruded from the consciousness by the occupation in enjoying all that is good: and thus the soul ... is conformed to ... the Divine nature; none of its habits are left to it except that of love.[54]

Macrina neither despised nor rejected desire. To put her views in terms more akin to the Song of Songs, desire was foreplay that ended when the soul achieved climax in love. Ephrem used the image of female sexuality to describe the quality of paradise:

Yes, Paradise yearns for the man whose goodness
makes him beautiful;
*   it engulfs him at its gateway,*
it embraces him in its bosom,
*   it caresses him in its very womb;*
for it splits open and receives him
*   into its inmost parts.*[55]

Sexual pleasure appeared frequently in discussions of *theosis* as a positive metaphor for the pinnacle of the soul's ascent to God—or God's descent into the depths of human life. The image of union in the garden in the Song of Songs, the story of the wedding at Cana, and the gender-crossing baptismal formula of brides of Christ suggested the connections between bodily pleasure in sex and the experience of God. Ephrem said,

> *He has left the heavens and descended,*
> *let us make holy for Him the bridal chamber of our hearts.*[56]
> *The Heavenly Bridegroom . . . has come down and invited all,*
> *And I too have been invited to enter His pure wedding feast.*[57]
> *The soul is Your bride, the body Your bridal chamber,*
> *Your guests are the senses and the thoughts.*
> *And if a single body is a wedding feast for You,*
> *How great is Your banquet for the whole Church!*[58]

The aim was the divinization of all aspects of human existence, a sensibility about the completeness of joy and the serenity of fulfillment.

IMAGES OF POWER

During Christianity's first millennium, visual images depicted sanctified women and men as dignified, strong, and beautiful. Mary, as the Mother of God, was enthroned in images like those of the goddess Isis. If she stood with the apostles, she was usually front and center, the largest, and therefore, the most important figure. Female saints were depicted, as were male saints, carrying victory wreaths, wearing white robes of glory, and gazing calmly and confidently at the viewer. Though the society subordinated women to men, churches apparently were disinclined to depict their subordination in the images of paradise on their walls.

The St. Apollinare Nuovo Church in Ravenna holds a striking example of gender parity on the walls of its rectangular basilica. King Theodoric, a Goth who ruled the Roman Empire, built it as a palace church around 520. His daughter, Queen Amalasuntha (498–535) held power first as regent for her son and later as queen.[59] Mosaics of life-size female and male saints process in lines on both sides of the walls of the nave from the entry door all the way to the chancel. On one side, twenty-two women (originally twenty-six), regal in stature, stride toward Mary, who is enthroned and holds the Christ child.[60] They wear elegant, embroidered gold tunics and carry wreaths of glory. Fringed gossamer veils cover their hands, cascading from jeweled crowns in their hair and falling over their shoulders. Their ruby slippers stand out in the emerald grass dotted with lilies and carnations. Sometime in the thirteenth to sixteenth centuries, the magi in their signature Persian outfits replaced four of the women at the head of the line, so that the three men now lead the procession to Mary, breaking the original gender symmetry of the images of men and women. On the other side of the nave, twenty-six men, just as large as the women, also process across a meadow filled with flowers and palm trees to the enthroned Christ, who, like his mother across the nave, is attended by angels.[61] Dressed

FIGURE 9. *St. Apollinare Nuovo Church, Ravenna, Italy. Nave left wall, mosaic. Late fifth century. Procession of Women Saints.*

in white tunics and topped by gold nimbuses, the men also hold crowns of leaves in their covered hands. Christ holds a scepter and raises his right hand in blessing.

The women and men process with the same dignity and beauty. Their names are written above them: Agatha, Thecla, Perpetua, Martin, Clement, Lawrence, and so on. Many died under persecution—burned, crucified, or slain in the arena. However, the martyrs were remembered on the church's walls as they lived and remained present to the living. They inhabited the meadows of paradise, resurrected, powerful and strong. These images suggest that Christians could imagine paradise as a realm without male dominance and female submission.

"For freedom Christ has set us free, submit no longer to the yoke of slavery," Paul had exhorted in Galatians 3, and the church walls said, "amen." Despite his emphasis on masculine virtue, even Clement of Alexandria was moved to say:

> Men and women share equally in perfection, and we are to receive the same instruction and the same discipline. For the name "humanity" is common to both men and women; and for us "in Christ there is neither male nor female."[62]

Christ had reopened paradise and restored humanity to its original dignity and equality.

This vision of the paradise garden was, however, contended throughout Christianity's first millennium. The church began in the second and third centuries to curtail the exercise of women's leadership as officeholders, teachers, and deacons, and by 441 the Synod of Orange forbade women's ordination. The Synod of Orlèans in 533 repeated the ban—obviously, some churches had ignored the first injunction.[63] Nonetheless, women were active as ordained deacons up through the sixth century, and are so again today in many church bodies, though not all. The contemporary Roman Catholic prohibition against women's ordination is based in the assertion that women cannot reflect the image of Christ.[64]

The asceticism of the fourth century desert fathers replaced the ideal of martyrdom with a masculine, heroic ideal of celibacy and physical austerities. Monastic life and ascetic practices, which rejected the norms of Roman citizenship and its core structure of the *pater familias*, became replacements for martyrdom for both men and women, but with distinctly gendered ideas of the role of virginity.[65] In the Eastern church, ascetic men living at the edge of the wilderness were believed to have purged their lives of "all hint of dark passions that ruled the world." Ascetic women were to submit to the guidance and leadership of such men.

With these changes in the understanding of martyrdom, bishops suggested that the infants whom Herod slaughtered were the first Christian martyrs. By the sixth century, the church in Rome had developed a Mass for the Innocents, celebrated immediately after Christmas.[66] Martyrs had been people whose exemplary faith defied the empire's power and exposed the impotence of its authority. They asserted their divinity through the exercise of freedom that resisted injustice and stood courageous against its idolatry of coercion and violence. With the new focus on infants, martyrs were identified with the powerless and unwitting victims of the powerful.

This new focus on the infants sanctified innocent victims. The more innocent and helpless the victims were, the more holy they were regarded. The ideal saint became someone who was childlike. To hold a position of authority compromised a person's moral claims. Having a choice and exercising power meant a person could have done otherwise than be good. If decision-making power was morally corrupting, the only moral position was to be helpless. The change in meaning paralleled the change in women's virginity from self-possessed power to subservience. The virgin martyr also became a powerless, innocent victim, instead of an ethically self-reflective, powerful person. In Christianity's second millennium, the idea of *theosis* as a community effort to do the work of God faded. Wisdom and experience sullied rather than advanced likeness to God. Knowledge of good and evil and the exercise of power would come to be associated with those outside of paradise. Paradise would become the garden of pristine innocence.

These new ideas of martyrdom shifted the view of humanity from that of the oppressed and marginalized who refuse to see themselves as powerless to that of those in power. When goodness is no longer wisdom but is innocence, the powerful can be deemed good if they identify themselves with helpless victims and protect them. Benevolent paternalism requires inequality: powerful, kindly helpers and powerless, grateful victims. Denying the agency and power of victims enhances the potency and importance of the powerful and makes dismantling the hierarchical power of paternalism unnecessary. In effect, when weakness and innocence are valorized as holy, communities are absolved of the necessity to create the social conditions for all people to gain power and exercise it with freedom and dignity. In Christianity's second millennium, Jesus as an abused and innocent victim, hanging dead on the cross, would become the image of holiness. But for a time—for nearly a thousand years—Christianity offered a different image of sanctity: the glory of God was humanity fully alive.

CHAPTER EIGHT

Hidden Treasures of Wisdom

Wisdom is radiant and unfading,
and she is easily discerned by those who love her.
She pervades and penetrates all things,
a breath of the power of God,
an image of God's goodness.
She renews all things;
In every generation she passes into holy souls
and makes them friends of God and prophets.
She is more beautiful than the sun.

WISDOM OF SOLOMON

Of the many ancient sites we visited in our research for this book, none was more beautiful than Hagia Sophia, the Church of Holy Wisdom in Istanbul. Built in the sixth century and converted to a mosque called Ayasofya in the fifteenth, Hagia Sophia is considered by many to be the greatest cathedral ever constructed.[1] In its vast, nearly square nave, the floor is an acre of ivory marble. Embedded in this expanse run four bands of green stone. Down the left and right sides of the nave, rows of tall, dark marble columns link the massive square gray pillars in each corner of the space, suggesting gravity and stately grace. Each column's capital blooms into filigreed marble acanthus vines and leaves that extend into arched spandrels, creating a canopy like a primeval tree arbor.

Across the nave from the imperial door, the towering apse rises high above the chancel. In its glittering gold conch, a beautiful mosaic of

Mary, Theotokos, gazes calmly and benevolently upon her visitors. She and the child on her lap appear tiny from the floor of the nave. On her right alongside the conch, the exquisitely lovely angel Gabriel is graced with resplendent eagle's wings; on the left are a few traces of the angel Michael. Mosaics of early Christian saints congregate along the walls of the nave above the columns.

As we moved into the center of the floor, we looked up at the upper women's balcony surrounding the nave on three sides. A border of columns marks the balcony, and more tiers of columns support a series of stacked half-domes, which drew our eyes up into the magnificent central dome. It is still an architectural wonder. Appearing far higher than its 180 feet, the wide, shallow stone dome arches 108 feet across. Forty windows ring its base and pour ethereal sunlight onto its inner surface. The dome seems to float like a parachute, the vault of the heavens both visible and mysterious at the same time. At the very top of each of the gray corner pillars that support the dome, an ancient image of a huge winged seraph guards the space below.

We climbed the long ramp up to the women's balcony and surveyed its elegant halls, lit by large windows. The balcony is level with the conch of the apse, and from one end of it, we could almost touch the mosaics of Mary and Gabriel we had seen from the floor far below. The enormous apparitions, at least fifteen feet tall, are breathtakingly beautiful at close range. They have stately, peaceful countenances, and Gabriel holds an orb in his right hand. As we continued around the balcony we found on one wall a thirteenth-century mosaic fragment of three life-size figures: Christ, Mary, and John the Baptist. It was the most beautiful *deisis* we had ever seen. A *deisis,* an image of prayer or intercession, is a composition that places Jesus between John and Mary, who look toward him, their heads slightly bowed as they intercede for humanity's salvation. The bearded, poignant face of Christ gazes out at the viewer with ineffable sweetness and compassion. According to legend, a tenth-century Russian delegation visited Constantinople to investigate whether Russia should adopt its form of Christianity. After attending the liturgy in Hagia Sophia, the ambassador remarked, "We

FIGURE 10. *Ayasofya, Istanbul, Turkey. Wall of women's balcony, mosaic. Thirteenth century. Deisis.*

knew not whether we were in heaven or on earth. . . . We only know that God dwells there among men." They reportedly became Byzantine Christians.[2]

The interior of Hagia Sophia is an icon of paradise. The rivers of Eden flow in green marble across the ivory floor, under the dome of sunlit heavens. We strolled among the groves of trees created by the marble columns and filigreed carvings of leaves and vines. Its space embraced us and surrounded us with signs on every side that earth is the dwelling place of God. Wisdom—God's presence—permeates all things. The early church believed the entire cosmos had been transformed by the presence of God in flesh. As Ephrem exulted, "The Lofty One became like a little child, yet hidden in him was a treasure of Wisdom that suffices for all."[3]

The apse image of Mary dates from around the ninth or tenth century. The angel Gabriel said to her, "Greetings, favored one! The Lord is with you. . . . Do not be afraid, Mary, for you have found favor with God. And now, you will conceive in your womb and bear a son, and you will name him Jesus. He will be great, and will be called the Son of the Most High" (Luke 1:28–32). In reflecting on her pregnancy, Mary magnified God by proclaiming a revolution of justice:

> *His mercy is for those who fear him from generation*
> *to generation.*
> *He has shown strength with his arm;*
> *He has scattered the proud in the thoughts of their hearts.*

He has brought down the powerful from their thrones,
and lifted up the lowly;
He has filled the hungry with good things, and sent the
rich away empty. (Luke 1:50–53)

Christianity emerged and grew in societies of economic injustice, slavery, and war. In the midst of struggle against the many forces of death, it offered a world of life, made known through the practices of wisdom. Holy Wisdom, displayed in the apse icon of the revolutionary Mother of God, reminded the faithful of the incarnation of wisdom in her many forms. The faithful felt, perhaps, in the church's spaces their hard-earned gift of life in paradise. Their paradise was neither perfect nor complete. It was complex and intermittent. At its best, it was the goodness of ordinary life, joyous and luxuriant. In an uncertain, troubled world full of pain and death and sorrow, the church offered spaces of respite where life might be loved and beauty appreciated. Paradise was where the work of justice and love continued, and where the revolution of values proclaimed by Mary guided the work of hardworking saints.

THE POWER OF ART

We had traveled to Istanbul to find, if we could, a corpse of the dead Jesus. No Crucifixion was depicted in Hagia Sophia. Instead, it confirmed that early Christians made paradise tangible in the art and architecture of their churches. Our journey into early Christian visual culture was a rewarding adventure for two Western Protestant theologians trained in the analysis of written texts and philosophical ideas. We began the adventure by looking at the images at length, as ordinary churchgoers might have done, and became convinced that the effort to understand the power of this art was crucial to a better understanding of Christianity in its first millennium.[4]

In looking at early art, we discovered that our backgrounds affected what we saw. Rita was raised for her first six years in a Japanese Buddhist family and in the linguistic forms of a pictographic, nonlinear language, and she experienced early Christian art differently from Rebecca, who was raised in a Western liberal Methodist family and the structures of English. Rita found herself drawn to the larger environmental scheme of the images, the sense, as it were, of the feeling and meaning of the whole. Her way of seeing the art led her to the insight that it was about paradise and that paradise was the key to its meaning. Rebecca was captivated by the people and creatures portrayed and by the vibrant colors that evoked luminous presence, and she focused on the characters and their stories. When first confronted with the paradise interpretation, she was unconvinced, but we both began to see the implications of paradise for understanding Christian salvation. Beginning with our shared surprise at the absence of images of a dead Jesus, our perceptions began to overlap until they cohered around the meaning of paradise.

Our journey into the early Christian visual world taught us to see more carefully in other ways. We recognized how powerfully images today dominate sighted people's lives. Perhaps because images are so numerous and pervasive, many of us fail to be conscious of their power or to relate to them with critical awareness. We live in a constant sea of images at home, at work, in cars and subways, on city streets, and in ads for virtually every object we purchase. We sit voluntarily poised for hours before screens, captivated by the beauty, horror, humor, pleasure, and sheer creativity of visual media. For those who are sighted, it may be difficult both to be aware of how deeply visual media affect us and to understand what it might be like to not be sighted and to be oblivious to their unconscious effects. Images can seduce us against our will and against our best interests as a society; and they can form the consciousness of the sighted in ways that deepen our responsibility for and love for life. The capacity to relate critically to images matters in a visually saturated society.

Ancient Christians understood that powerful images create a subjective change in committed viewers, what scholar Margaret Miles calls an initiation of knowledge and an awakening of *eros*, a transformation grounded in participation in the image. Such viewing involves attraction to the work, not detached observation of it.[5] Art lovers today see work in museums as objects to admire, but the impersonal, hushed crowds of strangers are not a congregation, and museums are rarely ritual environments. In addition, viewers may see an original work for only a few minutes and never see it again, whereas ancient viewers looked at images repeatedly. The ancient art still in churches today is also often in spare spaces—many ancient churches are now museums—and only fragments remain of the frescoes and dazzling mosaic art that once covered every inch of their upper walls. We see the remains of images without the chanting hundreds, the choreography of ritual, the curtains of sumptuous silk brocade, the robed clergy, the glittering gold chalices and patens, silver chandeliers, metal-encased altars, and smoky incense.

Ancient churches were rich and complete sensory worlds with physically demanding rituals. There were no pews, so everyone who could do so stood for the entire service, and worship services included frequent processional movement, which allowed the sighted to view again and again the panoply of images adorning the walls.[6] Instead of sitting in a theater and watching moving images, they moved themselves from image to image. Worshippers circulated in a crowded space for two to three hours. The images hovered above the stew of human bodies, lamp oil, incense, and foods brought by congregants for the Eucharist. Many participants fasted for a day, so that the first food they tasted was the Eucharist feast. The physical demands, repeated chanting, and communal interactions could produce altered states of consciousness. Dreams, trances, and visionary or ecstatic experiences were ordinary aspects of liturgical life and were among the ways images were experienced in the liturgy.

For early Christians, icons were sacramental. They made divine power present, just as relics of martyrs carried spiritual power. If blood and bone and bread and wine could be inspirited, they insisted, so too could glass, wood, and paint. A portrait of Christ engaged the viewer in a direct experience of God. To stand before an image of Mary, the

Mother of God, was to stand before holy power. In monasteries, the creating of icons was itself a sacramental act and spiritual discipline. In conveying presence, icons echoed an ancient sensibility. Rome's loyal citizens swore oaths before images of the emperor. Every new emperor issued coins with his image, and he sent statues or portraits of himself throughout the empire, where cities greeted his image with a triumphal *adventus,* as if the emperor himself had arrived, which, in effect, he had.

To convey spiritual presence, early Christian art moved toward a style that came to be called Byzantine, for the ancient Greek name for Constantinople. Figures in the art were formal and simplified on a flat surface, like styles found in Persia, Africa, and Asia. They differed considerably from the naturalistic, three-dimensionally molded classical traditions of Rome and Greece. The simplified anatomical forms in formal postures floated in plain backgrounds and conveyed an ethereal presence that was not strongly weighted. The Byzantine human figures addressed the viewer directly, inviting devotion, as they appeared to hover between earth and heaven.

People prayed to visual images of Christ, the apostles, and the saints for intercession on their behalf. These intercessors linked the world of the faithful on earth with God in the highest reaches of heaven, helping the faithful to reach divinity. Images of intercessors were reported to possess the power to heal by their very physical presence; they were tangible mediators of the power of the invisible Spirit to touch and transform life. John of Damascus witnessed to this power when he said: "I saw the human image of God and my soul was saved."[7]

ART AND EMPIRE

The power that art and architecture carry is not without complex and sometimes troubling ambiguities. Hagia Sophia's own history bears the marks of its long relationship to politics and religion. Constantine or his son built the first church on the site and Theodosius the second. This third edifice was constructed after the Theodosian church was burned in 532 during the Nika riots, which erupted between the Blue and

Green political parties at a chariot race in the Hippodrome. The Emperor Justinian (483–565) had decided to surrender his empire to the insurrection after it destroyed half the city and threatened him at his palace, but the Empress Theodora (500–548), a former burlesque actress in the Hippodrome who had risen to the heights of power, insisted that Justinian restore his authority. Procopius, a historian of the time, described the meeting of the remaining governing council, which was discussing how to flee the city. Theodora delivered an impassioned speech declaring that she preferred the shroud of royalty to a cowardly life of disgrace and humiliation. In response to her pressure, Justinian ordered the rioters massacred and reclaimed the empire. In the aftermath, Justinian and Theodora rebuilt the decimated city and constructed a cathedral far grander than its predecessors. Two pagan mathematicians designed the architecture—Justinian hired them after he closed their school in Athens and left them unemployed.[8]

Justinian and Theodora were the last to rule a Roman Empire both East and West. The subsequent East-West divide led eventually to the final split of Christianity in 1054 when the bishops of Rome and Constantinople excommunicated each other. The church split into different bodies, both claiming "catholic" identity; one was what came to be known as the Roman Catholic Church (the church of the West), and the other is what is now known as the Eastern Orthodox Church. In addition to these two, other groups of Christians—for example, in Ethiopia, Persia, India, and Syria—with their own languages and traditions, survive today. Until the fifteenth century, Hagia Sophia remained the cathedral of the bishop of Constantinople, the capital of the surviving half of the Roman Empire.

Architects, artists, and workers built the immense domed cathedral in an astonishingly short time, reportedly in only five years. They used expensive marbles, such as porphyry, and pieces of structures gathered from various parts of the empire. The columns still visibly lack uniformity, indicating hasty construction. The engineers did not wait for the mortar to dry before adding new layers to the pillars that would support the dome, which caused it to collapse within a few years. It was rebuilt to arch more directly down on its reconstructed support pillars and reinforced structurally. It continues to soar over the cavernous space.[9]

Hagia Sophia was a monument to a salvaged empire. Its sumptuous interior suggested that paradise was a gift the empire could deliver. Procopius wrote in 537 that the sanctuary was riveted with forty thousand pounds of silver, and Paul Silentary wrote in 563 that the altar table was gold. Every column capital, with its swirling acanthus vines, was gilded in gold. Tall silver lamps, shaped as conical trees, stood in the chancel. Hundreds of silver lamps, suspended on chains from cornices, lit the nave. They were shaped as perforated discs or crosses, filled with glass beakers of oil. Ten percent remains, perhaps, of the splendid mosaic art that once adorned the walls and dome.[10]

The cathedral was also a symbol to a traumatized city. In its dazzling, grand space, the feast of Resurrection proclaimed life restored, paradise here and now. Justinian was able to hold his empire, but his building ambitions cost him control of Italy when a massive plague struck his capitol city and he was unable to fund a military force that could hold Rome for the East. However, Constantinople survived nine hundred years after Justinian and Theodora built the great cathedral, and it remained a crossroad for cultural interaction between Europe and Asia. Christianity in the East developed complex, cosmopolitan attitudes toward other religions. The Eastern Empire shared borders and traded with equally sophisticated civilizations with their own religions. Christians in the East traveled trade routes that brought news of far-off lands, and they migrated as far away as China and India, where traces of Christianity survive from the seventh century. Their close proximity to and frequent interactions with Muslims required Eastern Christians to negotiate nuanced relationships with them. Eastern Christians shared with Muslims an interest in the works of ancient Greek philosophers and poets, and in the thirteenth century, Aristotle would return to Western Christianity via the Muslims in Spain, who passed him on to Thomas Aquinas. Later, the Muslim preservation of these pre-Christian Greek traditions would kindle the Renaissance and humanist Enlightenment in Europe.[11]

The Eastern Orthodox Church understood spiritual power as incarnated in the material life of the world, in many locations in life, not just in icons. Though the bishop of Constantinople was the emperor's spiritual advisor, and the emperor was the cathedral's pre-eminent Christian, Eastern Christians maintained forms of spiritual power distinct from the empire. Villages and remote provinces often had a variety of spiritual leaders, such as ascetics, monks, priests, and eccentric holy men. The Syriac Church continued its own language and theological traditions. The East did not follow a central leader, such as a pope, but remained an association of leaders called patriarchs. Nor did the East deem their empire or emperor especially "holy." The unity of their church lay not with formal, juridical authority. It could be discovered within the tensions of differences and theological disputations among the patriarchs as they met periodically at councils.

SHATTERED IMAGES

None of the original mosaics of Hagia Sophia have survived. They were destroyed in a series of iconoclastic controversies that rocked eighth-century Constantinople and reverberated throughout Christianity. Tensions surrounding the use of images, suspicion of graven images, charges of idolatry, and the destruction of temples and statues had erupted periodically in the ancient world. Why, however, the controversy carried such destructive vehemence in eighth-century Constantinople is difficult to pin down. The first outbreak of iconoclasm began in 726, when Emperor Leo III (680–741) removed a figure of Christ guarding the central gate to the royal palace and replaced it with a cross. He may have sought to undermine monasteries, which were centers of icon production and drained the empire's wealth and manpower at a time when Leo was waging major military campaigns to gain territories in Anatolia back from the Muslims.

Leo's iconoclastic acts raised the question of whether the emperor or only a council of bishops had the right to dictate religious practices.[12] Though Eastern Christianity integrated emperors into the church as highly elevated personages who had a say in church affairs, policies about creed, theology, and liturgical practices were usually left to the patriarchs. It was not unheard of for an emperor to call a church council and to influence theological statements of liturgical practices, but the relationship between church and empire was a negotiated process—it was neither a settled hierarchy nor a joint office held by one ruler. In addition, the East had a tradition of disputation and philosophical inquiry, with different forms of Christianity functioning alongside the church of the emperor. In areas distant from the capitol, these alternative Christianities sometimes functioned in resistance to the church in Constantinople, despite persistent attempts to quash them. However, after the fifth century, a patriarch's resistance to the decisions of an ecumenical council in major cities such as Alexandria and Antioch might result in his deposition and exile.

Conflicts among Jews, Christians, and Muslims appear to have fueled the iconoclastic debate. Two centuries before the controversy, Justinian had needed the bishop of Rome's help to hold Italy in the empire. To gain the bishop's favor, he instituted a persecution against Eastern Christians who rejected the dual nature of Christ voted at the Council of Calcedon in 451 by insisting that Christ had only a divine nature. Their opponents later called them Monophysites, from the Greek *monos* (one) and *physis* (nature). In the wake of Justinian's brutal strategy, many Monophysites later welcomed Muslim rulers who practiced religious tolerance. The assistance of disaffected Christians, as well as Jews, whom Justinian had also persecuted, aided Islam in the seventh century to spread from Syria into Egypt, territory where Monophysite Christianity was popular. In addition, Muslim expansion eastward into Mesopotamia and beyond began after the Roman Emperor Heraclius I (610–641) defeated Persia, which controlled the area east of the Euphrates. A century later, the iconoclastic Leo may have wanted to recruit Muslim soldiers to his army as he sought to restore a shrunken empire, or he may have sought to pacify the Jews and Muslims in territories he reconquered.

Church leaders were divided on iconoclasm. Iconoclasts jettisoned devotional practices, such as kissing icons and praying to them, and destroyed images. They rejected the idea that the inert matter of paint or wood could make Christ present. Only physical presences with voice and breath could reveal the Spirit of God. Images were lifeless.[13] The Eucharist alone, and not an image of it, was an acceptable representation of Christ's incarnation, iconoclasts insisted:

> The only admissible figure of the humanity of Christ, however, is bread and wine in the holy Supper. This and no other form, this and no other type, has he chosen to represent his incarnation. Bread he ordered to be brought, but not a representation of the human form, so that idolatry might not arise. And as the body of Christ is made divine, so also this figure of the body of Christ, the bread, is made divine by the descent of the Holy Spirit; it becomes the divine body of Christ by the mediation of the priest who, separating the oblation from that which is common, sanctifies it.[14]

The iconoclasts understood the dangerous power of images. To affirm that material life on earth incarnated the spirit of God risked offering divine sanction to people, places, objects and events that might not truly be of God. The power of images to evoke passionate feelings could be used to stir up hatred, squelch dissent, provoke resistance, or incite violence. Images could be turned into what we now call propaganda. People could be lulled into believing healing or justice would come through touching holy objects, ingesting the paint of icons, or journeying to sacred places. The Hebrew prophets had sounded warnings against idols, images, and rituals that took the place of feeding the hungry, clothing the naked, and working for justice. An iconoclast destroyed images not because they held no power, but because he believed they were idolatry. With great power came great responsibility for ethical uses of power, and images could be used unethically. Without leaders with educated, experienced, and critical capacities honed through years of experience, a community could go seriously astray. Without instruction and practice in how to understand and relate to the spirit incarnate in the world, people were a danger to themselves and others. The antidote to the dangers of incarnation, for the iconoclasts, was suspicion of idolatry and the cultivation of wisdom.

The iconophiles (lovers of icons) insisted that divinity had descended into the flesh and that the spirit of God permeated all matter, illuminating the whole world from within. If images could not make divinity present, neither could human beings or bread and wine. The monk John of Damascus said, "I adore the Creator of matter, who became matter for my sake, who was willing to live in matter and who, with matter, achieved my salvation."[15] Some Christian leaders used a pedagogical argument and justified the use of images by claiming they were biblical texts for teaching the illiterate masses. Others made the theological claim of incarnation; they asserted that images made the unseen present. They said the invisible God became visible through Christ, who was extolled as the *ikon* (image) as well as the *logos* (word) of God. They quoted John 1:18: "No one has ever seen God; the only Son, who is in the bosom of the Father, he has made him known." Thus Christ was the earthly icon of the divine Word that created life. Icons were also a dimension of *theosis*. Through icons, the presence of Christ became one with the worshippers. Gazing at the icon of Christ drew them near to God as gods seeing God. Icons were religious art, rather than art about religious subjects, icons as living power, not just art as illustrations of stories.

Irene, who ruled the empire as regent for her son, called the Seventh Ecumenical Council in 787 to restore the worship of icons. Seven iconoclastic bishops had to do public penance before they were admitted to the council. After a brief respite, the controversy resurfaced and raged another half-century. Theodora, another regent ruler, ended this second iconoclastic period in 843. During the controversies, much of the art of early Christianity was obliterated. Only traces remained, so that today, approximately half of all existing early Christian icons are found at the Monastery of St. Catherine at Sinai, a location so remote that the controversy did not breach its walls.[16]

In the wake of iconoclasm's final defeat, iconophile theologians interpreted the iconoclastic debate as being about incarnation itself. They believed the whole theological foundation of Christian life and salvation was at stake. Iconoclasts denied that the Spirit was in all things and that this earth revealed the Spirit of God. Iconoclasm desacralized the world, denuding it of power as paradise, and it made the material world mundane, devoid of religious significance. Eastern Orthodox iconographer and theologian Ouspensky says of the iconoclasts:

> By denying the human image of God, they denied the sanctification of matter in general and the deification of man in particular. In other words, by refusing to accept the consequences of the incarnation—the sanctification of the visible, material world—iconoclasm undermined the whole economy of salvation.[17]

After the iconoclastic controversy was resolved, new images filled Hagia Sophia. They revealed that tensions between imperial and spiritual powers were an ongoing struggle. Several ninth- to thirteenth-century mosaics of emperors and empresses show them making an offering to Mary as Theotokos or to Christ as Pantocrator, ruler of heaven. Above the central, imperial entrance, a mosaic of Constantine and Justinian shows them before an enthroned Christ, genuflecting humbly on hands and knees. Perhaps this was an attempt to remind the emperor of his proper relationship to the church. The current side door now used as a tourist exit was once where the emperor's bodyguards were required to wait for him, and, though it is no longer clear which it was, one door was reserved for the poor.

FROM CHURCH TO MOSQUE

In the fifteenth century, the Ottomans captured Constantinople and renamed it Istanbul, ending Christian rule. They converted Hagia Sophia into a mosque, called Ayasofya. The Ottomans so admired its architecture and beauty that they hired a talented architect named

Sinan (1491–1588), to build mosques in the same style. Sinan was raised in a Greek Christian family and converted to Islam after he moved to Istanbul as a soldier in the Ottoman military. He became the primary builder of mosques for the sultan and his empire. He followed an architectural plan created by Greek mathematicians a millennium before and designed more than two hundred mosques in Istanbul.[18]

Today, the experience of paradise that early Christians sought to create in places such as Ayasofya can most readily be found in Muslim mosques. The Jewish scriptures in Genesis that inspired early Christians to see churches as spaces of paradise were themselves inspired by even more ancient Sumerian stories. Whereas Christians eventually forgot their sense of paradise on earth, many forms of Islam maintained it. Muslims prayed in Ayasofya under the vast vault of heaven, kneeling on beautiful carpets. Since Islam prohibited depicting human images, they decorated their carpets with flowers and trees of life. Courtyards of mosques contain fountains, water channels, and other sources of water where worshippers carry out ritual ablutions of hands, mouth, nose, face, arms, head, ears, and feet in the symbolic waters of paradise in preparation for prayer.[19]

Ayasofya is, still, an icon of paradise as this life, in its complexities. It captures the translucent and fluid sense of paradise that holds contrary motions: earth and heaven, shadow and light, gravity and air, spirit and flesh. No longer an assertion of imperial largess and might, it bears the marks of its history. There are cracks in some of the walls and pillars, the columns' irregularly shaped bases, and the floor's worn paving slabs. Mosaic images are mostly fragments. The chancel platform orients to Mecca now, and the central dome surface displays elegant Arabic script where it once probably held an enormous image of Christ as Pantocrator. Beneath the winged seraphim on the four great pillars in the corners, large round shields of calligraphy interrupt the lines of architecture. Towering scaffolds obscure one side of the dome, where restorations are under way. In its venerable age, Ayasofya remains a testimony to the aspirations of Jews, Christians, and Muslims to recognize paradise on earth and to live wisely in it.

In the middle of the twentieth century, the Turkish government made Ayasofya a museum, reflecting its hybrid character as church and mosque. Today, pilgrims from all over the world and every religious tradition can see its light, stroll the arbors among its rivers, and rest in its spaces, contemplating the beauty and meaning stored in its silent walls, soft sunlight, and soaring dome.

POSTSCRIPT

The last day of our quest to find images of paradise in churches hidden among the desolate Kackar Mountains of northeastern Turkey, Erçun turned our little yellow *taksi* abruptly off the paved road onto a dirt track. Neither of us spoke Turkish, and Erçun spoke little English, so our hotel manager had given him an itinerary of places we wanted to visit. We set off each day unsure of exactly where we were going. Just after the turn, Erçun stopped at a grove of trees where a tiny old woman sat on the ground in the shade. A sheer black scarf covered her snowy hair, and the small coins dangling from its fringe shimmered as she looked up at our approach. We could see she was nearly toothless, and her black eyes sparkled in her wizened, brown face. We studied her dusty, full-length billowing black skirt and beautifully embroidered vest while she spoke to Erçun. He seemed to be asking her for directions to our destination, which we later learned were the monastery ruins of Şavşat-Tblesi.

After their highly animated conversation, she pulled herself up on a wooden walking cane, dusted herself off, and hoisted herself in the passenger seat next to him. The old woman continued to chat as we proceeded up the rocky, rutted road, which followed a rushing creek. The track crossed a dry streambed and veered away from the creek into nearby mountains.

As we climbed, the sunny sky turned gray and began to roil with black clouds. Fat raindrops plopped onto the windshield. The higher we ascended, the more fiercely it rained. Soon the windshield wipers hardly marked the sheets of water pouring over the cab. After a long climb, we emerged into what looked like a big meadow, barely visible through the torrent.

Ten bumpy minutes later, we stopped under a cluster of tall trees, and the old woman shook Erçun's hand. They said goodbye in Turkish, and she turned to smile at us and stepped out of the cab. Her stooped figure, leaning on her cane, limped away and faded into the curtain of rain. It appeared we had given her a ride home.

Erçun pointed into the opaque downpour. "Church," he said. The hazy silhouette of stone ruins stood just beyond the trees. It had been hot and sunny in Artvin, so we had brought no gear for rain. We covered ourselves as best we could and conducted a quick and cursory look at the ruins, which held little art beyond a few relief carvings on the crumbling walls and capitals. Disappointed and nearly soaked, we returned quickly to the cab.

The deluge ceased abruptly, and golden light leaked through the churning clouds. In the crystalline air, a rainbow straddled a vast rolling meadow below a ring of gray-blue peaks. Spread before us were acres of lush, emerald pastures and orchards dotted by swaying flowers and flocks of snowy sheep. The three of us sat in stunned silence in the cab for some time, simply gazing at what we had crossed unseeing as it now lay before us, vivid in the golden light.

Erçun retraced our route across this breathtaking valley. We rolled down our windows and passed small, carefully tended fields of cucumbers, tomatoes, grapes, peppers, beans, and onions. We smelled the wet grass and earth. Fruit trees sagged with ripe plums, peaches, and early apples. As we approached the turn that would take us down the mountain, we asked Erçun to stop. He pulled the cab next to some sheep and turned off the motor. In the moist stillness, we could hear the ticks of the cooling engine and the rip-click sound of the grazing sheep. On the opposite side of the valley, where we had found the ruins, we could see the village of Şavşat-Tblesi, nestled in the trees. An orange searchlight of sun streamed through a gap in the mountains and clouds, illuminating the ancient monastery stones. We paused a few moments to breathe in the fragrances brought by the breeze ruffling the grass and drank deeply of the valley. Then we turned down the mountain to return to Artvin. As we headed west, we could see crimson, gold, and mauve-streaked clouds billowing into a deepening indigo sky—our last glimpse of paradise as we rounded a switchback and the valley disappeared from sight.

Searching for images of paradise, we found the real thing. From ancient peoples in lands such as Turkey, Iran, Iraq, Egypt, and Israel, Christians inherited the idea that paradise is in this world. Our arduous journey told us that paradise is neither easy to find nor a guaranteed destination. But with a wise guide and intrepid driver, we found it is possible to arrive there.

PART TWO

FIGURE 11. *Gero Cross, Cologne Cathedral, Germany.*
Oak sculpture, life-size. Tenth century.

CHAPTER NINE

The Expulsion of Paradise

How did it happen that Christians wished to see their God
suffer and die? Who had released this gushing spring?
Who had thus struck the church in its very heart?

ÉMILE MÂLE

In Christianity's second millennium the Crucifixion expelled paradise
from earth. And Jesus died again. We found the corpse of Jesus in
northern Europe, in a side chapel of the enormous Gothic cathedral in
Cologne, Germany. The cool semidarkness and thick, tall stone pillars
of the vast cathedral evoke a primeval forest branching into a canopy of
arches that crisscross the high vaulted ceiling. Here, among the mottled
light and shadows, hangs the Gero Cross, the earliest surviving crucifix, sculpted from oak in Saxony around 960–970.[1]

The life-size work, gilded in gold, presents the crucified Christ
nearly naked. The loincloth, knotted around his pelvis, covers his
thighs. His gaunt legs are pushed up and turned at an angle from his
splayed feet, which are nailed to a block at the base of the cross. His slack
hands are nailed to wide planks of wood, and his distended arms strain
with the downward weight of his thin, sagging body. His hips pull away
from the cross, twisting his torso into an s-shaped slump, his belly pro-
truding over the top of his loincloth. His bare head hangs on his chest,
and his long hair is spread in waves across his shoulders. From below,
we could look up into his face. Beneath heavy brows, his eyes are
closed. His mouth gapes open. Deep lines scar his sunken face.[2]

Depictions of the crucified Christ proliferated in Europe in the eleventh century and became increasingly grotesque and bloody. New scenes detailed each step of torment—the flogging, the crown of thorns, the nailing to the cross, and the deposition of his body from the cross. By the end of the medieval period, Jesus was routinely displayed being tortured in a grim landscape. Saints became co-sufferers, burned alive, disemboweled, pierced with arrows, or mauled by wild beasts. At the threshold of nearly every Gothic cathedral, worshippers passed under a carving depicting the end of time. A stern Christ sat enthroned in judgment, presiding over a graveyard from which he divided the resurrected into the saved and the damned. Heaven was a walled city. Hell was a gaping maw of death, a huge serpent swallowing its human prey, a grinding machine, or a raging fire into which demons armed with pitchforks tossed anguished souls.

What brought about these changes? Why did Christians turn from a vision of paradise in this life to a focus on the Crucifixion and final judgment? How did images of terror, torture, and the desolation of the earth come to permeate the religious imagination of Western Christianity?[3]

A trail of clues led us to King Charles the Great, better known as Charlemagne (742–814), and his imperial ambitions. For three decades he waged a campaign of terror to subdue the Saxons on his northern border and force them at sword point to be baptized into his Latin version of Christianity. Descendants of the Saxons, baptized against their will, produced the Gero Cross and other early images of the crucified Christ, carved in life-size forms and placed at the center of worship.[4]

In this chapter, we unearth the story of imperial politics, religious ideas, and this new visual world that centered on death. To understand the emergence of the dead Christ in Christian imagery, we must recall the Saxon story and the devastations and tragedies that followed. It is also a story of resistance, a story of people who held on to paradise in this world in the face of an imperial campaign that tried to destroy it.

BAPTIZED IN BLOOD

The Old Saxons were an agrarian people, living on either side of the Rhine as it wended its way to the North Sea. Organized as a federation of small clans, each group was headed by a *drohtin* (local lord), to whom the clans swore loyalty. Through an annual assembly of tribal leaders, they practiced a form of democracy. Admired by the Romans for their skills as warriors, they built communities, *burgs* (forts), surrounded by wooden palisades. In times of war, their federation elected a chieftain whose duties concluded with the end of fighting.[5]

During Roman times, the Saxons had embraced Christianity, but their Christianity was a hybrid based in oral tradition rather than written texts. Their religious practices mixed pagan nature religion, which centered on great holy trees and sacred springs, with Christian folk traditions adapted from their early contact with Christians.[6] Historian Peter Brown describes their religious leaders exchanging pagan and Christian rituals, so that pagans baptized Christians and Christian priests sometimes presided at sacrifices to Thunor. The priests shared with pagans in ritual feasts and saw their Christian parishioners into an afterlife that blended Christian and pagan funeral traditions.[7]

Before Charlemagne's reign, missionary efforts to convert the Saxons to more "correct" forms of Christianity met with little success. In 590, Columbanus, an Irish monk, traveled into northern Europe and told the Saxons that they needed to perform penance for their corrupt practices.[8] Columbanus was concerned with sinful humanity's prospects after death, unlike more typical-sixth century Christians, such as Gregory of Tours, for whom paradise wafted into this world and bloomed in miracles of healing at shrines of the saints.[9] Columbanus threatened the Saxons. He said that at the moment of death, the divine judge stood waiting to assess each soul for its punishment or reward. The Saxons were unmoved by the salvation that Columbanus's otherworldly, future-oriented Christianity offered. They enjoyed life in this world and did not want to be rescued from it. A clash of cultures ensued.[10]

Boniface, an English monk, was as disturbed by the Saxons' impure Christianity as Columbanus had been. He traveled to Saxony in 719 with a papal commission to bring correct Christianity "for the enlightenment of the German people who live in the shadow of death, steeped in error."[11] He discovered, to his consternation, that baptisms had taken place in mangled Latin, so that priests apparently anointed people "in the name of the Father and the Daughter."[12] To demonstrate the superiority of his Christ and to sever Christian and pagan traditions, Boniface took an axe to the sacred oak of Thor.[13] Willibald described the incident:

> He attempted to cut down a tree of tremendous size which in the old time vernacular of the pagans is called the tree of Idsis, located in a place called Gaesmere, with the servants of God all standing close to him. As he, strengthened by his unswerving determination, cut the tree down, there was a great number of pagans present who kept on cursing this enemy of their gods under their breath with the greatest fervor.[14]

When Boniface cut down the tree of Idsis, Charles Martel's Frankish soldiers were on hand to enforce his threats. Martel (d. 741), called "the Hammer," was campaigning to expand the territory controlled by the Frankish aristocracy. He would successfully bring Paris and its surrounding region into his fold as well as Burgundy, and he would push back the advance of the Muslims in Spain. Martel used brutal and highly effective tactics: his troops looted towns, then burned them to the ground and slaughtered whole communities. His ambition was to create a new empire in Europe. His success, fulfilled when his grandson Charlemagne was crowned emperor of the west on Christmas Day, 800, earned Martel an empire named for him, *Carolus* (Charles) in Latin, the Carolingian empire.

After the breakup of the Western Roman Empire in the sixth century, Europe had fragmented into a patchwork of warring dynasties. The Merovingians had held the Frankish territories together for two centuries, but Martel's family dynasty, the Carolingians, replaced them in the eighth century and expanded the Frankish territories. The Saxons, their neighbors to the north and east of the Rhine, were closely related to the Franks and interacted with them in many ways. Though allergic to subjugation, beginning in the sixth century the Saxons paid annual tribute to the Franks—five hundred head of cattle a year. Their established territory was in the low-lying marshland around the Weser and Aller rivers, but early in the eighth century they began moving southward into the hill country around the River Lippe that flowed into the Rhine. This region would become the site of a century-long struggle for control. Treaties were repeatedly violated. In their historical records from the time, the Franks characterized the Saxons as a people "in revolt" and as "detestable pagans."[15] Missionary efforts and military actions alike aimed to bring the Saxons more fully into the Franks' sphere of influence.

Charlemagne (c. 742–814) followed on the heels of his grandfather, Charles Martel, and his father, Pippin III, and amplified their tactics against the Saxons. For thirty-three years, he terrorized them with military assaults designed to subdue them into allegiance to his growing empire and to force their religious conformity as a means to make treaties binding on them. His activities stand as the most brutal page in Christian missionary efforts in Europe.[16] For Charlemagne and the Carolingian warrior-aristocrats, the Resurrection cross of Christ symbolized the power that protected them in warfare and led them to victory. Priests traveled with the army, and before battles the army's preparation included religious rituals. The priests carried gold, jewel-encrusted crosses mounted on standards in procession through the troops—a sign of divine power and majesty and of Christ's victory over Satan and death. Soldiers shouted acclamations, *laudes regiae,* praising Christ who "vanquishes and rules" and appealed to heaven to protect their king and to "liberate his followers from evil, through the cross and passion."[17]

The shedding of human blood, however, remained a sin. On the night before every battle, long lines formed before the tents of the priests. Soldiers waited to confess their sins, lest they die in combat without having performed sufficient penance. Uneasily anticipating the fight to come, each soldier sought to whisper the deeds that burdened his conscience. Following their confessions, the army gathered in an open field or forest clearing to partake of the Eucharist.[18] Eating the sanctified bread and drinking from the holy chalice joined them to the body and blood of the all-powerful Christ, who assured victory over death. Armed with this sacred shield, they prepared to march into battle and emulate Christ's confrontation with evil.

Charlemagne launched his first campaign against the Saxons in 772. He took the Saxon fortress of Eresburg and then advanced to the headwaters of the Lippe, where the Saxons had built a great shrine. The Irminsul was a pillar or tree trunk that most likely represented Yggdrasil, the cosmic tree or tree of life. Saxons believed this tree held up the universe. Associated with the worship of Thor and Woden, the Yggdrasil tree formed the center of the Saxons' sacred practices. They may have intentionally erected the shrine in contested territory to assert sacred power that could repel Charlemagne's advance. Charlemagne's soldiers felled the tree, destroyed the shrine, and looted its silver. Then they rounded up the Saxon tribes hiding in the surrounding forests and forced baptism upon them under threat of death. The Franks' version of events said, "In great terror all the Saxons came to the source of the river Lippe . . . surrendered their land to the Franks . . . and were baptized."[19]

Saxon compliance was short-lived. Following their defeat, they retaliated by launching raids across the Rhine into the Frankish territory, burning churches and monasteries. The Franks counterattacked, and the Saxons again yielded in defeat. This pattern would repeat itself for decades. The Saxons broke fifteen treaties with the Franks within one thirteen-year period. The Franks fueled hostilities with stereotypes of the Saxons as kingless brutes who could not be trusted to keep an oath.[20] Converting them to "correct" Christianity would, Charlemagne believed, bind them to treaties of submission as members of Christ's body.

In *De conversion Saxonum,* a text from 777, some of Charlemagne's court theologians praised his "conversion" of the Saxons by comparing his victory to Christ's defeat of death through his crucifixion, descent into hell, and resurrection. In their view, Charlemagne's military victories replicated divine salvation. These events "belong to a single victory, by which the son of God 'took away the horrid accusations of infamous death,' 'washed away the crime of the world in the waves of the Jordon,' [and] 'marked the pious with the purple dye of his precious blood.' "21 Charlemagne used the legend of Constantine's cross to justify his campaign of violence.

In 782, Charlemagne intensified his efforts to control the Saxons by establishing a law code for them, the *First Saxon Capitulary.* It forbade the Saxons from engaging in their traditional religious activities and burial practices. The prescribed punishments were extreme. To refuse baptism or to eat meat during Lent merited the death sentence. The ensuing Saxon resistance killed several members of the Frankish aristocracy. Charlemagne retaliated at Verden and took forty-five hundred Saxons as prisoners. He ordered his soldiers to behead them all in a single day.22 The *Royal Frankish Annals* claim that theirs was a divine mission: "The more the Saxons were stricken by fear, the more the Christians were comforted and praised the Almighty God." In 804, Charlemagne deported ten thousand Saxons into Frankish territories. As late as 842, Saxons were continuing to rebel against Charlemagne's grandson.

The *Dream of the Rood,* a poem composed among the Anglo-Saxon Christians of Northumbria (western Britain) during this era, suggested their view of these wars. It evoked Saxon practices of ritual gatherings at holy sites in the forest around pillars or sacred trees. In the poem, a splendid paradise tree turned into a bloodied shrine.

> *I thought that I saw a splendid tree*
> *Lifted in the air and surrounded with light,*
> *The brightest of beams. All that beacon was*
> *Covered with gold . . .*

> *Yet through the gold I could glimpse*
> *The old torture: the right side of the tree*
> *Began to bleed. Sorrowing I beheld it*
> *At times drenched with gore.*[23]

Carolingian Christianity destroyed the Saxons' sacred natural places, and Carolingian preachers warned their Saxon parishioners away from pagan religious practices. They forbade them to worship at their former holy sites where they honored sacred springs, stones, and trees.[24] In building their new, "holy" empire, Charlemagne and his army jettisoned the Christian experience of this earth as being infused with divine presence and power, a religious sensibility that had been shared by Franks and Saxons. This hostility would have dire consequences for Europe's ecosystems by opening the forests for exploitation. Historians of the ecology of Europe indicate that the course of Carolingian missions among the Saxons was closely followed by deforestation.[25]

Not all Christian leaders supported Charlemagne's agenda. Alcuin (735–804), an Anglo-Saxon Northumbrian cleric in Charlemagne's court, objected to his strategies for "converting" the Saxons. Alcuin said preaching and scholarship—not arms—should be used. In this, he followed Pope Gregory I (540–604), who had advocated a gradual strategy for converting the pagans of the British Isles.[26] Alcuin may also have remembered the lingering scars from forced baptisms that had occurred in Britain. He argued, as did many other Christians, that Christ accomplished his victory by accepting the cross rather than by employing the sword. Christian acts of penitence were imitations of Christ's virtue, represented by his humility and pain. Nevertheless, Alcuin used battle imagery to speak of Christ and of the Christian life. In a letter to Paulinus of Aquileia, he called the two of them "comrades on Christ's battlefields and soldiers in one rank under the holy cross."[27] Use of such language came dangerously close to supporting war, and Christian leaders made efforts to clarify the difference between "spiritual warfare" and military action.

A group of bishops gathered along the Danube in the summer of 796 and protested Charlemagne's campaigns. Bishop Paulinus wrote to Charlemagne that a "military campaign . . . must not be confused with the war of the spirit: to defeat in battle was not the same as to convert."[28] A year after the bishops protested, Charlemagne issued the *Capitulatio de partibus Saxoniae,* the Law Code for the Saxon Territories. It reiterated the death sentence for those who sought to avoid Christian baptism. Charlemagne's sword obliterated the difference between fighting in the spirit and fighting in the flesh:

> From now on, should anyone hidden among the Saxons as a non-baptized person wish to remain in concealment, who disdains to come to baptism and wishes to remain a pagan, let him be put to death.

Charlemagne demanded loyalty oaths and required Saxons at baptism to vow, "I forsake all the Devil's works and words: Thunor, Woden and Saxnote and all the uncanny beings who are their companions." Charlemagne drew the boundary separating pagan and Christian. His laws for the Saxons made it a crime to transgress this boundary. Historian Roger Collins identifies Charlemagne's law codes as the origin of European notions of pure ethnic identities, defined as inescapable, essential traits.[29]

To subdue the Saxons into "correct" Christianity, Charlemagne installed his bishops and abbots to head cathedrals, monasteries, and schools throughout Saxony. The churchmen took possession of vast estates and became the people's landlords. They brought books and teachers and educated Saxons in Latin, in approved Christian literature, and in prescribed liturgical practices. They captured Saxon soothsayers and magicians and enslaved them in service to the new monasteries. Through these "colonizing monasteries," the Franks created institutions of control and instruction to solidify what warfare began.[30]

Preachers were part of the propaganda campaign as well. Sermons by Bishop Caesarius of Arles were translated into German and preached to the newly "converted" Saxons. A contemporary of Gregory of Tours, Caesarius did not share his confidence that paradise permeated this world. Instead, Caesarius stirred up anxiety over the danger of eternity in hell. Once, preaching a sermon on the Last Judgment, he locked his congregation in the church and told them that they would stand just so before Christ the judge: unable to escape. The Carolingians recycled his sermons to instruct the Saxons on the proper interpretation of their experience in Carolingian custody. Charlemagne's preachers told the Saxons, still seething from their humiliation and defeat, that his assaults on them were God's punishment for their pagan sinfulness. In one sermon, the crucified Christ spoke from the cross:

> I endured the blows and spit of those who mocked me; I drank vinegar mixed with gall; I was beaten with whips and crowned with thorns; I was fixed to a cross and wounded through the side. . . . Why have you afflicted me on the cross of your crimes? . . . Since, after all your wickednesses, you did not want to take refuge in the medicines of penitence, you do not deserve to escape the voice of condemnation. You and those like you will hear the words, "Depart from me, accursed ones, into the eternal fire prepared for the devil and his angels" (Matthew 25:41). And you will descend with the devil into hell's eternal fire, [because] captured by sweet snares and false gods, you have preferred the fire to me, your life.[31]

To the Saxons along the Rhine, this Christian theology arrived at the point of a sword. The cross—once a sign of life—became for them a sign of terror. Blood seeped through the gold. Within a few generations of their forced conversion, the Saxons hewed an image of the tortured and dead body of Christ hanging from the tree. Pressed by violence into Christian obedience, the Saxons produced art that bore the marks of their baptism in blood. In the Gero Cross, their once-sacred oak was carved into an elegiac effigy of brutalization. The *Dream of the Rood* described the tree's "conversion":

> *It was long ago—and yet I remember—*
> *the day I was hewed at the holt's end,*

stirred from my roots. Strong foes took me,
made me a spectacle, bade me raise sinners for them. . . .
Dark nails they drove deep inside me;
On me are the wounds still seen, open malicious wounds.[32]

DECLARE HIM KILLED

The Saxon frontier became a battleground between their more ancient forms of Christianity and Carolingian Christianity. The Carolingians fused church and state in new ways, altered the long-standing Christian prohibition against the shedding of human blood, and made Christianity a colonizing tool. In imitation of exaggerated legends about Constantine, ninth-century Carolingian Christians aligned the cross with military victory and laid the axe to the root of sacred trees. The more ancient forms of Christianity, represented by the Saxon pagan-Christian mix, venerated springs and sacred trees, as did pre-Carolingian Christianity throughout Gaul. "They brought down from heaven to earth a touch of the unshackled, vegetable energy of God's own paradise."[33] Christian rituals harnessed healing from the presence of the ancestors and the shrines of saints. They made paradise accessible in this world and located salvation in its healing balms. They celebrated the Eucharist as a sanctifying feast of life, hosted by the incarnate risen Christ.

The conflict between Carolingian and more ancient forms of Christianity came to a head in a struggle over the meaning of the Eucharist. To unify his "Holy Roman Empire," Charlemagne imposed a single Eucharistic rite across the territories he conquered. The new rite supplanted the older, non-Roman Gallican Rite that had been used throughout Europe before 800. The Gallican Eucharistic liturgy prayed:

Eternal God, You gave wonderful forms to the amazed elements: the tender world blushed at the fires of the sun, and the rude earth wondered at dealings of the moon. And lest no inhabitant should adorn all this, and the sun's orb shine on emptiness, your hands made from clay a more excellent likeness, which a holy fire quickened within, and a lively soul brought to life throughout its idle parts. We may not look, Father, into the inner mysteries. To you alone is known the majesty of your work: what there is in man, that the blood held in the veins washes the fearful limbs and the living earth; that the loose appearances of bodies are held together by tightening nerves, and the individual bones gain strength from the organs within.

But whence comes so great a bounty to miserable men, that we should be formed in the likeness of you and your Son, that an earthly thing should be eternal? We abandoned the commandments of your blessed majesty . . . and mourned the loss of the eternal comfort of your gift. But your manifold goodness and inestimable majesty sent the saving Word from heaven, that he should be made flesh by taking a human body, and should care for that which the age had lost and the ancient wounds. Therefore all the angels, with the manifold multitude of the saints praise him.

The proclamation of your magnificence, made in the starry realms, was revealed to your servants by a gift, not only to be known but also to be imitated.[34]

The new Carolingian Roman rite replaced this prayer with one that spoke of Christ as "a pure victim, a holy victim, an unspotted victim."[35] In the 830s, a group of monks living in Saxony asked the imperial court theologians for a clarification about the meaning of the Eucharist. In response, the Carolingian theologian Paschasius Radbertus, head of the Corbie monastery in northern Francia (where deported Saxons had been resettled under Charlemagne), composed *De corpore et sanguine Domini,* a tract on the Lord's blood and flesh. He offered an unprecedented interpretation: the consecrated elements were the material, historical body of Christ, and the bread and cup made the *crucified* blood and flesh of the Lord present. Paschasius explained, "No one who is sane believes that Jesus had any other flesh and blood than that which was born of the Virgin Mary and suffered on the Cross. And it is that very same flesh, in whatever manner, that should be understood, I believe, when he says: 'This is my body that is given for many,' and 'This is my blood.' " The Eucharist, he went on to explain, was the means by which "the lamb is sacrificed daily on the altar by the priest in memory of the sacred passion."[36]

Theologians in Saxony and elsewhere countered with the traditional doctrine: the glorified, resurrected body—not the crucified body —was present in the ritual. A Saxon monk, Gottschalk, refuted Paschasius unequivocally. Gottschalk had been denounced at the Synod of Quiery in 849 for his theological views on predestination; the Carolingians stripped him of his priestly office, flogged him, burned his texts, and imprisoned him at the Hautvillers Abbey until his death.[37] His views on the Eucharist were written during his confinement. Gottschalk argued that "at the last supper Christ gave his body and blood to his disciples 'before he suffered.' What he gave, therefore, was not the body that would be crucified." Gottschalk viewed the Eucharist elements as the heavenly Christ transferred to earth. Only heavenly things could be eternal and omnipresent. Christ's death could not be repeated. It did not have the status of a heavenly reality. Drawing on John 12:24–25 and I Corinthians 15:35–45, Gottschalk, according to historian Cecile Chazelle, "suggested that the crucified body of Christ, 'having been sown in death as a grain or seed of life,' rose up like the tree of life to offer its fruit 'to those who take it.' "[38]

In proposing that the Eucharistic elements were the literal body and blood of the crucified Christ, Paschasius interpreted the Eucharist as an encounter with Christ the judge. "For the cross of Christ was . . . lifted up as the tribunal of the judge," Paschasius wrote.[39] The new interpretation was embodied in the Roman rite that Charlemagne imposed throughout his empire. The Roman rite abandoned the Gallican rite's focus on the wondrous human body sanctified by Christ's incarnation. Scholar Rachel Fulton notes that for Paschasius, "To behold Christ's scars, the wounds and anguish that he suffered for humanity. . . would be a moment of terrible fear, of wailing and gnashing of teeth, of weeping and despair."[40]

In coming to the Communion table, worshippers would face the crucified Christ, who both exposed and condemned unrepentant sinners for their crimes. Sinners, enemies of God, dared not approach the Eucharistic feasts without having performed sufficient penance, or they would eat and drink damnation. As Paschasius said, "Behold, what does the sinner eat and what does he drink? Not flesh and blood useful for himself, but judgment."[41] Alcuin, the most renowned Carolingian theologian, made a similar claim writing in his treatise on the Trinity. He said that when Christ comes to judge the living and the dead, "the wicked will see him judging in the form in which he was crucified."[42] Archbishop Hincmar (845–882) further elaborated Paschasius's ideas, suggesting in *De cavendis* that the Mass was a reenactment of Christ's execution:

> "Declare him killed and offer him to be sacrificed in his mystery, . . . Kill! That is, believe him dead for sinners!" In the Eucharistic offering, Christ the fatted calf is daily immolated "for believers."[43]

Hincmar said that by eating the flesh and blood of the Crucifixion, repentant Christians obtained the benefit of Christ's sacrificial death on the cross, which redeemed the sins of humanity.[44]

By the late ninth century, Carolingian-illuminated manuscripts included Christ dead on the cross, his eyes closed and his blood flowing. Though not yet prominent in churches, these images of death appeared in texts used by priests in liturgies. Images of Christ's blood spurting from his side and filling a chalice were produced for the first time during this period. The dead Christ would appear in Rhineland churches within the second half of the tenth century and multiply throughout Europe in the ensuing centuries. By the fourteenth century, images would show Christ dying *in* a chalice.

The Carolingian theologian John Scottus Erigena (c. 800–880) reasserted the traditional Christian view, that "the consecrated bread and wine are transformed into Christ in the unity of his humanity and divinity, and therefore into the body and blood born on earth and risen from the dead."[45] He was part of the debate among ninth-century theologians during which a diversity of theological opinions were argued. But one significant point of contention stood out: either the Eucharistic elements made the incarnate, transfigured, risen, and glorified body of the living, eternal Christ present and united the church with the Resurrection, or the Eucharist reenacted the Crucifixion and made the bleeding, dead body of the past, historical Christ present, and united communicants with his suffering and dying.

The ensuing conflict would not be resolved until the eleventh century. With the triumph of a Eucharist that presented a dead body on the Communion table, death, instead of being defeated, became eternal. This innovation changed the ontological status of death. Whereas in the traditional Eucharist, Jesus had overcome death, never to die again, with Paschasius's Eucharist he entered a state of perpetual dying. Death, no longer in the past, became coeternal with life. Christ's dying became eternally present and began to haunt the Western European imagination, riddling it with a diffuse anxiety about existence, a terror of judgment, and a piety of holy suffering. Though some scholars interpret the change in the interpretation of the Eucharist as emphasizing Christ's vulnerable humanity and drawing him closer to human beings, in fact the change alienated him from humanity by changing the meaning of the human nature he revealed. Previously, Christ's incarnation revealed humanity's likeness to God and restored humanity's divine powers as first given in paradise. To be human was to become divine. Now, Christ's incarnation revealed humanity's mortality and powerlessness and its brokenness and suffering. To be human was to suffer and die.

The Carolingians inflicted their Eucharist on the people they conquered. Charlemagne's theologians said that Christ, dead on the cross, signified divine judgment against the Saxons' rebellious violence. These theologians blurred the ethical distinctions about who was a victim of violence and who was a perpetrator. They taught the Saxons that the correct interpretation of the Eucharist required them to see themselves as killers of Christ, accused and condemned unless they performed sufficient penance. Hence, it was Christian for the Saxons to submit to "Holy Roman" imperial violence, to be crucified like Christ. The Carolingians constructed a Christian piety that used violence to convert pagans and then taught its victims to regard their violation as justified and sanctified. As the ideas of Paschasius triumphed, the crucified Christ confronted communicants at every Eucharist, accusing them of killing him. Contemplation of his death evoked an intoxicating mix of gratitude and dread. To be an unrepentant, sinful Christian was to be judged a murderer by Christ the victim and judge. Those who knelt before the divine victim petitioned for mercy for their sins, hoping not to be condemned to hell.

SEPARATION FROM CHRIST

The Carolingian sanctification of the Crucifixion created theological confusions. On the one hand, the Carolingian victors saw the wounds of Christ as an accusation against the Saxons. On the other hand, Carolingian soldiers also faced judgment because shedding human blood continued to be regarded as a sin. Was it virtue to slay Saxons, or did the blood of their victims cry out against them? This conflict, enacted in a Eucharist focused on a bloody corpse, trapped warriors and their victims in cycles of unending, unmitigated guilt. The dead Christ made everyone sinful and blameworthy.

The Carolingian theology of the Eucharist drew humanity to the dead Christ and separated believers from the living Christ with his power to teach, heal, and give life to all. Jesus ceased to be the forerunner of humanity's own journey to divinity. Instead, he became a victim whose power lay in his suffering and its judgment against sinful humanity. Christ no longer offered love and abundant life but judgment to be feared and suffering to be repeated by the faithful. Salvation, once a community of life in paradise, now meant escape from guilt and punishment.

This Eucharistic system placed enormous control in the hands of the clergy. Their clerical office prevented their taking up arms or killing in war; instead they enacted ritual death. The slaying of Christ was the one murder that priests were sanctified and required to commit. At the same time, they were also the only ones authorized to prescribe penance to sinful human beings to atone for their crimes. The rest of sinful humanity, whether perpetrators or victims of violence, became fused together as murderers of Christ, the consummate victim of every sin, whose dying expiated sin. All alike were required to do penance to obtain the benefits of the Passion. The priests determined if sinners had done sufficient penance and absolved sinners of their crimes.[46]

The Christian consensus against killing began to fray when a few ninth-century clerics asserted that soldiers should not have to do penance. These preachers said Carolingian armies fought with Christ's support and assistance. Notable among this minority was Hincmar, who argued that those killed in war fought for "the peace of the kingdom" and should be regarded with favor, deserving of "prayers, offerings, and masses." Killing in war was an occasion for thanksgiving. Through it, Christ's blood cleansed sin.[47] However, this was a minority position for two more centuries.

The Carolingians reshaped the Eucharist in imperial terms and used it as a strategy for conquest. As victors, they blamed their victims' sinfulness for causing their own deaths and said God willed their deaths, which, by implication, meant that the victors did the will of God. With this interpretation, they absolved themselves of moral responsibility for violence and ceded power to those they harmed, in effect abnegating ethical choice and pretending they could not do otherwise. Moral confusions inevitably arose between conqueror and colonized, murderer and victim, harm and holiness, crime and punishment, and death and life. The Carolingians cut the connections between great power and great responsibility, and denied divine power in humanity, forfeiting their ethical obligations to protect life on earth. Christians lost their footing in paradise and began a precipitous slide into a pit of hell of their own making.

Was the Eucharist the crucified body or the resurrection of life?[48] The Carolingian Eucharist placed ritual murder at its center and a dead body on the altar of life. As a preventative for eternal damnation, Christ's oblation became a powerful image of forgiveness of sinners, but it offered little beyond relief from fear and guilt. The Carolingian Eucharist ceased to deliver life in its fullness, life everlasting, or fellowship with the risen Christ. This new theology of the Eucharist took away the life-giving love of Christ and made him a victim. His corpse's power to judge sin alienated Christians from communion with Christ and from the love and support of the community of the saints. It isolated individuals and left them terrified. By the middle of the eleventh century, Peter Damian (c. 1007–1072), a hermit-monk and later cardinal bishop of Ostia, would pray on Good Friday:

> I see you with my internal eyes, my Redeemer, affixed with the nails of the cross. I see you wounded with new wounds. . . . I thus implore [you] . . . I beg [you], I say with tears, by this sacrament of our redemption, do not cut me off, as I deserve, from the society of your elect. . . . Lord, sign my soul with the impression of this holy cross . . . deliver me wholly and entirely from your justice.[49]

The Christian trembled in the presence of the crucified Savior, guilty and overcome, begging for mercy. The anxious imperialist gaze had become the gaze of all Christendom.

A GOSPEL OF RESISTANCE

The Saxons resisted Charlemagne's Eucharist. If the crucified body of Christ was a sign of judgment, it was not a judgment upon them. It was a judgment upon their enemies. Scholar G. Ronald Murphy suggests that the Saxon struggle against subjugation is evident in their ninth-century poetry. They wrote their story of resistance in a German vernacular version of the Gospels, called the *Heliand* (the Healer), a mid-ninth-century epic in rhythmic verse marked for singing. A Saxon monk living in Fulda or Corvey was the probable author. Comprising seventy-one songs and nearly six thousand lines, the *Heliand* retells a version of Tatian's *Diatessaron,* a Syrian text that synthesized the four Gospels into one story and that Ephrem used as a version of Jesus's life.[50] To write in German instead of Latin, the official language of Carolingian Christianity, was itself an act of defiance. In addition, the *Heliand* depicts Christ as a resistance fighter and focuses the story on the activities of a loyal band of Saxon "thanes" or noble fighters.[51]

The common interpretation of the *Heliand* reads it as evidence that Charlemagne successfully subdued the Saxons and imposed Carolingian Christianity on them with the help of the Saxon aristocracy.[52] We find Murphy's discussion of its Saxon elements leads to a different assessment of it: the *Heliand* only *appears* to express compliance. A sense of this world as paradise pervades the *Heliand,* intimating an influence of Syrian Christianity—the tradition of Ephrem—on the Saxon poet.

We suggest that the *Heliand* is what scholar James C. Scott calls a hidden transcript of resistance. Strategies of resistance to imperial oppression are many, from armed revolt to suicide. One strategy is to feign submission while secretly maintaining a dissident identity. As an Ethiopian aphorism says, "When the great lord passes, the wise peasant bows deeply and silently farts."[53] This was the Saxon response to the Carolingians. They created art and poetry that preserved Saxon religious perspectives. The multivalences of art, poetry, and story—their ability to carry multiple meanings at once—allow for protest and compliance at the same time, in the same work. The Saxons produced such work to appear compliant with Carolingian Christianity, while telling the story of Jesus as a Saxon hero.

Sung in mead halls and monastery refectories, the *Heliand* thumbed its nose at Charlemagne's "Holy Roman Empire" and celebrated a Saxon life-affirming Gospel with paradise as its organizing core. The culture of the *Heliand* is not Carolingian and imperial; it is Saxon and tribal. The poem reaches into the past to depict an ethics of loyalty and camaraderie once practiced in traditional Saxon culture. Although Carolingian practices had outlawed and superceded much of that world, the *Heliand* employs the imagery of the *comitatus,* the band of warriors who swore their loyalty and valor to their local lord. Charlemagne outlawed such oaths and imposed a more hierarchical polity.[54]

The text introduces Christ as "the Best of healers, come here to the middle world to be a help to many, to give human beings an advantage against the hatred of the enemy and the hidden snare"(Song 1). The poem calls Jesus "God's holy Child, the good Chieftain" (Song 5). The word *drohtin* is used to designate Christ—the term for the local lord, the one to whom lifelong allegiance is owed. The *Heliand* does not refer to Christ using the term for their temporary war chieftain and distinguishes Christ and his men from the military might of *Romaburg* (Fort Rome) and the oppressive Carolingian empire.[55] In this contrast, the Saxon gospel focuses on the male culture of warriors in keeping with its probable audience of monks and the mead hall. It reflects admiration for a noble class of Saxon men who fight "Rome," but it glosses the New Testament's identification with the poor. Peasants are represented in the *Heliand* as beneficiaries of assistance from Christ's upper-class band.[56]

The text suggests striking parallels between the evil king Herod and Charlemagne. The poet hisses when Herod is on the scene. Herod is "the slithery-mouthed king, angrily talking with his men—he always enjoyed murder" (Song 7).[57] He is called "that loathsome man," "that moodily violent king," "that arrogant madman of an earl," "that cruel-minded king" who "was hoping, with the edge of the sword, to become the Child's murderer" (Songs 8–9). Murphy suggests the vivid portrayal of Herod's slaughter of the innocents mirrors the Saxon experience with Charlemagne:

> Then Herod sent a strict command throughout his kingdom, ordering his warriors . . . to march. He gave the order that by the strength of their hand they were to decapitate the boys around Bethlehem. . . . The king's warrior-companions did this horrible deed. Many a man was to die there in his childhood, innocent of any sin. Never before or since has there been a more tragic departure for young persons, a more miserable death. The women were

crying, the many mothers who saw their infants killed. Nor were they able to help them. Even if she held her own boy, little and loveable, tightly in her arms, the child still had to give up its life—in front of the mother. . . . The mothers were weeping. . . . The murderers killed the guiltless innocents, and didn't think a thing about the evil they were doing. (Song 11)

The Christ child escapes Herod's persecution with the help of Joseph and his warrior-companions. They flee "by night to Egyptland, to the green meadows by the best earth, where a river flows, the fairest of streams, northward to the sea—the mighty Nile" (Song 9). The Nile was one of the legendary rivers of Eden. The description of the "fairest of streams" fits the Rhine also as it flows northward to the sea, where the forested hills give way to the green plains—the home territory of the Saxons. Through this and many other telling details, the poem establishes a Saxon identity for Christ and Saxon lands as paradise.

The gospel itself carries instructions to the listener to read it as a dissident text. Christ counsels his warrior-companions to make use of the divine powers of awareness and memory in dealing with their enemies:

Keep your feelings opposed to them, stay intelligently face-to-face with them, just like the yellow snake, the colored serpent, when it becomes aware of its hated enemy, so that no one of the world-people can sneak up on you during the journey. You should take care that human beings are not able to twist the thoughts of your heart or your will. Be as truly against this, against their deceptive deeds, as one would be against enemies. (Song 22)

The *Heliand* moves toward a climax in Song 38 with the Transfiguration. Peter, James, and John climb "along the mountain face over rock and slope" until they come to "the place near the clouds." There, on the heights, Christ changes before their eyes:

His cheeks became shining light, radiating like the bright sun. The Son of God was shining! His body gave off light, brilliant rays came shining out of the Ruler's Son. His clothes were as white as snow.... Elijah and Moses came there to Christ.... There was a beautiful conversation, good words among men.... It became so blissful up on the mountain—the bright light was shining, there was a magnificent garden there and the green meadow, it was like paradise! (Song 38)

Peter exclaims that this would be a good place to live: "This is the home of happiness, the most appealing thing anyone could have!" When he says this, the clouds part, and the glory intensifies:

A cloud of light shone with a glistening glow and wrapped the good men in brilliant beauty. Then from the cloud came the holy voice of God; and the voice said to the heroes that this was His Son, the One He loved most of all the living, "I love Him very much in my heart, You should listen to Him—follow Him gladly!"

The sight is too much for the three disciples. They faint. Then "the Best of all healers touched them and told them not to be afraid of Him, 'Nothing at all of the wonderful and amazing things you have seen here will hurt you.'" They return to their senses, and accompany Christ down the mountain. He tells them to keep quiet until "I myself get up most gloriously from death, arise from my rest. After that you can go and ... tell the story throughout the middle world to many peoples—all over this wide world!"

This revelation of paradise forms the *Heliand*'s structural center. It is told in the middle of the poem and is echoed at the beginning and the end with similar language about brilliant beauty. On the night of the Nativity, "the darkness split in two in the sky, and the light of God came shining through" as an angel announced joyful news and "the shining people of God came down from ... the meadows of heaven ... [singing] a song as they wended their way through the clouds" (Song 5). On the morning of the Resurrection, the dark starlit night is sundered when, "brilliantly radiating, God's Peace-child rose up" and built "the road from this world up to heaven" (Song 68). Incarnation, transfiguration, and resurrection are, thus, the arc of the story—indicating that paradise is the source, the earthly dwelling place, and the ultimate home of Christ and his loyal followers.

Evil drives the narrative to its conclusion. Earthly enemies collude with Satan and Fate. Herod and others from Fort Rome attack, and Satan and his "little creatures" await their victims in their miserable, otherworldly realm called Hel, where they imprison the souls of the dead. In addition to Satan, *Wurd* (Fate) is an implacable, unchangeable divine force. Fate and Satan unite forces against Christ when he faces his enemies from Fort Rome. On the Mount of Olives, he struggles with his fear of death, but resolves out of loyalty to God to "take this chalice in my hand and drink it to your honor, my Lord Chieftain, powerful Protector!" (Song 57). Christ stands ready to meet his enemies who march up the Mount of Olives, "making a great din, angry armed men" (Song 57). Valiant Peter, without hesitation, draws his sword and injures a man. Blood gushes. "The men stood back—they were afraid of the slash of the sword" (Song 58). Christ tells Peter to put up his sword.

> We are not to become enraged or wrathful against their violence, since whoever is fighting is often killed himself by the edge of the sword and dies dripping with his own blood. We cannot by our deeds avert anything. (Song 58)

The *Heliand*'s Passion story unfolds as a battle with both the demonic earthly enemies from Rome and with Fate:

> Fate was coming closer then, the great power of God, and midday, when they were to bring His life-spirit to its death agony... they ordered warrior-heroes to use the edges of their battle-axes to make a mighty cross out of a hardwood tree with their hands.... There on the sandy gravel they erected the gallows... a tree on a mountain—and there they tortured God's Son on a cross. (Songs 64, 66)

The sandy gravel and a gallows tree evoke the landscape of the North Sea. Christ dies on the tree:

"I entrust My spirit into Your hands, into God's will," He said, "My spirit is now ready to go, ready to travel." The Chieftain of Mankind then bowed His head, the holy breath escaped from the body. As the Protector of the Land died on the ropes.... They found him already gone, His soul had been sent on the true road to the long-lasting light. (Song 67)

In death, Christ escapes captivity to both Fate and Satan. He slips away from his enemies and travels to God. He cannot win against evil or overcome fate with violence. He mounts the cross and through death, his spirit escapes his captors—outwitting them.

His followers take his body down from the cross and bury it in a Saxon grave—an earth mound covered with a stone slab—in clear defiance of Carolingian laws against the use of Saxon burial practices. Those who loved him, keep watch and grieve. "Many women were crying and beat their breasts. The horrible torture hurt their hearts, their Lord's death put them in deep sorrow" (Song 67). Roman soldiers are sent to guard the grave. In the dead of night, Christ's fugitive spirit returns to his corpse, right under their noses. "There was the spirit coming, by the power of God, the holy breath, going under the hard stone to the corpse!" (Song 68). He rises from the grave, a burst of dawning light, breaking the prison-bonds and setting free the captives in Hel's realm. He opens the road to the green fields of paradise. Saxon ancient religious traditions called the path to paradise the *bifrost*. They could see it on clear nights—the Milky Way, the route that the souls of the departed traveled to the meadows of God.[58]

Carolingian preaching had aimed to convince Saxons that they deserved to be conquered because of their crimes against Christ. The *Heliand* refuted their indictment. Christ was a Saxon. The Saxons were not killers of Christ and foes of God—Charlemagne's Holy Roman Empire killed him. In the presence of their Carolingian enemies, the Saxon

Christ delivered his clanspeople from captivity and preserved the Saxon paradise.

In the controversy over the Eucharist, the *Heliand* refuted the Paschasian theology and offered a dissident Eucharist. When Christ breaks the bread at the Last Supper, he begins by giving thanks for "the one who created everything—the world and its happiness" (Song 56). These words echo the Gallican Rite that Charlemagne supplanted, and references to the goodness of the Creation reverberate throughout the *Heliand.* It consistently speaks of this world as beautiful and shining with light. Those who follow Christ's teaching find fortune and happiness in this world. After giving thanks, Christ says:

> Believe me clearly... that this is My body and also My blood. I here give both of them to you to eat and drink. This is what I will give and pour out on earth. With My body I will free you to come to God's Kingdom, to eternal life in heaven's light. Always remember to continue to do what I am doing at this supper, tell the story of it to many men. This body and blood is a thing which possesses power.... It is a holy image: keep it in order to remember Me.... Always remember how I commanded you here to hold lovingness in your feelings toward one another. (Song 56)

The body and blood possess a "making-power," akin to the power of the Saxon runes, the power of God's Word, which is to say, the power to bring things into being.[59] The body and blood signify the power of divine creativity—the power of life. The *Heliand* reinforces this sacramental theology by the use of a puzzling pronoun in the Christmas story. The magi greet the newborn Christ child and bring him gifts. Then they "stand attentively, respectful in the presence of their Lord, and soon received It [the Child] in a fitting manner in their hands." Murphy notes that the original German does not immediately make sense, since "Him," rather than "It" would be the expected pronoun. However, he suggests that "It" has richer allusions, pointing to the moment in the Eucharist when the participant receives "It," the bread, "in a fitting manner in their hands."[60]

The *Heliand*'s Eucharist is a sign of the birth of Christ, of the incarnate Word, and of the life-creating power of his teaching. It uses Saxon runes and their magical power—perhaps the enslaved Saxon soothsayers and magicians are speaking here—to identify the Eucharist as a holy image, embodying the shining light of divine presence. A sharper alternative to the Carolingian theology of the Eucharist as a reenactment of the Crucifixion can hardly be imagined. For the poet of the *Heliand,* Jesus's crucifixion had no healing power. Those who did not love him in this life would not be changed by his death. Describing those who persecuted Jesus and witnessed his torture on the cross, the *Heliand* concludes:

> People saw these awesome things, but their slithery attitude had become so hardened in their hearts, that there was no sign shown them—be it ever so holy—that could ever make them trust any better in Christ's power. (Song 67)

HOLDING WHAT'S HERE

Around the time that a monk composed the *Heiland,* Dhuoda, a twenty-one-year-old noblewoman, married Bernard, duke of Septimania. Bernard's father had been Charlemagne's first cousin, and Bernard was a leading contender for high office. During his struggle for power, Bernard sent Dhuoda and their son, William, born in 826, to live in Uzès in southern France near Nimes. Dhuoda had to manage his estates and guard them against incursions from Spain.

In 841, Dhuoda had a second son. Bernard sent William to live in the court of King Charles the Bald, perhaps as a pledge of loyalty after Bernard had failed in a bid for power against Charles. Bernard then summoned his newborn son to Aquitaine and christened him Bernard. Dhuoda, abandoned in Uzès, financially struggling, in ill health, and bereft of her children, wrote a book for fifteen-year-old William.[61]

Her *Liber Manualis* provides a rare educated lay Christian voice from the Carolingian period, a voice original, subtle, and personal.[62] She offers us a picture of Christian life from outside the clerical church and Carolingian imperial Christianity. Unlike most women of the time, even noblewomen, Dhuoda was literate and wrote in Latin, though her poetry indicates a Germanic mother tongue and she may have been a Saxon.[63] She instructed her son in how to live a long and happy life. She uses literary devices—numerology, puzzles, word plays, acrostics, and poetry—that would have appealed to a clever son. She knew both the Bible and classical literature, and she drew from memory as she wrote, especially from the Hebrew Bible.[64]

Dhuoda's religious sensibilities, like those of the *Heliand*'s author, reflected Christianity's this-worldly, life-affirming traditions. Her Christianity, still centered on incarnation, was at the core of her advice to her son. Unlike the perspectives of the tribal culture of the *Heliand*, Dhuoda's were those of a mother in the Carolingian court who was desperate to protect the life of her son in politically unstable times when Charlemagne's sons vied for power. The book began with this prayer:

> *Divine Lord, high Maker of light, and Creator*
> *of heaven's stars, Eternal King, Holy—*
> *Deign to empower me, I entreat you,*
> *raising me high to be at your right hand*[65]
> *You center that enclose the whirling firmament,*
> *folding ocean and fields within your hand,*
> *To you I commend William, my son—at your command*
> *may well-being be lavished on him in all ways*
> *May he deserve to climb the highest peak,*
> *swift-footed, happy, with those who are yours.*
> *May his perceptions always be alert,*
> *open, to you; may he live blissfully for ever;*
> *When he's hurt, let him never burst into anger*
> *or wander away, severed from your friends;*
> *May your generous grace penetrate him,*
> *with peace and security of body and mind,*
> *In which he may flourish in the world, and have children,*
> *holding what's here so as not to lose what's there*
> *I . . . am asking you with all my strength: have mercy*
> *on him.*[66]

Dhuoda expressed her yearning, or *eros*, for God as a desire for holy embrace. She hoped for the infusion of peace and the flourishing of life. She did not reject this world for another, but joined the two, "holding what's here so as not to lose what's there." She hoped that William would ascend to divinity by a swift-footed and happy ascent with the saints of God and that he would be alert to recognize the Spirit of God in the world.

Though she presented normative courtly ideals of faith, morality, happiness, and beauty, Dhuoda was aware of the political realities her son faced. Her husband was embroiled in the feuds among Charlemagne's sons, Christians fought one another, and the empire executed pagans who refused to convert. Though Dhuoda's fate was largely tied to her husband's, he was, by her own description, not an ideal lord. She wrote that "to prevent his separating from you and me (as is the custom with many men), I feel I have gone heavily into debt."[67] She asked William to pray fervently and to ask all ranks of the clergy to pray for his father to learn to make peace and concord with other people, "if this is possible!"

While Dhuoda taught her son to have dignity and to be respectful and generous to others, she was clearly astute about both her husband's limitations and about the failures of priests. Violence had begun to creep into the life of the church, near its heart, paradise became uncertain, and *theosis* was less imaginable. Aware of the limitations of the church, she counseled her son to be generous, not judgmental, in assessing the clergy.

> Some priests have titles and powers that are so numerous and elevated that their dignity shines in the world, I ask you to render all the honor you can to those who are worthy. For if you notice some whose merit fails to come up to the standard of their holy estate, don't rashly judge them. Avoid heaping blame on their whole lives, as many people do. . . . God knows their hearts and all our hearts as we toil in the world.[68]

The strength to endure the sorrows of this life, Dhuoda said, came from loving it wisely and deeply. Love of this life required astuteness, discipline, prudence, and alertness, for though the Spirit of God was in the world, the world also inflicted great loss. Dhuoda seemed to know she would never see her son again when she sent the book to him in 843. She described her own ill health, sadness, and difficult circumstances. "Reverting to myself, I mourn.... As I sit all alone, racked with thought and wan... I do not see."[69] She told William what she wanted for her epitaph.

Dhuoda demonstrated a sense of her own spiritual power. She referred to herself in relation to her son as his *genatrix*, creator, a more active word than the traditional *mater*, mother. She identified herself as a creative force akin to God, as one who not only gave birth to her son but also taught him how to have a life worth living. She told William the means to life eternal: a constant face of inner joy. If he loved joyfully, those who preceded him into death would remain his intercessors, guarding him, and, when the time came, they would welcome him into the next world. "Love, venerate, welcome, and honor everyone, so that you may deserve the enjoyment of reciprocal benefit."[70] Her book was part of her creative activity. She sought to make him a skillful ruler and humble lover of God. Dhuoda knew that divine power protected her and she affirmed the power of the Spirit in the created world.

Surely, if sky and meadows were unfurled through the air like a scroll of parchment and if all the gulfs of the sea were transformed, tinged like inks of many colors, and if all earth's inhabitants born in the world from the beginning until now were writers (by some increase of human genius, an impossibility contrary to nature!), they would not be able to seize upon the grandeur, the breadth, the loftiness, and be able to tell the depth, of the sublimity, and divinity, and wisdom, and goodness, and mercy of him who is called God.

Furthermore. Trust that God is above and beneath, within and without, for he is higher, lower, deeper within and farther without. He is above, because he presides over us and rules us; he is sublime, and as the Psalmist says, "his glory is over all the heavens." He is beneath because he supports us all.... In him we remain always. He is deeper within, because he fills us all and satisfies us with good things ... He is farther without, because with his unassailable rampart he surrounds and defends and protects us all.[71]

The life of Christians was to conform themselves to the God in all things.

Dhuoda instructed William, born to privilege and danger, in the hope that he would survive the intrigues and wars of his day. Bernard was executed by Charles the Bald in 844. To avenge his death, William joined the Aquitanians and was killed in 848. We do not know if Dhuoda survived either husband or son. Her spiritual sensibilities still held, however, a taste that God dwelled within the human heart, leading it upward toward divinity, and a confidence in human capabilities to live in paradise in this life.

Two centuries after Dhuoda and within a hundred years after the creation of the Gero Cross, the Paschasian view of the Eucharist would become established doctrine in Europe. Denying this view would be heresy. This interpretation of the Eucharist defined every Christian who looked on the Crucifixion, either in images of the dead Christ or unveiled in the Eucharist, in precisely the same way: as someone who had crucified Christ and was judged by the blood of the cross. "An abnegation of inquiry" is how Fulton describes these developments.[72]

The ninth century's new focus on the crucified Christ coincided with a shift in the Christian prohibition against the shedding of human blood. For centuries, the church had taught that participation in warfare was evil, that killing broke the fifth commandment, and that soldiers were to perform penance to cleanse their souls from the stain of blood.[73] At the dawn of the Holy Roman Empire, Christianity began to lose its grip on the sinfulness of killing. A new age began—one in which the execution of Jesus would become a sacrifice to be repeated, first on the Eucharistic altar and then in the ravages of a full-blown holy war.

For the conquered Saxons, images such as the Gero Cross vibrated between public and hidden meanings. In its public display, the crucifix signaled Saxon submission to the Carolingian crucified Christ as the judge of humanity. As a hidden symbol of resistance, the image preserved the Saxons' experience at the hands of their oppressors. It unveiled Christ as a co-sufferer with them in their struggles with a colonizing empire. The image established a subversive kinship with Christ, who died at the hands of Rome just as Saxons died at the hands of Charlemagne. The death of Christ evoked grief, but he—and the Saxons—would outwit their tormentors. Whenever the arts of resistance exert their resurrecting power, imperial injustice is not the last word.

CHAPTER TEN

Peace by the Blood
of the Cross

The bishops raised their crosiers toward heaven, all present
stretched their palms to God, shouting with one voice "Peace!
Peace! Peace!": this was the sign of their perpetual covenant
which they had vowed between themselves and God.

RODULFUS GLABER, C. 1033

"Peace!" became the cry of people in towns and villages throughout
Europe in the tenth century. Charlemagne's warring descendants com-
peted for power, governed badly, and weakened the empire. As the empire fragmented, regional lords ruled over great feudal estates and
battled one another for dominance. By the time of the Gero Cross, the
fractious nobility were struggling to establish control and rekindle the
glory of the Carolingian empire. For ordinary people, daily life was often fraught with insecurity. Absent an effective government that linked
regions together and enforced a system of law, marauding gangs
roamed the countryside. They robbed and killed travelers on the road,
raped women, raided farms, and plundered monastery storehouses.

As looting and murder became common, church leaders sought to
quell the violence that threatened the empire's churches, monasteries,
and people. They tried to restore greater security, and the crucified
Christ and his promise of peace guided them. He made "peace by the
blood of the cross" the scriptures said (Col. 1:20). The church applied

the Carolingian Eucharist and its focus on Christ the victim and the judge to compel peacekeeping. Their strategies for doing so would result in tragedy—a story of passion for peace gone awry.

CONFINING PARADISE

In the face of the lawlessness that accompanied feudalism, the church in Europe followed two strategies of survival. The first strategy was to protect paradise in this world by increasingly confining it to circumscribed spaces in monasteries and convents. Ascetic retreats and cloistered religious vocations had developed very early in the church's history as one form of spiritual life especially removed from the burdens of the Roman *pater familias*. These special communities became increasingly important in Western Europe as walled havens of paradise. Cloisters were built around a square *hortus conclusus* (enclosed garden). Edged with shady, colonnaded walkways, the gardens were laid out in four quadrants, delineated by lines crossing in the middle—a ground plan indicating the four rivers of paradise. Often a fountain spurted at the center of the garden, filling a pool that flowed into four channels of water. Monastery gardens were planted with medicinal and culinary herbs, edible fruits, and fragrant flowers. The atrium of monastery churches carried the architectural term "paradise."[1]

Monasteries and convents located paradise within dramatically confined, miniature, and exclusive spaces. Life outside these gated communities was shadowed by hard labor and debt for many peasants, internecine battles among the nobles, and feudal wars. Seeking respite and safety, some laity retreated to monasteries for healing and rest, but this paradise was limited to those who had financial means to retire there. The cloistered life provided them access to spiritual practices and a taste of life in paradise, but monasteries and convents excluded the ordinary laity. For them, the church prescribed a piety of contrition, suffering love, and fear. Christ's promise, "*Today* you will be with me in Paradise," became a delayed promise for the majority of Christians.[2]

The church's second strategy of survival was to call peace councils.

[handwritten margin notes: B. peace councils — enforced by militias]

Around 975, Bishop Guy of Le Puy convened one of the first such councils. He assembled the region's soldiers, peasants, and roving gangs in an open field outside the city walls and entreated them to swear on the relics of the saints that they would desist from murder, rape, and looting and would keep the peace. He threatened to excommunicate all who raided monasteries and churches. To enforce his demands, the bishop recruited soldiers from the neighboring estates. Other bishops followed this strategy, eliciting oaths to protect the peace. The equivocating peace vow of Robert the Pious (996–1031) is an example:

> I will not infringe on the Church in any way. I will not hurt a cleric or a monk if unarmed. I will not steal an ox, cow, pig, sheep, goat, ass or a mare with colt. I will not attack a vilain [*sic*] or vilainese [*sic*] or servants or merchants for ransom. . . . I will not burn houses or destroy them unless there is a knight inside. I will not root up vines. I will not attack noble ladies traveling without husband nor their maids, nor widows or nuns unless it is their fault.[3]

Through such councils and vows, bishops began a movement called the *pax Dei* (Peace of God) to protect church property and the civilian population. Prayers and sermons at peace councils spoke of the bond of blood that united Christians through their sharing in Christ's blood at the Eucharist. This blood kinship obligated them not to shed one another's blood. As the Council of Narbonne in 1054 declared, "No Christian should kill another Christian, for whoever kills a Christian undoubtedly sheds the blood of Christ."[4] Those outside the body were another matter. The Peace of God excluded non-Christians. In a telling detail, the Council of Narbonne in 1054 used "Christian" where earlier Carolingian codes had condemned shedding the blood of a "human." The peace made by the blood of the cross drew a closed circle around the Christian community—cloistering the faithful within walls of obligation. Those outside were deemed to be of the devil, not of God. Killing them would come to be regarded as service to God.

In the eleventh century, the *treuga Dei* (the truce of God) employed an additional strategy. Church leaders negotiated truce days on which marauding bands agreed to abstain from their activities. The cease-fire was in force on all Sundays. Eventually, the church added the long weekend from Thursday through Monday morning, then saints' days and festival times, until, finally, the truce covered most of the year. By the Council of Narbonne, only eighty permissible fighting days remained.[5]

Over time, church leaders saw they could not enforce the peace by rallies, rituals, and vows alone, even with a backup force of soldiers, so they formed their own militias. In 1038, Andrew of Fleury described how the local church in Bourges employed a small army to attack a marauding band: "With the help of God they so terrified the rebels that ... the rebels scattered ... harried by divinely inspired terror."[6]

This use of violence had to be explained. Odo, the second abbot of Cluny (c. 879–942), developed a justification for the church's militias, even allowing monks to take up arms. In his *Vita Geraldi*, he created a model for the *miles Christi* (the warrior of Christ) who "did not lay aside arms but rather, moved by piety and charity, used arms in a way pleasing to God." Odo spoke of "fighting mingled with piety." He argued that such fighting had divine favor; for support, he drew on accounts of Israelite battles in the Hebrew Bible. Warriors against evil were doing *opus Domini* (the Lord's work).[7] Cluniac monks came to regard fighting for God as an aspect of their holy vows, which contributed to their attacking Muslims in Spain in 1085, though Pope Gregory VII (1023–1085) opposed their desire to reconquer it for Christianity.

Gregory VII did not oppose all wars, however. He offered soldiers two ways to gain everlasting life: they could give up their arms, or they could employ their arms in the service of the church. In 1074, he wrote, "For if, as some say, it is a noble thing to die for our country, it is a far nobler and a truly praiseworthy thing to give our corruptible flesh for Christ, who is life eternal."[8] Gregory promoted fighting for St. Peter as *fidelitas* (loyalty) to Christ. He ordered Count William of Burgundy to assemble a military force "to protect the freedom of the Roman Church [and to] to come hither with [his] army in the service of St. Peter." Military service was a way of imitating Christ and loving one's neighbors, "for as he laid down his life for us, so ought we to lay down our life for our brothers." Such charity was meritorious. Gregory made the remarkable suggestion that it might even suffice as penance for other sins. He failed in an attempt in 1074 to rally a military expedition against the Saracens (Muslims) in the east.[9]

In 1078, the Roman synod reaffirmed that military service incurred sins that required penance, but then qualified this teaching with an exception: a soldier "cannot perform true penance, through which he can attain eternal life, unless he lays down his arms and bears them no more *except on the advice of religious bishops for the defense of righteousness.*"[10]

In addition to the *pax Dei* and *treuga Dei*, with their military backups, church leaders emphasized a piety of fear, contrition, and supplication in the face of the terrible punishments God inflicted upon those who betrayed their vows to Christ. Life-size images of the Crucifixion appeared in churches throughout northern Europe to remind the faithful of their crime of killing Christ and to teach them fear of God's judgment. Liturgical prayers for Good Friday presented the tortured Jesus accusing humanity of killing him. These strategies sought to compel believers to submit to Christ the crucified judge and to keep their vows. The church threatened those who failed to do so with hell, which preachers described in frightening detail.

Devotional practices intensified fear of hell. When Princess Adelaide asked Bishop Anselm of Canterbury (1033–1109) for spiritual guidance, he compiled a series of daily prayers that began with the *Meditatio ad concitandum timorem* (meditation to stir up fear).[11] Reciting this prayer would train the heart:

> Horror! Horror! What is this that I gaze upon, where they live "without order, in eternal horror"? Ah, a confusion of noises, a tumult of gnashing teeth, a babble of groans. Ah, ah, too much, ah, too much woe! Sulphurous flames, flames of hell, eddying darknesses, swirling with terrible sounds. My soul, be exceedingly afraid; tremble, my mind; be torn, my heart.
>
> For I am fearful, knowing the wrath of the strict judge, for I am

a sinner, a prisoner deserving punishment. See, the accused stands before the tremendous Judge. He is accused of many and great offences. He is convicted. Terrible is the severity of the Judge. Torments without end, without interval, without respite, horrible tortures.[12]

Not all Christians welcomed images of the Crucifixion and this piety of fear. In the village of Vertus in Châlons, a local peasant named Leutard smashed a crucifix. In Orléans in 1022, clergy raised objections to an image of the Crucifixion; townspeople did so in Arras in 1025, and the nobility at Montefort d'Alba followed suit between 1027 and 1034.[13] One of the dissenting groups went so far as to insist that baptism was unnecessary for salvation and that worshipping the crucifix was idolatrous; they said Christian life should be focused on imitation of the apostles. When prosecuted for these offensive ideas, they testified that they sought "to abandon the world, to restrain our flesh from carnal longings, to earn our bread by the labor of our hands, to wish harm to none, to show loving-kindness to all."[14] Dissenting movements would grow in the twelfth century, with the rise of the Cathars and the Waldensians, who advocated ascetic disciplines and apostolic poverty and who rejected any shedding of blood. Peter of Bruys, a preacher in the south of France, repudiated all ceremonies and sacraments, advocated asceticism, and burned crosses in St. Gilles. He declared that the cross, as the instrument of Christ's death, should be condemned rather than worshipped.[15]

The official church fought dissent by emphasizing the Crucifixion even more and teaching the faithful that they needed to experience Christ's suffering to be saved. Bishop Gerard I (1013–1048) prescribed adoration of the crucifix. He insisted that holy thoughts and deeds were not sufficient for salvation because these relied on human will. The suffering death of Jesus was divine assistance that delivered the grace necessary for salvation. Gerard explained that those who adored the crucifix became conscious of the debt they owed God. He also argued that gazing at the dead body of Christ would protect people from harm:

We, traveling from the Egypt of carnal conversation through the desert of earthly exile to the land of celestial promise, are rid from our hearts of the venom of the ancient enemy through the sight of the Mediator hanging on the cross. For whoever will have gazed upon Christ through the image and passion of the son, that one will be able to evade the venom of the ancient enemy.[16]

In the transition to a new millennium, devotional practices escalated fear and stirred a greater urgency for repentance, as dread of an apocalyptic Last Judgment grew.[17] Adoration of the Crucifixion intensified into a mix of terror in the presence of the judge and passionate gratitude for Christ's sacrificial death that expiated sin. The crucified Savior aided the faithful in gaining the "land of celestial promise," imagined variously as paradise, the promised land, and the New Jerusalem. Religious imagination located these sites at a great physical distance, after death, or on the other side of the Final Judgment. Arduous pilgrimages to Jerusalem to see the places of Christ's torment became a popular mass movement in the eleventh century. Through their journey, pilgrims imitated Jesus's passage through pain and death, and the sites in Jerusalem sealed their identification with him.

Describing the 1026 pilgrimage of Richard, abbot of Saint-Vanne of Verdun, his contemporary biographer explained "how he passed thirsting through all these places, how he watered all of the places that he passed with fountains of tears." His penitential imitation of Christ's anguish and thirst allowed him to realize his desire "to suffer for Christ, to abide with Him, and to be buried that he might be granted through Christ to rise again in glory." His pilgrimage to Jerusalem culminated with viewing the historical locations of Jesus's passion and crucifixion. Seeing and touching these sights, Richard experienced the saving benefits of the crucifixion:

On the place of Calvary, he called to mind the Savior crucified, pierced with the lance, given vinegar to drink, reviled by those that passed by, crying out with a loud voice and yielding up his spirit—

when he reviewed these scenes, what pain of heart, what founts of tears do you imagine followed the pangs of pious reflection?[18]

For those who could not travel to Jerusalem, contemplation of art provided an alternative means to gain the benefits of Christ's torment. Detailed scenes of every aspect of Jesus's passion began to proliferate. They offered viewers a way to adore the corpse of Christ and weep for his gift of death. A mid-eleventh-century carved wooden relief in a small altar from the Rhineland holds one of the earliest Depositions— a depiction of Jesus's lifeless body being lifted down from the cross.[19] It shows a cross made of tree trunks. At the top left, a winged angel descends headfirst while swinging a censer of incense around the bowed head of Christ. Across from the angel, a man atop the crossbeam is releasing Christ's left hand. At his feet, another one pulls out the nail on his feet with a large pair of pliers. Mary holds her son's limp right forearm and bends her head as if to kiss his pierced palm. His body is falling into the open arms of Joseph of Arimethea who solemnly gazes up into his downcast face. John the evangelist stands opposite Mary next to the man with the pliers, looking down as if overseeing his work. The entire scene conveys sorrow for and devotion to the crucified Savior.

Peter Damian (c. 1007–1072) took crucifixion into his own flesh. Given humanity's sin, "What excuse can we offer? With what kind of defense can we clear ourselves?" he asked. Self-mutilation was his answer—the body was the only true possession that humanity could offer and the price Christ himself had paid for humanity's sins. Through physical austerities such as fasting, self-flagellation, and rejecting all creaturely comforts, a person could imitate Christ on the cross, escape torment in the afterlife, and gain paradise.

O happy exchange, where earthly wares are bartered for heavenly ones.... Blessed indeed the fair where one can buy eternal life ... where a short span of bodily affliction can buy the heavenly banquet.[20]

Peter's community bound their bodies with iron bands and beat themselves with scourges while reciting psalms. Peter defended these unprecedented practices against his critics:

> This is the Cross which we are commanded to bear after the Lord
> daily. He who carries it truly shares in the passion of his Redeemer.
> This emblem will separate the sheep from the goats in the last
> judgment. And the judge ... will recognize the mark as his own.
>   "There is no need, Lord, for you to order your officer to pun-
> ish me. . . . I have laid hands upon myself. . . . I have offered myself
> in place of my sins." ... This is the victim (*hostia*) which is
> sacrificed while still alive ... thus the victim of the human body is
> invisibly commingled with that unique sacrifice that was offered on
> the altar of the cross.[21]

Peter thought that to appear before Christ without wounds would
be to be damned. He put the body in pain at the center of salvation. His
piety sanctified his life as an orphan raised by relatives who abused him
severely. He rejoiced that on Judgment Day, "I shall be found signed
with this mark (*stigma*), so that having been configured to the Crucified
in punishment, I shall deserve to be the companion of the Arisen in
glory."[22] He had many followers.

FROM THE PEACE OF GOD TO THE WAR OF GOD

In November of 1095, Pope Urban II called a Peace Council in Clermont, France. Nobles, bishops, monks, and laity from across Europe responded to his summons. Addressing the gathering in an open field, the
pope announced a truce of God that was binding on all of Christendom.
An eyewitness, Fulcher of Chartres, reported that Urban then said:

> O sons of God, ... there still remains for you who are newly
> aroused by this divine correction, a very necessary work, in which
> you can show the strength of your good will by a further duty,
> God's concern and your own.[23]

Urban urged the crowd to take up arms and journey to Jerusalem to attack "the bastard Turks" who held "sway over our brothers." According to the version of Urban's speech later recalled by Baldric of Dol, Urban evoked the obligations of blood kinship, "Your own blood-brothers, your companions . . . are flogged and exiled as slaves for sale in their own land. Christian blood, redeemed by the blood of Christ, has been shed, and Christian flesh, akin to the flesh of Christ, has been subjected to unspeakable degradation and servitude." He said that the Turks had "shed blood like a river that runs around Jerusalem." He asked, "Upon whom does the task fall to avenge this, upon whom does it fall to relieve this, if not upon you?"[24]

In stirring up hostility against Muslims, Urban may have sought to improve tense relations with the Eastern church. The Western and Eastern churches had excommunicated each other in 1054. In March 1095, Urban received an envoy from the Byzantine emperor, Alexis Comnenus, appealing for military assistance to fight the Muslims in Anatolia (Turkey). At the time of Urban's First Crusade, however, Muslims in the East were not aggressively expanding their territories. Islamic kingdoms in Asia suffered from their own internal problems. Religious schism and political disunity had weakened their cultural and military strength. In the regions they controlled, Muslims were tolerant of Christians.[25] Anti-Muslim sentiment was not a strong feature of European life in the years leading up to the First Crusade. Even Pope Gregory VII had occasion to write a friendly letter in 1074 to an-Hasir, a Muslim leader in North Africa.

> We believe and confess one God, albeit in different ways, and we daily praise and revere him as the creator of the ages and the governor of this world. For as the Apostle says, "He is our peace, who makes both one" (Eph 2.14). . . . For God knows, that we love you sincerely to the honor of God, and that we desire your welfare and prosperity in the present life and in the world to come.[26]

Western pilgrims traveled to Jerusalem and the Holy Land throughout the eleventh century, returning with knowledge of Muslims there. They brought back reports of sophisticated Islamic societies with many admirable cultural achievements.[27]

The origins of Urban's call are best understood in terms of religious and political needs within Europe. Urban drove the call home, proposing that war against a common enemy could accomplish peace in Europe:

> Let those who are accustomed to wantonly wage private war against the faithful march upon the infidels. . . . Let those who have long been robbers now be soldiers of Christ. Let those who once fought against brothers and relatives now rightfully fight against barbarians. Let those who have been hirelings for a few pieces of silver now attain an eternal reward. . . . Let nothing delay those who are going to go![28]

Urban then pronounced the ultimate incentive: "Whoever goes on the journey to free the church of God in Jerusalem . . . can substitute the journey for all penance for sin."[29] With these words, Urban reversed nearly a thousand years of Christian teaching about the sin of shedding human blood. War ceased being a sin and became a way to atone for sin. Killing became a mode of penance, a pathway to paradise. Urban offered crusaders a mission so severe and a penance so complete that it could erase all their previous, current, and future sins and would deliver salvation.[30]

The church sought to keep peace in Europe, finally, by integrating violence into its own heart and sanctifying it. The story of Ralph of Caen, who became a crusader, captures the implications of this change:

> Day after day his prudent mind was in turmoil, and he burned with anxiety all the more because he saw that the warfare which flowed from his position of authority obstructed the Lord's command. For the Lord enjoins that the struck cheek and the other one be offered to the striker, whereas secular authority requires that not even relative's blood be spared. The Lord warns that one's tunic, and one's cloak, too, must be given to the man intending to take

them away; but the imperatives of authority demand that a man who has been deprived of both should have whatever else remains taken from him. Thus, this incompatibility dampened the courage of the wise man whenever he was given an opportunity for quiet reflection. But after the judgment of Pope Urban granted a remission of sins to every Christian setting out to overcome the gentiles, then at last the man's energies were aroused, as though he had earlier been asleep; his strength was renewed, his eyes opened, and his courage was redoubled. For until then, his mind was torn two ways, uncertain of which path to follow, that of the gospel, or that of the World.[31]

With the call of the First Crusade, the path of the Gospel became indistinguishable from "the World."[32]

The pope advocated "righteous warfare" as a form of love, "for it is charity to risk your life for your brothers." Their reward would be "the possession of the enemy. . . . You will make spoil of their treasures and return victorious to your own," according to Baldric of Dol.[33] In the life to come, crusaders would immediately receive remission for all their sin and gain the crown of glory. Historian Jonathan Riley-Smith observes that Urban made war a devotional activity, "a form of war-service which can be compared to saying a prayer."[34] Urban recruited murderers, thieves, and miscreants of all sorts, as well as faithful Christians, some strapped by debt or seeking fortune, and sent them east to die for their salvation. "May you deem it a beautiful thing to die for Christ in that city in which He died for us."[35] At the end of Urban's speech, by many reports, the crowd shouted "*Deus Vult!*": God wills it.[36]

THE GIFT OF DEATH

Archbishop Anselm of Canterbury completed the eleventh-century theological developments that led to the Crusades in his treatise *Cur Deus Homo* (Why God Became Man), published in 1098. He did not believe, as Peter Damian obviously did, that extreme personal pain was sufficient to atone for sin. Humanity's sins were far too grave for such compensatory measures. Anselm was haunted by the anxiety that even the imitation of Christ's crucifixion would not be enough to free sinners from the fires of hell. To answer the terrors he evoked with his devotional prayers "to stir up fear," he proposed that only God could resolve the dilemma and that he did so by becoming human to die on the cross.

Anselm was born to privilege in Aosta, south of Burgundy, but in adolescence he lost his beloved mother, the "anchor of his heart."[37] To escape his father's harsh and punitive behavior, he abandoned his inheritance at age 23. A few years later, he became a student of Lanfranc at the monastery of Bec in Burgundy. Lanfranc had decisively resolved the Paschasian debate about the Eucharist, establishing the Eucharist as the "real presence" of the crucified body of Christ. Anselm succeeded Lanfranc as the prior of Bec in 1063, and he became its abbot in 1078. He was called to Canterbury as archbishop in 1093, during a lull in a long-standing conflict between the church in England and King William Rufus. Rufus wanted the churches and monasteries to swear allegiance and donate their revenues to him rather than to the pope. Anselm opposed Rufus and became embroiled in the fray, which erupted intermittently through two popes, two kings, and two periods of exile. During his exiles, Anselm struggled to find resources to meet his community's needs. The conflicts trapped Anselm in a lifelong struggle with debt. During the course of these wrangles, Anselm became friends with Pope Urban II, who offered refuge and counsel. Anselm completed his treatise on the atonement in Italy during his first exile from England. While in Italy, Anselm and Urban camped out together to watch Roger of Apulia lay siege to Capua. Anthony Bartlett has observed that although "Eadmer [Anselm's companion and biographer] contrasts . . . the worldly pope and the humble archbishop, he passes absolutely no remark on the general picture of these two eminent churchmen so much at ease with a warrior aristocracy and assisting at a cruel act of war almost as entertainment."[38]

Unlike his predecessors and peers, Anselm did not base his theology on scriptural interpretation and disputation with other thinkers. Instead, he presented the question of humanity's salvation from eternal torment as a rational dialogue between himself and a student named Boso. Anselm argued with a relentless, constricting logic, like a snake squeezing its prey. He drew his analogies of sin and recompense from an emerging monetary system that, for many, resulted in crushing debt and the desperate struggle to pay it off. The obedient loyalty and honor due to feudal lords provided the framework of values for his thinking. God, for Anselm, was like such a lord who willed only what was just: "If, for example, God wills that it rain, it is right that it rains, and if He wills that some man be killed, it is right that he be killed." Because God's will is just, "every rational creature must be subject to the will of God.... This is the only and total honor which we owe to God and which God exacts of us. For only such a will produces works pleasing to God." Those who do not honor God with obedience dishonor God, and thus they sin. The sinner must "repay what he has plundered" and must "give back more than he took away."[39]

Sinners bore both the burden of repayment for their sins and the original sinfulness of human nature.[40] The devil may have offered temptation, but humanity chose to sin. Anselm believed God would punish human beings and bar them from heaven unless they had performed sufficient penance to fulfill their debt to God for their personal sins and their sinful nature. Humanity's level of debt for sin, however, was beyond any human capacity to repay it. Nonetheless, unless it was paid, none could enter heaven; all would go to hell. To override this double bind, God paid humanity's debt.[41] He became incarnate in Christ Jesus to die on the cross, offering the gift of his death to pay for humanity's crimes:

> The life of this man [Christ] was so sublime, so precious, that it can suffice to pay what is owed for the sins of the whole world.... Did He not give up His life for the honor of God? ... He freely gave to God for his honor [to] make compensation for all the debts of all human beings.[42]

As God, Christ could have willed not to die in his humanness, but he freely, without any necessity, willed to die to atone for humanity's sins. Because Christ was also human, he gave the gift of his death to his human kin. "The gift of death," not the gift of life, was the greatest gift that God could give. God took pleasure in this death. As a recompense for sin, the Crucifixion returned humanity's debt beyond any payment due to God. Christ's self-offering on the cross was so great it over-flowed with benefits to bless the rest of humanity. God owed the Son a reward for his sacrifice, but "the Son willed to give to another what is due to Himself." Like money in the bank, surplus grace went retroac-tively to pay for Adam and Eve and forward to redeem future sinners.[43]

What then, Anselm asked, could humanity offer in gratitude that would be of sufficient value to repay such grace? Humanity could ex-press its thanks by imitating the sacrifice that restored God's honor. By his gift of death, Christ gave "an example of dying for the sake of jus-tice." Anselm went on,

> There is nothing more bitter or more difficult for man to suffer for the honor of God voluntarily and without obligation, than death, and man absolutely cannot give himself more fully to God than when he commits himself to death for God's honor.[44]

With Anselm's theology of atonement, the Incarnation's sole pur-pose was to drive relentlessly to the act of dying. Though Anselm in-sisted the atonement was a free and willing act of God, not dictated by necessity, humanity could not be saved from the curse of having dis-honored God without the God-man's gift of death. Though he forbade his own monks from joining the Crusades, Anselm's doctrine of the atonement gave support for holy war. Christians were exhorted to imi-tate Christ's self-offering in the cause of God's justice. When authori-ties in the church called for vengeance, they did so on God's behalf. As Anselm wrote, "When earthly rulers exercise vengeance justifiably, the one who is really exercising it is the One who established them in au-thority for this very purpose."[45] God's will must be obeyed, *Deus Vult!*

Christ's resurrection became irrelevant. Anselm fails even to men-tion it in *Why God Became Man*. Constantine's mother, Helena, built the

Church of the Holy Sepulcher in Jerusalem as a shrine to the Resurrection. However, in the new spirituality that arose with the Crusades, the Holy Sepulcher became a gravesite for Jesus's dead body. A drawing of the church from the eleventh century shows that it was no longer an empty tomb; it contained a coffin with a body in it. A simple, twelfth-century sketch of the church's circular central ground plan depicts a long rectangular box in the middle of the innermost concentric ring of walls. Peering from above, as the aerial view shows, one can see Christ with his nimbus, lying full-length in a shroud.[46]

The Church of the Holy Sepulcher still commemorated the Resurrection, but by the eleventh century, the church's rituals had virtually reversed the traditions of Cyril's fourth-century Jerusalem. Instead of mourning the Crucifixion once a year and marking the Resurrection daily, the Resurrection slowly receded in importance. Resurrection had no place for Anselm in salvation because the only purpose of the Incarnation was to accomplish a saving death, and the precise purpose of Christ's being human was to die. "No soul could enter the heavenly paradise before the death of Christ," he wrote.[47]

Anselm did not construct his theology of death on cold-blooded reason alone. His popular devotional prayers, in addition to encouraging fear, shaped a piety of empathetic love that would develop further after his time. For an expression of unfathomable grief, he turned to Mary, the mother of all re-created things, who represented the grief of God, the creator of all things. "Most merciful Lady, what can I say about the fountains that flowed from your most pure eyes when you saw your only Son before you, bound, beaten and hurt?" He asked, "Mary, how much we owe you, Mother and Lady, by whom we have such a brother? What thanks and praise can we return to you?"[48] In this devotion to Mary, he read the Song of Songs as a speech between Mary and Christ, the story of a profound love in which each felt the suffering of the other. Mary was different from a contrite sinner who suffered in fear for his or her own sins and loved Christ out of self-interest. Her compassion was pure and for her son. In her grief, Mary, offered a mirror to the faithful of compassion and sorrow in its deepest, divine form. A harbinger of medieval devotion to Mary, Anselm referred to her as "Mother of the life of my soul." He prayed:

> What can I worthily tell of the mother of my Lord and God.... [You] showed to the world its Lord and its God whom it had not known. You showed to the sight of all the world its Creator whom it had not seen. You gave birth to the restorer of the world for whom the lost world longed.... [There] is no salvation except what you brought forth as a virgin.[49]

Mary's empathy for Christ's pain trained Christian feeling toward the Eucharist. Through a mother who loved so deeply she virtually died herself, Christians could approach the Eucharist with empathy for Christ's torment, as well as fear of Christ as judge. The Eucharist, received with trembling and heartbroken empathy, was at the heart of Anselm's piety. Consuming the bread and drinking the cup incorporated believers into the merits of Christ's death:

> This let thy heart *chew,* O man, this let it *ruminate,* this let it *suck,* this let it *swallow* when thy mouth receives the body and blood of the selfsame, thy Redeemer. Make this in this present life thy daily bread, thy viand and viaticum, for by means of this, and *by nothing except this,* shalt thou at once remain in Christ and Christ in thee.[50]

Anselm's theology and piety crystallized the religious foundation of the Crusades. "Peace by the blood of the cross" would become the path to unity among those who shared in Christ's blood, released for human consumption through his crucifixion. Those who shared in the bread and cup incurred obligations either to convert or to kill those who did not eat and drink with them. No one who stood outside the ritual circle of Communion was safe. This consuming vision of peace permeated Christian spiritual practices of the eleventh century. Killing and being killed imitated the gift of Christ's death, the anguish of his self-sacrifice, and the terror of his judgment.

TAKING PARADISE BY STORM

Urban commissioned Peter the Hermit to travel through the towns and cities of France and Germany to "preach the crusade." People followed Peter in droves, assembled arms, raised money (often by mortgaging lands), and formed an army "taking the cross." In public rallies, they vowed to give their lives to restore God's honor, and they sewed fabric crosses to their garments as a sign of this vow. Their first act was to travel to the Rhineland, where they attacked Jews. Peter preached on Good Friday in the Cologne Cathedral under the shadow of the Gero Cross. His sermon inspired the crusaders to force Jews to repent of murdering Christ and to accept baptism at the point of a sword. Many refused and were killed. Peter's preaching unleashed assaults on Jews that continued all spring—the first Christian pogrom against Jews.[51] Albert of Aachen described the May 25, 1096, massacre in Mainz:

> Breaking the bolts and doors, they killed the Jews, about 700 in number, who in vain resisted the force and attack of so many thousands. They killed the women, also, and with their swords pierced tender children of whatever age and sex.... Horrible to say, mothers cut the throats of nursing children with knives and stabbed others, preferring them to perish thus by their own hands.[52]

The crusaders killed approximately ten thousand Jews in the Rhineland in the spring of 1096—nearly a third of the Jewish population in Europe.[53] Only then did the waves of crusaders turn east. The crusading bands grew to include as many as a hundred thousand men, women, and children. A vanguard known as the People's Crusade, composed primarily of peasants, traveled overland by foot. They looted and rampaged along the way, and when they reached Hungary, Eastern Christians fought and killed them. Other bands followed, headed for Constantinople, only to be turned away by Christian leaders there who wanted nothing to do with their rapacious activities.[54] Anna Comnena, daughter of the Emperor Alexius I, described the Latin Christians as "no less devoted to religion than to war." She noted that Latin priests differed from the Eastern Christian leaders and that a

Latin Barbarian will at the same time handle sacred objects, fasten a shield to his left arm and grasp a spear in his right. He will communicate the Body and Blood of the Divinity and meanwhile gaze on bloodshed and become himself a "man of blood."[55]

Urban had many reasons to launch the Crusade. One may have been to offer salvation to the laity who had been demanding their own path to paradise in the eleventh century as paradise moved into cloistered communities. By taking the cross, lay people took on a life of poverty, austerity, and obedience, which paralleled the spiritual practices of monks and nuns. The journey to Jerusalem and service in battle became the people's pathway into paradise. Albert of Aachen, in his history of the First Crusade, told of a vision in which Christ appeared to a pilgrim in the Church of the Holy Sepulcher. Christ sent the pilgrim to bring the pope a letter demanding an armed pilgrimage to Jerusalem, explaining that for those who have "passed dangers and temptations, the doors of paradise will be opened."[56]

In the eleventh century, apocalyptic symbols were increasingly used to interpret contemporary times, places, and events, which were associated with the impending final battle of Armageddon and the New Jerusalem. At the turn of the millennium, the people of Orléans had a vision of a weeping crucifix and read it as a sign that their city was the New Jerusalem. Later in the century, Pope Gregory characterized his enemies as "the bellicose dragon" of Revelation 12. By the time of the call of the First Crusade, earthly battles were imagined in transcendent, cosmic terms.[57] For the crusaders, Jerusalem represented the apocalyptic promise of a new heaven and earth. Foretold in Revelation, the final battle between Christ and the Antichrist would defeat the enemies of God, and Jerusalem would arrive sparkling with jewels, a crystalline river, and healing trees. "Mourning and crying and pain will be no more" (Rev. 21:4), and the nuptials of Christ the bridegroom and his bride, the city, would consummate God's love for humanity. The terrestrial and celestial Jerusalem coalesced in a new way: not as a merging of present earthly blessing with the eternal, heavenly paradise, but as a merging of present war with future promises of a new and utterly different heaven and earth. The cataclysmic end of time was in the distant future *and* right now, because the Crusade could be imagined as struggles with Gog, the Antichrist, and Christians could become instruments of the divine purpose by destroying God's enemies and building the New Jerusalem.[58]

The waves of armed pilgrims who set out for Jerusalem in 1096 imagined their Crusade in just such apocalyptic terms. Death in battle enabled immediate entrance into celestial paradise. In the *Gesta Francorum*, "The Deeds of the Franks and the Other Pilgrims to Jerusalem," written during the First Crusade, the unknown author turns a crushing defeat into a moment of victory in what was not the first but certainly one of the best early examples of "spin." He claimed that the slain Christian soldiers won heaven by their cowardice and defeat:

> [The Turks'] attack was so fierce that our men began to flee over the nearest mountain, or wherever there was a path. Those who could get away quickly escaped alive, and those who could not were killed. On that day more than a thousand of our knights or foot-soldiers suffered martyrdom, and we believe that they went to Heaven and were clad in white robes and received the martyr's palm.[59]

When a Crusade reporter could turn humiliating defeat into glory, his capacity to distinguish between loss and victory and between death and life had evidently disappeared. Crusaders had nothing to lose and everything to gain; no price, therefore, was too great to pay.

After a long siege, the crusaders finally breached the walls of Jerusalem in 1099, and they believed the critical turning point for victory coincided with the hour of Jesus's crucifixion:

> On Friday at dawn we attacked the city from all sides but could achieve nothing, so that we were all astounded and very much

afraid, yet, when that hour came when our Lord Jesus Christ deigned to suffer for us upon the cross, our knights were fighting bravely on the siege-tower. . . . At that moment one of our knights, called Lethold, succeeded in getting on to the wall. As soon as he reached it, all the defenders fled along the walls and through the city, and our men went after them, killing them and cutting them down as far as Solomon's Temple, where there was such a massacre that our men were wading up to their ankles in enemy blood.

Following this divinely assisted "hour of power," the crusaders "rushed round the whole city, seizing gold and silver, horses and mules, and houses full of all sorts of goods, and they all came rejoicing and weeping from excess of gladness to worship at the Sepulcher of our Savior Jesus, and there they fulfilled their vows to him."[60] For these crusaders, the worship of God was indistinguishable from killing Muslims and plundering their homes. They saw their own acts, aligned with Jesus's crucifixion, as shimmering with divine blessing and bringing Judgment Day to fulfillment. If they exaggerated, the character of the exaggeration itself is a testimony to the mind-set of crusaders: rivers of blood in holy places gave glory to God. Muslim histories also recorded the taking of Jerusalem. Ibn al-Qalanisi reported:

The Franks stormed the town and gained possession of it. A number of the townsfolk fled to the sanctuary and a great host were killed. The Jews assembled in the synagogue, and the Franks burned it over their heads. The sanctuary was surrendered to them on guarantees of safety . . . and they destroyed the shrines and the tomb of Abraham.[61]

One ancient Muslim account of the fall of Jerusalem tells of refugees from Jerusalem arriving in Baghdad during the holy month of Ramadan. So great was their distress that they were relieved of the obligation to observe the holy fast. In the mosques at Friday prayers, they told the story of their ordeal, and the community wept with them.

BUILDING THE NEW JERUSALEM

Following the capture of the city in July 1099, Christians began building a New Jerusalem and establishing a Christian kingdom throughout the *Terrae Sanctae* (the Holy Land). The land they had conquered was home to a great diversity of peoples: Jews; Zoroastrians; Druze, Sunni, and Shia Muslims; and Nestorian, Maronite, Jacobite, and Eastern Orthodox Christians. The Latin Christians began by killing most of the Muslim inhabitants of the major cities such as Antioch and Caesarea. They spared Muslim peasants in the rural areas to preserve a labor force. Latin Christians installed themselves as governors and established regional ecclesiastical structures. Latin Christians tolerated Eastern Christians in subordinate roles. They relegated Jews and Muslims to the bottom of the pyramid of control. Their campaign marked the beginning of an apocalyptically inspired pattern of Christian pilgrimage, conquest and colonization. The pattern would later reach in new directions with the conquest and colonization of the New World.[62]

The Crusades dramatically changed Europe's economy. To mount their armies, landowners in Europe had to raise money. Lords released their serfs in exchange for cash. They borrowed heavily, mortgaging lands. One of the fastest ways to raise money was to cut down their forests and sell the timber. Church-sponsored taxation increased. These activities drained resources, but the resources of plunder and colonization flowed back to Europe from the Holy Land, and Europe experienced a period of economic growth in the twelfth century. The silver and gold taken by crusaders in the Holy Land greatly helped the rise of a middle class and the professional guilds. By robbing those they conquered of their treasuries of coins, crusaders provided an influx of money into mineral-poor Europe, lifting it from an agrarian trade system into a monetary economy. The new economic vitality contributed to the renovation of churches in Europe and the great flowering of Gothic architecture in the twelfth and thirteenth centuries.[63]

In Jerusalem, no expense was spared to build churches and shrines to mark the events of Jesus's life, death, and resurrection. Bernard of

Clairvaux (1090–1153) extolled the industry of the crusaders: "Once they have installed themselves in this holy house with their horses and their weapons, cleansed it and the other holy places of every un-Christian stain, and cast out the tyrannical horde, they occupy themselves day and night in both pious exercises and practical work."[64] Only the Church of the Holy Sepulcher in Jerusalem and the nearby basilica of Bethlehem were in working order when the city was conquered. Within ten years, the crusaders had built new churches all around Jerusalem. The Church of Mount Zion commemorated the site where Jesus celebrated the Last Supper and where the Holy Spirit descended at Pentecost. The Church of the Ascension was built on the Mount of Olives across the valley from the Holy Sepulcher.[65] Crusaders converted the Al-Aqsa Mosque, across a plaza from the Dome of the Rock, which commemorated Mohammed's ascension into the Temple of the Lord, to mark the presentation of the Christ child to the temple.

From 1099 to 1187—for 88 years—the Franks ruled the Holy Land, and, in the wake of their conquest and colonization, waves of settlers and pilgrims arrived. The closing pages of the *Gesta Francorum* presented a pastiche of holy places from the Bible and the life of Jesus that the pilgrims could visit. Like a travel brochure, the crusader's memoir invited others to come and see the many wonderful sites: the garden of Gethsemane, Adam's grave on Golgotha, the tomb from which Lazarus was raised, the site where Abraham offered his sacrifice, Solomon's temple, the tomb of Isaiah, "the place where God appeared to Moses in the burning bush," the place where Jacob wrestled the angel, the place where Mary the Virgin Mother and the other women "stood weeping and mourning when they saw the Lord hanging on the cross," and more.[66] Pilgrims came by the thousands. Armed and unarmed alike, their purpose was penitential: to endure the arduous journey, to touch the terrestrial holy sites, and perhaps to die in the very place where Jesus was crucified. In this way, pilgrims could repay their debt to God, escape the terror of hell, and assure their own safe passage to paradise.

Early in the twelfth century, the swarms included holy orders of fighting knights—an innovation in Christian monasticism. The Knights of St. John of Jerusalem were chartered in 1113 and the Knights of the Temple of Jerusalem (the Templars) in 1119. These orders defended the Holy Land, provided care for sick and indigent pilgrims, and protected the pilgrimage routes across Europe. Their emergence crystallized the effect of the crusading movements: monastic orders morphed into bands of armed knights and became, as one Crusade scholar put it, "monasteries on the march." The Holy Land was conquered and colonized by this new breed of monks: monks who killed for God as part of their vows of chastity, poverty, and obedience. The ⌐Templars⌐made the Temple of the Lord, the former Al-Aqsa Mosque, into their headquarters and decorated it as a shrine to themselves:

Of course the façade of this temple is adorned, but with weapons rather than with jewels, and in place of the ancient gold crowns, its walls are hung round about with shields. In place of candlesticks, censers and ewers, this house is well furnished with saddles, bits and lances. By all these signs our knights clearly show that they are animated by the same zeal for the house of God which of old passionately inflamed their leader himself when he armed his most holy hands, not indeed with a sword, but with a whip.[67]

The new religious imagination of medieval Christians impelled the destruction of everything for their salvation: lives, trees, cultures, and holy sites. Christians, Muslims, and Jews share ideas of holy war. However, the Christian version that emerged in the Crusades contained its own unique mixture of adoration for crucifixion and the gift of death, frenzied expectations of apocalyptic judgment, and an inability to distinguish between defeat and death or victory and life. Christian holy war and all that followed it turned an earthly address of paradise—the Holy Land—into a region to be conquered and colonized. Life on earth became a battle for the terrestrial paradise that could lead to celestial paradise in the hereafter. As the prophet Jeremiah wrote when Jerusalem fell to Babylon in the sixth century BCE:

V

> *From the least to the greatest of them,*
>> *everyone is greedy for unjust gain;*
> *and from prophet to priest,*
>> *everyone deals falsely.*
> *They have treated the wound of my people carelessly,*
>> *saying, "Peace, peace,"*
> *when there is no peace. (Jer. 6:13–14)*

CHAPTER ELEVEN

Dying for Love

You who love with a true love, awake! Do not sleep! The lark
draws towards us and tells us in its speech that the day of
peace has come which God in his great sweetness will give
to those who will take the cross for love of him and will suffer
pain night and day through their deeds. Then he will see who
truly loves him.

He who was crucified for us was not lukewarm in his love
for us but like a true lover and, for us, lovingly carried in great
anguish the Holy Cross.

TROUBADOUR SONG,
AUTHOR UNKNOWN, TWELFTH CENTURY

In the twelfth century, true love died. Images of Christ crucified came
to represent passionate self-giving love, manifested most fully in suffering and expiring for the beloved. Preaching, poetry, and popular songs
promoted crusading as an act of love. True lovers of Christ were to imitate his passion. Those who loved unto death would be transported to
paradise, which opened its gates for those who died for love. These developments shaped a new concept of Christian love that bound pity,
obedience, and desire into a potent and volatile mix that haunts modern Western culture's ongoing love affair with violence.

It was a century of contradictions. Preachers upheld gender norms,
emphasizing the weakness and frailty of women, even as their preach-

ing of the Crusades drained towns and monasteries of men and as strong, powerful women ruled in their place. Many women fought to defend their towns or joined the Crusades as prostitutes, cooks, or other servants. Some women even dressed as men, donned armor, and joined in battles.[1] The era was a time of frank acceptance and discussion of sexual matters, and although an emphasis on celibacy was growing, monks and priests kept lovers, and an occasional nun turned up pregnant. Legislation passed by the Second Lateran Council in 1139, which was called to end a schism in the church, also voted a policy of celibacy and prohibited marriage and concubinage for church leaders, both male and female. The church also separated the participation of nuns and monks in liturgy, prescribed plain dress for priests and monastics, and excommunicated laity who failed to pay their church tithes.

Paradise remained on earth in the world of the cloister, which also produced the most important religious leaders of the time. From that cloistered haven, we examine four figures. Two, Bernard of Clairvaux (1090–1153) and Hildegard of Bingen (1098–1179), are remembered as religiously and politically influential. Bernard was widely famous, and Hildegard produced an enormous body of work that included letters to emperors and popes; writings on medicine, science, and music; theology; and accounts of her personal mysticism. She and Bernard preached widely and supported crusading as a religious vocation. The other two, husband and wife, were the monk and teacher Peter Abelard (1079–1142) and Heloise (1101–1162), abbess of the Oratory of the Paraclete. They neither supported crusading nor accepted church ideas at face value, and thus they had little religious or political influence in their time. Abelard was twice excommunicated, and without Heloise's talent for administration and her commitment to him, we might not have any of his writing today. Abelard and Heloise became famous as lovers, but this romantic idea of them distorts her contributions. Heloise, we suggest, was a Christian woman who was not seduced by church pieties and who avoided both self-deception and the romance of suffering and violence that became a primary religious piety in this century. We attend to her strong dissenting voice at the conclusion of this chapter, but we begin with the twelfth century's religious superstar: Bernard, who most advanced a changed understanding of paradise that used the cloistered life as a monastic model for crusaders.

THE MARRIAGE OF EROS AND MARS

Bernard joined love and crucifixion completely. He sought to know Jesus Christ crucified directly through his personal contrition for sin. One of his hymns, "O Sacred Head, Now Wounded," still sung today in Western churches, illustrated this focus. It described Christ's head crowned with thorns as bliss and said, "though despised and gory I joy to call Thee mine." Christ's suffering was for the gain of sinners, "mine was the transgression, but Thine the deadly pain" Bernard took joy in hiding safely in the broken body "desiring thy glory now to see, Beside Thy cross expiring, I'd breathe my soul to Thee."[2]

Born to a noble family, Bernard lost his father in a Crusade battle; his mother died while he was a child. He defied his guardians and chose a monastic vocation, joining a small group of reformed Benedictines in Citeaux who formed the Cistercian order. When they decided to found a new abbey in Clairvaux in 1115, Bernard was chosen to be its first abbot. He wrote the rules of the order, was prodigiously successful in propagating monasteries, and became the most sought-out preacher and religious advisor of his time—at a time when monks, and a few abbesses such as Hildegard, regularly spoke to councils of bishops, cloistered communities, and gatherings of the laity. One of his monks was elected Pope Eugene III in 1145.

The monastery that Bernard built at Clairvaux was a plain, austere place that supported the disciplines of a secluded asceticism as if, in the words of Christoph Auffarth, "he were about to plant paradise anew."[3] He linked the *hortus conclusus* (enclosed garden) with the Garden of Love in the Song of Songs—a place of spiritual delight where the soul enjoyed mystical erotic union with God. His friend Hildegard regarded her convent in similar terms, speaking about the "greening of the soul." A contemporary described the grounds of Clairvaux:

Behind the abbey, and within the wall of the cloister, there is a wide
level ground: here there is an orchard, with a great many different
fruit-trees, quite like a small wood. It is close to the infirmary, and
is very comforting to the brothers, providing a wide promenade for
those who want to walk, and a pleasant resting-place for those who
prefer to rest. Where the orchard leaves off, the garden begins, divided into several beds, or (still better) cut up by little canals,
which, though standing water, do actually flow more or less.... The
water fulfils the double purpose of nourishing the fish and watering the vegetables.[4]

Here, in Bernard's garden of love, Christ could join in a lover's embrace with his bride—the monk.[5] There was no need for the monk to
embark on a long, physical pilgrimage to the Holy Land:

He has cast his anchor into the very port of salvation. His feet
already tread the pavements of the Holy Jerusalem. This Jerusalem which is linked with the heavenly Jerusalem and which is entwined with her in all the deepest feelings of the human heart is
Clairvaux.[6]

Because his core value was love, Bernard assured his monks they
need not live in fear, but in affection for their Lord. He was known for
his caring leadership of his community and his many friends. In sixty-
seven sermons on the Song of Songs, Bernard led his monks to follow
the path to mystical, erotic union with God, casting the feminine soul
as the seeker of God.[7] He lingered long over the meaning of enticing
scriptural phrases such as "his left arm is under my head, and his right
arm embraces me," and "let him kiss me with the kisses of his mouth."
He instructed his monks about the meaning of the Incarnation as a kiss
of the human and divine natures.

I must ask you to try to give your whole attention here. The mouth
that kisses signifies the Word who assumes human nature.... In

one sole instance the mouth of the word was pressed, that moment when the fullness of the divinity yielded itself to him as the life of his body. A fertile kiss therefore, a marvel of stupendous self-abasement that is not a mere pressing of mouth upon mouth; it is the uniting of God with man. Normally the touch of lip on lip is the sign of the loving embrace of hearts, but this conjoining of natures brings together the human and divine.... This was the kiss for which just men yearned... longing to taste that fullness of his.[8]

Human beings, Bernard said, had their origin in heaven, and longed to be reunited with their source. "I saw the holy city, the new Jerusalem, coming down out of heaven from God, prepared as a bride adorned for her husband," he said. "These two then have their origin in heaven—Jesus the Bridegroom and Jerusalem the bride." He told his monks that when they knew "the visible image and radiant comeliness of that supernal Jerusalem,"[9] they would be drawn to live as citizens of heaven. An armed pilgrimage to the Holy Land would suffice for those who could not enter the cloister, but from Bernard's perspective, the cloistered life provided the superior route to the New Jerusalem.[10] The monk should strive to be the beloved bride in the Song, who came from heaven and was modest, prudent, chaste, patient, compassionate, meek, holy, and humble of heart. These virtues made her pleasing to Christ and the angels. Bernard said, "With a love angelic in its fervor she shows herself to be a fellow-citizen with the saints and a domestic of God."[11]

Bernard's evocation of holy desire was reminiscent of imagery found in Ephrem of Syria and in Maximus the Confessor. However, Bernard's erotic mysticism introduced a dramatically different note.[12] Sufferings, which he called sweet, and torture, which he eroticized, were integral to his ideas of love. Bernard described God's beloved as wounded and disfigured, and he used her color to mark her as humiliated. In the Song of Songs, the bride says, "I am black and beautiful." Bernard noted that a black color could be beautiful, but dark skin was "a stigma," a source of "torment and taunts."[13] He likened the blackness of the bride to the infirmities of Paul. The bride shared with Paul in the scorn and the persecutions of the crucified Christ.[14] For Bernard, the bride's black skin was a sign of her deep pain and therefore her deep love, like the blows Christ endured on the cross.

> She is not ashamed of this blackness, for her Bridegroom endured it before her, and what greater glory than to be made like to him. Therefore she believes that nothing contributes more to her glory than to bear the ignominy of Christ. . . . The ignominy of the cross is welcome to the man who will not be an ingrate to his crucified Lord. Though it involves the stigma of blackness, it is also in the pattern of the likeness of the Lord.[15]

Torture and abuse marked the bride of Christ, who gloried in the cross of affliction because it united her to Jesus in mystical, erotic union. Bernard prayed that he would suffer similarly: "Sufferings are their joy equally with their hope. . . . Let me be not merely weak, then, but entirely resourceless, utterly helpless, that I may enjoy the support of the power of the Lord of Hosts!"

Cistercian life was a pilgrimage to the New Jerusalem, undertaken as prayerful adoration of the crucified Christ. Such adoration, Bernard said, folded Jesus to one's breast, just as the lover in the Song of Songs placed a "little bundle of myrrh"—a bitter herb—between her breasts. Bernard explained:

> As for me, dear brothers, from the early days of my conversion, conscious of my grave lack of merits, I made sure to gather for myself this little bunch of myrrh and place it between my breasts. It was culled from all the anxious hours and bitter experiences of my Lord; first from the privations of his infancy . . . and finally the dangers from traitors in the brotherhood, the insults, the spitting, the blows, the mockery, the scorn, the nails and similar torments that are multiplied in the Gospels, like trees in the forest, and all for the salvation of our race. Among the teeming little branches of this

perfumed myrrh I feel we must not forget the myrrh which he drank upon the cross and used for his anointing at his burial. . . . As long as I live I shall proclaim the abounding goodness contained in these events.[16]

Bernard never traveled to Jerusalem, but he supported armed pilgrimages to Jerusalem as a way for the laity to accomplish the union with God that his monks accomplished in the cloister. His valorization of pain as a sign of love translated directly into killing and being killed for Christ. In 1146, Pope Eugene III, Bernard's former monk, appointed him to preach the Second Crusade. Bernard used his considerable fame and influence to stir fervor, raise money, and recruit volunteers for the Crusade. Such papal appointments to rally support and form armies of pilgrims were important to the success of the pope's campaigns.

Bernard coined the term *malecide* (killing an evildoer) to describe the Crusades, in place of *homicide* (killing a human being) and claimed it fulfilled the ancient prophets who "foreshadowed the new knighthood" and promised the deliverance of Jerusalem from her enemies. However, Bernard cautioned, this earthly defeat of the "Saracens" (Muslims) must not blind people to the spiritual meaning of the Crusades: "Otherwise the tangible would supplant the intangible, material poverty would threaten spiritual wealth . . . the temporal glory of the earthly city does not eclipse the glory of its heavenly counterpart, but rather prepares for it."[17]

For Bernard, the Crusade forged a new form of love: ecstatic union with Christ's sufferings in life and death. Many have noticed the homoerotic dimensions of Bernard's interest in eros. Few, however, have discussed how he eroticized violence and pain. Love between same-sex people had long been appreciated by Christians, especially in the environments of monastery and convents.[18] However, the heterodox union of eros and violence was Bernard's own contribution, a marriage of Eros, the goddess of love, and Mars, the god of war. Cloistered monks and crusading knights both shared Christ's agony and humiliation. One served him through fasting, tears, and hard labor. The other served him with the physical hardships of long marches, hunger and thirst, and being pierced by arrows and swords. Both gave glory to God and were erotically joined to him as brides.

Bernard's religious imagery indicated traditional ideas of both race and gender. For him, the pitiable human body was dark-skinned, female, and crucified. As scholar Gay L. Byron notes, ancient writers used the color symbolism of black and Africa, especially Egypt and Ethiopia, to mean sin and evil, and dark women to suggest sexual licentiousness and filth.[19] For Bernard, black and female was a canvas on which to depict depravity and violence, which could be rescued by union with Christ. He did not, however, mean for his monks to take him literally. Bernard was incensed when his crusading knights began growing their hair long, adorned their helmets with plumes, and dressed their horses in silks. Symbolic womanhood might be holy, but real gender crossing offended him. He protested, "Are these the trappings of a warrior or are they not rather the trinkets of a woman?"[20] The true knight was to be

> formidable, rather than flamboyant . . . not quarrelsome, rash, or unduly hasty, but soberly, prudently and providently drawn up into orderly ranks. . . . The true Israelite is a man of peace, even when he goes forth to battle. Once he finds himself in the thick of battle, this knight sets aside his previous gentleness, as if to say, "Do I not hate those who hate you, O Lord; am I not disgusted with your enemies?" These men at once fall violently upon the foe, regarding them as so many sheep.[21]

By merging the warrior with the monk, Bernard lifted lay crusaders to the status of monks and turned monks into warriors. He wrote a defense of the Knights Templar, the order of fighting Cistercian monks who occupied the Al-Aqsa mosque in Jerusalem and made it their headquarters. He may also have been the author of their monastic rule. "A new knighthood has recently appeared on the earth," he said, "It ceaselessly wages a twofold war both against flesh and blood and against a spiritual army of evil." He called crusaders "God's ministers." Their slaughter was glorious service to God. If a Templar died in battle, Bernard explained, he gained paradise. He did not fear death: "No, he desires it. Why should he fear to live or fear to die when for him to live is Christ, and to die is gain?"[22] He sent the knights forth:

> Go forth confidently then, you knights, and repel the foes of the cross of Christ with a stalwart heart. . . . What a glory to return in victory from such a battle! How blessed to die there as a martyr! Rejoice, brave athlete, if you live and conquer in the Lord; but glory and exult even more if you die and join your Lord. Life indeed is a fruitful thing and victory is glorious, but a holy death is more important than either.[23]

For Bernard, killing, dying, and suffering were spiritual modes of communion with Jesus—aspects of salvation. He insisted that the "knight of Christ" could kill and die with confidence, "for he serves Christ when he strikes, and saves himself when he falls." His killing profited Christ, and his death profited himself.[24]

Monastic spirituality cultivated union with God. The Crusades offered the same to the laity. Bernard fused monks and warriors into a holy army and transformed the inebriating grace of paradise into a high-proof potion of eros, violence, and death. The Second Crusade that he preached with such fervor failed disastrously. When the crusaders were mowed down in Anatolia, Bernard, struggling to explain why God had allowed such horror, blamed the sins of the crusaders for their failures. Ironically, Bernard's own fame and persuasive preaching were responsible for the presence of many disorganized noncombatants who interfered with the professional military.[25]

Despite the failure of the Second Crusade, the call to "take the cross" continued, with hundreds joining subsequent Crusades and pouring their lives and their resources into dying for love. Cardinal Odo of Chateauroux called Christians into a Crusade in 1245 saying: "It is a clear sign that a man burns with love of God and zeal for God when he leaves country, possessions, house, children and wife, going overseas in the service of Jesus Christ. . . . Whoever wishes to take and have Christ ought to follow him: to follow him to death."[26]

THE GOLDEN CITY AND THE BEAUTIFUL BODY

Hildegard of Bingen (1098–1179) shared Bernard's ecstatic mysticism and love. She corresponded with him and also shared his enthusiasm for the Crusades. Her older brother led a Crusade against the pacifist Cathars in the south of France, and she supported his efforts. Crusading had given rise to powerful, educated, competent women who ruled in place of their absent husbands; famous abbesses, such as Hildegard, were their religious corollaries. She was a powerful and popular leader who highlighted her frailty and lowliness as a woman to preach a fierce message of human sinfulness, which she used to pressure rulers and popes to do what she thought best and to rally people to the church. She tended to consider her own desires the same as God's and to preach as if she spoke directly from a divine perspective. Among the more infamous controversies of her life was her inability to relinquish control of her most beloved nun, Richardis, who sought an abbess position. Hildegard implied that Richardis's early death was divine punishment for leaving her. Throughout her life, Hildegard maintained the class biases of her noble birth, prohibiting lower-class women from joining her community.[27]

Like Bernard, Hildegard was of a delicate physical constitution.[28] Her colleague Guibert wrote of her, "From the day of her birth this woman has been bound by grievous sickness as if in a net, suffering constant pains in her veins, bones, and flesh." Hildegard concluded that God sent her pain as direction for her creativity. "If the fierce physical pains I suffered had not been sent by God I could not have gone on living." She interpreted her pain as a sign that she was not in accord with God's will. She wrote that whenever "out of fear of people's reaction I did not follow the way God had pointed out, this physical anguish increased." However, she also seemed to be afflicted by sickness when she wanted to avoid a difficult duty or opposed something she was ordered to do. And she had visions. Early in her life, Hildegard sought Bernard's advice about how to interpret her mystical visions. He instructed her that she herself was the one who could best ascertain their meaning. Recording her visions and theological ideas eased her pain. "When I started writing I recovered my strength and rose up from my sick-bed." Whenever she preached, she upheld her authority to speak for God by claiming she spoke from her inner divine light.[29]

Hildegard shared Bernard's view of time, place, and history as moving toward an apocalyptic fulfillment, what a contemporary theologian might call a sense of "eschatological hope" (hope in final things). She approved of the persecution of heretics as preparation for the final resurrection and the completion of the New Jerusalem. Final salvation would be the *civitas aurea* (golden city), an image of the New Jerusalem as the transfiguration of the whole creation, lit from within by the fire of divine love. This city would be completed at the end of time, but even now its celestial blessings streamed into the world. "Rivers of living water are to be poured out over the whole world, to ensure that people, like fishes caught in a net, can be restored to wholeness."[30] With the arrival of the end times, "the whole world will exist in the full beauty of vitality and freshness," and once the beauty of earth was restored, so too would divine justice rule:

> Then people will experience the justice that the world so sadly lacked. . . . All weapons manufactured for purposes of death and destruction will be forbidden and the only tools, devices, and machinery permitted will be those that serve the cultivation of the land and are truly useful to humankind.[31]

Hildegard's apocalypticism may appear at odds with her life-affirming theology, for which she has become well known. She held them together as functions of the movement of time to the eschaton and of the separation of the cloister paradise from the sinful world outside. If Christians remained faithful to the means—celibacy, crusading, and piety—God would bring the end: a new age of beauty, justice, and peace. Like theologians of the earlier church, she celebrated Christ's incarnation as the sign that the Spirit of God had penetrated all human flesh and sanctified earthly life with incandescent beauty, but, until the end, these were limited to the cloister. The divine had originally inspirited even human sexual life. However, the celibate life was the higher spiritual calling in a sinful age.[32]

To motivate spiritual piety, Hildegard preached sermons of fierce condemnation and judgment of sin. She contrasted the corruption of her age with a vision of Jesus as "the most beautiful of human beings, the very image and essence of beauty."[33] Christians, if they repented and turned away from sin, could be *membra sui pulchri corporis* (members of his beautiful body). Though humanity's full splendor would come only on the last day, even now, in this life, Hildegard enjoined the wise to develop their capacity to see beauty. She affirmed Christ's incarnation as a manifestation of divine generosity and generativity that restored human divinity, rather than God's honor, which was Anselm's preoccupation. Hildegard's high view of humanity suggested that humans could be dignified, powerful beings endowed by God with responsibility for the well-being of all earthly life. Hildegard believed earthly life allowed Christians to grow in wisdom and to move toward the full restoration of "that beauty which Adam lost and which they will now have restored to them."[34]

Hildegard's theology shared Bernard's erotic mysticism of love, but not of Jesus crucified. Instead, she spoke of love as participation in divine *viriditas* (greening power). Hildegard developed a theory of medicine that regarded healing herbs, tinctures, spices and even poisons, when rightfully employed, as gifts from God and assurances that God was constantly coming to humanity's aid. In the mixture of beauty and tragedy that was the condition of life, God's mercy was an omnipresent greening power. She lived out principles of incarnation in her work as a healer, exorcist, scientist, and musician. She, like Bernard, related to those who sought her guidance and care with pastoral concern and love. Her work indicates that, even in the twelfth century and even

among those who saw crusading in religious terms, whiffs of the fragrance of paradise remained in cloisters to those who remained alert to
them:

I, the fiery life of divine essence, flame out over the beauty of the
fields, shine in the waters, and burn in the sun, moon, and stars.
With every breath of air I awaken all things to life.[35]

WHO WILL FORGIVE GOD?

Although nearly all church leaders supported the Crusades, including
accomplished women such as Hildegard, some dissented. The official
church persecuted opponents of the Crusades. Many dissidents, such
as the pacifist Cathars, rejected all or parts of church teaching on the
cross, baptism, the Eucharist, pilgrimage, swearing oaths, and the
death of Jesus. The church launched Crusades against them. In one famous incident in southern France, an abbot and leader of Cistercian
monk-soldiers was asked how to tell a heretic from a true follower of the
church. His reply: *"Caedite eos. Novit enim Dominus qui sunt eius"*
(Kill them all. The Lord will recognize His own), a novel interpretation
of 2 Timothy 2:19.[36] Though relatively few in number—and fewer after
many persecutions—religious opponents to the Crusades reveal what
was at stake in these ancient debates about ethics, war, and the will of
God that still haunt the Christian West today.

Peter Abelard was a critic of crusading and of Anselm's atonement
theology. Abelard had chosen to forgo feudal lordship to become a
teacher and scholar. From Brittany near Norman territory, he was the
eldest son of a nobleman who supported his intellectual aspirations.
Abelard became one of the most original ethical theorists of the twelfth
century and was among its greatest logicians, during a renaissance of
thinking in twelfth-century France.[37] During Abelard's time, Christians, Jews, and Muslims in Spain coexisted in some areas under Muslim rule and where they co-existed they interacted. Christians traveled
back and forth between France and Spain, bringing knowledge of the

sophisticated cultures in Andalusia, where Cordoba, the birthplace of the great Jewish scholar and doctor Moses Maimonides (1135–1204), was the largest city in western Europe. Muslim scholars had preserved the intellectual legacy of Aristotle and kept his books in their libraries, which informed the intellectual renaissance in France. Abelard wrote a dialogue among a Jew, Christian, and Muslim in which the latter, a philosopher, often represented Abelard's views.[38]

Abelard was part of a new system of urban church education outside monasteries and castles. He was a leader in this scholastic movement, which resulted in the founding of the University of Paris in the middle of the twelfth century. Bernard, on the other hand, was an opponent of any form of education that was not catechetical training for priests—discussions of logic and learning for their own sake grieved him. Bernard fiercely attacked Abelard's theological ideas and prosecuted him at the second trial at which he was excommunicated, though Bernard successfully avoided engaging his intellectually adroit opponent in a face-to-face debate. Abelard's style of disputation was the aggressive, competitive mode of debate developed in the schools rather than the contemplative and sermonic style of the monastery. Abelard's polemical gifts earned him powerful enemies, and his ideas challenged the scripture-based, traditional theologies of his day.[39]

Anselm's atonement theology struck Abelard as unreasonable and unethical. He dismantled its logical underpinnings:

> Indeed, how cruel and perverse it seems that [God] should require the blood of the innocent as the price of anything, or that it should in any way please Him that an innocent person should be slain —still less that God should hold the death of His Son in such acceptance that by it He should be reconciled with the whole world.[40]

Anselm's system, he noted, depended on the idea that God lacked something, that his honor had been diminished by human sin and needed to be restored.

Who would forgive God for killing his own son? Abelard asked. He asserted that God's perfection was not diminished by human sin, and his love was eternally boundless even for sinful humanity. The true lover did not need anything from the beloved. This divine generosity was a great contrast to Anselm's view of a God who required a payment to restore his own honor. For Abelard, Jesus's atoning death revealed the already completed and perfect divine love; it did not restore that perfection.[41]

If God did not need the gift of Jesus's death, was there still a reason for Jesus to die? Abelard answered yes. The atonement created a deeper love for God than would have been possible without it. God, being perfect in love and power, had created the best of all possible worlds. However, humanity needed to be transformed from fear to love. This was what Jesus's death made possible—a change of heart. For Abelard, the intentions of the heart mattered above all else; this was his great innovation in moral reasoning. The typical belief of his time was that inner urges or feelings—such as lust, murderous rage, or greed—were sinful. Abelard disagreed. These urges were not sinful in and of themselves. Everyone had such feelings; they were part of being human. Nor were actual acts sinful in and of themselves. If a person murdered someone but had not *intended* to do so, she or he was not culpable. People had to choose consciously to act against God's will. Because intention mattered, simply following divine commandments did not make people virtuous. They had to have an inner change of heart that went beyond mere obedience. People were to be judged moral or immoral based on their *intentions.* Only the final decision to commit an act was blameworthy, whether or not the act was completed. Similarly, even if persons disapproved of their own sinful actions, the fact that they decided to act made them immoral.[42]

Abelard also rejected ideas of original sin. He thought it illogical and beneath God to hold all humanity guilty for Adam's sin: human beings could not be blamed for something inherent in their nature that lacked any conscious intent. Sin was created by human choice and could not be inherited. Moreover, Abelard argued, Adam's sin seemed slight compared to other evils that human beings inflicted on one another. Adam bore responsibility for his own sin, just as every Christian must accept responsibility for her or his own sin. However, humanity still suffered the consequences of Adam's sin, just as people can suffer the effects of others' sins. Adam's sin made the atonement necessary, which helped humanity love more deeply.[43]

To experience the Crucifixion through the Eucharist, contemplation of images, or spiritual disciplines was to feel Christ's deep love. Through his suffering and death, Christ proved the extent of God's love for humanity, a willingness to endure anything on humanity's behalf. Such love was the supreme moral virtue. In seeing Christ's suffering on the cross, Abelard felt, people should be moved in pity to blame themselves, entreat forgiveness, and promise to make amends. One of his hymns for Good Friday captured this sentiment. It reflected on Jesus as he went to his death. Abelard described him as lonely because humanity was too sinful and pitiful to speak to him. "Ours were the sins, ... You take the punishment." Abelard asked that human hearts suffer as deeply as Christ suffered, and, by the grace of compassion, the repentant sinner could be made virtuous.[44] By opening their hearts to the innocent, suffering victim Christ, sinners felt contrition and sorrow, which were signs of conversion. In this contrition, human beings were bound to God by love and justified by Christ's blood.

Redemption occurred when the sinner turned away from the inclination to love self and felt overwhelming compassion for the victim of sin—Christ. Repentant sorrow flowed from selfless love rather than from fear of punishment. Both hope of reward and fear of punishment indicated self-interest, and they compromised pure, selfless love. Salvation restored the virtuous state of the soul, which loved so unselfishly that it would suffer unto death. Christians could then follow the moral example of the self-sacrificing Christ.[45] In taking on human nature and enduring its punishment, even unto death, Christ justified humanity through his blood. With this unique gift of grace, "he has bound us more closely to Himself by love, so that our hearts should be enkindled by such a gift of divine grace, and true charity should not now dread to endure anything for Him." Christ illuminated "our dark shadows and by word and example [he exhibited] the fullness of all virtues," inaugurating a new age of grace. As humanity's moral exemplar, Christ was patient in suffering, steadfast in prayer, perfect in obedience, and selfless in sacrificing for others.[46]

In keeping with the tradition that began with the ninth century Eucharist innovations that Paschasius articulated and Lanfranc sealed, Abelard saw Christ as the victim of human sin. Where Paschasius, Peter Damian, and Anselm emphasized repentance as a terrorized response to the fear of hell's torments, Abelard characterized repentance as brokenhearted love. The Crucifixion was the point of the deepest bonding love between God and sinners—an intense bond that mixed love and guilt, pity and repentance.[47]

Abelard's recognition of the plight of the Jews in his time best exemplified his emphasis on compassion for victims.[48] Abelard was less anti-Jewish than most of his contemporaries because, unlike many of his peers, he avoided characterizing groups of people as inherently evil or condemned. Abelard asserted that Jews and pagans were saved partly through their moral behavior. He arrived at this theological position through his ethics, rather than his theology of atonement. Abelard noted that though the Jews killed Jesus, they did not intend to kill the Son of God. They intended to protect their faith from someone they deemed dangerous to their God. Hence, their intent was not evil, and they were not culpable. This novel interpretation of sin was one reason he was charged with heresy. Seeing Jesus's suffering became, for him, a moral call to recognize injustice:

> To believe that the fortitude of the Jews in suffering would be unrewarded was to declare that God was cruel. No nation has ever suffered so much for God. . . . To mistreat the Jews is considered a deed pleasing to God. Such imprisonment as is endured by the Jews can be conceived by the Christians only as a sign of God's utter wrath. The life of the Jews is in the hands of their worst enemies. Even in their sleep they are plagued by nightmares. . . . If they

want to travel to the nearest town, they have to buy protection with high sums of money from the Christian rulers who actually wish for their death so that they can confiscate their possessions.[49]

Liberal Christian theologians in the nineteenth and twentieth centuries looked to Abelard as an attractive alternative to Anselm, whose theory of the atonement they found appalling. They rejected Anselm's God as unworthy of worship, an unethical father of judgment and harsh punishment, not of love. Abelard's theology seemed refreshingly different. "Come as a Redeemer not as an Avenger, as a God of clemency rather than of justice, as a merciful Father not as a stern Lord," Abelard prayed.[50] Abelard's theology set the stage for what would become liberal theology's basis for ethical action: compassionate pity for those who suffer, mixed with a deep sense of guilty responsibility, and an aversion to explicit uses of power.[51]

However, Abelard's love was a passive form of emotional bonding between sinners (humanity) and their victims (Christ and those who suffered like Christ.). Such a bond, esteemed as good, lacked any power to create, to decide, to resist sin, or to repair harm. He divided the triune God into three dimensions, God the Father as power, God the Son as wisdom, and God the Spirit as goodness. Power and wisdom invoked fear, whereas goodness elicited love, which was powerless:

There are two things that render us subject to God: fear and love. Power and wisdom produce fear, since we know that God is both able to punish and also that nothing is hid from Him. But love has its origin in goodness. If we hold that God is most good, then we have reason for offering Him the greatest love. . . . Goodness, in fact, is not power or wisdom, and to be good is not to be wise or powerful.[52]

Because he focused so sharply on selfless love, Abelard confused innocence and impotence with love and implied that no use of power could ever be loving. By making love an inner feeling and intention,

Abelard lost love as action on behalf of the beloved, based in wise uses of power. He did not see that loving action required power and wisdom. His emphasis on selfless love also meant that his total love for Christ the victim of sin involved embracing Christ's suffering without thought of himself. Abelard takes on Christ's pain. Now, instead of a victim of pain and someone to help him, there are two helpless victims of pain, Christ and Abelard. Abelard's love is the compassionate absorption and multiplication of suffering, not its alleviation. Abelard offers no ethical way to use power to stop harm. Rather, his form of love is unidirectional. Pain is absorbed and passed on by love; love is the contagion of pain.

With his interpretation of Jesus's atoning death, Abelard romanticized suffering and death and bonded the sinner and the victim of sin. Anselm had avoided this direct fusion by locating love and compassion through Mary, an innocent witness and lover, instead of directly via the sinner, the perpetrator of violence against Christ. Both made the death of Jesus his act of salvation, but Abelard, despite his emphasis on ethics, muddied distinctions more thoroughly between perpetrator and victim.

Abelard limited sin, love, and absolution to individual choice and intention, and he turned knowledge of self inward into awareness of intention. A person needed only Christ; relationships with others had nothing to offer that the individual had not already achieved internally. Those injured by sin played no necessary part in the process of repentance because the truly injured party was Christ. Though sinners might make restitution because of their contrition, a change of heart was what mattered. Restitution for those sinned against was not required for absolution.

Abelard acknowledged the inconstancy of the self, but he built his ethics of love on the subjective, self-conscious, self-absorbed self. The ideal of love, he said, was to sacrifice that self in love, so that it was totally given up to the other. Selfless love that required intention, however, begged the question of how love could exist without a self. Intentions and actions required a self-awareness and inwardness that, Abelard said, love sacrificed to the victim before the cross. Abelard's theology, finally, placed salvation on a foundation that constantly disappeared into the other. Hence his system of ethics and love oscillates between intense subjective introspection and self-denial and oblivion. He provided no means to assess conflicting individual decisions about what loving God or one's neighbor entailed, as if a compassionate and "good" person produced self-evidently selfless moral actions. In addition, for Abelard, communities were no longer essential to the process of transforming the sinner or healing the victim. He argued that God absolved individuals who had a change of heart; the church confirmed absolution outwardly, but it had already occurred inwardly through the Spirit. The individual's relationship to God rested in individual subjectivism at its most narrow, a form of self-scrutiny without grounding in anything beyond its own turning on itself.[53]

Abelard inspired intense feelings, even in his own time. His students admired him, and he was, when he met Heloise, a famous teacher in Paris. But Abelard's tendency to use his rapier intelligence to humiliate former teachers in discussion and to recruit students from these same duels alienated many.[54] When the scandal of his relationship with Heloise threatened his career, he turned to a monastic vocation to rehabilitate his reputation. In his monastic community, his morally strict administrative style made him unpopular with his own monks and prompted them to attempt to poison him. A failure at community life, Abelard provided no means for knowing the Spirit found in the community and in a sanctified world and no avenues for an individual to participate in the support of community as an experience of divine power. His peripatetic and difficult career meant his work was poorly preserved. Because of the controversies surrounding him, few others who followed him referred explicitly to his writing. He became much more famous for the tragic story of love in his life.

WHO TRULY LOVES?

The abbess in Abelard's life, Heloise, did not share his ideas of selfless love. Nor did she appreciate Bernard's support of the Crusades and his forms of erotic love. Heloise (c. 1098–1164), who was among the great abbesses of the twelfth century, rejected the spiritual pieties of both eros and war. The affair of Heloise and Abelard has been idealized from medieval times until the present as a great romance brought to a tragic and premature end by his castration. Heloise's own letters to Abelard likely constructed the popular legend and their mythic place in the pantheon of great lovers. Her letters, according to scholar Peter Dronke, place her squarely among the most rhetorically brilliant and compelling ancient writers on love. However, her actual relationship with Abelard was fraught with interesting tensions and differences in their thinking. Her differences from him offer us clues to a remarkable figure of the twelfth-century church whose model of human love resisted violence, false piety, and the romance of suffering. We find in her a voice of integrity, a steady and clear resistance to self-deception or self-pity, an honesty about human feelings of love and loss, and a commitment to responsible uses of power—in effect an antidote to the dangerous pieties erupting from the cloisters of her age. Heloise held, we suggest, firmly to the meaning of living in paradise, here and now.[55]

We know little about her family, only that she was under the care of her uncle Fulbert, who was a cathedral canon in Paris. He sent her as a child to be educated at the Argenteuil convent, near the city, where Heloise proved to be a dazzling student. She rapidly exhausted the learning available to her there and had, by age seventeen, gained fame for her literary knowledge. Her uncle arranged for Peter Abelard, then teaching at the Cathedral School in Paris, to come live with them and become her private tutor. The new educational system made intense demands on its teachers, who spent virtually every waking hour lecturing and grilling their students and functioning as mentors and advisors. The demands of marriage and family interfered with a teacher's success. Some people in church vocations, especially those in cloisters, regarded marriage as, at best, a burdensome distraction and, at worst, an indulgence of the morally weak. So most teachers, like Abelard, were celibate. The young, intellectually gifted Heloise and Abelard, twenty years her senior, became lovers. "Queens and great ladies envied me my joys and my bed,"[56] she wrote years later in her first letter to Abelard. She described his attraction to his many admirers:

> What king or philosopher could match your fame? ... When you appeared in public, who did not hurry to catch a glimpse of you, or crane his neck and strain his eyes to follow your departure? Every wife, every young girl desired you in absence and was on fire in your presence.[57]

They kept their affair secret. Heloise claimed pleasure at being his lover and did not wish to be married, "preferring love to wedlock, freedom to chains."[58] She regarded voluntary love as a stronger bond than marriage, which was a civil contract, not a church sacrament, at the time. Heloise did not regard marriage as a necessarily honorable estate; she observed that women often married for money, which she viewed as a form of prostitution. Unfortunately, however, Heloise became pregnant. Abelard sent her to his parents' estate and arranged for their son, Astrolabe, to be raised there.

Everything started to unravel when her uncle discovered the affair. He was furious with Abelard for having deceived him. In order to appease Fulbert's anger, Abelard proposed that he and Heloise marry but keep the marriage a secret for the sake of his career. Heloise refused. She asked if anything ordained by God, such as sexual intercourse, could be sinful and said that she would rather be his mistress than his wife. "God is my witness that if Augustus, Emperor of the whole world, thought fit to honor me with marriage and conferred all the earth on me to possess for ever, it would be dearer and more honorable to me to be called not his Empress but your whore."[59]

Abelard persisted. Against her own conscience, Heloise decided, out of love for him, to marry him but keep the marriage secret. Her uncle, however, made the marriage public to protect her reputation. Heloise stood by her promise to Abelard and said that her uncle was lying. Her uncle punished her severely, and Abelard, fearing for her well-being, sent her to her childhood convent for safety. This made her uncle even angrier because he believed Abelard had contemptuously cast her away as a worn-out affair. In retribution, Fulbert paid one of Abelard's servants to unlock the door of his sleeping room. Two men slipped in one night, pinned Abelard down, and castrated him.

The castration of a famous teacher was major news throughout Paris. After recovering, Abelard entered monastic life, attempting to start a community he called the Paraclete. Heloise remained at Argenteuil and became its prioress. When its land holdings fell into dispute, she moved her nuns and became head of the Paraclete community, which Abelard left to her when he moved away. In contrast to Abelard, Heloise was a successful administrator, and the Paraclete grew to have five subsidiary communities. She called on Abelard to function as her spiritual advisor through sporadic correspondence between them, and she collected his theological works. It is not clear, however, that they ever met in person after his castration.

Years after the scandal, Abelard wrote an autobiography called "The Story of My Misfortunes," in which he recalled the intimacies they shared:

> Under the pretext of study we spent our hours in the happiness of love, and learning held out to us the secret opportunities that our passion craved. Our speech was more of love than of books which lay open before us; our kisses far outnumbered our reasoned words. Our hands sought less the book than each others bosoms— love drew our eyes together far more than the lesson drew them to the pages of our text. . . . What followed? No degree in love's progress was left untried by our passion, and if love itself could imagine any wonder as yet unknown, we discovered it. And our inexperience of such delights made us all the more ardent in our pursuit of them, so that our thirst for one another was still unquenched.[60]

Abelard repented of his actions and said that his castration was justifiable punishment for having betrayed the trust of Heloise's uncle.

He characterized himself as a predator and said he had manipulated the uncle so as to take advantage of Heloise:

> Utterly aflame with my passion for this maiden, I sought to discover means whereby I might have daily and familiar speech with her. . . . For this purpose I persuaded the girl's uncle . . . to take me into his household. . . . He fell into my desires beyond anything I had dared to hope, opening the way for my love. . . . I should not have been more smitten with wonder if he had entrusted a tender lamb to the care of a ravenous wolf.[61]

Abelard's confession may have been a self-serving attempt to restore his reputation by sounding appropriately repentant and contrite. Heloise never spoke of their relationship as a source of shame, guilt, or dishonor. Nor was she enthusiastic about his suggestion that she should put love for God ahead of love for him. She entered religious life, she insisted, because Abelard asked her to, not out of any particular love for God. "No reward for this may I expect from God, for the love of Whom it is well known that I did not anything." When Heloise read Abelard's interpretation of their affair, she was incensed. She chided him for his self-absorbed self-pity, "the pitiful story . . . of the cross of unending suffering which you . . . continue to bear,"[62] and accused him of not loving her. "Tell me, I say, if you can—or I will tell you what I think and what the world suspects. It was desire, not affection, which bound you to me, the flame of lust rather than love."[63]

Abelard presented himself and Heloise as embodying an ideal of selfless love in their post-trauma relationship. "Each grieved most, not for himself, but for the other. Each sought to allay, not his own sufferings, but those of the one he loved."[64]

Heloise countered that he took her love for granted, but she did not understand love as selfless. Instead, she loved both boldly and with expectations of reciprocity. "If only your love had less confidence in me, my dear, so that you would be more concerned on my behalf! But as it is, the more I have made you feel secure in me, the more I have to bear with your neglect."[65] He failed to acknowledge that he owed her anything, she commented, even a letter! For her, love had a right to make demands; it was grounded in integrity, connection, and care. Abelard, in contrast, idealized a love that was unbounded by obligations, fears of punishment, or hopes of reward. For him, love was internalized as a condition of the heart—not a web of obligations and relationships.

Throughout her life, Heloise remained passionately devoted to and faithful to Abelard. She held out for love shared in the intellectual and spiritual dimensions that she thought Abelard could sustain. Challenging his self-absorption and sense of himself as a victim, she politely but pointedly noted that he used his own suffering to tell another man that his anguish was insignificant in comparison. He paid attention to the suffering of an acquaintance, Heloise noted, but ignored her and the community he founded:

> You cultivate a vineyard of another's vines which you did not plant yourself and which has now turned to bitterness against you. . . . You devote your care to another's vineyard; think what you owe to your own.[66]

In her fiery letter in response to his autobiography, Heloise said she was moved to tears by the recollection of his sufferings but that she regarded his focus on his tales of personal woe as a disruption of his capacity to meet the obligations of love, not only to her but to her community. However, she did not suggest that Abelard needed to be more selfless—she said he did not love enough because he was not open to receiving love. Heloise reminded him that he had neglected to call on others to help bear his burdens: "We beseech you to write as often as you think fit to us . . . with news of the perils in which you are still storm-tossed. We are all that are left you, so at least you should let us share your sorrow or joy."[67] And she herself made a request of him: "I beg you then to listen to what I ask—you will see that it is a small favour which you can easily grant. While I am denied your presence, give me at least through your words—of which you have enough to spare—some sweet semblance of yourself."[68]

Heloise understood compassion as something more than full

identification with another's pain and sorrow and the internalizing of the most abject, abyssal suffering. For her, compassion was more than subjective feeling, weakness, and devotion. Love required action. Heloise admonished Abelard:

> I do not want you to exhort me to virtue and summon me to the fight, saying, "Power comes to its full strength in weakness" and "He cannot win a crown unless he has kept the rules." I do not seek a crown of victory; it is sufficient for me to avoid danger, and this is safer than engaging in war.[69]

In contrast to Abelard, Heloise did not valorize weakness as the perfection of love. Her understanding of goodness was in its power: moral agency based on empathy that was grounded in resistance to violence, the alleviation of pain, acts of healing, and compassion. She did not confuse herself with Abelard's pain, even as she lamented his suffering. Her form of compassion maintained a tensile consciousness that combined empathy for another's pain with sufficient self-possession to be able to offer to someone mired in his own suffering a world beyond pain and helplessness, a world glimpsed in community and companionship—a world that offered, still, the possibilities of paradise. Her love was not afraid to make demands—it expected accountability and responsibility and understood that the best love was mutual. In her understanding and experience, love was a great power. In Heloise, true love lived.

Moreover, Heloise thought Abelard was wrong to dismiss erotic joy. Late in life, she reminded him of the pleasure he shared with her, and she grieved his castration. She did not support his conclusion that their sexual union was an unclean departure from the "spirit of the divines" or that it marred the "beauty of chastity." Abelard had come to assess his castration as a justified act of divine grace, saying, "how justly God had punished me in that very part of my body whereby I had sinned."[70] But Heloise asked him to remember their sensual union and to stay faithfully in relationship to her and to her religious community.

When Abelard died in 1141, on his way to Rome to defend himself at his excommunication trial, he had admirers and students who carried on his intellectual innovations, but few friends. Heloise sent a letter to the abbot at Cluny who was Abelard's superior at his death. She asked for a written statement of her husband's absolution "to be hung on his tomb," and she appealed for a position in the church for their son, Astrolabe.[71] Abelard's body was brought back to the Paraclete and buried there. Heloise ensured that he remained within the embrace of the community where she served as abbess until she died twenty-three years later.

Abelard, Heloise, Bernard, and Hildegard were harbingers of change in Western Europe that would long shape the modern world's understanding of love. Bernard's Christian faith, loving and yearning, pastoral and kind, had a Janus face of hatred for the "other" that sanctified killing for God as a form of love and exalted self-abasement as true love. Hildegard's affirmations of incarnation, the greening of the soul, could be glimpsed in cloistered life, but it could not overcome the horrors of the age. She held the beauty of Christ suspended beyond Bernard's world of Eros and Mars, until it could be fulfilled in the future. Abelard's scholasticism and use of logic were the first glimpse of education independent of the church; at the same time, his ideal of self-sacrificing love as the highest Christian moral achievement encouraged victims to acquiesce to violence in passive, forgiving love. Heloise stood in a long line of Christian dissenters who rejected the worship of violence, the demonizing of sexuality, and the valorization of suffering. She offered a love grounded in honesty, mutual care, obligation, and responsible uses of power.

While Heloise held out for love that was active, earthly, and mutual, Christianity moved increasingly toward love that was submissive, brokenhearted, and perpetually unrequited, always longing for final fulfillment. The church in western Europe had once been in love with the risen Christ, who joined his bride in the earthly garden of delight and helped her tend it. Beginning in the ninth century, she began to doubt her lover and took a violent Lord into her bed, lay with him, blessed him, and finally, took him into the Christian family by marrying him.

Erotically enthralled by her seductive abuser, the church spawned devotional pieties of fear, sorrow, torture, and death, whose progeny journeyed into the world determined to destroy their own shadows and neighbors. To solidify this unholy union, the church sacrificed her former love by killing him repeatedly and partaking of his mutilated body. She told herself that conquest, genocide, and the colonization of Jerusalem were God's will, a holy pilgrimage that would someday, if she sacrificed and suffered enough, deliver salvation, end the violence, and restore her to her first love. This delusional pattern would later carry conquistadors and pilgrims to the Americas and leave Jerusalem as one of the most contested cities on the planet. To assuage her broken heart and bleeding body, she told herself that such a marriage was good and pleasing to God. She hung, suspended in eschatological terror and hope, longing elusively for release, relief, and love's fulfillment. They did not come.

CHAPTER TWELVE

Escape Routes

Because the situation agrees with the beliefs of those holy and
wise theologians and all the signs strongly accord with this
idea, I am firmly convinced that the earthly Paradise truly lies
here, and I rely on the authorities and arguments I have cited.

CHRISTOPHER COLUMBUS,
letter to Ferdinand and Isabella,
from his third voyage

In a 1410 painting from an unknown artist in the upper Rhine area, three
men hang from crosses. They fill the upper half of the tall rectangle,
which has a plain, gold-colored background. Jesus's crucifixion dominates the scene; the thieves' crucifixions are half its size and set a little
behind it. The thieves are tied over the tops of their T-shaped crosses.
The crossbeams point to Jesus's chest, and below the thief on the left,
a red-robed old man holds a long spear piercing Jesus's side. The
blood spurting from the wound is the focal point of the scene of death.
Blood also drips from Jesus's thin, distended arms. A dense mass of
people cram the lower half of the painting and weigh it down.

The roiling crowd jams against the feet of the crosses, obscuring
their bases. A group of women dominates the lower left side. Among
them, Mary, the mother of Jesus, gazes adoringly at his pale, emaciated
corpse while on either side a woman tries to comfort her. On the right,
a haloed young man looks up in adoration at the dead Christ, while a
crowd of men huddle behind him, facing away. At the base of his cross,

a small, kneeling priest looks upward worshipfully. A monklike man wraps his arms around the base of the thief's cross on the right and stares at his tortured, broken body. The chaotic motion of the multitude pulls away from the graceful body of Christ lifting upward. The cross of Christ rises from the bottom of the rectangle, through the mass of bodies, and into the heavens where an angel reaches toward him. His head slumps forward in death, as it does on the Gero Cross.

This painting is a type that emerged in the late thirteenth century and became widespread in the fourteenth and fifteenth centuries. Such images appeared in the many chapels of cathedrals for the devotions of the faithful. Unlike earlier somber and subdued images of the Crucifixion, these images, usually called "Calvary," are marked by a large crowd of spectators—some cheering, some in awe, and some grieving—and great agony for the thieves. In this image, the broken and contorted bodies of the two thieves defy the limits of human anatomy. Both upper torsos loop unnaturally over the top of the cross bar, as if their shoulders have been dislocated. Their arms wrap around the bars as if they had no bones, and their deeply gashed shins bleed.[1]

THE SPECTACLE OF SALVATION

In Calvary images, the two thieves represent the stark choices that the torture and execution of Jesus presented to humanity. The good thief on his right, usually already dead, symbolized penitential suffering to gain redemption. The other, his body displayed as if he were a victim of medieval torture, warned of the punishments awaiting unrepentant sinners. Each thief suffered for a different reason, but both suffered the same agony, and the cauterizing power of violence was holy in both cases. The good thief had suffered enough torment in extremity and, thus, had atoned enough to gain paradise, whereas the bad thief would remain in perpetual hell. For the repentant, the greater the earthly pain, the sooner postmortem peace would arrive. In the thieves, we see humanity defined not as the image of God but as the victims of divine wrath, separated from God by the vast chasm of sin. To reach the shores

FIGURE 12. *Unter den Linden Museum, Colmar, France.*
Upper Rhine. Painting, c. 1410. Crucifixion.

of paradise promised, all had to endure the same punishment. Only the
saints survived, but one could hardly imagine their final destination, except as the end of torment.

Devotional literature encouraged Christians to identify with the
good thief and vilify the bad thief. Through meditation on such images,
Christians could attain "direct imaginative contact with the people and

events of the Passion," as surely as if they had crusaded to the Holy Land.[2] Merging themselves through prayer with images of Calvary, viewers empathetically took on the good thief's pain. His penance revealed their path. Contemplating the art, they became mystical crusaders who had taken the cross and journeyed to the New Jerusalem. The Franciscans, ardent supporters of crusading, particularly cultivated devotion to the good thief, dubbed St. Dysmas. They employed painters and sculptors to create elaborate Passion scenes that encouraged imaginative trips to the Holy Land. Paintings sometimes represented St. Francis of Assisi (1181–1226) as the good thief, his twisted body on the cross spattered by the blood still spurting from the dead Christ's wounded side.[3] When Francis embarked on a penitential mission to convert Muslims, his burning desire to be "torn limb from limb" fueled his journey.[4] His spiritual identification with the suffering of Christ was so intense that his body erupted in stigmata—his own hands, side, and feet reportedly bled.

In 1231, Pope Gregory IX made the torments awaiting the bad thief vividly real. He launched the Inquisition and licensed the church to use torture to discipline heretics and protect the faith. Instead of offering humanity freedom in Christ, the church kept the two divided and sought to control humanity. The Inquisition turned the crusading virtue of killing for God against Europe's own Christians, such as the Cathars. Heretics, who infected the body of Christ, became fagots for fires to purge the church.

Penalties and punishments proliferated for the faithful and unfaithful alike. The torments of the martyrs, like that of the good thief, became standard in devotional images. When we visited the early Christian art collection in the Museu Nacional d'Art de Catalunya in Barcelona, Spain, we saw the familiar images of Christ as Pantocrator, Mary as the Queen of Heaven, and the saints in glory. Then we stepped across the hall into the thirteenth- to fifteenth-century Gothic section. We expected the Crucifixions, but the images of martyrs took us aback. They were depicted being boiled or burned alive, disemboweled, speared, beheaded, stoned, devoured by beasts, tortured on a rack, and taunted by demons. Even with such vivid images, however, medieval theologians doubted that agonizing death was sufficient for gaining paradise. Despite the promotion of penitential suffering, uncertainty reigned. How could anyone know if she or he had performed sufficient penance to gain freedom from hell's terrors?

In the thirteenth century, postmortem paradise began to morph into purgatory.[5] The Second Council of Lyons in 1274 established that "purgatorial and purifying penalties" would take place after death for sinners who had failed to render full satisfaction for their sins before they died.[6] Once Christians died, they still had to be purged of every trace of sin before they could enter the heavenly paradise. The faithful saints sizzled in the flames of martyrdom, while the ordinary faithful stewed in purgatory before their final union with God. The living could pray for the dead, perform masses for them, or buy indulgences to lighten their purgatorial load. The church may have created these practices partly as a pastoral strategy to alleviate fears of hell and to offer hope for life beyond death. However, this focus on the dire fate of the dead meant that the deceased became a spiritual concern and financial burden to their survivors rather than a source of spiritual comfort and help to the living.

As purgatory heated up, the distance between heaven and earth stretched ever wider. Celestial paradise moved so far away that one could reach it only by following a long pilgrimage of penance and purgation. In the *Divine Comedy,* Dante (1265-1321) detailed his visionary pilgrimage through hell and up the steep mountain of purgatory. Earthly paradise, a tiny green patch at the summit of purgatory, was the last stop before stepping off earth to reach God in the stratosphere of angelic light. Guided by Virgil, then Beatrice, and finally by none other than superstar Bernard of Clairvaux, Dante's journey involved human struggle and love—an affirmation that something good in humanity led it toward God. However, the soul could attain union with God only when it left the earth, guided by the matchmaker who had married Eros to Mars.

By the fourteenth century, to die in an agony of torture had become a spiritual ideal. Public spectacles of torture and execution became popular, which the faithful could find repeated in Passion images. Sometimes in Calvary scenes, the bad thief is the only one of the three men left alive, writhing in agony. Often, he appeared to be screaming, his back was broken, and a piece of bone protruded from his cracked, bloody calf. The faithful could adore an image of horror that mirrored what lay just outside the cathedral doors and contemplate the escape promised to them if they could endure such pain. According to scholar Mitchell Merback, religious piety in this period veered "between serenity and shock, craving at once the sweet music of heaven and the stench and horror of Calvary." These polarized oscillations, between violent religious spectacle and loving, devout piety that adored such images, "simplify and vulgarize the holy."[7]

Western Europe became habituated to seeing torture and murder as sacred. Merback suggests that this piety of the outermost extremities of violence as redemptive was unique to western Europe. The agonized *corpus Christi* (body of Christ), seen in images and consumed in the Eucharist host, or bread, made salvific power present.[8] The Latin Mass, murmured by priests with their backs to the congregation, performed the murder of Jesus as a ritual sacrifice to God. Zeal for death's purifying power touched everyone. Executioners killed prisoners during public spectacles as dramatic reenactments of the death of the good thief. Crowds gathered to see hangings, beheadings, and torments on the wheel of torture, to be "eyewitnesses" to Calvary.

Convicted criminals sometimes acted the role of the good thief, expressing contrition, forgiving their executioners, and promising to intercede in heaven for the crowd. One chronicler reported that in Paris in 1411, when a condemned man implored his executioner to embrace him just before killing him, "there was a great multitude of people, who nearly all wept hot tears." Executed criminals had become martyr figures, and witnessing their deaths had become a way to salvation.[9] Spectators watched killings devotedly, as if they themselves were being torn limb from limb and thus escorted directly into paradise. By the mid-fourteenth century in Europe, Merback notes, Calvary was a standard scene on altars and captured a world in deep crisis, struggling both to understand and to escape the terrors of death that swept the continent.[10]

Holy wars and inquisitions were the church's strategies to bring peace, to purify the church, and to hasten the apocalypse. An *apokalypsis* (unveiling) arrived in western Europe in the middle of the fourteenth century, from the east, but it was not what the church had in mind. It began early in the century with rumors of massive pestilence in Asia. Western Christian leaders attributed the deaths of nearly half a million in China to their heathen status. They likened them to the Egyptians in Moses's time and said that plague was God's wrath upon them. Unfortunately for such theologians, by midcentury the pandemic had arrived in Europe from Asia and, within a few decades had marched up the continent from south to north, a fierce, consuming wildfire, fed by ancillary pestilences, famine, war, and climate change.[11]

Devastating plagues had struck before. For example, in 541–542 during the reign of Justinian, a global pandemic struck, and it did not fully subside until around 750. At its peak, the Byzantine historian Procopius reported, the daily death toll in Constantinople reached upward of ten thousand, and it eventually took 40 percent of the city. Reeling in its aftermath, Justinian lost control of the last united Roman Empire. That pestilence also killed, by some estimates, 40 to 60 percent of Europe.[12]

What was new about this fourteenth-century apocalypse? It unveiled the limits of a church whose only spiritual resources for responding to the epidemic were devotional pieties of intense suffering as the saving antidote to acute suffering. This catastrophic apocalypse would bring into being not a New Jerusalem but a new world built on escape routes, as Europeans sought ways to flee not only the plague but also the medieval pieties that sanctified suffering.

From 1347 to 1350, during the height of the plague, the horrors were unrelenting. Decimated communities left corpses to rot where they fell; mothers abandoned sick children; survivors lived in numb horror and exhaustion; and priests fled their flocks in terror, leaving Christians to die without the sacrament of penance. The piety of suffering compassion met its match. The only comfort the church gave its people was to say that such death made them holy, like the saving death of their Lord.

The apocalypse unveiled the limits of Christian ritual and theology. The official church proved impotent to help. It was one thing to meditate on images of Jesus crucified and to participate in Eucharistic rituals that symbolically reenacted his killing and consumed his flesh and blood. It was another to witness unbearable, unfathomable dying all around and live with the constant presence of rotting flesh and blood. It was one thing to believe a distant non-Christian world deserved the extremities of the wrath of God. It was another to watch the most innocent and devout die painfully before one's eyes without even the comfort of absolution.

The loss of priests was of such magnitude that unqualified and poorly trained men were ordained, including even the cowardly and avaricious. Ralph of Shrewsbury, bishop of Bath and Wells, who took refuge during the plague, circulated this in a letter in January 1349:

> Inasmuch as priests cannot be found who are willing out of zeal, devotion, or for stipend to undertake the care of the foresaid places, and to visit the sick and administer the Sacraments of the Church (perchance for dread of infection and contagion), many, as we understand, are dying without the Sacrament of Penance. We urgently enjoin that all who are sick of the present malady should make confession of their sins even to a layman, and, if a man is not at hand then to a woman. Such confession made to a layman in the presumed case can be most salutary and profitable to them for the remission of their sins, according to the teaching and the sacred canons of the Church.[13]

What could the faithful believe except that the world was ending?[14] In the wake of the plague, otherworldly apocalyptic fever spiked. Prognosticators linked symbolic images in Revelation with the events of their time to determine when the world would end and a new one would begin. Some terrified writers mapped the progress of the plague as an apocalyptic progression toward Armageddon, while also trying to find natural causes. Disasters were read as apocalyptic acts of God, steps on a timeline that would culminate in divine destruction of this evil realm before the birth of a new world. Natural and biblical explanations, laid side by side, made possible a "naturalizing" of apocalyptic expectations, a way of reading them not in relation to the descent of the eternally coexisting heaven come to bless the earth, but in relation to the forward-moving unfolding of history that would destroy this miserable world.[15]

Plague was not the only calamity. Decades of bad weather left many without food. The Hundred Years War reduced the peasant population who tilled the land; crop production declined. Other epidemics erupted: dysentery, chorea, influenza, leprosy, food poisoning, scurvy, smallpox, measles, diphtheria, typhus, and tuberculosis. Most were brutal and mysterious killers, and poor nutrition and cycles of starvation magnified human vulnerability. Over the course of the century, wars, epidemics, and disasters killed perhaps twenty million people or half the European population. Neither medicine nor exorcism could loosen the grip of death. The ecological, social, political, financial, and religious systems of Europe went into meltdown—what historian Kirkpatrick Sale characterizes as a "catastrophic collapse of all values."[16] For everyone, daily life was marked by fear, suffering, grief, and the stench of death. The fraying of social fabrics left little whole cloth for the survivors to patch life back together.

The fourteenth century's calamities undermined confidence not only in the church but also in the divine sovereignty it espoused. If such horror was part of a divine plan for salvation, the plan was beyond human comprehension or hope. If the wrath of God had caused such suffering against the faithful, divine power was indistinguishable from evil. If the calamities were outside divine control, no one was in charge of history, and no power transcended human agency in the world, making God irrelevant. Apocalyptic writing began to lose confidence in human abilities to understand the will of God on earth and implied that no power transcended history.[17] The most religiously devout persisted in a variety of futile efforts to halt the march of death, believing the calamities were the result of human sin. In outbreaks of atoning zeal, flagellants roamed towns, publicly whipping each other and people in the streets.

Catherine of Siena (1347–1380), a famous mystic, passionately believed a new Crusade would restore the church's authority and repair the social breakdown and chaos among Christians in Europe. She attempted in 1370 to persuade Pope Gregory XI to launch another Crusade, reiterating the theology that had justified the First Crusade:

> We are divided from one another in hatred and bitterness when we ought to be bound by ties of blazing divine charity—a bond so strong that it held the God-Man nailed fast to the wood of the most holy cross. . . . Make peace! Make peace! Make peace, and turn the whole war against the unbelievers. . . . We shall be freed—we from war and the divisions and many sins, and the unbelievers from their unbelief.[18]

A renewed devotion to killing unbelievers would deliver a gift to those who fought: "this sweet glorious wedding feast . . . full of joy, sweetness, and every delight."

Though she was unsuccessful at persuading the pope, Catherine's pious devotion to war as a response to social breakdown revealed how European society shaped not only a person's religious ideas but also the feelings and sensitivities of the age and its people. One finds in mystics of the time, including Catherine, great literature that extols peace and expresses profound compassion for the suffering of Christ. The bloody underbelly of such piety was the support for wielding the sword for Christ, killing evildoers, and seeking self-annihilation in ecstasies of dying love. To fulfill her desire to sacrifice for God, Catherine starved herself to death.

THE FIRST ESCAPE ROUTE: PRESTER JOHN

People found escape from post-plague Europe in popular tales of far-away lands where peace and health reigned. Among the most famous of such legends were stories of the kingdom of Prester John. In 1366, a collection of fables attributed to Sir John Mandeville began to circulate widely. They described Prester John as a Christian king of a rich, vast land, watered by the rivers of paradise and filled with its blessings. His palace and feasts were sumptuous, and "at all times burns a vessel of crystal full of balm, for to give good smell and odor to the emperor, and to void away all wicked airs and corruptions."[19] John's kingdom was a sign that paradise could still be found on earth, even if it was distant or elusive. As Prester John described his kingdom:

> We welcome all guests and pilgrims from other lands. There are no poor among us. There is no theft nor sycophancy nor greed nor divisions . . . No vice reigns among us. . . . There is an abundance of bread, wine, flesh, and all the things useful in sustaining human life . . . and no beast can enter it which is by nature poisonous.[20]

A fountain filled with "the grace of God and the Holy Spirit" preserved the youthfulness of anyone who bathed there. The tree of life grew nearby. Proper virtues of self-control and moderation required that sexual behavior be restricted to conceiving children.

The geographic location of Prester John's kingdom floated in European imaginations. Some tales placed it in Ethiopia, others in China or India. Still others located it in West Africa, perhaps deep in the interior up the Congo River. The kingdom was close to the headwaters, if not in the very environs, of earthly paradise. Some stories even suggested that Prester John would come to the aid of crusaders if he could be found.

Other versions, however, offered a scathing critique of crusading. John Mandeville's account of Prester John included a contrasting story of a "subtly deceitful" lord named Gatholonabes, who *appeared* to rule a paradise kingdom. His castle had a lush garden and halls adorned with precious jewels and gold. Beautiful young girls and boys offered sexual favors to visitors. The storyteller continues:

> When any good knight . . . came to see this royalty, [he] would lead him into his paradise, and show him these wonderful things . . . and he would let make divers instruments of music to sound in an high tower, so merrily, that it was joy for to hear . . . and then would he make them to drink of a certain drink, whereof anon they should be drunk. And then he would say to them that if they would die for him and for his love, that after their death they should come to his paradise . . . that if they would go slay such a lord, or such a man that was his enemy or contrarious to his list, that they should not dread to do it and for to be slain therefore themselves. For after their death, he would put them into another paradise, that was an hundred-fold fairer . . . and they should dwell with the most fair damsels that might be, and play with them ever-more. And thus went many diverse lusty bachelors for to slay great lords in diverse countries, that were his enemies, and made themselves to be slain, in hope to have that paradise.[21]

Beginning with the earliest Prester John legends that appeared in 1122, the stories offered a dissenting view of crusading. Just as paradise stories functioned in ancient times as critiques of kings and empires, Prester John's paradise critiqued rulers who called Crusades. Scholar Jacqueline Pirenne concludes that the Prester John stories began as a campaign

> inspired by the desire to move away from a Christianity marked by rivalries, ambitions, betrayals, fratricidal struggles, wars, massacres, and misery among the people; they were implicitly subversive, for they sketched a picture of a truly Christian empire.[22]

Despite these critiques, crusading continued to function as a route to paradise throughout the fourteenth century. Holy missions were proposed or pursued to convert Russians in Finland. Crusaders also sought to kill Cathars in Hungary, to defeat heretics in Bohemia, and to fight Muslims in Africa. They fought to regain control of the papal state in Italy, to occupy Cyprus, and to defend Constantinople.[23]

THE SECOND ESCAPE ROUTE: *TERRA PARIAS*

A new breed of crusaders emerged in the fifteenth century, inspired by tales of abundant lands, such as those of Prester John and Marco Polo's fabulous narrative. They set off in many directions looking for paradise on earth, determined to "discover" and colonize the "New World." A belief in paradise on earth inspired them, but they had abandoned hopes of entering it in this life. They believed they could plunder its environs in anticipation of the end of the world. They spoke of seeking fountains of immortality, gold and spices, lush vegetation, and precious jewels. They followed a crusading model of religious pilgrimage and colonization that began with Urban II's First Crusade to the Holy Land and reasserted Christian sovereignty over history, which moved toward a post-apocalyptic new world order. They called that new order many names: paradise, the promised land, the Garden of Eden, the New Jerusalem, the plantation of God, the New Canaan, Zion, and the kingdom of God. They would help make it happen. In the process, they would expand Christian Crusades against Muslims, Jews, and heretics into new territories. They would enslave and transport Africans, killing millions in the process, and they would decimate Native people already living in the "New World."[24]

Early in the century, Prince Henry the Navigator (1394–1460), son of King João of Portugal, launched an expedition down the coast of West Africa in search of Prester John's kingdom. Similarly, Vasco de Gama (c. 1469–1524) carried a letter of introduction to Prester John when he explored the coast.[25] Private financiers funded Henry's six ships, which sailed under the flag of the crusading "Order of Christ"— the surviving remnant of the Knights Templar. The crusaders did not find Prester John's paradise, but they did find gold, ivory, and spices, and they set up trading posts.

In 1444, Henry captured more than two hundred Africans, possibly Muslims, and brought them back to Lagos to sell as slaves.[26] His stated purpose was "to save their souls from perdition." The spectacle of the captured Africans arriving in port excited great interest. When Henry's boats docked in the Lagos harbor, thousands lined the streets to witness the parade of two hundred chained captives. Given their piety of vicarious suffering, the spectators apparently identified the Africans' tribulation with that of the thieves crucified with Christ—a form of penitential torture. As if participating in a ritual reenactment of Calvary, onlookers grieved and rejoiced that the captives, and they with them, were being redeemed from their sins. Before the Africans were auctioned in the public square, Henry presented one of them as a gift to the church. In the *Chronicle of Guinea,* a contemporary report of Henry's 1444 exploits, the writer Zurara described the auction as a harrowing scene in which families were torn apart. Evoking Jesus's cry from the cross and Mary's co-suffering with her son, he commented:

> What heart, however hardened it might be, could not be pierced by a feeling of pity at the sight of that company? Some held their heads low, their faces bathed in tears as they looked at each other; some groaned very piteously, looking towards the heavens fixedly and crying aloud, as if they were calling on the father of the universe to help them.... Mothers clasped their... children in their arms and lay face downwards on the ground, accepting wounds with contempt for the suffering of their flesh rather than let their children be torn from them.[27]

Zurara asserted that, for all its horror, the auction was for a good purpose. His hero Prince Henry had brought the infidel Africans to Portugal to liberate them and convert them to Christianity. Zurara prayed to "All-powerful Fortune":

> Place before the eyes of these miserable people some awareness of the wonderful new things that await them [at life's end] so that they

might receive some consolation in the middle of their present great distress.[28]

The Lagos auction marked the beginning of the Atlantic slave trade. Henry gave the profits to the church, and Pope Nicholas V blessed the crusading mission of the Order of Christ, which would grow rich from its activities in Africa. In his 1455 bull *Romanus Pontifex,* the pope praised Henry as one "greatly inflamed with zeal for the salvation of souls," a "true soldier of Christ" who attacked the enemies of "the life-giving Cross" residing in "remote and undiscovered places. . . namely the Saracens and all other infidels situated in Africa." He granted Henry's nephew, King Alfonso V of Portugal, the right

> to invade, search out, capture, vanquish, and subdue all Saracens and pagans whatsoever, and other enemies of Christ wheresoever placed, and the kingdoms, dukedoms, principalities, dominions, possessions, and all movable and immovable goods whatsoever held and possessed by them and to reduce their persons to perpetual slavery, and to apply and appropriate to himself and his successors kingdoms, dukedoms, counties, principalities, dominions, possessions, and goods, and to convert them to his and their use and profit.[29]

In 1482, the Portuguese built a ninety-seven-thousand-square-foot fortress at Elmina, their key foothold on the coast of Ghana. In 1637, the Dutch captured the Elmina "factory," as it was called, and for the next two hundred and seventy-four years, it imprisoned Africans to ship them to the New World as slaves. Visitors today can see its chapel, built over the women's dungeon. A quote from Psalm 132:14 hangs on a plaque over the chapel door: "For the Lord hath chosen Zion; he hath desired it for his habitation."[30]

Throughout the fifteenth century, mapmakers often included Prester John's kingdom or paradise on their maps. In 1492, the map-maker Martin Behaim drew a vast ocean between eastern Asia and western Europe. On this map, he included a long description of a few Pacific islands from Marco Polo's reports of his travels. The group included Cipangu, an ancient name for Japan. He marked it as having gold.[31] Until the middle of the sixteenth century, medieval navigation mapmakers often drew an island near China, which had a naked man and woman on it with a serpent-wrapped tree between them. Some explicitly labeled it paradise, and all wrote "forbidden" across it. Though they disputed the exact location of paradise, most put it in the east. Designations of the Pishon as the Ganges put paradise very far to the east, off the Asian coast somewhere.

Many medieval navigation maps were "oriented" with east, the direction of paradise, at the top. Oriented maps put Europe in the lower left corner and Jerusalem dead center. This orientation, unnecessary for navigation, reflected apocalyptic ideas that the world's history began with paradise in the east and would culminate in Jerusalem, at the center of the world. Such religious cartographies mapped dreams of conquest and colonization onto apocalyptic and messianic predictions circulating since the Crusades.

Cristobal Colon (he spelled his name many ways, but never, it appears, as Christopher Columbus) was among those who searched for paradise motivated by apocalyptic hopes. Colon set sail in 1492 looking for the home of the Ganges in India, where he hoped to find paradise. He knew paradise was closed, so he intended to take the wealth that flowed from its rivers. He wrote to King Ferdinand and Queen Isabella while on his third voyage and said he had found the earthly paradise.[32] Colon believed a new, Christian age was at hand and he would be one of its messiahs, precipitating Armageddon and a New Jerusalem.[33] With new apocalyptic speculations to inspire him, Colon anticipated the universal conversion of the final days around 1650. He derived his date from the early-fifteenth-century astrological writings of French Cardinal Pierre d'Ailly, the inspiration for many speculations about the timing of the end. Fictions depict Colon as a champion of scientific truth who proved the world was round instead of flat. The idea of the world as a round globe had existed since the time of the ancient Greeks and Romans. Medieval maps reflected knowledge of the earth as a sphere.[34] Colon's goal was fourfold: to reach the East by sailing west, to plunder the riches of the environs of paradise, to bring about the conversion of the "Indians," and to precipitate a Crusade to Jerusalem, where history would culminate.

In a letter urging Ferdinand and Isabella to undertake a Crusade, Colon cited d'Ailly as the source for his prediction of the end date. He claimed divine inspiration for his certainty that this new Crusade would succeed, and the royals may have agreed with him. Ferdinand and Isabella's *Reconquista* (re-conquest) defeated the Muslims in 1492 in Granada, ending centuries of interaction among Jews, Christians, and Muslims in Andalusia, and they reasserted a Christian Spanish crown over all of Spain. The same year, Spain killed or exiled all its Jews, as many as one hundred and fifty thousand in all. The Spanish, who had been for many centuries a multiethnic culture of Christians, Muslims, and Jews, subsequently made pork a national food.

The colonizing search for paradise, like King Midas, destroyed what it touched. Colon took a lush world of life and turned warm flesh into cold cash. He placed his first settlement on Hispaniola, where he found a stable, self-sustaining community of a million or more Taino natives. He built a colony and tried to convert the natives, taking some as slaves. He modeled his first approach to extracting the wealth of Hispaniola on the Portuguese plantations in Africa. He forced the natives into work camps and set impossible quotas of gold, which they could not extract from an island with thin jungle soils.

Bartolomé de las Casas, who arrived in Hispaniola in 1502, would spend his life protesting the cruel treatment of the indigenous peoples the Spanish conquered.[35] His firsthand account of "The Destruction of the Indies" detailed the atrocities:

> They forced their way into native settlements, slaughtering everyone they found there, including small children, old men, pregnant women, and even women who had just given birth. They hacked

them to pieces, slicing open their bellies with their swords as though they were so many sheep herded into a pen. They even laid wagers on whether they could manage to slice a man in two at a stroke, or cut an individual's head from his body, or disembowel him with a single blow of their axes.[36]

Sale comments that from the perspective of Bartolomé de las Casas, what most puzzled the Taino about the strange men who tried to enslave them was "not their violence, not even their greed, nor in fact their peculiar attitudes toward property, but rather their coldness, their hardness, their lack of love."[37] Twenty years after Colon first arrived in Hispaniola, his grim reaping left fewer than thirty thousand survivors. For personal gain and glory and in anticipation of the end of time, he plundered a world that was, by his own descriptions, the closest thing to paradise he could imagine. Colon and many who came after him were restless adventurers, dislocated from home and community life, a pattern long established by crusading. In attempting to escape the diseases, environmental devastations, and wars of Europe, they brought them to the Americas.

The history of the trade in enslaved Africans was bound up from its beginning with the fate of native peoples in the Americas and the crusading/colonizing escape route out of Europe. As Tainos slipped into the jungle or perished, Colon repopulated the labor force with enslaved African people. The first ships arrived in 1502. By the time the slave trade from Africa was abolished three centuries later, ten million to twelve million people had endured the brutal middle passage to provide free labor for the mines, plantations, households, and factories of the Western Hemisphere. Until 1620, only one European migrated to the New World for every five Africans brought by force. Only after 1830 did the percentage of Europeans exceed the percentage of Africans in North America.[38]

After the discovery of the Americas, the location of paradise on maps shifted from Iraq and India to the New World and then disappeared entirely. In 1507, Martin Waldseemüller sketched a map of the world with north at the top, Africa huge, and Europe small. He drew a long narrow strip of land across the Atlantic and marked it North and South America. Across the area where Mexico would be, he wrote *"Terra Parias"* (Paradise Land) and drew it with three unusual-looking rivers. By the mid-sixteenth century, a few maps of the Americas included pictures of slaves and of Europeans shooting native peoples. Paradise had disappeared.[39]

THE THIRD ESCAPE ROUTE: *SOLA SCRIPTURA*

In Basel, Switzerland, in 1529, attitudes toward and uses of images of the Crucifixion took a new turn. A Protestant crowd stormed the cathedral, tore down a crucifix, and paraded it through the city streets. In a parody of Lenten Passion plays, the mob taunted the image: "If you are God, help yourself; if you are man, then bleed." The city had divorced the Holy Roman Empire in 1501 and joined the Swiss Confederacy, becoming Protestant in 1529. Similar desecrations took place across Europe. Protestant Christians carried crucifixes into taverns and drowned them with beer. They threw them to the ground and urinated on them. In 1534 in Ulm, Germany, a crucifix was toppled from Our Lady's Gate, and a protester defecated into the statue's mouth. Elsewhere, sculptures of the crucified were put in stocks, subjected to mock tortures, decapitated, dismembered, and smashed.[40]

What prompted these assaults? For the protesters, crucifixes symbolized the church's fraudulent claim that it offered salvation through holy mysteries, sacraments, penitential rituals, and devotional images. The protesters said the church used dazzling silver and gold reliquaries to entice people into believing that adoring the saints and buying indulgences could free their loved ones from purgatory. The church displayed its worldly wealth with ornate interiors while disregarding the poor. Images of a dead and bleeding Christ dominated remote high altars where priests performed the sacrifice of the Mass, intoning long, elaborate liturgies and prayers in inaudible Latin with their gloriously robed backs to an uncomprehending laity.

Protesters dashed images of the Latin church to the ground as instruments of the devil. For too long, the church had captured people's senses and lured them into idolatry. Wherever the Protestant Reformation spread, a passion for iconoclasm accompanied it.⁴¹ Reformers not only sledgehammered stone crosses and burned crucifixes; they also smashed stained glass, broke altar rails, and whitewashed paintings. They sometimes even prohibited as idolatrous making the sign of the cross on the forehead of a child during baptism.

Charlemagne's Latin church had created an elite and inaccessible Christianity for the laity in a language no one spoke. At the end of the twelfth century, the church had banned vernacular translations of the Bible outright in response to rising dissident movements, such as the Cathars and Waldensians.⁴² Among the first harbingers of Protestant rebellion was the translation by John Wycliffe (1330–1384) of the Bible from Latin into English, which was condemned by the Oxford Synod in 1408. He also criticized many aspects of official medieval Christianity, including the authority of the papacy. Jan Hus (1373–1415) followed a half-century later with a Czech translation of many of Wycliffe's key ideas. Hus was burned at the stake for heresy, but he inspired a reformation in Bohemia, as well as an obscure Augustinian German monk named Martin Luther (1483–1546), who nailed his Ninety-five Theses on the door of Wittenberg Cathedral 102 years after Hus's execution.

The reformers used the Bible as their primary leverage against the Latin church. They translated the Bible in defiance of Rome, printed their translations, and put them into the hands of the laity. Some of them learned not only Latin and Greek but also Hebrew, so their translations were based on the original languages of the two Testaments. This escape route reached warp speed with John Gutenberg's invention of the printing press in Mainz in 1456. Printing made Protestantism as a mass movement possible, and Protestants made printing lucrative.

Waves of reform swept over Europe. Erasmus (c. 1469–1536), the leading Christian humanist of his day, published *In Praise of Folly*, satirizing civil and ecclesiastical corruption. A Dutchman living in Basel as a Roman Catholic, he advised prominent people and corresponded regularly with many others, including Martin Luther. Renaissance poets, philosophers, and artists sought escape from the dismal world of late medieval piety by turning back to the glories of classical Greece and Rome, and Erasmus called for a return to primitive and pure Christianity. His Greek New Testament was the first ever published, and it was the basis for many Protestant translations into vernacular languages.[43] Though he never left the Roman church and sought its reform from within, his work introduced a new angle of vision on "true" Christian community: as the innocent, uncorrupted, and pure Christian world before the fall of the church and society. He inspired Protestant reformers to reclaim this pure, Edenic Christianity of Jesus Christ.

Sola scriptura ("scripture alone") became the Protestant rallying cry: the text alone contained the unsullied Christianity for salvation. Protestants established programs to teach literacy, giving laity their own power to read and interpret the Bible. They focused on preaching to explain the meaning of the text. They believed that hearing the word of God preached opened a new channel of grace and freedom that the medieval church had clogged. By turning from the eyes to the ears, people moved from the corrupting influence of the visual and sensual to the saving word of God. The image oppressed, the word liberated.

Protestant churches were designed with one purpose in mind: audibility of the sermon. Those in France were called auditoria or temples to distinguish them from cathedrals and churches. The *temple de Paradis* (Temple of Paradise) in Lyon, France, was typical. It was a round, wooden, barnlike structure with simple, rough-hewn rafters and clerestory windows. Such temples restored the original, pristine church, according to John Calvin (1509–1564): "It is well known that among the ancients the position of the clergy was in the middle of the temples, which were usually round; and from that position...the things recited could be clearly heard and understood by all who were present."[44] Plaques bearing the dual commandment, called the Law of Love ("Love God with all your heart, and love your neighbor as yourself"), adorned the bare walls. Backless wooden benches focused all eyes toward a large, barrel-shaped pulpit. There was no visible Eucharist table.[45] In churches taken over from the Latin church, stained-glass windows not only presented idolatrous images but also blocked out light needed for reading. Records in 1630 at St. Edmund Church, Salisbury, report a decision to remove stained-glass windows "wherein God is painted in many places, as if he were creating the world . . . for that the said window . . . is very darksome, whereby such as sits near to the same cannot see to read in their books."[46]

Protesters also reformed the Latin Mass, especially its focus on blood sacrifice, which had included an elaborate preparation of the bread and wine to transform them into the real presence of the body and blood of Christ. A priest performed the ritual as a mystical spectacle of execution. According to reformers, the Mass used "magical mumblings." The laity had been included by virtue of the priest acting in their stead and received the full ritual with bread and wine only once a year. The most radical reformers rejected the ritual entirely and stopped performing it; others, such as Ulrich Zwingli (1484–1531), kept most of the Latin but reduced the ritual's significance. He insisted that because Christ was in heaven, the Mass was a symbolic memorial, and that true nourishment lay in the partaking through the word of God— that is, in the sermons.[47]

More moderate reformers, such as Luther, maintained the basic skeleton of the traditional Mass but urged that there be a vernacular liturgy. Service books of various Protestant versions began to appear, which allowed the laity to participate fully. Luther declared that Jesus's last meal with his disciples should be the framework for every Mass, but that any references to the ritual as a sacrifice and to the transubstantiation of the bread and wine into the real body and blood should be removed, and that the laity were to be served both elements at every Mass. He also drastically reduced the elaborate preparations of the elements for the ritual.

Martin Bucer (1491–1551) in Strasbourg, whom Luther had converted to Protestantism, renamed the Mass the "Lord's Supper" and greatly simplified it. He called the priest a "minister" or "pastor" and dressed him in a simple black gown, turned the table toward the congregation, emphasized the participation of the laity and the reading of the Gospels, and focused on preaching as the work of the Spirit. In his *Nine Propositions concerning the Holy Eucharist,* he said the elements lifted up the faithful to a real participation in the body and blood of the *heavenly* Christ, not the crucified. The prayers over the elements did not consecrate the elements as much as did the community partaking of them, who were lifted up to the risen Lord.[48]

John Calvin (1509–1564) stood out among reformers for the intensity of his iconoclastic convictions. Calvin rewrote the Ten Commandments to make "You shall not make graven images" a stand-alone injunction. He compared those who worshipped God through images to latrine cleaners mired in filth. "Hardened by habit, they sit in their own excrement, and yet believe they are surrounded by roses."[49] Though many reform movements emerged in Europe in the sixteenth and seventeenth centuries, including within Roman Catholicism itself, Calvin's legacy especially inspired movements for social reform, which spread from France to Holland to England to New England and South Africa. Calvinists sought to remake institutions in order to restore God's intention for Creation, to renew primitive Christianity, and to advance toward a new heaven and a new earth.

Calvin was, in many ways, an unlikely candidate to lead a religious movement. By his own admission, he had a bashful, "timid, soft, and pusillanimous disposition"—very unlike the earthy, voluble, and warm Luther.[50] Born a generation after Luther, he was the second son of the devout Jeanne Le Franc of Cambrai, who died while he was young, and of Gérard, a staff official in the Cathedral at Noyon, France. Calvin grew up among the upper classes his father served, with their aloof diffidence and reserve. He studied theology at the University of Paris, then law and classics at Orléans and Bourges. As a young man, he was "obstinately devoted to the superstitions of Popery," according to his own account, until "God by a sudden conversion subdued and brought my mind to a teachable frame." Having "received some taste and knowledge of true godliness," he visited reformers in France, where he became well known, and settled for two years in Basel to study theology and to master Hebrew.[51] While there, he wrote his *Institutes of the Christian Religion,* the first of many editions, which increased fivefold over the years. He wrote it to rally sympathy for executed Huguenot reformers.[52] In 1536, he was on his way to Strasbourg to fulfill his dream of being a scholar and writer for the Reformation when a war blocked his route, requiring him to detour through Geneva overnight. William Farel pressured Calvin to stay and help him reform the city. Calvin noted, "Whilst my one great object was to live in seclusion without being known, God so led me about through different turnings and changes, that he never permitted me to rest in any place, until, in spite of my natural disposition, he brought me forth to public notice." Apart from a stint in Strasbourg in exile, Calvin remained in Geneva until his death in 1564, struggling to make the city into the anti-Rome.

When Geneva became Calvinist in 1536, the reformers captured its cathedral, the Church of St. Peter. They stripped its interior of all statues, paintings, tapestries, and precious metal ornaments. The church still dominates the skyline of the city of Geneva, which sits at the southwestern tip of the crescent-shaped Lake Leman, the largest lake in central Europe. The Rhone glacier feeds its sparkling waters, and the snowy Alps ring its perimeter. When we visited the Church of St. Peter, its gray stone walls, plain wooden pews, and solitary high pulpit suggested to us an austere world of iron and ice. One of our religion professors once characterized this grim view of sensuality by imagining that when Calvin walked to the church every morning he held his Bible up to shield his gaze from the stunningly beautiful lake. As he walked, he said to himself, "Don't look! Don't look!"[53]

THE FOURTH ESCAPE ROUTE: RESURRECTING EDEN

We think, however, Calvin may have peeked occasionally. He believed paradise was still in this world. In contrast to Martin Luther, who thought that paradise was completely lost in the Flood and that the *imago Dei* in humanity drowned with it, Calvin held that earth "still bears the traces of this largesse of God."[54] Just as paradise was disappearing from navigational charts, Calvin introduced a map of Mesopotamia in his Genesis commentary, indicating signs of the location of paradise. The Bible he published also had a map with Adam, Eve, and a tree on it. Calvin explained that the world, as the handiwork of divine creation, was intended as good, and God's elect must care for it. Calvin believed that although sin had closed paradise, its original location could still be determined.

> For although I acknowledge that the earth, from the time that it was accursed, became reduced from its native beauty to a state of wretched defilement, and to a garb of mourning, and afterwards was further laid waste in many places by the deluge; still, I assert, it was the same earth which had been created in the beginning.[55]

In his Genesis commentary, Calvin followed this passage with a detailed discussion of the location of the four rivers in Mesopotamia. He concluded with a map to clarify the probable location of paradise somewhere near Babylon and Seleucia—present-day Iraq. There, he said, was "a region pre-eminent in beauty, in the abundance of all kinds of fruit, in fertility, in delicacies, and in other gifts."[56] This location bore the residues of paradise to show divine benevolence and the original goodness of the Creation.

Calvin's map of paradise was unique in mid-sixteenth-century Bibles and commentaries, but visual guides to locating paradise on earth soon became popular in Bibles. His use of a map staked out a theological position that rejected allegorical interpretations of paradise, which said that paradise was inner and spiritual or that it was not earthly at all but heavenly. Calvin asserted that paradise was materially real and on the earth, and it was the reason humanity should live as well as it could in this life. In a 1559 sermon, Calvin insisted:

> Thus, since the place is marked for us on earth, what good is it to fantasize and say that paradise is in the air or the circle of the

moon, or that it was eternal life? But the intention of Moses, or rather of the Holy Spirit, was to specify in full the goodness and love of God toward humanity.[57]

Calvin's map of paradise illustrated that the Creation manifested God's blessing and love. Both the dignity of humanity and the gracious providence of God were aspects of earthly life. For all of Calvin's austerity, he held that creation everywhere gave humanity a taste of God's goodness:

> We see, indeed, the world with our eyes, we tread the earth with our feet, we touch innumerable kinds of God's works with our hands, we inhale a sweet and pleasant fragrance from herbs and flowers, we enjoy boundless benefits. . . . There dwells such an immensity of divine power, goodness, and wisdom, as absorbs all our senses.[58]

Calvin affirmed that God could be known through the created world. "Let the world become our school if we desire rightly to know God," he said.[59] However, Calvin's observations of life and his attempt to reform an extremely unruly city led him to conclude that discovering God through the world was no simple matter. Human life was fraught with abuses of power and knowledge that confounded the human capacity to "taste and see that God is good." His commentary on Genesis laid the blame at the feet of Eve, who instigated the fall and exemplified the human dilemma. She was seduced by the devil "to know more than is right, and more than God allows" when she looked with desire on the tree of the knowledge of good and evil.

> This impure look of Eve, infected with the poison of concupiscence, was both the messenger and the witness of an impure heart. She could previously behold the tree with such sincerity, that no desire to eat of it affected her mind; for the faith she had in the word of God was the best guardian of her heart, and of all her senses. But

now... she corrupted both herself and all her senses, and depravity was diffused through all parts of her soul as well as her body.[60]

Eve had poisoned life in the present world. Humanity lived in a state of conflict, compromise, and struggle, longing for a paradise that could be remembered but not fully regained, glimpsed but not quite grasped. Calvin's remedy for this dilemma was administered through the precise channels by which Adam and Eve lost paradise: hearing and eating.[61] The Bible and the Lord's Supper were the divine means of grace.

The Bible provided a mirror "in which it was possible to perceive and contemplate human sin and curse, just as in a mirror people commonly look at the dirt and stains of their faces."[62] It made humanity's fallen, depraved, and helpless state visible, and it revealed both God's wrathful punishment and deliverance. Calvin wrote commentaries on every book of the Bible except Revelation, which he claimed not to understand. He understood the Hebrew Bible as the harbinger of divine mercy that culminated in Jesus Christ. He did not set Law and Gospel in opposition. He asserted that even the codes given in the books of Moses were a gift of God's grace and benevolence. The gift of the entire Word enabled humanity to be more moral.

Calvin's revised version of the Eucharist enacted the battle with sin and the proper training of the senses. He adopted Bucer's Eucharist in most respects, including the community's spiritual elevation to the risen, heavenly Christ. However, he dispensed with the prayers of intercession and thanksgiving prior to the meal and substituted an exhortation that was a "fencing of the table":

> We have heard, brethren, how our Lord celebrated his Supper
> with his disciples, thereby indicating that strangers, and those who
> are not of the company of the faithful, ought not to be admitted.
> Therefore, in accordance with this rule, in the name and by the
> authority of our Lord Jesus Christ, I excommunicate all idolaters,
> blasphemers, despisers of God, heretics, and all who form private
> sects to break the unity of the Church, all perjurers, all who rebel

against parents or their superiors, all who are seditious, mutinous, quarrelsome or brutal, all adulterers, fornicators, thieves, ravishers, misers, drunkards, gluttons, and all who lead a scandalous and dissolute life. I declare that they must abstain from this holy table, for fear of defiling and contaminating the holy food which our Lord Jesus Christ gives only to his household of believers.[63]

Calvin, like Bucer, also rejected the idea that the Mass was a reenactment of the killing of Jesus, which he associated with the "devilish" Latin church. Following Paul, he insisted that Christ was crucified only once, so his death could not be ritually repeated. Calvin emphasized its importance, however, as a reminder to Christians of their sin:

> We must necessarily be under great trouble and torment of conscience, when we consider who we are, and examine what is in us. For not one of us can find one particle of righteousness in himself, but on the contrary we are all full of sins and iniquities.... It follows that the wrath of God is kindled against us, and that none can escape eternal death. If we are not asleep and stupefied, this horrible thought must be a kind of perpetual hell to vex and torment us.[64]

Christians should prepare for the Lord's Supper by examining themselves and arriving at a state of sober self-knowledge. Though none was free of sin, and God graciously forgave, Christians were to approach the Lord's Table with humility and a resolve to improve. Calvin emphasized that Jesus suffered pain and humiliation for humanity. "He bore the weight of the divine severity ... wounded and afflicted by the hand of God; he experienced all the manifestations of the wrath and vengeance of God, so that he was forced to cry out because of his pressing distress, "Father, Father, why hast thou forsaken me?"[65] Unlike the tone of gratitude and celebration that characterized early Eucharists, Calvin's Lord's Supper began with the atoning death of Jesus as the preparation for what was promised. Those who partook were to remember the depths of pain and humiliation that Jesus endured on their behalf. Calvin excommunicated sinners instead of thanking God for salvation. Paschasius's terrible judge prepared communicants to partake of life among the elect.

Calvin made his Eucharist central to his moral reform of the city of Geneva. Against the Latin practice of offering the full Eucharist only once a year, he argued for a weekly Eucharist. Not attending services became a punishable offense in Geneva—by all accounts a rowdy, "free-swinging city" when Calvin arrived there.[66] Other prohibitions included gambling, adultery, dancing, drinking, and disruption of services, along with heresy and attempts to reinstate medieval church practices. Calvin emphasized the abyssal nature of human depravity— both his sister-in-law and stepdaughter were convicted of adultery.[67] Though he believed that the Holy Spirit, imparted at baptism, sealed the grace of God for the elect, Christians in present time had to work for sanctification as they lived between the pristine past and promise of heavenly glory to come after death or at the end of time. One reason Calvin was expelled from the city after less than two years there was resistance to his weekly Eucharist. When he returned after a few years of exile in Strasbourg, he reluctantly compromised with the city rulers by offering Eucharist four times a year.

Calvin intended for Geneva to manifest the primordial and millennial kingdom of God in its theocratic governance, its religious practices, and its culture. Geneva became a refuge for many reformers throughout Europe who had been persecuted by Rome. These exiles carried Calvin's ideas home when the coast was clear. Calvin's vast body of correspondence with other reformers also spread his reforming ideas. He thought that earthly rulers should create godly societies and that if they did not, Christians should resist and work to form a better world. Though he supported a state tied to the church, Calvin also held apart areas of responsibility to form a system of checks on abuses of power, not only between legal magistrates and church leaders, but also among various categories of church leadership and its treasury. Pastors administered sacraments and preached. With the elders, they admonished the erring. Teachers trained pastors and maintained correct views in the church. City magistrates were the elders, who appointed one another and governed the moral and religious life of the community. Finally, the deacons controlled the finances of the church and managed care for the poor and ill. Although the leaders of the church and city would ideally share responsibility for enforcing moral guidelines and prosecuting crimes, Calvin kept excommunication solely under church authority.

Calvin inspired his followers to imagine God's kingdom to be the antithesis of the wealth, power, and corruption of the Roman church. Whether the Calvinist religious imagination looked forward to the millennial arrival of God's final reign or backward to the restoration of the original paradise, the elect were to serve God by demolishing sinful things in this world and working to create life that was newly obedient to God's word. In Calvin's view, reform was a gradual process. The New Jerusalem would not be built in a day, nor would it simply be the work of human hands. Its establishment would never be complete on earth, but human effort now would prepare for its coming:

> The Kingdom of Christ is on such a footing, that it is every day growing and making improvement, while at the same time perfection is not attained, nor will be until the final day of reckoning. Thus both things hold true—that all things are now subject to Christ, and that this subjection will, nevertheless, not be complete until the day of resurrection because that which is now only begun will then be completed.[68]

When reformers called the pope the Antichrist, the epithet was more than an insult: it was a theological claim. The arrival of the Antichrist, in the form of the pope, meant that Satan's power had reached its zenith and that God would depose him. Christ would begin his millennial (thousand-year) reign on earth, and God would bring the final judgment and liberation of the earth from Satan's bondage. The new heaven and new earth would finally arrive. Calvinists, especially, inspired by an apocalyptic, reforming zeal, traveled to many parts of the world to realize their hopes.

In seventeenth-century England, Calvinist Puritans pursued social reform relentlessly. They condemned the rise of the fraudulent Roman church and an oppressive monarchy. They denounced the small number of landowners who controlled the lives of tenant farmers, took the fruits of their work, and kept them in poverty. They called church officials and civil authorities agents of hell. They railed against debtors prisons, accusing them of being the devil's work, and demanded release of the captives in Jesus's name. They even tried to instigate a revolution.

Calvinist Puritan Oliver Cromwell mustered his New Model Army to establish a new commonwealth in England, by force if necessary. Cromwell said, "I find this only good, to love the Lord and His poor despised people, to do for them, and to be ready to suffer with them, and he that is found worthy of this hath obtained great favor from the Lord."[69] *The Soldiers Catechism* of 1644 offered biblical justifications for "all that have taken up Armies in this Cause of God and his People."[70] Puritan soldiers celebrated their victories as fulfillment of God's command. Cromwell described one triumph: "Our men by the blessing of God . . . beat them from their standing. We killed about a thousand of them, and took, as we believe, about two thousand prisoners."[71]

John Milton, an ardent Puritan, served in Cromwell's government and defended the Puritan revolution. Along with other radical Puritans, he believed paradise could be restored through the destruction of the edifices and systems with which Satan had polluted the earth—most particularly the Catholic Church and the English monarchy. In Book I of *Paradise Lost,* Milton described how, at Satan's behest, a parade of idols issued from the pit of hell. The capital of Satan's realm was "Pandemonium" (demons everywhere)—a name Milton coined from the Greek.[72] All the depravities of popery were Satan's work:

> *By falsities and lies the greatest part*
> *Of Mankind they corrupted to forsake*
> *God the Creator . . .*

With gay Religions full of Pomp and Gold
And Devils to adore for Deities.[73]

Milton praised the Puritans who beheaded Charles I in 1649. However, in the aftermath of the English Civil War, reforms did not arrive. Cromwell made alliances with the old structures of power and abandoned the platforms for social reform that had inspired his army. Many radical Puritans felt betrayed. Religious dissent multiplied, and sects of Ranters, Levellers, Diggers, and Seekers continued to advocate for radical change. Within only a few years of publishing *Paradise Lost* (1667), Milton offered a chastened religious vision in his poem *Paradise Regained* (1671). Paradise could be restored, he suggested, through means other than bloodshed and government. Whereas in *Paradise Lost* Christ freed humanity from Satan's bondage by offering himself to be an atoning sacrifice, in *Paradise Regained* Christ defeated Satan through moral strength.[74] Struggling with Satan in the desert, Christ rejected the temptations of wealth and earthly power. In this way was

the Tempter foil'd
In all his wiles, defeated and repuls't,
And Eden rais'd in the wast Wilderness.[75]

Milton's turn to personal ethical strength as the route to paradise appeared in other mid-seventeenth-century writers—a century saturated with paradise literature.[76] A rebirth of enthusiasm for early Christian writings neglected during the medieval period influenced them as they had Milton. Writers often cited the Eastern thinker John of Damascus (c. 675–749), who viewed the human soul as a paradise inhabited by God, though they failed to notice that he also loved icons. Ephrem and Basil (330–379) also enjoyed a revival, as did Pseudo-Basil's homily on paradise. The homily pictured paradise as both a place and as an allegory for the realm of virtues: kindness, generosity, peaceableness, patience, and love. The Cambridge Platonist Henry More (1614–1687) published *Conjectura Cabbalistica*, in 1653, an allegorical interpretation of paradise. Like Ambrose, he associated the four rivers of paradise with the cardinal virtues. The tree of life, standing in the midst of the garden, represented the immortal human soul, and the tree of knowledge represented the human will. More also reinscribed Ambrose's view of gender. The primary challenges of life, in the view of the Cambridge Platonists, were to elevate masculine intellectual virtues and subjugate female sensuality.[77] In this way, virtue, in a properly ordered society in which men exercised dominion over women, could restore paradise.

Women had a different view. Once spiritual authority was freed from popery, clerics, and kings and resided in reading, hearing, and understanding the Word, any Christian might claim the authority of the Spirit, and many women did. Women emerged as preachers, prophets, and mystics. They published, agitated, witnessed, and started religious movements. In May 1649, arguing based on the Puritan principle that "all men were naturally born free, being the image and resemblance of God Himself," the women petitioned Parliament for their rights, declaring:[78]

We are assured of our Creation in the image of God, and of an interest in Christ, equal unto men, as also of a proportional share in the Freedoms of this Commonwealth.[79]

Female Christian reformers claimed spiritual power to petition for changes in public policy, especially on behalf of the poor, children, and prisoners.[80]

During this same era, people began to search for the original language of paradise—the pure language that Adam and Eve spoke in the garden before the Fall. Finding the language of Eden could hasten the millennium or return humanity to Eden's perfection. Some rejected the reigning theory that Adam and Eve spoke Hebrew, or perhaps Dutch. New theorists proposed finding the language of paradise farther east—in China, or better yet in the language of the Native Americans who inhabited the New World and lived closest to the state of "primitive man."[81]

In their longing for the original, pristine innocence of Eden and their ambition to hurry the millennium, nothing would prove more enticing to the English Puritans and radical reformers than creating the New World across the waters of the Atlantic. The New World became their consuming project, and their theology of paradise-past and paradise-to-come shaped the founding myths of North America. On the soil of what would become the United States, the compelling power and tragic limits of iconoclastic Protestantism unfolded. The hopeful European Protestants would seek to regain paradise by wiping away Satan's old world and claiming Christ's new one—by any means necessary.

The Puritans' master narrative envisioned them "crossing the Jordan" (the Atlantic) and occupying the "Promised Land" (New England). They thought of themselves as like the Israelites, a covenantal community, and they vowed to live in a righteous way in a land given to them by God. They united in the belief that the Protestant Reformation signaled the approach of the millennial reign of Christ, which would occur before the Final Judgment and the dawn of the New Creation. Edward Johnson (1598–1672), a Puritan who made the journey, said:

> Christ, the glorious king of his churches, raises an army out of our English nation, for freeing his people from their long servitude under usurping prelacy. And because every corner of England was filled with the fury of malignant adversaries, Christ creates a new England to muster up the first of his forces.[82]

More than twenty thousand Puritans crossed the Atlantic between 1620 and 1640 to be this apocalyptic army. They organized Plymouth Plantation and the Massachusetts Bay colonies of Boston, Charlestown, Dorchester, Roxbury, and Watertown. Thwarted in England, they set sail for the wilderness, excited that a pristine world awaited them across the sea.[83]

> The whole earth is the Lord's garden and he hath given it to the sons of men [to] increase and multiply and replenish the earth and

subdue it. . . . Why then should we stand starving here for the places of habitation . . . and in the meantime suffer a whole Continent as fruitful and convenient for the use of man to lie waste without any improvement.[84]

So spoke John Winthrop in 1629. He and other Puritans placed New England into a master narrative of primordial Creation fallen to sin and restored through millennial hope and holy war. As Edward Johnson exclaimed:

Oh yes! Oh yes! Oh yes! All you, the people of Christ that are here oppressed, imprisoned and scurrilously derided, gather yourselves together, your wives and little ones . . . be shipped for his service, in the western world. . . . This is the place where the Lord will create a new heaven and a new earth in new churches and a new commonwealth together.[85]

As the Puritans of New England settled into the New World, the constant flow of ships and news back and forth across the Atlantic would bring waves of militant, disillusioned, feminist, and pacifist reformers to North America. Each would form movements that imprinted themselves on land and people they called "wilderness," "the New Canaan," paradise, and "the Promised Land." They were thrust on North American shores by the trials and tribulations, the ambitions and hopes, the disruptions and disasters, and the visions of paradise that were their particular escape routes from Europe.

Pursued as an escape route, paradise was not a sacred place where Christians received with gratitude the wonders they discovered. Those seeking to escape to paradise moved too fast and too far into the future to find rest in this life and this world, or redemption among its peoples and places. In the New World, many escape routes would converge. It would not be a harmonic convergence.

CHAPTER THIRTEEN

Weeping Encounters

The chief began to weep over Perrot's head, bathing it with
his tears, and with the moisture that dripped from his mouth
and nose.

IOWA INDIAN welcome to
a French explorer, winter 1685

You tell us fine stories, and there is nothing in what you say
that may not be true; but that is good for you who come across
the seas. Do you not see that, as we inhabit a world so different
from yours, there must be another heaven for us, and another
road to reach it?

HURON INDIAN question to
a Jesuit missionary, 1635

The Algonquin peoples of the seventeenth century lived in the eastern coastal woodlands and the areas around the Great Lakes, fished the
waters, hunted in the forests, and farmed the rich soil. They used the
word "manitou" to convey their sense of life-giving forces everywhere.[1]
Often translated as "spirit," manitou referred to the distinctive powers
they experienced and respected in each living thing, in the environment,
and in human beings. Plants, rocks, birds, insects, animals, places, and
humans all had spirits that could be understood. Careful, astute observation of the spirit-filled world around them and reflection on such in-

formation guided their behavior and led to the accumulation of wisdom passed down through generations.[2]

The Algonquin used ritual to shape perception and meaning and to orient them to their world. Through rituals, they cultivated their awareness of the precise qualities of things and events, so that life could be negotiated with skill and sustained. They respected many ways of knowing truth: trances, dreams, and ecstatic experiences, in addition to practical observation. Rituals grounded their daily life and their trade relationships, political alliances, and approaches to war and peace-keeping.

Especially important to peaceful relationships was the Algonquian Feast of the Dead. The privilege of being the host tribe rotated among the groups, and the gathering began with each tribe making a ceremonial entrance. Over the course of several days, they performed rites to lament their dead. Then the tribes exchanged gifts, feasted, and danced. Scholar Robert L. Hall suggests that the main purpose of the ritual was "to establish, reestablish, or consolidate friendly relationships between villages or between nations."[3] Feasts of the Dead sustained intertribal treaties and trade. Through the gatherings, they shared lamentation and transformed loss into bonds of connection.

Lamentation for the dead also played a role in how Algonquin and many other native groups responded to strangers who arrived in their territories. They honored visitors with a ritual "weeping greeting" or "welcome of tears." In some versions of this lamentation ritual, the tribal members literally made the visitors wet from the flow of their eyes, noses, and mouths. Sinister magicians used such intimate bodily fluids to gain power over others; when the tribal members offered them voluntarily, they indicated their willingness to be vulnerable to the visitors and showed them both trust and respect. An adoption ritual accompanied this outpouring of lamentation to welcome the newcomers as replacements for the tribe's dead and to seal bonds of mutual assistance. A friendship feast and dancing followed. They concluded the ceremony with the smoking of tobacco from a ritually dressed pipe of peace. Such rituals were led by various leaders of a tribe, including chiefs and warriors, as well as women. The visitor would then be regarded as a member of the group. Indians also greeted old friends with weeping, using a ritual that mixed the joy of welcome with the sadness of the memory of those who had died since the friends had last met.

Lamentation/adoption rituals also were used in wartime. When tribes lost members in battle, they sometimes raided their enemies and took captives in retribution. They might torture some captives and kill the injured or weak, but they adopted others to replace their war dead.

When Indians encountered the Europeans, they employed their rituals to respond to the newcomers. French traders and explorers received the welcome of tears as they traveled up the St. Lawrence Seaway and across the Great Lakes. On one journey, Pierre Radisson and Medard Chouart des Groseilliers reported that an Eastern Dakota group in what now is Wisconsin stripped them and clothed them in buffalo and beaver skin cloaks. Then a group of men surrounded them and wept over their heads until they were wet, offered them the peace pipe, and perfumed them with its smoke.

A strategic ceremony of adoption took place in 1607 Virginia. Chief Wahunsenaca, leader of the Powhatan confederacy, was building alliances with other tribes as protection from the Spanish colonizers who had landed in Florida and ravaged Indian towns. He chose to employ the English settlers in the Jamestown colony as allies against the Spanish. As part of this strategy, Wahunsenaca welcomed Captain John Smith and made him a *werowance* (minor chief). The ritual took four days, during which time the Powhatan "captured" Smith and adopted him and, through him, the members of Jamestown. Wahunsenaca would have led the elaborate ritual, and if his beloved young daughter, Pocahontas (c. 1596–1617), "saved" Smith, she was performing an element in the adoption ritual, not a spontaneous act of love. Smith's report of the ritual indicates he failed to comprehend its meaning and the mutual obligations it entailed.[4]

Wahunsenaca expected the English to behave as members of the Powhatan confederacy. But the Jamestown colonists had other aims. They used their guns to frighten and coerce Indians as a means to gain land and take goods. They then left a few beads or copper jewelry and claimed to have "traded" for what they took. Wahunsenaca called the English to account for their failure to meet the kinship obligations implied by the ritual of adoption. In 1609, according to Smith, the chief admonished them:

> Why should you take by force that from us which you can have by love? Why should you destroy us, who have provided you with food? What can you get by war? We can hide our provisions, and fly into the woods; and then you must consequently famish by wronging your friends. What is the cause of your jealousy? You see us unarmed, and willing to supply your wants, if you will come in a friendly manner, and not with swords and guns, as to invade an enemy.... I, therefore, exhort you to peaceable councils; and, above all, I insist that the guns and swords, the cause of all our jealously and uneasiness, be removed and sent away.[5]

The opportunity for mutual alliance was lost on the Jamestown English. In 1612, the English abducted Pocahontas and demanded a ransom of weapons as part of a plan to subdue the Indians. Despite two payments, she was never released. The English killed Pocahontas's husband and sailed off with her. She was baptized, raped, and impregnated, forced to marry a coarse English commoner, and taken to England to raise money for the Virginia Company, which had financed Jamestown. According to Powhatan tribal history, she was poisoned on the return voyage; she was taken back to England for burial, and the English kept her young son. Wahunsenaca, overwhelmed with grief, died in 1618. More and more colonists arrived and killed his people for their fertile land. In 1622, the Powhatans rose against Jamestown and massacred more than three hundred settlers.

A LAMENTATION WELCOME

On the heels of the English at Jamestown, the Pilgrims arrived at Plymouth. Then waves of Puritans from England came to found the Massachusetts Bay Colony. The colonists may have heard about the attractiveness of the region from John Smith, who had described his travels in April 1614 through "the country of the Massachusett, which is the paradise of all those parts, for here are many isles planted with corn, groves, mulberries, savage gardens, and good harbors."[6]

Before the arrival of the Pilgrims, between 1616 and 1619, a major epidemic struck the Northeast coast. It killed up to 90 percent of the Abenaki, Pawtucket, Massachusett, and Wampanoag tribes. The plague had arrived with the European traders. In November 1620, the grieving and devastated Wampanoag watched from a distance as the English Pilgrims, among the most separatist and persecuted of all Puritan sects, arrived in one of the harbors of "the paradise of all those parts." The Wampanoag people had reason to be wary. An English shipmaster named Hunt had recently landed on the coast and captured nearly thirty people, whom he sold as slaves. A Pawtucket named Tisquantum, living with the Wampanoag, had been captured and enslaved and escaped after nine years in Spain and England.

The Wampanoag kept out of sight for months and observed the newcomers. Pilgrim search parties explored the coast and the woodlands but encountered no Indians. While "ranging and searching," Pilgrims came across two houses "which had been latterly dwelt in, but the people were gone." *Mourt's Relation,* a journal kept by Pilgrim Edward Winslow, described them as being made with tall saplings bent into the ground. In them, they found "wooden bowls, trays and dishes, earthen pots, handbaskets made of crabshells wrought together, also an English pail." They found traces of recent habitation including fresh deer heads and fish. In addition, they found baskets of parched acorns, silk grass, tobacco seed, and "sedge, bulrushes, and other stuff to make mats." They took what they needed, leaving the houses standing.[7]

The Pilgrims also stumbled upon a store of corn and helped themselves to many bushels. They discovered hunting traps and tracked the forest paths in search of villages. They rummaged through grave mounds and collected items they found useful. In some areas, they found signs of the devastating epidemic—remains of unburied bodies. One Pilgrim journal from the time noted that the "bones and skulls made such a spectacle . . . it seemed to me a new found Golgatha."[8] Entries in Winslow's journal suggested that the Pilgrims were both eager and terrified to meet the Indians. The Pilgrims lived in hope of help and fear of attack from "the savages" whose traces kept them alive. They were grateful for the stores of corn they found and took, "purposing, so soon as we could meet with any inhabitants of that place, to make them large satisfaction." They also recognized the danger of mistreating Indian burial sites, even though they scavenged through them: "We deemed them graves . . . and left the rest untouched, because we thought it would be odious to them to ransack their sepulchers."[9]

The land itself impressed them with its abundance, and they described it as the paradise they had anticipated:

> A goodly land . . . wherein are nothing but wood, oaks, pines, walnuts, beech, sassafras, vines, and other trees. . . . This bay is a most hopeful place, innumerable store of fowl . . . of fish in their seasons . . . abundance of mussels the greatest and best that ever we saw; crabs and lobsters, in their time infinite.[10]

Throughout the winter and early spring, the Wampanoag built bonfires near enough for the Pilgrims to see the smoke. One night, Winslow wrote, "We heard a great and hideous cry. . . . Their note was after this manner, 'Woach woach ha ha hach woach.' "[11] A few weeks later, a large party of Wampanoag came even closer, and lit a great bonfire near the Pilgrim's settlement. "A noise of a great many more was heard behind the hill but no more came in sight." William Bradford, the first governor of the Pilgrims, interpreted the several days of Wampanoag rituals behind the hill as a demonic effort to drive the Pilgrims away. The Pilgrims believed they were about to be attacked and prepared for battle.

They organized themselves into a military order, choosing Miles Standish as their captain.

While the Pilgrims were gathered in their meetinghouse to plan their defense, an adopted member of the Wampanoag tribe who spoke English—Samoset, who had interacted with English fishing stations along the coast of Maine—strode right up to the door and said "Welcome" in English. Then he asked for a beer. The astonished Pilgrims shared food and drink and talked with him into the evening. Samoset explained that the epidemic had killed most of the tribe and told the Pilgrims about the tribes in the region, their leaders, and their reasons for concern about the English.[12] A second welcome followed this diplomatic visit a few days later. With Tisquantum in the lead, the small envoy laid down their bows and arrows outside the town. The Pilgrims reported:

> They made semblance unto us of friendship and amity; they sang and danced ... they brought a little of their corn ... a little tobacco in a bag. .... Some of them had their faces painted black, from the forehead to the chin.[13]

The great Wampanoag sachem, Massasoit, arrived a few days later, accompanied by an entourage of sixty. He wore a "great chain of white bone beads about his neck, and ... a little bag of tobacco." His oiled body gleamed and his face was painted red. "All his followers likewise, were in their faces, in part or in whole painted, some black, some red, some yellow, and some white ... some had skins on them, and some naked, all strong, tall men." The Protestant Pilgrims, so averse to pomp and finery, did their best to respond in kind. They presented gifts and escorted their governor to greet Massasoit "with drum and trumpet after him, and some few musketeers. After salutations, our governor kissing his hand, the king [Massasoit] kissed him, and so they sat down."[14]

The meeting produced a peace treaty. The Wampanoag and the Pilgrims pledged not to harm or steal from one another and to aid one another if either was attacked. Massasoit shared tobacco with the Pilgrims—a ritual of deep significance for his people.[15] In the weeks following, the Indians set crops in the fields next to the Pilgrims, a sign that they had adopted the Pilgrims as a tribe within their confederacy. The alliance was important to the Wampanoag, who needed assistance to rebuild their own community devastated by plague and to protect against attacks from nearby enemy Narragansett tribes.

The relationship between the Wampanoag people and Pilgrims held for nearly half a century, as long as Massasoit lived. As the Pilgrims' community grew, however, their behavior increasingly baffled and outraged the Wampanoag. The Pilgrims interpreted the kinship agreement as a sign that they could impose their religion and laws on the Wampanoag. They saw the epidemic that killed so many Indians as a generous act of God. In their minds, divine intervention had prepared a place for them and justified their expansion of control. They regarded the Wampanoag exchange of gifts with them as an agreement to sell their land. Pilgrims began to arrest Wampanoag hunters for trespassing. Massasoit challenged them. He asked, "What is this thing you call property? . . . The woods, the streams, everything on it belongs to everybody and is for the use of all. How can one man say it belongs to him only?"[16]

Conflicts escalated over time, but from the start, the Pilgrims could not comprehend the Wampanoag as their kin. Pilgrim journals report with alarm that Wampanoag arrived at Plymouth expecting to stay in Pilgrim homes for several days and share their food. The Pilgrims turned them away from their doors. When the Wampanoag urged Pilgrims to stay in their village, the appalled Pilgrims sought to escape as fast as possible. Winslow's journal explained,

We desired to keep the Sabbath at home and feared we should . . . be light-headed for want of sleep, for what with bad lodging, the savages' barbarous singing (for they used to sing themselves asleep), lice and fleas within doors, and mosquitoes without, we could hardly sleep all the time of our being there; we much fearing that if we should stay any longer, we should not be able to recover home for want of strength.[17]

PARADISE THROUGH PURITAN EYES

The English had come to the New World on a mission to "raise Eden in the wilderness," not to form alliances with Indian tribes. To the Puritans, North America was virginal land—unspoiled by the corruptions of the Roman Catholic Church and the greed of the British aristocracy. While Pilgrim journals convey their need and appreciation for the Algonquian people as "neighbors," at the same time, they imagined the New World as empty of any "real" inhabitants, a pristine opportunity to create paradise anew. As William Bradford wrote:

> The place they had thoughts on was some of those vast and unpeopled countries of America, which are fruitful and fit for habitation, being devoid of all civil inhabitants.[18]

In the Pilgrims' religious imagination, "wilderness" was a place of trial and opportunity. Venturing into it was a contest against evil, a process of purification, and a pathway to the apocalyptic recovery of paradise. As mostly urban dwellers in England, most had little familiarity with rural life and possessed none of the skills needed to survive in unsettled virgin forests. They faced the first cold with little shelter, scant supplies, and many ill. Devoted to the guiding Word of God, they found themselves struggling for survival.[19]

Puritans, inheritors of Calvinist iconoclasm, distrusted their senses. Their religion had taught them that the world was filled with deceptive images, decoys from the devil.[20] Unlike the Algonquian peoples, for whom astute observation of the immediate world was a key to understanding whether manitou were sinister or friendly, the Puritans believed that scripture was the most reliable guide to truth. They interpreted the land and people of "New England" through the theological script provided by their Bible. The Indians were occasionally seen as innocent, original inhabitants of Eden to be treated as children. Sometimes they were seen as Canaanites, the illegitimate inhabitants of the promised land, who were to be vanquished and whose land was to be taken. Or they were viewed as the lost Jewish tribes, who were to be converted as preparation for the dawn of the millennium.[21] More often, they were regarded as agents of Satan whose presence in Eden was to be resisted or destroyed. Puritans relegated Natives to the status of beasts or demons in the shape of humans, part of a treacherous wilderness that they were to transform into a place of liberty for "those faithful saints and servants of God . . . that fled from the bloody prelates."[22]

For the Puritans, the times in which they lived were a test of faith that would earn them a future paradise as the covenanted elect. Hence, they could not relate to the New World without an ever-vigilant suspicion that called into question any unguarded embrace of present time, space, and people other than themselves. Thomas Shepard, one of the leading Puritan preachers from England, explained that in the Puritan's covenant "two eternities meet together." The covenanted elect see "the one before the world began" and enjoy that "which shall be our glory when this world shall be burned up and all things in it shall have an end." For the elect, eternal glory is "comprehended at hand near and obvious," and God's people are "sealed up daily unto all fullness of assurance and peace, in these evil times."[23] Unable to fully trust their senses or personal perceptions, Puritans viewed the land itself and the Native peoples through their longing for primordial purity and millennial restoration. To be thus "sealed up" within a covenantal community whose source of peace was outside of time and not of this world, the Puritans were ill equipped to engage with the real presence of "others" in the New World. New England's Native inhabitants could be nothing except outsiders to the covenant.

The Puritans constructed a world of hard group lines, strict ideologies, and suspicion of difference. Their habits of mind divided life into good or evil, sacred or profane, salvation or sin, elect or damned, and authority and obedience or rebellion and punishment. Long inured to violence and its religious and revolutionary uses, Puritans lived by what historian Richard Slotkin calls "the myth of regeneration through violence."[24] They related to the world and present time as a means to the end, which required identifying evil and destroying it. While some, such as the Pilgrims at Plymouth, had been persecuted in England, many had been leaders in Puritan reforms there, were highly educated, and came with charters from the Crown to form colonies. Some had been financed by merchants counting on economic gain.[25]

Their theology included war as a way to destroy evil and to fulfill God's purpose. In 1636, at the Mystic River in Connecticut, a Puritan militia massacred more than four hundred Pequot, including women and children, and burned their village to the ground.[26] Indian allies fighting with the Puritans cried, *Mach it! Mach it!* ("Enough!"), but they could not quell the total annihilation that ensued. The conflict had begun over control of the fur trade among the Dutch, French, Mohawks, and Pequot. Back at Plymouth Plantation, William Bradford regarded the massacre as an occasion for thanksgiving: "It was a fearful sight to see them thus frying in the fire ... but the victory seemed a sweet sacrifice, and they gave the prayers thereof to God, who had wrought so wonderfully for them, thus to inclose their enemies in their hands."[27]

Waves of colonists arrived from England. They chopped down the forests to build houses and churches and expanded farmland, planting their villages on the outskirts of Indian towns and crowding their already cleared, arable land. They consumed wood for building and heating at a pace unknown by the Algonquin peoples. Within a hundred years, the Puritans would denude the Eastern landscape of its great, ancient forests, and deplete or make extinct its wildlife in the rivers and forests.[28]

CONQUEST THROUGH CONVERSION

Following the Pequot massacre, the Puritans turned to converting the Algonquian peoples as a way to tame the wilderness and win the fight against Satan.[29] The Puritan's missionary ambition to Christianize the Indians was supported by the theory popular in Europe that the Indians were Jews, the lost tribes of Israel captured by Satan and in need of rescue and conversion. Their conversion was a necessary step before the Second Coming of Christ and the dawn of the New Creation, of which the Puritans were the vanguard.

When King Charles provided a charter to the Puritans to journey to America, he charged them to convert the Indians. John Eliot (1604–1690), a chartered English missionary, arrived in the Massachusetts Bay Colony in 1631 and made the Indians his life's work. He believed that the work of Christians "in these tumultuous days was to act as the Lord's instrument in bringing about Christ's rule—'whether by Councils or Wars, or otherwise,' " an apocalyptic view he kept all his life. Eliot saw commonalities to Christian practice in the Native practices. He thought the forest spirits of the Indians might be akin to angels. He recognized their concept of *manitowuk*—sacredness imbued in certain rituals and prayers. But they were deficient, he felt, in their capacity to understand sin.[30]

From the Indians' perspective, the Christian religion was hardly a religion at all. How could it be? They did not dance. They had no images. Spiritual presences were in scarce supply. Its practitioners appeared not to understand their own teachings. One sachem who steadfastly opposed Christianity told a missionary, "Go and make the English good first."[31] In response to Eliot's efforts to instruct them in "right beliefs," he reported that the Massachusett asked him "(1) What is the cause of thunder? (2) What causes the ebbing and flowing of the sea? and (3) What of the wind?" They also asked him to explain "why, given the good Lord's rule over all, strawberries are sweet and cranberries are sour." They challenged the sanity of the Christian God: "God made hell in one of the six days. . . . Why . . . did God make hell before Adam sinned?" and "If [sinners] repent in hell, why will God not let them out again?"[32] Eliot apparently thought these questions were asked in all sincerity, not as an intelligence test of the English.

Eventually, a small number of Natives became "Praying Indians." Eliot's own mission tracts, sent to his English financiers, reveal something of Indian resistance to and adaptation of Christianity for their own purposes. For example, upon first hearing him preach, Indians made demands for land, eventually suing in Massachusetts Bay Colony courts and gaining four thousand acres in the Natick area, despite the protests of the local colonists.[33] Eliot supported them by urging the colonial legislature to set aside land for a missionary village, "somewhat remote" and "set apart" from their former Native life and from the English colonies.

In 1650, the first Algonquian village called Natick (my land) was founded. By 1675 there were fourteen "praying villages" in the vicinity of the Massachusetts Bay Colony, home to around four thousand praying Indians. The praying towns gained Indians legal land rights, but they also isolated them from non-Christian Indians, requiring them to preserve cultural roots and relationships while under pressure to adopt Puritan culture.[34] The English expected the Natives to give up their egalitarian gender roles. Women were no longer to cultivate the "sacred sisters" in the fields—beans, corn, and squash. Men were to stop hunting and grow flax for the women to weave into clothes that could be sold to the English. The colonists came into the Indian towns to "instruct" them in proper industries "useful" to them, such as basket and broom making, and hired them to work as servants and farmhands. The Natives resisted the move into colonial houses, however, preferring to live in wigwams. They preserved elements from their own heritage and created new hybrid expressions of Christianity. The Massachusett Bible, translated by their efforts as much as Eliot's, simultaneously taught them Christianity and became a means of linguistic and cultural preservation.[35]

Just as the Puritans had segregated themselves from England in New England, the new Christian Indian villages were to be outposts of the millennium—exemplary biblical communities in the wilderness, preparing the way for the return of Christ and the dawn of the New Creation. This approach of keeping the Natives at a distance reflected the Puritans' inability to conceive of distinction and diversity without walls of separation. Thus, the Puritans created the first racially segregated communities, "reservations," as millennial cities chartered to fulfill Puritan dreams of paradise, a kind of cloister-garden gone awry. The isolation made Indians easy targets of colonists who remained deeply ambivalent about them. Scholar Andrea Smith notes that the praying towns were the beginning of the boarding school system that has continued to the present day. Boarding schools separated Native children from their home communities to "civilize" them. The record of physical, sexual, and cultural abuse in these schools has been criminal.[36]

Attempts to convert Indians to Christianity created an uneasy peace. Over the course of his many years with the Massachusett, Eliot broke with the Puritan doctrine that the church should be composed only of those who bore signs of being the elect of God. He welcomed all, "so as to keep the whole heape of chaff and corne together, only excluding the ignorant and prophane and scandalous."[37] His fellow Puritans did not welcome this inclusiveness, and they regarded with suspicion one among them who had learned to live with and respect the Indians. The Puritans relegated praying Indians to an inferior status among the elect, and they ostracized Indian sympathizers. Many Indian leaders, such as Massasoit, remained adamantly opposed to Christianity but continued to probe effective means to enable life to flourish in relationship to the colonists. However, the peace broke down in 1675. The murder of a praying Indian, John Sassamon, triggered the eruption of the worst war to take place on American soil.

PRELUDE TO WAR

John Sassamon was a bilingual, bicultural, second-generation Christian Indian who worked as an interpreter for the Puritans during the Pequot War in 1637. In exchange for English lessons, he taught Eliot the Massachusett language and helped Eliot translate the Bible, issuing the first Bible printed in North America so the Indians could "be wholly governed by the Scriptures in all things."[38] Sassamon participated in founding Natick and lived there for years as a teacher. In 1653, Eliot helped him attend Harvard, which he did only briefly before returning to Indian life as an advisor to a number of chiefs.

In 1661, Eliot sent Sassamon to Mount Hope in Rhode Island to start a mission among the Wampanoag after Massasoit—who had adopted the Pilgrims when they landed at Plymouth forty years before—died. Sassamon became the secretary to Massasoit's son Metacom, newly installed as the tribal leader. Like his father, Metacom had no interest in becoming a Christian. Reportedly, when Metacom had an occasion to meet John Eliot, he grabbed him by the lapels and said he "cared as little for his gospel as he did for the button on his coat."[39] Metacom recognized that conversion to Christianity meant political and cultural submission to the English. "If I become a praying sachem I shall become a poor and weak one, easily be trod upon by others . . . and I shall be a great loser by praying to God."[40] Working for Metacom, who had either adopted or been given the English name "King Philip," Sassamon wrote letters to the colonial governors urging them to honor treaties and deal justly with the Wampanoag. A few years earlier, the Pilgrims had taken Philip's older brother, Wamsutta, to Plymouth at gunpoint for questioning. The Pilgrims let him go, but kept his two sons as hostages. Wamsutta, seriously ill at the time, died before he made it home, and the Wampanoag held the English responsible for his death. King Philip expected the Puritans leaders to respect his people and honor their agreements. Receiving no satisfaction, he organized Indians to resist the English.

In late December of 1674, Sassamon, who had deep ties to both the English and the Wampanoag, told Governor Josiah Winslow of Plymouth of Philip's preparations for war. However, Sassamon's association with Philip made him suspect in the eyes of the English and some of the praying Indians. The governor dismissed the news as Indian hearsay and sent him away. Within a week, Sassamon disappeared. A month later, his body was found in a frozen pond. The Puritans decided to take seriously a possible uprising. They arrested three Wampanoag counselors to Philip, charged them with Sassamon's murder, and tried them before twelve English and six Indian jurors.

The most damning evidence emerged in court when Sassamon's exhumed and autopsied body was brought to the trial and reportedly bled afresh when approached by each defendant "as if it had been newly slain."[41] Whether in truth it was Indians or colonists who were responsible for Sassamon's murder has never been determined. Historian Jill Lepore suggests that Sassamon was a casualty of the cultural tensions that erupted into war and that made literate, bicultural praying

Indians especially suspected by all sides.[42] The three Wampanoag tried for his murder were convicted, and they were hanged in Plymouth on June 8, 1675.

The John Sassamon murder trial infuriated the Wampanoag. For fifty years, they had negotiated as the English encroached on their lands, depleted the forests and waters of wildlife, and expected them to abandon their lifeways and assimilate into English religion and culture. In the Pequot War, the English had shown themselves capable of unrestrained violence, which appalled the Indians. Now with the Sassamon trial, the English had asserted dominion over the law. They had drawn Indians into their court, their structures of justice, and had executed Indians—a development legal historian Yasuhide Kawashima terms "legal imperialism." King Philip recognized this as a final blow obliterating Indian self-determination.[43]

Sixteen days after the execution of the convicted Indians, Wampanoag warriors attacked Swansea and killed nine colonists. Two days later, English soldiers marching there from Boston saw a lunar eclipse with a shadow of something that looked Indian to them. They deemed it a sinister omen, portending a deadly war. Within a month of Sassamon's postmortem accusation, King Philip's War had begun. The Wampanoag warriors fought against the Puritans, against their Indian allies, and against the powerful eastern Mohawk who had been the Wampanoag's long-standing enemies. Had Philip not been fighting three wars at once, the history of the Puritans in North America might have ended in 1676. Instead, in the end, it would be the Indians—*all* the Indians—who were defeated.

In the course of the war, the Boston Puritans hastily rounded up Indians from the praying towns and interned them on Deer Island in the harbor. John Eliot strenuously objected, but his pleas went unheeded. The Christian Indians interned on Deer Island mostly froze or starved. At war's end, the Puritans sold the survivors into slavery.[44]

As the brutal fighting continued and Puritan losses mounted, Roger Williams, long a friend of the Wampanoag, thought his community would be spared. The Wampanoag burned Providence and his home to the ground. When, distressed and outraged, he demanded to know why they had betrayed him, they replied that they "were in A Strang Way," that the English had forced them to it, and that God was with the Indians. Williams condemned them and joined the English.[45] The Wampanoag's reply to him indicated that they understood the war as extraordinary. They described it as outside their cultural systems of war, an all-out cataclysm that, according to Williams's account, seemed even to them something beyond their ability to cease. On the other hand, the Puritans conceived of a God capable of total destruction and believed they were playing a role in hastening an all-encompassing, unavoidable apocalyptic transformation of the world.

On August 12, 1676, the English forces and their Indian allies killed Philip and butchered his body into quarters. They displayed his head on a stake in Plymouth and sent his hand as a trophy to Boston. The Puritans rounded up surviving Wampanoag and put them on ships to be sold as slaves in the Caribbean, where none would take them. They eventually shipped them to Africa and dumped the survivors in Tangier. Eliot wrote a letter pleading for their return. Further fighting continued until the Treaty of Casco in 1678 decreed an end to "King Philip's War." By the time it was over, nearly half of New England's ninety-five settlements had been laid waste, many burned to the ground. Approximately 17 percent of the English population was dead, and by most estimates nearly 50 percent of the Native population had perished from disease, starvation, or warfare.[46]

WAR AS CLEANSING

Even before the war was over, Puritan preachers began to interpret its religious meaning. As colonists desperately sought accurate news about the war, virtually all of it horrific, printed accounts—lurid and apocalyptic and mostly printed in England—waged their own war of words. Rev. William Hubbard wrote an account that depicted the Puritans as noble and good servants of God savagely attacked by brutes. His incensed rival Rev. Increase Mather (1639–1723), who beat him to print, agreed that the Indians were devil-possessed. His "Brief History of the War with the Indians in New England," published in 1676, exulted over the dismemberment of Metacom, likening it to how "Agag was hewed in pieces before the Lord," a reference to I Samuel 15:33. He called it God's doing that Philip "the perfidious and bloudy author of the War... was taken and slain," and he prayed, "So let all thine enemies perish, O Lord."[47] However, unlike Hubbard, Mather did not picture the Puritans as God's good servants. He interpreted the war as divine punishment for Puritan sins, and accordingly, tried to get the Massachusetts governors to condemn Hubbard's history. They refused, in effect sanctioning Hubbard's account, which was by far the more popular version.[48]

In Mather's view, the war was an instrument not only to cleanse New England of devilish Indians but also to purify the Puritans themselves. His history accused the Puritans of incurring divine wrath as Indian attacks because of Puritan apostasy, pride of apparel and hair, drunkenness, and swearing, as well as their leniency toward Quakers and their tolerance of "liberal" preachers such as John Eliot and his pro-Indian views.[49]

Puritan histories of the war, which proliferated as soon as it ended, failed to mention their treatment of Christian Indians with one exception: Daniel Gookin wrote an account that detailed the Indian's difficulties at the hands of the Puritans, but it languished unpublished for a century in the library of the Society for the Propagation of the Gospel in London. The heartbroken Eliot read it and remarked that he would leave the rest of the terrible story to be told "unto the day of judgment ... before the seeing eye of a glorious Judge."[50]

Increase Mather instigated and led the Massachusetts Puritans' 1679 Reforming Synod. The synod examined, among other things, the sins that had led God to unleash King Philip's War against them. The gathering concluded they were being punished for "a visible decay of the power of Godliness amongst many professors in these Churches." They urged people to redouble their pious practices: observances of the Sabbath, reading the Bible, and praying for God's Spirit to "rain down

Righteousness upon us." The synod ignored any of the reasons the Wampanoag themselves gave for their attacks. It never entered the Puritans' minds to consider repenting of their treatment of the Natives or the land. What mattered was the Puritan relationship to God. However, they did note that "Christians in this Land have become too like unto the Indians and we need not wonder if the Lord hath afflicted us by them."[51] What, we wonder, would have made them "too like unto the Indians"? Perhaps to lament the war as a tragedy or to care for the land and share its riches with one another—perhaps these might have been too like the Wampanoag. However, since the war was divine punishment, the correct Puritan response was stoic endurance, gratefulness for discipline, stricter control of their community, and more reading of the Bible, which some believed had magical powers to ward off death.[52]

The most popular and, in many ways, definitive Puritan interpretation of the war emerged in the "captivity narratives." Though some English captives "went native," others escaped, returned home, and wrote stories of their experiences. Mary Rowlandson published a detailed account of her experiences with Philip's tribe, at Mather's urging. In it, she tells how the Indians burned her house to the ground, killed her brother-in-law before her eyes, and shot her baby dead in her arms. They separated her from her husband and surviving children. She suffered the hardships of the hungry and harried Indians, who moved from camp to camp to avoid attack. While on this arduous winter trek, she reflected on the reasons for her miseries:

> I then remembered how careless I had been of God's holy time, how many Sabbaths I had lost and misspent and how evilly I had walked in God's sight, which lay so close unto my spirit that it was easy for me to see how righteous it was with God to cut the thread of my life and cast me out of His presence forever.[53]

Throughout her ordeal, she read her Bible and found comforting words of promise: God afflicts those whom he loves to make them understand they must depend solely on him for their hope and salvation.

"Yet the Lord still showed mercy to me and upheld me, and as He wounded me with one hand, so He healed me with the other." In her mind, the very horrors she had experienced were signs of divine care; in inflicting horror, God loved her. The Indians were agents of divine wrath, punishing her for her laxness in religious observances, and she must be grateful for such attention.

Rowlandson was ransomed and returned to her husband, and her family was reunited. She concluded her narrative by meditating on the spiritual lesson she drew from her captivity experience:

> I can remember the time when I used to sleep quietly without workings in my thoughts whole nights together, but now it is other ways with me. When all are fast about me and no eye open but His who ever waketh, my thoughts are upon things past, upon the awful dispensation of the Lord towards us. . . . I remember in the night season how the other day I was in the midst of thousands of enemies and nothing but death before me. . . . But now we are fed with the finest of the wheat. . . . Now I see the Lord had His time to scourge and chasten me. . . . We must rely on God himself and our whole dependence must be upon Him. . . . I have learned to look beyond present and smaller troubles and to be quieted under them, as Moses said, Exo. 14:13, "Stand still and see the salvation of the Lord."[54]

Haunted in the silent, still night by memories of horror, Rowlandson remembered Moses speaking to her as he spoke to the fleeing Israelites who stood on the shore of the Red Sea with Pharaoh's army on their heels.

Rowlandson's story, published in 1682, was the first English bestseller in the colonies, more popular, even, than the twenty-plus Puritan accounts of the war. By 1684, the historical accounts had ceased, and the captivity narratives took their place. Rowlandson's tenth edition was published in 1773. Returned captives created an entire genre of popular colonial literature, first-person stories that reinforced the barbarity of the Indians and promoted Christian trust in God's justice, grounding these claims in vivid descriptions of trauma. The narratives translated a large-scale drama of conquest and colonization into a highly personal, internal drama of struggle to be faithful to pious practices. Nothing mattered with respect to a society's treatment of others or the land. What mattered was inner trust in God's transcendent love in the midst of personal experiences of punishing sorrow and pain.

Life for Puritans was a razor's edge. Living on its dangerous verge required alertness to sin, without rest. The faithful of the covenant lived in anxious suspension, hypervigilant in present time, hanging by the thin thread of hope above horror and hell. They embraced memories of trauma as comfort that God had not abandoned them. God cared about them so much as to cause them pain for their own edification. Puritan religious piety could not teach the equilibrium and equanimity needed to heal from horror, to relinquish fear, to forgive their enemies or themselves, and to repair harm. They lacked the spiritual disciplines that taught them to observe the world carefully, to trust the senses, and to wonder at the beauty of the land.

This Puritan piety of danger, sin, and dislocation from space and time bore traces of the crusading spirit, the willingness to endure even death for God, knowing that such punishing pain was glory. The conquest and colonizing spirit launched in the grassy field outside Clermont, France, an ocean and half a millennium distant from Mary Rowlandson's front door had stowed away, making itself felt in her every waking moment. Unable to tell defeat from victory, she could define the worst humiliation and suffering as signs of divine favor. Once suffering became consolation and war was peace, there was no rest in this world.

Through their captivity narratives, Puritans traced their spiritual drama about God's wrath and grace onto their translucent consciousness of life in the New World and the war with the Indians. It was a strange overwriting, allowing them simultaneously to deny any sins against the Indians, even the praying Indians, and to feel blessed that they had been justly punished for their sins. They could describe the utter terrors of war while also being grateful for them. Trapped between horror and hope, they were unable to peer at the ghostly images at the edges of their consciousness, or grapple with doubts about their mission and their feelings of loss. Puritan religious sensibilities denied them access to lamentation, whose other side is resurrection, whose power is love, and whose fruit is peace.

"A THOUSAND YEARS IN HORROR, IF IT BE GOD'S WILL"

In the aftermath of King Phillip's War, repeated battles with Indians elicited further Puritan self-examinations. Puritan preachers emphasized that, at their deaths, individuals would be judged immediately and their final resting place in heaven or in hell sealed. Preachers wrung their hands, distressed at the laxity in religious life, especially among men because women had long been the majority of church members. Preaching increasingly emphasized personal sins, examination of individual faults, and anxiety over whether one was saved.

After decades of anxiety, the Great Awakening began. From 1735 to 1745, an intense revival movement took hold in the Connecticut Valley and spread across New England east and west, north to Maine, and south to Georgia. Men who set the revival in motion preached Calvinist ideas of providence and double predestination. Not only had God damned all sinners, a fate that preachers took pains to make vivid, but heaven awaited those whom God had already providentially elected—it was just not so easy to know if one was damned or elected.

Jonathan Edwards (1703–1758) became one of the movement's most compelling and influential leaders, remembered especially for his sermon "Sinners in the Hands of an Angry God." In his preaching, Edwards took pains to "awaken" his congregants to their state of risk and insecurity. Too many were unconcerned about the fate of their souls and unaware of their dependence on God:

> The God that holds you over the pit of hell, much as one holds a
> spider... he looks upon you as worthy of nothing else, but to be

cast into the fire. . . . And there is no other reason to be given why you have not dropped into hell since you arose in the morning, but that God's hand has held you up.[55]

Reports said Edwards's delivery was reserved and dispassionate. However, his words stirred up intense responses as he preached throughout the Connecticut Valley. As one witness described his preaching in Enfield, "the assembly appeared deeply impressed and bowed down with an awful conviction of their sin and danger. There was such a breathing of distress and weeping, that the preacher was obliged to speak to the people and desire silence, that he might be heard."[56]

Implicit in Edwards's preaching was a theology about how to see the world. His famous sermon is filled with biblical images that reflect Puritan life. To evoke the precarious nature of human existence, he spoke of axes wielded to the roots of trees, burning heaps of refuse, flooding rivers, and outbreaks of fire. He reminded them of attacks in the woods from hidden adversaries with bows and arrows. These events were "images" or "shadows" of divine action. Edwards held that "the works of God are but a kind of voice or language of God to instruct intelligent beings in things pertaining to Himself." The terror of an Indian attack, a flood, or a fire was more than an analogy to hell; it was an actual experience—in the mode of a shadow or image—of God's wrath.[57] Edwards pictured God as a threatening Indian:

> The bow of God's wrath is bent, and the arrow made ready on the string, and justice bends the arrow at your heart, and strains the bow, and it is nothing but the mere pleasure of God, and that of an angry God, without any promise or obligation at all, that keeps the arrow one moment from being made drunk with your blood.[58]

Fear of Indian attacks dominated Edwards's childhood. In February 1704, shortly after Jonathan's birth, Indians killed two of his cousins and took the rest of their family captive: his uncle John Williams, his aunt, four of his cousins, and two enslaved Africans. Daily prayers for their return marked Edwards's childhood. John Williams was re-

deemed after three years in captivity. In his best-seller, "The Redeemed
Captive Returning to Zion," Williams noted that being with the Indians was difficult, but the worst of it—the trial to which Williams devotes
the most pages—was that the Indians were allies of French Roman
Catholics:

> My [captor] took hold of my hand to force me to cross myself, but
> I struggled with him and would not suffer him to guide my hand;
> upon this he pulled off a crucifix from his own neck and bade me
> kiss it, but I refused once again. He told me he would dash out my
> brains with his hatchet if I refused.[59]

The Indians offered to release Williams's children if he would embrace
Catholicism. He refused. "I told them my children were dearer to me
than all the world, but I would not deny Christ and His truths for the
having of them with me."[60] Upon his release, Williams returned to
Boston and regained all his children but one. Williams's daughter Eu-
nice, seven years old when she was taken, remained with her captors,
married a Mohawk, and converted to Catholicism. Thirty-six years after her capture, she visited her brother Stephen and listened to Edwards preach, but it appears she was not moved by it.[61]

Edwards spent his career as a minister on the edge of the frontier,
like many of the men who preached the Great Awakening. The captivity narratives became, in revival preaching, a model of how to
understand God and respond in faith. God's punishing mercies were
frightening to those estranged from God, who experienced God's
wrath with terror. But the truly faithful should receive them with calm
happiness. For the elect, trauma was to be embraced as Mary Rowlandson had accepted captivity: an occasion to reflect on one's sins and
God's love.

Revival preachers saw the world in two ways: as a foretaste of
heaven, or as a foretaste of hell. For the sinner, this world tasted of hell.
For the saint, it had the savor of heaven—even when the circumstances
were hellish. To awaken his hearers to divine love, Edwards usually followed a terrifying sermon with a comforting one. He used the same im-

ages to console and to frighten. Water could be a rushing flood, a token of God's wrath. It could also be refreshment for the thirsty, the flow of God's goodness, a deep reservoir of boundless love. The state of a person's soul determined the way she or he experienced the world.

Edwards's most frequent examples of Christian piety were women. Women's daily lives gave them many occasions to be awakened to the danger of eternal torment—the risks of childbirth, the sorrows of children lost to early death, and endless work managing a household. In his own household, Edwards may have preached to his wife, Sarah, that she should submit to him, and perhaps enforced the message with actions as well as words. During January 1742, after the birth of her seventh child and while her husband was out of town preaching, Sarah experienced an intense awakening that seemed triggered by her sense of the town's ill treatment of her husband and by her conflict with a man whom her husband admired. She slipped in and out of rapturous states as she kept up her household duties. Then a guest preacher, Samuel Buell, came to town. Sarah secretly hoped he would not stir up the town as much as her husband had, but instead she became one of Buell's spectacular successes. Two weeks of spiritual rapture overtook her, which she described as "a ravishing sense of the unspeakable joys of the upper world." Having surrendered all jealousies to God, she could totally submit to ecstasy. Even her husband's abuse could not diminish her happiness—she had entered a realm over which he had no control whatever.

> I thought of myself being cast off by my nearest and dearest friends and as I had thought before of Mr. Edwards kicking me out of the house and finally casting me off, now I put it to myself how I could bear from him the worst treatment of me at home and thought that if he should turn to be most cruel to me and should horsewhip me every day I would so rest [in] God that it would not touch [my heart] or diminish my happiness. I could still go on in the performance of all acts of duty to my husband and my happiness remain whole and undiminished.[62]

She wanted to be able to experience with tranquility even "a thousand years in horror, if it be God's will." Records show that in December 1742, the local physician prescribed special drugs for the treatment of her "hysteria." But Sarah Edwards's ecstasy, intimately tied to pain, humiliation, and danger, gave her a new spiritual authority in her community, and it won over one of her husband's influential detractors.

For his role in the Great Awakening, Edwards became famous among those who preached the revival. In some circles, revival preachers were notorious. Charles Chauncy (1705–1787), great-grandson of the second president of Harvard and minister of First Church of Boston, was the leading cleric to attack the Great Awakening and, early on, was virtually its only critic. He traveled three hundred miles around New England to document its negative effects. He objected to its emotional manipulations, its anti-intellectualism, and its self-deceptions. He thought its emphasis on personal feelings and individual salvation through intense feelings of fear and contrition threatened the church. Chauncy advocated for the clear operation of reason and a religion of equanimity committed to traditional Puritan principles of covenant and church order. In the controversy over the revival, he successfully rallied the Boston community and its Massachusetts theocracy against the revival. His rationalism helped launch the Unitarian movement with its emphasis on the mind as bearing the image of divinity.[63]

The conflict over the Great Awakening fell along class and regional lines. In Boston, the old Puritan families, led by Harvard-educated clergy, were comfortable with the social order and economic relationships of their prosperity. Evangelical preachers attacked their social order. Advocates of the revival raised the less educated and less economically powerful to a higher sanctity than urban merchants and bankers and their clergy, whom Chauncy had recruited to oppose the revival. In the rural Connecticut Valley to the west, the epicenter of the revival, farmers and laborers were organizing a banking system that created paper notes for the poor, using land as loan collateral. The Boston merchant class opposed them with a competing, silver-based banking system, which prevailed. Historian Conrad Wright suggests that in the 1740s, a theological controversy over who would control sinners replaced the economic controversy of the 1730s over who would control debtors. Revival preachers, often poor or working class, offered sinners an ecstatic transformation that rejected the cold, economically powerful, educated elite, and their mildly rational, spiritless clergy. As they traveled the countryside, preaching in churches, they condemned ministers whom they characterized as unconverted. Since neither Harvard nor Yale would train them, the revivalists eventually formed their own school for the training of ministers, the College of New Jersey, which later became Princeton.

Yale-educated Edwards was not an unequivocal defender of the Great Awakening. He insisted that the movement's emotional ecstasies did not change the theological content of Puritan faith, and in this he differed from the itinerant revival preachers who stirred up opposition to the established church. Edwards sought to protect church life and moral instruction. He tried, for example, to force his congregation to adopt his plan for stricter membership requirements at a time when no one had joined the church in three years. His plan was such that in 1750, his Northampton, Massachusetts, congregation dismissed him after twenty-four years of service. He spent most of the rest of his life as a pastor and missionary to the Indians in Stockbridge, Massachusetts, and died in 1758 of a smallpox vaccination just months after becoming president of Princeton.

THE BESTOWER OF ALL BEAUTY

Edwards's defense of the Great Awakening was more sophisticated than were the attacks by rationalists such as Chauncy. Drawing on Augustine, Calvin, and the Cambridge Platonists, Edwards formulated a theology of beauty and sensibility to defend the religious importance of the affections.[64] Like Calvin, Edwards affirmed the world as a place of divine presence and a medium of God's communication. The created world had "the stamp" of divinity, and thus humanity could see divinity there. Human knowledge of beauty was the knowledge and experience of God in this world, where the elect received a blessed foretaste of eternity. It would be most fully realized in heaven, where the "unbosomed" Christ would embrace the elect, where they would "eat and drink abundantly, and swim in the ocean of love." In his eulogies for his most beloved protégé, David Brainerd, and for his beloved daughter Jerusha, Edwards described the joys of Puritan theology, its appreciation for divine grace and creativity, for God's great providence, and for the glory all could anticipate if they abandoned sin. He insisted that the deceased received this spiritual beauty instantly upon death and did not wait in limbo.[65]

Regenerated souls, filled with love for God and obedient to the scriptures, could see "the beauty of holiness." Edwards explained, "When the true beauty and amiableness of the holiness . . . that is in divine things, is discovered to the soul, it as it were opens a new world to its view."[66] In his *Personal Narrative*, he testified to just such a conversion in his own experience of walking in his father's pasture:

> Looking up on the sky and clouds, there came to my mind so sweet a sense of the glorious *majesty* and *grace* of God, that I know not how to express. . . . The appearance of everything was altered; there seemed to be, as it were, a calm, sweet cast, or appearance of divine glory, in almost every thing. . . . I often used to sit and view the moon . . . to behold the sweet glory of God . . . in the mean time singing forth, with a low voice my contemplations of the Creator and Redeemer.[67]

Awakened to God, the faithful could learn to distinguish between primary or superior beauty and secondary or inferior beauty. Secondary, or natural beauty, came from harmony within a being itself because of its natural properties. Secondary beauty, for example, would be our enjoyment of the earth's natural environment. Another secondary beauty was the joy that human beings experienced when they loved others. Primary beauty was God, who was the highest order of being, holiness, and excellence because only God could embrace all of being in a harmonious whole without any distortions. God was "the foundation and fountain of all being and all beauty," whose "being and beauty are, as it were, the sum and comprehension of all existence and excellence: much more than the sun is the fountain and summary comprehension of all the light and brightness of the day."[68]

God's perfect beauty was marked by love, the flow of generous, infinite, and ceaseless divine creativity. God's love was objective—it truly saw the being of another without deformity. The fullness of divine love also had to include the heart, or affections, as the enjoyment of being, because the experience of beauty without joy was partial, and God was complete and perfect. In this, Edwards understood the pleasure that came with knowledge and enhanced it, and he asserted that because God's knowledge of the world was whole and perfect, it included the affections. In human life, true holy affections were the direct gift of God. They infused the soul and transformed it into a new being whose foundation was in God, not in "natural man." The spiritual person was deeply moved by holy affections. God filled the heart, both through distress about sin and the excitement of faith. The active presence of holy affections was a sure sign of the saved, whose joy included self-love: " 'tis impossible for any person to be willing to be perfectly and finally miserable for God's sake."[69]

Edwards's understanding of the religious affections provided a place for tears of repentance. However, he offered little comfort for traumatic loss and its haunting nightmares. Instead, he proposed that even in frightening or difficult events, the regenerate saint saw God's majesty and mercy. Edwards testified:

> Before, I used to be uncommonly terrified with thunder, and to be struck with terror when I saw a thunder storm rising; but now, on the contrary, it rejoiced me. I felt God, so to speak, at the first appearance of a thunder storm; and used to take the opportunity, at such times, to fix myself in order to view the clouds, and see the lightnings play, and hear the majestic and awful voice of God's thunder, which oftentimes was exceedingly entertaining, leading me to sweet contemplations of my great and glorious God.[70]

Edwards said to mourners that grief was insignificant compared to eternal glory. Those who mourned too deeply doubted that God had taken those he loved to heaven. Edwards had regular bouts of depression, which he saw as an affliction from God to teach him sympathy for the afflicted to whom he had to preach the assurances of heaven.

Rather than engage people more deeply in the world, the Great Awakening lifted the soul beyond earthly life, to the "upper world." Edwards's earthly loves had always to point beyond themselves—to primary beauty—and, as he said, even the love of other human beings was "secondary beauty." To look through earth into heaven, through death into eternity, through the beloved into God was the spiritual ideal. To love in this way was always to have your heart, mind, and soul turned elsewhere, perpetually departing the present for something better. Edwards's beauty did not draw people into ethical engagement with life in this world, but moved them beyond the spirits in trees and clouds, dirt and rain, fish and deer, and bodies and winds. He asked them to dwell with one foot always in another, better world, not here, not now.

As Puritan Thomas Shepard had explained, God's people are "sealed up daily unto all fullness of assurance and peace, in these evil times."[71] Such a sensibility disconnected love from immediate, observant, astute engagement with life. It offered little inoculation against violence, and it counseled acceptance of violation as God's will. It encouraged "religion" to be a private state of the soul. If evil times could be escaped "in the spirit," there was little call to love this world, or to change it for the better, except to demonstrate one's moral virtue as proof of election. The Great Awakening's pathway to heaven abandoned love for the world, stepping from its small, green meadow of eros into an ecstatic retreat in the clouds.

ONE FINAL ESCAPE: COMMUNING WITH EXTINCTION

By the beginning of the nineteenth century, most New Englanders believed Indians were virtually extinct.[72] In a letter to Thomas Jefferson in 1812, John Adams wrote:

We scarcely see an Indian a year. I remember the Time when Indian Murders, Scalpings, Depredations and conflagrations were as frequent on the Eastern and Northern frontier of Massachusetts as they are now in Indiana, and spread as much terror.[73]

Washington Irving (1783–1859) read Increase Mather's account of King Philip's War and was disgusted by its applause for white atrocities. In his 1814 essay, "Philip of Pokanoket," Irving suggested that Philip was "a true born prince, gallantly fighting at the head of his subjects to avenge the wrongs of his family . . . to deliver his native land from the oppression of usurping strangers."[74] Irving urged his readers to overcome their prejudices against the Indians and to mourn how Philip died "without a pitying eye to weep his fall, or a friendly hand to record his struggle." His valorization of Philip was characteristic of Irving's interest in vanquished races of dark peoples as symbols of a glory both hopelessly lost and wistfully embraced. In the 1830s he wrote about the Moors of Spain in *The Alhambra,* noting that the palace and gardens in Granada, Spain, had been the place of their "terrestrial paradise."[75]

On December 15, 1829, one of the most successful plays in U.S. history, *Metamora; or the Last of the Wampanoags,* opened at the Park Theater in New York City. Irving's romantic valorization of the noble Philip had inspired it. For nearly half a century, somewhere on an American stage, the actor Edwin Forrest enacted the resistance and death of the great King Philip. His bellowing, fictional speeches proclaimed, "Our lands! Our nation's freedom! Or the Grave!" making Philip sound for all the world like Patrick Henry in his purported speech, "Give me liberty or give me death." By helping the audience identify with the noble and tragic Philip, Forrest could pit the Wampanoag sachem, defined as a true patriot, against brutal English tyrants loyal to England. Those tyrants were the ancestors of the audience, whom the play changed into the evil British they had fought in the War for Independence. In turning Philip into a sympathetic model of patriotism, the play transformed the white audience into "native" Americans, resurrecting Philip as a true "American." Without this appropriation of Native Americans, Euro-America was merely a land of British transplants. This transposition of identity made Philip English, more than it made whites Indians, effectively erasing Indians as a separate, still existing people.

As the fictional Metamora, Philip perpetually and ritually died to give citizens of the new United States of America an authentic, non-British identity. They partook of it by communing with his death. Rapturous audiences received with standing ovations Metamora's dying words:

My curses on you, white men! May the Great Spirit curse you when he speaks in his war voice from the clouds! Murderers! The last of the Wampanoags' curse be on you! May your graves and the graves of your children be in the path the red man shall trace! And may the wolf and panther howl o'er your fleshless bones, fit banquet for the destroyers! Spirits of the grave, I come! But the curse of Metamora stays with the white man![76]

As historian Jill Lepore's analysis has shown, Metamora's curse of the English colonists became their curse of their defeated British oppressors.

By "not seeing color," the white onlookers could whitewash their history and construct a new moral and heroic identity. Forrest's Metamora embodied the ideal robust, fierce, heroic American man and leader, nobly and aggressively protecting his land unto death. His audiences could identify themselves with this fictional Philip, rechristened Metamora, and become "native" Americans. This transformation required the absence of contemporary Indians to remind them of their own colonial history or call their appropriated identity into question.

Metamora's curse, which so moved audiences, did not alter policies in the United States towards Indians. *Metamora* opened a week before Andrew Jackson announced his plan for "Indian removal." A few months later, in spring of 1830, Congress voted for removal. The plan was to move the Indians out of the United States into the territories west of the Mississippi. Removal would finish off the many Indians still living on their own lands in the Southeast and those on reservations in New England. Where actual Indians still lived in the United States in large numbers, the identification with Indians as true Americans was not so compelling. The southern states, unlike New England, voted unanimously for removal. Andrew Jackson saw removal as part of a continuing campaign to subdue the Indians, and Forrest, a fan of Jackson, also supported removal. Other whites saw removal as a travesty and opposed it, while still others believed the new Republic had created a new and milder process of nation building that allowed the Indians to continue their lives in western territories. All used King Philip's War to support their positions. When removal came, a quarter of the Cherokee died on the Trail of Tears from Georgia to reservations in Oklahoma.[77]

Extinct Indians suited Edwin Forrest's purposes. Belief in extinction was a prerequisite for the transposition of identity that allowed Forrest to enact Metamora as a true American. Many white leaders, as well as French visitor Alexis de Tocqueville, declared, "All the Indian tribes who once inhabited the territory of New England . . . now live only in men's memories."[78] Through their romantic ideal of traditional, "wild," tragic, and now-extinct Indians, whites could supplant them with a new pure American identity by their identification with imaginary, not actual, Indians. Historian Brian Dippie observed, "The belief in a Vanishing Indian was the ultimate cause of the Indian's vanishing."[79]

At the same time, the attendance of a few actual Indians at performances of *Metamora* drew white audiences, who sought to witness "real" Indians authenticate the performance on the stage. Actual Indians functioned as experts who could verify the truth of an American identity uncontaminated by English colonists, though the actual Indians in the audience could not be regarded as uncontaminated. They were more like museum artifacts for the purposes of authentication. Few rapturous audiences appear to have seen the fundamental contradiction in this romantic construction of American identity or to have noticed that their very existence was cursed.[80]

Real Indians used *Metamora* to appeal to whites to take responsibility for their history, using whatever strategies seemed effective in furthering their struggle for land rights and against removal. In May 1833, Rev. William Apess, a Pequot Methodist minister, joined the Wampanoag in Mashpee, Massachusetts, to support them in their land claims against the state government. The Wampanoag adopted Apess, who helped them stir up support, protest, and go to court. The Mashpees tapped anti-removal sentiment in New England, and they were partly successful. The various Indian strategies were in keeping with what Native scholars, such as John Mohawk, have described as the one Native form of American philosophy: pragmatism, which flourished in North America long before the arrival of Europeans.[81]

Apess toured theaters to deliver a popular lecture he called *Eulogy on King Philip,* and he, like Forrest, created a stirring speech for Philip. However, his Philip did not speak as he was dying. Instead, he recited English crimes against his people as his grounds for war. His Philip judged, but did not curse, whites. Apess also contrasted the humane treatment that Puritan captives received among the Indians to the rape, exploitation, forced conversions and enslavement that the colonists inflicted upon the Indians.

I can hardly restrain my feelings to think a people calling themselves Christians should conduct [deeds] so scandalous, so outrageous, making themselves appear so despicable in the eyes of the Indians; and even now, in this audience, I doubt but there is men honorable enough to despise the conduct of those pretended Christians. . . . And then on the Sabbath day, these people would gather themselves together and say that God is no respecter of persons; while the divines would pour forth, "He says that he loves God and hates his brother is a liar, and the truth is not in him"—at the same time they are hating and selling their fellow men in bondage.[82]

He declared Philip "the greatest man that was ever in America."
Apess sought to call attention to contemporary Indian issues and to

motivate sympathy and action on behalf of actual Indians. He did not evoke nostalgia for extinct Indians or assuage white consciences. Apess described prejudice he had faced as an Indian and explained unjust legislation against Indians in the new Republic. He was also astute enough to know that many in his white audiences flocked to his performances not to hear him speak but to see a "real" Indian. To conclude his eulogy, he recited the Lord's Prayer in the Massachusetts language, which was often the one thing used to advertise his performance—his ability to speak Philip's language, not as a living tongue but as a historical artifact.

The restless Puritan impulse to build paradise and their obsession with their own piety and redemption remain in white supremacist culture in the United States. Preoccupied with its own needs and anxieties, it tends to regard those it oppresses and exploits as important only insofar as they can play a role in a script in which whites are the main characters. Locked within a biblically based master narrative, white society embraces African, Asian, Hispanic, Middle Eastern, and Native Americans as instruments of judgment and as agents of absolution. However, those shaped by such a culture tend to be primarily concerned with the state of their own souls—their guilt and their longing to be restored to innocence and their need to believe in their own goodness.

CHAPTER FOURTEEN

The Struggle for Paradise

"The woman thou gavest to be with me, she gave me and I did
eat," he whines—trying to shield himself at his wife's expense!
Again we are amazed that upon such a story men have built up
a theory of their superiority!
   Then flows what has been called the curse. Is it not rather a
prediction?

LILLIE DEVEREAUX BLAKE, *The Woman's Bible*, 1915

In the the nineteenth century, Christians in North America struggled
over the meaning of paradise. Those whose gender, race, or class had
acquainted them firsthand with Christianity's failures troubled the waters of their faith traditions. Diverse movements agitated for reform of
churches and society and worked to realize the Kingdom of God *"on
earth* as it is in heaven."
   Reformers forged vigorous and varied movements that found
beauty in the natural world, upheld the dignity and worth of all human
beings, and worked for justice and equality. They generated new visions
for community in North America. In the process, they dismantled doctrines of redemptive violence, and they challenged the idea that God
divided the world into the elect and the damned. Their claims of universal salvation resisted segregation; since all human beings would live
together in heaven, they should learn to live together on earth. Their efforts generated the conservation movement, women's suffrage, the New
Deal, and the Civil Rights Movement.

They were often unable, however, to connect one struggle for reform with another; for example, white abolitionists largely ignored lynching and white feminists argued over suffrage for blacks. Those fighting for economic justice overlooked the devastating impact of "progress" on the environment. Nonetheless, these movements shaped the society in enduring ways. They testify to the legacy of struggle, still incomplete, to dwell rightly in paradise here and now. Their commitments live on in the marrow of those today who love this world and who resist all the death-dealing forces in it.

Their efforts ignited conflicts. Those with vested interests in social and economic arrangements that privileged white men over others objected to changes that would make their wives and slaves their equals. Others argued against what they regarded as an overly optimistic view of human nature and objected to interpreting the Bible in the light of human reason and experience. They saw this world as a vale of suffering to be endured, escaped only through the atoning death of Christ and redemptive violence.

At the dawn of the twenty-first century, North American Christians are engaged in deep conflicts generated by the struggle for paradise.[1] Popular forms of Christianity that embrace redemptive violence and look to heaven in a world to come have become a major public and political voice for Christianity in recent decades. Reiterating Christian perspectives that echo imperial Christianity, they bless conquest and colonization, privilege those with wealth and status, sanction war against "evildoers," and exploit the environment. The paradise they offer is on the other side of the end of the world. Their apocalyptic expectations imagine that God's plan is to destroy this earth and rapture an elect few into heaven.

This blustery, reactive form of Christianity has long been resisted. In this chapter, we return to Genesis 1–3 to interpret the story of that resistance in the United States. We begin with movements that blessed the goodness of creation. We then describe efforts to affirm the glory of humanity in paradise. And, finally, we show how Christians wrestled with the evil that disrupts the best that life can be. In telling the story this way, we place contemporary Christianity in a four-thousand-year history of human beings struggling to live justly and well upon the earth.

AMERICAN BEAUTY

Nineteenth-century American Christians loved nature. The beauty of the earth stirred their spiritual desire for paradise, spoke to them of God's virtue, and helped them construct a sense of national purpose and identity.[2] Through love of nature they sought to return here and now to a pristine Eden that their own legacy of colonizing had destroyed.

Thomas Cole (1801–1848), the father of American landscape painting, depicted New England Protestant visions of nature. He saw it as having spread "a rich and delightful banquet" and said, "We are still in Eden."[3] Painting from his observations of the Catskills' forests, valleys, hills, and streams, his work suggested that nature held promises for pristine life in contrast to the cities, which he and some of his contemporaries increasingly regarded as fallen places. In the wilds of nature and in rural and town life, a more Edenic existence was possible. Like Jonathan Edwards, Cole viewed the natural world as a divine textbook, speaking of the beauty of God on the one hand, and the sinful folly of humanity on the other. The artist, like the preacher, was to call for awakening.

In Cole's "Expulsion from the Garden of Eden," the craggy cliffs and forest canopies of nature dominate. A tall, dark brown stone peak fills the center of the painting, reaching to its upper edge, and it divides the upper right from the left and bottom. The upper right quadrant has lush trees, a sunny sky, and flowing water. Sunlight from the right shoots through an arch that cuts through the bottom of the peak. The inner walls of the arch glow golden against the shadowed walls of stone surrounding it. The light from the arch illuminates two tiny human figures fleeing away from the light toward the lower left to a dark, murky area dominated by shadowed cliffs and barren trees bent by a fierce wind. The tallest of the miniature figures holds his left arm up across his forehead and in his right hand he holds the hand of the smaller figure, who is slumping in sorrow. Far above the fleeing pair, a mountain peak rises in the far distance, and rushing falls and tumbling water churn behind them.[4]

Cole sought to display the moral struggles of human life through the mirror of nature. Using "a clashing chiaroscuro," his richly shaded canvases, light on one side and dark on the other, were "a battleground for the warfare of good and evil."[5] Light, for Cole as for Edwards, opened the eyes to God. He wrote, "In the pure blue sky is the highest sublime. . . . There we look into the uncurtained, solemn serene—into the eternal, the infinite—toward the throne of the Almighty."[6]

When Cole painted at the beginning of the nineteenth century, the primeval forests of New England had all been felled, and all he knew were second-growth forests. Cole lamented the fallen trees that left "ghastly wounds" in the "green bosom of the woodland," and that symbolized civilization's defeat of nature.[7] Cole painted trees as if his images could raise them from the dead or protect them from further devastation. His trees were allegories for moral insight: the mighty can fall, new life can spring from old root, moral degradation can spoil Eden, and virtue can preserve it. Melancholic, romantic, sentimental, and moralistic, Cole located white American life within a nostalgic longing for Eden. God's voice spoke in nature, calling humanity to return.[8]

Henry David Thoreau (1817–1862) searched for the wilderness his own Puritan forebears had razed, nostalgic for the very thing his culture and ancestors had disregarded. He missed the Indians, too. He glimpsed their disappearing faces in the woods of New England—like spirit-ghosts in the trees—and melded them in his imagination with pristine nature itself. "The pine stands in the woods like an Indian," he wrote, "untamed, with a fantastic wildness about it, even in the clearings. . . . The pitch pines are the ghosts of Philip and Massasoit."[9] He sought out an Indian guide to show him how he could return to the woods, free from the hindrances of his society. *Walden* remains an all-time best-seller—perhaps even more popular than Hal Lindsey's apocalyptic fantasy, *The Late Great Planet Earth*. The two books are close cousins. Each of them is the product of a distinctively American

Protestant lineage that looks for paradise as a lost primordial wilderness or a longed-for new world that will transcend this one—at least for the elect few.

In his essay "Walking," Thoreau combined his nostalgia for the disappearing wilderness with a vigorous optimism that America would forge itself into a new world through its virile activism.[10] He notes the derivation of "sauntering" from Sainte-Terrer—a Holy Land pilgrim:

> For every walk is a sort of crusade, preached by some Peter the Hermit in us, to go forth and reconquer this Holy Land from the hands of the Infidels.... We should go forth on the shortest walk, perchance, in the spirit of undying adventure, never to return.[11]

Thoreau's crusade was westward—into the future. East was the Old World, to be forgotten across the Atlantic "Lethean stream." America was the white man's last chance. "If we do not have success this time, there is perhaps one more chance for the race left before it arrives on the banks of the Styx." He continued:

> The West of which I speak is but another name for the Wild, and what I have been preparing to say is, that in Wildness is the preservation of the world. Every tree sends it fibres forth in search of the Wild. The cities import it at any price. Men plough and sail for it. From the forest and wilderness come the tonics and barks which brace mankind.... The founders of every state which has risen to eminence have drawn their nourishment and vigor from a similar wild source.[12]

For Thoreau, the wilderness was America's salvation. Only by connection to its renewing purity and freedom could a self or society escape its sins. He scorned the "worldly miser" who surveyed, plowed, and built on the land but was oblivious to its beauty and sacredness. "Heaven had taken place around him, and he did not see the angels going to and fro, but was looking for an old post hole in the midst of paradise." But for those with holy vision, wilderness was the place to build the Holy Land and the New Eden. Thoreau celebrated the westward expansion of the American empire and armed his wilderness crusader with the weapons to build a new world: "not the sword and the lance, but the bush-whack, the turfcutter, the spade, and the bog-hoe, rusted with the blood of many a meadow, and begrimed with the dust of many a hard-fought field."[13]

Some among Thoreau's circle of influence sought to realize the ideal of a natural life by living in communities devoted to agriculture, spirituality, leisure, and social reform. For example, the Rev. George Ripley founded Brook Farm in 1841 to counter the corruption of cities and the alienation of industrialization. By creating a "colony" of life as it could and should be, this and similar Utopian efforts—more than a hundred in the nineteenth century—aimed to integrate spirit and body, as well as nature and human culture. Energized by a desire for the wild and free, these egalitarian communes sought to manifest Edenic life, and they offered a dissenting counterculture to the larger society. Brook Farm looked back to Eden—associated with pristine nature—and forward, Ripley explained, to "an order of society founded on the divine principles of justice and love, to a future age of happiness, harmony, and of great glory to be realized on earth." Brook Farm functioned as a gathering place for leading reformers and writers engaged in education, anti-slavery work, and women's rights, but it lasted only three years, collapsing under financial difficulties and leadership failures.[14]

Ralph Waldo Emerson (1803–1882) was invited to join Brook Farm, but he declined, as did his best friend, Thoreau. Each of them was too allergic to "society" to want to join even a Utopian one. Emerson invented a new approach to paradise. Instead of a temporal, material, or historical sense of innocent past and redeemed future, he created a spiritual structure for the individual soul to roam in its own interior, immaterial, natural spaces.

Emerson's early life was marked by a series of deaths: his father's death when he was eight; the death of his beloved and talented wife Ellen before she was twenty; the deaths of his brothers Edward and Charles; and, finally, the death of his five-year-old son, Waldo. A graduate of Harvard College and the son of a minister, Emerson had a brief ministerial career before abandoning any idea of a traditional Calvinist divinity and becoming a writer and lecturer.[15] Emerson wrote his influential book *Nature* in 1836, in the wake of Charles's death. His solace for grief was to exult in the moments when the soul was lifted through the sensual pleasures of the world into union with God. Like his ancestor Jonathan Edwards, he felt the beauties of the world pointed beyond themselves to divinity and could lead the soul to freedom and renewal:

The best moments of life are these delicious awakenings of the higher powers, and the reverential withdrawing of nature before its God. ... In the woods, we return to reason and faith. There I feel that nothing can befall me in life,—no disgrace, no calamity (leaving me my eyes), which nature cannot repair. Standing on the bare ground,—my head bathed in the blithe air and uplifted into infinite space,—all mean egotism vanishes. I become a transparent eyeball; I am nothing; I see all; the currents of the Universal Being circulate through me; I am part or parcel of God.[16]

Emerson distinguished himself from "theosophists" who have a "certain hostility and indignation towards matter" and asserted his loyalty to nature. "I expand and live in the warm day like corn and melons. Let us speak her fair. I do not wish to fling stones at my beautiful mother. ... I only wish to indicate the true position of nature in regard to man."[17]

Emerson thought in terms of relationships of dominance and subordination. His view of nature and redemptive wilderness exemplified a form of American romanticism that combined valorization of wildness with domination of the "wild." The subordinate position of nature, in particular, was a feature of its emanation from God through man. "The world proceeds from the same spirit as the body of man. It is a remoter and inferior incarnation of God."[18] For Emerson, the true position of "nature in regard to man" was akin to women's position with regard to men. Nature had little value in itself, but attained value as it reflected and supported man. "All the facts in natural history taken by themselves, have no value, but all barren, like a single sex. But marry it to human history, and it is full of life."[19] He associated woman's relation to man with the relationship of "the Orient" to the West. "I call her Asia," he said of his wife Lydia. In Emerson's time, the Boston transcendentalists had developed interests in Persian poetry and Asian cultures, which they regarded as mysterious, feminine, naturally religious, and soulful.[20]

Emerson embodied the colonial culture he inherited, which had turned to dark-skinned people as extensions of its own American identity. Nature, women, and the Orient were all there for godly Western men to dominate, subdue, consume, and subsume.

> Nature is thoroughly mediate. It is made to serve. It receives the dominion of man as meekly as the ass on which the Saviour rode. It offers up its kingdoms to man as the raw material which he may mold into what is useful. . . . One after another his victorious thought comes up with and reduces all things, until the world becomes at last only a realized will,—the double of the man. [21]

Emerson argued for the rights of American Indians and opposed slavery, but his framework of meaning did not disturb white male supremacy. The inequality among the races was "an indication that some should lead, and some should serve." [22]

> I think it cannot be maintained by any candid person that the African race has ever occupied or do promise ever to occupy any very high place in the human family. Their present condition is the strongest proof that they cannot. The Irish cannot; the American Indian cannot; the Chinese cannot. Before the energy of the Caucasian race all the other races have quailed and done obeisance.[23]

Emerson reduced paradise to the solitary soul capable of making extinct everything that troubled it. His view of the soul, which found itself in pristine wilderness, was made possible by a belief that Indians had vanished or were somewhat less than fully human. Emerson shared

Thoreau's nostalgia for the lost Indians. He wrote in 1845, "We in Massachusetts see the Indians only as a picturesque antiquity. Massachusetts, Sawmut, Samoset, Squantum, Nantasket, Narragansett, Assabet, Musketaquid. But where are the men?" When Emerson visited the California redwood groves in 1871 and was invited to name one of the giant trees, he christened it "Samoset" after the Indian who greeted the Pilgrims at Plymouth. In the safe remove of civilized white society, he urged white men to assume their proper place as creator gods. Just as Adam in the Garden of Eden had the power to name all things and was instructed to subdue the earth, Emerson saw the purified human soul as making paradise anew. He advocated wishful thinking as the way to change the world:

> All that Adam had . . . you have and can do. . . . Build therefore your own world. As fast as you conform your life to the pure idea in your mind . . . so fast will disagreeable appearances, swine, spiders, snakes, pests, mad-houses, prisons, enemies vanish; they are temporary and shall be no more seen. The sordor and filths of nature, the sun shall dry up and the wind exhale.[24]

The material world could be remade through man thinking a new, untroubled, and untroubling world into existence. The possibility was renewed with every birth: "Infancy is the perpetual Messiah which comes into the arms of fallen men, and pleads with them to return to paradise." That return was enacted in the "vast open spaces of untouched woods, virgin lands, and haunting wilderness" of the frontier, unpopulated by troublesome human beings. Emerson encouraged people to "see as though no one ever had seen before us." Emerson's regression to the primordial Eden skipped all the messy history in between and transported him to the pristine dawn of creation. Though he enjoyed the association of his friends and family, one senses in his idealist optimism a hunger for relationship beyond the surfaces of things —but absent any depths of engagement that might stir troubling emotions. His solitary, reborn soul seemed determined to flee from tragic and unredeemable history. It is as if he lived his entire life in a state of unresolved grief, unable to lament and, therefore, unable to love an ambiguous world.[25]

Emerson's essay *Nature,* in the end, was an evangelist's altar call to live a partial, disassociated life. Paradise could be regained, restored, or established anew in the transcendentalist world through the inner life of human beings. Emerson transported earthly paradise into a realm as imaginary as the "Metamora-phic" identity of Forrest's "native" American. Such a sense of paradise was remote from the real presence and obligations of a complex, demanding world, with actual inhabitants, habitats, and histories. Philosopher Cornel West has observed that for Emerson, "conversion of the world" remained related to "conquest and violence not solely because Emerson devalues those peoples associated with virgin lands, cheap labor, and the wilderness—e.g., Indians, Negroes, women—but also because for Emerson land, labor, and the wilderness signify unlimited possibilities and unprecedented opportunities for moral development."[26] Beauty mattered not because it drew individuals beyond themselves into community and justice making, but because the subjective self could consume it. When Emerson wrote his famous essay "On Self-Reliance," he was depending on the support and care of his wife, his mother-in-law, three servants, and a gardener—thanks to wealth he inherited from his first wife, Ellen. Cornel West exposes the parasitic character of such self-deception:

> The Emersonian self—much like the protean, mobile, performative self promoted by market forces—literally feeds off other people. It survives by means of ensuring and securing its own excitement and titillation. Nature itself becomes but a catalyst to the self's energies, a "means of arousing his interior activity."[27]

Not all nature lovers were as inwardly oriented as Emerson. The Universalist and Unitarian minister Thomas Starr King wrote a bestselling book on the White Hills of New England—more popular in its day than was *Walden.* Like Edwards and Emerson, he encouraged his readers to see divinity in the natural world and to read moral and spiritual lessons from the woods, mountains, and rivers. But he did more. He translated love for the beauty of the earth into active efforts to conserve the environment. He moved to California in the 1860s, and in the midst of advocating for racial equality and the abolition of slavery, working to keep California in the Union, and raising money for soldiers wounded in the Civil War, he wrote numerous articles for East Coast newspapers that described the beauty of the California redwood groves and the Sierra. His articles influenced Lincoln's decision to create the nation's first major environmental preserves—Yosemite and Mariposa Grove.

In many ways, the wilderness conservationists of the nineteenth century inspire today's environmental movements. They were, however, based on early Puritan models of separation and segregation. "Nature" and "wilderness" were romantic categories, separate from corrupting "civilization," society, and human institutions. In their romantic idea of nature, individual souls could restore themselves to what their own privilege and activities had destroyed. Industrialization created virtually unlivable conditions for many. People had to escape from civilization and history to "nature" to restore their souls. This segregation of the natural world from human settlement and civilization allowed capitalist growth and environmentally unsound practices to continue virtually untrammeled until the present, with America's spreading ex-urbs, strip malls, superhighways, and voracious appetite for oil.

Christians have struggled for a long time to create a just and peaceful society, the kingdom of God in the world. However, as many Christian social ethicists have noted in the last thirty years, Christians have had difficulty integrating commitments to global justice and peace with environmental responsibility. Where commitments to environmental issues take center stage, discussions of racism and sexism are often attenuated or absent. Where commitments to justice and nonviolence are strong, environmental issues are often neglected. Integrating environmental and social justice issues is difficult when the primary framework is one of nostalgia and hope. In this framework, the present is never enough. Though it is where we live, we inhabit this life aching for lost innocence and a better future self. This ache drives consumerism and supplies the unquenchable need for unnecessary products that have become deadly to ecosystems. We must be immediately attuned to what is here to relate ethically to actual ecosystems. Nostalgic visions of idealized nature or wilderness disconnect us from the everyday consumerism that causes us to do cumulative harm to environments. They cloister us away from noticing the minute-by-minute uses we make of resources and technology. They inhibit careful scrutiny of our spending patterns, emotionally driven consumerism, work habits, and leisure pursuits. Our longings for and personal escapes to "nature" often substitute for our working together to shape our homes, workplaces, and cities to be integrated, sustainable, humane environments. And they allow the privileged leaders of corporations and governments to ignore the way that environmental problems are the new face of racism, sexism, and poverty. Concrete, accurate information about actual effects and recommendations for policy changes and daily practices help, but we also require a spiritual discipline of being aware of our actions moment to moment to change what feeds engines of destruction.

The segregation of nature and civilization inherent in American romanticism replicates Puritan habits of dividing life in the search for paradise. Ever since Calvin included in his commentaries on Genesis a map indicating the earthly location of paradise, his spiritual descendants have sought to locate it or construct it in this world. However, as long as such efforts imagine paradise as purification and salvation as the ultimate and final separation of the pristine from the corrupt and the wild from the civilized, visions of paradise will foster disassociation from the present in all its complex demands. They will seek a realm in which the "good" shall be preserved and "evil" will be destroyed: "swine, spiders, snakes, pests, mad-houses, prisons, enemies vanish," as Emerson claimed. Life is actually sustained, however, by integration, interaction, and exchange in the present—it is ecological, not eschatological.

A GENEROUS JUSTICE

Commitments to God's generous justice and love began with the Universalists, whose roots extend back to seventeenth-century England. Leaders such as the prolific writer, mystic, and church founder Jane Leade (1624–1704) laid the groundwork. In her journals, published in 1697, Leade offered a spiritual vision of paradise as a realm in this life. She saw the church as the renewed garden of paradise, in which humanity's "beautiful diversity" flourished, and she taught that salvation was "accomplished through the life-giving power of God's love which embraced all people."[28] Other English Universalists, such as John Murray (1741–1815), brought their ideas of God's inclusive love to New England in the second half of the eighteenth century.[29] Judith Sargent (1751–1820), who married Murray after he came to America, became a leading voice for Universalism through her prolific writing and church work. In 1782, she published a catechism for parents to help instruct their children about the Christian faith. She acknowledged that she was stepping outside the traditional gender role for women "which custom hath circumscribed" and risked being "accused of arrogance, heresy, [and] licentiousness" for teaching theology. She made bold, nevertheless, to argue that all souls belonged to God and that all would be saved. "There is a day coming when the veil shall be taken from all hearts, and in the mountain of the Lord of hosts, the feast of fat things shall be made for all people." As a foretaste of this feast for all people, she taught that the Lord's Supper should not be regarded "as a figure of the sufferings of the Redeemer." Instead, the bread was a "gathering together of the many grains" into one loaf, so that when Christ said, " 'this is my body' . . . in him are collected the scattered individuals of humanity." The cup "holds up the oneness of the soul of Jesus with the spirits of the human race." Communion celebrated the connectedness of all human beings now and to come—none were left outside or cut off. Such inclusiveness obligated human beings to treat one another justly.[30]

Sargent Murray's teachings were a direct contradiction to the revival preaching prevalent in towns and villages throughout New England. The Universalist church she founded in America, along with her husband John Murray, rejected Calvinist ideas about the wrath of God, the transcendent distance of heaven, and double predestination—the election from the beginning of time of some to salvation and some to damnation. Instead of emphasizing the afterlife, Sargent Murray directed attention to making life in the present reflect God's love for all souls.[31]

Challenging the Calvinist idea that God would ultimately divide humanity into the saved and the damned had far-reaching social implications. Her teaching called into question social hierarchies based on gender distinctions. Through her extensive writings, Sargent Murray became one of America's earliest and most articulate advocates for women's equality and women's right to education. She reinterpreted the story of Eve, "that beauteous fair of paradise," to authenticate women's rights to education. In responding to the serpent's offer of the fruit of the knowledge of good and evil, "it doth not appear that she was governed by any one sensual appetite; but merely by a desire of adorning her mind; a laudable ambition fired her soul, and a thirst for knowledge."[32]

Hosea Ballou (1771–1852) followed Sargent Murray a generation later. A circuit-riding preacher in rural New England, Ballou proclaimed that God was not an angry father who needed his son to suffer to be appeased. He thought it immoral to say that God punished sinful humanity with violence.

> The belief that the great Jehovah was offended with his creatures to that degree, that nothing but the death of Christ, or the endless misery of mankind, could appease his anger, is an idea that has done more injury to the Christian religion than the writings of all its opposers, for many centuries. The error has been fatal to the life and spirit of the religion of Christ in our world; all those principles which are to be dreaded by men, have been believed to exist in God; and professors have been moulded into the image of their Deity, and become more cruel than the uncultivated savage![33]

Christians who professed faith in a violent God, he observed, imitated his violence and believed themselves justified. He also asserted that those who believed God condemned some people to eternal torment and others to eternal bliss found torture acceptable. Ballou characterized such theology as "Power moving on in front, exhibiting tyrannic majesty in every action; and meager justice in the rear, obsequiously pronouncing all right!"[34] Power as control was not Christian; it doubted the divine power of love to save the world and sanctioned those who used coercion and punishment instead of love and care for others.

Ballou was the eleventh child of Maturin and Lydia Ballou, farmers on the southwestern New Hampshire frontier. The Ballous had little formal education; they thought elite education straitjacketed the Holy Ghost. When Lydia died during Hosea's childhood, Maturin, a Baptist preacher, tutored his young son, who also briefly attended a Quaker school and an academy. Three of Maturin's sons, Ballou included, came to disagree with their father's Baptist view of divine grace, which restricted salvation to the predestined elect.

Hosea Ballou became a leading proponent of Christian Universalism. Universalists taught that no matter how much sin and death abounded, grace was greater. Nothing humanity might do could overcome the loving, generous grace of God. Death was not a punishment for sin, but a natural condition of human life, even before the Fall. Those who knew the love of God need not fear death because God's love "is stronger than death, which many waters cannot quench, nor the floods drown." God could be trusted to embrace all humanity; even in death, humans are in "the extended arms of heavenly love and divine benevolence."[35]

Ballou spent more than two decades traveling the frontier in Vermont, New Hampshire, and Massachusetts, preaching universal salvation and debating his Methodist and Calvinist opponents. His early writing shows the kind of religious ideas and disputes popular in the frontier towns of the new Republic. Ballou honed his intellectual and forensic skills at these public debates, which were a popular form of entertainment. Opponents fiercely and passionately contested crucial religious ideas, to the extent that audiences sometimes engaged in shouting matches, made threats of violence, and damaged property. Ballou's style of arguing, evident in his 1805 book, *A Treatise on Atonement,* was to concede the possible truth of his opponent's idea and to elaborate it. Then he dismantled it; he applied the doctrine in question to an example from human life, which exposed its weaknesses. For example, his opponents challenged his idea that salvation was not linked to individual character or faith. Without punishment for sin and incentives to be moral, why, they asked, should humans avoid sin and be saved? Ballou replied:

> Your child has fallen into the mire, and its body and garments are defiled. You cleanse it, and array it in clean robes. The query is, Do you love your child because you have washed it? or, Did you wash it because you loved it?[36]

These illustrations showed that it was slander to attribute to God behaviors that would be regarded as immoral in human beings, and knowing this, Ballou's every written objection to the atonement pointed to its depictions of a vengeful, violent, autocratic, or miserly God. He accused his opponents of making God the enemy of sinners by eternally banishing sinners "from heaven and happiness." He described the response of the thoughtful and sensitive to such threats:

> They have been so wrecked on this wheel of torture, as to be deprived of sleep and every kind of repose. . . . Awful dreams, fraught with the most terrifying imaginations, have corroded the mind. . . . A burning lake of fire and brimstone has been painted to the mind so clearly, that for several days together, the poor frightened soul would feel as if it were on the brink of a precipice, expecting the next moment to be the fatal one.[37]

The Universalist alternative to atonement theology emphasized God's all-embracing love and the beauty of Christ, who drew people to acts of justice and mercy and to happiness. Ballou suggested that, if the devil's goal was to have as many souls as possible miserable unto eternity, God's goal was human joy, in this life and the next. Ballou did not accept the idea that selfless devotion to God required enduring misery and sorrow in this life for happiness in the next. It was not selfish to want happiness because mutual, shared happiness was a greater happiness than a one-sided joy. For this reason, true happiness lay in seeking it not only for oneself but for every human being. Such fullness of happiness required promoting the common good, justice, and well-being for all, universally. In his reasoning about happiness, Ballou based the work of preaching the good news to the poor, outcast, imprisoned, and injured on an affirmation of life in this world, in the immediacy of loving relationships here and now. Hell was what human beings created in this world by cruelty and greed—not a realm of eternal punishment after death. Paradise was also available here and now, manifest in beauty and marked by relationships of justice and care.

By the middle of the nineteenth century, Universalism was a flourishing religious movement, especially strong among poor and middle-income whites in small towns and rural areas. Universalist Christians embodied their faith by working for social changes that rejected redemptive violence and expressed God's love for all souls. Unlike Calvinist Puritans, for whom social reform was a prelude to the apocalyptic end of time and involved purifying violence, Universalists embraced reform work that was aimed at fulfilling the prayer, "Thy will be done *on earth,* as it is in heaven." They employed means that replicated processes of life, such as nurture and growth. Love operated in tenderness, not terror. They advocated women's rights and were an early denomination to ordain women—Olympia Brown (1835–1926), Phebe Hanaford (1829–1921), and Augusta Jane Chapin (1836–1905). They worked to abolish slavery, and Universalist churches were often stops on the Underground Railroad through which runaway slaves were led to freedom. They opposed capital punishment and organized prison reforms on the theory that those who committed crimes should be rehabilitated and restored to society, not punished. They promoted

Christian pacifism. And they spoke out against the folly of believing that violence could beget peace.

Many nineteenth-century Christians came to reject the doctrine of the atonement and its sanctification of bloodshed. Among those who shared Ballou's views was Theodore Parker (1810–1860), a leading Unitarian minister, scholar, and social activist. In place of a wrathful, punishing God, Parker spoke of God as a loving father and mother, whose compassion and generosity nurtured humanity's moral development and called forth human capacities and powers that were deemed good. In contrast to those who focused on personal sins, Parker in particular understood sin in transpersonal ways. Social evils were sustained by four powerful social systems: economics, politics, education, and organized religion. The Christian "alleged revelation [of] salvation from God's wrath and eternal ruin, by the atoning blood of the crucified God" was the lynchpin of social injustice. He commented, "In this generation no American politician dares affront it."[38]

As an alternative to atonement theology, nineteenth-century Christians drew on Genesis 1–2 to reassert the idea that salvation restored the *imago dei* (image of God) in humanity. Women took the lead in asserting that paradise in this world was marked by egalitarian relationships, including those between women and men. Rooted in Methodist "holiness movements" and radical religious groups such as the Quakers and the Shakers, women claimed they were authorized by the indwelling spirit of God to live in freedom and dignity, to manifest their having been created in the image of God, and to be regenerated like Eve before the Fall.[39] Sectarian experiments to challenge the subordinating aspects of marriage, such as the Shakers, were part of the reforming impulses that characterized nineteenth-century Protestants, and women and sex were hotly contested religious issues, as they still are.[40] *Imago dei* theology inspired movements for abolition, prison reform, and peace, as well as for women's rights.

Moral philosophy, an emerging intellectual movement centered at Harvard Divinity School, also developed an *imago dei* theology. In sharp contrast to Calvinist notions of human depravity, a reverence for humanity as endowed with God-given "powers of the soul" marked the thought of the moral philosophers. Historian Daniel Walker Howe has called moral philosophy's blend of Christianity and Enlightenment philosophy "Puritanism without Calvinism."[41] Its most famous and influential proponent, Rev. William Ellery Channing (1780–1842), preached that the human capacities for reason, affection, imagination, will, creativity, aesthetic sensitivity, and moral conscience reflected the *imago dei.* He said that Christ came to restore the obscured image of God in humanity, the "impulse to what is divine within us." The divine likeness in humanity was found not in supernatural or miraculous gifts but in the human faculties of "understanding, conscience, love, and the moral will."[42]

Channing's parishioners applied his *imago dei* preaching to a range of issues. Margaret Fuller advocated for women's rights. Elizabeth Palmer Peabody started a movement for early childhood education that treated children with reverence. Horace Mann labored to establish free public education for all children, who without it would be inhibited from growing their souls. Lydia Maria Child protested Indian removal and agitated for an end to slavery. She pushed Channing to see that his theology required him to support the antislavery cause. However, Channing's elite Boston congregation was full of merchants whose wealth was built on the labor of slaves, and he was reluctant to call for abolition. For most of his ministry, he protected the comfortable life of his congregants and his affectionate relationships with them. When he finally took a strong, public antislavery stand in 1841, near the end of his life, it cost him his pulpit in a congregation he had served for nearly forty years.[43]

Though Channing eventually took a costly stand, his caution in publicly supporting abolition was typical of elite white Christians, who advocated some social reforms but balked at those that would disrupt their privileged identity as "true Americans." That identity, forged by genocide and slavery, maintained Anglo-Saxon economic, social, and political superiority in relationship to African Americans and Native Americans. Many, though morally troubled by slavery, were reluctant to relinquish its economic advantages. Slaveholding Quaker families in Maryland and Pennsylvania enjoyed wealth and prominence.[44] White women were just as inclined as white men to advocate for the end of slavery while also wishing to preserve racial hierarchies. Though many white women labored for a lifetime in the suffrage and abolitionist causes, white women's reform societies excluded black women.

Imago dei theology can go only so far in fostering human solidarity and changing power dynamics. It affirmed a common spark of divinity in every human; it provided a basis for rejecting social structures that inhibited the full exercise of God-given human powers; it undergirded human agency and activism; it fostered identification with the struggles of others. However, it only affirmed what is common to all humanity, not what is particular and different. Such theologies assumed that individuals seeing others as *like* themselves provided an adequate basis for human community, whereas in fact community requires recognizing others both as kin and as *other*, as distinct and valuable in their particularities. Color and gender blindness create white-out conditions that build systems of justice on reductionistic erasures of particularities and differences. The work of justice requires paying attention to how difference is used to justify oppression. It employs astute awareness of how oppressive systems grant privilege and seek to protect it at all costs. It engages those who have privilege in challenging systems from which they benefit, not just helping those "less fortunate."

In response to critiques of redemptive violence from Universalists and Unitarians, some Christians leaders reasserted the doctrine of the blood atonement. Congregationalist Horace Bushnell (1802–1876), a Yale graduate, thought that Ballou, Parker, and Channing had gone too far. He was close to them in many ways—his influential book *Christian Nurture* promoted the growth and development of children's spirits through the care of God's fatherly kindness, rather than the threat of divine punishment. He also agreed with the Universalist and Unitarian Christians that God was not a wrathful deity. However, Bushnell retained the concepts of atonement and redemptive bloodshed. He interpreted the Civil War as America's violent fate, an inescapable consequence of the nation's sins: "only blood, much blood, long years of bleeding, can resanctify what we have so loosely held and so badly desecrated." Advancing an Abelardian view of Christ's suffering in *The Vicarious Sacrifice*, he proclaimed God's compassionate identification with humanity's afflictions and pictured this loving God as a fellow sufferer. God's compassionate heart united him with humanity's painful existence and made God, like humanity, a victim of evil and sin.

The intimacy of shared pain was, for Bushnell, the essence of self-sacrificing love—the highest virtue was to *feel for* victims of sin:

> There is a cross in God before the wood is seen upon Calvary; hid in God's own virtue itself, struggling on heavily in burdened feeling through all the previous ages, and struggling as heavily now even in the throne of the worlds.... Let us come then not to the wood alone, not to the nails, not to the vinegar and the gall, not to the writhing body of Jesus, but to the very feeling of our God and there take shelter.[45]

Bushnell felt that humanity, frozen in hard-heartedness and selfishness, could be moved by the warm-blooded passion of God's vicarious suffering. Christ's sacrifice on the cross could save souls by enticing them to become like him, burdened in sorrow and pain by the sufferings of others, and moved to empathetic identification with even their enemies. Bushnell's suffering God recovered an orthodox affirmation of the atonement, and recentered social justice in benevolent paternalism.

It enabled them to see themselves as Godlike in their capacities for empathy, agency, and generosity—powers that should be used by the capable to assist the downtrodden, oppressed, and brokenhearted. Christian reformers understood themselves to be those with power, which they were to use to lift up the less powerful. To be sure, such paternalism often granted that all souls possessed Godlike capacities. The purpose of social reform was to remove barriers that prevented the oppressed from fully exercising their human powers.[46] But theology emphasizing God's benevolent paternalism blessed whites who emo-

tionally identified with black suffering; it praised men who sympa-
thized with women's subjugation; it valorized the privileged who found
wholeness by connecting with the poor. This sentimental bonding of
the "benevolent" elite with "victims" structured compassion as an im-
balance of power. Ironically, it required the ongoing existence of the
"helper" and "the helped"—a conundrum familiar, cloying, and an-
noying to those who have been targeted for assistance as the poor, oppressed, and pitied.[47]

Benevolent paternalism reasserted the centrality of Christ's crucifixion as an image of compassion and protected white supremacy.
Bushnell and many other elite liberals wanted a nurturing, co-suffering
God. However, since their positions of power and privilege spared
them from the soul-murdering, body-destroying consequences of slavery, they could demonstrate compassion for the victims of their systems
of power while still retaining the illusion of Anglo-Saxon superiority
over people of African descent. "Nothing can save the inferior race
but a ready and pliant assimilation," Bushnell asserted.[48] Assimilation
remains a framework of meaning that preserves both white supremacy
and benevolent paternalism. Paradise in this world cannot be honored
unless those with power and privilege release their grip on benevolent
paternalism.

Despite criticism, the rejection of the atonement and a commitment
to a this-worldly Christianity survived into the twentieth century.
Clarence Skinner (1881–1949), in *The Social Implications of Universalism*, published in 1915, pictured God as "a robust deity who likes his
universe, who hungers for fellowship, who is in and of and for the whole
of life." He taught that loving the world that God loves meant respect-
ing "the infinite variety of the forms of life," honoring that "human
beings exhibit the widest conceivable variety of physical and tempera-
mental differences" which must not be exploited. Loving the world
meant working to abolish injustice and to be motivated by joy "in the
beauties and riches of the earth." Optimistic, life-affirming religion recognized that "those who have faith in the world are the ones upon
whom rests the tremendous responsibility of redeeming the world."[49]

MORAL CLARITY ABOUT EVIL AND SIN

Living justly in this world requires people to name evil and sin accurately. Since the tenth century, Christian theology has often obfuscated violence, calling torment redemptive, sanctioning war as holy, deeming invasion to be liberation, and invoking self-annihilation as love. Precise recognition of that which harms life is a prerequisite for living in this world as paradise. The devil lurks in the paradise garden and must be confronted with astute analysis, as Cyril of Jerusalem taught in fourth-century Jerusalem.

In the early twentieth century, an astute analysis of evil was offered by "Social Gospel" Christians, who believed the purpose of Christian life was to "bring in the Kingdom of God"—to fulfill the prophetic vision that "earth might be fair and all men glad and wise."[50] The definitive theological statement of the movement came in 1917, at the end of World War I, when Walter Rauschenbusch (1861–1918), a Baptist minister and seminary professor, published *A Theology for the Social Gospel*. Rauschenbusch was clear that personal salvation for individual souls after death was not the point of Christian faith. He had little interest in an otherworldly heaven:

> In the present life we are bound up with [family] and children, with friends and work-mates, in a warm organism of complex life. When we die, we join—what? A throng of souls, an unorganized crowd of saints, who each carry a harp and have not even organized an orchestra.[51]

His work criticized Christian ideas that sanctioned war, racism, imperialism, economic injustice, and exploitation of the earth's natural resources. He was aware that Protestant missionary zeal frequently focused on the individual salvation of sinners while disregarding how mission work exported American cultural imperialism and promulgated oppressive social systems:

> It is essential to our spiritual honesty that no imperialism shall masquerade under the cover of our religion. Those who adopt the

white man's religion come under the white man's influence. Christianity is the religion of the dominant race. The native religions are a spiritual bulwark of defense, independence, and loyalty. If we invite men to come under the same spiritual roof of monotheism with us and to abandon their ancient shelters, let us make sure that this will not be exploited as a trick of subjugation by the Empires. As long as there are great colonizing imperialisms in the world, the propaganda of Christianity has a political significance.[52]

Rauschenbusch had a keen capacity to identify accurately how evil and sin operated, even in the guise of religion. He rejected the common Christian teaching that sin was rooted in rebellion against God's will. Rauschenbusch observed that "in actual life such titanic rebellion against the Almighty is rare. . . . We do not rebel: we dodge and evade. We kneel in lowly submission and kick our duty under the bed while God is not looking."[53] Sin mattered not because it disappointed, offended, or alienated God, but because it disrupted relationships of love and justice in human affairs. "We rebel against God and repudiate his will when we set our profit and ambition above the welfare of our fellows and above the Kingdom of God which binds them together."[54] For Rauschenbusch, selfishness was the root of all sin, and evangelical revivalism was selfish. Viewing sin as an individual failing alone was inadequate:

We rarely sin . . . alone. Science supplies the means of killing, finance the methods of stealing, the newspapers have learned how to bear false witness artistically to a globeful of people daily, and covetousness is the moral basis of our civilization.[55]

Rauschenbusch insisted that the death of Jesus did not redeem humanity from its sins. Rather, it revealed the character of transpersonal evil—collective sins that continue to put earth and its peoples at risk of crucifixion. Rauschenbusch enumerated six kinds of sin that combined to kill Jesus:

1. Religious bigotry: "The cause of untold social division, bitterness, persecution, and religious wars."

2. Graft and political power: "Those who are in control of the machinery of organized society are able to use it for selfish and predatory ends, turning into private profit what ought to serve the common good."

3. A corrupt legal system: "Even in free countries the judicial process can swiftly break conscientious convictions and the most cherished rights of democracy. In our own country the delays and appeals . . . set up a terrible inequality between the rich and poor."

4. Mob spirit and mob action: "Well dressed mobs are more dangerous than ragged mobs because they are far more efficient. Entire nations may come under the mob spirit and abdicate their judgment. . . . Sometimes the crowd turns against the oligarchy; usually the oligarchy manipulates the crowd."

5. Militarism: "With his arrest Jesus fell into the hands of the war system. When the soldiers stripped him, beat his back with the leaded whip, pressed the wreath of thorns into his scalp . . . when they blindfolded and struck him, asking him to prophesy who it was and spitting in his face—this was the humor of the barrack room."

6. Class contempt and class divisions: Economic systems amass wealth for the few and leave the poor bereft and despised. War profiteers killed Jesus. Unrestrained capitalism "directs the productive process of society primarily toward the creation of private profit rather than the service of human needs; it demands autocratic management and strengthens the autocratic principle in all social affairs; it has impressed a materialistic spirit on our whole civilization."[56]

Rauschenbusch placed the solidarity of God with humankind at the center of his theology. God was "the ground of social unity" and not the God of only one group or one nation. He objected to forms of

Christianity in which "full moral obligation stopped at the religious boundary line." To counteract the sins of nationalism, racial categorization, religious chauvinism, and economic exploitation, God must be conceived as "the all-pervading life . . . the ground of . . . spiritual oneness," and those who worship God must recognize "the consciousness of solidarity" to be of the essence of religion.[57]

Rauschenbusch called for solidarity but saw racism as a southern problem. As a German Baptist pastor in New York, he did not befriend black ministers. Another Baptist pastor would press his vision forward beyond segregation. His name was Martin Luther King Jr.

"NOT A PALE BLOODLESS, HEARTLESS THING"

Beginning under slavery, African American Christians created routes to liberation here and now—not beyond this world. They read the story of the Exodus as their story, a story of a God who supported freedom for slaves and blessed wilderness as a place of escape from oppression. Slave revolts in the late eighteenth century prompted whites to ban black churches among slaves and to force them either to attend white services, sitting at the rear of the church, or to attend separate services under the watchful eye of white guards and led by white ministers. At the end of the eighteenth century, free blacks formed their own churches, such as the African Methodist Episcopal Church and National Black Baptist Convention, which, along with the Quakers, Unitarians, Universalists, and other Protestants opposed to slavery, created and supported the Underground Railroad to freedom.[58]

Christian white supremacy reasserted itself with vehemence and violence. Some white supremacists lynched or murdered both rebellious blacks and the white abolitionists who helped them. Once the Civil War was over, lynching became a strategy to terrorize African Americans and their allies and reassert white power. Between 1882 and 1968, 4,743 murders were recorded, but many went unreported. They occurred in most states, though the largest number took place in Mississippi, Alabama, Georgia, Texas, and Louisiana, and around 80 percent of victims were black.[59]

Most Americans know something about lynching but imagine it as done by outlaws, drunken white men on a rampage, or by cowards under the cover of pale sheets and nightfall. In the face of documentation of white support for lynching, it is tempting to mystify violence, to insist it was "just" a small and aberrant minority who participated, or to resort to vague hand-wringing generalizations about the inherent violence in "human nature." But evidence shows that for many whites, lynching was a communal ritual to be attended in one's Sunday best and remembered as a special event. Many murders were planned well ahead. Newspaper ads announced the date, time, and place of the lynching. Schools closed so parents could bring their children. Professional photographers set up darkroom tents on site and produced souvenir postcards for the spectators, who paid ten times the price of a regular postcard for the images. Spectators posed for photos at midday, dressed as if attending a church picnic.[60]

The postcards resemble the pandemonium of late medieval Calvary images, with their depictions of torture and murder. In one chilling photograph, the limp corpse of a black man hangs in rags from a rope tied to a high tree branch. A crowd of white men, women, and children surrounds him. The women are in dresses; the suited men sport white boater hats. Some in the crowd gaze at the body in curiosity or self-congratulation. Others smile or cheer, many in family groups. In the foreground, three teenage girls in light-colored dresses huddle together. They stare in rapt attention at the hands of one of the girls. She holds a small piece of tattered cloth. The rag matches the ripped trouser leg of the man hanging from the tree. The horror of the image is its likeness to a picnic, as if the brutal murder of a human being were an ordinary, festive community gathering.

The reality of lynching testifies to how deeply Christian notions of redemptive violence are inscribed in the American psyche. As Hosea Ballou said, those who believe that God redeems the world through violence become cruel themselves. In 1931, in a blistering antilynching editorial in the *Baltimore Evening Sun,* H. L. Mencken condemned the festive crowds that gathered for a particularly gruesome execution in Maryland. Spectators had taken bones, clothing, and other grisly souvenirs, crowning their family mantles with infamy. Perhaps they sought to remember a time when they witnessed "good" triumph over "evil." Mencken's editorial cost the paper thousands of dollars in sales and canceled subscriptions.[61] The last lynching in the United States occurred in 1968, the year Martin Luther King Jr. was assassinated—within the lifetime of many reading this book.

Systems of privilege use public violence to maintain themselves, and they benefit from those who teach that selfless love acquiesces to violence. Just as Rome crucified Jesus to assert Roman supremacy over rebellious Jews in first century Palestine, lynching was a terrorist tool of white supremacy. The images call into question theologies that would see in such death an example of self-sacrificing love, rather than the attempt to kill love. Lynching images remind us of the chasm of difference between the reactions of the communities of the victims and the communities of the perpetrators. White communities openly celebrated with impunity, cheering the enforcers of their status. Black communities feared for their lives, hid their children, and prayed to their God for deliverance.

In the face of black suffering, some African Americans challenged traditional Christian pieties of atonement and an omnipotent deity. W.E.B. DuBois confronted God:

Keep Not Thou Silent, O God!
Sit no longer blind, Lord God, deaf to our prayer and dumb to our dumb suffering. Surely Thou, too, art not white, O Lord, a pale bloodless, heartless thing![62]

The Rev. Nathaniel Paul accused God of behaving like a white spectator at a lynching. He addressed God, making "the bold inquiry in this thy holy temple, why it was that thou didst look on with the calm indifference of an unconcerned spectator, when thy holy law was violated, thy divine authority despised and a portion of thine own creatures reduced to a state of mere vassalage and misery?"[63] Countee Cullen, a Harlem Renaissance poet and Methodist minister's son, rejected religious piety that promised liberation in a time to come, beyond the suffering of this life. In protest of the white, impassive God, he asserted he himself should be God: his body, his hands, feet, heart, all "this moving breathing frame of me" were more worthy of devotion. When human eyes close, "say then God dies."[64] These ways of saying "no" resisted oppression through affirmations of human dignity and power, not through valorizing innocent victims.

The greatest activist to say "no" to lynching was Ida B. Wells-Barnett (1862–1931). In the face of congratulatory white supremacy and its celebrations of lynching, she maintained a relentless campaign to stop it and was joined by DuBois, Frederick Douglass, and many others. Wells-Barnett was born in Mississippi six months before Emancipation, the oldest of eight. After her parents died when she was 16, she supported her siblings. To earn more money, she moved to Memphis, Tennessee, in 1881. A member of Beale Street Baptist Church, she launched her career as a journalist writing for a paper she co-owned and edited there, *The Free Speech and Headlight*. She wrote under the pen name "Iola."

When three of her friends were lynched in 1892, Wells-Barnett launched a major anti-lynching campaign using her paper and other publications to stir up protest and resistance. In one of her pamphlets, she described the lynching of a preacher, Elijah Strickland accused of conspiracy in the murder of a white man, Alfred Crawford:

> Sunday night, about 8:30 o'clock about fifteen men went to the plantation of Major Thomas and took Lige Strickland from the little cabin in the woods that he called home, leaving his wife and five children to wail and weep over the fate they knew was in store for the Negro. Their cries aroused Major Thomas, and that sturdy old gentleman of the antebellum type followed the lynchers in his buggy, accompanied by his son, W. M. Thomas, determined to save, if possible, the life of his plantation darky.[65]

Thomas, who had been in Congress and was a stalwart, distinguished citizen of the area, persuaded the men to vote unanimously to put Strickland in jail instead of killing him. Still, they hung him until dead after torturing him.

In her autobiography, *Crusade for Justice*, Wells-Barnett criticized northern white churchgoers for tolerating racism for fear of offending their white brethren.

> Our American Christians are too busy saving the souls of white Christians from burning in hell-fire to save the lives of black ones from present burning in fires kindled by white Christians.[66]

One of her antilynching editorials, published while she was traveling, excoriated the white community in Memphis for their tolerance of such crimes. She urged the black community to leave and make better lives elsewhere. Entire churches left. Two thousand people left in two months' time, and white businesses that were dependent on blacks suffered. White homemakers complained of the loss of domestic help. Wells-Barnett's paper was mobbed, and her friends warned her not to return, so she wrote for a time in exile in New York before settling in Chicago with her new husband, attorney Ferdinand Barnett, in 1895. There, she founded a club for African American women that opened the first kindergarten for black children. She also raised money to prosecute a police officer for killing an innocent black man and to help create the first black orchestra in Chicago. With Jane Addams, she successfully blocked the establishment of segregated schools in the city. Like DuBois, she opposed Booker T. Washington's accommodation strategies.[67]

Wells-Barnett, a deeply religious woman, likened herself to Joan of Arc and saw herself as a lone prophet. She had a profound faith in the power of truth to set people free and believed that if she compiled the evidence, proclaimed the truth, and held fast to her goal, change would follow. She regularly taught a Bible class at a settlement house she founded for African Americans in Chicago, just as she did at her church. She understood her life and that of the women of her generation as living in a kind of exile. Though they had escaped Egypt and slavery, they had not yet reached any sort of promised land. She saw her life as a great crusade for justice. Uncompromising and single-minded in her moral clarity and vision, she lacked the pastoral skills and attention to the present that created community and brought others along with her. By the end of her life, she was alienated even from those who had been her allies, including DuBois and other cofounders of the National Association for the Advancement of Colored People.[68]

Her oratory, flair for language, and passionate commitment to ending lynching and gaining justice for black women accomplished a great deal. She demonstrated the critical importance of naming violence and injustice clearly. By doing so, she cut through the illusion of redemptive violence and disrupted its unholy rituals of repeated tortures and crucifixions. Like many Christians committed to social change, she saw herself as a prophet, believing truth to be self-evident and persuasive if it were clearly declared.

Wells-Barnett and other courageous witnesses invoke outrage at carnage and sorrow for loss. They ask others to hold fast to the truth of what has occurred, and to sustain efforts to stop such injustice. They advance the sacred work of religious community: to shelter truth and accurate, integrative memory; to raise prophetic voices against injustice and violence; to organize communities to resist the principalities and powers of this world; and to make space for lamentation.

Deep mourning is not something a person can do alone. A high tide of grief can drown a stricken soul. Those who are too alone may find they can survive loss only by damping all feeling down. Closure of the heart protects against overwhelming sorrow and debilitating rage. One of the most important functions of religious community is to provide a container for grief. Held in the embrace of a community's rituals and traditions, grief can find its depth, anger can voice its anguish, and protest can fuel creative action that holds out the possibilities of restored and protected life even in the midst of or aftermath of injustice and tragedy.

Paradise is a place for the brokenhearted. Its accommodating environment can hold the sharp pieces of shattered lives, allowing sorrow and despair, incompleteness, rage, and struggle. Within the embrace of paradise—the realm of God's ongoing creativity, the realm of the

Spirit's all-permeating breath—those who suffer may find balm. The brokenhearted victims of violence, neglect, or abuse may find recovery. Life in paradise does not mean that conflict or despair or injustice are eliminated. It means that being present, fully feeling, and passionately engaged is possible and that the struggle for life can be sustained.

The challenge for those who are committed to life here and now is to keep the human heart open to truthful encounter with human-created horrors. What does it take for the privileged or protected to acknowledge and confront human acts of pitiless cruelty, torture, and humiliation? People can retreat into denial or turn away to protect themselves from being disrupted by injustice that seems not to touch them. Then they become anesthetized participants in systems that harm life. People need the art, ritual, journalism, and literature that hold such realities steadily before their eyes without moralizing simplifications or jeremiads that too quickly produce remorse without insight. If they turn away simply saying "How terrible!" condemnation becomes a dodge. It creates self-satisfied approbation while sidestepping the more difficult tasks of analysis and restorative action.

Emotional attentiveness is more possible when people ground their life in something more than outrage alone: in a deep affirmation of life's goodness, in epiphanies of life's beauty and the possibilities of grace. It is the embrace of life—the knowing of paradise in this life—that makes protest possible. One weeps because one has known beauty and love. The apprehension of paradise now provides a foundation for emotional aliveness and moral clarity—it fuels outrage, protest, and social critique. At the same time, it provides a basis for sustained activism in its acknowledgment of beauty and joy.

After World War II, African American church leaders, most notably Martin Luther King Jr., combined the burning passion for racial justice forged in the struggle against slavery and lynching with Social Gospel theology. The Social Gospel's focus on engagement with life here and now rather than salvation in an afterlife provided King with an antidote to his experience of black Baptist piety that counseled people to accept suffering and discrimination in this life and anticipate release and vindication in the afterlife. In addition, his study of Gandhi in graduate school and his friendship with the Vietnamese Buddhist Thich Nat Hanh, who organized nonviolent resistance to the U.S. war in his country, provided insight for King's development of methods of nonviolent resistance to oppression. King integrated these various strands of this-worldly salvation in his call for "beloved community." His clear analysis of the connections between racism and the Vietnam War testify to the enduring importance of prophetic critique. His concrete commitment to embody human solidarity and justice here and now reveal what it means to love the world.

THE COMMUNITY OF PARADISE

We can come to know the world as paradise when our hearts and souls are reborn through the arduous and tender task of living rightly with one another and the earth. Generosity, nonviolence, and care for one another are the pathways into transformed awareness. Knowing that paradise is here and now is a gift that comes to those who practice the ethics of paradise. This way of living is not Utopian. It does not spring simply from the imagination of a better world but from a profound embrace of this world. It does not begin with knowledge or hope. It begins with love.

To know paradise in this life is to enter a multidimensional spiritual-material reality, an interstitial place. Paradise is simultaneously this earth, a beautiful, luminous creation, and the realm of the dead, which is connected to the living but is separated by a thin veil through which the dead can pass to accompany, bless, or guide the living. Paradise is human life restored to its divinely infused dignity and capacity, and it is a place of struggle with evil and injustice, requiring the development of wisdom, love, nonviolence, and responsible uses of power. Paradise can be experienced as spiritual illumination of the heart, mind, and senses felt in moments of religious ecstasy, and it can be known in ordinary life lived with reverence and responsibility. Paradise is not a place free from suffering or conflict, but it is a place in which Spirit is present and love is possible.

Entering paradise in this life is not an individual achievement but is the gift of communities that train perception and teach ethical grace. Paradise provides deep reservoirs for resistance and joy. It calls us to embrace life's aching tragedies and persistent beauties, to labor for justice and peace, to honor one another's dignity, and to root our lives in the soil of this good and difficult earth.

Epilogue

I waited till this present season . . . that I might take and lead
you by the hand to the brighter and more fragrant meadows
of this present paradise.

CYRIL OF JERUSALEM, fourth century

We spent our last year of writing perched on the edge of an estuary
at the end of Wollochet Bay near Gig Harbor, Washington. The daily
tides accompanied the ebbs and surges of our spirits as we struggled to
wrestle four thousand years of history, theology, and sacred story into
this book. Rebecca's grandparents built the small log cabin where we
worked. Their ashes rest under the rhododendron by the boat dock. As
we plowed through yet another draft, tracked down still more pieces of
research, and discussed our deepening insights about new discoveries,
Rebecca's parents helped. At their beach home nearby, they hosted
nightly meals, an occasional evening of lively bridge, and frequent conversations about our research and conclusions.

In December, hurricane-force winds struck the area, felling huge
trees and causing power outages across the entire Pacific Northwest. Intense cold followed, and the surface of the bay froze over. It cracked and
popped as the tide withdrew, leaving beautiful, translucent, irregular
sheets of ice sparkling in the sunlight. Unable to recharge our comput-
ers or phones, we were required to stop writing, and instead, spent days
helping our neighbors clear trees and making the road passable. During our hiatus from work, Rebecca's eighty-year-old father, Bruce,

taught Rita to split wood, and we resorted to heating and cooking on the long-retired cast-iron wood-burning stove in the kitchen.

All summer, a bald eagle and curious harbor seal, whom we named Lucille, paid regular visits, and the chattering kingfishers, honking blue herons, and screeching gulls reminded us to stay present to the world right before us, "the paradise of all these parts," as John Smith once called a stretch of New England coastline. Rebecca's mother, Gretchen, said she likes, especially, to observe the wildlife around the Bay because they remind her that she is not the center of Creation. One warm afternoon at low tide, Bruce mused about the shape of the sun-baked mud flats, which he has observed nearly all of his life. He noted the many freshwater streams that crossed the expanse of sandy clay, strewn with shells and drying seaweed. As we looked, he pointed out that the streams converged into four main streams, which then flowed together down the channel of the bay into the great sea of Puget Sound, proving, of course, that Wollochet Bay is paradise. Bruce, a retired United Methodist minister, has always been appreciated for his impeccable logic in biblical interpretation.

We took breaks nearly every day to go walking. Along the rocky, barnacle-strewn beach we picked up stones, feathers, driftwood, and shells. The incessant peeping of osprey chicks reached us from their nest in the tall cedar across the bay, and we watched their parents diving expertly for fish. Wandering the roads through the mix of old farms, remnants of second-growth fir forests, and new McMansions, we scavenged blackberries and apples, fed the old mule, picked armloads of wildflowers, and stepped carefully around dead raccoons, squirrels, and birds, hit by cars speeding along the straight stretches of road. On the clearest days, we headed toward an area that affords us a splendid view of Mt. Rainier, a fourteen-thousand-foot-high glacier-covered volcanic peak that most locals just call "the mountain." One day, toward evening, rounding the crest by the horse farm, we stopped to admire the tall grasses of the fields catching the late sunlight and undulating gold and green in the soft wind. The dark woods, cool and dense, hugged the far side of the pasture. For a moment, we stood still in the presence of the breathing world.

Throughout our time here at Wollochet Bay, we have felt the moral ambiguities of life in an affluent consumer society. As we write the conclusion to this book, continual loud cracking and scraping noises across the bay accompany the clicking of our keyboards. A large yellow bulldozer consumes the old wooden cabins on the opposite shore; all that will soon remain is a pile of refuse on a dirt lot next to a small stand of firs. The bay is near the Narrows Bridge, which connects the Kitsap Peninsula to nearby Tacoma and Seattle, the closest large cities. Though a ballot measure to allot public funds for a new bridge failed, the county allowed a private company to build a second, even larger bridge, which will dramatically increase access to the peninsula.

Development fever has struck Wollochet Bay. "For Sale" signs litter the roads as property owners anticipate a real estate boom when the new bridge opens. Near the highway to it, new strip malls and a medical center are being built. Acres of forest have been cleared, and large, barnlike houses have slowly replaced small bungalows and cabins. Beautiful eelgrass once grew in the fresh streams of the mud flats, but fertilizers and pesticides have poured into the streams from the nearby golf course and lawns. Those poisons will only increase as more houses are built. Through the year, we have taken an ambiguous comfort in seeing only a few "sold" stickers, even on the signs that proclaim the lot or house is "price reduced." The sluggish rate of sales may slow the destruction of the trees and shoreline. However, we know that some residents, many of them older and retired, have to sell their property. They built their modest houses so they could spend the rest of their lives in this beautiful place, but they live on limited incomes and will not be able to afford the rising taxes.

Across the road a small wetlands was completely stripped of trees, probably illegally. The lot had been a boggy wood, which neighbors had made an effort to purchase together as a community park. Not enough people, however, were willing to help pay for it, so the denuded lot is now for sale at ten times what the neighbors once needed to buy it. The neighbor next to the lot, furious at its destruction, has posted a prominent sign saying "Buyer Beware!" It describes the lot's wetland classification, which makes it virtually impossible to build upon, and he proclaims bribes and greed destroyed the land.

At the nearby end of the bay, the residents saved the shoreline. Where the Artondale and Wollochet creeks empty onto the tidal mud flats, they bought the surrounding land and created a conservation area. A dense stand of old firs and maples rings fields of sea grasses, cut by streams. Kayakers snaking their way upstream duck under the fallen logs that crisscross the mouths of the creeks. During the very highest tides, the grasses are under water, and on warm days occasional jet skis and motorboats, breaking the speed limit, roar into the end of the bay. Flocks of Canada geese return to the estuary at sunset, honking enthusiastically as they glide in for a splashy landing. The estuary provides a shelter where they and many other water birds congregate and nest.

Late last summer, some large salmon splashed their way up Artondale Creek at the start of their annual run. A few days later, local Salish Indians brought a boat into the end of the bay and cast a net across it. Wollochet is their word for "happy clams." Descendants of the first inhabitants of the area, they have fished Puget Sound waters for centuries, though periodic conflicts have erupted when whites have resisted federal requirements that they honor the Native treaty rights. The Salish who visited last fall caught few fish, despite numerous attempts.

When Rebecca's grandparents built their cabin, they were among several Methodist families who spent summers on the bay. Like her, they had attended church camps where worshipping in the outdoor chapel, vespers around the campfire, and Bible study in the woods linked Christian life with appreciation for "God's world." During our year on Wollochet Bay, we haven't exactly camped, but we have lived more simply than usual. Our water surges into pumps from deep in the ground below us and, through a septic system, returns to it. We have eaten local products when we could get them and have hauled both our trash and our recycling to the local dump. We wear the same simple clothes several days in a row. We have not, however, even approximated living at minimal impact on the environment we find so beautiful.

What we've observed here at Wollochet Bay reflects the history of

Western culture, its habits, and its present problems. Similar observations, with different particulars, could be made of many places. Paradise
surrounds us "with its many delights," as Ephrem wrote. At the same
time, legacies of colonialism and habits of consumption—rooted in a
loss of awareness of paradise here and now—trouble the relationships
among human cultures and the environment.

PARADISE HERE AND NOW

In seeking to understand the history of Christianity's forgotten love for
this world, we have felt wonder, grief, horror, surprise, joy, dismay, and
delight on this pilgrimage through the past. We have struggled, over and
over, to understand the material we gathered and to come to terms with
what we discovered. We now both appreciate more deeply the value and
feel more acutely the limits of the religious traditions of Christianity that
are our heritage and our responsibility.

In reaching our conclusions and constructing this history of Western Christianity and paradise, we have sought to avoid falling into what
we know in our very bones is a self-defeating Protestant habit. That
habit searches history to retrieve a pristine, pure origin and separates
this precious kernel of truth from all the subsequent chaff that hides it.
The kernel of truth becomes the measure for judging everything that
followed as corruption and betrayal. From that purified kernel, the
Protestant habit constructs a vision for the future as a hope and enjoins
the faithful to labor tirelessly to bring the vision into being. In rejecting
everything between the pure past and the hoped-for future, Protestants
tend to identify themselves with an original goodness and to disasso-
ciate from the messy history and ambiguous institutions that their
forebears created and that ground present existence. However, this tendency forces us to view the past selectively and impose purity upon it
rather than to see its fullness, which is as complex, ambiguous, and diverse as any human endeavor ever is. Without the messy (as opposed
to pristine) past and all its people and years, we would not exist at all,
in this time, in this place, in our particular bodies, in these communi-

ties and institutions. History is our social and cultural DNA. We have
inherited it, and it shapes who we are. We have some measure of choice
in how we express it in our own lives, but how we creatively transform
it is the greater responsibility. We cannot lament and transform, however, what we reject or deny and refuse to engage.

The story of the garden in Genesis 2 lends itself, especially, to a habit
of longing for a pristine past and judging the present to be a corrupt age.
It functioned thus for the many Christians who settled the land now
called North America and shaped its dominant society both as a longing to retrieve the lost past and as a forward march toward the promised land, human progress, greater prosperity, and a better world. The
American Protestant structure of nostalgia and hope either retreats to
the past or runs toward the future without perceiving carefully where
we are. This relentless drive toward change, either as retrieval or
progress, characterizes much of American society and its values. Nostalgia and hope elide our responsibility for receiving the good around
us, for valuing it and relating ethically toward it.

This Protestant faith in pristine origins or in visions for the future
implicates us in self-annihilation or perpetual self-punishment. It encourages us to relate to the world around us with hypervigilance, to detect error, and to be suspicious of the present as the problem to be fixed
so that restoration or progress might prevail. We fall into believing that
we will be more completely and truly ourselves in an idealized future.
The alternatives to nostalgia and hope that we give ourselves are cyni-
cism, disillusionment, despair, and impotence.

Western Christianity has always stood at the open doors of paradise. However, it became unable to perceive what unfolded before it
and sought paradise elsewhere, leaving, in its wake, legacies of broken
hearts, traumatized bodies, and fractured cultures. The Puritans came
to North America to make themselves and paradise anew. Their religious ideas of time and human life have informed an American identity
that defines freedom and the pursuit of happiness as separation. Ideal
life is free from constraints on the exercise of individual conscience and
will; relationship to others inhibits individual rights. Pursuit of happi-

ness in this mode leaves life without deep, meaningful relationships of mutual responsibility and mutual knowing—life, finally, with little real presence or love and thus perpetually devoid of happiness. Such ideas foment resentment toward obligations and hostility toward limits on what individuals may acquire, use, and consume.

"Today you will be with me in paradise," Jesus said. But when Western Christianity removed paradise from today, placing salvation beyond, behind, or ahead of us—but not here and now—it disconnected life from full engagement in the present. In exile and always in search of paradise, Western Christianity has made humanity's location in time and space a problem. Preoccupied with being *lost*, Western souls are anxious for home, for grounding, for meaning, for contact, for communion, and for escape from present life, which can never measure up to our imaginary goals. This produces an eager greed for what others have and an insatiable desire for goods. Avarice takes place in countless small daily ways and interactions. It motivates large-scale programs of economic aggrandizement, military domination, and environmental exploitation. Western culture needs to face the origins of its hollowness and to relinquish its violent, colonizing habits.

What we need now is a religious perspective that does not locate salvation in a future end point, a transcendent realm, or a zone after death. Paradise is not withheld, closed, or removed from us. Realizing this requires us to let go of the notion that paradise is life without struggle, life free from wrestling with legacies of injustice and current forces of evil. Assuredly, we are in a world in which the struggle continues. However, it is also true that we already live on holy ground, in the presence of God, with bodies and souls sanctified by the Spirit's anointing, surrounded by the communion of saints. Our spiritual challenge is to embrace this reality: histories of harm are all around us, forces of evil operate within and among us, and yet everywhere the bushes are on fire, the risen Christ is with us on the road, the Spirit rises in the wind, the rivers of paradise circle the earth, and the fountain of wisdom springs up from the earth we tread, from this holy ground.

Another Christianity is possible. It begins when we understand that paradise is already present. We have neither to retrieve it nor construct it. We have to perceive it and to bring our lives and our cultures into accord with it. In writing this book, we seek to pass on this way of being Christian. One that will enhance our ability to live in this world, the one that has Wollochet Bay, our lovers, our families, our students and colleagues, our many friends around the world, and our hardworking, aging bodies in it. Paradise belongs to no one individual, not even to God, who shares it with us all, and we must learn to perceive it and to relate to it with ethical grace. Ethical grace is full-bodied life in the present— attuned to what is beautiful and good and responsive to legacies of injustice and currents of harm. For ethical grace to flourish, however, we require strong communities, rituals to train perception, and beauty to hold us and give us joy.

Sustaining communities must be at the forefront of our work, and we must accept that we have power and responsibility to foster life in them. To be both powerful and responsible requires us to be committed to the sometimes difficult, sometimes joyful relationships of human communities. They are the only way we come to perceive and act upon the world for a greater good that both includes and transcends our individual existence. People with strong commitments to strong communities make them happen. They create the institutional structures that enable communities to endure the comings and goings of individual lives, failures in leadership, and the difficulties that are inevitable in life. Communities of ethical grace sustain relationships that require us to share responsibility, act generously toward one another, and resist oppressive and dominating forces that separate human beings from each other and deny our powers of love and friendship. They value the distinctive gifts of individuals for the good of the whole and require us to be open and vulnerable to the many complex dimensions of life that support the survival and thriving of life on earth, in all its diversity.

Rituals are the core of every strong community's life. They are like the bones of a body's skeleton, the framework that holds things into a shape, giving form to a community's values and relationships. Humans ritualize everything that matters: eating, sex, death, meeting strangers, resolving conflict; they are our most significant forms of communication, more powerful than words. To live in paradise requires us to create the kinds of rituals that teach us to love the world and each other. Rituals guide us through the storm-tossed seas of the world—its principalities and powers and its addictive demons. The familiarity, structure, and rhythm of rituals create a container that can hold the conflicts and tragedies that touch every life and every community. Rituals enable us to express and survive pain, anger, lamentation, and despair, while being held by others who know that the other side of pain is healing, the other side of anger is forgiveness, the other side of lamentation is joy, and the other side of despair is wisdom. Sensually rich rituals, full of life, orient us to material and spiritual beauties, embedding us more deeply in love for the world and the many physical dimensions of paradise.

The eros of beauty calls to us and bids us be fully in the world, attentive to particularities, emotionally alive, open to grace, and responsive to injustice. Beauty can ground deeply ethical commitment and moral training, more so than visions and hope that drive us toward a future not yet in existence. The Spirit in Creation that is here now compels us to be mindful of everything we do. The visions we try to create and impose on reality often dissociate us from what we actually do day to day, minute by minute. "Everything belongs to the God of beauty," said Clement of Alexandria. One's response to the gifts of life already given, the beauty already here, makes all the difference.

Perhaps if we can learn how to worship and live within ethical relationships, here and now, we will see our way to honest disclosure about where we are and where we can go together to change unjust systems and institutions, to establish justice and peace, and to protect the created world. Perhaps if we are less concerned with whether we are proving our goodness or getting ahead, we will be better equipped to engage deeply with others because we value their presence with us. With training to be more attuned to the present, we might begin to measure our value by the quality of relationships we sustain rather than by the clarity or virtue of our visions. Having hope may be important, but it is more

Eco.-

important to arrive fully at "this present paradise before us" and re-spond to it with lives devoted to justice and care for the world.

We reenter this world as sacred space when we love life fiercely and, in the name of love, protect the goodness of earth's intricate web of life in all its manifold forms. We feast in paradise when we open our hearts to lamentation, to amplitudes of grief for all that has been lost and cannot be repaired. The beloved departed who have come before us draw near. The veil lifts between the living and the dead. We recommit ourselves to this world as holy ground when we remember the fullness of life that is possible through our communities, our life-affirming rituals, and our love of beauty. Thus immersed, we are more responsive to and responsible for life in this world. We give thanks for gifts of love that have been ours all along, an ever-widening circle of beauty, the Spirit in life. We enter fully—heart, mind, soul and strength—into savoring and saving paradise.

Acknowledgments

A project of this scope carries debts to a multitude of friends and colleagues, but first we thank all the scholars, past and present, whose work has made this project possible. Most are identified in the endnotes. For the dedicated readers who search endnotes looking for our intellectual conversation partners and resources, we have planted a few stray tidbits to make reading them a little more rewarding. We hope you enjoy them.

Here we mention just a few whose expertise and generosity have been essential to our work. We thank, especially, art historian Diane Apostolos-Cappadona for steering us toward the right churches and museums as we began to explore the mystery of Jesus's missing corpse and for being a willing conversation partner at several stages of this project. Others with expertise in religion and art who offered early advice include Margaret Miles and Frank Birch Brown. John Dominic Crossan encouraged us when we first began our work, and several scholars read drafts of chapters and gave us invaluable feedback, especially Joanne M. Braxton, Ibrahim Farajajé, Clark Gilpin, and Rick Lowrey. Other conversation partners over the course of the last five years have included John Cobb, James Cone, Peter Heltzel, Catherine Keller, and Kwok Pui Lan. Our research and discoveries in Turkey were greatly assisted in Istanbul by Mick McCain, who introduced us to scholars and sites, and in Artvin by Mehmet Karahan, a local historian and hotel proprietor, and by Erçun, our intrepid driver.

We have had the opportunity to present papers as we developed our ideas and received excellent feedback as well as encouragement from many colleagues. We thank, especially, the Association of Disciples for Theological Discussion; the Pacific, Asian, North American Asian Women in Theology and Ministry; the Center for Process Studies; the Ecumenical Association of Third World Theologians–U.S. Minorities Group; the Dialogue Group; and two program units of the American Academy of Religion: the Indigenous Traditions in the Americas Group and the Theology and Religious Reflection Section.

Many groups and organizations gave us chances to test our ideas with clergy, students, church people, and local communities. Among those to which we owe thanks are the Kellogg Lectureship at Episcopal Divinity School; the Festival of Homiletics; the Rauschenbusch Lectureship; the Christian Church (Disciples of Christ) Pacific Northwest Region; the Lutheran School of Theology in Chicago; the Graduate Theological Union Convocation Lectureship; the Religion Department of Indiana University in Pennsylvania; Open Hearts and Minds of Montgomery, Alabama; the Earl Morse Wilbur History Colloquium at the Starr King School; the Baptist Peace Fellowship; Kairos CoMotion of Wisconsin; the Columbus, Ohio, Council of Churches; the Voices of Sophia of the United Presbyterian Church; Call to Action; the Disciples Peace Fellowship; Progressive Christians Uniting; the Seattle University School of Theology and Ministry; clergy of the Evangelical Lutheran Church of America in the Upper Midwest; www.theooze.com; and local churches across the country, including Unitarian Universalist, United Methodist, Disciples of Christ, Presbyterian, and United Church of Christ congregations in Concord and Cambridge, Massachusetts; Chicago; Salt Lake City; Minneapolis; Appleton, Wisconsin; Portland, Oregon; Seattle; Ridgewood, New Jersey; and San Francisco, Berkeley, Palo Alto, and Davis, California. Knowing so many people waited patiently as we brought this project to fruition has inspired us through exhaustion and buoyed our spirits in the last dash to finish.

The initial research for this project began while Rita was a fellow at

Harvard Divinity School in 2001–2002, which gave us access to excellent scholars and one of the best theological libraries in the United States. In addition, the librarians at the Graduate Theological Union have been extraordinarily generous in assisting us in obtaining important resources and learning the computer technology to work with images. In the preparation of the manuscript for publication, we had the help of Rosemarie Buxton, who was able to use the Harvard Libraries to check our citations and obtain permissions. Justin Waters prepared the images for publication.

We thank especially the Starr King School for the Ministry and colleagues there who made this work possible: Thomas Smith, Kelly Flood, Dorsey Blake, Gabriella Lettini, Ibrahim Farajajé, David Dezern, Anita Narang, and David Sammons. The school granted Rebecca a sabbatical to complete the final draft and appointed Rita as a visiting scholar, which gave her access to the University of California Library system and its art history program, the Graduate Theological Union Library, and office support for faxing, computer support, photocopying, and mailing. The staff, trustees, students, and faculty at the school helped in countless ways, and we are deeply grateful for their cheering us on. In addition, the board of trustees at Faith Voices for the Common Good gave Rita a year's hiatus to finish the final draft, as well as constant encouragement.

We have had the gift of a great editor, Amy Caldwell, at Beacon Press. From the moment we first talked to her about our idea for the project in 2001, she has supported us with astute feedback, and she has been an enthusiastic advocate for our ideas. Her attention to good writing, the right story, the telling detail, the overall flow, and the organization of the ideas have been impeccable and strategically crucial. More important, we deeply appreciate her friendship, accompanying us through times of discouragement and the rare breakthrough.

A warm circle of family and friends have sustained our spirits. We thank the extended Parker family, who first read portions of this manuscript while on a summer boating trip in the San Juan Islands. Rebecca offers her deepest gratitude to Joanne M. Braxton for her generous friendship and labors of love in the final months of this project. Rita is grateful for the encouragement of many friends and colleagues, including Angella Current-Felder and members of the Women of Color Scholars Program of the United Methodist Church, JoAnne Kagiwada, Brian Sarrazin, Glenn Smith, and Kevin Vaughn.

We dedicate this book, in memoriam, to another great editor, the one who first taught us how to edit texts, when we were graduate students and research assistants at the Center for Process Studies in Claremont, California, and in whose company we became better acquainted as fellow students. Dorothy Hartshorne was a musician, an avid bird-watcher, a lover of the arts, an intrepid traveler, an excellent cook who loved a good dinner party and a good sherry late in the afternoon, a passionate friend, a marvelous and vivid storyteller, an attentive and gracious hostess, a quick wit, and a meticulous researcher who undertook late in her life a project on Buddhism in Japan with great respect and care for a culture and people so unlike her own. Her one piece of advice in marriage was "never bore each other!" This is good advice for friendships as well, and although we have been discouraged, aggravated, exhausted, joyful, and pleased, we have not been bored! Our friendship has not only survived five years of research, four major rewrites, and a year of intense work while we were crammed into one tiny cabin with two cats, it has also deepened and flourished. That is a great reward of this work for which we thank each other.

Notes

1. "Art in Late Antiquity," a course taught by Professor David Wright in the fall of 2002 at the University of California, Berkeley. Diane Apostolos-Cappadona, *Dictionary of Christian Art* (New York: Continuum Press, 1995).

2. *The Catholic Encyclopedia*, www.newadvent.org/cathen/09014b.htm, dates part of this image to the time of Constantine:

> The ancient apse, with mosaics of the fourth century, survived all the many changes and dangers of the Middle Ages, and was still to be seen very much in its original condition as late as 1878, when it was destroyed in order to provide a larger space for the ordinations and other pontifical functions which take place in this cathedral church of Rome. The original mosaics were, however, preserved with the greatest possible care and very great success, and were re-erected at the end of the new and deeper apse which had been provided. In these mosaics, as they now appear, the centre of the upper portion is occupied by the figure of Christ surrounded by nine angels. This figure is extremely ancient, and dates from the fifth, or it may be even the fourth century. It is possible even that it is the identical one which, as is told in ancient tradition, was manifested to the eyes of the worshippers on the occasion of the dedication of the church: "Imago Salvatoris infixa parietibus primum visibilis omni populo Romano apparuit" (Joan. Diac., "Lib. de Ecclesia Lat.," P.L. 194, 1543–1560). If it is so, however, it has certainly been retouched. Below is seen the crux gammata, surmounted by a dove which symbolizes the Holy Spirit, and standing on a hill whence flow the four rivers of the Gospels, from whose waters stags and sheep come to drink. On either side are saints, looking towards the Cross. These last are thought to belong originally to the sixth century, though they were repaired and altered in the thirteenth by

Nicholas IV, whose effigy may be seen prostrate at the feet of the Blessed Virgin. The river which runs below is more ancient still, and may be regarded as going back to Constantine and the first days of the basilica. The remaining mosaics of the apse are of the thirteenth century, and the signatures of the artists, Torriti and Camerino, may still be read upon them. Camerino was a Franciscan friar; perhaps Torriti was one also.

3.   A. Hilhorst, "A Visit to Paradise: *Apocalypse of Paul* 45 and Its Background," in *Paradise Interpreted: Representations of Biblical Paradise in Judaism and Christianity,* ed. Gerard P. Luttikhuizen (Boston: Koninklijke Brill, 1999), 128–139, text from p. 128. See also Ellen Bradshaw Aitken, who notes in "The Landscape of Promise in the *Apocalypse of Paul,*" in *Walk in the Ways of Wisdom: Essays in Honor of Elisabeth Schüssler Fiorenza,* ed. Shelly Matthews, Cynthia Briggs Kittredge, and Melanie Johnson-Debaufre (New York: Trinity Press, 2003), 153–165, that the text "motivates toward what it regards as the good and creates aversion to vice. . . . The deployment of landscape in the *Apocalypse of Paul* helps us to see that this is a text less about the future or present 'fate of the dead' and more about shaping the orientations and commitments of the Christian community in this life" (155).

4.   For example, the discovery and translation of the Gnostic Gospels have added enormously to what we know about female leadership and images of God in the early church, and feminist studies of the Bible and theology have cast new light on what traditional experts have claimed about the past. See, for example, early work on rethinking Christianity: Elisabeth Schüssler Fiorenza, *In Memory of Her: A Feminist Theological Reconstruction of Christian Origins* (New York: Crossroad Press, 1983); Elaine Pagels, *The Gnostic Gospels* (New York: Vintage, 1981); and Rosemary Ruether, *Sexism and God-Talk: Toward a Feminist Theology* (Boston: Beacon Press, 1983).

CHAPTER ONE: IN THE BEGINNING . . . PARADISE ON EARTH

1.   Unless otherwise noted, all biblical passages are taken from the New Revised Standard Version (NRSV). In the passage in the epigraph, we have inserted a more literal translation of the italicized words. Translations of this text are discussed in Ed Noort, "Gan-Eden in the Context of the Mythology of the Hebrew Bible," in *Paradise Interpreted: Representations of Biblical Paradise in Judaism and Christianity,* ed. Gerard P. Luttikhuizen (Boston: Koninklijke Brill NV, 1999), 19–36; and Phyllis Trible, *God and the Rhetoric of Sexuality* (Philadelphia: Fortress Press, 1975). For two historical surveys of the concept of paradise, see Jean Delumeau, *History of Paradise: The Garden of Eden in Myth and Tradition,* trans. Matthew O'Connell (New York: Continuum Press, 1995); and Gerard P. Luttikhuizen, ed., *Paradise Interpreted.*

2. See Harriet Crawford, *Sumer and the Sumerians,* 2nd ed. (New York: Cambridge University Press, 2004), for a general introduction to the society from the fifth to third millennia BCE. In chapters 2–3, Crawford notes that the earliest records from Sumer's settlements included a small minority of Akkadian people who can be identified by their names. Akkadian was a Semitic language, unlike Sumerian, and the Akkadians were perhaps earlier inhabitants invaded by the Sumerians or later sheepherding immigrants from the north. After 1800 BCE, Sumerian ceased to be a spoken language. She discusses, 16–36, variations in dating the defeat of the last Sumerian dynasty, based on texts and carbon dating. See also Samuel Noah Kramer, *Sumerian Mythology: A Study of Spiritual and Literary Achievement in the Third Millennium B.C.,* rev. ed. (Philadelphia: University of Pennsylvania Press, 1972); and *From the Poetry of Sumer: Creation, Glorification, Adoration* (Berkeley: University of California Press, 1979), 50–60. Kramer summarizes various theories of the origins of the Sumerians and the development of their social, religious, and political systems.

3. For the history and grammar of the Sumerian language, see Otto Edzard Dietz, *Sumerian Grammar* (Boston: Brill, 2003); and Marie-Louise Thomsen, *The Sumerian Language: An Introduction to Its History and Grammatical Structure* (Copenhagen: Akadamisk Forlag, 1983). Sumerian ceased, finally, to be used at all around the first century CE.

4. Genesis 11:31, "they went out together from Ur of the Chaldeans to go into the land of Canaan." Ur was the last capital of Sumer, conquered by the Babylonians (aka the Chaldeans). Dates for Abram and Sarai's migration vary from 2100 BCE to 1400 BCE. William F. Albright, "From the Patriarchs to Moses: From Abraham to Joseph," *The Biblical Archaeologist* 36 (1973): 5–33, suggests around 1800 BCE.

5. Kramer, *From the Poetry,* 1–16, notes that the stories vary and use different names for deities.

6. Ninhursag had a number of names, including Ki, Ninmah, and Nintu. Kramer, 27–29, *From the Poetry,* suggests that Ninhursag is an indication of the demotion of Ki at a time when the status of women also declined in Sumerian society from equality to subordination.

7. Kramer, *Sumerian Mythology,* 55, excerpts. See also Samuel Noah Kramer, *Enki and Ninhursag, a Sumerian "Paradise" Myth* (New Haven, CT: American Schools of Oriental Research, 1945).

8. Delumeau, *History of Paradise,* 5, describes the Sumerian ideas of paradise. For the location of Dilmun, see Noort, "Gan-Eden," 32, "the land Dilmun was known far beyond the boundaries of Sumer."

9. Harriet Crawford, *Sumer and the Sumerians,* 74–75, notes that some large temples had the bones of leopards or lions in their foundations.

10. Samuel Kramer: "She was worshipped under three aspects that at least on the surface seem unrelated, and even antithetical: as the Venus-goddess in charge of the bright Morning Star and Evening Star; as the goddess of war and weaponry, who

wrought havoc upon all who displeased her, and especially on the enemies of Sumer; as the goddess of love and desire who ensured the fertility of the soil and the fecundity of the womb" ("Adoration: A Divine Model of the Liberated Woman," in *From the Poetry*, 71–73). Kramer suggests she is the model of a liberated woman. In contrast to Kramer, Tikva Frymer-Kensky, *In the Wake of the Goddesses: Women, Culture, and the Biblical Transformation of Pagan Myth* (New York: Free Press, 1992), suggests that Inanna's various roles function in contrast to the traditional female roles and, by their contrast with bad examples, reinscribe proper gendered behavior. We think stories and symbols rarely function in one predictable way.

11. Kramer, *Sumerian Mythology*, 51–63.

12. Ibid., 98.

13. Frymer-Kensky provides a careful analysis of the gender dynamics of Sumerian myth in *In the Wake of the Goddesses*. Details of the curse are found in Samuel Noah Kramer and John Maier, "Enki and Ninhursag: A Sumerian Paradise Myth," in *Myths of Enki, The Crafty God* (New York: Oxford University Press, 1989), 22–30.

14. Harriet Crawford, *Sumer and the Sumerians*, chapters 4–5, discusses urban architecture and town plans in the rise of kings. Frymer-Kensky, *In the Wake of the Goddesses*, discusses the relationship of kingship to female subordination.

15. Kramer, *From the Poetry*, 58–70, discusses Sumerian hymns to their kings and their ideals of kingship, which were likely never really fulfilled.

16. Catherine Keller, *Face of the Deep* (New York: Routledge, 2003) draws possible links between this matricide and Genesis 1:1. She suggests that the Babylonian name Tiamat may be related to the Hebrew word *tehom*, meaning deep.

17. Jan N. Bremmer, "Paradise: From Persia, via Greece, into the *Septuagint*," in *Paradise Interpreted: Representations of Biblical Paradise in Judaism and Christianity*, ed. Gerard P. Luttikhuizen (Boston: Koninklijke Brill, 1999), 1–20; and Noort, "Gan-Eden," 21.

18. Marina Belozerskaya, *The Medici Giraffe and Other Tales of Exotic Animals and Power* (New York: Little, Brown, 2006), 3–10, describes ancient Persians and animals during the time of Alexander the Great.

19. Bremmer, "Paradise," 8. See also Delumeau, *History of Paradise*, 5.

20. Mary Boyce, *Zoroastrianism: Its Antiquity and Constant Vigour* (New York: Mazda, 1992); John R. Hinnells, *Zoroastrian and Parsi Studies: Selected Works of John R. Hinnells* (Burlington, VT: Ashgate, 2000); and Jonathan Z. Smith, ed., *The Harper-Collins Dictionary of Religion* (San Francisco: HarperSanFrancisco, 1995), 1150–1151.

21. Keller, *Face of the Deep*, suggests that Genesis 1:1 can also be linked to the Babylonian versions of the Sumerian stories. She also discusses the relational quality of Creation, in which God is depicted not as creating from nothing, ex nihilo, as some early church teachers argued, but from the deep.

22. Translation in this section is taken from Trible, *God and the Rhetoric of Sexuality*, 16–17, with Hebrew transliterations inserted.

23. Richard H. Lowrey, *Sabbath and Jubilee* (St. Louis: Chalice Press, 2000), 82, notes:

    Themes of natural abundance and personal self-restraint stand at the heart of the story. It portrays a created world fundamentally benevolent and able to produce enough to sustain prosperous human life. This theme of natural abundance is coupled, however, with a theme of self-restraint. God's own precedent weaves rest into the fabric of the universe. Periodic self-limitation, deliberate relinquishment of power to work the world and control it, is by Sabbath example a cosmic principle. Creation climaxes and finally coheres in Sabbath rest. It is the glue that holds the world together.

24. Trible, *God and the Rhetoric of Sexuality,* 72–99. Gale Yee, *Poor Banished Children of Eve: Woman as Evil in the Hebrew Bible* (Minneapolis: Augsburg Fortress, 2003), discusses the consequences of blaming Eve for sin.

25. Trible, *God and the Rhetoric of Sexuality,* 144–165.

26. Translation of Amos 9:15 is from Shalom M. Paul, *Amos: A Commentary on the Book of Amos,* in *Hermeneia: A Critical and Historical Commentary on the Bible,* ed. Frank Moore Cross (Minneapolis: Fortress Press, 1991), 288. Paul discusses the blessings of bounty and security in relation to ancient Mesopotamian literature and parallel biblical passages such as Ezekiel 28, which explicitly references Eden. See especially pp. 288–295.

27. Maya Lin, an architect and sculptor, attributes this quote to Martin Luther King Jr. Before the monument was public, families of the slain were allowed to see it. Many wept, and Lin described their tears as becoming part of the waters of justice that flow over the monument. Her work on this monument and the Vietnam Memorial in Washington, DC, is documented in the 1995 Academy Award–winning film about her, *Maya Lin: A Strong Clear Vision.*

28. Renita Weems, *Battered Love: Marriage, Sex, and Violence in the Hebrew Prophets* (Minneapolis: Fortress Press, 1995).

29. In the palace of Sargon II (721–705 BCE), creatures with the face of a man, the wings of an eagle, and the legs, horns, and trunk of a bull guarded the entrance to the throne room. Descriptions and visual examples of ancient art reflected in Ezekiel's vision can be found in Michael Avi-Yonah and Emil G. Kraeling, *Our Living Bible* (New York: McGraw-Hill, 1962), 216–222.

30. The earliest surviving example is the apse mosaic of St. Pudenziana, Rome, which was likely created near the beginning of the fifth century to thank God for sparing the church from the sack of Rome in 410. It depicts the torsos of four winged creatures: a man, a lion, an ox, and an eagle. The four beasts of the apocalypse of John (Rev. 4:6–8) refer to imagery of God's presence from Ezekiel. The presence of these creatures in early Christian art more likely related to Ezekiel because the prophet books were far more accepted and used in the early church than was Revelation. The accent, thus, is on the presence of God. When the iconography develops to represent the four evangelists, the Gospels symbolize divine presence.

31. This paradise image of a life-giving river flowing from the sanctuary has Canaanite as well as Mesopotamian precedents. The image is also found in Joel 3:18, Zechariah 14:8, and Revelation 22. Psalm 46:4 also suggests the image: "There is a river whose streams make glad the city of God, the holy habitation of the Most High." Psalm 65:9 presents the river of God watering the whole earth, filling it with abundance.

32. Zoroastrian apocalyptic ideas became especially prominent in medieval Christianity and continue in some strands of conservative Christianity but are not emphasized in Jewish religious ideas. Hinnells's *Zoroastrian and Parsi Studies* is especially helpful in its discussion of the history of scholarship on Zoroastrian and of Boyce's prominent and controversial place in it.

33. Gary A. Anderson, "The Cosmic Mountain: Eden and Its Early Interpreters in Syriac Christianity," in *Genesis 1–3 in the History of Exegesis: Intrigue in the Garden,* ed. Gregory Allen Robbins (Lewiston, NY: Edwin Mellen Press, 1988), 187–224. The history and description of the second temple, which Herod completely rebuilt in 19 BCE, can be found at www.jewishencyclopedia.com.

34. Jacob Milgrom, *Leviticus: A Book of Ritual and Ethics* (Philadelphia: Fortress Press, 2004), and *Leviticus 1–16: A New Translation with Introduction and Commentary* (New York: Doubleday, 1991) notes two views in Leviticus. One locates holiness in the Jerusalem temple and its activities. The other view regards the whole land of Israel, with multiple sacred sites, as a coextensive sacred realm inhabited by the presence of God the Creator who is worshipped by ceremonial acts and by keeping the covenant. Proverbs describes Wisdom as permeating the created world and teaches that ethical action is the mark of those who honor her. These traditions do not isolate paradise in one location.

35. For a discussion of the temple as paradise, see Anderson, "The Cosmic Mountain."

CHAPTER TWO: IN THE BEGINNING ...
GOD SO GENEROUSLY LOVED

1. Jan N. Bremmer, "Paradise: From Persia, via Greece, into the Septuagint," in *Paradise Interpreted: Representations of Biblical Paradise in Judaism and Christianity,* ed. Gerard P. Luttikhuizen (Leiden, Netherlands: Koninklijke Brill, 1999), 1–20, summarizes some of the paradise traditions that influence Christian texts.

2. Matt. 14:13–21, 15:32–39; Mark 8:1–9; Luke 9:10–17; and John 6:1–13.

3. The Priscilla catacombs date to the late third century. These and similar catacomb images of the feast table are variously interpreted by scholars. Some suggest that the images represent a Christian practice of holding feasts with their dead in the catacombs, as pagans did. The link between the New Testament feeding stories and the evolution of Eucharistic practices is complex. For a detailed discussion of the relationship between the images and the historical issues of liturgical practice, see Andrew McGowan, *Ascetic Eucharists: Food and Drink in Early Christian Ritual Meals*

(Oxford, UK: Clarendon Press, 1999), 127–142. For a study of multiple sacred meal traditions and the development of Christian Eucharistic practices, see Dennis E. Smith, *From Symposium to Eucharist: The Banquet in the Early Christian World* (Minneapolis: Fortress Press, 2003).

4. John Dominic Crossan, *The Birth of Christianity: Discovering What Happened in the Years Immediately after the Execution of Jesus* (San Francisco: HarperSanFrancisco, 1998), 444.

5. The various uses of the two terms are described in Barbara Rossing, "(Re)claiming Oikoumene? Empire, Ecumenism, and the Discipleship of Equals," in *Walk in the Ways of Wisdom: Essays in Honor of Elisabeth Schüssler Fiorenza*, ed. Shelly Matthews, Cynthia Briggs Kittredge, and Melanie Johnson-Debaufre (Harrisburg, PA: Trinity Press, 2003), 74–87. She notes that English versions often translate both terms as "world." J. Edward Wright, *The Early History of Heaven* (New York: Oxford University Press, 2000), chap. 4, notes that the understanding of the earth as a sphere was well established in Greek and Roman ideas by the second century BCE.

6. J. E. Wright, *Early History of Heaven,* discusses West Asian cosmologies, such as those of Sumer and Israel, with a vault of the heavens, the flat disk of earth, and the underworld. He argues that the Greek and Roman cosmologies of a globe and planetary orbits, plus the Platonic idea of an immortal soul, led to the development of heaven as the afterlife for good souls and the underworld as a place of punishment. Though this idea of the afterlife may have emerged in this time, heaven also continued to be connected to this life through the visitations of spirits and heavenly beings and travel to its realms by those in this life. The use of "Kingdom of the Heavens" in Matthew and "heaven" in John carry a strong this-worldly emphasis and describe how life should be on the earth, as it is in heaven, not only after people die and go there.

7. Examples in Ravenna include the vault of the dome in the Mausoleum of Galla Placidia, midnight blue with gold stars; the arch in the Archiepiscopal Chapel, blue with silver and gold stars; and the top of the chancel vault in St. Vitale, a circle of blue. Clouds with the hand of God reaching through are found in many places, including at St. Vitale and St. Apollinare church in Classe.

8. J. E. Wright, *Early History of Heaven,* 109: "Persian astrology also spread throughout the Mediterranean world, and astrology had become so popular in Rome by 139 BCE that the authorities tried to curtail it." Thomas F. Mathews, *The Clash of the Gods: A Reinterpretation of Early Christian Art* (Princeton, NJ: Princeton University Press, 1993), 143–150, discusses scholarly interpretations of the dome of heaven in early Christian art. He observes that Christians distanced themselves from Roman views of the heavens and fate, rejecting ideas of a cosmos controlled by the planets and stars as imagined in Roman astrology. Instead of Roman astrological signs or symbols of the seasons, Christians placed images symbolizing Christ (the lamb, the Pantocrator), the angels, and the saints (stars) in the dome. They emphasized human freedom rather than fate.

9. John Dominic Crossan, *The Historical Jesus: The Life of a Mediterranean Jewish Peasant* (San Francisco: HarperSanFrancisco, 1993), and *Who Killed Jesus? Exposing the Roots of Anti-Semitism in the Gospel Story of the Death of Jesus* (San Francisco: HarperSanFrancisco, 1996); Obery Hendricks, *The Politics of Jesus: Rediscovering the True Revolutionary Nature of Jesus' Teachings and How They Have Been Corrupted* (New York: Doubleday Books, 2006); Richard Horsley, *Jesus and Empire: The Kingdom of God and the New World Disorder* (Minneapolis: Fortress Press, 2002).

10. The Romans controlled the entire grain supply of Italy. In the time of Julius Caesar, 25 percent of the population of Rome received a free dole. Such welfare systems function to keep the poor from disrupting an empire's economic practices that channel great wealth into the hands of an economic elite. Bruce W. Winter, *Seek the Welfare of the City: Christians as Benefactors and Citizens* (Grand Rapids, MI: Wm. B. Eerdmans, 1994), 168–177, discusses Roman officials' practice of providing feasts to the citizenry and the early Christian response to this practice.

11. Jews, Christians, and pagan Greek philosophers all use *logos* as an important concept. Daniel Boyarin notes in *Border Lines: The Partition of Judaeo-Christianity* (Philadelphia: University of Pennsylvania Press, 2004) that distinct traditions separately labeled as Jewish or Christian were slow to develop, and the idea of religion as a belief system separate from culture and society only gradually emerged after the time of Constantine in the middle of the fourth century CE. Christians and Jews, as we now call them, comprised so many diverse groups that they were often indistinguishable until well into the fourth century. They often argued with each other as apostates or competing factions of one tradition, not as separate religions.

   Much of the Christian literature layers Jesus's stories and sayings onto the Hebrew texts as commentaries. Bart D. Ehrman's *Lost Christianities: The Battles for Scripture and the Faiths We Never Knew* (New York: Oxford University Press, 2003) discusses some of the politics and processes that divided Jews, Christians, and pagans, which eventually produced the Christian canon. He notes that the New Testament took nearly four centuries of dispute and controversy to develop. In the process of its early formation, some sects wrote alternative scriptures that rejected Judaism and the Hebrew books entirely. Erhman suggests that the deep roots in antiquity that Judaism afforded Christianity worked to the survival advantage of "orthodox" Christianity and the final New Testament. Elaine Pagels, in *The Gnostic Gospels: A New Account of the Origins of Christianity* (New York: Random House, 1979), and *Beyond Belief: The Secret Gospel of Thomas* (New York: Random House, 2003), comments on the orthodox tradition from the perspective of texts not included in the biblical canon and their theological perspectives.

12. Boyarin discusses at length in *Border Lines* the Jewish ideas of Logos, found especially in Philo and captured in the first chapter of John, as a Midrash on Genesis. He suggests that Philo may have invented the Middle Platonism found in John. Our

somewhat different study of the northern Israelite influences on John is found in Rita Nakashima Brock and Rebecca Ann Parker, "Enemy and Ally: Contending with John's Anti-Judaism," in *Walk in the Ways of Wisdom: Essays in Honor of Elisabeth Schüssler Fiorenza,* ed. Shelly Matthews, Cynthia Briggs Kittredge, and Melanie Johnson-Debaufre (Harrisburg, PA: Trinity Press, 2003), 166–180.

13. Burton Mack first acquainted us with the link between *logos* and *sophia* when we studied with him in 1979. Boyarin, in *Border Lines* (93–111), discusses the history of scholarship associating word and wisdom, its advantages and its problems. He argues persuasively for a reading that keeps John's use of *logos* clearly grounded in Jewish concepts and interpretive practices. On p. 95 he comments, "I wish to argue . . . that the Logos of the Prologue. . . is the product of a scriptural reading of Genesis 1 and Proverbs 8 together. This reading will bear out my conclusion that nothing in Logos theology as a doctrine of God indicates or even implies a particularly Christian as opposed to generally Jewish, including Christian, kerygma."

14. Tikva Frymer-Kensky, *In the Wake of the Goddesses: Women, Culture, and the Biblical Transformation of Pagan Myth* (New York: Free Press, 1992), discusses the variety of goddesses present in the Bible. J. E. Wright writes that "as early as the eighth century BCE . . . Jews settled as mercenaries in service of the Pharaoh . . . [and] seem to have worshiped, in addition to Yahweh, the gods and goddesses Anat and Bethel, as well as the Egyptian god Chnum" (*Early History of Heaven,* 69).

15. Exodus 3 revealed the power of the names of divinities. At the burning bush on Mt. Sinai, Moses told God that, if he claimed that the God of the Israelites sent him, he needed to know God's name (v. 13). The ancient personifications of Word and Wisdom captured this power of language and truth. Without being able to specify by name the deity a people worshiped, they would have no access to its spiritual power.

16. For example, I Enoch 42:2, a Jewish text from the end of the second temple period says, "Wisdom went out to dwell with the children of the people, but she found no dwelling place. So Wisdom returned to her place and she settled permanently among the angels."

17. Boyarin, *Border Lines,* 104. On p. 102, he comments: "We need to read John carefully against the background of this twin concern for theodicy and revelation."

18. The descent of God onto Sinai, the holy mountain, and Moses's ascent/descent as a mediator between heaven and earth is a theme throughout the Torah. See for example, Exodus 19, 24, and 34. Wayne Meeks discusses the motifs that connect Moses and Jesus in his book *The Prophet-King: Moses Traditions and the Johannine Christology* (Leiden, Netherlands: E. J. Brill, 1967). Scholars have detected motifs of ascent and descent in John's Gospel as reflecting the pattern of Jesus's travels to and from Jerusalem. The pattern of the Gospel as a whole is a descent/ascent from and to heaven. Jacob's dream, Genesis 28:12–15, bears traces of the Mesopotamian ziggurats that replicated the cosmic mountain and paradise. The Hebrew word usually trans-

lated "ladder" also has the connotation of "stairway" or "ramp." See the *Oxford Annotated Bible with the Apocrypha,* edited by Herbert G. May and Bruce M. Metzger (New York: Oxford University Press, 1977), 35; and *Study Helps to the Holy Bible,* New Revised Standard Version (Nashville: Thomas Nelson, 1990), 25.

19. This theme is especially strong in early Syriac Christianity but is reflected throughout the early theologians of the church. We discuss its relationship to baptismal theology and practices in chapter 5. For more on the "robe of glory," see Seely J. Beggiani, *Early Syriac Theology: With Special Reference to the Maronite Tradition* (Lanham, MD: University Press of America, 1983), 15–21; and Sebastian Brock, *The Luminous Eye: The Spiritual World Vision of Saint Ephrem the Syrian* (Kalamazoo, MI: Cistercian Publications, 1985), 85–99.

20. J. Edward Wright, *Early History of Heaven,* 72–85, discusses Yahweh in relation to other deities.

21. Peter Brown, *The Rise of Western Christendom: Triumph and Diversity A.D. 200–1000* (Malden, MA: Blackwell, 2003), 59.

22. This interpretation of John 3:16 appeared established by the late fourth century. Augustine interpreted John 3:14 ("just as Moses lifted up the snake in the desert") to be an allegory for Jesus's crucifixion (based on John 12:32–33). Many interpreters followed suit. However, Augustine did not narrow the incarnation to Jesus's "dying for us." That narrowing occurred in the eleventh century. We contend that reading John's Gospel to imply that Jesus was given (*edoken*) to the world in order to be crucified imposes a theological framework on the Gospel that the Gospel does not share.

23. The Gospel of John uses the Greek verb for "give" (*didomi;* past tense, *edoka*) sixty-three times, several times with gifts from God. God gives all things to Jesus (John 3:35), including life, authority, glory, and the bitter cup (John 18:11). God gives the "Comforter" (John 14:16). Jesus gives water (John 4:14), food (John 6:51), a new commandment (John 13:34), peace (John 14:27), the word of God (John 17:8), and bread and fish (John 21:13). Jesus's death is not a gift given by God. From the moment Pilate hands him over to be crucified until his Resurrection appearances, the Gospel makes no use of the verb for "give." Other New Testament texts use *paradidomai,* "is handed over," to speak of the betrayal of Jesus, such as I Corinthians 11:23. The use of the passive voice can indicate that God has ordained the event. Acts 4:30 makes this assumption explicit: "And in truth both Herod and Pilate were gathered together in this city with the Gentiles and the peoples of Israel against your holy servant Jesus, to do whatever your hand and your degree had foreordained to be done." In contrast, John 19:11 uses *paradidomai* to speak of Judas's "great sin" in handing Jesus over to Pilate. Thus John contradicts any suggestion that those who betrayed Jesus were fulfilling God's plan.

24. Richard A. Horsley, in *Jesus and the Spiral of Violence: Popular Jewish Resistance in Roman Palestine* (Minneapolis: Fortress Press, 1993), 70–71, says of the Pharisees, "They must have been torn between maintaining what role and local influence they

still held, and being resentful at the alien domination that had diminished their own traditional role."

25. For a discussion of the Samaritan elements in the Gospel, see Rita Brock and Rebecca Parker, "Enemy and Ally."

26. Jarl E. Fossum, *The Name of God and the Angel of the Lord: Samaritan and Jewish Concepts of Intermediation and the Origins of Gnosticism* (Tübingen, Germany: Mohr, 1985), 84, explains that Yahweh "inhabits the earthly temple, but not in person; he is present through the agency of his name." And on p. 126, Fossum writes, "Moses was the possessor of the Divine Name, and the eschatological prophet who was going to be like him would also be the owner of the Name." John Bowman, *Samaritan Documents Relating to Their History, Religion, and Life* (Pittsburgh: Pickwick, 1977), 3, notes that, in their liturgical practices, Samaritans chanted the "ten words of creation." The first word is "let there be light," the last was the divine name, given to Moses at the burning bush.

27. Sandra Schneiders, *Written That You May Believe: Encountering Jesus in the Fourth Gospel* (New York: Paulist Press, 1979), 137, notes that the Hebrew prophets characteristically depicted religious apostasy as female harlotry or adultery. The Jews at the time believed that the Samaritans had worshipped five Assyrian gods in their temple. The woman's matter-of-fact response to Jesus's observation about her "husbands" indicates this was not a judgment of her personally but a statement about the people she belonged to. "As anyone familiar with the major commentaries on the Fourth Gospel knows, the treatment of the Samaritan woman in the history of interpretation is a textbook case of trivialization, marginalization, and even sexual demonization of biblical women, which reflects and promotes the parallel treatment of real women in the church."

28. John 6:41, 8:12, 10:11, 11:25, 14:6, 15:5. Each of these "I am" statements includes a long discourse on its meaning.

29. For a comprehensive survey of the Bible's anti-imperial message, see Obery Hendricks, *The Politics of Jesus: Rediscovering the True Revolutionary Nature of Jesus' Teachings and How They Have Been Corrupted* (New York: Doubleday, 2006).

30. Biblical scholars have studied and debated these themes in detail. For discussions of Jesus's community as a community of resistance to oppressive power, see especially Elizabeth Schüssler Fiorenza, *In Memory of Her;* Richard A. Horsley, *Jesus and the Spiral of Violence,* chap. 8, "The Renewal of Local Community, I: Egalitarian Social Relations," and chap. 9, "The Renewal of Local Community, II: Social-Economic Cooperation and Autonomy"; and John Dominic Crossan, *Birth of Christianity,* chap. 23. The history of these resistance practices in Jewish communities of resistance to Rome is especially important to note, and is treated extensively by Horsley and by Crossan.

31. The classic Greek texts are Aristotle's *Nicomachean Ethics* and Plato's *Lysis.* The principle found in John 15:13, "Greater love has no man than that he lay down his life for his friends," is a standard definition of the true friend in the Greek literature.

Equality and mutuality mean that a true friend will not hesitate, for example, to jump into a lake to save a drowning friend (a favorite example in the friendship literature). This suggests that for John's Gospel, the risks Jesus took that led to his crucifixion were expressions of friendship, not self-sacrificing acts of obedient submission to God's will. True friendship has political import: Greek philosophy makes it the foundation of democracy.

32. Mary Hunt, *Fierce Tenderness: A Feminist Theology of Friendship* (1991); Elizabeth Johnson, *Friends of God and Prophets: A Feminist Theological Reading of the Communion of Saints* (New York: Continuum Press, 1998).

33. John is particularly concerned with authorized power and conferred rights. The *logos* confers the right to be born of God (John 1:12). Jesus is the one who has the right to lay down his life—no one has the right to take his life from him (John 10:18). God gave Jesus authority over "all flesh" to give eternal life (John 17.2). Jesus's power, in short, is the authority to relate people to God, to exercise sovereignty over his own life, and to give others eternal life.

34. We believe that the Gospel has its origins in a Samaritan or similar northern Israelite community hostile to Jerusalem and its Jewish leaders. The bitter division evolved through a long history of competing responses between Samaritans and Jews regarding how to negotiate the pressures of imperial domination. For a more detailed scholarly analysis of the Samaritan aspects of the Gospel, see R. Brock and R. Parker, "Enemy and Ally."

35. The Passion narratives differ in many details and in tone and theologies. Jesus appears stoic, even serene, in John's Gospel. His outcry of abandonment, quoting Psalm 22:1, is in Matthew 27:46 and Mark 15:34. In Luke 23:46, Jesus commends his spirit to God before breathing his last. John places his death on a Thursday; the other Gospels place it on Friday. John, unlike the other Gospels, does not have a Last Supper with the words of institution, "this is my body . . . this is my blood." For a major study and bibliography on Passion narrative scholarship, see John Dominic Crossan, *The Cross That Spoke: The Origins of the Passion Narrative* (San Francisco: Harper and Row, 1988). For archaeological evidence regarding crucifixion practices in the first century, see Crossan, *Birth of Christianity*, 523–525 and 542–545. For details from ancient literary sources, see Martin Hengel, *Crucifixion in the Ancient World and the Folly and the Message of the Cross* (Philadelphia: Fortress Press, 1977).

36. Erich Gruen, *The Last Generation of the Roman Republic* (Berkeley: University of California Press, 1974): 20–22.

37. Methods and practices of crucifixion are discussed in Crossan, *Who Killed Jesus?*, and in Horsley, *Jesus and Empire*.

38. Paolo Giglioni, fig. 2, "Cristo deriso: graffito del Palatino. Nell'ingiuriosa iscrizione in Greco si può leggere: 'Alessameno adora Dio,' " *La Croce e il Crocifisso: Nella Tradizione e Nell'arte* (Rome: Liberia Editrice Vaticana, 2000).

39. Peter's sermon in Acts 3:12–26 recounts Jesus's crucifixion and resurrection and makes an appeal—like a speech to a jury that has unjustly condemned a man—that the people of Jerusalem should reconsider their verdict. "You killed the author of life, whom God raised from the dead . . . repent, therefore, and turn again, that your sins may be blotted out, that times of refreshing may come from the presence of the Lord" (Acts 3:15, 19).

40. Contemporary theology continues to represent such views. Miroslav Volf, for example, in *Exclusion and Embrace: A Theological Exploration of Identity, Otherness, and Reconciliation* (Nashville: Abingdon Press, 1996), 291–292, says, "By suffering violence as an innocent victim, he took upon himself the aggression of the persecutors. He broke the vicious cycle of violence by absorbing it. . . . the sacralizing of him as victim subverts violence." Similarly, Douglas John Hall, "Theology of the Cross: Challenge and Opportunity for the Post-Christendom Church," in *Cross Examinations*, ed. Marit Trelstad (Minneapolis: Fortress Press, 2006), 257, writes, "The theology of the cross is a theology of love, not power. . . . Love . . . to achieve its aim must become weak." We disagree with these theological perspectives because they contravene assumptions of power by the oppressed and suggest that life can be saved by passivity. Not so. Nonviolent resistance is not passivity. Furthermore, Jesus was not innocent: his actions were in violation of the laws of the Roman Empire, and Jesus was aware of this. He was guilty of the charges against him, even if he did not do anything that was morally wrong.

41. Constantina-Nadia Seremetakis, "The Ethics of Antiphony: the Social Construction of Pain, Gender, and Power in the Southern Peloponnese," quoted in Crossan, *Birth of Christianity*, 541. Kathleen Corley, quoted in Crossan, *Birth of Christianity* (528), writes in her forthcoming book, *Gender and Jesus: History and Lament in the Gospel Tradition*, "Women have in past and present times habitually keened and mourned the dead. Many of these lament traditions in fact sustain a poetic genre that goes back in some cases . . . thousands of years. . . . The Passion narrative itself could have its roots in the formal context of repeated, sung storytelling, which could have preserved basic details of the tale of Jesus death. . . . I am suggesting that the Passion narrative had its origins in a grass-roots liturgical context dominated by women and ordinary people." In chapter 26, "Exegesis, Lament, and Biography," Crossan surveys and discusses Corley's thesis, drawing on the scholarship of Gail Holst-Warhaft, Seremetakis, Marianne Sawicki, Margaret Alexiou, and Anna Caraveli-Chaves. He comments, on p. 541, "What is at stake in female lament is an alternative mode of power that protests the general injustice of death over life but also the particular injustice of men over women." He concludes that women's "ritual lament is what changed prophetic exegesis into biographical story" (573), suggesting that women's lament practices are what produced the Gospel form as a whole.

42. Marianne Sawicki, *Seeing the Lord*, quoted in Crossan, *Birth of Christianity*, 539.

CHAPTER THREE: SO GREAT A CLOUD

1. John Dominic Crossan, *The Birth of Christianity: Discovering What Happened in the Years Immediately after the Execution of Jesus* (San Francisco: HarperSanFrancisco, 1998), xiv. Crossan notes (xvii) that visits from the dead remain a commonly reported phenomenon in the contemporary United States and are considered nonpathological by the American Psychiatric Association. For ancient ideas of the afterlife, see Jean Delumeau, *History of Paradise: The Garden of Eden in Myth and Tradition*, trans. Matthew O'Connell (New York: Continuum Press, 1995), 6–8.

2. Jon Davies, *Death, Burial, and Rebirth in the Religions of Antiquity* (London: Routledge, 1999), writes, "[Resurrection] was a matter of necessity if the injustice of the Roman world was to be transcended" (123). Jewish and Christian concepts of resurrection were formulated in response to the violence of the Roman Empire. See also 110–114.

See Eibert J. C. Tiggelaar, "Eden and Paradise: The Garden Motif in Some Early Jewish Texts (1 Enoch and Other Texts Found at Qumran)," in *Paradise Interpreted: Representations of Biblical Paradise in Judaism and Christianity*, ed. Gerard P. Luttikhuizen (Leiden, Netherlands: Brill, 1999), 37–62. In the Hebrew scriptures, the realm of the dead, Sheol, was under the earth, dark, and unpleasant. By the first century BCE, the Jewish afterlife was associated with the "abode of the righteous." I Enoch described a journey to many regions of the cosmos, including a place in the east called the "paradise of the righteous." Edenlike, it was somewhere on earth. Enoch also has visions of separate realms after death for the righteous and the sinful—an afterlife division largely absent from the Hebrew Bible.

Testament of Abraham, quoted in Davies, *Death, Burial, and Rebirth*, 87. See also Joachim Jeremias, "παραδεισος" (paradeisos), in *Theological Dictionary of the New Testament*, Vol. 5, ed. Gerhard Kittel, trans. Geoffrey W. Bromile (Grand Rapids, MI: Wm. B. Eerdmans, 1967), 765–773. Jeremias discusses the development of Jewish ideas of paradise as the abode of the righteous and notes the presence of the idea in the New Testament.

Written in Greek between 20 and 54 AD, the fourth book of Maccabees interprets the second century BCE revolt of Jews against Greek rule as reason and emotional control triumphing over folly and violence.

3. *The Didascalia Apostolorum* 1979:175–176, quoted in Davies, *Death, Burial, and Rebirth*, 197. The *Didascalia* was likely composed around 250 in Syria. The New Testament suggests an afterlife zone in Jesus's parable of the rich man and Lazarus, Luke 16:19–31. After dying, Lazarus is "carried by angels to Abraham's bosom." Jeremias, 769–771, interprets "Abraham's bosom" as a version of "the hidden paradise as the abode of the righteous dead" and notes the occurrence of related ideas in 2 Cor. 5:8; Phil. 1:23; Acts 7:59; John 12:26, 14:2; 2 Tim. 4:18; Heb. 12:22; Mark 13:27.

4. Cyril Vogel, "The Cultic Environment of the Deceased in the Early Christian Period,"

in *Temple of the Holy Spirit: Sickness and Death of the Christian in Liturgy,* trans. Matthew J. O'Connell (New York: Pueblo, 1983), 259–276. Feasting with the dead was a common practice in many religions of antiquity.

5. See Isabel Moreira, *Dreams, Visions, and Spiritual Authority in Merovingian Gaul* (Ithaca, NY: Cornell University Press, 2000), 18–34. Belief in dreams that accessed paradise was grounded in the story of Adam, whom God put to sleep in the garden. Actually, there may be many in addition to Monica who would prefer to never see Augustine again, alive or dead.

6. For the conditions of life in late antiquity, see Peter Brown, *The Body in Society: Men, Women, and Sexual Renunciation in Early Christianity* (New York: Columbia University Press, 1988), 5–32.

7. David Wright, professor of "Art in Late Antiquity" at the University of California, Berkeley, discussed the images and provenance of the Via Latina Catacomb, closed to the public, in a lecture in October 2002.

8. This early period of Jewish-Christian interaction is discussed in Daniel Boyarin, *Dying for God: Martyrdom and the Making of Christianity and Judaism* (Stanford, CA: Stanford University Press, 1999), and *Border Lines: The Partition of Judeo-Christianity* (Philadelphia: University of Pennsylvania Press, 2004); and in Clark Williamson, *Has God Rejected His People: Anti-Judaism in the Christian Church* (Nashville: Abingdon Press, 1982). Jews and Christians enjoyed friendly relations, despite efforts by the church to separate them, well into the fifth and sixth centuries. They regarded each other more as heretical versions of each other rather than as separate traditions. The closeness of their relations is revealed by the fact that beginning in Elvira, Spain, in 300 CE, the church passed formal decrees forbidding associations between Christians and Jews. Church leaders attempted to prohibit them from intermarriage, mutual hospitality, blessings of fields, visits to each other's homes, and shared feast days.

9. Thomas Mathews, *The Clash of the Gods: A Reinterpretation of Early Christian Art* (Princeton, NJ: Princeton University Press, 1993), discusses some of the political implications of the images.

10. Jan N. Bremmer, "Paradise: From Persia, via Greece, into the *Septuagint*," in *Paradise Interpreted: Representations of Biblical Paradise in Judaism and Christianity,* ed. Gerard P. Luttikhuizen (Boston: Koninklijke Brill, 1999), 14.

11. In Greek, "Jesus Christ, God's Son, Savior," creates an acrostic, *ichthus,* which in Greek means fish.

12. T. Mathews, *Clash of the Gods,* 54–91.

13. Ibid., 124.

14. For discussion of the shepherd model of leadership that distinguished it from Roman authority, see Christopher Pitts, "Patron and Pastor: The Economy of Authority Present at Nicea as a Discursive Intersection between Empire and Church," master's thesis (Berkeley, CA: Graduate Theological Union, 2005). The apostles are

often shown as sheep. Cyril of Jerusalem, commenting on Song of Songs 6:3, Luke 15:5–6, 23:40, and Psalm 119:176, pictures the good thief crucified with Christ as a sheep: "I am come to feed My sheep in the gardens [Cyril says Golgotha was a garden]. I have found a sheep, a lost one, but I lay it on my shoulders, for he believes, since he himself has said, I have gone astray like a lost sheep: Lord remember me when Thou comest in Thy kingdom." See *A Library of the Fathers of the Holy Catholic Church: Anterior to the Division of the East and West*, translated by members of the English Church (London: J.G.F. and Rivington, 1845), lecture 13.31, p. 159.

15. Tertullian, *On the Resurrection of the Flesh*, chap. 63, "Conclusion. The Resurrection of the Flesh in Its Absolute Identity and Perfection. Belief of This Had Become Weak. Hopes for Its Refreshing Restoration under the Influences of the Paraclete." Available at www.tertullian.org.

16. Tertullian, quoted in Arthur J. Droge and James D. Tabor, *A Noble Death: Suicide and Martyrdom among Christians and Jews in Antiquity* (San Francisco: HarperSan-Francisco, 1992), 129.

17. Bernadette Brooten, *Love between Women: Early Christian Responses to Female Homoeroticism* (Chicago: University of Chicago Press, 1994), 314–320.

18. Brown, *Body in Society*, 28: "A thing of the natural world, the body was expected to speak of its own needs in an ancient, authoritative voice. It was only prudent to listen at times. The tolerance that was extended to the body in late classical times was based on a sense that the antithesis to the animal world, the city, was so strong that, once made, the claims of the city were inexorable."

19. Origen, quoted in Arthur J. Droge and James D. Tabor, *A Noble Death: Suicide and Martyrdom among Christians and Jews in Antiquity* (San Francisco: HarperSan-Francisco, 1992), 149.

20. Origen, *On First Principles*, 152–153. Quoted in Delumeau, *History of Paradise*, 31.

21. Tertullian, *De testimonio animae*, quoted in Vogel, *Temple of the Holy Spirit*, 334 n. 74; Origen, *De oratione* 31, 5, quoted in Vogel, *Temple*, 334 n. 79.

22. Boyarin, *Dying for God*, notes the similarities in Judeo-Christianity developments of the idea and analyses and the differences in evolution of the martyr idea as the two diverged, especially in relation to ideas of gender, heterodoxy, and power.

I propose that we think of martyrdom as a "discourse," as a practice of dying for God and of talking about it, a discourse that changes and develops over time and undergoes particularly interesting transformations among rabbinic Jews and other Jews, including Christians, between the second and the fourth centuries. For the "Romans," it didn't matter much whether the lions were eating a robber or a bishop, and it probably didn't make much of a difference to the lions, either, but the robber's friends and the bishop's friends told different stories about those leonine meals. . . . 1. A ritualized and performative speech act associated with a statement of pure essence becomes the central action of the martyrology. . . . 2. In late antiquity, for the first time the death of the martyr was conceived of as the fulfilling of a religious mandate per se. . . . 3. Powerful erotic elements, including visionary experience, were introduced into martyrology at this time . . . These eroticized elements produce effects that have to do with sex and gender systems, as well. (94–96)

Boyarin suggests that this third element eroticized death (107). On this point, we differ from him. Death was not eroticized; rather the eros of love and community are held as "strong as death" (Song of Sol. 8:6), representing a life-affirming, not death-eroticizing, faith.

23. Peter Brown, *The Rise of Western Christendom: Triumph and Diversity A.D. 200–1000* (Malden, MA: Blackwell, 2003), 66. See also Boyarin, *Dying for God*, which discusses the development of martyrdom from the second century BCE to sixth CE and its role in the mutual formation of Judaism and Christianity as they negotiated their understandings of each other.

24. Joyce Salisbury, *Perpetua's Passion: The Death and Memory of a Young Roman Woman* (New York: Routledge, 1997), discusses the history of child sacrifice in Carthage, 49–57, 124–134; and the ties of Jews and Christians, 59–62.

25. Judith Perkins, *The Suffering Self: Pain and Narrative Representation in the Early Christian Era* (New York: Routledge, 1995), chap. 4; and Salisbury, *Perpetua's Passion*.

26. Patricia Wilson-Kastner, G. Ronald Kastner, Ann Millin, and Rosemary Rader, trans. and ed., "The Acts of Perpetua and Felicitas," in *A Lost Tradition: Women Writers of the Early Church* (New York: University Press of America, 1981), 1–32. Quote from p. 21. The majority of scholars believe the journal accounts are authentic and were expanded from Perpetua's notes.

27. "The Acts of Perpetua," quoted in Jan N. Bremmer, *The Rise and Fall of the Afterlife* (London: Routledge, 2002), 58.

28. Wilson-Kastner et al., "Acts of Perpetua," 24–25.

29. For some of the gender-disrupting aspects of this story, see Virginia Burrus, "Word and Flesh: The Bodies and Sexuality of Ascetic Women in Christian Antiquity," *Journal of Early Christian Studies* 2, 2 (Summer 1994): 27–49; Elizabeth Castelli, "'I Will Make Mary Male': Pieties of the Body and Gender Transformation of Christian Women in Late Antiquity," in *Body Guards*, ed. Julia Epstein and Kristina Straub (New York: Routledge, 1992), 29–49; and Mathew Kuefler, *The Manly Eunuch: Masculinity, Gender Ambiguity, and Christian Ideology in Late Antiquity* (Chicago: University of Chicago Press, 2001).

30. Wilson-Kastner et al., "Acts of Perpetua," 30.

31. Perkins, *Suffering Self*, 111–112.

32. Christine Trevett, *Montanism: Gender, Authority and the New Prophecy* (New York: Cambridge University Press, 1996), chap. 1, discusses many of the names their opponents directed at the New Prophecy. Andrew McGowan, *Ascetic Eucharists: Food and Drink in Early Christian Ritual Meals* (New York: Oxford University Press,

1999), 102, notes the Eucharistic features of Perpetua's vision. Milk, curds, and cheese were used in early Eucharists. He suggests that the vision may also relate to her baptism, as milk was often given at the first Eucharist to symbolize new birth. Peter Dronke argues in *Women Writers of the Middle Ages: A Critical Study of Texts from Perpetua (†203) to Marguerite Porete (†1310)* (Cambridge: Cambridge University Press, 1984) that the cheese indicates a pagan practice signifying embryonic life, taken from Aristotle. "What Perpetua is given with her morsel of cheese is her destiny, her celestial birth—with its inevitable corollary of physical death" (9).

33. Peter Lampe and William Tabernee, *Pepouza and Tymion: The Discovery and Archaeological Exploration of a Lost Ancient City and an Imperial Estate in Phrygia,* is scheduled for publication in 2008.

34. Tertullian, *Apologeticum,* 40. Tertullian criticized the peculiar procedures used by the pagan authorities against the Christians. Christianity, he argued, was a philosophy, but pagan philosophers, unlike Christians, were not forced to make a ritual sacrifice to the emperor. Some philosophers even denied the existence of gods without penalty. Ordinarily, the authorities applied torture to force a confession, but the Christians were tortured to obtain a denial of their Christian identity or to compel them to make the ritual sacrifice to prove their denial. They could be executed simply for saying, "I am a Christian." Tertullian also refuted vile suspicions circulated against Christians.

35. Tertullian's idea of original sin is found in *De Anima,* 41.

36. Barbara Rossing, *The Rapture Exposed: The Message of Hope in The Book of Revelation* (New York: Basic Books, 2004), chap. 5.

37. Catherine Keller, *Apocalypse Now and Then: A Feminist Guide to the End of the World* (Boston: Beacon Press, 1996), suggests that once Constantine befriended the church, Revelation lost its political punch as a this-worldly critique of empire, and interpretations shifted to a more cosmic antiworld reading of its descriptions of horror. She defines the apocalyptic habit as one that

> manifests itself as the performance of an apocalypse script, which is in most cases written out as a text, and acted out in multifarious secular and subliminal practices. . . . This pattern, always adjacent to suffering, rests upon an either/or morality: a proclivity to think and feel in polarities of "good" versus "evil"; to identify the good and to purge the evil from oneself and one's world once and for all, demanding undivided unity before "the enemy"; to feel that the good is getting victimized by the evil, which is diabolically overpowering; to expect some cataclysmic showdown in which, despite tremendous collateral damage . . . good must triumph in the near future with the help of some transcendent power and live forever after in a fundamentally new world. . . . Most often within this pattern, the extremes of innocence and of vice are coded as impersonally feminine, while the active agencies of good and evil are figured as masculine heroes and their enemies. . . . I am talking about a habituated and reactive tendency, collec-

tively instilled and readily acted out in individual bursts of self-righteous certainty: we may "do an apocalypse" in our most intimate relations as well as in our most visionary politics. (11)

38. Josephus, *War*, 6.300–309, quoted in Barbara Rossing, "Prophets, Prophetic Movements, and Voices of Women," in *A People's History of Christianity*, Vol. 1, ed. Richard A. Horsley (Minneapolis: Fortress Press, 2005), 265.

39. Davies, *Death, Burial, and Rebirth*, summarizing the report of Dio Cassius, 112.

40. Josephine Massyngberde Ford, *Revelation, Anchor Bible Commentary Series* (New York: Anchor Doubleday, 1975), 242, makes the case that the whore of Babylon is Jerusalem and that the book includes a history of the Roman and Jewish wars. Many mainstream biblical scholars regard Revelation as a drama pitting Christian-Jewish communities against the Roman Empire, which destroyed the second temple in 70 CE. For an extensive study, see Elisabeth Schüssler Fiorenza *The Book of Revelation: Justice and Judgment*, 2nd ed. (Minneapolis: Augsburg Fortress, 1998). Also see Rossing, *Rapture Exposed*, and Keller, *Apocalypse Now*.

41. Keller, *Apocalypse Now*, 44–46, 75–77, discusses the misogyny in such female images. The witch-hunts would later murder thousands of women, often based on suspicion of their ties to Satan. See also Anne Barstow, *Witchcraze: A New History of the European Witch Hunts* (San Francisco: HarperSanFrancisco, 1995); and Deborah Wills, *Malevolent Nurture: Witch-Hunting and Maternal Power in Early Modern England* (Ithaca, NY: Cornell University Press, 1995).

42. Rossing, *Rapture Exposed*, chap. 7.

43. Alfred North Whitehead, *Process and Reality: An Essay in Cosmology* (New York: Macmillan, 1929), 404.

44. Doris Lessing, *The Four-Gated City*, bk. 5, *The Children of Violence* (New York: Harper Perennial, 1995).

45. Roger Rees, *Diocletian and the Tetrarchy* (Edinburgh: Edinburgh University Press, 2004). Diocletian created an administrative system of Caesar Augusti in the East and West, each with a subordinate Caesar, which was called the Tetrarchy.

46. Joyce E. Salisbury, *The Blood of the Martyrs: Unintended Consequences of Ancient Violence* (New York: Routledge, 2004), 21.

47. J. Salisbury, *Perpetua's Passion*, 73.

48. Pitts, "Patron and Pastor," discusses Diocletian's administrative reforms and his use of religion in his administration.

49. Gregory Dix quotes the entire report in *The Shape of the Liturgy* (London: Dacre Press, A. and C. Black, 1960), 24–26. See Mary Rose DAngelo, "Veils, Virgins, and the Tongues of Men and Angels: Women's Heads in Early Christianity," in *Women, Gender, Religion: A Reader*, ed. Elizabeth A. Castelli (New York: Palgrave, 2001), 389–419, for a discussion of the veils for virgins who spoke in churches.

50. *Martyrium Polycarpi* 18, quoted in Vogel, "Cultic Environment of the Deceased," 331 n. 50.

51. Brown, *Rise of Western Christendom,* 162–163.
52. Kathleen McTigue, "They Are with Us Still," in *Singing the Living Tradition* (Boston: Beacon Press, 1993), 721.

CHAPTER FOUR: THE CHURCH AS PARADISE IN THIS WORLD

1. "The Passion of St. Theodore the Recruit," *Bibliotheca Hagiographica Latina* 8077, www.ucc.ie/milmart/BHL8077.html, describes the confrontation: " 'Are you willing to offer sacrifice or do you want to be tortured still further by me?' In reply blessed Theodore said confidently to the governor . . . 'Do you not fear the Lord who gave you this power, through whom kings rule and tyrants obtain land, but compel me to desert the living God and worship lifeless stones?' Then the judge, with much shuffling of papers, said to the holy martyr, 'What do you want? To be with us or with your Christ?' To which the holy martyr replied . . . 'I have been, am, and shall be with my Christ.' "

2. Gregory's description is found in Vasiliki Limberis, "The Cult of the Martyrs and the Cappadocian Fathers," in *Byzantine Christianity, A People's History of Christianity,* Vol. 3, ed. Derek Krueger (Minneapolis: Fortress Press, 2006), 42, 44, 45. Saints' images evolved from funerary art and from portraits of the dead in paradise in the catacombs. For a discussion of this evolution, including depictions of Christ presiding over the martyrs, see Hans Belting, *Likeness and Presence: A History of the Image before the Era of Art,* trans. Edmund Jephcott (Chicago: University of Chicago Press, 1994), 78–98.

3. Lactantius, "Edict of Milan," *De Mort. Pers.,* in Henry Bettenson and Chris Maunder, eds., *Documents of the Christian Church* (Oxford: Oxford University Press, 1999), 17. Though it is commonly believed that Constantine created a state religion, in fact he instituted religious tolerance with favoritism toward Christianity: "When we, Constantine and Licinius Emperors, . . . decided . . . the worship of God ought rightly to be our first and chiefest care, and that it was right that Christians and all others should have freedom to follow the kind of religion they favoured; so that the God who dwells in heaven might be propitious to us and to all under our rule . . . all . . . are to be allowed the free and unrestricted practice of their religions."

4. George Long, "Codex Theodosianus," in *A Dictionary of Greek and Roman Antiquities,* ed. William Smith (London: John Murray Press, 1875), 302–303.

5. *Panto* means "all," *krateo* means "to sustain," and *krator* means "dynamic power." The Septuagint translates the Hebrew El Shaddai (God of the Mountain) as Pantokrator. Paul in 2 Corinthians 6:18 quotes the Septuagint to describe the presence, governance, and love of God. For a discussion of how early Christian art avoided portraying Christ in Roman imperial iconography, see Thomas Mathews, *The Clash of the Gods: A Reinterpretation of Early Christian Art* (Princeton, NJ: Princeton Uni-

versity Press, 1993). Before Mathews, the prevailing theory in twentieth-century art history read post-Constantinian Christian imagery as a capitulation to the imperial cult.

6. Lawrence was executed, most likely by beheading, by Emperor Valerian, who ordered the execution of Rome's Christian priests, deacons, and bishop in 258. Ambrose said Lawrence was burned to death on a gridiron—an oral tradition. Lawrence was extolled for his assistance to Rome's poor and for protecting the church's sacred books from being confiscated by Rome.

7. Irenaeus, *Against Heresies,* quoted in George Hunston Williams, *Wilderness and Paradise in Christian Thought: The Biblical Experience of the Desert in the History of Christianity and the Paradise Theme in the Theological Idea of the University* (New York: Harper and Row, 1962), 30.

8. Irenaeus, *Against Heresies,* in *Early Christian Fathers,* Vol. 1, ed. Cyril C. Richardson (Philadelphia: Westminster Press, 1953), 391–392.

9. Irenaeus, *Against Heresies,* quoted in G. H. Williams, *Wilderness and Paradise,* 31.

10. Theophilus of Antioch, quoted in Vladimir Kharlamov, "Deification in the Apologists of the Second Century," in *Theōsis: Deification in Christian Theology,* ed. Stephen Finlan and Vladimir Kharlamov, Princeton Theological Monograph Series (Eugene, OR: Pickwick Publications, 2006), 78.

11. Origen, *On First Principles,* quoted in Jean Delumeau, *History of Paradise: The Garden of Eden in Myth and Tradition,* trans. Matthew O'Connell (New York: Continuum Press, 1995), 16.

12. Gary Anderson, "The Cosmic Mountain: Eden and Its Early Interpreters in Syriac Christianity," in *Genesis 1–3 in the History of Exegesis: Intrigue in the Garden,* ed. Gregory Allen Robbins (Lewiston, NY: Edwin Mellen Press, 1988), 187–224, discusses the linguistic impact of various translations.

13. Hippolytus, *Fragmenta in Hexameron,* quoted in Delumeau, *History of Paradise,* 16–17.

14. See Delumeau, *History of Paradise,* 1–14, for the range of early church positions.

15. Ibid., 6–8.

16. Ibid., 10–11, for Justin Martyr's defense. Bart D. Ehrman, in *Lost Christianities: The Battles for Scripture and the Faiths We Never Knew* (New York: Oxford University Press, 2003), discusses how the Christians who traced their lineage through Judaism and the Hebrew Bible were eventually more successful than those who used only the Christian texts as their sources for sacred scripture and ideas, 112: "In the fields of philosophy and religion, as opposed to the field of military technology, it was the *old* that was appreciated and respected, not the new. One of the most serious obstacles for Christians in the Roman mission field was the widespread perception—and it was entirely valid—that the religion was 'recent.' Nothing new could be true. If it were true, why was it not known long ago? How could it be that no one until now has understood the truth? Not even Homer, Plato, or Aristotle?"

17. Two translations of Ephrem's poems exist in English, *Saint Ephrem: Hymns on Paradise,* trans. Sebastian Brock (Crestwood, NY: St. Vladimir's Seminary Press, 1990); and *Ephrem the Syrian: Hymns,* trans. Kathleen McVey (New York: Paulist Press, 1989). For a brief account of his life and times, see Sebastian Brock's introduction to his translation, 7–75. In addition, see Brock's *The Luminous Eye: The Spiritual World Vision of Saint Ephrem the Syrian,* rev. ed. (Kalamazoo, MI: Cistercian Publications, 1992); and Robert Murray, *Symbols of Church and Kingdom: A Study in Early Syriac Tradition,* rev. ed. (Piscataway, NJ: Gorgios Press, 2004). For discussions of several ancient hagiographies of Ephrem, containing some fabrications, see Brock's introduction to *Saint Ephrem,* 11–25.

18. Syriac, a form of Aramaic, was used in Anatolia, Armenia, Georgia, India, Arabia, Palestine, and Persia. Although most Western scholars today study early Christianity as represented in Greek and Latin texts, the ancient church had three important languages: Greek, Latin, and Syriac. Ephrem enjoyed a revival in the West in seventeenth- and eighteenth-century England. John Wesley spoke of Ephrem as his favorite ancient Christian writer.

19. Jerome, quoted in S. Brock, introduction to *Saint Ephrem,* 12.

20. Sozomen, *Lausiac History,* quoted in S. Brock, introduction to *Saint Ephrem,* 15–16.

21. Christopher Buck, *Paradise and Paradigm: Key Symbols in Persian Christianity and the Bahā'ī Faith* (Albany: State University of New York Press, 1999), 45–62, discusses Ephrem in the context of his struggles and disagreements with Marcion, Bardaisan, Mani, the Arians, the Chaldeans, the Jews, and Julian.

22. Ephrem, *Hymns on Paradise,* quoted in S. Brock, *Luminous Eye,* 163.

23. Ephrem, *Hymns on Paradise,* in S. Brock, *Saint Ephrem,* 158. Historians disagree on the roots of Syriac Christianity in Nisibis. For a comprehensive discussion of its complex history, see R. Murray, *Symbols of the Church and Kingdom,* 3–23. He reports that the history suggests Gnostic, Jewish, and Hellenistic influences. A strong argument can be made that Syriac Christianity began as a Jewish Christian sect. For an overview of this literature, see note 13 in Kathleen McVey's introduction to *Ephrem the Syrian.*

24. Ephrem, *Hymns on Paradise,* in S. Brock, *Saint Ephrem,* 81.

25. Ephrem, quoted in S. Brock, *Luminous Eye,* 152–153. Brock notes that paradise is an eschatological image for Ephrem that is "other" from space and time. In our reading, for Ephrem the eschatological character of paradise does not postpone it in time or remove it from space—it permeates space and time. While remaining "other," it is also here and now and is accessed in various ways. See Brock, introduction to *Saint Ephrem,* 49–57, for a detailed discussion of the landscape of paradise and its meaning for Ephrem. The paradise mountain was variously understood as a physical place, as a metaphor for the blessedness of the whole earth, as a spiritual reality "other" than time and space but permeating them, as the sanctuary of God's presence—and more.

26. Ephrem, *Hymns on Paradise,* in S. Brock, *Saint Ephrem,* 109–110.

27. See Bettenson and Maunder, *Documents,* 22.

28. Robin E. Waterfield, *Christians in Persia* (New York: Harper and Row, 1973), 19–20. See also McVey's introduction to *Ephrem the Syrian,* 12–23. Persia persecuted Christians far more extensively than even Rome had done: when Constantine asked King Shapur II to protect Christians in Persia, his request put them under suspicion of being sympathizers with Persia's most hated enemy. For the importance of elephants and Persian wars, see Marina Belozeskaya, *The Medici Giraffe and Other Tales of Exotic Animals and Power* (New York: Little, Brown, 2006), 3–48.

29. Ephrem, *Carmina Nisbena,* in McVey, *Ephrem the Syrian,* 18.

30. Ephrem, *Hymns against Julian,* in McVey, *Ephrem the Syrian,* 247.

31. Ibid., excerpts, 221–222.

32. Buck, *Paradise and Paradigm,* 7.

33. Ephrem, *Hymns on Paradise,* in S. Brock, *Saint Ephrem,* 57.

34. Ephrem, *Hymns on Virginity,* in McVey, *Ephrem the Syrian,* 401–402.

35. See Murray, *Symbols of Church,* 104–113.

36. Ephrem, *Hymns on Paradise,* in S. Brock, *Saint Ephrem,* 111.

37. Ephrem, *Letter to Hypatius,* quoted in S. Brock, *Luminous Eye,* 167.

38. Ephrem, *Heresies* 10:9, quoted in S. Brock, *Luminous Eye,* 166.

39. Quotes from Ambrose, *Paradise,* in *Saint Ambrose: Hexameron, Paradise, and Cain and Able,* trans. John J. Savage (New York: Fathers of the Church, 1961), 287–298.

40. Virginia Burrus, *Begotten Not Made: Conceiving Masculinity in Late Antiquity* (Stanford, CA: Stanford University Press, 2000); and Mathew Kuefler, *The Manly Eunuch: Masculinity, Gender Ambiguity, and Christian Ideology in Late Antiquity* (Chicago: University of Chicago Press, 2001) discuss the formation of this new masculinity in the fourth century. Ambrose, *Paradise,* 301, says, "Note the fact that man was created outside Paradise, whereas woman was made within it. This teaches us that each person acquires grace because of virtue, not because of locality or of race. Hence, although created outside Paradise, that is, in an inferior place, man is found to be superior, whereas woman, created in a better place, that is to say, in Paradise, is found to be inferior."

41. Ambrose, *Paradise,* 297, links the physical geography of the Nile with symbolic virtues and associates black skin with sin. "The meaning of Ethiopia in Latin is 'holy and vile.' What is more lowly, what is more like Ethiopia, than our bodies, blackened, too, by the darkness of sin?" For a discussion of this race discourse, see Gay L. Byron, *Symbolic Blackness and Ethnic Difference in Early Christian Literature* (New York: Routledge, 2001).

42. Theodoret, *Ecclesiastical History,* 5.17–18, in William Stearns Davis, ed., *Readings in Ancient History: Illustrative Extracts from the Sources,* 2 Vols. (Boston: Allyn and Bacon, 1912–13), Vol. 2: *Rome and the West,* 298–300.

43. Ambrose wrote to Theodosius, "For it is no matter of wonder that a man should sin,

but this is reprehensible, if he does not recognize that he has erred, and humble himself before God . . . Put away this sin from your kingdom, for you will do it away by humbling your soul before God. You are a man, and it has come upon you, conquer it. Sin is not done away but by tears and penitence. . . . Conquer [the devil] whilst you still possess that wherewith you may conquer. Do not add another sin to your sin by a course of action which has injured many. . . . He who accuses himself when he has sinned is just, not he who praises himself." *Letter of St. Ambrose*, in *Library of Nicene and Post Nicene Fathers*, 2nd ser., Vol. 10, trans. H. De Romestin (New York: T&T Clark, 1896), 450–453.

44. Theodoret, *Ecclesiastical History*, in Davis, *Readings in Ancient History*, 300, described how Theodosius "prayed neither in a standing, nor in a kneeling posture, but throwing himself upon the ground. He tore his hair, struck his forehead, and shed torrents of tears, as he implored forgiveness of God."

45. Augustine, *Confessions*, trans. J. G. Pilkington, in *Basic Writings of Saint Augustine*, Vol. 1, ed. Whitney J. Oates (New York: Random House, 1948), 113.

46. G. H. Williams, *Wilderness and Paradise*, 33–35, contrasts Eusebius to those in the fourth century who maintained a sense of what Williams calls "the church as a provisional paradise." He writes:

> Eusebius chose to extinguish entirely the motif of paradisic harmony in the Marcan version, and . . . pictured Christ as crushing by his divine virtue the asp and the adder, the lion and the dragon in the wilderness. With this concept of Christ as Victor . . . Eusebius readily imagined Constantine completing the resolute action of the Saviour in crushing by force of arms the demons of divisiveness, disorder, and the depraved cults. Commingling the imperial and his own Episcopal ideal of the Christian commonwealth, Eusebius . . . brought about the eclipse of the Old Catholic interpretation of Jesus among the animals in the wilderness in Mark 1:13 as the New Covenantal Adam in Paradise, which is the Church. (34)

47. Augustine, *Confessions*, in Pilkington, *Basic Writings*, 252.

48. Ibid., 234, 239, 241.

49. Augustine, *The Literal Meaning of Genesis*, trans. John Hammond, Vol. 2 (New York: Newman Press, 1982), 36–37.

50. Johannes Van Oort, "Augustine's City of God: Background and Importance for Christianity in a Postmodern Europe," lecture, Nov. 3, 2005, University of Malta. Summary at http://home.um.edu.mt/philosophy/activities.html. "Augustine can be said to have been in love with the world, a world he called a smiling place (Sermon 169.4)." In his view of the church he "creates a complex moral map that offers space for loyalty and love and care. . . . Augustine also torments cynics who disdain any project of human community, or justice, or possibility. . . . Wisdom comes from experiencing fully the ambivalence and ambiguity of the human condition."

51. Augustine, *The Literal Meaning of Genesis,* Vol. 2, 157.

52. Like other great thinkers who produce a body of work over a long lifetime, Augustine kept changing his ideas, even producing a list of all his works and his reconsideration of them near the end of his life in *The Retractions, Fathers of the Church: Saint Augustine: The Retractions,* trans. Mary Inez Bogan (Washington, DC: Catholic University of America, 1999). His third commentary on Genesis is from this later, more mature stage in his life, whereas *Confessions* was written midcareer. He also began some works midcareer but completed them much later, which means they also contain internal tensions. Among these is *The City of God,* trans. Marcus Dods, in *Nicene and Post-Nicene Fathers of the Christian Church,* Vol. 2, ed. Philip Schaff (Grand Rapids, MI: Wm. B. Eerdmanns, 1956).

53. Augustine, *City of God,* 13.21.

54. Johannes Van Oort, in *Jerusalem and Babylon: A Study of Augustine's* City of God *and the Sources of His Doctrine of the Two Cities (Supplements to Vigiliae Christianae)* (Leiden, Netherlands: Brill Academic, 1991), comments:

> A Christian state as Eusebius saw it is out of the question for Augustine, as is a Christianization of the emperorship. . . . There are no permanent empires here on earth. Not even Christian ones, although through the mercy of God there are Christian emperors. Only the city of God is firm and permanent. On earth she sojourns under different worldly powers, always as an alien. She uses and appreciates earthly peace . . . for in Babylon's peace is her peace. . . . [But] there is essentially no difference between the era following Constantine and the one preceding it. Now, too, the Church is in peregrination; now, too, it is being persecuted. Being a member of the Church still means: enduring, suffering, bearing. . . . The persecutions by Satan and the fallen world are still going on. . . . It is only in the hope of eternal life that all this can be endured. (160–163)

55. Augustine, *City of God,* 3.14.

56. See Phil. 2:5–11. This early letter, sent by Paul from prison to the church in Philippi, includes a very early confessional prayer which asserted that Jesus was divine and took human form.

57. *Testament of Levi* 1:1–13, quoted in G. H. Williams, *Wilderness and Paradise,* 31.

58. The *Book of the Cave of Treasures,* a third-century Syriac text, quoted in R. Murray, *Symbols of Church and Kingdom,* 261: "Adam was priest and king and prophet, God brought him into paradise that he might minister in Eden."

59. Richard Rubenstein, *When Jesus Became God: The Epic Fight over Christ's Divinity in the Last Days of Rome* (New York: Harcourt, Brace, 1999), suggests that differences between the Nicene and Arian positions was partly determined by the religious contexts of the bishops. In the West, pagan polytheism prevailed. In the East, Jewish monotheism supported subordinating Christ to God. Rubenstein uses the form of a

historical novel to describe the violence in Alexandria and the ongoing conflicts, including Constantine's vacillations and Athanasius's tactics for holding power.

60. The 325 creed reads, in part:

> We believe in one God the Father All-sovereign, maker of all things visi-
> ble and invisible; And in one Lord Jesus Christ, the Son of God, begotten of
> the Father, only-begotten, that is, of the substance [from the innermost being]
> of the Father, God of God, Light of Light, true God of true God, begotten not
> made, of one substance [sharing one being] with the Father, through whom
> all things were made, things in heaven and things on the earth; who for us
> men and for our salvation came down and was made flesh, and became man,
> [taking on himself all that makes man] suffered, and rose on the third day,
> ascended into the heavens, is coming to judge the living and dead. ("The
> Nicene Creed," in Bettenson and Maunder, *Documents*, 27)

61. Peter Brown writes in *The Rise of Western Christendom: Triumph and Diversity A.D.
200–1000 (Malden, MA: Blackwell, 2003):

> The position that "won" at Nicaea strengthened the hand of Christian bish-
> ops to judge and discipline Roman emperors. It placed the Church in a position
> of power over the Empire. Whether this would be to the good depended on what
> the bishops did with their newly solidified power. Nicaea offered some clues:
> among the decisions of the council were condemnations of Jews. This was an ill
> portent of things to come: a willingness by Christians to use the power of law to
> constrain and control the lives of Jews. . . . By the end of the fourth century the
> "Arian Controversy" was narrated in studiously confrontational terms: it was as-
> serted that "orthodox" bishops had defeated "heretics"; and in so doing, they
> had offered heroic resistance to . . . the threats of "heretical" emperors. (77–80)

62. In *Begotten Not Made*, Burrus points out that the divinization of humanity constructed masculinity with greater aggression and uses of power.

63. Rubenstein suggests in *When Jesus Became God* that the Arian position, had it won,
might have allowed Christians and Jews to evolve as compatible siblings. Daniel Boyarin, *Border Lines: The Partition of Judeo-Christianity* (Philadelphia: University
of Pennsylvania Press, 2005), argues that the decision to move toward doctrinal uniformity was the key difference to emerge, rather than the content of the theologies.
Rabbinic Judaism maintained an ability to hold conflicting positions together and
continue traditions of disputation that distinguished it from post-Constantinian
Christianity. Margaret R. Miles, *The World Made Flesh: A History of Christian
Thought* (Malden, MA: Blackwell, 2005), summarizes what is known of Arius's views
and approach, 70–72, 92–93.

64. "[Christ] being the deifying and enlightening power of the Father, in which all things
are deified and quickened, is not alien in essence from the Father, but coessential (*ho-

moousios) . . . if He was Himself too from participation, and not from the Father His essential Godhead and Image, He would not deify." Athanasius, *De synod.*, quoted in Jeffrey Finch, "Athanasius on the Deifying Work of the Redeemer," *Theōsis: Deification in Christian Theology*, ed. Stephen Finlan and Vladimir Kharlamov, Princeton Theological Monograph Series (Eugene, OR: Pickwick Publications, 2006), 105.

65. Rubenstein, in *When Jesus Became God*, describes in vivid detail the disputes and riots that accompanied the Nicene controversies, as well as imperial indecision.

66. In *The Clash of the Gods* (114), Thomas Mathews dismantles the commonly held view that this and similar images assimilate Christ into an imperial figure. Such an interpretation is a product of pre–WWII German, Austrian, and Russian scholars (Ernst Kantorowicz, Andreas Alfoldi, and André Grabar) who were nostalgic for lost empires in Europe. He writes, "The three imperial states in which they were raised, and which they fought valiantly to defend, they saw crumble ignominiously in the horrible chaos of the First World War. . . . A call to greatness in the model of past imperial accomplishments is implicit in their scholarship" (19).

67. For a discussion of Christian resistance to Roman claims of dominance through its use of geographic imagery, see Barbara Rossing, "(Re)claiming *Oikoumenē?* Empire, Ecumenism, and the Discipleship of Equals," in *Walk in the Ways of Wisdom: Essays in Honor of Elisabeth Schüssler Fiorenza*, ed. Shelly Matthews, Cynthia Briggs Kittredge, and Melanie Johnson-Debaufre (Harrisburg, PA: Trinity Press, 2003), 74–87. See also Ellen Bradshaw Aitken, "The Landscape of Promise in the *Apocalypse of Paul*," in *Walk in the Ways of Wisdom*, 153–165. Christian apocalyptic descriptions of the new creation or the 'land of promise,' such as the popular third century *Apocalypse of Paul*, placed Christianity in direct competition with Rome's claims, and fostered resistance to Rome. She comments, "The ideal age was presented in order to motivate action in this world. In the age of Augustus and his successor, the aim was to uphold the exercise of *imperium* in the Roman world through instilling Roman values and practices. With the *Apocalypse of Paul*, these same rhetorical strategies, deployed to construct a picture of paradise and the landscape of promise, provided a means of shaping the ethical identity of the Christian community living in the here-and-now" (165).

68. T. Mathews, *Clash of the Gods*, notes that Christians regarded imperial opulence with irony and outrage:

> The reaction of Synesius was pure outrage. Arriving in Constantinople . . . seeking relief for his native province, he found the emperor Arcadius so laden with his consular garments that he appeared insulated from all contact with his subjects. "When do you think the Roman Empire reached its apogee?" he asked the emperor. "Was it when you wrapped yourself in purple and gold and bound your brow with stones and imported pearls? . . . You have made yourself into a gold-spangled masterpiece like a peacock. . . .

You glitter under the load like some prisoner bound in gold chains ... who is unconscious of his suffering and does not even know he is bound, deceived by the great expense of his surroundings." Christ was never so clad. (192)

69. Gary A. Anderson, in *The Genesis of Perfection: Adam and Eve in Jewish and Christian Imagination* (Louisville, KY: Westminster John Knox Press, 2001), writes on the *Genesis Rabbah* 19:7:

> The real home of the Shekinah (divine presence) was in the realm below, not the heavens above. When Adam sinned, it departed to the first level of the heavens. With Cain, it departed to the second; the generation of Enosh, to the third; the generation of the flood, to the fourth; the builders of the tower of Babel, to the fifth; with those of Sodom, to the sixth; and with the Egyptians in the days of Abraham, to the furthest remove possible, the seventh heaven. But over against these sinful generations, seven righteous persons arose: Abraham, Isaac, Jacob, Levi, Kohath, Amram, and Moses. They brought the *Shekinah* from the seventh heaven back to the realm of earth. ... With Moses, at the top of Mt. Sinai ... the divine presence again resides on earth. In one tradition, the power of the angel of death was removed from Israel. The effects of the fall were undone. Paradise had been regained. (14, 19)

Many of the saints and images in St. Vitale reflect the story of faith told in Hebrews 11, the theophany of Ezekiel 1, as well as images of the Creation from Genesis and Revelation. Moses is shown on Mt. Sinai as well as before the burning bush.

CHAPTER FIVE: THE PORTAL TO PARADISE

1. Sources for this chapter include Allen Cabaniss, *Pattern in Early Christian Worship* (Macon, GA: Mercer University Press, 1989); Peter Cramer, *Baptism and Change in the Early Middle Ages, c. 200–1150* (New York: Cambridge University Press, 1993); Thomas M. Finn, *From Death to Rebirth: Ritual and Conversion in Antiquity* (New York: Paulist Press, 1997), which surveys the range of earliest practices in Rome, Syria, and North Africa; Kilian McDonnell, *The Baptism of Jesus in the Jordan* (Collegeville, MN: Liturgical Press, 1996), which examines multiple meanings of baptism in the early church, focusing on the primacy of Jesus's baptism in the Jordan as key to the church's interpretation of baptism rather than of his death and resurrection; Margaret Miles, *Carnal Knowing: Female Nakedness and Religious Meaning in the West* (Boston: Beacon Press, 1989); Hugh M. Riley, *Christian Initiation: A Comparative Study of the Interpretation of the Baptismal Liturgy in the Mystagogical Writings of Cyril of Jerusalem, John Chrysostom, Theodore of Mopsuestia, and Ambrose of Milan* (Washington, DC: Catholic University of America Press, 1974), which studies fourth-century baptismal rites, comparing the four in his title; E. C. Whitaker and Maxwell E. Johnson, *Documents of the Baptismal Liturgy* (Collegeville, MN: Litur-

gical Press, 2003), which provides original baptismal texts organized by regions and languages; and Patricia Wilson-Kastner, G. Ronald Kastner, Ann Millin, Rosemary Rader, eds. and trans., *A Lost Tradition: Women Writers of the Early Church* (New York: University Press of America, 1981).

2. Cyril of Jerusalem, quoted in Finn, *From Death to Rebirth*, 9–10.

3. Dura-Europas was rediscovered in the mid-twentieth century. "The Dura church ranks with major finds in the catacombs, Asia Minor and North Africa, among the most important discoveries in Christian archaeology. Alone its date, approximately AD 232, makes it the earliest Christian building yet found" (William H. C. Frend, *The Archaeology of Early Christianity: A History* [Minneapolis: Fortress Press, 1996]). For a discussion of the much larger nearby synagogue and its frescoes, see Joseph Gutmann, ed., *The Dura-Europos Synagogue: A Re-evaluation (1932–1992)* (Atlanta: Scholars Press, 1992). Yale University owns the Dura baptistry frescoes. Slides of the original excavation and the display at Yale were shown in a lecture by Professor David Wright, "Art in Late Antiquity," Department of Art History, University of California, Berkeley, September 6, 2002.

4. Ephrem, *Crucifixion,* quoted in Sebastian Brock, *The Luminous Eye: The Spiritual World Vision of Saint Ephrem,* rev. ed. (Kalamazoo, MI: Cistercian Publications, 1992), 34.

5. Excerpts from *Odes of Solomon,* in McDonnell, *Baptism of Jesus,* 151. See McDonnell's discussion (149–153) of scholarly opinions about the dating and original language of the odes. J. H. Bernard argues for reading the odes as baptismal texts. Many place the text in mid-second-century Syria.

6. McDonnell observes, "Paradise begins now, here on earth, and is not a promise of a distant future. The images are of some kind of immediate experience and transformation" (*Baptism of Jesus,* 150).

7. Riley writes in *Christian Initiation,* "The candidate, in what he says and does and in what is said and done to him, is enlightened. . . . Not through abstract instruction, but through concrete engagement in physical symbolic action the candidate performs his rite of passage" (1).

8. Irenaeus, *Against Heresies,* V.20. 2. Quoted in George Huston Williams, *Wilderness and Paradise in Christian Thought; The Biblical Experience of the Desert in the History of Christianity and the Paradise Theme in the Theological Idea of the University* (New York: Harper, 1962), 30.

   For discussions of ritual as a significant aspect of religious life, see Tom Driver, *The Magic of Ritual: Our Need for Liberating Rites That Transform Our Lives and Our Communities* (San Francisco: Harper San Francisco, 1991); and Gordon W. Lathrop, *Holy Ground: A Liturgical Cosmology* (Minneapolis: Fortress Press, 2003). Lathrop makes a case for Christian ritual as a mode of orientation in time and space that has ethical implications for how humanity can live justly on the planet, understanding earth as holy ground.

9. Egeria, in Wilson-Kastner et al., *Lost Tradition,* 77. Scholars debate the dating of Ege-

ria's journal, with the fourth century as a strong possibility, specifically c. 381–384, during Cyril's time. See Maxwell Johnson, "Reconciling Cyril and Egeria on the Catechetical Process in Fourth-Century Jerusalem," in *Essays in Early Eastern Initiation,* ed. Paul F. Bradshaw (Bramcote, UK: Grove Books, 1988). For a bibliography of scholarship on Cyril, see Whitaker and Johnson, *Documents of the Baptismal Liturgy,* 26–27. For an introduction to Cyril, see Edward Yarnold, *Cyril of Jerusalem* (London: Routledge, 2000). Cyril's *Catechetical Lectures,* which were given to candidates for baptism, provide extensive information on baptismal practices and their meaning in fourth-century Jerusalem. For a translation of the complete lectures, see Cyril, *The Catechetical Lectures of S. Cyril, Archbishop of Jerusalem,* anonymous trans., in the series *A Library of Fathers of the Holy Catholic Church* (Oxford, UK: John Henry Parker, 1845). Brief excerpts from the lectures, in a modern translation, can be found in "The Catecheses of Cyril of Jerusalem," in *Springtime of the Liturgy: Liturgical Texts of the First Four Centuries,* ed. Lucien Deiss, trans. Matthew J. O'Connell (Collegeville, MN: Liturgical Press, 1979), 267–289. In this chapter, unless we note otherwise, quotations from Cyril's lectures are from the 1845 Oxford translation, with slight modifications made by the authors to modernize the English.

10. Finn, *From Death to Rebirth,* 3; and Michel Dujarier, *A History of the Catechumenate: The First Six Centuries,* trans. Edward J. Haasl (New York: Sadlier, 1979), 44–45. The terms for the stages of baptism varied; these are the terms used in Jerusalem.

11. Egeria, in Wilson-Kastner et al., *Lost Tradition,* 128.

12. Yisrael Shalem, "Jerusalem: Life throughout the Ages in a Holy City," www.biu.ac.il/JS/rennert/history_5.html. After 135, the Romans repopulated the city by importing pagan Hellenists. They allowed uncircumcised Christians to live in Jerusalem but excluded circumcised Christians—dividing Christian Jews from Christian Gentiles. Jews, including Christian Jews, remained in the regions around Jerusalem. They bought land back from the Romans and reestablished towns. When the Roman legion left, those who moved into the city were likely from the surrounding countryside.

13. Eusebius, *Life of Constantine* 3.28, quoted in Yarnold, *Cyril of Jerusalem,* 12. Yarnold comments, "This account by Eusebius of these events is remarkable for his systematic refusal to speak of Golgotha or the wood of the cross" (12).

14. For a fuller discussion of "finding" the "true cross," see James Carroll, *Constantine's Sword: The Church and the Jews, A History* (Boston: Houghton Mifflin, 2001), 197–207. In his sermon on the death of Emperor Theodosius, given in 395, Ambrose credited Helena with this discovery and extolled it as a sign that the Jews had been vanquished: "The church manifest joy, but the Jew blushes. Not only does he blush, but he is tormented" (Ambrose quoted in Carroll, 201). Whenever an emphasis on the Crucifixion emerged, Jews were accused of being Christ-killers.

15. Egeria, from Wilson-Kastner et al., *Lost Tradition,* 113.

16. Cyril, *Catechetical Lectures* 15.12, 26, 33.

17. The story of Cyril selling Constantine's gifts is reported in the preface to the 1845 Oxford edition of Cyril's *Catechetical Lectures*, iv. Acacius, the bishop of Cesarea and an Arian, was in conflict with Cyril over several matters. He used Cyril's selling of Constantine's gifts to discredit Cyril in the eyes of Constantius II, the current emperor, who was Arian in his theological outlook.

18. Yisrael Shalem comments on Julian's efforts, "At this time we may find the beginnings of Jewish reverence for the Western Wall. Graffiti carved on the Western Wall bearing a messianic verse from Isaiah may have been written at this time. In Exodus Rabba, Rabbi Aha states that 'the Shechina (divine presence) never departed from the Western Wall.' Another midrash from this period claims that the Western wall was built with donations form the poor and therefore could not be destroyed" (*Jerusalem: Life through the Ages in a Holy City* at www.biu.ac.il/JS/rennert/ history_7.html).

19. Hippolytus in Dujarier, *History of the Catecumenate*, 50. The list is in "The Apostolic Tradition." See Whitaker and Johnson, *Documents of the Baptismal Liturgy*, 4–5, for an overview of the current scholarly literature on Hippolytus's writings. The text is no longer considered exclusively third century or Roman. It "may well reflect a synthesis or composite text of various and diverse liturgical patterns reflecting even diverse ecclesial traditions, some quite early and others not added until the time of its final redaction," in the fifth century (4). According to Deiss, *Springtime*, 123–127, Hippolytus was a leading writer and preacher in third-century Rome. Appalled by the Pope's laxity, he had himself elected bishop of Rome, making him the first antipope, and founded an alternate church. During Maximus's persecution, he and Pope Pontian were arrested and sent to the mines (Roman extermination camps). There, they abdicated their offices, reconciled to each other, and died as martyrs, ending the schism.

20. Bart D. Ehrman, *Lost Christianities: The Battle for Scripture and the Faith We Never Knew* (New York: Oxford University Press, 2003), 230, notes that Easter was a movable feast, and its time had to be set by the bishop. The most famous letter setting the time of Easter is Bishop Athanasius's Festal Letter of 367, in which he also identifies Christian books in the number and order that eventually became the Western canon of the New Testament.

21. Cyril, *Catechetical Lectures* 1.1, in Deiss, *Springtime*, 274–275.

22. Tertullian, *On the Resurrection of the Flesh*, quoted in Miles, *Carnal Knowing*, 30.

23. Egeria, in Wilson-Kastner et al., *Lost Tradition*, 117.

24. Athanasius, *On Virginity*, quoted in Miles, *Carnal Knowing*, 42. Similarly, Augustine in *Sermon 207* (Miles, 42): "The temptations of the world, the snares of the devil, the suffering of the world, the enticement of the flesh, the surging waves of troubled times, and all corporal and spiritual adversities were to be overcome by almsgiving, fasting, and prayer. As you presented your bodies to sin as the instrument of iniquity,

so now you may present your members to God as instruments of justice." See Miles, *Carnal Knowing,* 24–52, for an extensive discussion of the role of fasting and the body in baptism.

25. Cyril, *Catechetical Lectures* 6.35.

26. Cyril, *Catechetical Lectures* 4.7.

27. John Chrysostom, *Biblical Homilies,* quoted in Riley, *Christian Initiation,* 120. For baptism as an athletic contest, see Riley, 27, 49, 116, 120, 193, 199–202, 206, 208–209.

28. John Chrysostom, *Baptismal Instructions,* quoted in Dujarier, *A History of the Catechumenate,* 96.

29. Clement of Alexandria, *On Spiritual Perfection,* in Henry Chadwick and John E. L. Oulton, eds., *Alexandrian Christianity: Selected Translations of Clement and Origen* (Philadelphia: Westminster, 1954), 94.

30. Ibid., 124.

31. Ibid.

32. Cyril, *Catechetical Lectures,* in Deiss, *Springtime,* 272.

33. Ibid., 272–273.

34. For survey and study of exorcism in antiquity, see Wendy Cotter, *Miracles in Greco-Roman Antiquity: A Sourcebook* (New York: Routledge, 1999), 75–127.

35. Cyril, *Catechetical Lectures* 19.2–4, in Deiss, *Springtime,* 277.

36. Ibid.

37. Cotter, *Miracles in Greco-Roman Antiquity,* 106. Greco-Roman-Egyptian traditions lacked ideas of Satan, apocalyptic cataclysms, and hell, but some Christians regarded demons as lackeys of a lord, such as Satan or Beelzebub, who would be punished at the end of time with all his legions. Lackeys of Satan represented an apocalyptic sign of the impending battle of good and evil, visions found in Jewish post-exilic documents, such as I Enoch from the second-century BCE and the book of Jubilees from the first century BCE. However, many Jewish teachers regarded such ideas as heretical, since they were borrowed from Persian Zoroastrianism. Apocalyptic texts lacked individual exorcisms altogether—the defeat of evil forces was placed in a larger war of powerful forces. Those forces acted more like armies than garden-variety demons subject to the everyday power of a healer. The ordinary powers of exorcists were irrelevant in symbolism that imagined a final battle against evil that would defeat one's imperial oppressors. The New Testament and early Christianity contain both views of demons, apocalyptic and everyday, though a strong temporal apocalyptic sensibility is much more pronounced in the medieval church. For example, during the sixth-century rule of Justinian, the Eastern Roman Empire experienced a devastating time of plague, but it was not understood as an apocalyptic end of the world, a common interpretation of plague in fourteenth-century western Europe. "Only when we see that a Christian narrator has taken pains to include some of these distinctive [apocalyptic] features [of prophecies of judgment and punishment] in a Jesus exorcism story may we conclude that the meaning of the exorcism as well as its

implications for the role of Jesus is meant to be situated against the unusual cosmo-logical expectation of apocalypticism."

38. Cyril, *Catechetical Lectures* 4.6.

39. Cyril, *Catechetical Lectures* 1.3.

40. Cyril, *Catechetical Lectures* 4.1.

41. Egeria's report indicates that even during worship services public debate about theological ideas occurred. See Wilson-Kastner et al., *Lost Tradition*, 129.

42. This was the Arian-Orthodox controversy, which Constantine called the Council of Nicaea in 325 to settle, but the debate continued throughout the fourth century and beyond. Cyril was a semi-Arian in his early years and became increasingly orthodox over the course of his life.

43. Cyril, *Catechetical Lectures* 12.15.

44. Cyril, *Catechetical Lectures* 13.2, 31. For Cyril, the tree of Jesus could refer to the Crucifixion, but never in separation from the Resurrection. He explains that Christ's resurrection took place in the springtime and renewed the Creation. "Is not the earth now full of flowers, and are they not pruning the vines? . . . This is the season of the creation of the world: for then God said, 'Let the earth bring forth grass, the herb yielding seed after his kind.' And now, as thou seest, every herb is producing seed. . . . At that time, God said, 'Let us make man in Our own image, after Our likeness': and the 'image' he received; but the likeness, by his transgression, he defaced; at that very season then in which he lost it, did his restoration also come to pass. At the same season in which created man was cast out of paradise for his disobedience, was believing man brought into it again" (*Catechetical Lectures* 14.10). "The Tree of Life, therefore, was planted in the earth, that the earth which had been cursed might enjoy the blessing, and that the dead might be released" (*Catechetical Lectures* 13.35).

45. Cyril, *Catechetical Lectures* 13.38.

46. Cyril, *Catechetical Lectures* 13.4. Cyril on the cross: "Let us not then be ashamed of the Cross of Christ; but though another hide it, do thou openly seal it on thy brow: that the devils beholding that princely Sign, may flee far away trembling. . . . For if, when crucified and buried, He had remained in the tomb, then we had shame: but now He who was crucified on this Golgotha, hath from the Mount of Olives on the East ascended into heaven" (*Catechetical Lectures* 4.14). For Cyril, in contrast to Anselm in the eleventh century, the Crucifixion by itself does not free humanity from sin; the Resurrection does: "If Christ be not risen, we are yet in our sins" (*Catechetical Lectures* 13.17).

47. Egeria, in Wilson-Kastner et al., *Lost Tradition*, 110, 126. "Vigil is kept in the Anastasis that the bishop might read that place in the Gospel which is always read on the Lord's Day, that is, the resurrection of the Lord. . . . At the tenth hour, which here is called *licinicon*, which we call *Lucernare* . . . all light lamps and candles and it is very light. The light is not brought in from outside, but is taken into [from?] the interior of the cave, where within the enclosure by night and day a lamp is always lit." Egeria

describes this as a daily practice. The ever-burning light is a sign of the living presence of the resurrected Christ.

48. McDonnell, *Baptism of Jesus*, 202–235, points out that Paul's baptismal theology in Romans 6:4 was used infrequently until the fourth century, except by Origen. For this shift and Cyril's resistance, see his chapters, "Calvary Threatens the Dominance of Jordan—Institution" and "The Threat of Sacramental Imagination and the Jordan's Tenacity—Institution." Cyril's third catechetical lecture is on Romans 6:3–4. Though Paul's text speaks of being baptized into Christ's death and buried with him, Cyril's lecture is almost entirely based on Jesus's baptism in the Jordan. He barely mentions the Crucifixion, and, in one place where he does, his point is that baptism cleanses even the sin of crucifying Christ. "Ye have killed the Prince of life. What salve is there for so great a wound? . . . Behold the power of Baptism! If any of you hath by blasphemous words crucified Christ; if any of you hath through ignorance denied Him before men; if any of you, through wicked works, hath led to the doctrine's being evil spoken of, let him be of good hope in repenting" (*Catechetical Lectures* 3.15). Any notion that the Crucifixion was *the* saving event is entirely absent in Cyril.

49. Gregory of Nyssa, *Catechetical Oration* and *On the Baptism of Christ*, quoted in McDonnell, *Baptism of Jesus*, 129. See McDonnell for the idea that all rivers have been blessed by Christ's baptism, 61; all rivers circulate to and from paradise, 146–150; baptism as the reenactment of Jesus's baptism in the Jordan, 125–126; Origen's association of baptism with death and resurrection, 201–203; baptism as womb, 101–106; baptism as cosmic re-creation, 50–68. For Ephrem's teaching, among others, on the garment of light, see Sebastian Brock, *The Luminous Eye: The Spiritual World Vision of Saint Ephrem the Syrian*, rev. ed. (Kalamazoo, MI: Cistercian Publications, 1992), 85–97; and McDonnell, *Baptism of Jesus*, 128–144.

50. Cyril, *Catechetical Lectures*, in Deiss, *Springtime*, 274.

51. Cyril, *Catechetical Lectures* 4.5.

52. Augustine, *The First Catechetical Instruction*, trans. Rev. Joseph P. Christopher (Westminster, MD: Newman Bookshop, 1946), 14, 25.

53. Robert Wilken, *The Spirit of Early Christian Thought: Seeking the Face of God* (New Haven, CT: Yale University Press, 2003), 39.

54. Cyril, *Catechetical Lectures* 1.1, in Deiss, *Springtime*, 275.

55. Cyril, *Catechetical Lectures* 20.2, in Deiss, *Springtime*, 279.

56. Cyril, *Catechetical Lectures* 19.4, in Deiss, *Springtime*, 277.

57. Cyril, *Catechetical Lectures* 19.9, in Deiss, *Springtime*, 278. In the fifth-century baptistery of Saint Lawrence was the inscription "Turn your vessel back toward the shores of Paradise," found in "Klasmata," in Lucien Deiss, *Springtime of the Liturgy: Liturgical Texts of the First Four Centuries*, trans. Matthew J. O'Connell (Collegeville, MN: Liturgical Press, 1967), 264. Riley (*Christian Initiation*, 33, 63–66) notes that in some rituals the vow was: "I enter into your service, O Christ. I engage myself by vow, I believe, and am baptized." In Jerusalem, the vow was, "I believe in the Fa-

ther, and in the Son, and in the Holy Spirit, and in one baptism of *metanoia*—trans-formation." Riley places the acts in this order: (1) renunciation of Satan and profession of Christ; (2) removal of clothes and pre-baptismal nointing; (3) immersion in the font and confession of faith; and (4) post-baptismal anointing. See Riley's synoptic charts (comparing Cyril, Ambrose, Chrysostom, and Theodore) for detailed outlines of the liturgical acts, 41, 86, 104, 153, 161, 193, 225, 300, 357, 359, 413.

58. Finn writes in *From Death to Rebirth,* "Early Christian baptism had clearly in view adults; yet infants and children (and the incapacitated) were not thereby excluded.... Where circumstance dictated, the Church's faith could supply for the faith of the individual, and, in any case, early Christians did not think that God was hemmed in by the sacraments" (15).

59. Riley, *Christian Initiation,* 150.

60. Cyril, *Catechetical Lectures* 16.12.

61. Cyril, *Catechetical Lectures* 21.1, 2, in Deiss, *Springtime,* 282.

62. Ambrose, *The Sacraments,* quoted in Riley, *Christian Initiation,* 440. Though these words are from Ambrose, a near contemporary of Cyril, they reflect the fondness for interpreting baptism with texts from the Song of Songs, which Cyril uses throughout his catechetical lectures.

63. This is Ambrose's version of the Twenty-third Psalm. See Finn, *From Death to Rebirth,* 61.

64. Cyril, *Catechetical Lectures* 29.1.

65. For a comprehensive discussion of the significance of different foods used in the diversity of early church Eucharist practices, see Andrew McGowan, *Ascetic Eucharists: Food and Drink in Early Christian Ritual Meals* (Oxford, UK: Clarendon Press, 1999).

66. Cyril, *Catechetical Lectures* 1.4, in Deiss, *Springtime,* 276.

67. Hippolytus, *Apostolic Tradition,* in Deiss, *Springtime,* 145.

68. Clement of Alexandria, *Paedagogus,* in Deiss, *Springtime,* 116–117.

CHAPTER SIX: THE BEAUTIFUL FEAST OF LIFE

1. The description and discussion of the Eucharist that follows here is based on the mid-fourth-century practices in Jerusalem. Jerusalem, a pilgrimage site, had a liturgy that reflected traditions from Egypt, Asia Minor, and Syria. For a detailed overview of key issues with respect to Cyril's Eucharistic practices, sources, and innovations, see Karl J. Burreson, "The Anaphora of the Mystagogical Catecheses of Cyril of Jerusalem," in *Essays on Early Eastern Eucharistic Prayers,* ed. Paul F. Bradshaw (Collegeville, MN: Liturgical Press, 1997), 131–152. Additional sources consulted include R.C.D. Jasper and G. J. Cuming, eds., *Prayers of the Eucharist: Early and Reformed* (Collegeville, MN: Liturgical Press, 1980); Paul F. Bradshaw and

Lawrence A. Hoffman, eds., *The Making of Jewish and Christian Worship* (Notre Dame, IN: University of Notre Dame Press, 1991); Lucien Deiss, ed., *Springtime of the Liturgy: Liturgical Texts of the First Four Centuries,* trans. Matthew J. O'Connell (Collegeville, MN: Liturgical Press, 1967); Dom Gregory Dix, *The Shape of the Liturgy,* 2nd ed. (London: Adam and Charles Black, 1945); Andrew McGowan, *Ascetic Eucharists: Food and Drink in Early Christian Ritual Meals* (Oxford, UK: Clarendon Press, 1999); Dennis E. Smith, *From Symposium to Eucharist: The Banquet in the Early Christian World* (Minneapolis: Fortress Press, 2003); and J. H. Srawley, *The Early History of the Liturgy,* 2nd ed. (Cambridge: Cambridge University Press, 1949).

2. Hippolytus, in Deiss, *Springtime,* 148.

3. Ibid., 149.

4. McGowan, in *Ascetic Eucharists,* discusses the variety of foods used and forbidden in early Eucharists. Quotes from pp. 206–207. He asserts that there was considerable diversity in how holy meals were understood and ritualized. He discusses the ways in which the foods used reflected "dissident diets" that had social and political implications especially concerning Roman imperialism and its sacrificial system.

5. Excerpted from the *Apostolic Constitutions,* in Lucien Deiss, *Springtime of the Liturgy: Liturgical Texts of the First Four Centuries,* trans. Matthew J. O'Connell (Collegeville, MN: Liturgical Press, 1979), 229–231 (full text 228–235), a compilation of late-fourth-century liturgical texts that originated in Syria or Constantinople.

6. Examples in Deiss, *Springtime,* 73–94, 113–119, of ancient Christian Eucharistic practices that make no reference to the Crucifixion include the *Didache* (first century), the "Great Prayer" of Clement of Rome (first century), the descriptions of Justin Martyr (second century), and the liturgical prayers of Clement of Alexandria that may reflect late-second-century Eucharistic practices in Alexandria.

7. *Anaphora of Addai and Mari,* as early as the third century, in Deiss, *Springtime,* 161.

8. Cyril, *Catechetical Lecture* 17.15, in *The Catechetical Lectures of S. Cyril, Archbishop of Jerusalem,* anonymous trans., in the series *A Library of Fathers of the Holy Catholic Church* (Oxford, UK: John Henry Parker, 1845).

9. Ephrem, *Faith 10:12, 17,* quoted in Sebastian Brock, *The Luminous Eye: The Spiritual World Vision of Saint Ephrem the Syrian,* rev. ed. (Kalamazoo, MI: Cistercian Publications, 1992), 112, 108.

10. Cyril, *Catechetical Lectures* 4.3, 5.7, 5.21, quoted in Edward Yarnold, *Cyril of Jerusalem* (London: Routledge, 2000), 63. See pages 41–42 for a discussion of the absence of the words "This is my body, broken for you. This is my blood, poured out for you" in Cyril's Eucharist.

11. Augustine, *Sermon 227,* quoted in Margaret Miles, *Carnal Knowing: Female Nakedness and Religious Meaning in the West* (Boston: Beacon Press, 1989), 41.

12. Ephrem, *Virginity,* quoted in S. Brock, *Luminous Eye,* 105–106.

13. Cyril, *Catechetical Lecture 23,* in Deiss, *Springtime,* 289. "With care, sanctify your

eyes by contact with the sacred body. . . . Then sanctify yourself further by sharing in the blood of Christ. And while your lips are still wet, touch them with your fingers and sanctify your eyes, your forehead, and your other senses."

14. Augustine, *Confessions,* quoted in Carol Harrison, *Beauty and Revelation in the Thought of Saint Augustine* (Oxford, UK: Clarendon Press, 1992), 135.

15. Origen, *Peri Archon,* in Alejandro Garcia-Rivera, *The Community of the Beautiful: A Theological Aesthetics* (Collegeville, MN: Liturgical Press, 1999), 171–172. Recent scholarship moves away from older, more dichotomous body/spirit readings of Origen. See, in addition to Garcia-Rivera, Robert J. Hauck, " 'Like a Gleaming Flash': Matthew 6:22–23, Luke 11:34–36, and the Divine Sense in Origen," *Anglican Theological Review* 36 (Fall 2006).

16. Ambrose, *Paradise,* in Gesa Elsbeth Thiessen, ed., *Theological Aesthetics: A Reader* (Grand Rapids, MI: Wm. B. Eerdmans, 2004), 58.

17. Carol Harrison, *Beauty and Revelation in the Thought of Saint Augustine* (Oxford, UK: Clarendon Press, 1992):

> Augustine breaks with an anti-material, spiritualizing emphasis in his doctrine of man and the Fall. Man is also said to bear the form or beauty of God, in the image of God in his mind, and in his body. Like Creation, in so far as he turns toward God he receives form and beauty, in so far as he turns away from him, he becomes deformed and ugly. . . . God's entry into time and history and his assumption of a human body in the Incarnation absolutizes . . . those aspects of earthly existence to which Augustine the spiritualizing philosopher might have been tempted to give a secondary place. . . . The world will be saved by beauty: it is saved by God, who is Beauty, and by the revelation of Himself as Beauty, in His Creation. . . . Such revelations save because they meet man in the temporal, into which he has fallen, and because of their beauty evoke in him a love for their source. . . . Thus, he is himself reformed, made beautiful, or saved. (272–273)

18. Tertullian, *On the Soul,* in Thiessen, *Theological Aesthetics,* 55–56.

19. Judith Herman, *Trauma and Recovery: The Aftermath of Violence from Domestic Abuse to Political Terror* (New York: Basic Books, 1992), discusses post-traumatic stress disorder.

20. Augustine, *Confessions* 10.28.39, in Carol Harrison, *Beauty and Revelation in the Thought of Saint Augustine* (Oxford, UK: Clarendon Press, 1992), 169. See Harrison for an interpretation of Augustine's tricky combination of both distrust and respect for beauty and the senses. See also Albert Hofstadter and Richard Kuhns, *Philosophies of Art and Beauty: Selected Readings in Aesthetics from Plato to Heidegger* (Chicago: University of Chicago Press, 1964), 172–173, which notes that Augustine spoke of all living things as embodiments of number and rhythm, a metaphysics of beauty that he worked out in his *De Musica.*

21. Aristotle's theory of music makes the connection between music and the shaping of moral character. Augustine follows suit. See Aristotle, *Politics* 8.5, in Hofstadter and Kuhns, *Philosophies of Art and Beauty*, 134.

22. Ephrem, *Hymns on Virginity*, in *Ephrem the Syrian: Hymns*, trans. Kathleen McVey (New York: Paulist Press, 1989), 401–402.

23. The problematic, "Beauty is in the eye of the beholder," is attributed to a variety of sources, but actually appeared first in Margaret Wolfe Hungerford's 1878 novel, *Molly Bawn*. The idea was argued by Hume in "Of the Standard of Taste," in *Essays Moral, Political and Literary*, rev. ed. (Indianapolis: Indiana Liberty Classics, 1987). Hume said that beauty is "no quality in things themselves." It exists only "in the mind of things that contemplate them." For many ancient Christians, beauty was also in the things—not only in the mind.

24. Macrina, "On the Soul and Resurrection," in Amy Oden, ed., *In Her Words: Women's Writings in the History of Christian Thought* (Nashville, TN: Abingdon Press, 1994), 50.

25. Irenaeus, *Against Heresies*, 4.7, bk. 3. *The Writings of Irenaeus*, Vol. 1, trans. Rev. Alexander Roberts and Rev. W. H. Rambaut, in *Ante-Nicene Christian Library: Translations of the Writings of the Fathers Down to A.D. 325*, Vol. 5 (Edinburgh: T and T Clark, 1868). Altered to substitute "human being" and "humanity" for "man" and "men."

26. Evagrius the Solitary, quoted in Justin Sinaites, "The Sinai Codex Theodosianus: Manuscript as Icon," in *Holy Image, Hallowed Ground: Icons from Sinai*, ed. Robert S. Nelson and Kristen M. Collins (Los Angeles: J. Paul Getty Museum, 2006), 76.

27. Anestis G. Keselopoulos, *Man and the Environment: A Study of St. Symeon the New Theologian*, trans. Elizabeth Theokritoff (Crestwood, NY: St. Vladimir's Seminary Press, 2001), 142. For a full discussion of the "transfiguration of the world," see chap. 5, "The Transfiguration of the World in Christ," 141–171. See also Leonide Ouspensky, *Theology of the Icon* (Crestwood, NY: St. Vladimir's Seminary Press, 1978), 215–221. Eastern Orthodox theology usually interprets the Incarnation as inaugurating the transfiguration of the world. It will be fulfilled at the end of time, but is also a present reality now, manifest in icons, attained through the Eucharist, and enacted in stewardship of the earth and love of neighbor.

28. D. E. Smith, *From Symposium to Eucharist*, 283–284, discusses the relationship between sacred banquets and ethical obligations in the ancient world. "Ethics in early Christianity was largely social ethics, and social ethics discourse was founded primarily on banquet ideology. . . . Since the meal was an occasion in which community was the focus, behavior was defined according to that which enhanced the community as a whole. Categories such as friendship and pleasure, both basic components of the proper banquet, were invoked as the basis for appropriate behavior."

29. The prayer is an approximation of what was said over the Eucharist table, based on

recollections of witnesses, though names have been altered to preserve people's privacy. The congregation had a weekly Eucharist.

30. Excerpts from the *Didache* can be found in Deiss, *Springtime*, 74–76. Scholars have debated whether the text is first or second century, but the earlier dating is preferred and generally accepted. Jasper and Cuming, *Prayers of the Eucharist*, 20.

31. Clement of Rome, "Letter to the Corinthians," in Deiss, *Springtime*, 82–83. The editor discusses his likely dates and historical attestations to his succession from Peter.

32. Saint Justin, in Deiss, *Springtime*, 93–94.

33. Hippolytus, *The Apostolic Tradition*, in Jasper and Cuming, *Prayers of the Eucharist*, 35.

34. Hippolytus, *The Apostolic Tradition*, in Deiss, *Springtime*, 130–131. See n. 23 for the relationship to Irenaeus.

35. Excerpts from *The Apostolic Constitutions*, in Deiss, *Springtime*, 232–233, show this:

> He who makes all things that are begotten . . . who is born from all eternity . . . He lived a holy life, taught with uprightness, drove from the midst of men "every disease and every infirmity." . . . He shared our food, our drink, our sleep. . . . Having brought his entire work to completion, He was betrayed by the man who was corroded by wickedness, And delivered into the hands of the impious by treachery. He suffered painfully at their hands. . . . He was nailed to the cross. . . . He underwent death. . . . He was buried, the giver of life. . . . Thus did he break the bonds of the devil and free men from deceit. He rose from the dead on the third day and remained with his disciples for forty days. He ascended to the heavens.

36. Cyril, *Mystagogical Catechesis*, in Yarnold, "Introduction," *Cyril of Jerusalem*, 41.

37. This is a topic of scholarly debate. Though Cyril makes reference to the New Testament idea that Jesus died as a propitiation for sin, his description of the Eucharist makes no mention of the words of institution "This is my body, broken for you; this is my blood," and so on. Various theories have been proposed to explain this absence. See Yarnold, "Introduction," *Cyril of Jerusalem*, 41–42. See also Burreson, "Anaphora of the Mystagogical Catecheses," in *Early Eucharistic Prayers*, 145–148.

38. Recent scholarly studies of the Eucharist, such as McGowan, *Ascetic Eucharists*, and D. E. Smith, *From Symposium to Eucharist*, emphasize the diversity of early Christian meal practices and their social/cultural contexts and histories.

39. Melito of Sardis, *Homily on the Pasch*, in Deiss, *Springtime*, 105–106. Writing around 170, Melito also, according to Deiss, "shows himself as the first promoter of a certain solidarity between the empire and the Christian religion" (98).

40. Ibid., 103, 106–107.

41. James Carroll, *Constantine's Sword: The Church and the Jews, A History* (Boston: Houghton Mifflin, 2001), documents the history of Christian violence against Jews. On p. 7, he identifies Melito of Sardis as the beginning of a history of vitriol that

culminated with the Holocaust. He sees Christian ritual practices as a part of the problem.

42. Alexander Schmemann, *The World as Sacrament* (London: Darton, Longman, and Todd, 1966), summarizes the Eastern Orthodox view: "The joyful character of the Eucharist must be stressed. For the medieval stress on the crucifixion while not a wrong one, is certainly one-sided. The liturgy is, before everything else, the joyous gathering of those who are to meet the risen Lord and to enter with him into the bridal chamber ... it is heaven on earth according to our Orthodox tradition; it is joy ... which alone is capable of transforming the world" (34–35).

   Liturgical renewal movements in Western Christianity, begun in the 1960s, have focused, to some extent, on the Eucharist as a Resurrection feast that grounds social ethics. Only feminist reworkings of Christian liturgy have gone as far as early Christianity towards reimagining baptism and Eucharist as life-centered rituals. For example, the World Council of Churches mid-decade celebration of churches in solidarity with women, "Re-Imagining," in November 1993 in Minneapolis, made extensive use of women's research in liturgy and theology; see *Bring the Feast; Songs from the Re-Imagining Community* (Cleveland, OH: Pilgrim Press, 1998). See also Diann Neu and Mary Hunt, *Women-Church Source Book* (Washington, DC: WATERworks Press, 1993); and Marjorie Procter-Smith and Janet R. Walton, eds., *Women at Worship: Interpretations of North American Diversity* (Louisville, KY: John Knox Press, 1993).

43. Pseudo-Dionysius, *The Divine Names,* quoted in Thiessen, *Theological Aesthetics,* 34–37.

44. Macrina, "On the Soul and the Resurrection," quoted in Oden, *In Her Words,* 57.

45. Margaret Miles explains in *Image as Insight: Visual Understanding in Western Christianity and Secular Culture* (Boston: Beacon Press, 1985): "In the theory of vision described by Augustine ... for an object to be seen by a viewer, this fire [within the body] must be projected in the form of a ray that is focused on the object, thereby establishing a two-way street along which the attention and energy of the viewer passes to touch its object. A representation of the object, in turn, returns to the eye and is bonded to the soul and retained in the memory" (7).

46. Gertrud Schiller discusses the Last Supper images in *The Passion of Jesus Christ,* Vol. 2 of *Iconography of Christian Art,* trans. Janet Seligman (Greenwich, CT: New York Graphic Society, 1972), 30–32.

47. Irenaeus, *Against Heresies* 4.18.5.

48. Excerpted from a first-century prayer from Clement of Rome, in Deiss, *Springtime,* 83–84.

49. Keselopoulos, *Man and the Environment,* 167–168, makes the link between Eucharist, beauty, paradise, and ecological stewardship.

50. Vine Deloria, *God Is Red: A Native View of Religion,* 3rd ed. (Golden, CO: Fulcrum, 2003), 296. Deloria notes (297–300) that Supreme Court Justice William O. Douglas

offered a response to this plea in his dissenting position in *Sierra Club v. Morton.* "Earth should be represented in the courts by spokespersons whose intimacy with specific places gave them knowledge of their value and their needs. . . . The problem is to make certain that the inanimate objects, which are the very core of America's beauty, have spokesmen before they are destroyed."

CHAPTER SEVEN: GODS SEEING GOD

1. The idea that humanity could manifest divinity was common in the ancient world. For this cultural context, see Stephen Finlan, "Second Peter's Notion of Divine Participation," in *Theōsis: Deification in Christian Theology*, ed. Stephen Finlan and Vladimir Kharlamov, Princeton Theological Monograph Series (Eugene, OR: Pickwick Publications, 2006), 33–36.
2. Quotes from Ephrem's *Nisibene Hymns*, quoted in Sebastian Brock, *The Luminous Eye: The Spiritual World Vision of Saint Ephrem the Syrian* (Kalamazoo, MI: Cistercian Publications, 1985), 152–153, and his *Hymns on Virginity*, also in *Ephrem the Syrian: Hymns*, trans. Kathleen McVey (New York: Paulist Press, 1989), 455.
3. Clement of Alexandria, excerpts, quoted in Robin Margaret Jensen, *Understanding Early Christian Art* (New York: Routledge, 2000), 43. See also Clement, *On Spiritual Perfection*, trans. John Ernest Leonard Oulton, in *Alexandrian Christianity*, Library of Christian Classics, Vol. 2 (Philadelphia: Westminster, 1954): "And since the east symbolizes the day of birth, and it is from thence that the light spreads, after it has first 'shone forth out of darkness,' aye, and from thence the day of the knowledge of the truth dawned like the sun upon those who were lying in ignorance, therefore our prayers are directed towards the rise of dawn" (120).
4. Basil, quoted in Georges Florovsky, *The Eastern Fathers of the Fourth Century*, trans. Catherine Edmunds, Vol. 7 of *Collected Works of Georges Florovsky* (Belmont, MA: Notable and Academic Books, 1987), 104–105.
5. In 42 BCE, Julius's heir Octavian declared him the *Divus Iulius* (Divine Julius) and himself Caesar Augustus *Divi Filis* (Son of a God).
6. Ephrem, *Hymns on Paradise*, in *Saint Ephrem: Hymns on Paradise*, trans. Sebastian Brock (Crestwood, NY: St. Vladimir's Seminary Press, 1990), 117. For further discussion, see Finlan, "Second Peter's Notion of Divine Participation," 41.
7. Bishop Kallistos of Diokelia, quoted in Georgios I. Mantzaridis, *The Deification of Man: St. Gregory Palamas and the Orthodox Tradition*, trans. Liadain Sherrard (Crestwood, NY: St. Vladimir's Seminary Press, 1984), comments: "This phrase from the Old Testament, quoted by our Lord Himself (Jn 10:34), has deeply marked the spiritual imagination of [Eastern] Orthodoxy. In the Orthodox understanding Christianity signifies not merely an adherence to certain dogmas, not merely an exterior imitation of Christ through moral effort, but direct union with the living God,

the total transformation of the human person by divine grace and glory—what the Greek Fathers termed 'deification' or 'divinization' (*theosis, theopoiesis*)" (7).

8. On Harnack, see Jeffrey Finch, "Athanasius on the Deifying Work of the Redeemer," in *Theōsis: Deification in Christian Theology,* ed. Stephen Finlan and Vladimir Kharlamov, Princeton Theological Monograph Series (Eugene, OR: Pickwick Publications, 2006), 106. Finch defends Athanasius against Harnack. We think incarnation-centered theologies do make the apex of the Christian proclamation that Christ has reopened paradise by his incarnation and resurrection, not by the Crucifixion.

9. Clement, *Spiritual Perfection,* in *Alexandrian Christianity,* 129, 128.

10. Athanasius, as quoted by Bishop Kallistos in Mantzaridis, *The Deification of Man: St. Gregory Palamas and the Orthodox Tradition,* trans. Liadain Sherrard (Crestwood, NY: St. Vladimir's Seminary Press, 1984), 7. Athanasius explained, "For as the Lord, putting on the body became man, so we men are deified by the Word as being taken to him through His flesh, and henceforth inherit life everlasting" (Athanasius, quoted in Jeffrey Finch, "Athanasius on the Deifying Work of the Redeemer," 119).

11. Gregory of Naziansus (aka Gregory the Theologian), quoted in Florovsky, *Eastern Fathers,* 114; quote made inclusive. The early theologians varied with respect to how divinization related to earthly existence. In Florovsky's view, for Gregory, "the goal of human life lies beyond the earth and beyond the senses. Man is a 'new angel' who has been put on earth, and he must rise to the heavens and the radiant realm of the elect" (118). Even if this is the final goal, its first steps are to be realized within the body of earthly existence, beginning with baptism. Gregory, quoted in Florovsky, *Eastern Fathers,* 119, writes, "Everyone who belongs to the celestial ranks is transformed into a god by the sacraments."

12. Gregory of Nyssa, quoted in Elaine Pagels, *Adam, Eve, and the Serpent* (New York: Random House, 1988), 101.

13. Cyril of Alexandria, quoted in Walter J. Burghardt, *The Image of God in Man according to Cyril of Alexandria* (Washington, DC: Catholic University of America Press, 1957), 160–163.

14. Georges Florovsky, *The Byzantine Fathers of the Sixth to Eighth Century,* trans. Raymond Miller, Anne-Marie Döllinger-Labriolle, and Helmut Wilhem Schmiedel, Vol. 9 of *The Collected Works of Georges Florovsky* (Vaduz, Europa: Büchervertriebsanstalt, 1987), 245. Florovsky is summarizing the views of Maximus the Confessor (c. 580–661). Florovsky reports that Maximus was tried "as an enemy and criminal of the state" for denying imperial power in matters of faith (211).

15. Symeon the New Theologian, quoted in Eric D. Perl, " . . . That Man Might Become God: Central Themes in Byzantine Theology," in *Heaven on Earth: Art and the Church in Byzantium,* ed. Linda Safran (University Park: Pennsylvania State University Press, 2002), 49–50. Quote is excerpted and arranged for ease of reading.

16. Tertullian quoted in Elaine Pagels, *Adam, Eve, and the Serpent* (New York: Random

House, 1988), 32, 50. Pagels writes, "The boldest Christians not only defied pagan society to the death but also set out to create in its place a new social order—what Tertullian called 'the Christian society'—based upon a new religious ideology and a new vision of human nature." See pp. 32–50 for a discussion of the "new vision of human nature" that fueled resistance to Rome and the church's growth as an alternative society. That new vision was rooted in the interpretation of Adam and Eve as prototypes of human responsibility and freedom. Clement, quoted in Pagels, 39, expressed it as the idea that Christ's divinity now "pervades all humankind equally . . . deifying humanity."

17. Ephrem, *Hymns on Paradise,* in S. Brock, *Saint Ephrem,* 80.
18. Ibid., 87, 79.
19. The pinnacle of Ephrem's paradise mountain was home to the Shekinah—the shining presence of God. In Hebrew, *Shekinah* is a feminine noun. This image was *not* the throne of an emperor lording it over the entire inhabited world, nor was God an autocratic dictator. The waters that flowed from Shekinah's mountain defined the world as paradise. The church provided a geography and source of power very different from Rome's, and the downtrodden of the earth shared these as the creative, healing, loving power of God.
20. Irenaeus, *Against Heresies,* in Vol. 1 of *Early Christian Fathers,* ed. Cyril C. Richardson (Philadelphia: Westminster Press, 1953), 348.
21. Ibid., 366 (excerpt).
22. Ibid., 359–369.
23. Ambrose, *Paradise,* in *Saint Ambrose: Hexameron, Paradise, and Cain and Abel,* trans. John J. Savage (New York: Fathers of the Church, 1961), 314.
24. Augustine, *Sermon to Catechumens on the Creed,* 7:15.
25. Ibid., 8:16.
26. Tertullian, *On Idolatry* 19.3, quoted in Louis J. Swift, *The Early Fathers on War and Military Service* (Wilmington, DE: Michael Glazier, 1983), 41–42.
27. Athanasius, quoted in Jean-Michel Hornus, *It Is Not Lawful for Me to Fight: Early Christian Attitudes toward War, Violence, and the State,* rev. ed., trans. Alan Kreider and Oliver Coburn (Scottdale, PA: Herald Press, 1980), 71. Athanasius himself was accused by his fellow bishops of murdering a theological opponent; he fled when called to trial and never faced charges. In other writings, quoted in Swift, *Early Fathers on War,* 95, he took the position that "killing the enemy in battle is both lawful and praiseworthy."
28. For Ambrose's views of war, see Tomaž Mastnak, *Crusading Peace: Christendom, the Muslim World, and Western Political Order* (Berkeley: University of California Press, 2002), 63. Augustine, in *The City of God* 1.21, discussed exceptions to the divine law "Thou shall not kill": the law applies except when war has been authorized by a just ruler or when a person has experienced, as Abraham did in the command to kill Isaac, "a special intimation from God Himself." Augustine argued that war could be just if

it was undertaken out of love. He based this argument on the example of a parent who uses corporeal punishment to discipline a child.

29. Mastnak writes in *Crusading Peace:*

> Traditionally, the Church had been averse to the shedding of blood. *Ecclesia abhorret a sanguine* was a principle ever present in patristic writings and conciliar legislation. Participation in warfare was regarded as an evil; killing transgressed the Fifth Commandment; the stain of blood burdened Christian conscience. Even if a Christian stained his hands with blood in a just war, he still sinned. ... Even killing a pagan was homicide. From the fourth century to the eleventh century, the Church as a rule imposed disciplinary measures on those who killed in war, or at least recommended that they do penance. (16)

30. *Canons of Hippolytus,* Canon 14, quoted in Swift, *Early Fathers on War,* 93.

31. Jerome, *Commentary on Ecclesiastes,* 10:11.

32. *The Irish Penitentials with an Appendix by D. A. Binchy,* ed. Ludwig Bieler (Dublin: Dublin Institute for Advanced Studies, 1963), 99, excerpted.

33. John Chrysostom, quoted in Pagels, *Adam, Eve,* 103, agreed with Irenaeus's view of God's persuasive, nonviolent character. Irenaeus said, in *Against Heresies* 5.1.1, "The Word of God ... acted justly even in the encounter with Apostasy itself, ransoming from it that which was his own ... by persuasion, not by the use of force, that the principles of justice might not be infringed, and, at the same time, that God's original creation might not perish" (*Documents of the Christian Church,* ed. Henry Gettenson and Chris Maunder [New York: Oxford University Press, 1999], 33).

34. Ambrose, *Paradise,* in Savage, *Saint Ambrose,* 325–342.

35. For a discussion of religious sexual and gender practices, see the Brandeis University Feminist Sexual Ethics Project at www.brandeis.edu/projects/fse. An essay on early Christianity by Bernadette Brooten is posted at www.brandeis.edu/projects/fse/christianity/chris-index.html.

36. Jerome, quoted in Matthew Kuefler, *The Manly Eunuch; Masculinity, Gender Ambiguity, and Christian Ideology in Late Antiquity* (Chicago: University of Chicago Press, 2001), 285.

37. For discussions, see Virginia Burrus, *Begotten Not Made: Conceiving Manhood in Late Antiquity* (Stanford, CA: Stanford University Press, 2000); and Kuefler, *Manly Eunuch.*

38. Augustine, *Enarrationes in Psalmos,* quoted in Carol Harrison, *Beauty and Revelation in the Thought of Saint Augustine* (Oxford, UK: Clarendon Press, 1992), 259.

39. Augustine, *Confessions,* quoted in Kuefler, *Manly Eunuch,* 140.

40. See Elisabeth Schüssler Fiorenza, *In Memory of Her: A Feminist Theological Reconstruction of Christian Origins,* 2nd ed. (London: SCM Press, 1995); and Karen Jo Torjesen, *When Women Were Priests: Women's Leadership in the Early Church and*

the *Scandal of Their Subordination in the Rise of Christianity* (San Francisco: HarperSanFrancisco, 1993). See Ann Wire, "The Social Functions of Women's Asceticism in the Roman East," *Images of the Feminine in Gnosticism* (Minneapolis: Fortress Press, 1988), 309–323, for one approach to the difficulty of determining the relationship between texts that speak of women apostles and the actual lives and leadership of women in the early church.

41. See Stephen J. Davis, *The Cult of St. Thecla: A Tradition of Women's Piety in Late Antiquity* (Oxford: Oxford University Press, 2001), for a discussion of Thecla's extensive influence. Davis assembles evidence of extensive devotion to the saint, beginning with the second-century apocryphal *Acts of Paul and Thecla,* which gave her prominence for many centuries. The monastery of St. Tekla in Maaloula, Syria, is a destination for both Christian and Muslim pilgrims. The Coptic collection in the Louvre Museum in Paris contains artifacts with her image. See also the essay and bibliography at gbgm-umc.org/umw/corinthians/theclabackground.stm.

42. For scholarship on women priests, bishops, deacons, and apostles in early Christianity, see Ute E. Eisen, *Women Officeholders in Early Christianity: Epigraphical and Literary Studies,* trans. Linda M. Maloney (Collegeville, MN: Liturgical Press, 2000). Her exhaustive study of inscriptions and papyri establishes "that women were active in the expansion and shaping of the Church in the first centuries: they were apostles, prophets, teachers, presbyters, enrolled widows, deacons, bishops and stewards. They preached the Gospel, they spoke prophetically and in tongues, they went on mission, they prayed, they presided over the Lord's Supper, they broke the bread and gave the cup, they baptized, they taught, they created theology, they were active in care for the poor and the sick, and they were administrators and managers of burial places" (224). See also Antoinette Clark Wire, *The Corinthian Women Prophets: A Reconstruction through Paul's Rhetoric* (Minneapolis: Fortress Press, 1990).

43. Elaine Pagels, *The Gnostic Gospels* (New York: Vintage Books, 1979), 76–81, discusses the role of Mary in this tradition.

44. Quotes from *The Gospel according to Mary* are found in Amy Oden, ed., *In Her Words: Women's Writings in the History of Christian Thought* (Nashville: Abingdon Press, 1994), 18–20, with the exception of the reference to the place of rest in the Aeon of silence. That can be found in *New Testament Apocrypha,* Vol. 1: *Gospels and Related Writings,* ed. Wilhelm Schneemelcher, trans. R. M. Wilson (Philadelphia: Westminster Press, 1963), 342.

45. See Karen King, "The Rise of the Soul: Justice and Transcendence in the Gospel of Mary," in *Walk in the Ways of Wisdom: Essays in Honor of Elisabeth Schüssler Fiorenza,* ed. Shelly Matthews, Cynthia Briggs Kittredge, and Melanie Johnson-Debaufre (Harrisburg, PA: Trinity Press, 2003), 239, 240–243. King says the text "invites the reader to discern the true character of power as it is exercised in the world. It insists that ignorance, deceit, false judgment, and the desire to dominate must be

opposed by accepting the Savior's teaching and refusing to be complicit in violence and domination." She adds,

> Religious teaching that points the soul toward peace in the afterlife is often seen not only as *apolitical,* but as *antipolitical,* an escapist ideology that serves only to distract people from real political struggle by focusing on interior spiritual development and flight from the material world with all it troubling demands. . . . Viewed as a purely external event, ascent could be pure escapism. But before the soul can ascend it must be prepared to face the powers of Darkness, Desire, Ignorance, and Wrath. This preparation involves recognizing one's own true spiritual nature, accepting the truth revealed in the teachings of the Savior . . . and eschewing violence in any form. The capacity to overcome evil requires that one has perceived the Good-beyond-evil and molded oneself to its image and nature . . . This discernment does not advocate escape from the world, but transformation of the world through the disciples' mission, which leads to the practice of the kingdom of the gospel of the Child of true Humanity. This practice is possible only for those disciples who have themselves overcome the rule of the unjust powers in their own lives.

46. For a discussion of the classification of sexual acts in the ancient world, see Bernadette Brooten, "Nature, Law, and Custom in Augustine's 'On the Good of Marriage,' " in *Walk in the Ways of Wisdom: Essays in Honor of Elisabeth Schüssler Fiorenza,* ed. Shelly Matthews, Cynthia Briggs Kittredge, and Melanie Johnson-Debaufre (Harrisburg, PA: Trinity Press, 2003), 181–193. For a study on virginity as an ascetic practice versus women's subjugation to men, see Elizabeth A. Clark, "Ascetic Renunciation and Feminine Advancement: A Paradox of Ancient Christianity," *Anglican Theological Review* 63 (1981): 240–257. For a critical assessment of problems with "the bride of Christ" as a liberating image for women, see Elizabeth Castelli, "Virginity and Its Meaning for Women's Sexuality in Early Christianity," *Journal of Feminist Studies in Religion* 2 (1986): 61–88. Many of these topics are also considered by Kuefler in *The Manly Eunuch.*

47. Mary Foskett, *A Virgin Conceived: Mary and Classical Representations of Virginity* (Bloomington: University of Indiana Press, 2002), discusses ideas of virginity in Luke and in the second-century *Protoevangelium of James.*

48. The early church fathers—most of whom found women's leadership threatening—gave various meanings to virginity, and contemporary historians continue to debate its meaning. See Susanna Elm, *Virgins of God* (Oxford, UK: Clarendon Press, 1994), and Foskett for studies of virginity in the early church that are sensitive to the specific and changing meanings of virginity in a variety of locations.

49. Peter Brown, *The Rise of Western Christendom: Triumph and Diversity A.D. 200–1000* (Malden, MA: Blackwell, 2003), 174. For a history of marriage, see John Witte

Jr., *From Sacrament to Contract: Marriage, Religion, and Law in the Western Tradition* (Louisville, KY: Westminster John Knox Press, 1997). Witte says that the early church regulated the behavior of married members and discouraged clerics from marriage after the fourth century. He also discusses the various Protestant models of marriage that moved from sacrament to covenant to contract. In most cases, couples who declared themselves married were regarded as such. See also E. J. Graff, *What Is Marriage For? The Strange Social History of Our Most Intimate Institution* (Boston: Beacon Press, 2004).

50. Ephrem, *Hymns on the Nativity,* in *Ephrem the Syrian,* 215.

51. Ephrem, excerpts from *Hymns on Virginity,* in *Ephrem the Syrian,* 356–360.

52. Virginia Burrus, "Word and Flesh: The Bodies and Sexuality of Ascetic Women in Christian Antiquity," *Journal of Early Christian Studies* 2, 2 (Summer 1994): 45–51.

53. Ibid., 48–49.

54. Macrina, "On the Soul and Resurrection," in Oden, *In Her Words,* 59.

55. Ephrem, *Hymns on Paradise,* quoted in S. Brock, *Saint Ephrem,* 85.

56. Ephrem, *Armenian Hymn,* quoted in S. Brock, *Luminous Eye,* 114.

57. Ephrem, *Hymns on Virginity,* quoted in S. Brock, *Luminous Eye,* 124.

58. Ephrem, *Hymns on Faith,* quoted in S. Brock, *Luminous Eye,* 125.

59. A. Daniel Frankforter, "Amalasuntha, Procopius, and a Woman's Place," *Journal of Women's History* 8 (Summer 1996): 41–57.

60. It is likely that there were originally twenty-six women, now twenty-two. Three magi appear to have been added at a later date, at the head of the line, presenting their gifts to the Virgin, and replacing four women. Of course in real life it would take eight wise men to replace four women.

61. Christ is never seated on an imperial throne. The Jupiter throne indicates he is the highest God. During renovations in the nineteenth century, the open book with the inscription "Ego sum Rex gloriae" (I am the King of Glory) was changed into a scepter, conforming more to the image of Christ as ruler of heaven and earth.

62. Clement of Alexandria, *Paidagogus,* quoted in Pagels, *Gnostic Gospels,* ch. 3, note 92.

63. Kuefler, *Manly Eunuch,* 148–151. In *Women Officeholders* (184–185), Eisen documents the centuries-long process that led to the full outlawing of women's ordination in the Western church.

64. As Reverend Maureen Dickmann, a former Catholic, noted, "You don't have to *be* like Jesus to be ordained; you just have to pee like Jesus."

65. These changes began after persecution had ended. Bishops retold the legends of the martyrs, changing details to suit their own purposes, and shifted the locus of the martyrs' spiritual power from shrines to churches. Until the time of Ambrose, martyrs were buried near the places where they died and pilgrims visited them to draw spiritual power from their material remains and experience the concentration of paradise in this world. Ambrose set a precedent for change when he moved the remains of Proteus and Gervais to the cathedral in Milan. His precedent placed even the power of

martyrs under the authority of his church, and churches gradually became the primary spaces where paradise entered this world, as martyrs' remains were moved into them or churches were built on top of them.

66. On the slaying of innocents, see Peter Cramer, *Baptism and Change in the Early Middle Ages, c. 200–1150* (New York: Cambridge University Press, 1993), 133. The first written record of the Mass is found in the Leonine Sacramentary, dating from about 485.

CHAPTER EIGHT: HIDDEN TREASURES OF WISDOM

1. See Cyrus Mango, *Hagia Sophia: A Vision for Empires* (Istanbul: Ertuğ and Kocabiyik, 1997), xliv, for a description and discussion of the interior. See also Rowland J. Mainstone, *Hagia Sophia: Architecture, Structure, and Liturgy of Justinian's Great Church* (New York: W. W. Norton, 1997).

2. Eric D. Perl, " . . . That Man Might Become God," in Linda Safran, *Heaven on Earth: Art and the Church in Byzantium* (University Park: Pennsylvania State University Press, 2002), 54.

3. Ephrem, "Hymns on the Nativity," in *Ephrem the Syrian: Hymns,* trans. Kathleen McVey (New York: Paulist Press, 1989), 100.

4. Our training in arts and media many years ago in graduate courses with Professor Jack Coogan was helpful in this preparation. We have found Suzanne Langer's works in aesthetics and Margaret Miles's study on the meaning of images of great value. In addition, we have appreciated guidance from Diane Apostolos-Cappadona.

5. Margaret R. Miles, *Image as Insight: Visual Understanding in Western Christianity and Secular Culture* (Boston: Beacon Press, 1985), 141–145.

6. "While modern church-goers park themselves in pews like spectators at a cinema, the early church was without seats, and the liturgy of the Eucharist was dominated by processional movement" (Thomas Mathews, *The Clash of the Gods: A Reinterpretation of Early Christian Art* [Princeton, NJ: Princeton University Press 1993], 170).

7. John of Damascus, quoted in Leonide Ouspensky, *Theology of the Icon* (Crestwood, NY: St. Vladimir's Seminary Press, 1978), 174.

8. J.A.S. Evans, *The Age of Justinian: The Circumstances of Imperial Power* (New York: Routledge, 2000) describes Theodora's historical significance. Carolyn L Connor, *Women of Byzantium* (New Haven, CT: Yale University Press, 2004) begins her comprehensive study of women with Thecla and devotes an entire chapter to Theodora. Eva Cantarella, *Pandora's Daughters: The Role and Status of Women in Greek and Roman Antiquity,* trans. Maureen B. Fant (Baltimore: Johns Hopkins University Press, 1984), 136–164, discusses the Justinian laws about women that Theodora may have influenced, including those ending forced prostitution, prohibiting the use of

male guards for imprisoned women, and expanding divorce rights. She is credited with improving the legal status of women in a number of ways.

9. Mango (*Hagia Sophia: A Vision*) and Mainstone (*Hagia Sophia: Architecture*) describe the cathedral's history and construction. Mango has an extensive collection of photographs and early drawings.

10. Perl, " ... That Man Might Become God," 54.

11. See Peter Brown, *The Rise of Western Christendom: Triumph and Diversity A.D. 200–1000* (Malden, MA: Blackwell, 2003), 267–320 and 383–406.

12. Patricia Karlin-Hayter, "Iconoclasm," in *The Oxford History of Byzantium* (New York: Oxford University Press, 2002).

13. Alain Besançon's *The Forbidden Image: An Intellectual History of Iconoclasm*, trans. Jane Marie Todd (Chicago: University of Chicago Press, 2000), traces the very long philosophical and religious roots of iconoclasm and notes its contemporary forms.

14. "Epitome of the Definition of the Iconoclastic Conciliabulum, Held in Constantinople, A.D. 754," in *Medieval Sourcebook: Iconoclastic Council, 754*, available at www .fordham.edu/halsall/source/icono-cncl754.html.

15. John of Damascus, in Ouspensky, *Theology of the Icon*, 154.

16. Robert S. Nelson and Kristen M. Collins, eds., *Holy Image Hallowed Ground: Icons from Sinai* (Los Angeles: The J. Paul Getty Trust, 2006).

17. Ouspensky, *Theology of the Icon*, 147, 174.

18. Almut von Gladiss, "The Ottoman Empire: Architecture," in *Islam: Art and Architecture*, ed. Markus Hattstein and Peter Delius (Königswinter, Germany: Könemann, 2004), 549–550.

19. Oleg Grabar, "Art and Culture in the Islamic World," in *Islam: Art and Architecture*, ed. Markus Hattstein and Peter Delius (Königswinter, Germany: Könemann, 2004), 39.

CHAPTER NINE: THE EXPULSION OF PARADISE

1. For multiple examples, in chronological order, of the emergence of images depicting the Crucifixion, see Gertrud Schiller, *The Passion of Jesus Christ*, Vol. 2 of *Iconography of Christian Art*, trans. Janet Seligman (Greenwich, CT: New York Graphic Society, 1972), figs. 321–395, 455–494. In her discussion of the images (88f), Schiller uses the term "Crucifixion" for any image that shows Christ on the cross, alive or dead. We use the term "Crucifixion" only for images that depict Jesus suffering on the cross or dead. We were looking specifically for large-scale images on public display in places of worship, in which Christ is clearly dead with his eyes closed.

Before the tenth century, small depictions of Christ on the cross appeared in illuminated manuscripts, on ivory book covers, and on tiny amulets. Only an elite few would have been able to see or own these precious objects, and they usually depicted

Christ alive, with open eyes. An eighth-century icon from St. Catherine's Monastery in Sinai has survived; it measures about nineteen by ten inches and depicts Christ standing on a platform mounted on the cross. He stands upright, as in Resurrection images, but his eyes are closed. For a reproduction and brief discussion of the Sinai icon, see Robert S. Nelson and Kristen M. Collins, eds., *Icons from Sinai: Holy Image, Hallowed Ground* (Los Angeles: J. Paul Getty Museum, 2006), 129. In a side chapel of Rome's St. Maria Antiqua, a wall painting that dates to the eighth century also portrays Christ on the cross. As in the Sinai icon, he stands erect, fully clothed in purple, not slumped or suspended from the cross. Unlike the Sinai icon, his eyes are open. His torturers are shown wounding his side with a spear. He stands alive between Mary and John, who pray to him as the crucified and risen Christ.

2.   Schiller (*Passion*, 141) notes that the Gero cross is unprecedented: "The Death of Christ is here an elemental occurrence. It was never presented thus in Byzantine art, not even in the monumental mosaics of the eleventh century.... Its historical significance lies in its representation of suffering in its extreme physical consequences."

3.   There are two standard answers to these questions. One is that earthly existence became horrendously miserable in the medieval period, and Christian art changed to reflect these realities and to promise release in a world after death. However, life for early Christians was no less arduous and uncertain. They contended with war, epidemics, imperial persecutions, and early death. Europe's disastrous fourteenth century of plagues and famines was worse than anything before in Europe. Fourteenth-century art reflects the horror experienced, but images of Christ in agony had emerged three centuries earlier. Ellen Ross suggests in *The Grief of God: Images of Suffering Jesus in Late Medieval England* (New York: Oxford University Press, 1997) that Christianity became more sensitive to human suffering at the dawn of its second millennium and thus came to favor images of a passably human, suffering Christ over an impassive, transcendent Christ. Rachel Fulton, *From Judgment to Passion: Devotion to Christ and the Virgin Mary, 800–1200* (New York: Columbia University Press, 2002), offers a more complex view. She discusses the emergence of the Crucifixion images as a shift toward Christ as a judge and victim. This change, which first took place in connection with the conversion of the Saxons, advanced at the turn of the millennium in connection with rising expectations of the end of time, which, in tandem with new forms of devotion to Mary, led to a piety of empathy with suffering. In *The Crucified God in the Carolingian Era: Theology and Art of Christ's Passion* (Cambridge: Cambridge University Press, 2001), Celia Chazelle presents a multisided and detailed study of these shifts in attitude toward the Crucifixion in ninth-century Carolingian theology, liturgy, devotion, art, and imperial ambitions.

4.   Archbishop Gero of Cologne commissioned the cross, but the artist is unknown.

5.   The Romans admired the Saxons and recruited them into their armies. Writing in 95 CE, Tacitus described the warrior ethic in his *Germania:* "Both prestige and

power depend on being continually attended by a large train of picked young warriors, which is a distinction in peace and a protection in war. . . . On the field of battle it is a disgrace to a chief to be surpassed in courage by his followers, and to the
followers not to be equal to the courage of their chief. . . . To defend him and protect
him, and to let him get the credit for their own acts of heroism, are the most solemn
obligations of their allegiance. The chiefs fight for victory, the followers for their
chief" (quoted in Anthony W. Bartlett, *Cross Purposes: The Violent Grammar of
Christian Atonement* [Harrisburg, PA: Trinity Press, 2001], 113).

6. The early history of Christianity among the Saxons is difficult to reconstruct with any
   certainty. Peter Brown, in *The Rise of Western Christendom: Triumph and Diversity
   A.D. 200–1000* (Malden, MA: Blackwell, 2003), cites archeological evidence from regions ranging from Strasbourg to Stuttgart that indicates the presence of Christian
   churches, insignia, and ornaments dating to four centuries before the Carolingian
   "conversion" of the Saxons. See Brown, 410–411, 413. The figure of Christ and
   Woden/Odin are linked in the ancient Norse epic, the *Hâvamâl,* suggesting a hybrid
   of Christianity and older pagan traditions in the North, though the poem's dating is
   uncertain.

7. Brown, *Rise of Western Christendom,* notes that the Saxons in Britain already had
   adopted Christian ideas and practices before they were missionized in the late sixth
   century: "The issue was not whether Christianity would 'come' to a world that knew
   nothing of it. Christianity was already there and the Saxons knew it. What was at stake,
   rather, was not only 'whether' the various Saxon groups would accept Christianity,
   but also, once they did, 'which' Christianity it would be and 'how' it could be thought
   as having come to them" (342). Also see p. 420.

8. Brown, *Rise of Western Christendom,* 250, says for Columbanus there was no sense
   "in which Paradise, though lost, might yet still linger in the mind, tantalizing the soul
   like the subtle whiff of the scent of fresh, ripe apples in a malodorous world." See
   Brown, 257–266, for a discussion of how concern for the fate of the soul after death
   emerged in Europe in the sixth-century aftermath of the collapse of the Roman Empire, a significant factor in Christianity's gradual turning away from a focus on paradise in this life.

9. Brown, in *Rise of Western Christendom,* discusses Gregory's sense of paradise in this
   world:

> Paradise stood very near to a sixth-century Christian such as Gregory. It
> was no abstract heaven, but rather a place of super abundant vegetation,
> jewel-like in its radiance and bright color. . . . Holy men and women, dwellers
> of Paradise, stood ready, in all places, and even in the most out-of-the-way ar-
> eas, to help Catholic worshipers in their everyday needs. . . . Paradise itself
> came to ooze into the world. Nature itself was redeemed. . . . Gregory allowed
> sacrality to seep back into the landscape of Gaul. The countryside found its

voice again, to speak, in an ancient spiritual vernacular, of the presence of the saints. Water became holy again.... Trees also regained some of their majesty. (161–165)

10. James C. Russell contends in *The Germanization of Early Medieval Christianity: A Sociohistorical Approach to Religious Transformation* (New York: Oxford University Press, 1994) that such a clash was predictable: "When representatives from an eschatological, other-worldly, future-oriented Christianity confronted members of a past-oriented, this-worldly Germanic society, offering salvation from a world from which the Germanic peoples did not desire to be saved, fundamental problems were inevitable" (177).

11. Papal commission to Boniface, quoted in Brown, *Rise of Western Christendom*, 20.

12. "A Bavarian priest performed his baptism *In nominee Patria et Filia.* He had confused both case and gender. Boniface doubted that such a baptism was valid" (Brown, *Rise of Western Christendom*, 420).

13. Brown, *Rise of Western Christendom*, 83, notes that Christian missionary assaults on sacred trees began as early as the fourth century when Martin of Tours (335–c. 400) launched conversion efforts in the Loire valley, hewing down forest sanctuaries. Martin, whose grave would later become a major pilgrimage site, destroyed temples in the countryside as exorcisms. Boniface was not simply attempting to force Christianity on "pagans." Characterizing them as "pagan" was a later Carolingian appellation for any enemy of the empire. The empire also characterized Saxons as "Saracens," a term usually regarded as applying specifically to Muslims; "Saracens," like "pagan," became the general term for "other" or "enemy." See Tomaž Mastnak, *Crusading Peace: Christendom, The Muslim World, and Western Political Order* (Berkeley: University of California Press, 2002), 116. Brown, in *Rise of Western Christendom*, emphasizes that "it was not to convert a totally pagan population but, rather, to end an age of symbiosis between pagans and Christians that Boniface decided ... to cut down the mighty Oak of Thunor at Geismar. This oak had stood at a joining point between half-Christian Hesse and the pagan Saxons" (420–421). Later, Boniface had the Saxons' sacred oak sawed into planks and used them to build a church dedicated to St. Peter. In 754, North Sea pirates killed him, and Boniface, who reportedly did not fight against his attackers, became recognized as a martyr. But G. Ronald Murphy comments in *The Saxon Savior: The Germanic Transformation of the Gospel in the Ninth-Century Heliand* (New York: Oxford University Press, 1989), 14, that Boniface was hardly an embodiment of gentleness. He left a tradition of non-accommodating missionary methods based on a powerful and even ruthless personality.

14. *Bonifatii Epistolae,* quoted in Murphy, *Saxon Savior,* 14.

15. *Chronicarum continuationses* 19, quoted in Mastnak, *Crusading Peace,* 100.

16. Murphy, *Saxon Savior,* 11.

17. Chazelle, *Crucified God,* 20.

18. Chazelle notes that reading from an illuminated prayer book, the priests gazed on an

image of Christ, alive on the cross, arms outstretched. Blood spurted copiously from his side. His large, open eyes stared from the page into the eyes of the liturgists. Above him, two angels hovered with wings like peacock feathers, symbols of the Resurrection. The Gellone Sacramentary, dated to 790–c. 804, in which this image is found, exemplifies art and liturgy from the Carolingian Court. See Chazelle, *Crucified God*, 86–94.

19. *Royal Frankish Annals,* quoted by Murphy, *Saxon Savior,* 21.

20. The conflict between the Saxons and the Franks primarily was a clash between a tribal confederacy and an empire. "Christian" came to mean "Frank" and "pagan" came to mean "Saxon," even though forms of Christianity were present in both regions.

21. *De conversione Saxonum,* quoted and discussed in Chazelle, *Crucified God,* 20.

22. Heinrich Himmler erected a Nazi shrine at Verden to the forty-five hundred Saxons. White supremacist movements today sometimes frame themselves as pagans or neo-pagans, victims of imperial violence who seek to preserve the purity of their blood. The categories of "pure" and "impure" were no more accurate in the eighth century than now, and then as now, they function to justify violence. An Internet search for "Irminsul," the ancient Saxon sacred tree, leads to white supremacist sites.

23. Anonymous, "The Dream of the Rood," trans. Stephen Cox, in *The New Testament and Literature: A Guide to Literary Patterns* (Chicago: Carus, 2006), 325, lines 4–8, 17–20.

24. Roger Collins, *Charlemagne* (Toronto: University of Toronto Press, 1998), 53.

25. In *The Rise of Western Christendom,* Peter Brown reflects on the consequences of Christian missionizing among the European pagans:

> It seems to me that the most marked feature of the rise of the Christian church in western Europe was the imposition of human administrative structures . . . at the expense of the landscape itself. St. Martin attacked those points at which the natural and divine were held to meet: he cut down the sacred trees, and he broke up the processions that followed the immemorial lines between the arable and the non-arable. His successors fulminated against trees and fountains, and against forms of divination that gained access to the future through the close observation of the vagaries of animal and vegetable life. They imposed rhythms of work and leisure that ignored the slow turning of the sun, the moon, and the planets through the heavens, and that reflected, instead a purely human time, linked to the deaths of outstanding individuals. What is at stake in sixth-century Gaul . . . is nothing less than a conflict of views on the relations between man [*sic*] and nature. (124–125)

26. Writing to Mellitus on his way to Britain, Pope Gregory outlined a strategy of patient persuasion:

> The temples of the idols among the people should on no account be destroyed. . . . We hope that the people, seeing that their temples are not destroyed, may abandon their error and, flocking more readily to their ac-

customed resorts, may come to know and adore the true God. And since they have a custom of sacrificing many oxen to demons, let some other solemnity be substituted in its place.... For it is certainly impossible to eradicate all errors from obstinate minds at one stroke, and whoever wishes to climb to a mountain top climbs gradually step by step, and not in one leap. (Bede, *Historia Ecclesiastica*, 1.30, quoted in J. Russell, *Germanization*, 185–186)

27. Fulton, *Judgment to Passion*, 19. Mastnak discusses Carolingian religious attitudes regarding war and Alcuin's protests that church leaders should be "preachers, not predators." Mastnak argues that the Carolingians did not develop a full-blown concept of holy war. See *Crusading Peace*, 67–71.

28. Peter Cramer, *Baptism and Change in the Early Middle Ages, c. 200–1150* (New York: Cambridge University Press, 1993), 186.

29. Roger Collins, *Early Medieval Europe: 300–1000* (New York: St. Martin's Press, 1991), notes:

> As Christianity was introduced and then imposed on the Saxons ... there are no grounds for seeing these as representing ancestral customs or traditional laws amongst them. In other words these are Frankish rules that the Saxons were required to abide by.... A number of other indications exist that show the Franks of the late eighth century trying to "tidy up" their neighbours and to impose firm ethnic identities on them and give them distinct customs and laws. They seem to have been, from our perspective, strangely anxious to think of their neighbours and also non-Frankish groups within their own territories as being distinct *gentes* or peoples. (275)

30. For a detailed discussion of how the Carolingian empire and the Carolingian church colluded in colonizing activity, see Collins, *Charlemagne*, 102–124. "Colonizing monasteries" is Collins's term.

31. Caesarius of Arles, excerpted, quoted in Fulton, *Judgment to Passion*, 58–59.

32. *Dream of the Rood*, lines 24–27, 42–43.

33. Brown, *Rise of Western Christendom*, 164.

34. Excerpts from the Immolatio and Post-Sanctus from the Gallican Rite can be found in *Prayers of the Eucharist: Early and Reformed*, ed. R.C.D. Jasper and C.J. Cuming, 3rd ed. (Collegeville, MN: Liturgical Press, 1990), 148–149. The editors write, "The name 'Gallican' strictly applies to the rite used in France until its supersession by the Roman rite completed by Charlemagne c. 800; but it is used in a wider sense to include ... a family of non-Roman Latin rites. All these rites tend to show more traces of Eastern influence than does the native Roman rite.... Some of the prayers are clearly of great antiquity, predating the Roman canon in its historic form" (147).

35. Roman rite, in Jasper and Cuming, *Prayers of the Eucharist*, 161. The language that refers to Christ as a sacred victim is not entirely new. It appears in the earlier Mozara-

bic rite, and its introduction is attributed to Leo the Great, bishop of Rome from 440 to 461. The emphasis on Christ as a sacred victim and the imposition of this one rite throughout the empire are new. Early Christian insistence that the Eucharist is a "sacrifice without blood" disappeared.

36. Paschasius, quoted in Fulton, *Judgment to Passion*, 13. For discussions of *De corpore et sanguine Domini* see Fulton, 3, 12–16, 55–59; and Chazelle, *Crucified God*, 215–225. Chazelle, in particular, notes the controversy regarding the new idea of the Eucharist as a reenactment of the Crucifixion.

37. Chazelle, *Crucified God*, 168. Gottshalk (c. 803–869) held to a theory of double predestination: God predestined some to salvation and others to eternal damnation. The Crucifixion, once and for all (not to be repeated ritually), secured eternal life for the elect. Gottshalk's archenemy was Hincmar, who interpreted the Eucharist as a reenactment of the Crucifixion, and he also opposed Paschasius. Fulton comments in *Judgment to Passion*, "Gottshalk . . . explicitly accused Paschasius of advocating a cannibalistic realism in which Christ suffered torture at the celebration of each and every Mass" (14).

38. Chazelle, *Crucified God*, 230–231.

39. Paschasius, quoted in Fulton, *Judgment to Passion*, 57.

40. Fulton, *Judgment to Passion*, 58.

41. Paschasius, quoted in Fulton, *Judgment to Passion*, 56.

42. Alcuin, quoted in Fulton, *Judgment to Passion*, 57.

43. Hincmar, quoted in Chazelle, *Crucified God*, 218–219.

44. Chazelle, *Crucified God*, 225.

45. John Scotus Erigena, quoted in Chazelle, *Crucified God*, 227.

46. Gary Macy notes in *Treasures from the Storeroom: Medieval Religion and the Eucharist* (Collegeville, MN: Liturgical Press, 1999), 151, that by the twelfth century, manuals on the meaning of the Eucharist explain that the priest, in his ritual gesture of stretching his own arms wide at the Communion table, sacrifices himself along with Christ.

47. Sarah Hamilton, *The Practice of Penance: 900–1050* (Rochester, NY: Boydell and Brewer, 2001), 191.

48. See Chazelle, *Crucified God*, 209–238, for a detailed and nuanced discussion of additional factors in the debate: predestination, eschatology, and theories of representation.

49. Peter Damian, quoted in Fulton, *Judgment to Passion*, 105.

50. On the probable authorship, sources, and dating of the *Heliand*, see Fulton, *Judgment to Passion*, 26–27; and Murphy, *Saxon Savior*, 11–13.

51. For translations, textual notes, and commentary on the *Heliand*, see Murphy, *Saxon Savior*; G. Ronald Murphy, trans., *The Heliand: The Saxon Gospel* (New York: Oxford University Press, 1992); and James E. Cathey, ed., *Hêliand: Text and Commentary* (Morgantown: West Virginia University Press, 2002).

52. Brown, *Rise of Western Christendom*, 2003, 451–452; and Fulton, *Judgment to Pas-*

sion, 26–48. The *Heliand* is commonly read as a text that imports a warrior culture into Christianity. See Anthony W. Bartlett, *Cross Purposes: The Violent Grammar of Christian Atonement* (Harrisburg, PA: Trinity Press, 2001), 105–116. Bartlett regards the Saxon warrior culture as one of the sources of the violence of the later Christian Crusades. Bartlett's view accords with James Russell's in *The Germanization of Early Medieval Christianity* (167–168) and with the influential thesis of Carl Erdmann in *The Origin of the Idea of Crusade* ([Princeton, NJ: Princeton University Press, 1977], 19–20) that the Germans brought war "as a form of moral action" into Christianity, in contrast to Christian origins which were peace-loving. This thesis reflects strong anti-German sentiments. Though the *Heliand* assuredly represents a warrior culture, we think it is important to locate Christianity's turn to holy war more particularly with Carolingian imperial aggression.

53. James C. Scott, *Domination and the Arts of Resistance: Hidden Transcripts* (New Haven, CT: Yale University Press, 1990) is the basis of our interpretation of the Saxon response to the Carolingians. He quotes this aphorism as the book's epigraph.

54. See D. H. Green, *The Carolingian Lord: Semantic Studies on Four Old High German Words* (London: Cambridge University Press, 1965), 354–363. Green traces how, under Carolingian pressure, the Old Saxon polity of loyalty and reciprocity became a hierarchical polity of obedience to the emperor and to a ruling class.

55. Murphy, *Saxon Savior,* 17.

56. The *Heliand*'s association of Charlemagne with the Roman Empire is discernable in textual details. These include references in lines 339–374 to Carolingian church taxes and, in lines 4121–4157, the use of the term "bishop" when the text speaks of the high priest, Caiphas; the Saxon term for "priest" was different. See Cathey, *Héliand: Text and Commentary,* 157, 220. "The author of the *Héliand* wanted to be sure that any analogy between the Roman occupation of Jewish lands and Charlemagne's of Saxon lands would be quite obvious," Cathey writes (157). The *Heliand* reflects Saxon class hierarchies, for example, in the absence of Mary's Magnificat, and in its depiction of the feeding of the multitude as a gathering of earls and warriors—not peasants and common folk.

57. All *Heliand* quotations are from Ronald Murphy's translation.

58. Murphy, *Heliand,* 191. The *bifrost* could also be seen in rainbows. Murphy writes in *The Saxon Savior,* "The monk-poet has cleared a gentle path for his Saxons, a path on which they can overcome their conquerors through the very religion brought by the conquerors and, in a real sense, overcome the 'Christians' with Christ. In Christian spirituality they can escape their captivity by the Franks and even rise again to a new life. They need not fear the loss of their knighthood, for the *Heliand* has shown them a new type of *comitatus* loyalty" (115).

59. Murphy, *Heliand,* 207.

60. Murphy, *Heliand,* comments in his footnotes on the translation: "This beautiful if obscure line merits closer observation. . . . The 'It' causes difficulty for translators,

since the previous reference to Christ in the last sentence was to 'Him' as 'their Lord,' thus requiring 'Him' rather than 'It' as the expected pronoun of reference" (26 n. 43). "It" was a rich allusion to "Child" and made the scene an allegory of the Mass, when the communicant received the wafer in the hand.

61. Primary sources for this account are Peter Dronke, *Women Writers of the Middle Ages: A Critical Study of Texts from Perpetua (†203) to Marguerite Porete (†1310)* (Cambridge: Cambridge University Press, 1984); Dhuoda, *Handbook for William: A Carolingian Woman's Counsel for Her Son,* trans. Carol Neel (Lincoln: University of Nebraska Press, 1991); Dhuoda, *Liber Manualis: Handbook for her Warrior Son,* Cambridge Medieval Classics 8, Marcelle Thiébaux, ed. and trans. (New York: Cambridge University Press, 1998), 44–45. Marcelle Thiébaux, trans. and intro., *The Writings of Medieval Women: An Anthology,* 2nd ed. (New York: Garland, 1994).

62. Carol Neel, "Introduction," Dhuoda, *Handbook for William: A Carolingian Woman's Counsel for Her Son,* trans. Carol Neel (Lincoln: University of Nebraska Press, 1991), xi–xiv.

63. Dronke, *Women Writers of the Middle Ages,* 37.

64. Neel, "Introduction," xvi.

65. Dhuoda, *Liber Manualis,* 43–45.

66. Dronke, *Women Writers of the Middle Ages,* 42.

67. Dhuoda, *Liber Manualis,* 227.

68. Ibid., 121–123.

69. Dronke, *Women Writers of the Middle Ages,* 52.

70. Dhuoda, *Liber Manualis,* 113.

71. Ibid., 67–69.

72. Fulton, *Judgment to Passion,* 140.

73. Mastnak, *Crusading Peace,* 16.

CHAPTER TEN: PEACE BY THE BLOOD OF THE CROSS

1. See Christoph Auffarth, "Paradise Now—But for the Wall Between: Some Remarks on Paradise in the Middle Ages," in *Paradise Interpreted: Representations of Biblical Paradise in Judaism and Christianity,* ed. Gerard P. Luttikhuizen (Leiden, Netherlands: Brill, 1999), 176–178; and George Hunston Williams, *Wilderness and Paradise in Christian Thought: The Biblical Experience of the Desert in the History of Christianity and the Paradise Theme in the Theological Idea of the University* (New York: Harper and Brothers, 1962), 47–57. Williams notes (48) that Honorius of Autun, a twelfth-century encyclopedist, explained that the cloister was a paradise because it replicated the portico of Solomon—the courtyard of the temple in Jerusalem—where the first apostles preached the good news and taught Christians to share their goods in common.

2. Monastic communities ordinarily excluded lay people, but they sometimes took in abandoned children, and the destitute sought alms there. The orphans might be raised to take holy orders, or they and the destitute might work as unpaid servants. See John Boswell, *The Kindness of Strangers: The Abandonment of Children in Western Europe from Late Antiquity to the Renaissance* (Chicago: University of Chicago Press, 1982). Boswell notes that abandonment rates hovered around 20 to 40 percent of all live births in the period he studied. Parents of all classes left unwanted children in public places or donated them to the church.

3. Quoted in Roland Bainton, *Christian Attitudes toward War and Peace: A Historical Survey and Critical Re-Evaluation* (New York: Abingdon Press, 1960), 110–111.

4. First canon of the Council of Narbonne, quoted in Tomaž Mastnak, *Crusading Peace: Christendom, the Muslim World, and Western Political Order* (Berkeley: University of California Press, 2002), 37. Mastnak offers an extensive and detailed analysis of the evolution of such peace councils and church strategies, and he revives the thesis that these strategies were critical to the emergence of the Crusades.

5. Mastnak, *Crusading Peace,* 4–6.

6. Ibid., 45.

7. Ibid., 17.

8. Gregory to Matilda of Tuscany, quoted in Mastnak, *Crusading Peace,* 32.

9. Quotes in this paragraph are from Mastnak, *Crusading Peace,* 17–19. For his discussion of Gregory VII, see pp. 79–90.

10. Quoted in Mastnak, *Crusading Peace,* 30. Emphasis added.

11. Quoted in Rachel Fulton, *From Judgment to Passion: Devotion to Christ and the Virgin Mary, 800–1200* (New York: University of Columbia Press, 2002), 172.

12. Quoted in Fulton, *Judgment to Passion,* 175, excerpts. This instruction is found in Anselm's dedicatory letter accompanying prayers he sent to Princess Adelaide around 1072.

13. Fulton, *Judgment to Passion,* 81.

14. From a synod held in Arras in January 1025, discussed in Fulton, *Judgment to Passion,* 83–84.

15. Williston Walker, *A History of the Christian Church,* 3rd ed. (New York: Charles Scribner's Sons, 1970), 227–232.

16. Gerard, quoted in Fulton, *Judgment to Passion,* 85.

17. Fulton suggests that apocalyptic anxieties were a defining feature of piety in this period. We think the piety was part of a great mix of social and political changes in western Europe that began with Carolingian imperialism. Apocalypticism intensified further from the fourteenth to sixteenth centuries.

18. Biographer of Richard, abbot of Saint-Vanne, quoted in Fulton, *Judgment to Passion,* 66–67.

19. See Gertrud Schiller, *The Passion of Jesus Christ,* Vol. 2 of *Iconography of Christian Art,* trans. Janet Seligman (Greenwich, CT: New York Graphic Society, 1972), fig. 554.

20. Peter Damian, quoted in Fulton, *Judgment to Passion*, 96–97.

21. Ibid., 103.

22. Ibid., 105. On pages 93–94, Fulton describes Peter's early life as marked by abuse. Orphaned as a small child, he was raised by relatives who "fed him with slops, clothed him with rags, kicked him and beat him, and eventually turned him out as a swineherd to live with the pigs. . . . It seems reasonable to suggest that Peter's childhood left him with a lingering sense of personal distress." Harsh treatment of children was not unusual; Anselm's father was brutal to him when he was a child. Fulton discusses (466–467) the importance of the body in medieval piety. Our previous work analyzed the link between child abuse and theologies of redemptive violence. See Rita Nakashima Brock, *Journeys by Heart: A Christology of Erotic Power* (New York: Crossroad, 1988); Rita Nakashima Brock and Rebecca Ann Parker, *Proverbs of Ashes: Violence, Redemptive Suffering, and the Search for What Saves Us* (Boston: Beacon Press, 2001).

23. For a comprehensive discussion of the major contemporary accounts of Pope Urban's sermon at Clermont, see Penny J. Cole, *The Preaching of the Crusades to the Holy Land, 1095–1270* (Cambridge, MA: Medieval Academy of America, 1991), 1–36. The primary sources she discusses are Fulcher of Chartres, *Gesta Francorum Jerusalem Expugnantium*; Robert the Monk, *Historia Hierosolymitana*; *Gesta Francorum* (The Deeds of the Franks); Balderic of Dol; Guibert de Nogent: *Historia quae dicitur Gesta Dei per Francos*; and *The Privilege of Urban to the Pilgrims*, December 1095. The latter is all we have in Urban's own words. The other reports of his speech are reconstructions by early crusaders, representing the interests and viewpoints of the times.

24. Baldric of Dol, in Edward Peters, ed., *The First Crusade, the Chronicle of Fulcher of Chartres and Other Source Materials* (Philadelphia: University of Pennsylvania Press, 1998), 29–32.

25. Carole Hillenbrand, *The Crusades: Islamic Perspectives* (Chicago: Fitzroy Dearborn, 1999), 33.

26. Quoted in Mastnak, *Crusading Peace*, 86.

27. Hillenbrand, *Crusades: Islamic Perspectives*, 15. It is unlikely that these pilgrims added fuel to anti-Muslim hostility in the West, since their direct experience would not have substantiated enmity. In addition, Muslims, Christians, and Jews, though experiencing sporadic tensions and occasional military skirmishes, often interacted peacefully. They lived together in many places, especially in Spain and southern Italy.

28. Fulcher of Chartres, in Peters, *First Crusade*, 65–67.

29. *The Privilege of Urban to the Pilgrims*, in Peters, *First Crusade*, 37.

30. Jonathan Riley-Smith, "The State of Mind of Crusaders to the East, 1095–1300," in Jonathan Riley-Smith, ed., *The Oxford Illustrated History of the Crusades* (Oxford: Oxford University Press, 1995), 77, 82.

31. Quoted in Peters, *First Crusade*, 12.

32. The thesis that the crusades were primarily motivated by Christian piety was first proposed in the 1950s by C. Erdmann. For a discussion of Erdmann's now widely accepted thesis, see H.E.J. Cowdrey, "Pope Urban II's Preaching of the First Crusade," in *The Crusades: The Essential Readings*, ed. Thomas F. Madden (Oxford: Blackwell, 2002), 17–20.

33. Quotes from Peters, *First Crusade*, 32.

34. Riley-Smith, "State of Mind," 77.

35. Baldric of Dol, quoted in Cole, *Preaching of the Crusades*, 14.

36. The Crusades cannot be adequately understood as a response to external threats to Europe, as an expression of a preexisting anti-Muslim sentiment, or as an eruption of inevitable human propensities for violence. They embodied a new religious ideology, promulgated through preaching, ritual, and pageantry. Pope Urban II sought to strengthen "the peace" among Christians by characterizing Jews and Muslims in totalitarian religious terms as evildoers. They were the enemy of Christians, whom Urban characterized as blood kin. Mastnak, *Crusading Peace*, 93–95, comments: "Latin Christians found their way to themselves as Christendom through peacemaking. . . . Peace commended the Christian brotherhood, *fraternité*, to go to war against those who were not of the Christian family. Thus Christian society became conscious of itself through mobilization for holy war."

37. Anselm, *Why God Became Man and The Virgin Conception and Original Sin*, trans., intro., and notes by Joseph M. Colleran (Albany, NY: Magi Books, 1969), 2.

38. Anthony Bartlett, *Cross Purposes: The Violent Grammar of the Christian Atonement* (Harrisburg, PA: Trinity Press, 2001), 95. Bartlett examines the relationship between Anselm's theology and the Crusades. Though we do not subscribe to Bartlett's adherence to the theories of René Girard, we appreciate his work, which links atonement theology and the Crusades. James Carroll, *Constantine's Sword: The Church and the Jews* (Boston: Houghton Mifflin Press, 2001), 284–289, also makes this connection in his discussion of Anselm.

39. Anselm, *Why God*, 84–87.

40. Anselm, like Augustine, speaks of two kinds of sin. Sin that "arises from our nature" and sin "arising from the person." Anselm's distinction between "original" and "personal" sin is laid out in *The Virgin Conception and Original Sin*. See Anselm, *Why God*, 167–211.

41. Anselm, *Why God*, 113–116 and 155: "The restoration of humanity . . . could not be accomplished unless man paid to God what he owed for sin. But this debt was so great that, although man alone owed the debt, still God alone was able to pay it. . . . Hence it was necessary that God assume human nature into the unity of his person."

42. Anselm, *Why God*, 155, 156.

43. Ibid., 145–146.

44. Ibid., 160, 136.

45. Ibid., 86.

46. Jonathan Riley-Smith, ed., *The Oxford Illustrated History of The Crusades* (New York: Oxford University Press, 1995), 115.

47. Anselm, *Why God,* 147, 146.

48. Anselm, quoted in Fulton, *Judgment to Passion,* 204, 192.

49. Ibid., 203. Fulton discusses Anselm's devotion to Mary, tracing the themes of Mary's co-suffering back to the ninth-century Carolingian theologian Hrabanus Maurus and noting the new developments in Anselm's prayers (195–243). "The translation of the crucified Judge into the suffering man went hand in hand with the translation of the queenly Intercessor into the grieving Mother—and this mutual translation was and is nowhere more urgent or visible than in Anselm's prayers" (205).

50. Anselm, *Op. omn.,* quoted in George Hunston Williams, *Anselm: Communion and Atonement* (St. Louis: Concordia, 1960), 56–57. Williams comments, "Each believer by penitential-Eucharistic incorporation into the universal Man of sorrows daily pays the *iustitia* due to God. In other words, the *meritum* of Christ's death can be repeatedly and individually returned by the believer in the divine office which is at once the re-enactment of the action on Calvary and the individual participant's payment of due honor to God . . . through daily incorporation in the self-sacrificing *corpus* on the altar" (51–52). For Anselm, ritual eating of Christ's sacrificed body would gradually incorporate the believer into Christ's glorified and resurrected body. In this way, the Resurrection is not completely absent from Anselm's piety, though it is absent from *Why God Became Human.* Williams discusses the importance of Anselm in the evolution of Marian piety (37–38) and, overall, makes the case that *Why God Became Human* is the logical theological outcome of shifts in sacramental theology that began in the ninth century. These shifts diminished baptism as entrance into paradise beginning now and elevated the Eucharist as the reenactment of the Crucifixion, which incorporated Christians into his saving death.

51. Carroll, *Constantine's Sword,* 250, 251.

52. Albert of Aachen, quoted in Thomas Asbridge, *The First Crusade: A New History* (Oxford: Oxford University Press, 2004), 88.

53. Bartlett, *Cross Purposes,* 106, and Carroll, *Constantine's Sword,* 248. Both agree that the historical trajectory to the Holocaust began with these early pogroms.

54. See Asbridge, *First Crusade,* 40–82, for a discussion of Urban's political preparations in advance of the gathering in Clermont and of the diverse groups—from nobility to peasants—who responded to the call. We have focused on the complex religious motivations for crusading. These are key factors, but political and economic motivations are also part of crusading's massive appeal.

55. Mastnak, *Crusading Peace,* 147.

56. Auffarth, "Paradise Now," 174.

57. For discussion and examples, see Bernard McGinn, *Apocalypticism in the Western*

Tradition (Aldershot, UK: Variorum, 1994), art. III, 277-278; and Fulton, *Judgment to Passion*, 64-71.

58. Mastnak, *Crusading Peace*, 46-47, writes that crusaders "carried images of Jerusalem and the holy places with them. . . . They moved within the mental world those images formed. . . . What the pilgrims saw in their minds' eye was the heavenly Jerusalem, the sacred city from the Book of Revelation. . . . The nets entangling Jerusalem were not merely symbolic. Before the turn of the eleventh century, Jerusalem fell to Christian forces. Those who destroyed it, the army of the new chosen people, had already built an image of the New Jerusalem in their minds' eye."

59. *Gesta Francorum: The Deeds of the Franks and the Other Pilgrims to Jerusalem*, ed. Rosalind Hidd (London: Thomas Nelson and Sons, 1962), 40.

60. Ibid., 91.

61. Quoted in Hillenbrand, *Crusades: Islamic Perspectives*, 64-65.

62. For a discussion of the colonizing of the "Holy Land," see Jonathan Phillips, "The Latin East, 1098-1291," in Jonathan Riley-Smith, ed., *The Oxford Illustrated History of the Crusades* (Oxford: Oxford University Press, 1995), 112-140.

63. For a discussion of the financing of the Crusades, see Simon Lloyd, "The Crusading Movement: 1096-1274," in Jonathan Riley-Smith, ed., *The Oxford Illustrated History of the Crusades,* (Oxford: Oxford University Press, 1995), 54-65. Lloyd acknowledges that "it is impossible to know whether the economic stimulus stemming from the expenditure for the crusades was outweighed by the disruption that crusading also caused to economic life" (65). For details of changes in the economy of western Europe from the tenth to the thirteenth centuries, see R.H.C. Davis, *A History of Medieval Europe: From Constantine to Saint Louis,* 2nd ed. (London: Longman Group, 1988), 371-381; and David Nicholas, *The Evolution of the Medieval World: Society, Government, and Thought in Europe, 312-1500* (London: Longman Group, 1992), 273-275, 283-319. Nicholas notes that "the Crusades strengthened the internal economy of western Europe by increasing the availability of money. . . . The Christians captured substantial hoards of Muslim coin in Palestine, Spain and Sicily. . . . The greatest impact of the Crusades may well have been not the promotion of east-west trade but the stolen Muslim coin creating the basis for the commercial capitalism of twelfth-century Europe" (274).

64. Bernard, *Liber ad milites Templi,* 5 (www.the-rb.net/encyclop/religion/monastic/bernard.html), p. 7.

65. Byzantine iconography retained its emphasis on the Incarnation, Transfiguration, and Resurrection. Latin Christians often hired Byzantine artists to decorate the interiors of the Holy Land shrines, and the beauty of churches in Constantinople and the Holy Land led to a renaissance of Byzantine-style art in the West. Christians endeavored to plant the New Jerusalem in Europe by building replicas of the church of the Holy Sepulcher in their home cities and by restoring Byzantine-style mosaics.

66. *Gesta Francorum,* 98-101.

67. Bernard, *Liber ad milites,* 5.

CHAPTER ELEVEN: DYING FOR LOVE

1. For general cultural trends, see Fiona Maddock, *Hildegard of Bingen: Woman of Her Age* (New York: Doubleday Books, 2001) and Susan B. Edgington and Sarah Lambert, *Gendering the Crusades* (New York: Columbia University Press, 2002).

2. Bernard of Clairvaux, trans. James W. Alexander, www.igracemusic.com/hymnbook/hymns/009.html. Rachel Fulton, *From Judgment to Passion: Devotion to Christ and the Virgin Mary, 800–1200* (New York: Columbia University Press, 2002), 302–309, notes that although Bernard is famous for heightening devotion to Mary, he in fact said little about her.

3. Christoph Auffarth, "Paradise Now—But for the Wall Between: Some Remarks on Paradise in the Middle Ages" in *Paradise Interpreted: Representations of Biblical Paradise in Judaism and Christianity*, ed. Gerard P. Luttikhuizen (Leiden, Netherlands: Koninklijke Brill, 1999), 176.

4. At www.gardenvisit.com/got/6/2.htm.

5. For discussions of popular love poetry in the twelfth century, which shaped the context for Bernard's interpretation of the Song of Songs, see Michael Routledge, "Songs," in Jonathan Riley-Smith, ed., *The Oxford Illustrated History of the Crusades* (Oxford University Press, 1995), 91–111; and David Nicholas, *The Evolution of the Medieval World: Society, Government, and Thought in Europe, 312–1500* (New York: Longman, 1992), 329–334. See also Caroline Walker Bynum, *The Resurrection of the Body in Western Christianity, 200–1336* (New York: Columbia University Press, 1995); and Caroline Walker Bynum and Paul Freedman, eds., *Last Things: Death and the Apocalypse in the Middle Ages* (Philadelphia: University of Pennsylvania Press, 2000).

6. Bernard, quoted in Karen Armstrong, *Holy War: The Crusades and Their Impact on Today's World* (New York: Anchor Books, 2001), 205.

7. For a discussion of Bernard's unique use of this text and the relationships between Christian mystical ideals of love and the courtly love that emerged in the same period, see Jeanne Nightingale, "Inscribing the Breath of a Speaking Voice: *Vox Sponsae* in St. Bernard's Sermons on the Canticles and in Chrétien's *Erec et Enide*," in *Courtly Arts and the Art of Courtliness: Selected Papers from the Eleventh Triennial Congress of the International Courtly Literature Society, University of Wisconsin–Madison, 29 July–4 August 2004*, ed. Keith Busby and Christopher Kleinhenz (Rochester, NY: Boydell and Brewer, 2006). We read this paper in unpublished form, sent to us by the author at our request.

8. Bernard, *Commentary on the Song of Songs*, Sermon, *The Works of Bernard of Clairvaux: Song of Songs I,* trans. Kilian Walsh (Kalamazoo, MI: Cistercian Publications, 1981), 9–10.

9. Bernard, *Commentary*, Sermon 27.4.7, in *The Works of Bernard of Clairvaux: Song of Songs II*, trans. Kilian Walsh (Kalamazoo, MI: Cistercian Publications, 1983), 79–80.

10. Fulton suggests that around 1033, a millennium after the Crucifixion, fears escalated over the Last Judgment and the symbolism of Jerusalem. When the new age had not arrived, fervent fears of final judgment and hopes of deliverance assumed new forms, which likely intensified interest in the Crusade to Jerusalem as an attempt to bring a new heaven and earth. Though apocalypticism was a factor in these developments, Tomaž Mastnak, *Crusading Peace: Christendom, the Muslim World, and Western Political Order* (Berkeley: University of California Press, 2002) locates the forces of change in the feudal wars and "peace" movements of the church of the Middle Ages.

11. Bernard, *Commentary,* Sermon 27.4.7, *Songs II,* 81–82.

12. By way of contrast: Ephrem associated the wedding of Christ and his bride with the triumphal entry into Jerusalem, with the baptism of Jesus, with the feast of the Resurrection, with Jesus's first miracle at the wedding in Cana, with his parables of the wise and foolish virgins, with the baptismal vows that Christian take, and with Mary and the incarnation. See Sebastian Brock, *The Luminous Eye: The Spiritual World Vision of Saint Ephrem the Syrian* (Kalamazoo, MI: Cistercian Publications, 1985), 115–130. What Ephrem does *not* do is associate erotic spirituality with the Crucifixion. Rather, he associates the wounded side of Christ with the opening of paradise: "Through the side pierced with the sword I entered the garden fenced in by the sword." Brock, 84, notes that the association of this wound with bridal imagery occurs in later poets, not Ephrem.

13. Bernard, *Commentary,* Sermon 25.1.3, *Songs II,* 52.

14. Bernard, *Commentary,* Sermon 25.5, *Songs II,* 53.

15. Bernard, *Commentary,* Sermon 25.8, *Songs II,* 56. Bernard comments in 25.3 that when the bride reaches heaven, her glorified body will become white. Speaking of Paul in 25.8, he writes, "This the Doctor of the Nations is reputed abject, dishonorable, black, beneath notice, a scrap of this world's refuse . . . though black without he is beautiful within."

16. Bernard, *Commentary,* Sermon 43.3, *Songs II,* 221–222.

17. Bernard, *Liber ad milites Templi,* 3, trans. Conrad Greenia, www.the-orb.net/encyclop/religion/monastic/bernard.html.

18. John Boswell, *Same-Sex Unions in Premodern Europe* (New York: Vintage Books, 1995).

19. Gay L. Byron, *Symbolic Blackness and Ethnic Difference in Early Christian Literature* (New York: Routledge, 2002).

20. Bernard, *Liber ad,* 2.

21. Ibid., 4.

22. Ibid., 1.

23. Ibid., 1.

24. Ibid., 2.

25. In fact, they likely failed because of Bernard's ability to stir up passion and to recruit widely for the war. Simon Lloyd, "The Crusading Movement 1096–1274," in

Jonathan Riley-Smith, ed., *The Oxford Illustrated History of the Crusades* (New York: Oxford University Press, 1995), notes:

> Large numbers of noncombatants took the cross and departed, especially on crusades to the Holy Land, thereby causing immense problems. In particular, they placed intolerable strains on available food supplies, exacerbating, if not causing, the famine situations that developed on the march to the East and the consequent staggering rise in prices of foodstuffs. They also posed a major problem for discipline and organization, and contributed not a little to the developing friction with the Byzantines, the crusaders' supposed allies, all the time consuming resources which would otherwise have been available to others more useful than themselves.
>
> This is starkly clear from eyewitness accounts of the First and Second Crusades, and the experience prompted monarchs who led the Third Crusade to take steps to prevent the participation of a host of non-combatants. But neither they nor later crusade leaders who followed suit were entirely successful; crusader privileges and the lure of the Holy Places were so potent that crusading, at least to the Latin East, retained its considerable popular appeal.

Over time, crusading would embed itself into feudal society as the activity of entire estates and family lines, or across regions that regularly supported crusading and not only sent knights and other combatants but also funded them.

26. Quoted in Lloyd, "Crusading Movement," in Riley-Smith, *Oxford Illustrated History,* 36.
27. Peter Dronke, "Hildegard of Bingen," in *Women Writers of the Middle Ages: A Critical Study of Texts from Perpetua (†203) to Marguerite Porete (†1310)* (Cambridge: Cambridge University Press, 1984), 144–171, offers a nuanced discussion of her class biases and the Richardis affair. He also discusses the many contradictions of Hildegard's life, as well as her dazzling contributions to music, medicine, and theology. For a discussion of her religious use of the Crusades, see Miriam Rita Tessera, "Philip Count of Flander and Hildegard of Bingen," in Edgington and Lambert, *Gendering the Crusades,* 77–93.
28. For a study of Hildegard's life and calling, rooted in her infirmities, see Dronke, "Hildegard of Bingen," 144–171.
29. Quotes in this paragraph are from Hildegard and Guibert, found in Heinrich Schipperges, *The World of Hildegard of Bingen: Her Life, Times, and Visions,* trans. John Cumming (Collegeville, MN: Liturgical Press, 1998), 53.
30. Hildegard, quoted in Schipperges, *World of Hildegard,* 140.
31. Ibid., 145.
32. Where Hildegard stood on sex is unclear. She seems to have held both a positive view of it in Eden and typical religious views of sin and sex. Explicit sexual information was available to Hildegard in manuals and in frank conversations about sex among

women, according to Maddock, *Hildegard: Woman of Her Age,* 9–12. According to Dronke, "Hildegard of Bingen," 175, she speaks descriptively in her writings of sexual intercourse: "When a woman is making love with a man, a sense of heat in her brain, which brings with it sensual delight, communicates the taste of that delight during the act and summons forth the mission of the man's seed." Schipperges writes in *The World of Hildegard* that Hildegard saw the sexual joining of humans as generated by the power of God working in them. Life was intended in God's *plantation prima* (initial planting) to be a garden of earthly pleasures. He quotes Hildegard as saying, "Full joy in life should prevail between man and woman: that perfect love that already flowered in the first human couple" (80). Maddock and others suggest this was not her view of sex in this life. She believed sin corrupted it, and it would not be fully restored until the eschaton.

33. Schipperges, *World of Hildegard,* 82.
34. Ibid. Hildegard says,

> Human beings are at the center of the world's structure, and are more important than all other creatures that depend on it. People may be small in stature, but their souls make them powerful. They have their heads erect and their feet on firm ground, and this dual ability to think and act enables them to control and accomplish both higher and lower things. The effects of what they do with their right and left hands are felt throughout the universe, because their inner power makes it possible for them to exploit its potential. . . . Just as the human heart is concealed in the body, so the body is surrounded by the powers of the soul, which reach out over the whole world. Righteous people live in awareness of God and see him in all his works.

35. Hildegard quoted in Schipperges, *World of Hildegard,* 68.
36. Caesarius of Heisterbach, *Caesarius Heiserbacencis monachi ordinis Cisterciensis, Dialogus miraculorum,* ed. J. Strange, Vol. 2 (Cologne: J. M. Heberle, 1851), 296–298. Caesarius (c. 1180–1250) was a Cistercian master of novices. He attributes this comment to Arnaud-Amaury, whose fighting monks massacred thousands of men, women, and children in 1209 in a campaign against the Cathars, opponents of the Crusades in Béziers, France. The phrase can be found on T-shirts popular among U.S. military units such as the Marines, Army Rangers, and Special Forces. The shirts say, "Kill 'em all and let God sort 'em out." Google lists many suppliers of them.
37. Abelard is noted in philosophy for his logic, his ethics, and his refinement of the method of dialectic, a mode of reasoning that used logic to examine contradictory ideas and resolve them. Abelard is credited with bringing dialectic into discussions of doctrine, thereby inventing the discipline of theology as a philosophical pursuit independent of church teaching. It had previously been focused on biblical interpretation, explication of doctrine, polemics against heretics, catechetical instruction, and apologetics. See Constant J. Mews, *Reason and Belief in the Age of Roscelin and Abelard* (Burlington, VT: Ashgate, 2002).

38. Peter Abelard, *Collationes,* ed. and trans. John Marenbon and Giovanni Orlandi (New York: Oxford University Press, 2001). The editors suggest that the philosopher was likely Ibn Bājjah (Avempace), a famous Spanish Muslim (d. 1138) who "had the reputation of having rejected the authority of sacred texts and basing himself on reason alone. . . . There was in Islam in Abelard's day an established tradition of *falsafah,* of the study of philosophy on the basis of the ancients, especially Aristotle, which was regarded as a pursuit quite distinct from that of *kalām,* Muslim scholastic theology" (li). Abelard describes the philosopher as a circumcised descendant of Ishmael, and the philosopher sometimes expresses Abelard's own positive assessment of pagans. For an assessment of Abelard's philosophy, see Daniel F. Blackwell, *Non-Ontological Constructs: The Effects of Abelard's Logical and Ethical Theories on His Theology: A Study in Meaning and Verification* (New York: Peter Lang, 1988).

39. Abelard's writing has not been well preserved and he tended to leave works unfinished. Blackwell discusses his deontological thinking, and George P. Fedotov, in *Peter Abelard: The Personality, Self-Consciousness, and Thought of a Martyr of "Enlightenment"* (Vaduz, Liechtenstein: Büchervertriebsanstalt, 1988) sees him as a harbinger of the Enlightenment. Kathleen M. Starnes, *Peter Abelard: His Place in History* (Lanham, MD: University Press of America, 1981), 104–106, notes his contributions to theology, especially his dialectical method.

    John Marenbon, *The Philosophy of Peter Abelard* (New York: Cambridge University Press, 1997), offers a thorough, careful assessment of his constructive work in philosophy and theology. He draws a sharp line between Abelard's ontology and his ethics and suggests that the ontology was not nearly as influential in his thinking as the ethics. He shows how Abelard reinterprets orthodoxy according to his creative ethical positions rather than rejecting orthodox ideas outright.

    Other writers who have attempted to systematize and relate Abelard's thinking to Enlightenment categories and to orthodox theology include Leif Grane, *Peter Abelard: Philosophy and Christianity in the Middle Ages* (London: George Allen and Unwin, 1970); J. Ramsay McCallum, *Abelard's Christian Theology* (Merrick, NY: Richwood, 1976); Richard E. Weingart, *The Logic of Divine Love: A Critical Analysis of the Soteriology of Peter Abelard* (Oxford, UK: Clarendon Press, 1970); and Paul L. Williams, *The Moral Philosophy of Peter Abelard* (Lanham, MD: University Press of America, 1980).

40. *Epist. Ad Romanos* 2, 835D–836A, cited in P. Williams, *Peter Abelard,* 156.

41. Abelard took Paul's language of divine justice in Romans 3, which demands the blood of Christ, and shifted it from justice to love. Abelard says, "To show forth His justice, that is His love, which, as has been said, justifies us before Him, that is, by exhibiting His love for us, or convincing us how much we ought to love Him, [He] spared not even His own Son for us." *Epist. Ad Romanos,* 2, 833 Ab, cited in P. Williams, *Peter Abelard,* 157.

42. See Marenbon, *Philosophy of Peter Abelard,* 256.

43. Peter Abelard, *Peter Abelard's Ethics,* intro. and trans. D. E. Luscombe (London: Oxford University Press, 1971), 81.

44. Abelard, Hymn 44, excerpts, from *The Hymns of Abelard in English Verse,* trans. Sister Jane Patricia (Lanham, MD: University Press of America, 1986), 69.

45. See Peter Abelard, *Römerbriefkommentar,* Vol. 2, intro. and trans. Rolf Peppermüller (New York: Herder, 2000).

46. Abelard, *Epist. Ad Romanos,* quoted in P. Williams, *Peter Abelard,* 159.

47. Despite his statements on the atonement, Abelard's work evidenced conflicts about its necessity for salvation, according to McCallum in *Abelard's Christian Theology.* Abelard's strong emphasis on ethical intent led him to assert that both Jews and pagans could be saved if they lived by good moral intentions and worshipped one God. To make this claim, Abelard extended the idea of natural law to the non-Christian people of his own time. To emphasize pagan salvation, he painted a highly idealized picture of pagan philosophers and their societies.

48. James Carroll, *Constantine's Sword: The Church and the Jews* (Boston: Houghton Mifflin Press, 2001), 294, suggests that if Abelard's theology had prevailed, the fate of the Jews in Europe would have been better. For Abelard, Carroll says, God is not "the monster God who needs . . . to be paid back in blood, the blood sacrifice of an only Son. Rather, the cross is an epiphany of the permanent and preexisting love of God that needs nothing from the beloved except existence." Abelard said, however, that since the crime of the Jews was so heinous, they deserved the punishments visited upon them, especially the destruction of Jerusalem by Titus, who is one of Abelard's heroes. Abelard, quoted in McCallum, says, "Titus, son of Vespasian, . . . avenging the Lord's death, was of such good disposition that, when late at night he recalled at supper that he had no good deed to his credit during the day, he would remark: 'My friends, this day I have lost a day' " (*Abelard's Christian Theology,* 65).

49. Abelard, *Collationes,* quoted in James Carroll, *Constantine's Sword,* 295. The Jew helped build the argument that culminated in the Christian's debate with the Muslim, who sometimes expressed Abelard's own positive assessment of pagan philosophers.

50. Quoted in Carroll, *Constantine's Sword,* 294.

51. Followers of René Girard have argued that Jesus, by absorbing violence and becoming a victim, unveiled mechanisms of violence. For example, Anthony W. Bartlett, *Cross Purposes: The Violent Grammar of Christian Atonement* (Harrisburg, PA: Trinity Press, 2001), offers as an alternative to Anselmian redemptive violence. His alternative—though not identified as Abelardian, but with Girard—resonates with Abelard. It valorizes the saving power of a victim. He writes that in Jesus's death,

> a limitless response of trust and surrender on part of the victim broke the pattern, provoking something entirely new in the repertoire of human possibility . . . his fidelity to his redemptive project in the midst of lethal persecution, achieved not in bitter defiance but in fathomless yielding. . . . It is the

compassionate response of Jesus in his abyssal discontinuity, the impossibility that he makes possible, that opens the doors of boundless love between individuals through mimesis of that response. . . . [It is] the abyssal isolation of Jesus where the time-shattering possibility of love, of absolute gift, is generated. . . . Abyssal subjectivity made possible by Christ . . . becomes the mode of personal existence called love. . . . When Christ breathes his final breath on the cross, without asking God to avenge him, he plunges God into the abyss of non-retaliatory love. . . . Here, then, is the intense radicalism of the Christian project, the glory of the individual sustained in the self-surrender of love stretching out endlessly. (257–260)

52. McCallum, *Abelard's Christian Theology*, 46, 88.

53. Marenbon, *Philosophy of Peter Abelard*, 281, notes especially the inability to address conflicting intentions as a weakness of Abelard's emphasis on love of God and intent, as well as the problem of accounting for actions, which "we do not think about but for which it is reasonable to think we are fully responsible."

54. Marenbon (*Philosophy of Peter Abelard*), Mews (*Reason and Belief in the Age of Roscelin and Abelard*), and Starnes (*Peter Abelard: His Place in History*) discuss the controversies surrounding Abelard and the criticisms of his former teachers and other enemies.

55. Peter Dronke, "Heloise," in *Women Writers of the Middle Ages*, 107–142. Some scholars still debate whether Heloise actually wrote these letters. Dronke makes a strong argument for her authorship. Heloise lived at a time that witnessed the rise of powerful women. The era also saw the development of romantic troubadours, some of whom opposed the Crusades through their songs and extolled erotic, sexual love. If Heloise did not write the letters, they nonetheless reflect values and a perspective that were conceivable for women in the twelfth century and that present a marked contrast to the devotional piety of Anselm, Abelard, and Bernard. Dronke also argues that Heloise taught Abelard her "Italianate" epistolary writing style. For other studies of Heloise, see Constant J. Mews, *The Lost Love Letters of Heloise and Abelard: Perceptions of Dialogue in Twelfth-Century France* (New York: St. Martin's Press, 1999); and *The Letters of Abelard and Heloise*, trans. and intro. Betty Radice (Hammondsworth, UK: Penguin Books, 1974).

56. Heloise to Abelard, First Letter, *Letters of Abelard and Heloise*, 115.

57. Ibid.

58. Ibid., 113–114.

59. Ibid., 114.

60. Peter Abelard, *The Story of My Misfortunes*, trans. Henry Adams Bellows (New York: Macmillan, 1972), chap. 6. Abelard's motives for his interpretation of his failed marriage are suspect, since he was trying to gain a teaching appointment at the Cathedral School in Paris, after years of ostracism and exile, by depicting himself as adequately repentant of his affair. He may, on the other hand, have depicted himself thus to make

Heloise an innocent victim of their affair. Marenbon writes in *The Philosophy of Peter Abelard* that he thinks Heloise softened Abelard's abstract ethical theory (and his idealization of pagan society and monastic life) by forcing him to think in terms of practical ethics and the ambiguous limits of human moral behavior, even in monastic communities.

61. Abelard, *Historia Calamitatum,* chap. 6, trans. Henry Adams Bellows (Medieval Sourcebook, www.forham.edu/halsall/basis/abelard-histcal).

62. Heloise to Abelard, First Letter, *Letters of Abelard and Heloise,* 109.

63. Ibid., 116.

64. Abelard, *Historia Calamitatum,* chap. 6.

65. Heloise to Abelard, First Letter, *Letters of Abelard and Heloise,* 117.

66. Ibid., 112.

67. Ibid., 110.

68. Ibid., 116.

69. Heloise to Abelard, Second Letter, *Letters of Abelard and Heloise,* 135.

70. Abelard, *Historia Calamitatum,* chap. 8.

71. Heloise, "Letter (167) to Peter the Venerable," *Letters of Abelard and Heloise,* 285.

CHAPTER TWELVE: ESCAPE ROUTES

1. For numerous examples of the emergence of Calvary scenes in painting and sculpture, beginning in the late thirteenth century, see Mitchell B. Merback, *The Thief, the Cross, and the Wheel: Pain and the Spectacle of Punishment in Medieval and Renaissance Europe* (Chicago: University of Chicago Press, 1998). See Gertrud Schiller, *The Passion of Jesus Christ,* Vol. 2 of *Iconography of Christian Art,* trans. Janet Seligman (Greenwich, CT: New York Graphic Society, 1972), figs. 505–525, for a chronologically arranged series of images.

2. Merback, *Thief, Cross, and Wheel,* 43. Discussing thirteenth- to sixteenth-century Crucifixion scenes, Merback explains: "The physical pilgrimage to the Holy Land or its European surrogate, limited in time and space, was to be matched if not surpassed in the believer's lifetime by countless mental journeys, interior visualizations of the personages, places and events which comprised the corpus of sacred narratives. Among these narratives, the story of the Passion demanded, and rewarded, the most intensive mental efforts at 'mystical witnessing.' . . . [Artworks] were expressly designed to facilitate such acts of 'mystical witnessing' " (46).

3. See Merback, *Thief, Cross, and Wheel,* 218–242, for an extensive discussion of Franciscan piety, patronage of Passion art, and the function of images in devotional practices. The Franciscans supported crusading—as spiritual devotion and as action in the world. After 1220, they were responsible for preaching the Crusades and collecting crusading taxes, though Saint Francis preferred to convert the Muslims rather than to kill them.

4. Francis "longed to offer to the Lord his own life as a living sacrifice in the flames of martyrdom." The "fruit of martyrdom had so attracted his heart that he desired a precious death for the sake of Christ more intensely than all the merits from the virtues." Bonaventure, *Life of Francis*, 9. 5–6, quoted in Thomaž Mastnak, *Crusading Peace: Christendom, the Muslim World, and Western Political Order* (Berkeley: University of California Press, 2002), 188.

5. The classic study of the origins of purgatory and its apogee in Dante's *Divine Comedy* is Jacques Le Goff, *The Birth of Purgatory* (Chicago: University of Chicago Press, 1984). For a critical assessment of Le Goff, see Jan N. Bremmer, *The Rise and Fall of the Afterlife* (London: Routledge, 2002), 64–69. Bremmer disputes Le Goff's view that early Christian texts such as the "Acts of Perpetua" reflect a nascent concept of purgatory.

6. Postmortem purgatorial and purifying penalties appeared as a formal doctrine in the Second Council of Lyon in 1274. See Paul McPartlan, "Purgatory," in Adrian Hastings, Alistair Mason, and Hugh Piper, eds., *The Oxford Companion to Christian Thought: Intellectual, Spiritual, and Moral Horizons of Christianity* (New York: Oxford University Press, 2000), 582–583.

7. Merback, *Thief, Cross, and Wheel*, 19.

8. Ibid., 20–21.

9. In *The Thief, the Cross, and the Wheel* (152), Merback describes an eighteenth-century public execution in which a soldier, condemned for killing another soldier, was executed as if he were being martyred. He sang the *Salve Regina* after being fixed to the torture wheel, and invited the crowd to join him. They sang hymns with him as they watched him die.

10. Merback (*Thief, Cross, and Wheel*, 41–68) relates public executions and torture to the emergence of iconography depicting them as crucifixions. Jacqueline E. Jung describes public executions in "From Jericho to Jerusalem: The Violent Transformation of Archbishop Engelbert of Cologne," in *Last Things: Death and the Apocalypse in the Middle Ages*, ed. Caroline Walker Bynum and Paul Freedman (Philadelphia: University of Pennsylvania Press, 2000), 60–82.

11. Kirkpatrick Sale, *Christopher Columbus and the Conquest of Paradise* (New York: Alfred A. Knopf, 1990). See also Norman F. Cantor, *In the Wake of the Plague: The Black Death and the World It Made* (New York: HarperCollins, 2001).

12. Lester K. Little, ed., *Plague and the End of Antiquity: The Pandemic of 541–750* (New York: Cambridge University Press, 2006) is a comprehensive interdisciplinary study.

13. Excerpted from George Deaux, *The Black Death: 1347* (New York: Weybright and Talley, 1969), 119–120. Cantor, *Wake of the Plague*, explains that the loss of priests "had the unanticipated effect of driving the spread of the Lollards, the feared radical heretics whose founders came out of Oxford seminars, especially John Wycliffe's, to attack church leadership, and ecclesiastical morality, and to question even the efficacy of the Sacrament of the Mass. The Lollards also aroused fear and anger in the established Church by allowing women to preach in their communities" (207).

14. Laura A. Smoller, "Of Earthquakes, Hail, Frogs, and Geography: Plague and the In-vestigation of the Apocalypse in the Later Middle Ages," in *Last Things: Death and the Apocalypse in the Middle Ages,* ed. Caroline Walker Bynum and Paul Freedman (Philadelphia: University of Pennsylvania Press, 2000).

15. Ibid. Smoller writes that efforts to understand the black plague sometimes stretched logic as people combined apparently inconsistent explanations:

> Fourteenth-century authors clearly set the outbreak of pestilence in an apocalyptic frame of interpretation, mapping plague's progress in a course that paralleled the eschatological geography of the *mappaemundi* and high-lighting the disease's outbreak with apocalyptic signs.... On the other hand, the same authors offered an interpretation of plague ... as a completely nat-ural phenomenon.... In their indecisive ambiguity, they refused to set the problem in terms defined at century's beginning, in which the apocalypse was to have nothing whatsoever to do with natural causes.... Doubtless these au-thors were terrified and sought to understand the overwhelming disaster around them in any and every way possible, even in ways deemed to be in-compatible. In their very human reactions to plague, these writers reopened the door to naturalizing the apocalypse. (186–187)

16. Sale, quoting Egon Friedell, in *Conquest of Paradise,* 37.

17. Claudia Rattazzi Papka, "The Limits of Apocalypse: Eschatology, Epistemology, and Textuality in Commedia and Piers Plowman," in *Last Things: Death and the Apoca-lypse in the Middle Ages,* ed. Caroline Walker Bynum and Paul Freedman (Philadel-phia: University of Pennsylvania Press, 2000), 233–256.

18. Catherine of Sienna, quoted in Mastnak, *Crusading Peace,* 340–346.

19. Mandeville on Prester John, chap. 33, in *Medieval Sourcebook,* www.fordham.edu/halsall/source/mandeville.html

20. Prester John legends from the twelfth to fourteenth centuries quoted in Jean Delumeau, *History of Paradise: The Garden of Eden in Myth and Tradition,* trans. Matthew O'Connell (New York: Continuum Press, 1995), 76, 80–81. For a detailed discussion, see the chapter titled "The Kingdom of Prester John," 71–96.

21. Mandeville on Prester John, chap. 33.

22. Jacqueline Pirenne, quoted by Delumeau, *History of Paradise,* 75. Some versions soft-ened Prester John's political critique, and such versions helped feed the fantastic and avaricious hopes of early crusading explorers and colonists, as we note below. The stories' power as social critique did not evaporate, however. Prester John returned in nineteenth-century African American movements for liberation and justice. As the ruler of an ancient Christian kingdom in Africa, he authenticated an African Ameri-can Christian identity that protested Euro-American dominance and justified back-to-Africa movements.

    Ibrahim Farajajé, an expert on African diaspora movements comments in per-sonal correspondence June 16, 2007, to the authors,

There are ideational connections between the Prester John story and the [Marcus] Garvey Movement. It played a part in the symbolic universe of Ethiopianism because it was believed that the Prester John story showed the high esteem in which "Ethiopia" (I use the quotation marks since this is more than just the country as we know it today) was held in antiquity and in the "Middle Ages." The fact that the late Emperor Haile Selassie was seen as the sign of the beginning of an eschatological in-gathering to "Zion" of peoples of African descent was not without its connections to the Prester John story. What is perhaps even more interesting is that the Prester John story was not at all used in Ethiopianism as a sign of how Islam could be vanquished; in fact, its value lay not in its role as a signifier of Christian resistance to Islam but rather in showing to a white-supremacist colonizing "Christian" Europe the value of Africa.

23. A chronological list of these Crusades can be found in Jonathan Riley-Smith, ed., *The Oxford Illustrated History of the Crusades* (Oxford: Oxford University Press, 1995), 397.

24. Delumeau, *History of Paradise,* 97–116.

25. Tudor Parfitt refers to Vasco da Gama carrying letters for Prester John in "Hebrew in Colonial Discourse," *Journal of Modern Jewish Studies* 2.2 (October 2003): 159–172. Jacqueline Pirenne (whose work is summarized in Delumeau, *History of Paradise,* 91–93) suggests a connection between Henry the Navigator and Prester John. See also Peter Russell, *Prince Henry "the Navigator": A Life* (New Haven, CT: Yale University Press, 2001), 120–127.

26. See P. Russell, *Prince Henry,* 239–263. We speculate that some of these Africans were Muslims because they were present in West Africa, and Henry regarded his journey as a crusade against infidels and Saracens (Muslims) in Africa. For this history, see Sylviane A. Diouf, "African Muslims in Bondage: Realities, Memories, and Legacies," in *Monuments of the Black Atlantic: Slavery and Memory,* ed. Joanne M. Braxton and Maria I. Diedrich (Münster, Germany: LIT Verlag, 2005), 77–89. Diouf notes: "Between the early 1500s and 1860s, West African Muslims from Senegal, Gambia, Mali, Guinea, Sierra Leone, Liberia, Côte d'Ivoire, Ghana, Bene, and Nigeria were shipped to the New World. They probably represented from 10 to 15 per cent of the 12 to 15 million Africans swept away by the transatlantic slave trade" (77). See also Sylviane Diouf, *Servants of Allah: African Muslims Enslaved in the Americas* (New York: New York University Press, 1998).

27. Zurara, *Chronicle of Guinea,* quoted in P. Russell, *Prince Henry,* 242.

28. Ibid., 244.

29. Excerpts from *Romanus Pontifex,* papal bull, January 5, 1455, available at www .romancatholicism.org/popes-slavery.htm

30. In a personal communication, Professor Joanne M. Braxton, director of the Middle Passage Project of the College of William and Mary, pointed out that while many re-

fer to these fortifications, some of which still dot the West African coastline, as "castles," European slave-trading companies called them "factories." Europeans who engaged in this highly lucrative but risky business on the slave coast were called "factors"; many of these "factors" died after being exposed to diseases for which they had little or no tolerance. Yet millions of enslaved Africans died in the dreaded Middle Passage. See "African Odyssey," an exhibition of photographs posted at www .wm.edu/middlepassage/. See also Tom Feelings, *The Middle Passage: White Ships, Black Cargo* (New York: Dial Books, 1995).

31. Martin Behaim, map n. 92c, Biblioteque Nationale de France in Paris, collection of medieval maps. See also Valerie Flint, *The Imaginative Landscape of Christopher Columbus* (Princeton, NJ: Princeton University Press, 1992); and Alessandro Scafi, *Mapping Paradise: A History of Heaven on Earth* (Chicago: University of Chicago Press, 2006). Scafi, especially, offers an engrossing and thorough study of many centuries of mapping, from ancient to modern.

32. Flint, *Imaginative Landscape,* 216–224.

33. Sale, *Conquest of Paradise,* 7–27.

34. Alessandro Scafi, *Mapping Paradise,* 254–255, discusses the influence of Ptolemy's *Geography* on maps from late antiquity forward.

35. Bartolomé de las Casas trained in law, moved to Hispaniola in 1502, and became a Dominican priest. His writings are a primary source for Colon's first journal, which survives in las Casas's transcription. Jill Lepore, *Encounters in the New World: A History in Documents* (New York: Oxford University Press, 2000), 75–78, offers excerpts of a public debate in 1550 between las Casas and Spain's royal historian, Juan Ginés de Sepúlveda, over the Spanish treatment of the Indians in the New World. Las Casas argued for their humanity and freedom and believed they deserved to be converted to Christianity. Sepúlveda contended that their conquest and enslavement as "apes," "cruel barbarians," "inferior to the Spanish" was justified. Luis N. Rivera-Pagán notes that Las Casas's last act was to appeal to the pope on behalf of the peoples of the New World, imploring the Spanish to repent and offer restitution for the crimes of their conquests. In the native people he saw "Jesus Christ . . . not once, but a thousand times whipped, insulted, beaten, and crucified." In an attempt to redress the sufferings of the Taino, Las Casas proposed replacing their decimated numbers with African slaves. He later repented for this, but his plan helped establish the Atlantic slave trade. See Rivera-Pagán, "A Prophetic Challenge to the Church: The Last Word of Bartolomé de las Casas," inaugural lecture, Henry Winters Luce Professor in Ecumenics and Mission at Princeton Theological Seminary, April 9, 2003, www .lascasas.org/Rivera_Pagan.htm, p. 3. Jill Lepore, *The Name of War: King Philip's War and the Origins of American Identity* (New York: Vintage Books, 1999), says that Las Casas's scathing characterizations of Spanish cruelty were translated into English and used by the English to valorize themselves over against the terrible Spanish.

36. Bartolomé de las Casas, *A Short Account of the Destruction of the Indies,* ed. and trans. Nigel Griffin, intro. Anthony Pagden (London: Penguin Books, 1992), 15.

37. Sale, *Conquest of Paradise,* 25.

38. Albert J. Raboteau, *Canaan Land: A Religious History of the African Americans* (New York: Oxford University Press, 2001), 4–7; and Lepore, *Encounters,* 125–145.

39. Maps number 90c and 97c, respectively, in the Biblioteque Nationale de France, Paris.

40. Merback, *Thief, Cross, and Wheel,* 283.

41. Philip Benedict, "Calvinism as a Culture?" in *Seeing beyond the Word: Visual Arts and the Calvinist Tradition,* ed. Paul Corby Finney (Grand Rapids, MI: Wm. B. Eerdmans, 1999), 29, quotes the Heidelberg Catechism (1562), which systematized the teachings of the Calvinist Reformation and required Protestants to memorize the following questions and answers:

> Should we, then, not make any images at all?
>
> God cannot and should not be pictured in any way . . .
>
> But may not pictures be tolerated in churches in place of books for unlearned people?
>
> No, for we must not try to be wiser than God, who does not want his people to be taught
>
> by means of lifeless idols, but through the living preaching of his word.

42. Jaroslav Pelikan, *Whose Bible Is It? A History of the Scriptures through the Ages* (New York: Viking Press, 2005) is a lively, accessible history of the formation of the various Bibles and how they are read.

43. The Earl Morse Wilbur Rare Book Collection of the Starr King School for the Ministry in Berkeley, California, has one of the rare surviving copies of this Greek New Testament.

44. Quoted in Raymond A. Mentzer Jr., "The Reformed Churches of France and the Visual Arts," in *Seeing beyond the Word: Visual Arts and the Calvinist Tradition,* ed. Paul Corby Finney (Grand Rapids, MI: Wm. B. Eerdmans, 1999), 205.

45. Such temples also included plaques of the Ten Commandments. A picture of the *temple de Paradis* can be found in *Seeing Beyond the Word,* plate 21.

46. Margaret Aston, "Puritans and Iconoclasm, 1560–1660," in *The Culture of English Puritanism, 1560–1700,* ed. Christopher Durston and Jacqueline Eales (London: Macmillan, 1996), 108. On page 96, Aston quotes Thomas Cranmer as saying, "Either they be no books, or, if they be, they be false and lying books, the teachers of all error," in his *Homily against Peril of Idolatry.*

47. For a summary of different Protestant rituals, see R. C. D. Jasper and G. J. Cuming, trans. and eds., *Prayers of the Eucharist: Early and Reformed* (Collegeville, MN: Liturgical Press, 1992), 177–314.

48. Jasper and Cuming, *Prayers of the Eucharist,* 204–205.

49. Quoted in Philip Benedict, "Calvinism as a Culture?" 28.

50. John Calvin, "The Author's Preface, John Calvin, to the Godly and Ingenuous Readers, Greeting," in *John Calvin: Selections from His Writings,* ed. and intro. John Dillenberger (Missoula, MT: Scholars Press, 1975), 28.

51. Ibid., 26.

52. Ibid., 27.

53. Ronald Huntington used this illustration in a course on the history of religions that Rita took at Chapman University in 1971.

54. Max Engammare, "A Portrait of the Exegete as a Geographer: The Map of Paradise as a Hermeneutical Instrument in Calvin and His Contemporaries," in *The Earthly Paradise: The Garden of Eden from Antiquity to Modernity,* ed. F. Regina Psaki (Binghamton, NY: Global Publications, Binghamton University, 2002), 229–230.

55. John Calvin, *Commentaries on the First Book of Moses Called Genesis,* trans. John King (Grand Rapids, MI: Wm. B. Eerdmans, 1948), 119.

56. Calvin, *Genesis,* 122.

57. Engammare, "Portrait of the Exegete," 215–234. Engammare discusses Calvin's map of paradise and indicates that Calvin's purpose was more than illustrative or informative.

58. Calvin, *Genesis,* 57.

59. Ibid., 60.

60. Ibid., 151.

61. Ibid., 154: "So long as they, firmly believing in God's word, freely suffered themselves to be governed by Him, they had serene and duly regulated affections.... But after they had given place to Satan's blasphemy, they began, like persons fascinated, to lose reason and judgment; yes, since they were become the slaves of Satan; he held their senses bound."

62. Calvin, *Institutes,* in *Selections from His Writings,* 270.

63. John Calvin, "The Form of Prayers and Manner of Ministering the Sacraments according to the Usage of the Ancient Church," in R.C.D. Jasper and G.J. Cuming trans. and eds., *Prayers of the Eucharist: Early and Reformed* (Collegeville, MN: Liturgical Press, 1992), 216.

64. Calvin, "Short Treatise on the Holy Supper of Our Lord Jesus," section 7, in *Selections from His Writings,* 511. In section 35, "The Sacrament Not a Sacrifice," Calvin refutes the idea that Jesus dies at every Eucharist.

65. Calvin, *Institutes,* in *Selections from His Writings,* 291.

66. John Dillenberger, "An Introduction to John Calvin," in *John Calvin: Selections from His Writings,* ed. and intro. John Dillenberger (Missoula, MT: Scholars Press, 1975), 5. Much of this summary of Calvin's life is taken from the introduction and "The Man and His Life," 21–44.

67. Ibid., 8: "Calvin's youngest brother, Antoine, had lived in the household since the original flight to Geneva. Antoine's wife was found guilty of adultery with Calvin's manservant. Divorced as a result, Antoine again married.... Calvin's step-daughter,

who had lived with Calvin and his wife in Geneva prior to her marriage, was also found guilty of adultery."

68. Quoted in Joy Gilsdorf, *The Puritan Apocalypse: New England Eschatology in the Seventeenth Century* (New York: Garland, 1989), 7.

69. Oliver Cromwell, quoted in C. H. Firth, *Oliver Cromwell and the Rule of the Puritans in England* (Covent Garden, UK: Putnam, 1901), 192.

70. See Maurice Ashley, *Oliver Cromwell and His World* (London: Thames and Hudson, 1972), 43, for a facsimile of the title page.

71. Cromwell, quoted in Firth, *Cromwell and the Rule of the Puritans,* 202.

72. Milton, *Paradise Lost,* bk. 1.705–750 (New York: Odyssey Press, 1935).

73. Ibid., excerpts, bk. 1.367–373.

74. In Milton, *Paradise Lost,* bk. 3.145–340, Christ offers himself to be the atoning sacrifice. Verses 3.235–240 read: "I offer, on mee let thy anger fall;/Account mee man; I for his sake will leave/Thy bosom . . . and for him lastly die . . . on me let Death wreck all his rage." All heaven rejoices at Christ's self-sacrificing love.

75. John Milton, *Paradise Regain'd* (Menston, UK: Scholar Press, 1968), bk. 1.5–7. Milton calls Satan the "thief of paradise" in 1.600. George Hunston Williams says of the redemptive scheme in *Paradise Regain'd,* "Milton ascribed to God the plan to 'exercise' Jesus in the wilderness that he might there, against the assaults of Satan, fashion the disciplines or instruments of spiritual warfare. . . . Paradise was in fact regained when Christ 'the glorious Hermit' went into the wilderness and from his cave of meditation raised it by his redemptive presence to become an Eden" *(Wilderness and Paradise in Christian Thought: The Biblical Experience of the Desert in the History of Christianity and the Paradise Theme in the Theological Idea of the University* [New York: Harper and Brothers, 1962], 77–78).

76. Joseph E. Duncan, *Milton's Earthly Paradise: A Historical Study of Eden* (Minneapolis: University of Minnesota Press, 1972), 89–115, surveys the multitude of books, pamphlets, and tracts on paradise themes. "Paradise saturated" is Duncan's characterization of the century's literature.

77. Ibid., 259.

78. John Milton, *Tenure of Kings and Magistrates,* quoted in Firth, *Cromwell and the Rule of the Puritans,* 233.

79. Petition quoted in Patricia Crawford, *Women and Religion in England 1500–1720* (London: Routledge, 1993), 211.

80. Ibid., 133–134, gives examples from 1640 to 1660. Mary Cary agitated to reduce infant mortality rates. In 1641 and 1642, women petitioned for peace. In 1649, Leveller women petitioned for release of prisoners, and seven thousand Quaker women petitioned Parliament to end tithes—high taxes that harmed the poor. Crawford notes that radical men reacted to women's leadership with repressive moves. See her discussion of the conflicts involving Martha Simmonds and George Fox, 173–180, and the decline of women's leadership within Quakerism after 1670, 193–197.

81. Kristen Poole, *Radical Religion from Shakespeare to Milton: Figures of Nonconfor-*

mity in Early Modern England (Cambridge: Cambridge University Press, 2000), 149–150.

82. Edward Johnson quoted in Perry Miller, ed., *The American Puritans: Their Prose and Poetry* (Garden City, NY: Doubleday, 1956), 29.

83. Miller, *American Puritans,* 1–5, 20–21. The Pilgrims were radical Puritan separatists who believed the true church consisted of "visible saints" in covenant with one another. They were persecuted in England for the treasonous step of "separating" from the national church. They were in conflict with the more moderate "presbyterian" Puritans in England who merely wanted to depose the king and eliminate all the bishops in order to reform the national church—not separate from it. Those who founded the Massachusetts Bay Colony were not as bold as the Pilgrims in stating their goals, but they shared their views, apparently somewhat surreptitiously in the beginning.

84. Quoted in Ronald Takaki, *A Larger Memory: A History of Our Diversity, with Voices* (New York: Little, Brown, 1998), 32–33.

85. Quoted in Miller, *American Puritans,* 29–30.

CHAPTER THIRTEEN: WEEPING ENCOUNTERS

1. Key sources for the discussion of native peoples include Robert L. Hall, *An Archaeology of the Soul: North American Indian Belief and Ritual* (Urbana: University of Illinois Press, 1997); Ronald Niezen, *Spirit Wars: Native North American Religions in the Age of Nation Building* (Berkeley: University of California Press, 2000); Neal Salisbury, *Manitou and Providence: Indians, Europeans, and the Making of New England, 1500–1643* (New York: Oxford University Press, 1982); and Vine Deloria Jr., *Spirit and Reason: The Vine Deloria Jr., Reader,* ed. Barbara Deloria, Kristen Foehner, and Sam Scinta, foreword by Wilma P. Mankiller (Golden, CO: Fulcrum, 1999). "Algonquin peoples" refers to a language family that included many of the tribes first encountered by English Pilgrims and Puritans on the East Coast of the present-day United States and by the French in the sixteenth and seventeenth centuries who traveled up the St. Lawrence Seaway, across the Great Lakes, and down the Mississippi.

2. Vine Deloria Jr. writes in *God Is Red: A Native View of Religion,* 3rd ed. (Golden, CO: Fulcrum, 2003): "The task of the tribal religion . . . is to determine the proper relationship that the people of the tribe must have with other living things and to develop the self-discipline within the tribal community so that man acts harmoniously with other creatures. The world that he experiences is dominated by the presence of power, the manifestation of life energies, the whole life-flow of a creation . . . The awareness of the meaning of life comes from observing how the various living things appear to mesh to provide a whole tapestry" (87).

3. Hall, *Archaeology of the Soul,* 1–38, notes that Feasts of the Dead were widespread throughout the Americas. Quote from p. 38.

4. At the conclusion of the ritual, John Smith returned to Jamestown, where he was arrested, tried, and sentenced to death. The arrival of Captain Newport from England saved his life. See Dr. Linwood "Little Bear" Custalow and Angela L. Daniel "Silver Star," *The True Story of Pocahontas: The Other Side of History* (Golden, CO: Fulcrum, 2007) for the Powhatan account. The authors are a historian and keeper of oral tradition for the descendants of the Powhatan and a Ph.D. candidate at the College of William and Mary, respectively. According to Powhatan history, Pocahontas, because she was a child, would not have been present during any of the four-day ritual. Smith's account was written long after the events occurred.

5. Wahunsonacock quoted in Peter Nabokov, *Native American Testimony: A Chronicle of Indian-White Relations from Prophecy to the Present, 1492–2000* (New York: Penguin Press, 1999), 72.

6. Captain John Smith quoted in Ronald Dale Karr, ed., *Indian New England 1524–1674: A Compendium of Eyewitness Accounts of Native American Life* (Arkansas City, KS: Gilliland, 1999), 27. For multiple early descriptions of New England through the eyes of Europeans, see Howard S. Russell, *Indian New England before the Mayflower* (Hanover, NH: University Press of New England, 1980), 10–11.

7. Thomas Morton, *Mourt's Relation: A Journal of the Pilgrims at Plymouth* (1622), ed. and intro. Dwight B. Heath (Bedford, MA: Applewood Books, 1963), 6. The book, which Morton published in England, is a firsthand account, apparently by several authors, of the Pilgrims' experiences from November 1620 through November 1621. Heath comments that it is "almost certain that the principal author was Edward Winslow, although it is generally believed that William Bradford also had a hand in the effort" (xiii).

8. Morton, quoted in N. Salisbury, *Manitou and Providence*, 103. See pages 101–106 for a full discussion of the epidemic and its aftermath. Salisbury interprets the unburied bodies as a sign that the plague had led to cultural and spiritual breakdown.

9. Morton, *Mourt's Relation*, 21.

10. Ibid., 38–39.

11. Ibid., 4, 9.

12. Ibid., 50–52. Our narrative has condensed events that reportedly took place over several hours on March 16, and several weeks of Indian and Pilgrim activities preceded the arrival of Samoset.

13. Ibid., 15, 17.

14. Ibid., 18.

15. Hall, *Archaeology of the Soul*, 1. It is not possible to be certain of the meaning of the Indians' actions from a native perspective. But from what is known of Native approaches to strangers and captives as replacements for their dead, it is plausible to interpret the Wampanoag ritual as a form of lamentation/adoption. Neal Salisbury comments, "Bradford wrote that, before approaching the English, the Indians gathered 'for three days . . . to curse and execrate them with their conjurations.' But this

description betrays his fear of witchcraft as it was understood by Europeans rather than a comprehension of Indian beliefs and customs. More likely the Pokanoket [alternative name for Wampanoag] were ritually purging themselves of their hostilities toward the English as a prelude to their diplomatic reversal" (*Manitou and Providence,* 114).

16. Massasoit, quoted in Russell Bourne, *Gods of War, Gods of Peace: How the Meeting of Native and Colonial Religion Shaped Early America* (New York: Harcout, 2002), 33.

17. Winslow, quoted in N. Salisbury, *Manitou and Providence,* 118. By 1698, when Cotton Mather wrote *Magnalia Christi Americana,* his history of Puritan New England, the Puritans were telling themselves—without foundation—that, in the Plymouth Treaty, Massasoit and the tribe "entered into a firm agreement of peace with the English, but also they declared and submitted themselves to be subjects of the King of England." Quoted in Bourne, *Gods of War,* 30–31. Bourne comments, "One searches the original document in vain for any support of that reading."

18. Quoted in Perry Miller, ed., *The American Puritans: Their Prose and Poetry* (Garden City, NY: Doubleday, 1956), 12.

19. George Hunston Williams, "Fleeing to and Planting in the Wilderness in the Reformation Period and Modern Times," in *Wilderness and Paradise in Christian Thought: The Biblical Experience of the Desert in the History of Christianity and the Paradise Theme in the Theological Idea of the University* (New York: Harper and Brothers, 1962), 65–97.

20. John Cotton wrote, "The devil decoyed those miserable savages [to New England] in hopes that the Gospel of the Lord Jesus Christ would never come here to destroy or disturb His *absolute empire* over them." Quoted in Ronald Takaki, *A Larger Memory: A History of Our Diversity, with Voices* (New York: Little, Brown, 1998), 32.

21. For a discussion of European interpretations of Native Americans, see Wilcomb E. Washburn and Bruce G. Trigger, "Native Peoples in Euro-American Historiography," in *The Cambridge History of the Native Peoples of the Americas,* Vol. 1: *North America Part 2,* Washburn and Trigger, eds. (New York: Cambridge University Press, 1996), 1–124. Rousseau's eighteenth-century romanticized "noble savage" was two centuries in the making.

22. Thomas Shepard, quoted in Miller, *American Puritans* 25. Shepard, an outspoken Puritan silenced by Archbishop Laud, arrived in the Massachusetts Bay Colony in 1635. Miller calls him "one of the four or five greatest preachers in the first generation" (22).

23. Thomas Shepard, "The Covenant of Grace," in Miller, *American Puritans* 148–149.

24. Richard Slotkin writes in *Regeneration through Violence: The Mythology of the American Frontier, 1600–1860* (Middletown, CT: Wesleyan University Press, 1973), "The first colonists saw in America an opportunity to regenerate their fortunes, their spirits, and the power of their church and nation; but the means to that regeneration ultimately became the means of violence, and the myth of regeneration through violence became the structuring metaphor of the American experience" (5).

25. By the time the men of the colonies organized a revolution against the English Crown in 1776, they were among the richest, most elite of its people, and they elected one of the richest men in the colonies as their first president.

26. For a detailed description of the Pequot War, see Bourne, *Gods of War,* 51–67.

27. Quoted in Howard Zinn, *A People's History of the United States: 1492–Present* (New York: Harper Perennial, 2003), 15.

28. See Evan Eisenberg, *The Ecology of Eden: an Inquiry into the Dream of Paradise and a New Vision of Our Role in Nature* (New York: Vintage Books, 1998), 240–261.

29. As Joy Gilsdorf says in *The Puritan Apocalypse: New England Eschatology in the Seventeenth Century* (New York: Garland, 1989), the Puritans did not see these ambitions as separable: "In some ways the combined promise and threat of the Indian was even more disturbing for the Puritans than the wilderness itself. For the Indian was the human embodiment of the "wilderness-condition." . . . He was a continual reminder of what man would be without the benefit of the Word of God. . . . Clearly the Indian like the physical wilderness had to be improved and made fruitful if the puritans were to flourish in their sanctuary" (120).

30. John Eliot, quoted and discussed in Gilsdorf, *Puritan Apocalypse,* 82–84, 121. See also Kristina Bross, *Dry Bones and Indian Sermons: Praying Indians in Colonial America* (Ithaca, NY: Cornell University Press, 2004).

31. Ninigret, called "an old crafty sachem," by Increase Mather, addressed these words to the missionary Matthew Mayhew. Quoted and discussed in Yasuhide Kawashima, *Igniting King Philip's War: The John Sassamon Murder Trial* (Lawrence: University Press of Kansas, 2001), 143.

32. John Eliot recorded the Indians' questions. See Bourne, *Gods of War,* 127, and Niezen, *Spirit Wars,* 36.

33. Bross writes in *Dry Bones:* "Although the final ruling favors the Natick Indians, it also foreshadows later treatment. Natick had retained its lands by virtue of its inhabitants' favored status as symbols of New England's sacred purpose. When the Praying Indians ceased to embody millennial promise, New England authorities withdrew their 'encouragement,' and the converts were left vulnerable to the avarice and antagonism of their English neighbors" (45).

34. Bross writes: "Close reading of the mission tracts reveals both individuals who found in Christianity the means to understand better their colonized position as well as those who never ceased to resist the demands English evangelists placed on them. We can see moments in which the English preachers are taken aback by the persistence of Indian interlocutors, and we can see examples of Indians who learned to use Christianity and scripture to negotiate their place in the English colonial order" (*Dry Bones,* 21).

35. Bross, *Dry Bones,* 52–83, discusses the complex cultural interactions involved in translation and its modes of dissent and cultural preservation.

36. Andrea Smith, *Conquest: Sexual Violence and American Indian Genocide* (Cambridge, MA: South End Press, 2005), 37, notes, "For the most part, schools prepared

Native boys for manual labor or farming and Native girls for domestic work. Children were also involuntarily leased out to white homes as menial labor. . . . The primary role of this education for Indian girls was to inculcate patriarchal norms into Native communities so that women would lose their place of leadership in Native communities."

37. Bourne, *Gods of War*, 132.

38. Eliot, quoted in Gilsdorf, *Puritan Apocalypse*, 82–84, 121. This Sassamon-Eliot translation, *Mamusee Wunneetupanatamwe Up-Biblum God Naneeswe Nukkone Testament Kah Wonk Wusku Testament*, was the first Bible published in the New World.

39. Niezen, *Spirit Wars*, 37.

40. Metacom, quoted in Kawashima, *Igniting King Philip's War*, 61.

41. Jill Lepore, *The Name of War: King Philip's War and the Origins of American Identity* (New York: Vintage Books, 1999), 23.

42. Ibid., 21–26.

43. Kawashima, *Igniting King Philip's War*, 111–129, concludes,

> It was the Sassamon case that suddenly and flatly destroyed the principle of legal co-existence, forcing the Indians to conform to English law. . . . Christianization, which meant not only conversion but also Europeanization, would force the Indians to change their way of life. . . . Now, Philip feared, the missionary activities would take a more aggressive course if formally endorsed by the Plymouth government. . . . The Sassamon case, which sparked King Philip's War, was not merely a triggering incident but a legal manifestation of the primary cause of the war, the final culmination of not only legal conflict but more general confrontation between the colonists and the natives in southern New England. (125, 129)

44. See William Apess, "Eulogy on King Philip," in Colin Calloway, ed., *First Peoples: A Documentary Survey of American Indian History*, 2nd ed. (Boston: Bedford/St. Martin's, 1999), 129–132, for a nineteenth-century Native view of the war. All sides committed atrocities against noncombatants. Apess acknowledged Philip's brutality. However, he noted that Philip's war tactics were no worse than those committed by whites and made the case that in many respects, as a warrior, Metacom showed more humanity and restraint than did the colonizers. Native women captured by the English were violated. They were forced to betray their kin or were brutally killed. But the Indians did not violate women. Using the testimony of captive Mary Rowlandson, Apess defended the Indians: "It appears that Philip treated his prisoners with a great deal more Christian-like spirit than the Pilgrims did, even Mrs. Rowlandson, although speaking with bitterness sometimes of the Indians, yet in her journal she speaks not a word against him." Apess noted that in the aftermath of the war, the English kept none of their promises to their Indian allies. He protested, "It was only, then, by deception that the Pilgrims gained the country, as their word has never been fulfilled in regard to Indian rights."

45. Lepore, *Name of War,* 120, reports the confrontation in Providence. Unlike Lepore, we do not consider the war as extraordinary for the Puritans.

46. Lepore describes the fate of the Indian slaves in *Name of War,* 168–170. Bourne, in *Gods of War,* 156, summarizes the devastations of the war. No other war on American soil has been marked by as high a proportion of the total population killed.

47. Increase Mather, in Calloway, *First Peoples,* 126–127.

48. For a discussion and analysis of colonial writing about the war, see Lepore, *Name of War,* 48–70.

49. Bourne, *Gods of War,* 157.

50. Lepore, *Name of War,* 45.

51. Quotes from the Reforming Synod cited by Gilsdorf, *Puritan Apocalypse,* 131–132; and in Alden T. Vaughan and Edward W. Clark, eds., *Puritans among the Indians: Accounts of Captivity and Redemption* (Cambridge, MA: Harvard University Press, 1981), 14.

52. Lepore mentions the belief in the magical powers of Bible reading in *Name of War:* "Seventeenth-century New England was . . . 'a world of wonders' in which belief in the occult coexisted with church theology and in which books were both especially valuable and especially magical. . . . One colonist sat in the town common reading the Bible in the midst of an Indian attack, believing he couldn't be killed that way (instead, he was the single casualty of the day)" (54).

53. Mary Rowlandson, "The Sovereignty and Goodness of God," in Vaughan and Clark, *Puritans among the Indians,* 38.

54. Ibid., 74–75.

55. Jonathan Edwards, "Sinners in the Hands," in *Jonathan Edwards: Representative Selections, with Introduction, Bibliography, and Notes,* ed. Clarence H. Faust and Thomas H. Johnson, 2nd ed. (New York: Hill and Wang, 1962), 165–166.

56. Faust and Johnson, "Introduction," *Jonathan Edwards: Representative Selections,* xvii.

57. Conrad Cherry, *Nature and Religious Imagination: From Edwards to Bushnell* (Philadelphia: Fortress Press, 1980) quotes Jonathan Edwards as writing: "Death temporal is a shadow of eternal death. The agonies, the pains, the groans and gasps of death, the pale, horrid ghastly appearance of the corpse, its being laid in the dark and silent grave, there putrefying and rotting and becoming exceeding loathsome and being eaten with worms (Isa. 66.24), is an image of the misery of hell. And the body's continuing in the grave, and never rising more in this world, is to shadow forth the misery of the eternity of hell" (31).

58. Edwards, "Sinners in the Hands," 163–164.

59. John Williams, "The Redeemed Captive Returning to Zion," in Vaughan and Clark, *Puritans among the Indians,* 186.

60. Ibid., 196.

61. George M. Marsden, *Jonathan Edwards: A Life* (New Haven, CT: Yale University Press, 2003), 219.

62. Ibid., Sarah Edwards quoted on 245–246. Details of the Edwardses' lives are taken from Marsden's biography, 246–247, 320–323, 511–512. Marsden comments on the passage quoted in the text:

> In our era, when traditions of martyrdom and submission have been all but lost . . . it is difficult to view such experiences in their own context. The temptation today is to speculate on what the passage about horsewhipping reveals about Sarah's psyche or about the Edwardses' relationships. Before doing that, however, we should be reminded that trained psychologists and psychoanalysts often hear many hours of testimony from patients without being able to diagnosis [*sic*] the roots of their problems. So one should not jump to a conclusion based on a fragment. Nevertheless, if one holds to a realistic view of human nature (as Calvinists themselves do), one should acknowledge that there are dark sides to every human and to every human relationship, even if we lack the evidence for identifying the specifics. The one thing that is clear from this passage is that the Edwardses valued submission far more than it is usually valued today. (246–247)

63. Conrad Wright, *The Beginnings of Unitarianism in America* (Boston: Starr King Press, 1955), 36–58.

64. Edwards's ideas are analyzed in Roland A. Delattre, *Beauty and Sensibility in the Thought of Jonathan Edwards: An Essay in Aesthetics and Theological Ethics* (New Haven, CT: Yale University Press, 1968), which attempts to systematize the relationships among primary and secondary beauty, the role of sensibility and the affections, and the primacy of consent and of relational being in God, as opposed to unitary being.

65. See Marsden, *Edwards: A Life,* 326–331, quotes from "True Saints, When Absent from the Body, Are Present with the Lord," 327.

66. Edwards, quoted in Cherry, *Nature and Religious Imagination,* 59, 61.

67. Edwards, "Personal Narrative," in Edwards, *Representative Selections,* 60–61.

68. Jonathan Edwards, "The Nature of True Virtue," quoted in Delattre, *Beauty and Sensibility,* 35.

69. Jonathan Edwards, "Miscellanies," quoted in Delattre, *Beauty and Sensibility,* 37.

70. Edwards in Cherry, *Nature and Religious Imagination:* "Wherever we are, and whatever we are about, we may see divine things excellently represented and held forth. And it will abundantly tend to confirm the Scripture" (61).

71. Thomas Shepard, "The Covenant of Grace," in Miller, *American Puritans,* 148–149.

72. Indians lived in New England—on reservations. Kawashima writes in *Igniting King Philip's War:*

> The Indian villages, in which most of [the surviving Praying Indians] went to live, were after the war turned into reservations, which colonial governments used as a means to control Indians effectively. . . . The Indian reservation never

became an integral part of the political system of the colony. It was outside the political divisions of the colony and thus did not attain the status of township, the basic political and territorial unit in colonial New England ... a new set of regulations began to control various activities of the Indians in their daily life. They were even placed under a curfew law in their own land! Nor were the Indians given the chance to become citizens. (154)

73. Lepore, *Name of War*, 207. She discusses the use of the myth of the extinct Indian in the construction of American identity in chapter 8.

74. Ibid., 196–197.

75. *Washington Irving: Bracebridge Hall, Tales of a Traveller, the Alhambra* (New York: Library Classics, 1991). The opening paragraph of chapter 3, "The Palace of the Alhambra," said it was "the royal abode of the Moorish kings, where, surrounded with the splendors and refinements of Asiatic luxury, they held dominion over what they vaunted as a terrestrial paradise, and made their last stand for empire in Spain."

   Renato Rosaldo, *Culture and Truth: The Remaking of Social Analysis* (Boston: Beacon Press, 1993), calls white longings for lost dark races destroyed by white conquest "imperialist nostalgia," which allows white guilt about their own atrocious behavior to be subsumed into sorrow and longing that restore their sense of being good people.

76. Lepore, *Name of War*, 191, 193. The Patrick Henry–like phrase is quoted on 197.

77. Calloway, *First Peoples*, 220–256, relates removal to Jefferson's policies. See also Grant Foreman, *Indian Removal: The Emigration of the Five Civilized Tribes of Indians* (Norman: University of Oklahoma Press, 1989); and Ronald N. Satz, *American Indian Policy in the Jacksonian Era* (Norman: University of Oklahoma Press, 2002). Indian removal forced thousands of Southeast Indians—the Chickasaw, Choctaw, Creek, Seminole, and Cherokee—west of the Mississippi. More fragmented, less powerful tribes in the Northeast—Shawnees, Ottawas, Potawatomis, Sauks, and Foxes—were also removed. Of these other tribes, approximately half would die of disease, starvation, and exposure.

78. Alexis de Tocqueville, quoted in Calloway, *First Peoples*, 229.

79. Brian Dippie, quoted in Lepore, *Name of War*, 211.

80. One who noted the implicit self-contempt was the Massachusetts Congressman Edward Everett, who asserted that, in applauding, the audience accepted that the introduction of "the civilized race into America" was wrong, and that "the whole of what is now our happy and prosperous country ought to have been left as it was found, the abode of barbarity and heathenism." Quoted in Lepore, *Name of War*, 206.

81. Before his death in 2006, John Mohawk was planning a book project on the Indian roots of pragmatism. Cornel West, in his otherwise perceptive study of American pragmatism, *The American Evasion of Philosophy: A Genealogy of Pragmatism* (Madison: University of Wisconsin Press, 1989), neglects its Indian connections.

82. William Apess, "Eulogy on King Philip," in Calloway, *First Peoples*, 127–136.

CHAPTER FOURTEEN: THE STRUGGLE FOR PARADISE

1. For information about concerted efforts to destroy progressive Christianity or move it rightward, see the National Committee for Responsive Philanthropy Publications, *Axis of Ideology: Conservative Foundations and Public Policy,* March 2004, and *Funding the Culture Wars: Philanthropy, Church, and State,* February 2005, both available at www.ncrp.org/publications/index.asp; Stephen Swecker, *Hard Ball on Holy Ground* (Charleston, SC: BookSurge, 2005); and Andrew J. Weaver, "When Good News Is Bad News, or Working on a Coup D'etat," available at www.talk2action.org/story/2006/3/24/175239/669.

2. Diane Apostolos-Cappadona, an art historian and expert on nineteenth-century American art, makes this point in *The Spirit and the Vision: The Influence of Christian Romanticism on the Development of Nineteenth Century American Art* (Atlanta: Scholars Press, 1995):

   > The search for an iconography and mythology that identified and authenticated the singularity of the American experience was premised on the recognition of the American wilderness. The transformation of the Wilderness into Nature, and of the Virgin Land into the Garden of Eden, issued from the artistic and religious interpretations. American artists and theologians recognized the appropriateness of the landscape as the singular characteristic which defined 'America.' ... The nineteenth-century interest in the wilderness was a variation of the Puritan understanding of their 'errand into the wilderness' which was the basic premise that the American landscape was created by God as a gift to this specially chosen group of peoples. (55)

3. Thomas Cole, quoted in Charles L. Sanford, *The Quest for Paradise: Europe and the American Moral Imagination* (Urbana: University of Illinois Press, 1961), 144.

4. This painting can be seen at the Museum of Fine Arts in Boston.

5. Sanford, *Quest for Paradise,* 144.

6. Cole, quoted in Sanford, ibid., 145.

7. Ibid., 147.

8. "In the American forest we find trees in every stage of vegetable life and decay—the slender sapling ... the giant in his prime ... the hoary patriarch of the wood—on the ground lie prostrate decaying trunks that once waved their verdant heads in the sun and wind" (Cole, quoted in Sanford, *Quest for Paradise,* 147–148).

9. Thoreau, quoted in Edwin S. Fussell, "The Red Face of Man," in *Thoreau: A Collection of Critical Essays,* ed. Sherman Paul (Englewood Cliffs, NJ: Prentice-Hall, 1962), 152.

10. For a discussion of "Walking" in light of the whole body of Thoreau's work and his religious perspectives, see David M. Robinson, *Natural Life: Thoreau's Worldly Transcendentalism* (Ithaca, NY: Cornell University Press, 2004), 148–161.

11. Henry David Thoreau, "Walking," in Ralph Waldo Emerson and Henry David Thoreau, *Nature Walking*, ed. and intro. John Elder (Boston: Beacon Press, 1991), 72–73.

12. Ibid., 87, 94–95.

13. Ibid., 80, 102.

14. Ripley, quoted in Sterling F. Delano, *Brook Farm: The Dark Side of Utopia* (Cambridge, MA: Belknap Press, 2004), xvi. Delano provides a comprehensive study of the vision and difficulties of Brook Farm. He notes, xiv, that "one hundred nineteen communal and utopian societies were established in the United States between 1800 and 1859."

15. Emerson's intellectual lineage extends back to Jonathan Edwards, who taught Samuel Hopkins, who was the minister for William Ellery Channing, Emerson's tutor while he was a student at Harvard.

16. Emerson, "Nature," in *Selections from Ralph Waldo Emerson,* ed. Stephen E. Whicher (Boston: Houghton Mifflin, 1957), 43, 24.

17. Ibid., 49, 48.

18. Ibid., 38, 50.

19. Ibid., 33.

20. See Emerson, *Selections,* 478: "The idea of the Orient had always strong emotional connotations for Emerson: it meant mystery, large faith, feminine passivity, and religious contemplation, thus contrasting with the active, masculine West; it stood for the life of the Soul." Emerson's second wife, Lidian, and his daughter, Edith, became women's rights activists, and his friend Margaret Fuller was a strong advocate for women's equality. Eventually, after much prodding from many women in his life, Emerson lent his support to the cause of women's suffrage. See Robert D. Richardson Jr., *Emerson: The Mind on Fire* (Berkeley: University of California Press, 1995), 534.

21. Ibid., 38.

22. Emerson quoted in Cornel West, *The American Evasion of Philosophy: A Genealogy of Pragmatism* (Madison: University of Wisconsin Press, 1989), 31. Emerson wrote to President Van Buren in 1835 to protest the removal of the Cherokee Indians from their land. He protested the Fugitive Slave Law in 1859. West, 20–21, sees Emerson's social activism as impotent—a characterization that Emerson agreed with.

23. From Emerson's journal, quoted in West, ibid., 30.

24. Emerson, "Nature," in *Selections,* 56.

25. Ibid., 53. West writes: "Emerson's notion of vision wipes the temporal slate clean not in order to stop or transcend time but in order to be at the beginning a new time, just as his exhilarating walk through the woods and wilderness locates him on the edge of new space that is on the frontier" (*American Evasion,* 19).

26. West, *American Evasion,* 19–20. He quotes the following passage from Emerson scholar Michael Lopez: "For Emerson, war *was* 'the Father of all things.' The world

512 Notes to Pages 386–391

was 'a battle-ground, every principle . . . A war-note.' . . . In Man's 'lapsed estate' the

crises which try his edge can appear as 'the natural history of calamity' rather than
that natural history of growth by which the universe proceeds and metamorphoses
itself. War was with 'the highest right' because it mimicked nature's tendency to
'break up the old adhesions' and allow 'the atoms of society to take a new order.' "

27. West, *American Evasion,* 27. The last phrase is from Emerson.

28. For a scholarly study, see Julie Hirst, *Jane Leade: Biography of a Seventeenth-Century Mystic* (Hants, UK: Ashgate, 2005).

29. The first generation of Universalists in America took the position that Jesus's death on the cross was "once and for all"—he never would have to die again, nor would any soul have to endure eternal punishment for sin. The second generation of Universalists, exemplified by Hosea Ballou, rejected the doctrine of the atonement as a payment to God for humanity's sins and affirmed the salvation of all souls based on the generous, all-inclusive character of God's love. Judith Sargent Murray laid the groundwork for Ballou with her teachings that religious authority derives first of all from observation of life, with scripture as supplemental, and her rejection of any association between the Eucharist and Christ's crucifixion. A scholarly history of Universalism can be found at www.online.sksm.edu/resources.php.

30. Judith Sargent Murray, *Some Deductions from the System Promulgated in the Page of Divine Revelation, Ranged in the Order and Form of a Catechism, Intended As an Assistant to the Christian Parent or Teacher* (Norwich, CT: John Trumbull, 1782). Bonnie Hurd Smith has edited the text, which can be found at www.hurdsmith.com/judith/catechism.htm.

31. J. S. Murray's "Catechism" reversed Jonathan Edwards' view of nature as the "second book of revelation." She instructed children that their primary source for coming to know God was their observation of the world around them:

"When you behold the effects of love, manifested in rain, sunshine, seed time and harvest, you ought to conclude there is a power divine, though to you invisible; and further, that that power is all good, all gracious, and mighty."

In response to the children's question, "But did you not inform me that God had revealed himself by express declaration in the sacred scriptures?" She responds, "Yes, the volume of inspiration may serve as a supplement to that of nature." To bolster her point, she gave the example of an "aboriginal of this country" who decided to accept the teachings of Christianity because they accorded with observation of the world.

32. Judith Sargent Murray, "On the Equality of the Sexes," *Selected Writings of Judith Sargent Murray,* ed. Sharon M. Harris, Women Writers in English 1350–1850 (Oxford: Oxford University Press, 1995), 12–13.

33. Hosea Ballou, *A Treatise on Atonement* (Boston: Skinner House Books, 1986), 104–105.

34. Ibid., 75.

35. Ibid., 242.

36. Ibid., xix.

37. Ibid., 126.

38. Theodore Parker, "Experience as a Minister," *Theodore Parker: An Anthology*, ed. and intro. Henry Steele Commager (Boston: Beacon Press, 1960), 350–351. Parker names the four social forces: "the organized trading power"; "the organized political power . . . commonly controlled by the trading power"; "the organized ecclesiastical power, the various sects which . . . all mainly agree in their fundamental principle of vicariousness—an alleged revelation, instead of actual human faculties, salvation from God's wrath and eternal ruin, by the atoning blood of crucified God"; and "the organized literary power, the endowed colleges, the periodical press." On calling God "Mother," he writes, "I have called God Father, but also Mother . . . to express more sensibly the quality of tender and unselfish love, which mankind associates more with Mother than aught else beside" (347).

39. See Nancy Hardesty, *Women Called to Witness: Evangelical Feminism in the Nineteenth Century*, 2nd ed. (Knoxville: University of Tennessee Press, 1999), for a study of the relationship between evangelical holiness movements and nineteenth-century movements for temperance, women's education, women's suffrage, abolition, and related social justice work. See Joanne M. Braxton, *Black Women Writing Autobiography: A Tradition within a Tradition* (Philadelphia: Temple University Press, 1989), 49–79, for a specific study of Nancy Prince, Jarena Lee, Rebecca Cox Jackson, Sojourner Truth, and Harriet Tubman.

40. Experiments in new forms of community and sexual relationships abounded in the nineteenth century. For a study of one, the Oneida Community, see Spencer Klaw, *Without Sin: The Life and Death of the Oneida Community* (New York: Penguin Press, 1993).

41. Daniel Walker Howe, *The Unitarian Conscience: Harvard Moral Philosophy, 1805–1861* (Middletown, CT: Wesleyan University Press, 1988), 137.

42. See William Ellery Channing, "Likeness to God," *William Ellery Channing: Selected Writings*, ed. David Robinson (New York: Paulist Press, 1985), 161, 162, 157, 159.

43. Jack Mendelsohn, *Channing: The Reluctant Radical* (Boston: Little, Brown, 1971), 268–269, describes the breach that divided Channing and his congregation.

44. See James Thomas Flexner, *An American Saga: The Story of Helen Thomas and Simon Flexner* (New York: Fordham University Press, 1993). Other Quakers who also enjoyed wealth and privilege actually paid their slaves recompense and freed them.

45. Horace Bushnell, *The Vicarious Sacrifice*, quoted in Gary Dorrien, *The Making of American Liberal Theology: Imagining Progressive Religion 1805–1900* (Louisville, KY: Westminster John Knox Press, 2001), 169.

46. For example, William Ellery Channing, "Address on the Anniversary of Emancipation in the British West Indies," (1842), in *The Works of William E. Channing, D.D.* (Boston: American Unitarian Association, 1877), 909: "The great right of a man is,

to use, improve, expand his powers, for his own and others' good. The slave's powers belong to another, and are hemmed in, kept down, not cherished, or suffered to unfold. If there be an infernal system, one especially hostile to humanity, it is that which deliberately wars against the expansion of men's faculties, and this enters into the essence of slavery."

47. McKanan, *Identifying the Image of God,* studies the place of sentimental identification with victims in Christian social reform in the nineteenth century. He sees sentimental identification as a positive way for "even bitter enemies to recognize their common humanity," 215. We share his enthusiasm for religiously based social reform but see significant problems with utopian idealism and benevolent paternalism. The former begins with what could be, whereas we would ground Christian social activism in care for what is already present in this world. The latter preserves structures of oppressor and oppressed by transforming them into structures of helper and helped.

48. Bushnell, *Christian Nurture,* (1860, 3rd ed.), quoted in Dorrien, *Making of American Liberal Theology,* 139. Dorrien discusses Bushnell's Anglo-Saxon, Puritan chauvinism and his racism, saying that for Bushnell "America was the hope of the world because it was founded and built by a superior Christian race devoted to liberty and Christian civilization. To believe in America was to have faith that American Protestants and their northern European families of origin would remake the world in their image, progressively pushing the weaker races 'out of the world, as in the silence of a dew-fall' " (140).

49. Clarence Skinner, *The Social Implications of Universalism* (Boston: Universalist Publishing House, 1915), quotes from 21, 24, 47, 43, 50. Skinner's extravagant confidence in human abilities to shape life led him to a number of questionable conclusions. He believed, for example, in eugenics.

50. This line is from the hymn "Turn Back, O Man" by Clifford Bax (1886–1962). It appears in many Christian hymnals. In 1908, a group of mainline U.S. Protestant denominations formed the Federation of Christian Churches and issued a Social Creed, drawing from documents generated by its Methodist and Presbyterian members. The creed set forth an agenda for reform, anticipating nearly all the issues addressed by the New Deal.

51. Walter Rauschenbusch, *A Theology for the Social Gospel* (New York: Macmillan, 1917), 235. See also Christopher Hodge Evans, *The Kingdom Is Always Coming: A Life of Walter Rauschenbusch* (Grand Rapids, MI: Eerdmans, 2004).

52. Ibid., 186.

53. Ibid., 48.

54. Ibid.

55. Ibid., 49.

56. Ibid., 111, for the last quote. The rest is a summary of pages 244–261.

57. Ibid., 186, 187, 185, 186.

58. C. Eric Lincoln and Lawrence H. Mamiya, *The Black Church in the African American Experience* (Durham, NC: Duke University Press, 1990).

59. Hilton Als, Jon Lewis, and Leon F. Litwack, *Without Sanctuary: Lynching Photography in America,* ed. James Allen (Santa Fe, NM: Twin Palms, 2000); Philip Dray, *At the Hands of Persons Unknown: The Lynching of Black America* (New York: Random House, 2002); and James W. Trelease, *White Terror: The Ku Klux Klan Conspiracy and Southern Reconstruction* (Baton Rouge: Louisiana State University Press, 1995).

60. Als, Lewis, and Litwack, *Without Sanctuary,* is about these postcards.

61. The story of Mencken and his paper's courageous antilynching campaign is found in Marion Elizabeth Rodgers, "H. L. Mencken: Courage in a Time of Lynching," *Nieman Reports* 60, 2 (Summer 2006), available at www.neiman.harvard.edu/reports/06-2NRsummer/p74-0602-rodgers.html.

62. W.E.B. DuBois, "Litany at Atlanta," quoted by M. Shawn Copeland, "Wading through Many Sorrows," in *A Troubling in My Soul: Womanist Perspectives on Evil and Suffering,* ed. Emilie M. Townes (Maryknoll, NY: Orbis Books), 126.

63. Quoted by William R. Jones, *Is God a White Racist? A Preamble to Black Theology* (Boston: Beacon Press, 1998), 35.

64. Countee Cullen, quoted in ibid., 33.

65. Ida B. Wells-Barnett, "Lynch Law in Georgia," pamphlet, June 20, 1899, in the Daniel Murray Pamphlet Collection (Library of Congress).

66. Ida B. Wells-Barnett, *Crusade for Justice: The Autobiography of Ida B. Wells* (Chicago: University of Chicago Press, 1970). See also Braxton, *Black Women Writing Autobiography,* 102–138.

67. Patricia A. Schechter, *Ida B. Wells-Barnett and American Reform, 1880–1930* (Chapel Hill: University of North Carolina Press, 2001).

68. Emilie Townes, "Ida B. Wells-Barnett: An Afro-American Prophet," *Christian Century,* March 15, 1989, 285, provides a nuanced assessment of her remarkable achievements and interpersonal failures to build coalitions.

Index

Page numbers in italics refer to illustrations

Saint